BEN KIERNAN was born in Melbourne in 1953, and graduated from Monash University in 1974. He was tutor in Southeast Asian History at the University of New South Wales from 1975 to 1977, and earned his Ph.D. in History at Monash in 1983. His work has appeared in the *Journal of Contemporary Asia*, the *Bulletin of Concerned Asian Scholars*, and *Southeast Asian Affairs* (Singapore). He has spent seven months in Kampuchea since the fall of the Pol Pot regime, and is co-author (with Chanthou Boua) of *Peasants and Politics in Kampuchea, 1942-1981* (London, Zed Books, 1982) and co-editor (with David P. Chandler) of *Revolution and Its Aftermath in Kampuchea* (Yale University, 1983).

How Pol Pot Came To Power

A History of Communism in Kampuchea, 1930-1975

BEN KIERNAN

VERSO

London · New York

British Library
Cataloguing in Publication Data

Kiernan, Ben
  How Pol Pot came to power.
  1. Kampuchea — Politics and government
  I. Title
  959.6′04   DS554.8

First published 1985
© Ben Kiernan 1985
Reprinted 1986
Reprinted 1987

Verso
UK: 6 Meard Street, London W1V 3HR
USA: 29 West 35th Street, New York, NY 10001-2291

Filmset in Bembo by
Swanston Typesetting, Derby

Printed in Great Britain by
Thetford Press Limited
Thetford, Norfolk

ISBN 0 86091 097 0
     0 86091 805 X (pbk)

Contents

for Joan and Peter

The Story of El Salvador
The Silence of Hiroshima
Destruction of Cambodia
Short memory, must have a short memory.

Midnight Oil, *10,9,8,7,6,5,4,3,2,1.*

Acknowledgements

My greatest debt is to Chanthou Boua, who supported me both emotionally and financially during the five years of researching and writing this book. Moreover, innumerable discussions with her have enlightened my understanding of Khmer society, politics and language. Her ignorance of and aversion to history, on the other hand, provided a healthy counterbalance to my own fetish for the past tense.

David P. Chandler has been an inspiring teacher and patient friend for over a decade. My intellectual debt to him is large, and I hope it is reflected in these pages.

I also wish to thank the staff of the National Library, the Tuol Sleng Museum and Archives, the Institute of Social Sciences, and the Ministries of Information and Foreign Affairs in Phnom Penh; the Archives d'Outre-Mer in Paris and Aix-en-Provence; the Monash University Library; and the Olin Library at Cornell University.

My colleagues and teachers at the History Department, Monash University, and the School of History, University of New South Wales, were a source of great challenge and encouragement. I would particularly like to thank Ian Black, Fritz Buchler, the late Prescott Clark, Ian Copland, Nguyen Dien, John Ingleson, John Legge, Jamie Mackie, Michael Pearson and Merle Ricklefs. I also owe a considerable debt to Pam Sayers and to my fellow students in the Centre of South-East Asian Studies, Monash University, and to the Christopher Reynolds Foundation.

During two years of field work and research abroad, many people, now friends, provided help and hospitality without which my work would have been impossible. These include the people of Phluang village and a large number of Khmer refugees in France. Special thanks are due to Laor Rampaneenin, Chhun Tong, Poeu Veasna, Keo Vong Sully, Ouch Sean and Keng Vannsak, as well as to John McAuliff, Anthony Barnett, Victoria Butler, Timothy Carney, Murray and Linda Hiebert, Jacques Nepote, Gareth Porter, Bill and Julie Southwood, John Taylor, Serge Thion, Maarten and Sima van Dulleman and Michael

Vickery. Most helpful of all in this respect were many friends in Kampuchea, particularly Sok Sokhun, Nil Sa'unn, Seng Chum, Chum Bun Rong and Sar Sambath.

I need to thank Chanthou Boua and Michael Vickery for providing me with their translations of Hu Nim's and Non Suon's 'confessions'; and Stephen Heder for providing me with transcripts of many of his interviews, which supplement my own, and with other materials.

I wish to thank, finally, the hundreds of Khmers who contributed to the compilation of this history by giving their recollections in interviews. I would also include those who wrote out their life stories under torture in Tuol Sleng political prison from 1976 to 1978. Although these people were forced to confess to grotesque charges of treason in the process (which invariably ended with their execution), their labours produced unique insights into the origins and dynamics of their movement, and historians of Kampuchea owe them a special debt. In what follows I have attempted, as far as is practicable, to let the Khmer sources (both oral and written) speak for themselves, and I hope that, in cases of long quotations or stilted political jargon, the reader will understand what they all went through, and bear with them.

Introduction

A certain euphoria came over Phnom Penh just towards the end of the war at the thought that the fighting was soon to be over. And many people seemed almost ready to welcome the communist troops (which is what eventually happened after the surrender). There were some who went into a panic, however, or wondered whether they should leave if possible. One of these was a friend who had previously been in the Khmer Rouge, and who had always hitherto been prepared to speak frankly in their favour. As the 'Liberation' forces came nearer to victory, his attitude changed to fear, and when he saw that there was no possibility of his leaving he seemed to sink into dejection. When I reminded him of his previous remarks, he said pathetically that he had only been joking. Why else did I think he had left the Khmer Rouge? Of course he disliked communism.

Nobody knew what to expect but this man knew something more than the rest. He seemed to have just remembered it — and I wondered what it was.

James Fenton, 'The Bitter End in Cambodia'.[1]

When the 'Khmer Rouge' marched in to Phnom Penh on 17 April 1975, their ruthlessness surprised most observers. So did the fact that they had triumphed. Communism, like brutality, had long been considered alien to the Khmer people, something that could only be imposed by outsiders. Of course, outsiders had played a critical role in the 1970-75 war; for the last two years, however, it was fought almost entirely by Khmer armies, republican and communist (see Chapter Eight). Further, the Communist Party of Kampuchea (CPK) regime of Pol Pot quickly established a reputation for obsessive secrecy. Not only were all foreigners other than Chinese either expelled from the country, shut up in half a dozen embassy compounds, or, in a handful of cases, shepherded around on guided tours in which they were forbidden to talk to ordinary people;[2] but also, for its first two years in power, the regime published almost no information about itself. Even when the CPK 'declared itself' to the world in September 1977, the membership of its Central Committee, for instance, remained almost entirely unknown to outsiders. Timothy Carney's seminal work, *Communist Party Power in Kampuchea* (1977), based on the surprisingly few captured documents and defectors' accounts from the war period, [3] was one of the rare sources of information about the

CPK and its history. And of course conditions inside the country made it impossible, to say the least, for Khmers themselves to obtain or publicize such information; refugees, therefore, had little to say about the internal dynamics of the movement that had caused them to flee. But it was not only the *modern* history of Khmer communism that was shrouded in mystery.

The CPK's victory came twenty-five years to the day after 200 delegates assembled in Kampot province on 17 April 1950, and formed the communist-led Unified Issarak ('Independence') Front (UIF), ushering in the first period of significant growth of Khmer communism. The next year, 1951, saw the official formation of the Khmer People's Revolutionary Party (KPRP), backbone of the UIF and predecessor of the CPK itself. By the Geneva Conference of 1954, the Khmer communist movement had become a serious political force, a direct product of France's refusal to grant independence to the components of Indo-China – Vietnam, Kampuchea and Laos. As a result of the Conference, King Norodom Sihanouk's government secured international recognition, and the French withdrew. So did the Vietnamese troops who had been backing the KPRP. A thousand of the most experienced KPRP cadres, fearing Sihanouk's repression, followed them to north Vietnam; this opened up critical opportunities for a new, 'domestic' communist leadership, as we shall see. When Sihanouk proclaimed Kampuchean neutrality in foreign affairs soon afterwards, the local Khmer communists, like their counterparts in Vietnam and China, restrained their opposition to his regime. All three communist parties, not to mention Sihanouk himself, or the French, now found it prudent to maintain silence about the role played by the Khmer communists in the struggle for independence. As we shall see in Chapter Three, the KPRP had led not Kampuchea's only anti-colonial resistance movement, but the major one; however, for compelling international reasons, the early history of Khmer communism was very difficult to write. Nor did Western observers delve deeply into the subject. Most, sympathetic to Sihanouk's fiercely independent regime, tended to regard Khmer communism as limited to 'several hundred' Vietnamese proxies.[4] (The fact that after 1954 the KPRP, whatever its political loyalties, received little or no material aid from Hanoi, and was staffed by ethnic Khmer, was overlooked.) An exception was Wilfred Burchett; although a personal friend of Sihanouk, Burchett provided what was not merely the first book in any language on Khmer politics, *Mekong Upstream* (1957): for many years it was the only detailed account of the local communist movement.

Only with the overthrow of the CPK regime by the Vietnamese army in 1979 has it become feasible to attempt a history of that movement. Firstly, the archives of the former political prison, Tuol Sleng, have been made accessible to outsiders by the new government of the People's Republic of Kampuchea (PRK); they contain much rare and valuable documentation on the CPK, mostly in the form of confessional autobiographies, extracted under torture, of communists suspected of dissidence.[5] The most revealing is probably that of Vorn Vet, who had held the No. 5 position in the CPK Politburo until his arrest in 1978; but there are hundreds of others. Secondly, it has become possible for journalists and scholars to interview (in many cases unsupervised) large numbers of Khmers, including veteran communists as well as opponents of the new communist regime. This has become possible also on the Thai border, where more than 200,000 refugees and the remnants of the CPK's Democratic Kampuchea (DK) regime have gathered in search of foreign sanctuary and support. Finally, although much of the material in the National Library in Phnom Penh (for instance all newspaper runs) disappeared at some point after 1975, most of the political records of the French colonial regime during the First Indo-China War have survived there, and at the same time more have been made available in France. This material has not, to my knowledge, been examined by historians. I have attempted to make use of all these sources of information in the pages that follow.

During the course of my research I interviewed at length well over five hundred Khmers, including a hundred refugees in France, who had lived through all or most of the 1975-79 period in Kampuchea. I reached the conclusion that roughly one and a half million perished during those years, that is, more than a fifth of the country's population. Although I will not be dealing with that period here (I intend to make it the subject of a second study), the importance of uncovering the origins of the regime that presided over this disaster is clear.

In the 1940s, when Khmer communism first emerged, where did those wishing to secure their country's independence from France turn? Kampuchea was a small country which was the subject of complex international contention, and there were many potential foreign allies. The most important Khmer nationalist of the early 1940s, Son Ngoc Thanh, looked first to Japan as the 'Liberator and Defender of the Yellow World' (see Chapter Two), and from 1952 to the USA (Chapter Four), without success in either case. Poc Khun, who in 1940s founded the first Khmer Issarak Committee, and Leath Muon, Kampuchea's first woman nationalist, both began their political careers in western Kampuchea in collaboration with an expansionist Thailand. They too soon became disillusioned. On the other side of the country, the Khmer communists of the period, led by Son Ngoc Minh (a pseudonym – no relation to Thanh), turned to Vietnam, a regional power traditionally as ambitious as Thailand but whose communist movement had by 1945 become the major political force in Indo-Chinese resistance to French rule. And it was the Vietnamese communists who eventually delivered the death-blow to the colonialists at Dien Bien Phu in 1954. As their movement developed its momentum towards this goal, so did that of the Khmer communists, under the tutelage first of the Indo-China Communist Party (ICP) and then, from 1951, of the Vietnam Worker's Party (VWP). (See Chapters Three and Four.)

But other alternatives were also tried. Some attempted to rely on Khmers alone, and to drive out foreign intruders of all stripes; in 1949, 'boiling over with revolutionary spirit, with love for their country, race and religion', rebel leaders such as Puth Chhay provided early and violent echoes of the nationalist/racialist cause that much later pre-occupied and eventually destroyed the Pol Pot regime. The first formal Khmer political party was the Democratic Party, founded in 1946. Like Poc Khun and Muon, in their different ways, the Democrats soon tried to open another road to independence by (unsuccessfully) attempting to unite all the Khmer anti-French groups, whatever their foreign backing. When in 1949 the Democrats and another rebel warlord, Achar Yi, produced the first signs of Kampuchean non-alignment, they immediately attracted the interest of the only Asian power yet to become involved in Kampuchean affairs — China. (See Chapter Three.)

The Democrats were stifled by colonial and royal repression, but it was their path that its beneficiary Norodom Sihanouk chose to follow in order to maintain the country's independence, after he had secured power in 1954–55. Although very much a latecomer to the nationalist movement, Sihanouk quickly recognized the strategic stake that so many powers believed they had in his small country. This suited the strategies of the Vietnamese and Chinese communists, but repelled the United States, which sought pro-American counter-weights to Sihanouk's 'unreliable' policies. All it could come up with in this period was Son Ngoc Thanh, who by then, partly because he had failed to obtain support in the anti-French war, was a spent force on the Khmer political scene. The other opposition, the Khmer communists, was now unable to obtain foreign material support, and swung behind Sihanouk's nationalism. This is why Non Suon, whose political career demonstrated many of the problems encountered by the Khmer communist movement, could be described by a conservative French commentor in the early 1960s as 'rather odd but docile'.[6] However, some of the younger, most militant communists planned to take up arms against Sihanouk; they claimed that neither his regime nor their own movement was independent of foreign control. The tribulations and divisions of Khmer nationalism now became those of Khmer communism. The Saloth Sar (Pol Pot) strand of communism, which tended to reject all foreign influences and pressures but particularly those of the Vietnamese, increasingly took on the characteristics of such movements as those led by Puth Chhay and Achar Yi, and likewise attracted Chinese interest. The rise of the Pol Pot group also broached an issue which, like most Khmer political issues (including communism itself), had originated in the ranks of the Buddhist clergy: the struggle between traditionalism and modernist change, between faith and science, and at least in its inchoate beginnings, between countryside and town. (See Chapter One.) But the inter-communist struggle emerged only in the 1960s, and it is to this period that we now turn.

The problems facing the Khmer communist movement in the 1960s resembled those of the Communist Party of India (CPI).[7] Like the Khmer People's Revolutionary Party, the CPI had emerged from the struggle against colonialism as a serious political force, and also found itself confronting a nationalistic, neutralist government which followed generally conservative policies. The contrast in the ways in which the two movements dealt with their respective situations is instructive.

The CPI split in the early 1960s over differing perceptions of the nature of the Indian state, and over the Party's links with

Moscow. The radical, breakaway group, the CPI (Marxist), took the view that independence had not affected the activities of foreign monopolies in India. The old guard CPI disagreed, holding that independence was a 'historic event', and called for a 'broad anti-imperialist front' with the national bourgeoisie.[8] The radical CPI(M) sought only a worker-peasant alliance with the petty bourgeoisie. Now all these issues similarly divided Khmer communists in the 1960s, with the Pol Pot group taking a stance similar to that of the CPI(M), rejecting close ties with Hanoi analogous to those of the CPI with Moscow.

But here the analogy ends. Both Indian parties agreed in 1964 that the time was not yet ripe for social revolution. Even the radicals affirmed the importance of a legal political struggle.[9] It was left to a third group, the Naxalites, who broke away from the CPI(M), to stage an armed insurrection. And it was the Naxalites who threw in their lot with Beijing,[10] while the CPI(M) remained neutral in the Sino-Soviet split (and the CPI, pro-Soviet).

By contrast, the Pol Pot group in Kampuchea adopted not only an underground, insurrectionary strategy, but also close ties with Beijing. Under their leadership, the Communist Party of Kampuchea was the Khmer Naxalite movement. It also, as we shall see in Chapter Six, produced contortions similar to the Naxalite view that the government of India was 'a lackey of US imperialism and [sic] Soviet Social-Imperialism'.[11] At the same time the actions of the Pol Pot regime in power from 1975 to 1979 echoed the words of the Naxalite leader Charu Mazmudar, when he said: 'The annihilation of the class enemy is the higher form of class struggle'.[12]

At its April 1968 Plenum, the CPI(M), which had won over most of the pro-Moscow CPI's following, had again rejected the strategy of 'people's war', and criticised both the USSR and China for interfering in other Parties' affairs. This view was vindicated over the next couple of years as the Naxalite movement was ruthlessly crushed by the Gandhi government, and the CPK rebellion in Kampuchea reached an impasse in 1969 from which only the Chinese and Vietnamese communists (because they won the allegiance of the CPK's declared enemy, Sihanouk) could rescue it. In the words of one man involved as a student in the Naxalite movement: 'Our theory that repression by the bourgeois state will make the masses revolutionary, and increase their resistance to the state, failed ...'[13]

In the meantime, however — and this is part of the tragedy of modern Kampuchea — another theory had failed, this time in Indonesia. The Communist Party of Indonesia (PKI), rejecting the strategy of armed struggle, had hoped for a gradualist programme of reforms backed by President Sukarno, but this hope was thwarted by the abortive coup of September 1965 and its aftermath, which demonstrated Sukarno's powerlessness to protect his allies. The world's third largest Communist Party disappeared overnight in an orgy of bloodletting which claimed over half a million lives. Pol Pot was in Beijing at the time; he is unlikely to have been impressed with the strategy of the PKI, or with the achievements of the CPI(M). He saw the Chinese road as the path to success, and upon his return home he took up Mazmudar's doctrine 'of annihilating class enemies through guerrilla actions' in rural areas.

For its part, the CPI(M) pursued its gradualist strategy and soon won elections for the government of several Indian states, notably the populous West Bengal, which it rules as this is written and has done almost without interruption since the late 1960s (except during periods of federal intervention). Successes on this scale were probably never possible in Kampuchea; nevertheless, in the early 1960s the Khmer communist counterparts of the CPI and CPI(M) did have something to show for their willingness to participate in the Sihanoukist state, as we shall see in Chapter Six.

But even at that stage Pol Pot had already rejected such participation, and this is inadequately explained either by the events in Indonesia or by important differences between the Indian and Kampuchean cases. One difference, the far greater development of democratic institutions in India, was perhaps offset by India's far greater social problems, which would have fuelled communist impatience for revolution more than any aspect of Kampuchea's condition would have galvanized the CPK. Secondly, the small size of Kampuchea (in relation to Vietnam) compared to that of India (in relation to the USSR), certainly strengthened the CPK's desire to avoid domination by the Vietnamese Party (just as it did Sihanouk's foreign policy of making China 'Cambodia's best friend'). But the CPK decision to go to the other extreme, and unlike the CPI(M) to reject Party ties with Hanoi and Moscow to the profit of Beijing, has quite different causes. It was not so much independence that Pol Pot wanted for his party in this period, as independence from the Vietnamese; this desire was reinforced, of course, by the fact that many of his potential Party rivals had received Vietnamese training during the First Indo-China War and many others were doing so in Hanoi at the time.*

Sihanouk's close relationship with China, in combination with his development of secondary education for the first time in the country's history, channelled a *new political phenomenon* – large numbers of politically aware students and teachers – in the direction of Maoism. Most would have been unaware of the problems emerging between Hanoi and Beijing, but at any rate there seemed no reason to reflect on this, or to protest the difficulties Sihanouk placed in the way of contacts with Vietnam (north or south), while sympathy with communism in China was allowed to flourish among Kampuchean youth unhindered. And it did flourish, ironically owing partly to the US intervention in Vietnam. But the very newness of this educated element in Kampuchean cultural life blocked the development of an independent left-wing tradition similar to that of the CPI(M), or, say, the Vietnamese Trotskyists and even Communists in their attempts to remain neutral in the Sino-Soviet split. One need go back no further than the 1950s to find that, in the absence of a modern educational system, it was former Buddhist monks like Son Ngoc Minh and others who bore much of the burden of leadership in the Kampuchean struggle for independence, much more than in any other South-east Asian Buddhist country. In Burma, of course, modern anticolonialism had begun with the formation of the Young Men's Buddhist Association in 1906, but it had already become predominantly secular by the 1930s.[15] In terms of its size and culture, Burma provides a closer analogy to Kampuchea than either India or Indonesia, and this difference is therefore crucial. As the only non-maritime country (apart from Laos) in nineteenth century South-east Asia, Kampuchea came under Western influence much later than the others, and to a much lesser degree. But more of this later.

To discover the important reasons for which Pol Pot adopted the strategy he did in the 1960s, we must look both to his own intellectual and cultural background and that of his closest

* A third difference from the Indian case is that, as Dilip Hiro has pointed out, the foreign policy of the Indian governments tended to 'placate' the pro-Moscow forces in India,[14] while Sihanouk leaned towards China rather than towards the ideological homeland of the KPRP old guard, Vietnam. In each case it was the *neighbouring* communist power which was regarded as more dangerous by the government.

comrades; and also to the fact that his Party allies (like Mok) as well as alternative Party leaders (like So Phim), had had very little education at all, let alone a modern one. (It was this which made an educated Marxist like Hou Yuon an exceptional figure.) In their different ways both factors were products of French colonial rule and its bolstering of traditionalism to stifle modernization, as was Sihanouk's monarchical autocracy. (It was only in the late 1940s that Khmers, among them Pol Pot and Hou Yuon, began to study in France in any significant number, and this was at the height of the struggle for independence.) It is fruitful, for instance, to ask what was the impact on Kampuchean political culture when in the 1930s the French banned the Vietnamese Cao Dai religion because it threatened to undermine the Khmers' 'traditional hatred for their former despoilers'; or when in 1945 the country's republican Prime Minister Son Ngoc Thanh was dragged off 'by the scruff of the neck' into exile in France. Naive collaborator with the Japanese though he was, few Prime Ministers have been treated in such a way. (One might also add both Thanh's failure, after his return home in 1951, to obtain the US support he sought for independence, and his success in obtaining it *after* independence.)

Subsequent events served to intensify the bitterness of those Khmers who had wanted to see their country enter the modern world and hoped for independence to usher in a new era. Many of their hopes were dashed when the International Control Commission certified as 'correct' Sihanouk's dictatorial elimination of opposition political parties from the National Assembly during the elections of 1955. (See Chapter Five.) But they were in many cases obliged to support Sihanouk a decade later when the US sent half a million troops into the country next door. Sihanouk managed to keep the Vietnam War at bay until his overthrow in 1970, but long before then his country's freedom of manoeuvre had become severely limited. The US intervention in Vietnam drained and polarised Kampuchea both economically and politically as early as 1966, and this worked to the advantage of Pol Pot when he returned from China in that year and ordered preparations for a full-scale revolt (1967-70, see Chapter Seven).

The latter was nothing compared with the war of 1970-75, a war which arose from the Vietnam conflict as well as from the local anti-Sihanouk insurgency (even though Sihanouk was now an 'ally' of the CPK). It developed its own fratricidal dimension and smashed Khmer society almost beyond recognition. Up to half the population became refugees. Until late 1973, the most destructive factor involved was the US air force, whose carpet bombardment of populated rural areas gave enormous impetus to peasant fury at the very time when the Pol Pot group was mobilizing its dictatorship against more moderate elements of the revolution, beginning with the Khmer communists who had returned from Vietnam. (See Chapter Eight.) This bombing, which the CIA's Chief Strategy Analyst in Saigon at the time, Frank Snepp, describes as 'the centre-piece of the Administration ceasefire strategy',[16] helped lay the groundwork for ten more years of continuing warfare in Indo-China.

As the Kampuchean civil war dragged on through 1974 and into 1975, the CPK leaders, headed by Pol Pot, strengthened their hold over the communist movement, and this enabled them, upon victory, to carry out one of the greatest forced population movements of modern times – the evacuation to the countryside of the two million inhabitants of Phnom Penh, the news of which was as yet unknown when James Fenton wrote the article quoted at the beginning of this Introduction. With this began a new and increasingly tragic era in Kampuchean history. The unexpected end of the old Cambodia owed a great deal of its bitterness not only to international pressures on the country, but also to what had been happening inside the Khmer communist movement since the early 1960s. This movement, an important factor in domestic politics from the early 1950s, needs to be analyzed in detail and this book is an attempt to do that.

But first it is necessary to consider the social context in which the communist movement grew. Two factors seem to be important: the material social environment, particularly in the countryside, and the intellectual environment.

Modern education in the Kampuchean context has been described as a 'sociological detonator'.[17] This is probably true of the 1960s, but it is important to remember how dry the powder had been kept during ninety years of French rule. In the nineteenth century, most male Khmers spent a period of at least three months (and up to many years) studying in a Buddhist pagoda, or *wat*. However, as one commentator has written: 'There is good reason to believe that the common training acquired by young Cambodians at the pagoda was merely a coloration that quickly washed off and that, in practice, illiteracy was rather widespread. As for 'secondary' and 'higher' education, it catered for no more than several hundred — perhaps several dozen — students per year.'[18]

After 1870 the French made a mild attempt at introducing modern public education, but by 1888 this system had reached its peak with 23 teaching staff, and the number declined to 7 in 1900, when the only remaining primary school for Khmer students was that in Phnom Penh.

A new effort was made from 1903. There were 160 modern primary schools with 10,000 students by 1925, when Khmer-language school books began to be used. But even by 1944, when 80,000 Khmers were attending modern primary schools, only about 500 Khmer students per year completed their primary education certificate. Those enrolled even now made up less than 20 per cent of the male school-age population (few females were enrolled). In the same year, 1944, there were only 1,000 Khmer secondary students. The first high school, the Lycée Sisowath in Phnom Penh, offered a full secondary education only after 1933. Even by 1953 there were still only 2,700 Khmer secondary students, enrolled in eight high schools. (There were of course no universities.) Only 144 Khmers had completed the full Baccalauréat by 1954. The number of primary students had risen to over 200,000 by 1950, but this was still only a small percentage of the school-age population. And in the meantime traditional *wat* schools had been marginalized.[19] So had classical Khmer literature, which, for reasons mostly related to the turmoil of the 1830s and after, had almost disappeared by the late nineteenth century.[20] But the first Khmer prose novel was not published until 1938, and the genre really took root only after 1950.[21] The contrast with Vietnam was stark.

It is clear, then, that the French colonial period (1863-1954) saw a severe decline in traditional intellectual institutions, but did not provide a compensatory development of a modern education system. By the time independence was achieved, only a tiny elite had gained a secondary education, and most of those with a primary education were still teenagers.

One of the major achievements of 'the Sihanouk years' (1954-1970) was the rapid advance of the educational system, which increased in size by 25 per cent each year. That the improvements were more quantitative than qualitative does not invalidate the point that by 1970 nearly all Khmers had the

opportunity of acquiring basic literacy. Still, partly because of
the barren legacy of the French, the enormous expansion was
destabilizing.

The eight high schools in 1953 increased to fifty-four in 1962,
and two hundred in 1967. Enrolments increased tenfold to 27,000
in 1962, and to 150,000 in 1967. Three universities had opened by
1962 and there were nine in 1968, with over 11,000 students. By
1967 there were already over one million educated youth, 20 per
cent of the Khmer population.[22]

These people have been described by a French scholar as 'a
mass of pseudo-intellectuals'.[23] If this was true, they can hardly
be fully blamed for it. The cultural climate under Sihanouk was
such that 'no serious work of history, politics, economics or
literature' appeared in the Khmer language from 1954 to 1970[24]
— or almost none. (Interestingly, 200 novels were published in
the years 1965 and 1966 alone.) Secondly, much of the Khmers'
education was based on inappropriate French text books, and
most of it was non-technical: 'their image of modernism (was)
restricted to the Chinese shops in the main street of the province
capital.'[25]

Finally, the inability of most educated youth, partly because of
the undeveloped economy, to find qualified employment,
together with their detachment from traditional culture, proved
an explosive combination. 'This education tended to create a
larger and larger core of 'detribalized' young people, who no
longer identified with their cultural context, their hierarchy and
their political symbolism. This led therefore to a rupture
between the State and the youth.'[26]

The intellectual atmosphere of the 1960s, in combination with
Sihanouk's close relationship with China, was fertile soil for an
inchoate revolutionary ideology such as Maoism.

But what of the villages whence these youth had come?
Obviously many of them turned to radicalism because of
injustices they had seen there, or poverty they would have to
endure should they be obliged through lack of employment to
return home.

There was never a rigid class structure in the countryside.
Kampuchea before 1970 has even been called 'an almost perfect
rural democracy'.[27] This was true in so far as there was a
relatively equitable distribution of land, at least in the 1950s
(stark contrast to the situation in Vietnam). Between 1950 and

1970 the percentage of farming families who owned no land and lived as tenants or sharecroppers increased from 4 per cent to 20 per cent.[28] Nevertheless, even the later figures are relatively low. Landlordism never really became an explosive national issue in Kampuchea, although Pol Pot later stressed that it was crucial.

Figures from both 1929-30 and 1962 show that the 'middle' half of the farming population owned about half the cultivated land. There were smaller groups of both landlords or rich peasants, and poor peasants. The latter were significant in number by 1962. (31% of the farming families then owned less than one hectare – which made them very poor, given the low rice yields of one tonne per hectare – and all their land represented only 5% of the total cultivated area.) But they were still a minority of the peasantry, and probably remained so in 1970.

Their future role in the 1970s revolution was probably very significant, but it should be borne in mind that even though land was only *relatively* evenly distributed, the vast majority of peasants always owned some land, and even by 1970 the majority still owned enough for a family farm unit.

Nearly all peasants, however, had serious problems obtaining credit and repaying debts. Not surprisingly, since money was usually lent at 12% interest per month, and credit available from rural shopkeepers (overwhelmingly Chinese and Sino-Khmer) returned 10 to 20% per month. Three detailed surveys of significant indebtedness in the Kampuchean countryside between 1952 and 1966 found that it affected 75%, 50% and 67% of peasants respectively.

So rural living standards were always low, despite the richness of the countryside, generally well-watered and with a low population density. Most consumer goods were not usually within the reach of peasants, nor was modern farming equipment. Obviously there was a potential for many peasants to welcome serious reforms, such as the abolition of usury and the establishment of marketing cooperatives, as well as a more equitable redistribution of land.

But as we have seen there was also a much smaller but still significant number of peasants with no land (or very little), and few other enduring ties to their village community. These people, who increased in number when war came in 1970, and particularly their teenage children, might have been expected to *xvi*

welcome a far more radical social upheaval which promised a
direct reversal of their status in relation to the rest of the rural
community.

This discussion of the material and intellectual social context
does not tell us much about the leadership of the Khmer
communist movement. As we shall see in Chapter One, the
movement's initial leadership was primarily Buddhist and rural
in background, while the Pol Pot group was primarily urban and
French-educated. The story of how the latter took the place of
the former, and how each in turn managed to mobilize a
substantial following, is the subject of this book.

Notes

1. *New Statesman*, 25 April 1975.
2. See for instance Richard Dudman, 'Cambodia: A Land in Turmoil', St.Louis
   Post-Dispatch, 15 January 1979, pp.1B–8B.
3. Carlyle Thayer has noted: 'The contrast with Vietnam during the years of US
   involvement there is startling. Captured Viet Cong documents, testimony of
   defectors, and even declassified intelligence reports were widely distributed'.
   See 'New Evidence on Kampuchea', *Problems of Communism,* May-June 1981,
   pp.91-96, at p.91.
4. Maurice Laurent, for instance, claimed that Khmers had made up only 'about
   a tenth' of the 4,000-5,000 communist anti-French rebels active in the country
   (the rest being Vietnamese). In a note published in the same book, however,
   the French commander at the time put Khmer participation in the
   5000-strong 'Viet Minh' forces at fifty per cent, and at a majority in the case of
   'Khmer Viet Minh'. As we shall see in Chapter Four, the actual strength of the
   Khmer communist armies was much closer to 5,000 than to 500. Laurent,
   L'Armée au Cambodge et dans les pays en voie de développement du sudest asiatique,
   Paris, PUF, 1969, pp.45,71,290. See also Prince Sihanouk's statement on
   p.252, below.
5. See 'Bureaucracy of Death', *New Statesman*, 2 May 1980.
6. André Tong, *Sihanouk: La fin des illusions*, Paris, 1972, p.68.

7. Much of what follows is taken from Dilip Hiro, *Inside India Today*, London, 1976.
8. Hiro, *Ibid.*, pp.130, 135-6.
9. *Ibid.*, p.148.
10. *Ibid.*, p.150.
11. *Ibid.*, p.153, quoting a CPI(M-L) statement of April 1969. cf. p.224–5, below.
12. *Ibid.*, quoting Mazmudar in *Liberation*, December 1969.
13. *Ibid.*, pp. 151,164.
14. *Ibid.*, pp.134, 138.
15. See U Maung Maung, *From Sangha to Laity: Nationalist Movements of Burma, 1920-1940*, Australian National University, Manohar, 1980.
16. *Decent Interval*, Penguin 1977, p.61.
17. Jacques Nepote, 'Education et développement dans le Cambodge moderne', *Mondes en Développement*, no. 28, 1979, pp. 767-792, at p.782.
18. *Ibid.*, p.770.
19. *Ibid, passim.* (And Michael Vickery, *Cambodia 1975-1982*, Boston, South End Press, 1984, p.18.)
20. *Ibid.*, p.785. But see reference in Note 21, for details. A periodical of Khmer classical and Buddhist literature, *Kambuja Suriya*, started up in 1927.
21. Hoc Dy Khing, 'Le Développement ecónomique et la transformation littéraire dans le Cambodge moderne', *Mondes en Développement'*, no.28,1979, pp.792-801, at p.796.
22. Nepote, *op.cit., passim.*
23. *Ibid.*, p.782.
24. Charles Meyer, *Derrière le sourire khmer*, Paris, Plon, 1971, p.181.
25. Nepote, *op.cit.*, p.783.
26. *Ibid.*, p.784.
27. Jean Delvert, 'La paysannerie Khmère avant 1970', *Mondes en Développement*, no.28, 1979, pp.732-749, at p.739.
28. The information that follows is drawn from 'Socio-Economic Structure, 1930-70' in the Introduction to Ben Kiernan and Chanthou Boua, *Peasants and Politics in Kampuchea, 1942-81*, London, Zed Press, 1982, pp.4-13.

The Origins of Khmer Politics:
Kampuchea between the Wars

On January 14, the anniversary of the deaths of Liebknecht, Rosa Luxemburg and Lenin, there were no demonstrations or leaflets distributed in Cambodia.

French Sûreté report, 1934[1]

The French Protectorate in Kampuchea, to which King Norodom gave his hesitant assent in 1863,[2] provoked unsuccessful rebellions led by the former Buddhist monks Achar Sva (1864-66) and Pou Kombo (1865-67) and by the King's half-brother Prince Si Votha (1876-77), all of whom also laid claim to the throne. In 1884, French Governor Charles Thomson attempted to persuade Norodom to sign a convention providing for a number of thoroughgoing reforms which France would 'judge it useful to introduce'. When Norodom proved unwilling, Thomson summoned troops and brought three gunboats up the Mekong from Saigon and, as the gunboats stood off the royal palace, he burst into the King's chamber with a detachment of soldiers. Norodom signed. Within six months, rebels, led in part by Si Votha, had established control in most of the country and were threatening the capital. But, as Milton Osborne has written,[3] crucial to the revolt was the role played by provincial officials, who wanted to defend traditional values but also to protect their own social pre-eminence and their right to collect taxes and maintain slaves. For similar reasons they felt threatened by French proposals to introduce private property in land, and to reduce the number of *srok* (districts). The authority they wielded brought virtually the entire Khmer structure into conflict with colonial rule, in both its imperialist and its reformist aspects. Osborne continues: 'In fact, as French sources well show, it was not until France had concentrated some four thousand troops in Cambodia and gained the assistance of the

King and his forces that a shaky calm was achieved, at the end of 1886.'[4]

Si Votha died, unsubdued, at his remote jungle camp in Kratie province in 1892. French control steadily encroached on all spheres of Khmer life and met with little further resistance. Ruling first through a despondent Norodom, and after 1904 through his much more malleable brother, King Sisowath, the French managed to reinforce the traditional image of the monarchy, by such measures as the construction of a large new Royal Palace, while at the same time strengthening their own economic and political hold on the country. In 1916, up to a hundred thousand Khmer peasants marched to Phnom Penh to ask the King to relieve tax and corvée burdens upon them, but most returned home peaceably once Sisowath had given them vague assurances on these matters. This demonstration differed significantly from the 1885-86 uprising, however, in that some of the protestors then assaulted the houses of provincial governors and local officials. The attackers lost seventeen dead in three incidents in the eastern provinces of Kompong Cham and Prey Veng.[5]

In most of South-East Asia, the 1920s and 1930s were a period of considerable unrest. The communist revolts of 1926-27 in Indonesia, the Saya San rebellion of 1930-32 in Burma, the Sakdalista rebellion of 1935 in the Philippines, the Nghe-Tinh Soviets of 1930-31 in Vietnam, and Kommadan's insurgency in Laos (1910-37) all combined to give colonialism a profound shock and in some senses laid the groundwork for successful independence movements after World War Two. In uncolonized Thailand, too, the 1932 coup against the monarchy brought real changes. By contrast, the same period in Kampuchea has been termed 'the years of colonial calm';[6] in a rare outburst of anti-colonialism there in 1925, the Khmer peasants of Krang Leav, Kompong Chhnang province, assassinated a French official, Resident Félix Bardez, who had come to collect taxes during the New Year festival.[7]

But the increasing unrest in neighbouring Vietnam was beginning to have an influence on some members of the Khmer Buddhist community. In November 1922, 'a religious demonstration consisting of a procession of 200 Vietnamese and Cambodian monks' took place in the mountains of the border province of Chaudoc. Ostensibly this was a ceremony to mourn victims of a boat accident on the Bassac River the previous year;

French intelligence suspected nevertheless that 'it might also have a hidden political motive', and dispatched agents to investigate. They reported that 'several individuals considered suspect by the Sûreté' (the Security Service) had used the occasion to 'make requests of the inhabitants in order to raise money in the hope that it would one day be used in the cause of revolution'.[8]

The 1920s: Renovated Indo-Chinese Buddhism

Khmer Buddhism was on the threshold of a major internecine struggle[9] which later played a part in the development of a local anti-colonial movement. Theravada Buddhism in Kampuchea had first been divided by the introduction of the royalist Thommayut Order from Thailand in 1864.[10] Its Khmer founder, Preah Saukonn, had spent most of his life in a Bangkok monastery; the order, which zealously advocated a return to the strict application of Buddhist doctrine, also became known for its close links with the Thai royal family, and made little headway in Kampuchea outside royalist and upper-class circles. Nor did it play the modernizing role it assumed in Thailand.[11] By the 1950s, all but 92 of the 2,650 Khmer *wats* (monasteries), including all village ones,[12] remained associated with the less strict, populist Mohanikay Order.

The establishment of the Higher School of Pali in Phnom Penh in 1914[13] gave impetus to new religious studies, and by the 1920s a rift began to develop *within* the Mohanikay Order itself. The more traditionalist monks were opposed by a modernist group who were 'influenced by western science and alerted to a critical attitude [and] wanted to renew the understanding of the Canonic Texts'.[14] It was through these monks, later known as the Thommakay faction,[15] that Khmer Buddhism first assumed a political role.

An early sign of the rift was probably the dispute within the Buddhist hierarchy over the editing of the first Khmer dictionary.[16] In 1915, King Sisowath appointed a commission of twelve religious scholars and prominent personalities to undertake what proved to be an eight-year task. Only six of them appear to have participated actively in the compilation of the Dictionary, including the Commission's Secretary, Preah Sila-sangvar Hak, a leader of the Mohanikay Order from Phnom Penh's Wat Unnalom. Hak may well have belonged to the modernist faction. In its first meetings, according to its adviser George Coedès,[17] the Commission adopted several reforms in the Khmer spelling system. Another French scholar, Louis Finot, wrote at the time: 'The new spelling achieves appreciable progress by simplifying certain complicated letters and by establishing a more exact correspondence between the Khmer words and their Pali or Sanskrit prototypes.'[18]

However, according to Coedès, writing in the 1930s, the reformers failed to consult the Council of Ministers, which led to much opposition from 'conservatives in principle (there are many in Cambodia)'.[19] The Council opposed the reforms, but the dispute dragged on; a primary school teaching manual printed in the new system was banned, and finally, after a 'small war' which continued throughout 1926, the Council arrested printing of the now completed Dictionary.[20] The King then appointed a new commission, which included only one of the previous six active members and a different Mohanikay representative, which rejected the reforms after two meetings. The Dictionary was completely revised, and finally appeared in 1938. By that time, however, and especially since the foundation of the Buddhist Institute in 1930, the modernist faction had become dominant, and a Thommakay dignitary was soon elected leader of the Mohanikay Order.[21]

Inspired by French scholarship and enlightenment, but repressed by French colonial officialdom through its buttressing of Khmer traditionalism, the best minds of Khmer Buddhism — and arguably of contemporary society — had to find their own way into the twentieth century.

According to a Khmer scholar, Khy Phanra, the dispute between the modernist Thommakay and traditionalist Mohanikay adherents 'was lively and burst out periodically'. 'It took the divisions within the body of the clergy and within the community of believers right down to the pagoda level. Undoubtedly it must have damaged the prestige of the traditional religious order, at the moment of the appearance of Caodaism which claimed to renovate Buddhism.'[22]

Founded in 1921, the Vietnamese Cao Dai sect, which attempted to unify the philosophies of Buddhism, Taoism, Confucianism, spirit-worship and Christianity, began to expand rapidly in Saigon in 1926.[23] In March 1927 its leaders established a 'Holy City' outside Tay Ninh on the Kampuchean border. (It was in Tay Ninh, with its mixed Khmer-Vietnamese population, that Pou Kombo's anti-French uprising had begun in 1865; the following year Pou Kombo had defeated the King's army in eastern Kampuchea with a force of 5,000 rebels, including over 700 Vietnamese.[24]) The French authorities regarded the Cao Dai sect as another anti-colonial movement which aimed to 'bring Vietnamese and Cambodians together', an interpretation perhaps justified in view of what Khy Phanra calls the 'insistent crusade of Caodaism into Cambodia' which began at the end of 1926.[25]

The sect's Pope, Le Van Trung, claimed that Caodaism represented 'Renovated Indo-Chinese Buddhism', and advocated mutual aid among Khmers and Vietnamese to solve material problems.[26] A statue was erected in Tay Ninh purporting to be of the Neak Mian Bon, a figure who in Khmer folk tradition would one day arrive to end all misery. This statue, of a man on a white horse, was in the eclectic Cao Dai practice also identified with the Buddha, and with a Khmer prince whose reincarnation was imminent. It faced in the direction of Phnom Penh. By the end of 1926, large numbers of Khmers, often including entire families and sometimes led by the village monks, were making pilgrimages to the statue.

In early 1927, between two and three hundred Khmers arrived at Tay Ninh daily.[27] Crowds camped around the statue; in June, 5,000 Khmers were reported to have prostrated themselves before it.[28]

The accession to the throne of Sisowath's son Monivong, in August 1927, caused consternation; some of the Khmer pilgrims at Tay Ninh sought an answer from Cao Dai leaders as to why the Norodom branch of the royal family had been bypassed. It was announced that the prince on horseback would, in response to certain incantations, leap into the heavens and take possession of 'his capital', ushering in an era of prosperity. He was now identified as Pou Kombo.[29]

Official attempts to prohibit the exodus at first proved ineffective. The Minister of Religion and the chiefs of both Buddhist Orders in Kampuchea had all denounced Caodaism in May and June. But in November, 8,000 Khmers attended a Cao Dai festival at Tay Ninh.[30] The next month, a proclamation by Monivong was, according to Phanra, 'posted in all the pagodas and subdistrict offices in the affected region'. It described Caodaism as a heresy created by the Vietnamese in order to exploit Khmer naivety, and stressed the King's right to the throne.[31] It did have some impact, but in June 1928, when the Cao Dai claimed that a new king would appear to the Khmers at Tay Ninh, nearly 10,000 Khmer pilgrims made their way there.[32] In the same year other Khmers explained the reason for their visit as follows: 'We have heard that an all-powerful being is here who will reduce our moral and physical misery, diminish our taxes, give land to the poor and heal all diseases. We have come because we are unhappy and believe in the mercy of the all-powerful being.'[33]

Early the next year the pilgrimages began again, and in October 1929 the Cao Dai Pope emphasised the socio-economic factors in a letter to the French Resident-Superior: 'We even have to feed the Khmer pilgrims who remain in our domain for a period ... The recent poor harvest and floods in Cambodia have plunged the Khmer people into real misery. All these calamities have driven the Cambodians to come and ask for the hospitality of our pagoda ... We ask you to have pity on their misery.'[34] But there were also political factors. According to Khy Phanra, in their propaganda the Cao Dai 'attempted to awaken nationalist feeling in the Cambodians, and their activities took an anti-French course; leaflets and speeches therefore promised the converted the imminent arrival of a virtual Garden of Eden, with no taxes or levies and the country rid of the French presence.'[35]

In comparison with the state of affairs in 1916, traditional loyalty to the throne was now under severe pressure, and, as much as any revival of it, legal sanctions such as heavy prison sentences[36] threatened by the King and the colonial authorities, together with police surveillance of the border, brought about a gradual decline in the number of Khmer pilgrims from 1929. Even so, in response to 'secret propaganda', two hundred Khmers went to Tay Ninh for the 1931 Christmas festival, and others made their way there in 1933.[37] However, the 'very firm' attitude[38] adopted by the authorities to these later movements prevented any further occurrences: the Khmer pilgrims were either interrogated, or prosecuted for 'participation in a non-recognised religion' and 'failure to observe police regulations'.[39] From that time onward only Vietnamese were allowed to practice Caodaism. In 1937, a large Cao Dai temple was inaugurated in Phnom Penh,[40] but by then the sect had once again become foreign to nearly all Khmers. Nevertheless the affair had shown that large numbers of Khmers did not view Vietnamese culture solely as something thrust on their ancestors during the Vietnamese invasion of the 1830s.

The French were naturally as concerned as the King about the early implications of the movement. According to Khy Phanra: 'The spread of Caodaism to Cambodia also threatened, in the mind of the Protectorate, to neutralise the 'traditional antagonism' which divided the Khmers from the Vietnamese, and then to unite them in common action against the colonial power.'[41] Phanra quotes one French official as saying that the Khmers' 'strong national sentiment and traditional hatred for their former despoilers [the Vietnamese] constitutes a double immovable wall which must block all subversive projects ...' Another talked of the need, in the same cause, 'to withdraw Cambodian Buddhism from all foreign influence'.[42] Ironically, French attempts in the early 1940s to reshape Khmer Buddhism contributed to the rise of a conscious strand of Khmer nationalism not averse to co-operation with Vietnamese. But the ideology of those Vietnamese was not Caodaism.

The 1930s: The Indo-Chinese Communist Party

As elsewhere, economic crisis struck Kampuchea in the early 1930s, after a decade of expansion of the agricultural economy. (There was still almost no industrial sector.) The world-wide depression meant that rice could not be sold abroad, and its price fell dramatically; the timber industry came to a halt; dried fish production foundered; and finally a poor harvest in 1932 together with the rapid devaluation of the piastre brought social problems of such an order that one French official wrote: 'The least administrative or fiscal blunder would antagonize the masses and risk the most distressing consequences.'[43]

In eastern Kampuchea, particularly Kompong Cham province, were the rubber plantations French companies had established in the 1920s. Nearly all the workers were indentured labourers from Tonkin (north Vietnam), but they also included Chinese, Vietnamese from the south (Cochinchina), local Stieng tribespeople, and Khmers. According to French records: 'The Cambodians are recruited either among the inhabitants of surrounding villages, or among people in an irregular situation because of the taxes, who find temporary refuge in the plantations.'[44]

In 1927, these Khmers were reported to be 'calm',[45] but they cannot fail to have noted the resistance put up by Vietnamese workers and the punishments meted out to them: 'Already 450 coolies have fled. Most of them have been recaptured and sent back to Memut, and have undergone punishment that should frighten the rest.'[46]

Not surprisingly, the first communists reported to be active in Kampuchea were Vietnamese. On 22 October 1929, militants active in Phnom Penh and several provincial capitals were arrested by the Sûreté. They included members of three different anti-colonial organisations — Ho Chi Minh's *Thanh Nien* (Revolutionary Youth League) founded in 1925, the Annam Communist Party, and the Vietnam Nationalist Party (VNQDD). As a result of these arrests, the Sûreté claimed that 'revolutionary agitation in Cambodia had been almost entirely annihilated'.[47]

The Vietnamese communist movement was unified the next year with the formation, in February, of the Vietnam Communist Party (*Viet Nam Cong San Dang*), and a VCP cell soon began operating in the Chup rubber plantations in Kompong Cham.[48]

Then, in early April 1930, the first Chinese Communist Party (CCP) cell in Kampuchea was established in Kampot province (the region of the greatest concentration of Chinese residents),[49] with the co-operation of the VCP.[50] The founder was Huynh Nghi, who was recruited by a resident of Phnom Penh, Lao Hun, apparently a Vietnamese-born Chinese. The cell met in a Kampot barber shop established specifically for the purpose. (Huynh Nghi also established 'The General Union of Cambodian Workers' (*Cao Mien Chong Kong Houy*), which he told local Chinese was a mutual aid association similar to one formerly run by the Kuomintang's Kampuchean branch.) By the end of the month, the cell comprised five members, all of whom distributed leaflets, supplied to them from Phnom Penh by Lao Hun, in the streets of Kampot on May Day. Three more cells were soon formed in small towns nearby. On 21 July, Nghi returned to Phnom Penh for more literature.

Lao Hun introduced him to a Vietnamese activist, and to a former teacher of Chinese characters named Ta Nien, a portrait painter in Phnom Penh. Nien is described in separate sections of the same Sûreté report as both Vietnamese and Chinese.[51] It seems that he was an escapee from the Kuomintang repression of the Canton Commune in 1927; he may have arrived by way of Saigon. Nien gave Nghi copies of leaflets in both Vietnamese and Chinese to be reproduced for distribution on 1 August. Nghi and Hun returned to Kampot the next day, where they printed six hundred copies of the leaflets and fifty posters. Hun returned to Phnom Penh with about half of these, and others were sent to the three district cells in Kampot.

On the night of 31 July, three hundred leaflets and fifty posters were distributed and displayed in five towns in Kampot province. Three cell members were arrested on the spot, however, and this led to thirty-six further arrests. Huynh Nghi and Lao Hun each received five years' gaol and ten years' exile, and ten others also received gaol sentences.[52] The Sûreté regarded this affair as 'proof of the Sino-Vietnamese alliance' designed to engineer 'co-penetration' of Kampuchea by the two communist parties, but was unable to identify the agent reponsible for liaison between them.[53]

It is interesting that in Phnom Penh *on the same night*, some of the same leaflets were distributed by the first Khmers known to have become involved in communist activities.[54] Ben Krahom, a 24 year-old coolie at the Electricity Works, two teenage Vietnamese from the Collège Sisowath, as well as two teenage Khmers from Saravann monastery, Sau Mel and Prak Sim, and Krahom's Vietnamese wife were all arrested after distributing a significant number of leaflets. They had also hung from the trees three red banners 'with Soviet emblems' which bore slogans in Vietnamese calling on the population to establish 'a workers' government'.

The leaflets were also in Vietnamese, but one was signed 'The General Union of Cambodian Workers'; it called for the overthrow of the Kuomintang in China, and protested against the increased taxes to which local Chinese were subjected. The leaflet and others also urged the struggle of the proletariat against imperialism. Some were signed 'Communist Party, Executive Committee for Cambodia' and others 'Communist Youth League Committee for Cambodia' or the 'Provisional Executive Committee for Cochinchina'.

Krahom and his wife said in court that they had been given the leaflets by two Vietnamese, a guardian at the Electricity Works and a travelling hairdresser (confessions which do not seem to support their simultaneous claim that they thought they were distributing cinema programmes). Sau Mel and Prak Sim said they had been given them by a Vietnamese accountant. A Sûreté search of the homes of these three Vietnamese yielded no evidence of their involvement. Krahom and the two Vietnamese youths were sentenced to eighteen months' gaol, their two

Khmer companions to one year.[55] They all disappeared from sight at this point.

In October 1930, the VCP changed its name to 'Indo-China Communist Party' (ICP) (*Dang Cong San Dong Duong*), at the first plenary meeting of its Central Committee in Hong Kong. The change was made in response to a Comintern directive which stressed internationalism, and ran counter to views expressed by Ho Chi Minh at the February meeting — he was not present at the October one — to the effect that the word 'Indo-China' implied too broad a scope for Vietnamese communist activity.[56] Ho Chi Minh's own response to the Comintern's directive was to support a proposal from the VCP Committee in Central Vietnam that the name should not be changed until similar committees had been established in Laos and Kampuchea.[57] The October meeting rejected this, however, and stressed that despite social and ethnic differences the three countries of Indo-China were of necessity 'closely related to one another politically and economically'.[58] But it seems true that the continuing Vietnamese nationalist character of the ICP, expressed in a Party newspaper in February 1931, required as a minimum not the triumph of *communism* throughout Indo-China, but that of independence movements: 'If the Vietnamese revolution succeeds but French imperialism is lurking in Laos and Cambodia, the revolutionary power in Vietnam will be shaky.'[59]

This strategic appraisal, though combined intermittently with proletarian internationalist policies to sponsor and assist Khmer communists in times of common military struggle against outside powers, remained the cornerstone of the Vietnamese communist view of Kampuchea for the next half century.[60]

Even as the Hong Kong meeting ended, revolutionary activity recommenced in Kampuchea, as did French repression. During October 1930, leaflets were distributed and meetings held among Vietnamese residents in Phnom Penh and in five villages of Svay Rieng. In the same month, on the anniversary of the establishment of the Chinese Republic, five CCP flags, and leaflets in Vietnamese calling for a general strike and demonstrations in support of the Nghe Tinh Soviets, were found in Svay Rieng and Prey Veng. Seven ethnic Vietnamese were arrested, one of whom was sentenced to eight months' gaol and another to three. The *father* of a Phnom Penh suspect was also arrested and died in prison.[61]

On the night of 6 November, the eve of the thirteenth anniversary of the Russian Revolution, Phnom Penh was lashed by a violent storm and suffered an electricity blackout. Soon after, leaflets were found at the port, in the Post Office letter-box, and in the town centre. They appealed for a revolt and gave a brief history of the Russian Revolution, and were signed by the 'Communist Party, Provisional Executive Committee for Cochinchina'. A Vietnamese mechanic was held responsible but could not be found, and two pedicab drivers who had assisted him also disappeared. Two weeks later, more communist leaflets were discovered in Svay Rieng.[62]

But the repression was having its effect. The Indo-China Communist Party and its affiliated organizations were already suffering from the violent French repression of the Nghe Tinh Soviets, and Kampuchea served largely as a place of asylum. But there were difficulties there too. On 10 March, a report by a leader of the 'Chinese Special Committee' of the ICP in Saigon lamented: '*Cambodian Special Committee:* After the work of 1 August last year, this Committee was destroyed by our enemies and up to now has not been able to be re-organized. Although I have written to the responsible cadres on several occasions, inviting them to recommence their work, I have received no report. This is apparently due to the change of address of the correspondents or to transfer of these cadres. I have also decided to send delegates to inspect the work in different localities in order to restore the sections in Cambodia ... and reinforce the political leadership, but because of lack of funds these plans are difficult to implement.'[63]

On 16 March, the ICP Executive Committee for Cochinchina 'ceased distributing tracts in Cambodia on the occasions of revolutionary anniversaries'.[64] Nevertheless, on 31 March and 5 April, after a worker at the Russey Keo Electricity Plant had been killed in an industrial accident, leaflets appeared at work-sites calling for an electricity workers' strike, improved conditions and higher wages.[65] The Vietnamese students at the Phnom Penh technical school staged a strike which ended only when four ringleaders were arrested and the rest threatened with dismissal.[66] In Kampot, 'propaganda in the prisons' led Khmer guards at Kompong Trach gaol to desert with three prisoners.[67]

However, during March and April 1931, almost all the members of the ICP Central Committee were arrested, and even the regional committees were dispersed.[68] Leaflets found in the streets of Phnom Penh calling on the proletariat to celebrate May Day, had been distributed a day late.[69] This proved to be the last such incident in Kampuchea for some time. By the end of May the Sûreté was able to report that 'calm had continued to reign in the Cambodian capital and provinces', claiming it had made a 'clean sweep of all the revolutionary organizations' there.[70] This claim had most truth in the case of the Chinese Communist Party.

In February 1932, a number of people from Cochinchina went to Phnom Penh to try to establish a Trotskyist cell there. They were immediately expelled and sent back to Cochinchina.[71] It would seem that the revolutionary vacuum was now filled by a semi-autonomous 'Transbassac Committee' of the ICP, founded by 'nine members of peasant origin' who were 'local agitators'[72] in western Cochinchina. This area, comprising Travinh, Soctrang and Rach Gia provinces, had come under Vietnamese rule well over a hundred years before but still had a large Khmer population, known in Kampuchea as Khmer Krom or 'Lower Khmers'.

The Transbassac Committee took charge of ICP activities both here and in Kampuchea, and seems to have been responsible for recruiting the first Khmer party member. This was Thach Choeun, who was born in the Mekong Delta in 1904 and joined the ICP in 1932 while working as a fisherman on the Tonle Sap. The ICP assigned him an unknown political 'mission' there.[73] The Party's programme, elaborated in 1932, included not only the defeat of French colonialism, but also 'the overthrow of the indigenous dynasties, the court of Annam, the kings of Cambodia and Laos, with all the mandarins and notables [and] confiscation of all their possessions'.[74] But anti-colonial activity of any kind in Kampuchea remained minimal, despite the ICP's call for a 'fraternal alliance of all the peoples of Indo-China' and its promise of 'the right of the Cambodians, Laotians and all other peoples of Indo-China freely to manage their own affairs'.[75]

Meanwhile, some ICP leaders who were outside the country at the time of the Nghe Tinh uprisings had been undergoing training at the University of the Toilers of the East, in the Soviet Union. One, Tran Van Giau, soon managed to return to Vietnam and began to rebuild the ICP structure in Cochinchina.[76] During 1933 he was able to do so in the east and centre of the colony.[77] Giau was arrested and gaoled towards the end of that year, but he reappears later in the story. A Sûreté official wrote in 1934: 'It is because of the efforts of the Transbassac Committee that we have seen the reactivation of communist activity in Cambodia. This push towards the north stems from the agitators hunted down by the repression, who are offered very hospitable asylum by their compatriots now noticed in Cambodia. In exchange the Cochinchinese escapees bring them propaganda newspapers and brochures. There is no cause for surprise at the ease with which communist bases have been created in the provinces of Kampot, Prey Veng and Takeo, where cells and agricultural unions appear to have been established. The border that separates Cochinchina from these provinces is purely symbolic.'[78]

The same source noted, however, that 'propaganda in Cambodia is directed only at peasants of the Annamite race', while in Phnom Penh 'a workers' union has been created, whose members are recruited principally among railway employees'. 'We have not yet come across a single case of contamination of Cambodians'[79] — only later, it seems, did Choeun's activities come to light. In November 1933 the Sûreté did report a case of agitation among Khmer farmers: 'A certain number of tobacco growers, particularly in the Kompong Cham region, intend to create a Union of Mekong Growers, following the lead of the analogous Cochinchinese organization ... One of the immediate aims of this Union would be to assure protection for the growers against the actions of the *Manufacture Indochinoise des Cigarettes*, which fixes the selling price of tobacco at its whim.'[80]

However, there was no ostensible sign of communist involvement in this. In contrast, the Chup cell of the VCP, now part of the ICP, still consisted only of ethnic Vietnamese workers even though Khmer workers were apparently taking some part in local industrial action.[81] For most of the 1930s, revolutionary activity in Kampuchea remained limited to ethnic Vietnamese — whether rubber plantation workers, petty officials, skilled workers in the towns, or peasants along the border — and to members of the Chinese community. The words of a Sûreté official, written in 1929, still held true: 'In fact the Cambodians, in spite of the proximity of the Vietnamese and Chinese, have not yet learnt to organize meetings to hatch conspiracies. They know how to gather together only on pagoda feast-days and for funeral ceremonies, which are not very suitable for intrigues.'[82]

The spirit of intrigue and adventure, as with social unrest, found its expression chiefly in rural banditry, which became endemic in Kampuchea in the 1930s. But most of the bandits' exploits were acccomplished at the expense of fellow Khmers and rich Chinese, rather than the French administration. Ravaging the countryside at will in groups of up to fifty, they specialized in robbery, murder, rape and cattle-stealing. In Kompong Chhnang in 1936, four bandit groups joined forces and took a blood oath of mutual loyalty until death, becoming 'like five fingers of the same hand' and resolving to admit no others into their select brotherhood. Members wore amulets, and shirts bearing mystical symbols ensuring invulnerability. The leader of these bands, who, according to the French-language paper *Le Khmer*, had received a good education, was a man named Som. On visits to his native village he would saunter around 'in broad daylight, his rifle in a sling ... flouting the sub-district authorities, who feared him, with impunity'. Som's followers had only five rifles, but a more critical weakness was the fact that the local villagers joined the Sûreté in hunting them down through the forest.[83]

One of the most formidable bandit leaders was Prak So. From his base in the forest of Dauntey in Kompong Cham (which much later was the headquarters of the Khmer communist leader of the Eastern Zone, So Phim), he terrorized whole provinces. While on the run So found refuge in a pagoda and, in *Le Khmer's* words, had the advantage of the 'native telegraph' which 'travels faster than the transmissions of our most modern radios'. But again, it was fellow Khmers, in the service of the French, who gained So's confidence and managed to disarm and execute him in December 1935.[84]

Within weeks, one of So's 'faithful lieutenants', Ouk Chell, who had escaped from prison in 1932, assumed So's mantle. His name quickly became feared 'by the peaceful Cambodian populations in Kratie, Svay Rieng, Kompong Cham, Prey Veng and Kampot provinces' — a wide area indeed. *Le Khmer* reported that Chell's deeds (for which he was sentenced *in absentia* to forty-nine years' hard labour), his skill in constantly eluding the forces of order, and 'the terror which he made reign over the Cambodians' earned him the popular title of Luong Chell (King Chell), an interesting comment on contemporary perceptions of royalty. Fear of his terrible reprisals meant that 'no Cambodian' would serve as guide or informant in the hunt for the 'King of the Bandits'. But Chell was eventually killed in February 1936 after being surprised in his jungle hut; a Khmer official who had done survey work in that area, and had befriended the Phnong tribespeople there, was able to secure their help in tracking Chell down. According to *Le Khmer*, 'the good news spread and the terrorized inhabitants uttered a sign of relief'.[85]

The contrast between this and the political turmoil in the Chinese community in Kampuchea could not be more striking. As reported by the Sûreté in mid-1931, the latter was closely linked to events in China itself: 'What, therefore, has been the attitude of the local Kuomintang to the communist propaganda? In our last annual report, we expressed the fear that the conflict noted within the KMT party between the employers, mostly loyal to the Nanking government, and the workers, won over to the cause of Wang Ching-wei, could easily be resolved in favour of the extremists. This did not occur, firstly because of the lack of leaders capable of co-ordinating the masses and seizing power; secondly, and especially, because the workers, disgusted with the capitalist policy followed by the local KMT leaders, ended up breaking completely with a party that trampled underfoot its primitive democratic organization and no longer responded to the aspirations of the proletariat. Some of them did not even hesitate to solemnly affirm their contempt for the policy followed, and thus 220 partisans of the extremist Cantonese leader tendered their resignations to the local KMT.'[86]

In an interesting reversal of political rhetoric, Semaun, the Indonesian delegate to the Comintern, in this period described in a much more pessimistic fashion the problems faced by communists in Kampuchea, where the organization 'remained weak in the development of revolutionary work': 'Most of the enterprises ... are still in the hands of Chinese who, during strikes and disorders among the local Malay [sic] population, benefit from the protection of the French authorities and are able to replace their Malay workers with Chinese coolies.'[87]

Although two CCP cells in Kompong Cham and one in Kratie survived the 1930 repression and its aftermath,[88] Chinese communist activity now dropped off dramatically. Only a single meeting in Phnom Penh, attended by twenty members of the 'General Union of Chinese Workers' in May 1938, was reported by the Sûreté; the theme of the address was the overthrow of imperialism and capitalism.[89] Leadership of that struggle, to the extent that it existed, had in Kampuchea passed definitively to the ICP.

Tran Van Giau was released from gaol in February 1934, but found himself on account of this considered suspect by his comrades.[90] Perhaps in an attempt to win the confidence of the Transbassac Committee, he tried to develop the ICP on a decentralized basis, and confided 'secret documents' to the 'Travinh group', in an ethnically mixed part of the western delta. He planned to hold a general assembly of the ICP in Saigon, in order to reunify the movement and choose a delegate to the next Comintern Congress in Moscow. 'With this purpose in mind, he instructed a female militant — a proven liaison agent — to negotiate in Phnom Penh the sending of a representative of the communist organizations of Cambodia, but the leaders in Phnom Penh were still under the influence of the denigration campaign against Tran Van Giau and refused to participate in the projected 'general assembly".[91]

It was in this context that the ICP leaders then wrote an important 'letter to comrades in Cambodia', which stressed: 'There is no question of a separate Cambodian revolution. There is only a single Indo-Chinese revolution. Indo-China being under the domination of a single imperialist government, all the revolutionary forces must be unified and grouped under the direction of a single party, the ICP. Cambodia does not have the right to a separate Cambodian communist party. The communists there must unite and create a regional committee which will be placed under the leadership of the ICP Central Committee. To create a Cambodian communist party would harm the revolution by dividing the forces of the proletariat, and by breaking the leadership of unity of the ICP, it would be to fall into the trap of the policy of racial division, set by imperialism.'[92]

The 1932 ICP programme was now re-interpreted as encouraging 'the freedom of unification and centralization of the military and economic forces of the liberated peoples'.[93]

In June 1934 Tran Van Giau redoubled his efforts to win the co-operation of the Transbassac Committee. He eventually succeeded, after the latter ran into serious trouble from August onward and a number of its leading members were arrested. Delegates from ICP organizations in Cochinchina, Annam and Kampuchea met in Cholon on 7 November, and formed the ICP 'federal committee for Southern Indo-China'. The Transbassac Committee merged with this ICP structure, becoming the regional committee for western Cochinchina (including Travinh) and retaining responsibility for communist activity in Kampuchea.

By this time, according to Vietnamese sources, there were five communist cells in Kampuchea — in Phnom Penh, Kandal, Kompong Cham and Kratie.[95] Their activities involved about a hundred people. The Sûreté, for its part, had information on three Party members, sixty members of affiliated clandestine worker and peasant unions, and three 'liaison stations', all in Phnom Penh and Kandal, in particular Loeuk Dek district.[96] This district was inhabited mainly by Vietnamese peasants regarded by the French as 'knockers' (*frondeurs*), who 'voluntarily join in all forms of opposition to the government'.[97]

Tran Van Giau, together with a representative of communists in Kampuchea,[98] almost certainly an ethnic Vietnamese, then left for the ICP's First Congress in Macao in March 1935. Resolutions submitted to the Congress included an attempt to analyse the minority nationalities of Indo-China. These were divided into three categories: tribal groups that lived in a 'primitive and natural' economy; those that were 'feudal with vestiges of the tribal system'; and peoples such as the Khmer and Lao whose economies were characterized by 'nascent capitalism with many vestiges of feudalism'. As for their political rights, the 1932 ICP programme was re-stated: 'After the eviction of the French imperialists from Indo-China, these minorities will have the right to manage their own affairs up to and including the right to secede and form an independent state and to adopt the political regime of their choice. The worker peasant and soldier Soviet government of Indo-China undertakes not to interfere in their internal affairs.' The eventual aim was a 'Union of Soviet Republics of Indo-China'; each people would be free to join on 'a basis of liberty and equality' and, while co-operating in foreign affairs and defence matters, would 'enjoy complete autonomy within their territorial limits'. The Union would form part of a 'World Union of Soviets'.[99]

In the real world, the small communist organization in Kampuchea was seriously threatened. On 15 May 1935, the Sûreté raided a pharmacy in Loeuk Dek and arrested four militants. Sixteen subsequent raids in Phnom Penh led to several more arrests and to the capture of numerous party documents. By June, the three leading communists in Kampuchea, including Chau Van Giac, a member of the federal committee for

Southern Indo-China, were arrested, along with about ten members of agricultural and workers' unions and four women. Giac was sentenced to two years gaol and five in exile. The Sûreté reported 'the almost complete destruction of the party organization in Phnom Penh'.[100] Thach Choeun, perhaps still the only Khmer ICP member, fled to Cochinchina and took a job at a print-works in My Tho.[101]

In the first half of 1936, the French reported 'no clandestine revolutionary activity' in Kampuchea.[102] But in May 1936, the more tolerant Popular Front government took office in Paris with the support of the French Communist Party, and soon afterwards rubber-plantation workers in Chup and Thmar Pitt staged a strike.[103] In July the ICP plenum launched a 'new semi-legal stage' in its development.[104]

After Chau Van Giac's release from gaol, he and other Vietnamese activists made several attempts to re-establish the ICP in rural Kampuchea, but they were all tracked down and deported, while the Khmer population, according to Sûreté reports, showed 'complete indifference'.[105] In November and December 1936 there were protests and strikes among rubber-plantation workers and Chinese garage workers in Phnom Penh, and even among pedicab drivers, who were probably Khmer, but these were not considered by the Sûreté to be indicative of a 'social movement'.[106]

The ICP was now publishing legal newspapers in Hanoi, which were 'read in the five countries of the Union', their influence extending 'well beyond' Tonkin. *Le Travail*, for instance, had 'numerous subscribers' in Phnom Penh, but it is unlikely that many would have been Khmers.[107] Two years later, the Sûreté reported that even a Trotskyist journal, *Thang Muoi* ('October'), was being circulated and sold in Phnom Penh, but again, by Vietnamese rather than Khmer activists.[108]

The Rise of the Modern Khmer Elite

As we have seen, more than fifty years of colonial rule had seen the establishment in Kampuchea of only one secondary educational institution, the Collège Sisowath, which became a High School only in 1935.[109] Around 1899, the French explorer and administrator Auguste Pavie had taken ten or more Khmers to study in France, and at his request a special section of the prestigious École Coloniale in Paris had been established for

Indo-Chinese students. But in 1905, apparently, only one Khmer was enrolled there, and the reason is perhaps made clear by an account of the preparatory school, by Prince Phetsarath of Laos: 'Because I had studied only to the level of the second grade of elementary school, I could hardly keep up with the other students. I couldn't understand anything the teacher taught and found it a waste of time. There was no way to keep up with the Vietnamese students who had already had secondary schooling in Vietnam. The academic level my brother Chitarath and I found at the École Coloniale had long been a problem for Lao and Cambodian students who had come there before us. Because of this, those who returned home after three or four years at the École Coloniale had only a little knowledge – not commensurate with the time they had spent studying.' The following year, King Sisowath arrived on a visit from Phnom Penh and enrolled two of his sons and a Khmer official at the École. Although a tutor was soon provided, the three Khmers lasted only a year, and returned home in July 1907. It was only Sisowath's third son (the future King Monivong), whom he had enrolled in a military academy, who continued his studies in France.[110] The others left with Phetsarath's brother, who had been 'frightened' by punishments that Phetsarath had received for making complaints and suggestions about their education without consulting the school's principal.

It is fruitful to compare this experience with that of students from Burma, the third Southeast Asian Buddhist country under colonial rule. (Of course, Kampuchea was colonized much later than Burma, but that still does not explain fifty years of colonial neglect.) In 1908, six Burmese students returned to Rangoon after qualifying in England as barristers; they joined the proto-nationalist Young Men's Buddhist Association, which had been founded in 1906 and gave rise to a vernacular newspaper, *Thuriya* ('The Sun'), in 1911.[111] The emergence of a Kampuchean counterpart only came twenty-five years later. (In that year, 1936, there were less than sixty thousand Khmer students in *primary* schools.)

The almost total lack of modern education in Kampuchea under French rule had severe implications for Khmer society and politics once the country had emerged into the twentieth-century world in the 1940s. 'Intellectuals' were few and far between. But, in the second most economically backward country in East Asia, they constituted not only a motive force for change in their own right but also, in a real sense, a 'separate class'. (This even became a political issue in the Pol Pot period.) For a long time they were easily kept in place by the forces of conservatism and traditionalism. Where they did manage to act independently in politics, they often displayed a certain contempt for their uneducated compatriots. But, partly because intellectual activity was traditionally associated with monks, they also attracted enormous prestige and deference. And these tendencies affected the communist movement as much as they did other sections of society.

Modernism was repressed as a matter of routine by colonialists and royalists alike. This often provoked great bitterness among educated people, who were forced to bide their time. Finally, with the rapid expansion of the education system in the 1960s, they got their chance, as we shall see in later chapters.

Just as the founding of the Higher School of Pali made an impact on national life, so the outbreak of World War I in the same year provided Khmers with an unprecedented view of the international scene. When in 1915 King Sisowath appealed to his people to pray for the French army, the reaction reported by French officials was one of belief that the colonial forces were weakening, while the general mobilization of civil servants gave Khmers the impression that the French lacked manpower.[112] Indeed, an unknown number of Khmers were sent to fight alongside French troops in Europe. After the return of these riflemen at the end of the war, French officials in the provinces stipulated that they should disperse as quickly as possible and would not be permitted to organize future social reunions.[113] But at least one man, an interpreter for the troops named Pach Chhoeun, became an important figure of emergent Khmer nationalism twenty years later, as we shall see. In the meantime, however, he established himself in a garage business in Phnom Penh.

Another Khmer who had fought in France, Khim Tit, chose a different career and joined the colonial service. By 1945 he was governor of Kampot province, and threw in his lot with the traditional elite. In the summer of that year, when the royal family and others felt that the traditional political structure was under threat, Khim Tit called in the French to re-establish their dominance. (Pach Chhoeun, by contrast, then requested Vietnamese communist assistance. See Chapter Two.) In the late 1940s, Tit joined a pro-monarchist, authoritarian political movement — headed by Lon Nol (President of the Khmer Republic in the 1970s) — which nevertheless strongly advocated independence.

It was the royal family which produced the founder of the first conservative political party, Prince Norindeth. He was a grandson of both the half-brother kings, Norodom and Sisowath. (Norodom Sihanouk was a great-grandson of both.) In 1946, Norindeth founded the Liberal Party, which was both pro-French and 'dedicated to the maintenance of the status quo'.[114]

In the 1920s a small number of Khmer Krom, benefitting perhaps from the French citizenship granted to the inhabitants of Cochinchina (a Colony, rather than a Protectorate like Kampuchea), made their way to France to obtain a higher education. They included a founder of modern Khmer nationalism, Son Ngoc Thanh. Born in Travinh in 1908, Thanh attended primary school there and in Saigon, before going to France for secondary education in Montpellier and Paris. He completed a teaching diploma there and studied law for a year at the University of Paris, returning to Indo-China in 1933. After working briefly as a clerk at the Phnom Penh Library, he became a magistrate in Pursat, then a public prosecutor in the capital and finally Deputy Director of the Buddhist Institute.[115] It was presumably during this period that Thanh met Pach Chhoeun; in 1936 the two men established the first Khmer-language newspaper, *Nagaravatta* (Pali for 'Angkor Wat'). As Michael Vickery has written, this newspaper 'advocated very moderate reforms: more Cambodian participation in commerce, greater educational opportunities, equal treatment for Cambodians and French, all of which probably worried the traditional Cambodian elite more than the French, since their realization would have undermined the old oligarchy.'[116]

The rift between Khmer traditionalists and modernists that we have seen in the religious sphere was beginning to appear elsewhere too; like the rift between Pach Chhoeun and Khim Tit, it was a political current that, in the final days of World War Two, would cut right across that of independence.

Nagaravatta was of course an expression of subdued anti-colonialism; it publicized the occasional overt example of French oppression, daring enough at the time. But its world-view was, in Vickery's words, 'strictly shopkeeper capitalist and nationalist'; it urged Khmers 'to go into business in order to break the monopoly of the other ethnic groups and thereby strengthen the position of the Khmer within their own country'.[117] This perception of Khmer nationalism (and modernism) was to make leaders of the *Nagaravatta* group receptive to the appeal of Japanese fascism, or as Son Ngoc Thanh later termed it, 'National Socialism'. But unlike other sections of the emergent Khmer elite, Thanh's group was not at all anti-Vietnamese. In 1938, Thanh founded the *Yuvasala,* a youth organisation 'started for the explicit purpose of fostering fraternal relations between the two traditionally hostile peoples'; in the 1940s Thanh favoured the teaching of the Vietnamese language in Khmer schools, seeing it as a channel for the introduction of the modernizing ideas that had developed in Vietnam.[118] While mainly preoccupied with ousting French rule, Thanh and his followers saw Thailand rather than Vietnam as the most predatory of Kampuchea's neighbours.

Thailand had seized the north-west and northern Khmer provinces of Battambang, Siemreap and Stung Treng in 1794; only in 1907 did a Franco-Thai treaty secure their return to the Protectorate. In the late nineteenth century, the Thai had appointed a local Chinese named Keo as chief of the district of Samrong (later Oddar Meanchey province). After the cession of the territory, Keo's son Leath established a cattle ranch, a rare commercial enterprise in Kampuchea at the time. Leath married Thoeup, a member of the small Kuoy tribe in the north of Kompong Thom; their daughter Muon, born in 1900, grew up as an illiterate cow-girl on the ranch. Her adopted younger brother, Kao Tak, who was also part-Chinese, married a Sino-Khmer woman from Surin, a principally Khmer province across the border in north-east Thailand; he was accorded Thai nationality. Muon and Tak, with their racially diverse backgrounds, later played key roles in the anti-colonial struggle: Tak, who became a stock merchant in the 1930s, worked closely with the Thai (and later with Son Ngoc Thanh), while Muon adopted a more independent stance, as we shall see in the next chapter.[119]

Other influences from Thailand were also at work, especially after the 1932 coup had established a constitutional monarchy there. Vietnamese communist sources suggest that the development of Khmer anti-French feeling in the north-west, although still rather mild, was not hampered by fear of the re-establishment of Thai domination.

In 1933 the people of Battambang rose up against taxation. In the

first five months of that year, French soldiers and police involved
in the repression fought insurgents on seven occasions ...

Of note was a movement led by two progressive monks, Achar
Miet and Achar Prinh, in the 1933-35 period. Achar Miet joined
the Buddhist Order in Siam and was influenced by the progressive
democratic movement in Siam at that time. When he returned to
Kampuchea he and Achar Prinh called on the people to struggle
for democratic reforms. On the occasion of a Bon Kathen
religious festival, they organized a meeting to protest the
repressive and exploitative regime of French colonialism. The
demonstration was repressed. Achar Miet was arrested. Shortly
afterwards Achar Prinh died of illness.

There is no documentary evidence to show that these spontaneous movements were connected with the Indo-china Communist Party. But the progressive thought content of these
movements clearly expressed the revolutionary demands of
Kampuchea in the new era.[120]

And it was in Thailand that the Khmer Issarak ('independence')
movement was to be founded, in 1940, by Poc Khun, whom we
shall meet in the next chapter.

Around 1939, Son Ngoc Thanh, Pach Chhoeun and others
began visiting different *wats* and talking to the monks about the
intellectual 're-awakening' of the Khmer, as well as discreetly
criticizing French rule.[121] According to one of the group,
Bunchhan Mul, 'the most prominent character of all' was
Chhoeun: 'Pach Chhoeun was the only one who visited many
places – many more than the others. That is why people knew
him, recognized him more easily and liked him more than the
others. There were some places he could not get to, but the
people came and carried him to the agreed meeting place.'[122]

It is probably coincidental that the ICP member Thach
Choeun, who had returned from Cochinchina in 1937 and
become a monk in Takeo, now left the *wat* in 1939, becoming
chief of the ICP for Svay Rieng province.[123] The ICP was
described by its Central Committee in 1938 as 'very weak' in
Kampuchea[124] and nothing is known of Choeun's later activities;
although he almost certainly read the newspaper, he is unlikely
to have had close connections with the *Nagaravatta* group.
However, one of Son Ngoc Thanh's fellow members of the
Buddhist Institute, a Pali teacher from Kompong Speu named
Achar Sok,[125] did later join the communist movement in
Kampuchea; in fact, under the name of Tou Samouth, he
eventually assumed its leadership. (Another student at the

Buddhist Institute at that time was Huynh Cuong, a Khmer Krom from Travinh. Cuong, who was Secretary of the Cochin- china Khmer Buddhist Association from 1943, graduated from the Buddhist Institute in Phnom Penh in 1945. He later became an inspector of Pali schools and pagodas in the Western Mekong Delta. In 1962 he was elected to the NLF Central Committee. Cuong now represents a Khmer Krom constituency in Viet- nam's National Assembly, of which he is a vice-chairman.)

Another Khmer Krom who gained a French education in the 1930s was Lam Phay, who under the name Chan Samay later became a senior member of the Khmer communist movement. A brother-in-law of Son Ngoc Thanh, Samay spent ten years in France;[126] he did not move to Phnom Penh on his return, however, but remained for the time being in Cochinchina, where he joined the communist Viet Minh in the 1940s. A more respectable career was that of Son Sann, who came from a wealthy landowning family of mixed Khmer-Vietnamese ances- try in Travinh. His father Son Sach was called to an official post in Phnom Penh by Sisowath Souphanouvong, one of the princes who had briefly studied at the École Coloniale in Paris. Sann himself graduated with a Diploma of Higher Commercial Studies in Paris in 1933 (his brother Son Qui became a surgeon); he was appointed Deputy Governor of Battambang province two years later, and of Prey Veng in 1937. He went on to found the National Bank of Cambodia in 1955, held various ministerial posts in the Sihanouk period and was for a short period Prime Minister (1967-68). Now in his seventies, Sann is currently head of the anti-communist Khmer People's National Liberation Front (KPNLF) on the Thai-Kampuchean border.[127]

A similar trajectory was that followed by Lon Nol, who was born in 1913, the grandson of a Khmer Krom from Tay Ninh. His maternal grandfather was governor of Prey Veng, and his father Lon Hin made his name there 'pacifying' bandits on the Vietnamese border. Hin then served as a district chief in Siemreap and Konpong Thom, while Lon Nol received a secondary education at the Lycée Chasseloup-Laubat in Saigon from 1928 to 1934. (The young man who was later to be King Norodom Sihanouk, arrived at the same school several years after.) Lon Nol's first post was as a magistrate, but he soon became a district official in Kompong Cham. According to his official biography, he acquitted himself well by 'conciliating' and then 'pacifying' successive anti-colonial uprisings among the inhabitants of the Bos Khnor area in 1939. He rose through the administration and by early 1945 was Deputy Governor of Kompong Cham.[128] He too held important posts, in particular in the Armed Forces, throughout the Sihanouk period, which he helped end in 1970. Lon Nol was President of the Khmer Republic until its defeat five years later by the Communist Party of Kampuchea (CPK) headed by Saloth Sar (Pol Pot) who, although he never held an official government post, came from a similarly privileged but rather more sheltered background.

Saloth Sar was born on 19 May 1928 (The Year of the Dragon), in Prek Sbauv village, Kompong Svay district, Kompong Thom province. He was the youngest of seven children. His father Phen Saloth and mother Sok Nem owned nine hectares of rice land, three hectares of garden land, and several pairs of buffalo, which in most parts of Kampuchea would have made them 'rich peasants'. However, according to Saloth Sar's elder brother Loth Suong, some of the villagers owned fifty to a hundred hectares, and others very little at all, and Saloth was therefore a 'middle peasant'. Suong says he employed no servants but worked his land with the help of two of his sons and some adopted nephews, calling on normal mutual aid arrangements *(prowas dai)* with other villagers at harvest time.[129] The family's average annual production was about six tonnes of paddy,[130] enough for the rice needs of twenty or more people. Their tile-roofed house, one of the largest in the area, looked out across the Sen River seven kilometres downstream from Kompong Thom city.[131]

Rich or poor, the people of Prek Sbauv were rarely completely destitute. The River Sen was well stocked with fish, and coconut and mango trees lined its lush banks, beyond which stretched unusually large rice-fields each more than half a hectare in size. The poorest families owned two or three such fields as well as chickens, ducks and pigs. Near the Saloth family home was a small Chinese shop, the only one in the area, which sold coffee, rice, wine and a few consumer items; after each harvest Chinese merchants would gather outside it and buy paddy from the richer Khmer farmers.[132]

There was no Buddhist *wat* in Prek Sbauv. The nearest one, where Phen Saloth made merit by sponsoring festivals, was up river near Kompong Thom, opposite the French Residence of the time. It was a *wat* of the Thommayut sect, and reflected the strong local influence of the Khmer royalty. For at this very *wat*, sixty years before Saloth Sar was born, inhabitants of the area had drawn the anti-monarchical, anti-French rebel Pou Kombo into a trap and executed him.[133]

Since then, the people of Kompong Svay have been considered, in the words of Laau Thouk, to be 'quiet, kindly, neither turbulent nor deprived, and very pro-royalist'; quite unlike the people of the nearby Baray district, a much poorer area with a long tradition of rebellion. Nevertheless, in 1929, the year after Saloth Sar was born, a French official may have captured, in different ways, the spirit of both districts when he wrote that of the whole country, the inhabitants of Kompong Thom were 'the most deeply Cambodian and the least susceptible to our influence'. A fitting birthplace for a man who was to call himself the 'Original Khmer'.[134]

Laau Thouk asserts that at one point in the 1930s, King Sisowath Monivong came to Kompong Thom with his entourage and visited the Saloth family home. Sar's three surviving brothers deny that the visit occurred, but it is *possible* that it did, for their cousin Luk Khun Meak was one of Monivong's principal wives,[135] their sister Neak Moneang Roeung was a minor consort of the king, and Loth Suong himself began working in the protocol office of the palace in 1930. The connection seems to have been Phen Saloth's elder sister, Neak Cheng, who at first worked as a servant in the palace, and then married Chhim Long, secretary to a French Resident. (Long may also have had royal connections since he was born near the former palace at Oudong.) Their daughter Meak grew up as a palace dancer, and became the first of King Monivong's wives to bear him a child without succession rights (a boy named Kossarak).[136]

In 1922, the twelve-year-old Loth Suong was sent by his father to Phnom Penh, where he entered a monastery, presumably to complete his schooling. In 1928, Meak brought him to work for her in the palace; he married another dancer, Chea Samy. His sister, Loth Saroeung, came to the capital at the age of fifteen and soon became one of Monivong's thirty or forty concubines;[137] her title of Neak Moneang signified that she was a commoner admitted into the royal entourage.

In 1978, perhaps in an attempt to hide his background, and without revealing the fact that his real name was Saloth Sar, Pol Pot told Yugoslav journalists: 'I am from a peasant family; during my childhood, I lived with my parents and helped them in the agricultural work. But after, according to custom, I lived in a pagoda to learn how to read and write. I spent six years in a pagoda and I was a monk for two years.[138]

According to three of his brothers, Sar never worked in the fields at home.[139] At the age of six he too was sent to Phnom Penh and for one year was a novice at Botumvodey monastery, the religious centre of the small, royalist Thommayut order. When he was eight years old, with the help of Luk Khun Meak, Saloth Sar began his schooling at the École Miche, a private Catholic shool, and spent the next six years there.[140] He lived in a large house in Trasak Paem Street with Suong, Samy and Meak, and seems to have had a rather strict upbringing. Sbong Saksi, who also grew up with close connections with the palace and was then the girl next door, recalls that Suong 'was very serious, and would not gamble or allow children such as myself to play near his home', although Samy 'did gamble and play with me a little'.[141]

It was a closeted, conservative, and at times (at least where the King was concerned) decadent environment. The Palace personnel and their relatives, then the principal Khmer community in the capital (which had a population of only 100,000), lived quite apart from the Chinese shop-keepers and Vietnamese workers and officials who formed the majority of Phnom Penh's inhabitants;[142] this may well have reinforced in the 'Original Khmer' a deep sense of his ethnic identity.[143] At the same time, emergence from such a narrow atmosphere into that of a genuinely Khmer bustling market town in 1942 was probably something of an eye-opener, and rather sudden exposure after the isolation of the monarchical culture. At the age of fourteen, apparently because he failed the entrance examination to a Phnom Penh school, Saloth Sar was sent for his intermediate education to Kompong Cham city, where he spent the next six years in the Norodom Sihanouk High School.[144]

Little is known about Sar's schooling in Kompong Cham, but he very probably met students from a variety of backgrounds. One of them may have been Hu Nim, a future member of the CPK Central Committee, who enrolled in the same school in 1946.[145] Nim was born of landless peasant parents in a village on the Mekong in 1930, but he and his mother were soon abandoned by his father; they took shelter first in a *wat* and then with various relatives in different parts of the area where Lon Nol was district chief. Forty years later, in a Pol Pot prison, Hu Nim wrote: 'My mother and I wandered aimlessly from place to place, selling our labour ... She made *akao* cakes and exchanged them for rice to feed our stomachs. Later she was remarried, to a poor peasant ... Because her husband was poor she sent me to live in Wat Mien. An old monk named Nhep Nauv brought me up and looked after me like a son from that time on.'[146]

Hu Nim was then twelve years old. Nauv had nine other boys in his care, but he managed to get Nim an education — at first in Wat Mien, then (with the help of a government scholarship) at a local primary school, then at high school in the provincial capital. For his first two years in the city Nim lived in another *wat*, until he won a scholarship which paid for his board at the high school. It was also in Kompong Cham that he met his future wife, Var Yat, whose father was a jeweller and paid for him to finish his secondary education at Sisowath High School in Phnom Penh. There he lived with a monk in Wat Unnalom, the religious centre of the majority Mohanikay Order, before pursuing his studies in France in the mid-1950s.[147]

Another future communist leader of peasant background, who unlike Hu Nim received little formal education, was Heng Samrin, now President of the People's Republic of Kampuchea. Born in 1934 in the Kompong Cham border village of Anlong Kres (which in the 1960s was a major sanctuary for Khmer revolutionaries, including So Phim), Samrin became involved, like many others in the area, in the illicit cattle trade across the Vietnamese border in the 1950s. This brought him into contact with the Vietnamese communists, and he took up the revolutionary cause in 1959.[148]

By the time Hu Nim arrived in Sisowath High School in 1950, it had already become the training centre for the Khmer educated class, many of whom, like Nim himself, were to become communists. One of the earliest of this generation of students was Ieng Sary, later a member of the CPK Politburo. Born into a mixed Khmer-Chinese landowning family in Travinh, Sary arrived in Phnom Penh around 1943.[149] His future wife, Khieu Thirith, daughter of a Battambang judge related to the royal family, enrolled at Sisowath one class below him.[150] Her elder sister, Khieu Ponnary, became the first Khmer woman to obtain the Baccalauréat, and was to marry Sary's friend Saloth Sar in 1956. The Khieus' cousin, Mey Pho, became a palace clerk in the early 1940s; in 1945 he was to help launch a coup attempt that signalled the beginning of the anti-colonial resistance, and he later joined the ICP.[151] Another cousin, Chhan Sokhom, became a Minister in the Sihanouk and Lon Nol governments, and a brother, Khieu Tham, was Lon Nol's ambassador to Berlin.

Another child of a judge who attended the school was Khieu Samphan,[152] President of Democratic Kampuchea from 1976 to 1979. Among the Sisowath students who went on to study in France and to become leading communists, one of the few from a less well-to-do background was Hou Yuon; his peasant father grew rice and tobacco on the Mekong in Kompong Cham, not far from the birthplace of Hu Nim.[153] Some of the future Democratic Kampuchea leaders, of course, did not attend Sisowath: Son Sen, whose parents were small landowners in Travinh, arrived in Phnom Penh in 1946 and went to the Teacher Training School there, as did another Khmer Krom, Chau Seng.[154] And Saloth Sar, who returned from Kompong Cham in early 1948, began studying carpentry at the Russey Keo Technical School, where he was a boarder, on the outskirts of the capital. After one year he received a scholarship, apparently not through any royal connections,[155] to undertake a two-year technicans' course at the *École Française de radioélectricité* in Paris.[156] He arrived in France in September 1949.[157]

Others who passed through Sisowath in the 1940s, were later educated in France and became prominent CPK members included Rat Samuoeun, Touch Phoeun, Ros Chet Thor and Thiounn Prasith.[158] Prasith and his three brothers, all of whom were to become Ministers of Democratic Kampuchea, came from by far the most privileged background. The Thiounn brothers are in fact direct descendants of two of the most powerful families in the Khmer administration in the first half of the twentieth century. (See genealogical chart, Figure 1.)

Further, the Thiounn brothers were nephews of Bunchhan Mul, who was himself a nephew of Poc Khun. Their aunt brought a second and closer connection: she married Khun's brother, whose daughter — their cousin — married Prince Monireth, Sihanouk's uncle. (It was Monireth's father, King Monivong, who took Pol Pot's sister and cousin as consorts in the 1930s.)

The original Thiounn was a commoner who studied French in Phnom Penh and entered the colonial service in 1883. Playing the role of what might be called a 'comprador feudalist', he rose quickly to become Second Secretary to the Council of Ministers in 1891, Secretary-General in 1899, and Minister of the Palace in

1902.[159] Sihanouk once recalled him in these terms: '[A] veritable little king, as powerful as the French Résidents-Supérieurs of the period. He passed out titles and positions, and dipped into the Crown Treasury to look after his children and grandchildren, who were raised as princes.'[160]

Thiounn finally retired in 1941, six years after his son Thiounn Hol had become Secretary-General of the Council of Ministers. Hol's four sons were Prasith, Thioeunn, Mumm and Chum. Their mother, Bunchhan Moly, came from another powerful family. Her father (and Bunchhan Mul's) was a district chief in Kandal province; in the early years of the century he had married Poc Loun, grand-daughter of the then Prime Minister, Poc. Poc, too, owed his position to French patronage: he faced royal opposition partly because he was descended from another man of the same name who had served as a pro-Thai regent from 1796 to 1810, after the Thai seizure of Kampuchea's north-west provinces in the late 1700s.[161] Loun's brother Poc Khun was to do the same in 1941, as we shall see. A great-nephew of Poc Khun was Poc Deuskomar, who became a leader of the urban Khmer left in the 1960s. Also related was Douc Rasy, a leader of the intellectual right in the same period.

Thiounn Thioeunn and Thiounn Chum were both sent to study in Hanoi from 1942 to 1945; their attitude to France and Japan during this period is not known, but they noted, according to their 1979 account, that 'Vietnamese intellectuals spoke of Angkor as their own'.[162] After the war the two men went on to Paris, where Thioeunn completed a degree in medicine and Chum a doctorate in law. Their brother Mumm gained a doctorate in science there, and the fourth brother Prasith was also sent to study in France, where he remained for over twenty years. All developed left-wing contacts there, but their nationalism was fierce. In fact they refused to meet Ho Chi Minh. Chum recalls: 'In Paris during the Fontainebleau Conference, in July 1946, we were called to the Vietnamese delegation. 'You will pay your respects to Uncle Ho', they said. But we answered, 'He is not our 'Uncle Ho'. They then said, 'We are brothers. You should pay your respects'. But we did not do it. Socialism was only a cover. We said to the representatives of the Yugoslavian Youth Federation: 'It is not right that a country as fertile as Kampuchea should have such a small population'.[163]

'Socialism was only a cover' is of course a reference to Vietnamese attitudes, but it seems just as appropriate to those of

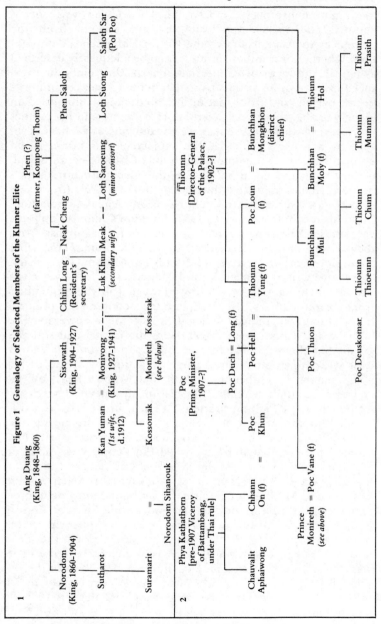

Figure 1 Genealogy of Selected Members of the Khmer Elite

the Thiounn brothers. Their political worldview was one of national and racial grandiosity, evident enough from the references to Angkor and to the size of Kampuchea's population. Whether or not these attitudes can be adequately described as feudal, the form of Khmer nationalism they embodied was specific: it was quite distinct from that of the Khmer communists in this period, and from that of the 'bourgeois nationalist' Son Ngoc Thanh, whose goals were more concrete and his politics much less sensitive to Vietnamese patronizing, as we have seen. But, by a process which is the subject of this book, it did eventually become the dominant strand of Khmer communism, under the leadership of Saloth Sar (the 'Original Khmer'). It is ironic as well as tragic that the brief period of his rule (from 1975 to 1979) saw a substantial reduction in Kampuchea's population.

On his return from Paris in 1952, Thiounn Chum set out on a very successful business career, as a 'comprador capitalist'[164] (in the parlance of his 1979 socialist cover). Thioeunn, on the other hand, sided with the left, as did Prasith and Mumm. Their sister, however, married Chhean Vam, headmaster of Sisowath High School in the late 1940s. Having graduated in the humanities from Paris as early as 1940, Vam became a conservative political figure after independence. When the CPK came to power in 1975, both he and Chum were driven from the capital and suffered greatly like the rest of the former urban population, but Vam at least was 'apparently spared from execution by virtue of his wife's name'.[165] Thioeunn, Prasith and Mumm had now all emerged as high-ranking officials in the new Democratic Kampuchea (DK) administration.[166] Then, in 1978, Chum was recalled to the capital and put in charge of organizing the country's finances. The next year, after the Vietnamese army had invaded the country and established the People's Republic of Kampuchea, Chum joined the exiled DK Cabinet as Minister of the Economy. With Mumm as Minister for Science, and Thioeunn as Minister for Health, the Thiounn family held three of the ten portfolios in the ousted regime, while Thiounn Prasith was its Ambassador to the United Nations.[167] Meanwhile, Son Sann was organising the rightwing KPNLF, also on the Thai border. He appointed Chhean Vam as his deputy, and the stage was set for an anti-Vietnamese coalition.[168] Members of the DK side also included men who had been Vam's students at Sisowath — Khieu Samphan, Ieng Sary, and the latter's wife Khieu Thirith — as well as Saloth Sar (Pol Pot) and Son Sen.

Formally announced in 1982, and headed by the former King Norodom Sihanouk, the coalition reunited the remnants of a small political elite whose members had a great deal in common, in spite of over thirty years of fragmentation and civil war. But it was an exiled coalition, and the country they now set their sights on reconquering was not the Kampuchea of the 1930s and 1940s.

Notes

1. Archives D'Outre-Mer (AOM), Aix-en-Provence, France. Cambodge 7F 14(1), 'Notes mensuelles', January 1934.
2. Milton E. Osborne, *The French Presence in Cochinchina and Cambodia: Rule and Response, 1859–1905,* Cornell University Press, 1969, p.183.
3. *Ibid.,* pp.222, 207.
4. *Ibid.,* p.213.
5. Milton E. Osborne, 'Peasant Politics in Cambodia: The 1916 Affair', *Modern Asian Studies,* 12, 2, 1978, pp.217–243 at pp.224–25.
6. Milton E. Osborne, *Politics and Power in Cambodia,* Melbourne 1973, p.24.
7. See David P. Chandler, 'The Assassination of Resident Bardez: A Premonition of Revolt in Colonial Cambodia', *Journal of the Siam Society,* 70 (1982) pp.35–49.
8. AOM, Aix-en-Provence. Cambodge 7F 15(1), Direction de la Sûreté, Rapport annuel 1922-23, p.4.
9. Khy Phanra, 'Les Origines du Caodaisme au Cambodge, 1926–1940', *Mondes Asiatiques,* 3, automne 1975, pp.315–348 at p.321.
10. *Ibid.,* See also Osborne, *The French Presence, op.cit.* p.255.
11. David J. Steinberg, *et al, Cambodia: Its People, Its Society, its Culture,* HRAF Press, New Haven, 1959, p.70; and Osborne, *The French Presence,* p.293.
12. *Ibid.* and F. Martini, 'Organisation du clergé bouddhique au Cambodge', *France-Asie* (Saigon), Special Issue, November-December 1955, pp.416–424 at p.417.
13. Upasaka Purusakara, 'Le peuple cambodgien est plus bouddhiste que ses bonzes', *Indochine Sud-Est Asiatique,* 31, July 1954, pp.25–31, at p.26.
14. Khy Phanra, *op. cit.,* p.321.
15. Steinberg, *op. cit.,* p.70.
16. G. Coedès, 'Dictionnaire cambodgien', *Bulletin de l'Ecole Française de l'Extrème-Orient,* 38, 1938, pp.314-21.

17. *Ibid.*, p.317.
18. *Ibid.*
19. *Ibid.*, p.318.
20. *Ibid.*
21. Steinberg, *op. cit.*, p.71.
22. Khy Phanra, *op. cit.*, p.321.
23. *Ibid.*, p.316–17.
24. Jean Moura, *Le Royaume du Cambodge,* Paris, 1883, Vol. II, pp.159, 162.
25. Khy Phanra, *op. cit.*, p.318. From Kampuchea, the sect later spread into Laos as well. Geoffrey Gunn, personal communication.
26. *Ibid.*, pp.321–22.
27. *Ibid.*, pp.322–24.
28. Osborne, *Politics and Power*, p.29.
29. Khy Phanra, *op. cit.*, pp.323–34.
30. *Ibid.*, pp.325, 323.
31. *Ibid.*, p.325.
32. *Ibid.*, p.324.
33. *Ibid.*
34. *Ibid.*, pp.326–27.
35. *Ibid.*, p.326.
36. *Ibid.*, p.327.
37. *Ibid.*, p.328. These Khmers came from Svay Rieng, Prey Veng and Kompong Cham.
38. *Ibid.*, p.329.
39. *Ibid.*, p.332.
40. For an account of this ceremony see Gabriel Gobron, *Histoire et philosophie du Caodaisme,* Paris 1949, pp.87–109.
41. Khy Phanra, *op. cit.*, p.330.
42. *Ibid.*, pp.330–31.
43. *Ibid.*, p.320.
44. AOM, Aix-en-Provence. Cambodge 3E 4(4), Rapports politiques trimestriels, 15 April 1927.
45. *Ibid.*
46. *Ibid.*
47. *Ibid.* Cambodge 7F 15, Direction de la Sûreté, Rapport annuel 1930–31, p.1.
48. W. J. Duiker, *The Rise of Nationalism in Vietnam, 1900–1941,* Ithaca 1976, p.216.
49. *Ibid.*, p.215.
50. AOM, Aix-en-Provence. Cambodge 7F 15, Direction de la Sûreté, Rapport annuel, 1930–31, pp.12-16, p.4.
51. *Ibid.*, pp.14, 4.
52. Eleven members escaped and were sentenced *in absentia.* Ta Nien also got away, just as the police were entering his apartment, and was later identified in Swatow by the Hong Kong police. *Ibid.*, p.5.
53. *Ibid.*, p.4.
54. *Ibid.*, pp.9-12.
55. *Ibid.* Wilfred Burchett has noted the coincidence that Ho Chi Minh often disguised himself as a travelling hairdresser in this period. See *The China Cambodia Vietnam Triangle,* Chicago 1982, p.10. According to official archives at Aix-en-Provence, Ho's father was then an occasional visitor to Phnom Penh. David P. Chandler, personal communication.
56. Duiker, *op. cit.*, pp.214-16.

57. See D. Gareth Porter 'Vietnamese Policy Towards Kampuchea, 1930-1970' in David P. Chandler and Ben Kiernan (eds.) *Revolution and its Aftermath in Kampuchea,* Yale 1983, p.59.

58. *Ibid.,* p.60.

59. *Ibid.* Porter cites *Cong Nong Binh* ('Worker, Peasant and Soldier') 6 February, 1931. Reprinted in Tran Huy Lieu, *Lich Su Tam Muoi Nam Chong Phap* ('A History of Eighty Years' Resistance to the French'), Vol. 2, Hanoi 1958.

60. *Ibid.* It is interesting to note the 1958 statement by Tran Huy Lieu, in this period a senior ICP official: 'Each country has concrete conditions. . . different from the others. . . Thus, the parties. . . cannot be pressed into the same mould, from name to political line, though they are following the same path.'*Lich Su Tam Muoi Nam Chong Phap,* p.36–37.

61. AOM, Aix-en-Provence. Cambodge 7F 15, Direction de la Sûreté, Rapport annuel 1930–31, p.17–20.

62. *Ibid.,* pp.20–22.

63. *Ibid.,* pp.3–4.

64. *Ibid.,* p.4.

65. *Ibid.,* pp.23–25.

66. AOM, Paris. Slotfom III, dossier 48. 'Les Associations antifrançaises et la propagande communiste en Indochine', 2e quinzaine et avril 1931, p.44.

67. *Ibid.,* p.43.

68. Duiker, *op. cit.,* p.229.

69. AOM, Paris, Slotfom III, dossier 48, p.43.

70. *Ibid.* and AOM, Aix-en-Provence, Cambodge 7F 15, Direction de la Sûreté, Rapport annuel 1931–32, p.1.

71. *Ibid.,* p.2.

72. AOM, Paris, Slotfom III, dos. 59, Note periodique no. 31, 2e trimestre 1934; and dos. 54, Note periodique no. 35, 2e trimestre 1935.

73. AOM, Aix-en-Provence. Cambodge 7F 29(2). *Note sur l'organisation politique et administrative du Viet-Minh au Cambodge,* Direction des services de securité du Haut Commissariat en Indochine. December 1952, p.23. Hereafter cited as *Note.*

74. Programme de 1932, in *Partisans,* no. 48, juillet-août 1969; first published in *l'Internationale communiste,* 30 Juillet 1932. Cited in Pierre Rousset, *Communisme et nationalisme vietnamien,* Paris 1978, pp.199–200.

75. *Ibid.* According to Gareth Porter, *op. cit.,* p.88, the French words found in the translation of the document, *union* and *nationalités,* do not represent the meaning of the Vietnamese original.

76. Duiker, *op. cit.,* p.235.

77. AOM, Paris. Slotfom III, dos. 54, Note périodique no. 35, 2e trimestre 1935.

78. *Ibid.,* dos. 54, Note périodique no. 31, 2e trimestre 1934, pp.18–19.

79. *Ibid.*

80. AOM, Aix-en-Provence. Cambodge 7F 14(1), Direction de la Sûreté, Note mensuelle, November 1933.

81. Author's interview with Nguyen Xuan Hoang, Hanoi, 4 November 1980.

82. AOM, Aix-en-Provence. Cambodge 7F 15 C(7), Sûreté report 1928–29.

83. *Le Khmer,* Phnom Penh, 1 February 1936, pp.2, 5.

84. *Ibid.,* 28 December 1935, p.1: 1 February 1936, p.2.

85. *Ibid.,* 29 February 1936, p.1.

86. AOM, Aix-en-Provence. Cambodge 7F 15, Direction de la Sûreté, Rapport annuel 1930–31, p.5.

87. AOM, Paris. Slotfom III, dos. 56. March 26, 1936 (?). 'Traduction d'un rapport soumis à la section coloniale du Comité executif de l'International communiste'. Semaun represented the communists of Indo–China, Indonesia and the Malay Archipelago.

88. *Ibid.*, dos. 59, n.d.

89. *Ibid.*, Slotfom VIII, dos. 11.

90. *Ibid.*, Slotfom III, dos. 54, Note périodique no. 35, 2e trimestre 1935, p.28.

91. *Ibid.*, dos. 52, Note périodique, no. 31, 2e trimestre 1934.

92. *Ibid.*, dos. 53 (?), Note périodique no. 32, 3e trimestre 1934, annexe 10. Cited in Rousset, *op. cit.*, pp.200–202.

93. *Ibid.*, annexe 5. Cited in Rousset, *op. cit.*, p.201.

94. AOM, Paris, Slotfom III, dos. 54. Note périodique no. 35, 2e trimestre 1935, pp.28–33.

95. Tan Huyen and Pham Thanh, *Dat Nuoc Campuchia*, Hanoi, QDND, 1980, p.113; and Tim Hieu, *Dat Nuoc Campuchia Anh Hung*, Hanoi 1979, p.69.

96. AOM, Paris, Slotfom III, dos. 54, Note périodique no. 35, 2e Trimestre 1935, p.77, note 1.

97. AOM, Aix-en-Provence. Cambodge 7F 14(1), Direction de la Sûreté, Note mensuelle, avril 1934.

98. AOM, Paris, Slotfom III, dos. 54. Note périodique no. 35, 2e trimestre 1935, p.30, and Duiker *op. cit.*, p. 238.

99. AOM, Paris, Slotfom III, dos. 94, annexe 7. 'Urgent tasks', point no. 6. Cited in Rousset, *op. cit.*, p.201.

100. *Ibid.*, dos. 54, Note périodique no. 35, 2e trimestre 1935, p.89; and no. 36, 3e trimestre 1935, p.77.

101. *Note, op. cit.*, p.23.

102. AOM, Paris, Slotfom III, dos. 54, Note périodique no. 39, April 1936.

103. *Ibid.*, dos. 59, Note périodique, no. 47, December 1936, p. 55.

104. Duiker, *op. cit.*, p. 242.

105. AOM, Paris, Slotfom III, dos. 54, Note périodique no. 42, July 1936, p.30; no. 44, September 1936, p.41; no. 46, November 1936, p.35; no. 47, December 1936, pp.53–54.

106. *Ibid.*, pp.55–56.

107. *Ibid.*

108. AOM, Aix-en-Provence. Cambodge 7F 14(1), Direction de la Sûreté, Note mensuelle, November 1938, p.2.

109. *le Khmer*, 18 May 1936, p.1.

110. *Iron Man of Laos: Prince Phetsareth Ratanavongsa*, by '3349'. Translated by John B. Murdoch. Cornell University South–east Asia Program, Data Paper no. 110, 1978, pp.13–14.

111. U Maung Maung, *From Sangha to Laity: Nationalist Movements of Burma, 1920–1940,* Australian National University, Manohar, 1980, p.3.

112. AOM, Aix-en-Provence. Cambodge 3E 8(2), report from Prey Veng, 3e trimestre, 1915.

113. *Ibid.*, 3E 12(2), report from Svay Rieng, 1er trimestre 1920.

114. David P. Chandler, *A History of Cambodia*, Westview Press, 1983, p.177.

115. 'Etat Civil (de Renseignements)' in the *Son Ngoc Thanh Papers* donated to the Monash University Library by Chana Samudavanija, 1981.

116. 'Looking Back at Cambodia', *Westerly*, 4, December 1976, pp.14–28 at p.15.

117. 'Cambodia: The Present Situation and its Background', April 1973 typescript, 50 pp. at p.4.

118. V.M. Reddi, *A History of the Cambodian Independence Movement, 1863–1955.* Tirupati, Sri Venkatesvara University, 1973, p.107. Also Michael Vickery, personal communication.

119. AOM, Aix-en-Provence. Cambodge 7F 29(7), *Etude sur les mouvements rebelles au Cambodge, 1942–52,* 136 pp. at annexe, pp.19, 24. (Hereafter cited as *Etude.*) Also author's interviews with relatives of Muon and Tak.

120. Tim Hieu, *op. cit.,* pp.69–70. I am grateful to Paula Simcocks for the translation.

121. *Etude,* op. cit., p.3.

122. Bunchhan Mul, *Kuk niyobay* ('Political Prison'), Phnom Penh, Apsara Press, 1971. A partial translation of this work can be found in Ben Kiernan and Chanthou Boua, *Peasants and Politics in Kampuchea, 1942–81,* London 1982, 401pp., at pp.114–126.

123. *Note, op. cit.,* p.23.

124. Porter, *op cit.,* p.61.

125. *Note, op. cit.,* p.24, and author's interview with Chea Soth, who lived and worked with Samouth from 1949 to 1951. Phnom Penh, 22 October, 1980.

126. *Note, op. cit.,* p.24. See also the Pol Pot Regime's *Livre Noir,* Phnom Penh 1978, p.23.

127. 'Biographie de Monsieur Son Sann', Document no. 07 of the Khmer People's National Liberation Front *News Bulletin,* November 1979, p.18.

128. *Revue de l'Armée,* no. 1, September, 1970, pp.12–15. I am grateful to Michael Vickery for drawing my attention to this and other sources of information about Lon Nol, namely: *Bulletin Administratif du Cambodge,* 1929, p.978; *Journal Officiel du Cambodge* 27 September 1945, p.788; and *Cambodge,* no. 40, 10 May 1945.

129. Author's interview with Loth Suong, Phnom Penh, 9 July 1980. On the other hand, Laau Thouk, who grew up in the neighbouring village and knew Saloth Sar 'very well' ('we often played together as boys'), remembers Phen Saloth as a landowner well-liked in the area, who employed thirty or forty labourers at harvest time, kept a large granary, and often sponsored village religious festivals. He also says that Saloth owned thirty or forty buffalo. (Information drawn from author's interview with Laau Thouk, Paris, 9 February 1980.)

130. Loth Suong, *op. cit.*

131. Laau Thouk, *op. cit.,* and author's interviews at Prek Sbauv, 14 October 1980.

132. Laau Thouk, *op. cit.*

133. According to Jean Moura, Pou Kombo's revolt of 1865–67 'turned the small Khmer kingdom upside down' and made him master of all but the royal capitals of Oudong and Phnom Penh. But the population of the Kompong Svay area, the seat of one of the five 'regional kings' (*sdach tran*) of Kampuchea, wrote a letter to Pou Kombo inviting him to be their chief and pledging him their loyalty. In November 1867, Pou Kombo and over a hundred followers arrived from the eastern provinces which he had conquered in their entirety, and camped 100 metres from the monastery at Kompong Thom. Moura takes up the story: 'The next morning, in fact, the entire population began to move very early. The men exhorted and jostled one another tumultuously beside the pagoda. Pou Kombo stood below the sacred fig tree, surrounded by his men massed several deep around him and determined to defend their chief to the last. The struggle began and quickly became fierce: the women were on the spot, too, urging on their men, bringing in ammunition, reloading the weapons and looking after the

38

wounded'. Pou Kombo escaped alone, but was pursued into the centre of a lake by two slaves of the former *sdach tran* who waded out and subdued him with clubs. He was beheaded, and his head was sent to Phnom Penh and publicly exhibited there the next day. *Le Royaume du Cambodge.* Paris 1889, Vol. 2, pp.167–69.

134. AOM, Aix-en-Provence, Cambodge 3E 6(2), report from Kompong Thom, 1929. The 'Original Khmer' (*khmae da'em*) is the pseudonym Saloth Sar used in his handwritten contribution to a Khmer student magazine in Paris. *Khemara Nisit,* no. 14, August 1952. Keng Vennsak, personal communication. See chapter four below.

135. A traveller's account published in 1928 records that the title Luk Khun signified 'the king's favourite', and intriguingly tells the story of a peasant girl from Kompong Thom who rose to this position. See Harry Hervey, *Travels in French Indo–China,* London 1928, pp.111–116.

136. Loth Suong, *op. cit.,* and author's interview with Sbong Saksi, Paris, 27 January 1980.

137. Loth Suong, *op. cit.*

138. *Interview of Comrade Pol Pot. . . to the Delegation of Yugoslav Journalists in Visit to Democratic Kampuchea.* Phnom Penh, March 1978, pp.20–21.

139. Loth Suong, *op. cit.,* and author's interviews with Saloth Seng and Saloth Nhep, Kompong Thom, 14 October 1980. According to an official biography broadcast on Pyongyang Radio, Pol Pot 'engaged in farming with his parents from 1937 to 1939' (US, CIA *Foreign Broadcast Information Service* (FBIS) IV, 4 October 1977, p.H38). However, his brothers say he left home for Phnom Penh in 1934 and never returned.

140. Loth Suong, *op. cit.*

141. Sbong Saksi, *op. cit.*

142. *Le Khmer* of 3 August 1936 breaks down the capital's population as follows: 48,000 Khmers, 21,000 Chinese, 28,000 Vietnamese, 3,500 Chams and 1,500 French.

143. A traveller in Phnom Penh in the 1920s found 'surprisingly few Cambodians' in 'a swarm of people that made the late afternoon throb with colour', and also noted 'the absence of many Cambodians in the bazaars' of the city. Hervey, *op. cit.,* p.106.

144. Loth Suong, *op. cit.*

145. Hu Nim's 'confession', *I would like to tell the Party in full about my biography,* Tuol Sleng prison, 2 May 1977.

146. *Ibid.* Part of what follows is confirmed and supplemented by the author's interview with Nhep Nauv, Prey Totung, 4 August 1980, and with other locals, including former classmates of Hu Nim, on the same day.

147. *Ibid.*

148. *Democratic Kampuchea News Bulletin,* n. 012/79, 26 February 1979; and *The Kampuchean People's Revolutionary Council,* NUFSK Information Service, Phnom Penh, January 1979, p.3.

149. François Ponchaud, *Cambodia Year Zero,* London, Allen Lane, 1978, p.172.

150. 'Interview with Madam Ieng Thirith', by Mukundan C. Menon, New Delhi, November 1979 (no publication details), p.4.

151. See next chapter.

152. Ponchaud, *op. cit.,* pp.199, 173.

153. Author's interview with Ung Bunhuor, Yuon's brother-in-law, Sydney, 21 November 1977.

154. *Contrôle des étudiants boursiers, op. cit.* See note 158.
155. According to *Le Monde* (9 January 1979), he obtained it 'on the recommendation of a mandarin of the royal palace'. Loth Suong denies this.
156. Loth Suong, *op. cit.*
157. *Contrôle des étudiants boursiers, op. cit.* See note 158.
158. Ponchaud, *op. cit.*, p.173, and also *Contrôle des étudiants boursiers: Carnet no. 1, France (1946–50),* copy kindly supplied by Stephen R. Heder.
159. *Nagaravatta,* no. 302, 27 September 1941, and *Bulletin Administratif du Cambodge,* 1902, p.135. I am grateful to Michael Vickery for providing me with these references and much of the information that follows.
160. *Les Paroles de Samdech Preah Norodom Sihanouk,* Phnom Penh, Ministry of Information: October–December 1967, p.811. Speech on 19 October, 1967.
161. On the Poc family, see Milton Osborne, *Before Kampuchea*, Sydney 1979, ch. 8.
162. Quoted in Jan Myrdal, 'Why is there Famine in Kampuchea?', *South-east Asia Chronicle,* no. 77, February 1981, pp.16–18, at p.17.
163. *Ibid.*
164. Ibid., p.18.
165. *Far Eastern Economic Review,* 9 November 1979, p.42. An uncle of the Thiounns and his family also escaped mistreatment, 'thanks to the recommendations of Thiounn Thioeunn'. Y Phandara, *Retour à Phnom Penh,* Paris 1982, p.151.
166. Thiounn Thioeunn was Minister of Health, Thiounn Mumm was Minister of Energy, and Thiounn Prasith was head of the Asia Department of the Foreign Ministry. See epilogue.
167. *Le Monde,* 28 December 1979, p.5.
168. *Far Eastern Economic Review, op. cit.,* 'A New Link Forms in the Chain', by John McBeth, pp.41–42.

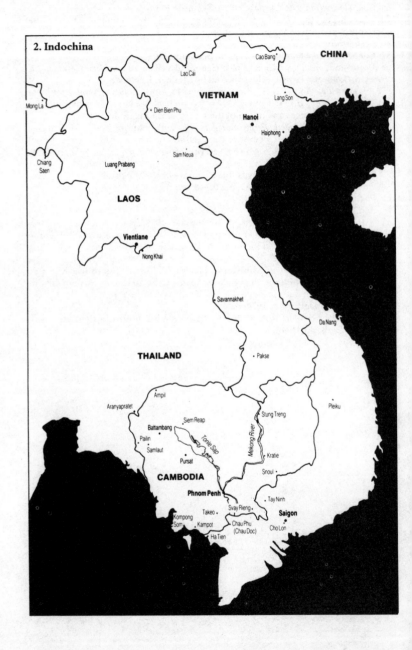

2. Indochina

Contending Colonialisms:
1940-49

*Many Thais acted as leaders of the Khmer Serei [Khmer Issarak] in helping
Cambodia to get rid of France. But even if these people were Thai, they
were good Cambodians as well. They loved Cambodia more than the
Cambodians themselves.*

Samniant Khanthachawana in *Siam Rath*,
Bangkok, 30 June 1970.

In November 1939, the Sixth Plenum of the ICP Central
Committee had resolved that Japanese Fascism and French
Imperialism were equally inimical to the peoples of Indo-
China.[1] In May–June 1940, Nazi Germany invaded France, and
the new Vichy regime there agreed on a policy of collaboration.
In Phnom Penh, Son Ngoc Thanh's group quickly approached
the French Resident-Superior Thibadeau and, while professing
sympathy for France, asked for 'the restitution of Cambodia to
the Cambodians' on the grounds that France was no longer able
to protect the country.[2] In September 1940, Japanese troops
began to move into northern Indo-China. (Two divisions arrived
in Kampuchea in May the next year.) Emboldened by this
display of Asian force, the editors of *Nagaravatta* are reported to
have grown increasingly frank in their criticism of French rule,[3]
still intact but enjoying an uneasy relationship with the Japanese
troops.

However, in November an equally emboldened Thai army
invaded the north-west of Kampuchea and after some fierce
fighting took control of Battambang and Siemreap provinces,
with the exception of a French garrison at Angkor Wat and
Siemreap town. Their takeover was legitimitized with Japanese
backing by a Peace Treaty signed in Tokyo in March 1941. The
Thais now made use of the first Khmer Issarak ('Khmer
Independence') Committee. This had been set up in Bangkok in
December 1940 by Poc Khun, former director of a Battambang
pawnshop who had been dismissed on discovery of accounting
irregularities and had fled to Thailand in 1939.[4] Khun was both
descended from, and related by marriage to, officials who had
served Bangkok in an earlier period of Thai suzerainty (see the

genealogical table in Chapter 1). He now became the representative of Battambang in the Thai parliament. Siemreap, now called 'Phibun Songkram province' after the pro-Japanese Thai leader, was represented by Yat Hwaidi, a Khmer born in the Thai border province of Surin.[5]

These developments worried the *Nagaravatta* group. According to French intelligence: 'Son Ngoc Thanh and Pach Chhoeun decided to create a political organization capable at the right time of claiming independence for Cambodia from the Japanese and with their support resisting new Thai advances on Cambodia. They sounded out students and merchants and began recruiting followers among the lower classes of the population who would work towards neutralising the French by surprise.'[6]

The main activists were Achar Hem Chieu, a teacher at the Higher School of Pali in the capital, and Achar Nuon Duong, a graduate of the school. *Nagaravatta* began publishing Khmer translations of articles from the Japanese press agency Domei. These were often censored by the French authorities, and on several occasions, according to Thanh, Pach Chhoeun asked for 'advice and directives' from the Japanese consul in Phnom Penh, and was briefed on Tokyo's policy towards Kampuchea.[7]

In April 1941, following the death of King Monivong, the French authorities placed the eighteen-year-old Norodom Sihanouk on the Khmer throne. The next month, the Central Committee of the ICP met for its Eighth Plenum at Pac Bo in Tonkin, and formed the 'League for the Independence of Vietnam' (or Viet Minh); it also resolved to help set up a 'League for the Independence of Cambodia', and another for Laos. It was planned that these three separate national fronts would form a federal 'League for the Independence of Indo-China'.[8] But the ICP observed that there was 'still no trace of a Party'[9] in Kampuchea. Anti-French mobilization of any kind was still in its infancy there, and was divided into contending groups under the influence of the Thai and Japanese governments. Worse, these governments were allied to one another (as Japan was to Vichy France) and unlikely to favour the interests of Khmers at the expense of an ally. And the Khmers themselves were feeling their way in a totally changed situation. Early in 1942, *Nagaravatta* cautiously advised its readers that 'so far Pétain's policy seems to be good for us'.[10] This hope proved illusory.

Soon after, the French authorities introduced the Gregorian calendar (and even planned a new romanized script for the

Khmer language[11]), arousing the ire of many monks. Thanh then decided to attempt a pro-Japanese coup. He contacted Lieutenant Ochi, Commander of the Japanese police in Phnom Penh, who is reported to have encouraged him in the idea.[12]

But on 18 July 1942, the French arrested Achar Hem Chieu and Nuon Duong for preaching anti-French sermons to Khmer troops in the colonial army, in preparation for the revolt. Chieu was summarily defrocked without, as was required by religious law, first having been judged by his fellow monks. Thanh took refuge in the home of a Japanese captain,[13] and decided that a demonstration of protest was necessary. As he later wrote to the Japanese 'Commander-in-Chief of the Independence Organizations of the South Seas': 'Because our movement and our preparations for a coup d'état against the French with the promised support of the Imperial Army had already almost reached their maturity, it was imperative that the French should not succeed in extinguishing them without a demonstration of their vitality.'[14]

At 10 a.m. the next day, according to Thanh, 'we received confirmation from the General Staff in Saigon that the Japanese Army and Police in Phnom Penh would help us and be present with us at our demonstration'.[15] Much to Thanh's later regret, however, he did not inform the Japanese Consul in the capital. The Japanese captain insisted that the demonstration be peaceful; if unsuccessful in its demands the crowd was supposed to march to the Japanese Police Headquarters and ask them to intervene.[16]

Thanh says he gave the Japanese copies of demands to be submitted to the French. These included the release of the detainees, reorganisation in all fields of public life, close economic collaboration with Japan to aid the war effort, tax reduction, and a Constitution providing for a 'National Socialist Monarchy'.[17]

At six o'clock the next morning, 20 July, at least one thousand to two thousand people, including at least five hundred monks mainly of the Thommakay sect,[18] gathered behind the Royal Palace. Son Ngoc Thanh remained in the Japanese police headquarters but his liaison agent, Bunchhan Mul, who participated in the demonstration, has described what happened: 'People came out of Langka, Unnalom and other monasteries and met behind the palace, with Pach Chhoeun as leader courageously striding out in front. The demonstrators paraded bravely, harbouring no illusions. French, Khmer and Viet-namese spies walked alongside, but they were pale and scared of the demonstrators. (The French spy named Sambraige was more careful than the others.) Everyone walked towards the office of the Resident Superior.

When the demonstrators got there they stopped; people were everywhere to the west of Wat Phnom, opposite the Hotel Royal, with a banner in front of them. First of all, Pach Chhoeun came forward to describe the events to some French officials who were waiting for us on the steps. Pach Chhoeun asked to see the Resident-Superior.'[19]

The French immediately closed the front door, swept Chhoeun out through the back of the building, and took him away in a car. Part of the crowd dispersed when King Sihanouk's father, Prince Suramarit, and a leading monk assured them that the detainees would be released and that the authorities would examine the question of independence.[20] But others attempted to break into the building, and a riot ensured. The several hundred police who were present used batons, while the demonstrators had sticks, stones, and rivets tied to elastic leads, which they used as missiles; monks struck police with their umbrellas, 'leading to many injuries', according to Mul, but there were apparently no deaths. Two truckloads of Japanese soldiers arrived during the riot but did not intervene.[21]

Over the next few days, the number of arrests reached approximately two hundred.[22] Thanh later claimed to the Japanese that only ten of his active militants had been captured,[23] but the organization was small and in fact severely disrupted; those who escaped arrest — including Ros Yoeun, later a leading Issarak figure — fled to Thailand.[24] Others took refuge in the countryside. One, Chan Dara, ended up working for the Japanese in Stung Treng province, in the far north-east.[25] Another, a teacher of Pali at Unnalom monastery named Achar Mean, fled to Kompong Chhnang; there he entered Yeay Tep monastery[26] and also established clandestine contact with the overseas branch of the ICP in nearby Thai-controlled territory. Another monk, Achar Pres, took to the Cardamom mountains of southern Battambang; deciding that 'the peaceful road to independence had failed', he attempted to 'wake up' the people and begin a more concerted armed resistance.[27] Achar Pres, who seems to have taken the name of an anti-royalist rebel leader in the 1860s, later worked closely with the ICP, while

Achar Mean was the first Khmer to join it after the war, under the name 'Son Ngoc Minh'.

With the help of the Japanese, Son Ngoc Thanh secretly made his way to Battambang and then to Bangkok. He wrote to the Japanese Prime Minister Tojo, asking for immediate intervention on the basis of a four-point programme: immediate release of all the Khmer political prisoners, 'military occupation of Cambodia by the Imperial Army throughout the period of reorganization of the Kingdom', close economic collaboration between his country and Japan, and French concession of 'Cambodia to the Cambodians' accompanied by a complete change of government.[28] In another letter to the Japanese Consul in Phnom Penh, Thanh claimed: 'After several weeks of reorganization we are still capable of recommencing all posssible activity: *attentats*, guerilla war, terrorism and the distribution of leaflets, provided that we have *the formal agreement of Japan and the directive* indicating in what direction we must take our movement.'[29]

He advocated 'reorganization of Cambodia in accordance with the New Order instituted by the Empire of the Rising Sun',[30] but the Japanese response was cautious. On 4 August he asked whether 'I should go to Tokyo or remain here to recommence activity until Cambodia is independent and the Imperial Army effectively occupies the Khmer Kingdom'.[31] Still, in a third letter, to a Japanese official in Saigon in October, Thanh showed he was not disheartened: 'All of us, monks and lay people, are quite attached to Japan in the cause of Cambodia's independence, knowing that we can form with all the other states of yellow Asia a compact bloc around Japan, the Liberator and Defender of the Yellow World.'[32]

But his hopes for effective Japanese aid faded quickly. On 19 December, Pach Chhoeun, Hem Chieu ('still preaching', according to Bunchhan Mul) and Nuon Duong were sentenced to death by a French military tribunal in Saigon. This was commuted by the Vichy regime to a life sentence with hard labour, on Poulo Condore off the coast of South Vietnam. Mul and his brother were sentenced to five years there and fifteen years exile from Kampuchea.[33] Thanh left Bangkok on 22 January 1943 in a Japanese military aircraft, and arrived in Tokyo four days later. He then made clear to his supporters the significance of this: *'We must wait.* Only Japan's complete victory in Asia will resolve all the Asian problems to which the lot of our

Cambodia is linked.'[34]

On 26 April, he wrote: 'I have asked you to collaborate in all fields with the Japanese authorities wherever you meet them. I have also shown you who are our enemies: on one side the French, on the other the Thais. Our sole support, our liberator, can therefore only be Japan ... The Japanese principle is cooperation and not colonization or an armed protectorate, the imperialism of the old order ... Japan assumes leadership of the movement, the coordination of the operation, and the maintenance of peace and equilibrium ... Your work in Battambang therefore consists of developing close relationships with the Japanese consulate, of forming a compact bloc behind this consulate.'

But again, general Japanese strategy had priority. Referring to the pacts linking Japan with Vichy France and Thailand, he continued: 'However you must not push things as far as upsetting the current general situation ... The international circumstances do not yet permit Japan to openly resolve the Khmer (Indo-Chinese) problem.'[35] On 25 July, in a letter to Ros Yoeun, Thanh even attempted to draw encouragement from the close relationship between Japan and the enemy Thailand: 'Quite recently Japan has just given four Malay states and two Shan states to Thailand: I think that with this they are signalling, to that last belligerent and frenzied imperialist, Asian equilibrium in these regions. So confidence in Japan – let us remain firm and ready behind the Imperial Army: Asia (for us our Cambodia) can only be rebuilt by it and led by the Empire of the Rising Sun.' He then spelled out what he understood to be his country's future: 'From the opinion of Japanese non-official circles, it transpires that the position of our Cambodia should be [that of] a buffer state between Thailand and the Vietnamese states. Its status would perhaps take the form of an autonomous state under Japanese supervision, like Manchukuo for example.'[36]

This is an interesting analogy. Thanh must have known that Tokyo had settled about half a million Japanese in Manchukuo since the 1920s. (They were now planning similar settlement schemes in Burma.) Although the spectre of such settlement — by Vietnamese — haunted the more racially sensitive Khmer nationalists, Thanh's position was genuinely pan-Asian.

But at the very least he was extremely naive. To the extent that he was now a prisoner of the situation, that could have been avoided earlier by a decision to go underground in Kampuchea (or to stay in Thailand independently), as others did, rather than to seek Japanese protection that was not available to others. In any case, he would have found many sympathizers in the Khmer countryside even if he had not taken to the mountains or jungle.

Not only did Thanh, unlike Ho Chi Minh, fail to foresee Japan's long-term imperialist intentions or the fact that it would eventually lose the war; he also misconstrued Japan's short-term intentions in 1942. There is no reason to believe that Thanh was any less patriotic than Indonesia's Sukarno, who also collaborated with Japan. But Thanh was a victim of Tokyo's four years of co-existence with the French in Indo-China — a policy quite different from the instant Japanese destruction of the Dutch administration in Indonesia in 1942, which allowed Sukarno to take centre stage. In Kampuchea, as in Vietnam and Laos, bourgeois nationalists were not provided by Japan with any such space in which to establish themselves. But unlike those of Vietnam and Laos, the leading nationalist of Kampuchea sat out most of the war in Tokyo. Thanh became a captain in the Japanese army. For public purposes the Japanese described him as a Burmese, and he assumed the name Chayo (Khmer for 'Hurrah').

In the meantime, however, the Khmer political prisoners were developing international contacts of a different kind. Also on Poulo Condore were a large number of Vietnamese communist prisoners, who 'had been politically educated for a long time [and] treated one another like brothers', according to Bunchhan Mul. 'The Vietnamese were hospitable to the Khmer political prisoners ...[They] were happy to see us serving sentences [and] said that when we all unite to bash the heads of the French, the French could not bring 'our Khmer brothers and sisters' to bash them. This was the idea of rebellion for common interest that the Vietnamese woke up to and started before we did ... The Vietnamese political prisoners, at that time, looked after Achar Hem Chieu, Nuon Duong and Pach Chhoeun very well. Why? Because it added to their strength and was in their interest too.'[37]

The Vietnamese in nearby cells included senior Viet Minh leaders Ton Duc Thang and Pham Van Dong. According to them, Hem Chieu's heroism in the prison led to sanctions which brought on his early death,[38] from illness, in October 1943. He was forty-six.[39]

On the Thai-Kampuchea border, the first Khmer resistance

organizations were established in 1944 in Battambang, by the ICP and the Communist Party of Thailand. Membership was small, but those involved included Achar Pres, and a young practitioner of traditional medicine from Battambang named Sieu Heng, who later rose quickly through the communist ranks.[40]

Meanwhile, the Japanese had put one of Thanh's followers, Chan Dara, 'in charge of all the workers in Stung Treng province', according to Dara's autobiographical account. They discreetly informed him of Thanh's presence in Japan, and recruited him into the Imperial Army. But only in March 1945 were they ready to move against the French. Dara, writing in the third person, describes what he saw, in Stung Treng, of the Indochina-wide Japanese coup: 'At six o'clock one evening, four Japanese, including two Lieutenant-Colonels and two youths, asked Chan Dara to walk with them and gave him a sword and a knife. Chan Dara was then told to go to eat, but not to sleep, because they had something to do that night. Chan Dara readied himself according to the orders. [On 9 March] 1945, on Friday at 10.00 that night, we were informed that we had to arrest the French. So in two hours, the Japanese encircled and arrested all French citizens in Stung Treng province. In Kratie province, the French fought against the Japanese all night, were defeated and placed in detention by the Japanese ... The Japanese victory over the French in Cambodia took only an estimated twenty-four hours.'[41]

In the ensuing anti-French euphoria in Phnom Penh, members of the ethnic Vietnamese community,[42] as well as Khmers now released from gaol,[43] assisted in the destruction of the French apparatus. But like the July 1942 crackdown, this new upheaval brought some recruits to the communists. For instance, a Khmer soldier in the French army, Sok Saphai, escaped and fled to Vietnam, where he joined the Viet Minh underground.[44] He reappears later in our story as an Issarak leader.

A third incident around this time had a similar effect. On 7 February 1945, US B-29 warplanes had bombed part of Phnom Penh. Bombs fell in front of Unnalom monastery, killing twenty monks and a large number of other people.[45] Tou Samouth, then a Professor of Pali at the monastery, took fright and fled into the countryside.[46] He too made his way to Vietnam and, like other monks who had also participated in the 1942 demonstration, began working with the ICP.

Under Japanese pressure, Sihanouk declared independence on 13 March; at a Khmer New Year ceremony a month later, he praised 'the Empire of the Rising Sun, the Liberator of the Asian People'.[47] However, surprisingly perhaps, it was *another* six weeks before Son Ngoc Thanh could return from Tokyo, which he did on 30 May. He was made Foreign Minister. He also began organizing the training of Khmer militia units (involving about a thousand youths) under Japanese supervision, similar to the Peta forces in Indonesia.

On 20 July 1945, a large crowd gathered by the Mekong for a ceremony at Wat Unnalom commemorating the 1942 anti-French demonstration. Anti-colonial heroes from Pou Kombo to Hem Chieu were honoured. The new nationalism was not only linked with hitherto repressed undercurrents of the past, however. It also revealed a strong sense of modernity, which anticipated a future that would sweep away traditional backwardness. Son Ngoc Thanh's militia commander expressed it this way: 'I am convinced that my compatriots and myself are the best Cambodian troops because we have been chosen from among the intellectuals.'[48]

But members of the government were not so chosen. Among Ministers in the new Cabinet, only Thanh had any nationalist or reformist/modernist credentials. The others were, in Sihanouk's words, 'best-known previously, in bourgeois Phnom Penh society, for their pro-French zeal'.[49] Royal powers, too, were actually increased. The Japanese presumably considered this the most expeditious method of consolidating their local support as the Allied armies approached. All that was too much for a group of seven young Khmer officials with militia training. One of them recalled, years later, how they were 'dissatisfied with a government filled with old traditionalists and wanted genuine nationalists brought in'[50] and a greater role for Son Ngoc Thanh. On 9 August, these seven youths stormed King Sihanouk's palace during the night in an attempt to force his abdication, shooting and wounding his secretary in the process. They also arrested almost the entire Cabinet except for Thanh, who became Prime Minister the next morning.

Whether the Japanese were involved in the coup itself remains a moot point. But, whatever their role, it was an important event in Khmer history, for three reasons.

Firstly, it was supported by many Buddhist monks and by the Association of Former Students of Sisowath High School, which until the 1940s was the only post-primary school in the entire country.

A crowd of fifty students had gathered in the school grounds during the night, ready to participate in the events taking place in the Palace next door.[51] (One of those students was Keng Vannsak, who later went on to study in England and in France, where he invented the Khmer typewriter, and helped introduce Pol Pot to Marxism; in the 1950s he became a leading political figure, as we shall see, and in the 1960s he was Dean of the Faculty of Arts of Phnom Penh University.) In one sense, the coup was the tip of the small but solid iceberg of modern Khmer political thinking; in another, it resembled, again on a small scale, the *pemuda* movement of Indonesia's militant youth in the same period. It was the clarion call to anti-colonial resistance, and gave it a distinctly modernist tone, unlike the traditionalist re-awakening of the previous five months.

Secondly, in an inexplicable act of betrayal, Son Ngoc Thanh immediately released the former ministers and arrested the seven young coup-makers. Some of the seven, however, escaped from gaol within months, and in later years five of them were to work with or in the Indo-China Communist Party. (They were Mey Pho, Mao Sarouth, Neth Laing Say, Mam Koun, and Hem Savang. We shall come across them again in the next chapter.) Further, according to French intelligence, Achar Mean (Son Ngoc Minh) took part in the insurrection also.[52] This is not confirmed, but if true it helps explain why future cooperation between him and Thanh proved difficult. By the end of the year Achar Mean was working with the ICP as well; in Vietnam, where the Viet Minh were leading the August revolution which swept the country after the Japanese capitulation, he met up with Tou Samouth (Achar Sok), and they worked together to recruit among the Khmer Krom. These two ex-monks were the founders of Khmer communism.

Thirdly, the 9 August coup not only exposed internal rifts in Khmer nationalism, but also had a traumatic effect on the young King Sihanouk (who has despised Thanh ever since), and on other sections of the traditional elite. Defence Minister Khim Tit, for instance, was soon to visit Saigon and request the return of the French to quell the 'unrest' in the country.[53]

Son Ngoc Thanh wished to improve relations with the Vietnamese (and all 'yellow-skinned' peoples).[54] He recognized Ho Chi Minh's Democratic Republic of Vietnam (DRV) when it was proclaimed in Hanoi on 2 September,[55] and, in the hope of obtaining its support, allowed it to establish a mission in Phnom Penh.[56] Over the next month Thanh's government made several calls for Khmers to cooperate 'sincerely and fraternally' with the Vietnamese.[57] Thanh also dispatched a young Sino-Khmer graduate of Sisowath High School called Ea Sichau on a journey to seek Chinese aid.[58] Soon after, leaders of the Viet Minh in Cochinchina contacted Thanh (through his brother Son Thai Nguyen in Vietnam), in an attempt to coordinate resistance to the returning French. According to the Viet Minh military commander, Nguyen Thanh Son, Thanh accepted their proposal and sent a return delegation for talks; however, this delegation 'committed an error' by demanding, as a precondition for cooperation, the return to Kampuchea of the long-lost Travinh and Soctrang provinces.[59] Negotiations broke down over the issue. The French had little trouble in re-establishing their authority in Kampuchea; they arrested Son Ngoc Thanh on 15 October and sent him into exile first in Saigon and then in France.

In an unpublished interview with Anthony Barnett, the Allied Commander in Kampuchea, Lt. Col. E.D. Murray, has described Thanh's arrest, which he himself planned 'very carefully and very secretly' in cooperation with the French General Leclerc. Murray, who arrived in Phnom Penh on 8 October, did not meet the Khmer Prime Minister until the arrest took place a week later. He recalls: 'Everything was always done, it has always rather puzzled me, by my chum, the Defence Minister [Khim Tit] ... It's strange now, why the hell I didn't have the Prime Minister come and see me ... This Prime Minister chappie was against the King.'

Murray noted that Khim Tit, by contrast, was committed to the royal family. Finally Murray summoned Thanh to his headquarters, and then went to fetch Leclerc from the airport. 'Poor little Prime Minister thought Leclerc was welcoming him and got up to sort of say 'How lovely'! He was taken by the scruff of the neck by this [Leclerc's] gunman, bundled into the car and off. I never saw them again.' Ea Sichau, for his part, was stopped by the French at the Vietnam-China border.[60]

Pach Chhoeun, who had become Thanh's Minister of the Economy in August, managed to escape to Vietnam, accompanied by Chau Sen Cocsal, governor of Kompong Cham province, and seven Khmer district chiefs. Others who followed them into the ranks of the Viet Minh included Hem Savang, one of the seven young men involved in the 9 August coup, who escaped from gaol in December.[61] At the same time, according to French intelligence: 'Numerous Vietnamese from Phnom Penh and the provinces, fearing troubles and incidents with the Cambodians as well as reprisals on our part, fled to Cochinchina, to their provinces of origin.'[62]

Many of them also joined the Viet Minh, with whose help Pach Chhoeun established a Khmer Issarak Committee along the border. Although it enlisted the support of many monks in the distribution of its propaganda (Pach Chhoeun claimed a local following of six thousand Khmer Krom)[63] and recruited several hundred youths into its armed forces,[64] this Committee collapsed after only four months, when the French re-established control of the border areas and the Committee's Triton headquarters. Chau Sen Cocsal surrendered to the French in February 1946.[65] Pach Chhoeun did likewise in April, depressed at the setback and disillusioned with the 'very cool' Viet Minh response to his December request for Vietnamese support for an attack on Phnom Penh.[66] Some of the Committee's followers then joined the army of the Viet Minh, who were already sending the ethnic Vietnamese fugitives back to Kampuchea to recommence their activities. Others such as Hem Savang joined the Bangkok-based Khmer Issarak Committee after making their way to western Kampuchea or to Thailand. There Savang met up with Mey Pho, a former palace clerk who had also been involved in the August coup, and had also escaped from gaol in December.[67]

The Thai civilian government under Pridi Phanomyong was sympathetic to the cause of Kampuchean independence from France, and in early 1946 also permitted the establishment in Bangkok of a DRV mission, headed by Tran Van Giau, the senior communist leader. At one point in that year, Pridi arranged for the handing over of a barge carrying twenty tonnes of carbines, US weapons supplied to the Free Thai movement during the war.[68] However, when Pridi was overthrown by Phibun Song-kram, a wartime collaborator with the Japanese, in a military coup in November 1947, Thai-Vietnamese cooperation came to an end.

Many of the key figures in the Khmer communist movement began their activities at this time. In 1946 Son Sichan, a Kampuchean-born Vietnamese who had been district chief of

Peamchikang in Kompong Cham, recruited Ney Sarann, then a subdistrict clerk in Svay Rieng, and Keo Meas, a fourth-year student at the Phnom Penh Teachers' Training College. They were soon joined by Nhem Sun, an *adjudant-chef* in the French army.[69] Son Ngoc Minh and Tou Samouth recruited supporters among the Khmer Krom on the basis of anti-colonial solidarity, and travelled to Thailand to buy arms with funds supplied by the Viet Minh. They made contact with Mey Pho and other members of the Issarak Committee there, and recruited more supporters in Thai-held Battambang and Siemreap. It was in Thailand, under the auspices of its overseas branch, that Son Ngoc Minh joined the ICP, in October 1946. Tou Samouth followed suit in Kampuchea at the end of the year. (Mey Pho joined in 1949, in the Dangrek mountains on the northern Thai-Kampuchean border, along with a former district official from Battambang named Hong Chhun.)[70] But already in June 1946, a mixed Khmer-Vietnamese resistance command had been set up in Battambang; its political commissar was Neth Laing Say,[71] who with Mey Pho, Hem Savang and four others had staged the palace coup of August 1945. Also in June, a sum of 150,000 piastres raised from voluntary contributions among the people of Battambang, had arrived at Poc Khun's office in Bangkok. He brought 150 Japanese guns and ammunition, several automatic weapons, and grenades, which he sent to the Issarak forces in Battambang, which now numbered about a thousand with three thousand supporters.[72] One well-armed, three hundred strong mixed Khmer-Vietnamese force was led by a former sergeant in the Thai army named Dap Chhuon, rebel Prince Norodom Chantaraingsey, a woman called Leath Muon, and Son Ngoc Minh; on 7 August they briefly seized the city of Siemreap and killed seven French officers.[73]

This success heralded increased Vietnamese and leftist influence in the Thai-based Issarak Committee. In late 1945, the Committee of twelve members had included only one who was sympathetic to the Vietnamese communists — Mey Pho.[74] But this Committee had fallen apart through internal dissension, and another was created in early 1946 at the Bangkok home of its founder Aphaiwong, brother-in-law of Poc Khun and former Thai governor of Battambang. Known as Korocho, or the Committee of National Union (*Kana Ruom Cheat*), it eventually recruited most of the members of the disbanded Issarak Committee, but subsequently itself collapsed, partly because even its three sub-committees were headed by Thai officials.[75] With varying degrees of enthusiasm these Thai tried to use the Issarak movement to retain (and later recover) control of Battambang and Siemreap.

Yat Hwaidi, the local Thai Education Supervisor, later wrote that he had 'tried to tell the pupils and the people': 'We are Thai and we are brothers. But we had to be separated because of French colonialism. Now we are gathered together on one piece of land. We have a Thai King as our leader.'[76] One of Hwaidi's associates at that time was Kao Tak, a stock merchant from Siemreap, and adopted brother of Leath Muon.

In December 1946, Thailand was forced to relinquish control of Battambang, Siemreap and Stung Treng; Hwaidi says that at this time, Kao Tak 'invited me to a meeting in the Battambang market'. People at this meeting, which was attended by Aphaiwong, Dap Chhuon, and two other leading Thai officials, expressed the fear that 'the French would oppress as before'. Hwaidi says: 'The people were under Thai control for six years. They like Thailand and want to be under Thailand ... I agreed to be a major advisor of the Khmer Issarak ... I drank the water of allegiance with Mr. Dap Chhuon and Mr. To Lim Trakun [Kao Tak] and helped to give them ideas.'[77]

But the Thai were also good businessmen. French intelligence reports: 'After having waited in vain for the free delivery of arms promised by the Thai authorities, these rebel chiefs [in Battambang] decided to go ahead themselves with purchasing the arms that they needed. Korocho was formed at this point to take in hand this lucrative trade which constituted the bulk of its activities.[78]

Nevertheless, the liberation cause had developed its own momentum and broadened its scope beyond the traditional Khmer-Thai relationship. Prince Phetsarath, a Lao Issara leader then in exile in Bangkok, has described the increasing cooperation between the independence movements of South-east Asia. He wrote in the third person:

> During the same period, Vietnam, Cambodia, Burma and Indonesia were [like Laos] also thinking of national liberation. The Cambodian leader was the Governor of Siemreap [Poc Khun ?] ...
> Since the national liberation movements of five countries competed in the purchase of guns, the prices of bootleg weapons increased manyfold. The Prince then arranged a secret meeting of

representatives of the five countries, the outcome of which was an agreement on two important points:

Point 1. Investigation of places to buy bootleg guns: if any of the countries found weapons sources, they would be the sole buyers and others would not compete. When their needs were met, the other countries would buy. Countries without money would be helped. For example, the Cambodian national liberation group found a source of weapons but had no money. The Lao group loaned them 5,000 *baht*. At that time, the Cambodians could not pay, but such help was to be repaid in the future.

Point 2. Because various groups in the five countries were doing different things for national liberation, it had been impossible to cooperate in the beginning and this was why the enemy had the advantage. However it was clear that for Laos, Vietnam and Cambodia, France was the common enemy. In view of this situation, the following three [sic] subsidiary agreements were made:

1. Anyone from any of the countries could hide in the area of the other countries, but they had to be under the authority of that country. For example, if Vietnamese entered Laos, they had to be accompanied by Lao.

2. Laos and Cambodia had small populations and were unable to fight large battles, but they would work as guerrilla bands seeking every possible opportunity to weaken the French. They would stay in Cambodia and Laos and not join forces with Vietnam. However, the Vietnamese, with their large population, would take whatever opportunity to use their strength to destroy the French in Vietnam. Whenever the Vietnamese fought a large battle, the Cambodians and Lao would begin guerrilla warfare to harass the French as much as possible.[79]

Meanwhile, the Lao Issara and Khmer Issarak representatives in Bangkok were working on a joint memorandum to the UN Secretary-General, requesting his help in obtaining independence from France. According to the American representative in Bangkok, Edwin F. Stanton, Viet Minh ('Vietnam Government') representatives were 'drawn into' the preparation of the final draft, which was handed to Stanton in early January 1947 by Prince Souphanouvong (who in 1975 became President of the Lao People's Democratic Republic). Stanton cabled this summary of its contents to Washington: 'The memo as finally drafted is a fairly objective presentation of the views and aspirations of the three states. Perhaps the two most significant features of the document are firstly, advocacy of a United States or Federation of the countries of South-east Asia comprising Burma, Siam, the

Malay Federation, the United States of Indonesia, Vietnam, Cambodia and Laos, and secondly that the memo is a joint document signed by representatives of free Cambodians, free Laos and the Vietnam Government ... The Vietnam Government by radio and through its various agents has naturally been working among free Cambodians and free Laos in an effort to enlist their open support against the French, and there are numerous indications that these efforts have met with a favourable and in some instances an enthusiastic response.'

Stanton pleaded with the State Department to use its good offices to ensure that the memorandum was considered by the UN Security Council at an early date; otherwise, he predicted, there would be 'general chaos' in Indo-China. The reply from Washington, however, was as follows: 'The Department approves efforts to secure info concerning current developments in Indo-China but does not consider the Department the proper channel to transmit memoranda to SC from 'free' groups claiming to represent nationalist movements of Indo-China. You should therefore return the document in question.'[80]

Souphanouvong received his letter back unopened. Phetsarath recorded: 'The Lao group finally concluded that America was reluctant to impose upon the French and would do nothing to make the French lose face.'[81] The Khmer Issarak must have drawn the same conclusion; but it was a lesson that other nationalists, in particular Son Ngoc Thanh — still in enforced exile in France — had yet to learn.

In May 1947, two of the fourteen Korocho Committee members, Ros Yoeun and Mey Phorin, were shot by the Thai for insubordination, after they had refused instructions to raise funds by pillage.[82] Another surrendered to the French at Poipet with 280 men and a good deal of equipment. They were followed by several hundred other defectors in Battambang, and a similar number in Kompong Chhnang, including 102 women.[83] But there were more serious signs of the political degeneration of the Issarak movement. In the words of the Indian historian V. M. Reddi, alleged 'Francophiles became the targets of Issarak hatred and persecution'. In November 1946, 'in Keiey Puoy village, where the majority of inhabitants were Catholics, situated about 8 km. to the south of Battambang, more than one hundred inhabitants fell victim to the Issarak sword. At the same time, however, an American pastor, Reverend Ellison, who was arrested by mistake, was released.'[84]

Despite all this, the anti-French military struggle was hotting up. Colonel Yves Gras, a French military officer, later reported Issarak losses of 500 killed and 136 arms captured in the month of May 1947 alone, but noted that the Issarak movement in the north-west had not been defeated: 'It had even developed, thanks to its support from Siam and the Viet Minh, to the point of creating a serious problem in Cambodia.' In Battambang, Siemreap and the Dangrek mountains, Gras estimated that there were in all 1,200 armed Issaraks, supported by 'Viet Minh reinforcements of about the same numbers'.[85]

But Neth Laing Say was killed in an ambush in Kompong Speu in October 1946; and in late 1947 Chantaraingsey, Mey Pho and Hem Savang withdrew from Korocho.[86] Sieu Heng did the same, and with a hundred followers began operating south of Battambang 'in theory under Viet Minh command but with broad autonomy'.[87] Another member, Prak Sarin, made his way to Svay Rieng and began working with the ICP there.[88]

Throughout Indo-China a struggle was developing along the lines described by Phetsarath and Edwin Stanton. In the second half of 1947 French intelligence reported that combined Lao-Vietnamese insurgent units had established sanctuaries and bases in both Siemreap and Battambang, where they were joined by four hundred Thai, led by a suspected communist, who fled their country after the November 1947 coup.[89] Soon afterwards, a rebel unit under Souphanouvong's control in Laos was reported to be commanded by a Khmer.[90]

However the biggest force representing Khmer nationalism and modernism in this period was not the guerrilla movement but the Democratic Party. (There were of course haphazard contacts between the two.) It had been founded by Prince Yuthevong soon after his return home from Paris (where he had been a member of the Socialist Party) in March 1946. In Constituent Assembly elections that September, the Democratic Party won 50 of the 67 seats. However its ideals of independence and democracy proved very difficult to realize in the face of the combined opposition of the French, the King and the traditional economic elite. Yuthevong's premature and allegedly mysterious death in a French hospital in July 1947 was a blow to the Democrats, but they again won easily in the elections for the National Assembly in December that year. Although they failed to jeopardize seriously the French grip on Kampuchea, the Democrats continued to attract many of the best of the Khmer intellectual elite and for some years also remained the most popular political party in the country.

On 1 February 1948, the Issarak movement formed a Khmer People's Liberation Committee (or KPLC; in Khmer, *Kana Cheat Mouta Keaha Mocchim Nokor Khmer*). Chantaraingsey declined to join, considering it to be 'pro-Viet Minh'.[91] Although the KPLC and its armed forces were headed by Dap Chhuon, a traditional warlord rather than a left-wing nationalist, at least five of its eleven leaders — Hong Chhun, Mey Pho, Sieu Heng, Leav Keo Moni, and Muon — were sympathetic to the Vietnamese communists and four of them were soon to join the communist party. Two other members of the KPLC Committee were its military 'political commissar', Mao Sarouth, and the man responsible for foreign affairs, Hem Savang, both of whom had taken part in the August 1945 palace coup. Their views quickly became clear too. According to French intelligence: 'The influence of the Viet Minh is in fact very obvious in the drafting of articles published in the French-language organ of the KPLC, *Indépendance*, whose tone contrasts with the much more monotonous Cambodian journal, *Ekareach*, designed for the Khmer masses.'

The first manifesto of the KPLC stated: 'French imperialism is on the wane. It will meet its death at the hands of fraternal combat by the three peoples, Lao, Vietnamese and Cambodian. An Indo-Chinese Front for Independence is therefore an immediate necessity. The Khmer people must follow the path traced by democratic and anti-colonial humankind.'

Dap Chhuon and Ho Chi Minh exchanged congratulatory messages.[92] Chhuon's own armed forces numbered eight hundred guerrillas,[93] including several hundred led by Kao Tak and former bamboo seller, Leav Keo Moni. Sieu Heng's forces had also joined the KPLC, making it a formidable problem for the French in Kampuchea's north-west. On 27 April 1948, a mixed Khmer-Vietnamese force led by Hong Chhun and including Kao Tak and Leav Keo Moni, attacked the Phnom Penh-Battambang train, 'caused several casualties, and took ten French lives'.[94]

Meanwhile, on the other side of the country, Son Ngoc Minh returned from a trip to Thailand where he had gone to purchase weapons with funds supplied by the Viet Minh. He bought enough to equip a largely Khmer company at Bay Nui across the Vietnamese border from Takeo.[95] At the end of 1947 he

established the Liberation Committee of South-east Kampuchea, but seems to have left it to another former Khmer
monk, Keo Moni (not to be confused with Leav Keo Moni), who
joined the ICP in that year and began recruiting a Khmer armed
force in Prey Veng.[96] In 1948, Son Ngoc Minh became Chief of
the Military Affairs Committee of the 'Joint Khmer-Vietnamese
Forces in the 10th War Zone' (the South-west), and in March
established the Liberation Committee of South-west
Kampuchea.[97] In April, joint Khmer-Vietnamese Liberation
units were formed; according to a French source, these were
composed of Vietnamese and unknown Cambodians liberated
from internment on Poulo Condore in 1945.[98] Around the same
time, Long Reth, a Khmer law student at Thammasat University
in Bangkok, working part-time as a clerk in the Ministry of
Foreign Affairs, was recruited by Muon and joined the Communist Party of Thailand.[99] He moved back to Battambang and
soon transferred to the ICP. (In 1960, under the name Nuon
Chea, he became deputy secretary of the Communist Party of
Kampuchea.)

By late 1948, the combined Khmer resistance had divided the
country into four military zones: the South-east, headed by Keo
Moni; the North-east, under Son Sichan; the South-west, under
Son Ngoc Minh; and the North-west, under Dap Chhuon as
head of the KPLC.[100] Apart from Dap Chhuon, all were members
of the ICP and had established Liberation Committees closely
linked with it. (The ICP also had a North-western branch, headed
by Sieu Heng.) The KPLC did not (or not yet) have such links,
although a French intelligence report lamented that in this
period, 'The Khmer Issarak leaders who had just shaken off Thai
tutelage were inclined to accept that of the Viet Minh instead'.[101]

In early 1949, the KPLC became the Khmer National Liberation
Committee, or KNLC (*Kana Kamathikar Khmer Sang Cheat*); it was
reported by French intelligence to have 'rid itself of elements
considered too pro-Viet Minh'.[102] It is true that Sieu Heng, at
least, transferred east and, according to Bernard Fall, became
chief of the Viet Minh's 'Central Office South', with 'jurisdiction
over Cambodia, South Vietnam and South Central Vietnam' —
not an insignificant post.[103] But the new KNLC Committee of
seven, elected in January 1949, and headed by Dap Chhuon and
his deputy Kao Tak, still included three close allies of the Viet
Minh: Mey Pho, Leav Keo Moni and Muon. They took charge of
the KNLC's Information, Economy and Treasury branches

respectively.[104] In February, Muon was reported to be distributing medicines in villages in Siemreap, and, having obtained authorization from Dap Chhuon to requisition ox-carts to transport fish and rice to Thailand,[105] to have sold them and bought eighty rifles for Chantaraingsey's forces in the southwest.[106] She was obviously attempting to forge unity among all Issarak groups.

But Dap Chhuon's authoritarian style was rapidly alienating many of the KNLC's other leaders and members, [107] and in February he had already begun secretly putting out feelers to the French to arrange an accommodation.[108] Bunchhan Mul, disillusioned with Chhuon's brutality, quit the movement and returned to Phnom Penh.[109] Leav Keo Moni broke away with a hundred men,[110] and in April Kao Tak followed with four hundred.[111] In early July Chhuon invited Mao Sarouth and Hem Savang to a meeting, and had them assassinated.[112] In elections later that month, he was replaced as KNLC leader by Poc Khun,[113] who had founded the first Issarak Committee in Bangkok in 1940. Three other leaders, also 'accused of having mistreated the population too much', were expelled.[114] Dap Chhuon finally surrendered to the French in September 1949 with three hundred armed followers and a number of 'female auxiliaries'. He was immediately named Commander-in-Chief of the 'Franco-Khmer Corps' in the Siemreap-Kompong Thom 'Autonomous Sector', by the colonial government.[115]

This was a serious blow to the Khmer independence movement, as well as to the revolutionary movement that was just beginning to develop within it. The continuing political isolation of Khmer communists is illustrated by the account of Chea Soth (now Minister of Planning in the PRK), who had made contact with Dap Chhuon in 1946 but then returned home to Prey Veng, where he joined Tou Samouth in 1949. 'There were only Vietnamese, Viet Minh, living with us. We worked with them and they explained things to us. I did not even know what communism meant. If anybody had asked me whether I was afraid of communism then, I would have said 'yes'.'[116]

But the groundwork for a communist movement had been laid, and the trend towards colonial emancipation was also irresistible, Issaraks cannot fail to have noted the success of independence movements in the Philippines (1946), India (1947), Burma (1948), and Indonesia (1949), to say nothing of the communist victory in China. The longer the French attempted to maintain their control of Indo-China by force, the stronger the communist elements in the independence movements there would become.

Notes

1. W.J. Duiker, *The Rise of Nationalism in Vietnam*, 1900-1941, Cornell University Press, Ithaca, 1976, p.262.
2. According to Thanh, Thibadeau replied 'verbally' that should France become so unable he 'would be the first to hand over Cambodia to us'. Letter from Son Ngoc Thanh to the Japanese consul in Cambodia, undated. In the *Son Ngoc Thanh Papers*, donated to the Monash University Library by Chana Samudava-nija, 1981.
3. Archives D'Outre-Mer (AOM), Aix-en-Province, France. Cambodge 7F 29(7), *Etude sur les mouvements rebelles au Cambodge, 1942-52*, 136 pp., at p.3. (Hereafter cited as *Etude*.)
4. *Ibid.*, annexe, p.20.
5. *Ibid.*; and 'Norodom Sihanouk and the Khmer Issarak', by Yat Hwaidi, *Bangkok Democrat*, 25 May and 1 June 1970.
6. *Etude*, op. cit., p.4.
7. A second letter, also undated, from Son Ngoc Thanh to the Japanese consul in Cambodia, *Son Ngoc Thanh Papers, op. cit.*
8. Tran Huy Lieu, *Lich Su Tam Muoi Nam Chong Phap* ('A History of Eighty Years' Resistance to the French'), Hanoi, Van Su Dia, Vol. 2, book 2, pp.71-77, at p.76. I am grateful to Huynh Kim Khanh for this reference.
9. D. Gareth Porter, 'Vietnamese Communist Policy towards Kampuchea, 1930-1970', in David P. Chandler and Ben Kiernan (eds.) *Revolution and its Aftermath in Kampuchea*, New Haven 1983, p.62.
10. Michael Vickery, 'Cambodia: The Present Situation and its Background', April 1973 typescript, 50 pp., at p.4.
11. This was introduced in 1943.
12. *Etude, op, cit.*, p.4.
13. Bunchhan Mul, *Kuk niyobay* ('Political Prison'), Phnom Penh 1971.

62

14. *Son Ngoc Thanh Papers, op. cit.*
15. *Ibid.*, letter to the Chief of Staff of the Japanese Imperial Army in Indo-China, undated.
16. Bunchhan Mul, *op. cit.*
17. *Son Ngoc Thanh Papers, op. cit.*, 'Mémoire sur l'entretien avec le Gendarmerie', attached to first letter to the Japanese consul in Cambodia.
18. David J. Steinberg, et al., *Cambodia: Its People, Its Society, Its Culture*, HRAF Press, New Haven, 1959, p.72. Steinberg gives no source for his statement that it was 'certain members of the Thommakay' who were 'permitting themselves to be concerned with political affairs'.
19. Bunchhan Mul, *op. cit.*
20. *Son Ngoc Thanh Papers*, second letter to the Japanese consul in Cambodia.
21. Bunchhan Mul, *op. cit.*, and *Son Ngoc Thanh Papers, op. cit.*
22. 'Mémoire sur l'entretien avec le Gendarmerie', *Son Ngoc Thanh Papers, op. cit.*
23. *Ibid.*
24. *Etude, op. cit.*, annexe, p.4.
25. 'A Khmer Issarak Leader's Story', typescript translation by Timothy Carney of Chan Dara's autobiographical sketch written in 1974. 8pp. at p.1.
26. *Ibid.*, p.5. Also author's interview with Chea Soth, Phnom Penh, 22 October 1980.
27. Author's interview with Krot Theam, who later studied under Pres. Melbourne, 2 December 1976.
28. *Son Ngoc Thanh Papers, op., cit.*
29. *Ibid.*, second letter to the Japanese consul in Cambodia. Emphasis in original.
30. *Ibid.*
31. *Ibid.*, letter to M. Chin, 4 August 1942.
32. *Ibid.*, letter from 'the Representative of the Nationalist Party for the Independence of Cambodia' (Thanh) to Matusita, Director of Dainankoosi, Saigon, 1 October 1942.
33. *Etude, op. cit.*, pp.4,5.
34. *Son Ngoc Thanh Papers, op. cit.* Emphasis in original.
35. *Ibid.*
36. *Ibid.*,
37. *Kuk niyobay, op. cit.*
38. Norodom Sihanouk, *Souvenirs doux et amers*, Paris 1981, pp. 109-110.
39. *Kuk niyobay*, op. cit.
40. Krot Theam, *op. cit.*; and author's interview with Andrew Antippus, who interviewed Sieu Heng in 1970. Washington, March 1980.
41. Chan Dara, *op. cit.*
42. AOM, 7F 29(2). *Note sur l'organisation politique et administrative Viet-Minh au Cambodge*, Direction des services de sécurité du H.C. en Indochine, December 1952, p.1. (Hereafter cited as *Note*.)
43. Bunchhan Mul, *op. cit.*
44. Author's interview with Sang Lon (Chen Lon), Kandol Chrum, 7 August 1980.
45. *Rajabangsavatar brah Norodom Sihanouk* (RNS, the chronicle history of King Sihanouk, 1949), pp.491-92. I am grateful to David P. Chandler for bringing this information to my attention. Reddi, *op.cit.*, p.87, gives a figure of 600 civilian dead from the bombing. (See note 47.)
46. Chea Soth, *op. cit.*
47. V.M. Reddi, *A History of the Cambodian Independence Movement, 1863-1955*,

Tirupati, Sri Venkatesvara University, 1973, p.91. (He cites Sam Sary, *Le Grand Figure de Norodom Sihanouk,* Phnom Penh 1955, p.4)

48. *Ibid.,* p.97.
49. Norodom Sihanouk, *Souvenirs doux et amers, op.cit.,* p.106.
50. Vickery, 1973, *op. cit.,* p.5.
51. Keng Vannsak, personal communication.
52. *Note, op. cit.,* p.23.
53. Reddi, *op.cit.,* p.108. On Khim Tit, see Sihanouk, *op. cit.,* p.110, and *Echo du Cambodge,* 23 October 1940.
54. RNS, *op. cit.,* pp.564ff.
55. Reddi, *op.cit.,* p.108.
56. *Ibid.*
57. *Ibid.,* and RNS, *op.cit.,* p.533.
58. *Etude, op. cit.,* annexe, p.19.
59. Nguyen Thanh Son, interview with author, Ho Chi Minh City, 28 October 1980.
60. *Etude, op. cit.,* annexe, pp.1, 19.
61. Nguyen Thanh Son, *op. cit.,* and *Etude, op. cit.,* p.8.
62. *Note, op. cit.,* p.1.
63. Reddi, *op. cit.,* pp.151-52.
64. Nguyen Thanh Son, *op. cit.*
65. *Etude, op. cit.,* annexe, p.11.
66. Reddi, *op. cit.,* p.152, note 34, and *Etude, op. cit.,* annexe, p.2.
67. *Etude, op. cit.,* annexe, p.10.
68. A Viet Minh captain, accompanied by a Thai police official, discreetly sailed the boat down the Chaophraya River and then motored off into the Gulf of Siam. The Thai policeman was Chana Samudavanija. Personal communication, Bangkok, 19 August 1981.
69. *Livre Noir: Faits et preuvres des actes d'agression et d'annexion du Vietnam contre le Kampuchea,* Phnom Penh, Ministry of Foreign Affairs of Democratic Kampuchea, September 1978, p.24. Also author's interview with Tea Sabun, Phnom Penh, 23 August 1980; and 'Khmer Communist Rallier Keoum Kun', unclassified Airgram to Department of State from US Embassy, Phnom Penh, 13 January 1972, p.8.
70. The preceding information comes from the author's interview with Nguyen Xuan Hoang, Hanoi, 4 November 1980.
71. *Etude, op. cit.,* annexe, p.7.
72. *Ibid.,* pp.21, 43.
73. King Sihanouk immediately protested to the French High Commissioner for Indo-China, d'Argenlieu, correctly claiming that the attack had been facilitated by Thailand. Reddi, *op.cit.,* p.121.
74. *Etude, op. cit.,* p.19.
75. *Ibid.,* pp.19-20.
76. Yat Hwaidi, *op. cit.*
77. *Ibid.*
78. *Etude, op. cit.,* p.21.
79. *Iron Man of Laos: Prince Phetsarath Ratanavongsa,* by '3349'. Cornell University South-east Asia Program Data Paper No. 110, 1978, pp.41-42.
80. US Department of State, *Foreign Relations of the United States: 1947,* vol. 6, 1976 (?), p.92, 'The Minister in Siam to the Secretary of State', 7 January 1947.
81. *Iron Man of Laos, op. cit.,* p.42.

64

82. *Etude, op. cit.,* pp.21-22. (This was confirmed to the author by informed Kampuchean sources.)
83. *Ibid.,* and Reddi, *op. cit.,* p.136, note 75.
84. Reddi, *op. cit.,* p.122.
85. *Histoire de la guerre d'Indochine,* Paris 1979, pp.231-32.
86. *Etude, op. cit.,* annexe, p.7; p.22.
87. *Ibid.,* annexe, pp.24-25.
88. *Ibid.,* p.20. Also Archives Nationales, Bibliothèque Nationale, Phnom Penh; Ministère de l'Intérieure, Divers, file no. 2, 'Takeo', reports 'Prak Sarun' as a 'Viet Minh/Khmer Issarak' leader in Svay Rieng in June 1952.
89. I am grateful to Geoffrey C. Gunn for this information, which is contained in an unpublished draft of his Ph.D. dissertation, *Colonialism, Communism and Nationalism in Laos, 1930-54.* He cites Archives d'Outre-Mer (AOM), Aix-en-Provence, France. F16, Sûreté Fédérale, 16 June 1947, and F17, 16 March-16 April 1948.
90. P.F. Langer and J. J. Zasloff, *North Vietnam and the Pathet Lao,* Harvard University Press, 1970, p.43. See also the roles of Son Ngoc Minh and Sieu Heng, p.59 of this book.
91. *Etude, op. cit.,* pp.23, 49.
92. *Ibid.,* pp.23-24.
93. *Ibid.,* p.23.
94. Reddi, *op. cit.,* p.155.
95. Nguyen Thanh Son, *op. cit.*
96. *Ibid.,* and Nguyen Xuan Hoang, *op. cit.*
97. *Etude, op. cit.,* p.100.
98. Pierre Christian, 'Le Viet-Minh au Cambodge', *Indochine Sud-est Asiatique,* February-March 1952, p.73.
99. Nguyen Xuan Hoang, *op. cit.,* and Chana Samudavanija, *op. cit.*
100. Chea Soth, *op. cit.*
101. *Etude, op.cit.,* p.24.
102. *Ibid.,* p.25.
103. Bernard B. Fall, *The Viet-Minh Regime,* Cornell University South-east Asia Program, Data Paper no. 14, April 1954, pp.44, 55.
104. *Etude, op. cit.,* p.25
105. Archives Nationales, Bibliothèque Nationale, Phnom Penh. Ministère de l'Intérieure, Divers (henceforth MID). *Rapports sur la situation politique de divers khets, fin décembre 1948 à fin 1949.* Report by Governor of Siemreap, 9 February 1949.
106. Author's interview with Muon's relatives, Kao Thao and Virayuth Puckdinukul, Bangkok, 19 August 1981.
107. MID, *Rapports ..., op.cit.,* Governor of Siemreap to Ministry of Interior, 27 July 1949.
109. *Etude, op. cit.,* p.52.
109. *Kuk niyobay, op. cit.*
110. *Etude, op. cit.,* annexe, p.26.
111. *Ibid.,* pp.25, 46.
112. *Kuk niyobay, op. cit.,* pp.86-88, and *Etude, op. cit.,* annexe, p.10.
113. *Etude, op. cit.,* p.25.
114. MID, *Rapports ..., op. cit.,* Governor of Siemreap to Ministry of Interior, 27 July 1949.
115. *Etude, op. cit.,* p.52, and Reddi, *op. cit.,* p.162.
116. Chea Soth, *op. cit.*

3
Contending Nationalisms: 1949–52

We did not fight the French. That is just what has been said. We fought Phnom Penh soldiers. The French were in Phnom Penh. There were only one or two Frenchmen in the soldiers' camp, no more. But in history they say we fought the French.

A Khmer peasant, former Issarak, 1980

The East and South-West

One of the earliest Viet Minh documents captured in Kampuchea by the French provides an insight into both the motivation and the style of Vietnamese communist operations there. Dated 30 April 1949, the statutes of the League for National Salvation of the Vietnamese Residents in Cambodia point out that Khmer and Vietnamese revolutionary organizations 'must live side by side to help one another, to exchange initiatives and lessons drawn from experience, to help the two peoples to understand one another, to realise in deeds Khmer-Vietnamese friendship, to conclude on the basis of equality an alliance between the two peoples in the struggle against the reactionary French colonialists, invaders of Cambodia and of Vietnam.'

The same document goes on to show how revolutionary power should be allocated in Kampuchea. It claims that Khmer sympathizers had agreed to the following:

a. In the localities inhabited entirely by Vietnamese, the latter may take part in the Government of their localities.

b. In the localities populated by Cambodians and Vietnamese where the Cambodian element forms the majority of the population the Vietnamese may occupy auxiliary posts in the Government of their localities to aid the Cambodian authorities and conciliate the interests of the Vietnamese with those of the Cambodians.

c. The internal administration is entirely the province of the Cambodian government and is assured by the Cambodians.[1]

In this period, the Viet Minh and the Khmer communists were also attempting to form alliances with the disparate Khmer groups that had emerged to combat the French in the East and South-west. At first, such alliances were merely *de facto*. In the words of a Viet Minh circular dated June 1949: 'A single Cambodian people's front should not be created immediately, for the movement is still too weak and such a front would not be able to work effectively.'[2]

It is in this context that Son Ngoc Minh is first mentioned in French official correspondence (at least by that name, which he adopted either to give the impression that he was a brother of Son Ngoc Thanh, or as a symbol of unity between the latter and Ho Chi Minh, by combining their names into one). In July 1949, Son Ngoc Minh was reported to be based in Chhouk district, Kampot province, at the head of a 'well-armed band of about three hundred, including women ... equipped with a hospital where all the wounded of other rebel bands are cared for'.[3]

One such band was that led by Puth Chhay, 'a cheap hoodlum' (*un vulgaire voyou*) according to French sources, who had been gaoled for a month in 1934 on an assault charge, interned for a year in 1944, and also charged with theft and gambling.[4] Chhay emerged in September 1948 as chief of a small mixed Khmer Issarak/Viet Minh band in Kandal province, and a 'member of the Khmer Issarak/Viet Minh Committee of Vinh Thanh'.[5] In two incidents in September and October 1948, Puth Chhay shot dead four members of the police and Security forces (Sûreté), and the authorities put 10,000 piastres on his head.[6] Another such figure was Huu Thinh, a sub-lieutenant from the colonial garrison at Takeo, who deserted in August 1948 with eight well-armed riflemen, and joined a band loyal to Son Ngoc Minh at Baset in Kompong Speu.[7] Thinh was reported to be 'the only Cambodian admitted into the Viet Minh camp at Damrey Romeal to report and execute orders'.[8]

On 12 January 1949, a combined force of three hundred rebels led by Puth Chhay, a Vietnamese from Takeo named Huynh Thinh, and Son Ngoc Minh's followers Ngin Hor and Keo Moni from Prey Veng, attacked Sa'ang district office in Kandal. (In the ensuing clashes, Keo Moni was wounded and captured.[9]) The situation in South-east Kampuchea was summed up in a February 1949 report from the governor of Kandal: 'The rebel grip has extended across the Bassac to the right bank and is tending to spread west and encircle the capital more and more tightly. Prek Thnaot has been threatened, and if this movement continues Kompong Kantuot is now subject to an eventual attack. A similar spread towards the north is noticeable on the East side, based from Lovea Em district. The rebels, who are stationed there permanently, are extending their actions towards Khsach Kandal district starting with the regions along the Tonle Tauch river.'

The police were ordered to withdraw from the administrative post of Vihear Suor to avoid loss of arms to the rebels.[10] On 28 February, a confidential report made by the Phnom Penh Police claimed that general command of these Issaraks was exercised by Chea Keo.[11] A former bazaar proprietor in Phnom Penh, Keo spoke Khmer, Vietnamese, French, Thai and Lao, and had been 'known to the police for a very long time'. 'He was a disciple of a Vietnamese monk known as 'Thay Nam', now living in a cave on Nha Bang mountain (Chaudoc). Thay Nam appears to be considered a local master of the occult capable of transforming all things and to be about 100 years old. Kruu ['Master'] Keo, who had and still has personal influence over the Vietnamese and Cambodian masses, even in religious circles, now commands an important band of Khmer Issarak and Viet Minh.' He and his two lieutenants, a former monk from the Pali School in Phnom Penh and an unnamed woman, 'pass themselves off as teachers in the art of sorcery and claim to be capable of making people invulnerable, and with their mystical signs can make them avoid rifle bullets. Won over by this manoeuvre, many inhabitants, mostly military deserters, escaped prisoners and individuals sought by the Law, are enrolling in Kruu Keo's band.'[12]

The report noted that Keo had received arms from the Viet Minh, and had also managed to acquire weapons locally. Keo had established units in seven districts, totalling over 2,500 men, according to the report. The most important force under Keo's command was said to be a band of five hundred men with modern arms stationed on the border of Takeo and Kandal, where they were digging fortifications. 'Small groups of from six to fifteen armed men belonging to these bands appear to have been assigned to raise taxes, watch over the subdistrict officials, and gather intelligence on the movements of the Army and the Administrative Authorities ... As for taxes, the levy for the Takeo area is 6 piastres per inhabitant, and for Kandal it varies between 12 and 100 piastres per head depending on the person's wealth.'[13]

The variation should perhaps have been seen as evidence of less organizational coherence, and a more modest role for Chea Keo, than the report suggests: in Prey Veng in July, Tou Samouth and his Vietnamese deputy collected taxes averaging 5 piastres per inhabitant.[14]

Similarly, Nop Pen, a former corporal in the colonial army and ex-agent of the Sûreté, was credited in the same report with building up a rebel army of over 2,300 men in Kampot and southern Takeo, including three hundred Khmer Issarak and Viet Minh in Prey Nup (the rest were all apparently Khmer).[15] In fact, though, as the governors of those provinces pointed out, the largest of these bands were actually led by Meas Vong, a Khmer Krom working with the Viet Minh as 'representative of the Government of the South-west', and by another revolutionary, 'the big Khmer Issarak chief Nhem Sun', a native Khmer. Nop Pen and a hundred of his followers joined forces with them in April 1949.[16]

Huu Thinh's forces were now estimated to number eight hundred men spread throughout Kompong Speu.[17]

The largest Issarak force, according to the police report, was that led by Prince Norodom Chantaraingsey based in Battambang, but as we shall see this was in fact the army of the KNLC, itself still not a very coherent organization. The report estimated this force at nearly five thousand, including 850 Khmer Issarak, 460 Viet Minh, 3 Europeans, 6 Japanese, 210 Thais, 200 Sino-Cambodians, 640 members of mixed 'Khmer Issarak and Viet Minh' units, and hundreds of others whose allegiance was unspecified. They were active from Battambang to Prey Veng.[18]

In all, then, about 10,600 rebels were said to be confronting the French throughout Kampuchea by early 1949. 'It seems to be exaggerated',[19] a French official scribbled on the police report at the time, but the regular detailed intelligence reports from the provincial governors confirm the scale of the Issarak movement.[20] However, at this stage it comprised poorly-armed, vulnerable concentrations of forces rather than entrenched guerrilla units. Interestingly, the police estimate specifies less than a thousand Vietnamese, and although at this point all groups benefited from Viet Minh advisers and weapons supplies, the discernible Vietnamese role seems to have been limited.

Achar Yi and the Democratic Party — Primitive Neutralism

The Khmer members of the ICP were in no sense unchallenged leaders of the independence movement. In the South-east, for instance, Keo Moni was flanked by Chan Dara, a military commander who had participated in the 1942 demonstration and then escaped to join the armed forces of the Japanese. Chan Dara emerges in a French report from Prey Veng dated 24 January 1949 (soon after Keo Moni's capture) as chief of a 'rebel committee for southern [sic] Cambodia', based in Kompong Trabek with Ngin Hor. Nearby in Peam Chor was another band, led by a Vietnamese and said to be composed of '10 legionaries, 50 or 60 Cambodians, 130 Tonkinese, and 100 young Tonkinese women', while in the north of Prey Veng, another five hundred rebels 'infested' the Tonle Tauch valley.[21] In March, the Vietnamese concubine of a Sûreté agent in Banam was arrested by rebels and taken blindfold to their camp. 'She saw she was surrounded by hundreds of Khmer Issarak/Viet Minh rebels, the majority of whom were Khmer Issarak and Vietnamese and Khmer women. The big chief was an old Issarak, aged about forty [Chan Dara's age at the time].'[22]

Of course, this Vietnamese woman may have been a double agent, and her 'kidnap' staged in an attempt to delude (or perhaps impress) the authorities as to the extent of Khmer collaboration with the Viet Minh. Double agents, it seems, were not lacking. Soon after, for instance, on the exhortation of an Issarak who had 'surrendered' and enrolled in the government forces, military authorities released Keo Moni, who immediately rejoined the resistance.[23] On 17 April, he and Ngin Hor are reported to have led an attack by forty 'Khmer Issarak Viet Minh' on a new government post in Peam Chor, and then to have 'begun recruitment of seven hundred individuals to carry out a second attack'.[24] Three weeks later, the governor of Prey Veng reported a large mixed rebel band massed in Peam Chor and said to number a thousand to two thousand, the vast majority of them Khmer.[25]

Clearly it was not difficult to find recruits, or chiefs, but unity among the latter was another question. At this very moment, Chan Dara was reported to have decided to go to Phnom Penh and surrender;[26] he was apparently impressed with the proclamation in December 1948 of 'the independence of Cambodia within the framework of the French Union'.[27] Many now believed, at least temporarily, that the struggle was over. In an autobiographical sketch written in 1974, Chan Dara says that in this period 'the Khmer Issarak and the Viet Minh began to have increasingly stronger and greater differences on the matter of nationalism ... The Khmer Issarak proclaimed that all Khmer should rise up ... to fight and kill all Vietnamese and drive them back to Vietnam ... No Vietnamese were permitted to live in Kampuchean territory any more ... the Viet Minh troops dispersed until none were left.'[28]

However, Chan Dara did not surrender but moved to Kompong Chhnang (where the archives of twenty seven subdistricts, and one district office, had recently been put to the torch by rebels)[29] and began organizing an Issarak army there. It is possible that he himself was eclipsed in the confrontation he described in Prey Veng; he certainly changed his mind about the 'independence' proclamation, as did many others; and he later re-appeared in the Son Ngoc Minh camp. In his 1974 account he pointedly makes no mention of Keo Moni at any stage.[30] But Chea Soth, who says he had been travelling the country 'searching for the revolution' since 1946 and finally joined Tou Samouth in Prey Veng in 1949, recalls: 'In Prey Veng at that time there were many types — Puth Chhay, Achar Yi, Chan Dara, Keo Moni and Tou Samouth — but they were not united. It was difficult to know who were the real Issaraks, the loyal revolutionaries, and who were the bandits and robbers.'[31]

According to French intelligence, 'the split commenced towards the end of March'.[32] Instrumental in the conflict was a band of three hundred men led by a former member of Dap Chhuon's bodyguard named Achar Yi, a 'quack sorcerer' who 'walked around with a fan in his hand'.[33] More recently, Yi had been a local electoral agent for the Democratic Party. In 1948 he was entrusted by Ieu Koeus, President of the Assembly, with a secret mission to form 'an autonomous defence group' in Lovea Em district. But Yi's forces soon became perhaps more autonomous than had been intended: not only did they attack government posts and Viet Minh forces alike in order to procure arms, and burn several Vietnamese fishing villages, massacring some of the inhabitants; they burned down a number of Khmer pagodas of the modernist Thommakay sect of the Mohanikay order, making it clear that the nationalist cause was not the sole issue.[34] According to the governor of Kandal: 'This band, which is hostile to the modernist Mohanikay sect and to religious

reform measures, has burnt Pratray Beydak [Tripitaka] manu-
scripts in several pagodas of Khsach Kandal. It is to be feared that
the crimes of this band, numerous in membership but poorly
armed, may provoke fratricidal struggles between the Cambodians of the traditionalist and modernist Mohanikay sects.'[35]

In May 1949, Democratic Party emissaries warned Achar Yi:
'All Cambodians must unite for the independence of the country
and must not kill one another. They must not burn villages, and
in particular they must respect religion and holy places.'[36] On 11
June, Yi received a Democratic Party delegation, which included
a Chinese claiming to be a representative of the CCP in Phnom
Penh, who said he brought the support of the Chinese
communists. In a ceremony in Lovea Em three days later, an
interesting proclamation was read: 'This resistance movement
exists in all big countries such as France, Russia, America, China
... The communists in these countries work for the glory of their
country and the welfare of the people. We must not let our
country be invaded by the Viet Minh, even though they are
patriots in their own.'[37]

The Viet Minh were not described as communists, and there
was of course no mention of Indo-Chinese solidarity. Six days
later, according to the governor of Prey Veng, Yi and three
hundred followers confronted and defeated a Viet Minh force in
the north of the province, and the next month some of them
proclaimed in Peam Ro district that they had come 'to massacre
the local Vietnamese, Viet Minh or not'.[38] Perhaps Chan Dara,
whose account parallels this, was with them. But not all Issaraks
shared such ethnic antagonism (or the religious anti-modernism
that went along with it), at least in southern Prey Veng, closer to
the Vietnamese border.

In June 1949, Ngin Hor's band of forty Khmer Issarak and
eighty Viet Minh was reported to have left Ba Phnom for Peam
Ro 'in order to talk with the Catholics, beside the Church'. The
Catholics were of course Vietnamese. Even in Prey Veng district,
to the north, a Kampuchean-born Vietnamese commanded a
force of two hundred Khmers and fifty Viet Minh. Meanwhile,
four hundred 'Viet Minh/Khmer Issarak', led by a Khmer, were
camped to the south in Peam Chor; and in Svay Rieng district, a
'Khmer Issarak Viet Minh Committee' was formed, with two
hundred members of both nationalities, led by a Cao Dai
adept.[39] Confrontation between the two different expressions of
Khmer nationalism was avoided, however, when Achar Yi was

72

captured by the government during an operation in September and sentenced to ten years' hard labour by a Phnom Penh Military Tribunal.[40]

Also in September 1949, King Sihanouk dissolved the National Assembly. He was presumably under French pressure, but as Michael Vickery has pointed out, the Democrats had 'angered the King and local conservatives who preferred to put law and order before either parliamentary government or independence'.[41] Their ideas were best expressed by the 'king's representative', Nhek Tioulong, who proclaimed around this time: 'Independence has been obtained ... All citizens without distinction of rank must show themselves to be citizens of an independent country. For that, there is only one thing to do — Work. Officials, be loyal and faithful servants of the State and of the People. Farmers, be good farmers; artisans, try to be good artisans.'[42] Of course, independence was far from being obtained, but when it eventually came, the traditionalist attitude to Khmer society would remain, as this statement makes clear. The issue of traditionalism still cut across that of independence.

Further, the Democratic Assembly had opposed the commitment of Khmer troops to the French struggle against the Viet Minh in Vietnam itself, pointing out that their country must live at peace with its neighbours.[43] Seen in conjunction with its simultaneous opposition to Viet Minh involvement in Kampuchea even while the French remained there, the policies of the Democratic Party and its Issarak offshoots provide the first indication of Kampuchean neutralism. Fostering this attitude later became an objective of the new Chinese Communist government, as it attempted to secure its own influence in Kampuchea through the establishment of an independent bulwark to that of both the West and the Vietnamese. But evidence for this, or for Vietnam–China tension remains slight in the 1949-54 period.[44] An intelligence report from 1952 described 'a large group' of Issaraks and Chinese who were stopping highway traffic in Pursat and 'ostentatiously displaying not only the Issarak flag but also the Chinese communist one. The size of this band seems to betray the aim of propaganda, for the simple waylaying of cars does not justify this deployment of forces.'[45] By Geneva, however, these Issaraks and the Democratic Party had lost whatever Chinese support they had had to a nationalist of more recent vintage, King Sihanouk himself.

In January 1950, the Democrat leader Ieu Koeus was assassinated in the Party headquarters by a member of the entourage of the conservative politician, Prince Norindeth, who fled abroad. According to French intelligence, the subsequent police enquiry, led by another conservative who had defected from the Democrats to take part in the new government, was 'extremely suspect'.[46] Following as it did the death of the Democrats' founder and previous leader, Prince Youthevong, this left the Party in considerable disarray. With Son Ngoc Thanh still in France, where he had been joined by Pach Chhoeun in 1948, the Democrats were unable to find a leader who could unite their disparate membership, now divided into as many squabbling cliques as the Issaraks themselves. (The same was, of course, true of the pro-French conservatives, who formed six revolving-door cabinets over the next two years.)

Puth Chhay — 'Country, Race and Religion'

Achar Yi had declared his loyalty to Puth Chhay,[47] who was involved in a similar conflict with the Vietnamese and Khmer communists in Takeo and Kandal. In late January 1949, rebels in Kandal had begun to respond to the proclamation of 'independence' and to appeals for their surrender. There was a 'sudden change in their attitude', however, 'following counter-propaganda on the part of the Khmer Issarak chiefs coming from Prey Veng and especially the pressure from the Vietnamese'.[48] At this point, Chhay began to pose as a 'defender of the Khmer population against the exactions of the Vietnamese'. But he retained his links with the latter and kept up the fight against the government.[49]

The situation deteriorated rapidly when Puth Chhay launched an attack on Bati district capital. 'Everywhere the rebel activities are generalized, and to avoid the catastrophe, we must react quickly and forcefully. In short the scenario is dark, in fact dramatic.'[50] But relief was in sight.

In March 1949, the government military commander in Loeuk Dek, Sub-Lieutenant Savang Vong, mysteriously deserted with his men after simulating a Viet Minh attack on his post. While the French put a price of 20,000 piastres on his head, Ngin Hor provided Savang Vong with 'a bicycle and 10,000 piastres'. But Vong immediately separated from Hor and the Viet Minh, and joined up with Puth Chhay.[51] In April, Huu Thinh did likewise, and Chhay then proclaimed himself 'Commander of the

Cambodian Army'. In May, he began to arrest and execute Viet Minh agents in four districts. Chan Dara apparently attempted to mediate, but without success.[52] After escaping a Viet Minh ambush, Puth Chhay took revenge by massacring another sixty Vietnamese in Kandal.[53] The governor wrote on 10 June: 'The week has been characterized by the massive infiltration of Viet Minh bands, supported by Ngin Hor's and Keo Moni's partisans in Lovea Em, Kandal Stung, Loeuk Dek and Kien Svay. These bands intend to eliminate Puth Chhay's.'[54] Puth Chhay's followers reacted by burning Vietnamese villages in Lovea Em, kidnapping Vietnamese in Sa'ang, and massacring others taken as hostages.[55]

Within a month, it was reported that 'the Viet Minh leaders of the 8th Zone had sent ... about 200 to 350 men commanded by Tou Samouth, in search of the band of Puth Chhay, to eliminate them'. On 8 July Samouth, Ngin Hor, Keo Moni, Chan Dara, Vong Kan and Khieu Ten joined up with Vietnamese forces led by Dinh Van Lan. According to the governor of Prey Veng: 'Dinh Van Lan is the chief of this band, but his powers are restricted because of the presence of other Viet Minh chiefs in the band.'[56]

Significantly, 'the other Viet Minh chiefs' were all native-born Khmer. They were joined two days later by a band of two hundred Viet Minh led by 'Say, a Cambodian from Cochinchina'.[57] In October 1949, in the first acknowledged Vietnamese intervention in the country, large units of 'Viet Minh Troops to Help Cambodia', under the command of Nguyen Thanh Son, moved into Kampot and Kompong Speu. They brought Viet Minh forces in Kampuchea to a total of three regiments, about three thousand troops.[58]

This show of force was not all that put paid to Chhay's ambitions. Huu Thinh and Savang Vong, who were reported to be 'disgusted with the atrocities committed by Puth Chhay', broke with him in September and created an independent band. Then Chhay was wounded in the stomach during a naval bombardment, and put out a rumour that he was dead, 'to obtain a respite'.

From that point on, Chhay's area of activity gradually became restricted to northern Kompong Speu and southern Kompong Chhang. The communists had cleared the South-east Zone of rivals. According to Bernard Fall, 'the whole South Vietnam Zone Command of the Vietnam People's Army transferred its headquarters to Prey Veng province. . . finding it quieter than tightly-controlled South Vietnam'. Sieu Heng's 'Central Office South' (see page 59) followed them there, bringing its radio transmitter 'The Voice of Free Cambodia', which broadcasted in both Vietnamese and Khmer.[59]

In December 1950, Chhay offered to surrender in return for command of an autonomous sector in Kandal and Kompong Speu, but was rebuffed by the government. He did achieve a ten-day truce, however, and organized a large festival at Ang Pagoda in Kompong Speu, which was attended by Huu Thinh, Savang Vong, Chantaraingsey, and even by officials from Phnom Penh. Then, on 28 January 1951, Huu Thinh came to see him with eight bodyguards; suspecting betrayal, Chhay had them all massacred. He stepped up his levying of taxes, forced recruitment, and acts of terrorism. His forces were soon variously estimated by government sources to number from 600 to 1,200 men, and he showed 'rare energy', especially against the Viet Minh.[60]

In fact, confronted by his difficulties, Chhay was developing a well-defined political position and soon began to call himself leader of the 'Khmer Issarak Committee of the Central Zone'.[61] On 18 June 1952, his forces met and decided unanimously to suppress their 'police' units in Kandal province, which were censured for their 'anti-religious crimes, abuse of their authority over the population, and encouragement of gambling'.[62] Racial violence, however, was apparently overlooked. Two days later, fifty of Chhay's followers opened fire with automatic weapons on a gathering of the Cham [Muslim] community in Kandal, killing eighteen people and wounding ten.[63] This incident, like Chhay's earlier massacres of Vietnamese, foreshadowed policies towards ethnic minorities on the part of the Pol Pot regime (in particular the leader of its 'Central Zone', Ke Pauk) in the 1970s. So did the following tract signed by Chhay, distributed in December 1952: 'Do not forget so quickly everything that is Khmer! Do not lose hope! The Khmer Issarak Committee of the Central Zone began the revolution with a few weapons, has maintained it and now possesses them in plenty. Eliminating it will not be at all easy. Friends, do not sway with the wind or worry about the movement of the tides. The Khmer Issarak of the Central Zone still preserve all the fullness of their unity. They are still boiling over with revolutionary spirit, with love for their country, race and religion.'[64] Apart from the reference to

Buddhism, this could have been a broadcast of 'The Voice of Democratic Kampuchea'.

Norodom Chantaraingsey and Savang Vong — Comprador Warlords

There was little sign of such political development in the activities of Prince Chantaraingsey. Although in February 1949, as we have seen, the Phnom Penh police reported him to be the leader of widely scattered forces totalling five thousand men, his control over these units was in fact tenuous; he had been away from their Battambang headquarters for eight months, and returned there only briefly in July when he joined the KNLC as its official 'Supreme Army Chief'. In June 1948, as it turned out, Chantaraingsey had established himself in the backwoods of Pursat and Kompong Speu with three or four hundred followers.[65] By 1952 he had built up a force of between seven hundred and a thousand, of whom about four hundred were armed, but his area of operations, like that of Puth Chhay, became increasingly circumscribed. He 'refused to leave his fief', broke with the KNLC, developed relations with the governor of Kompong Speu, and allowed government forces to move through his sector,[66] but clashed frequently with those of the Viet Minh, Puth Chhay and Savang Vong.

In February 1950 Savang Vong received a personal letter from King Sihanouk inviting him to surrender. 'His conditions (assignment of a sector in Kompong Speu where he would have complete liberty of manoeuvre) were rejected by the government. However they were tacitly accepted because since then Savang Vong has collaborated with the province chief of Kompong Speu in the repression of Viet Minh activities.'[67] His four hundred followers were able, according to French intelligence, to 'defend rather effectively' his small sector in the south of Kompong Speu and part of Takeo, against the Viet Minh,[68] but not against the government, whose forces enjoyed 'unhindered movement' there by December 1951.[69] A May 1952 intelligence report concluded: ' An opium addict, and sickly, Savang Vong is not a very dynamic element in the Khmer Issarak line-up.'[70] But he still had a part to play, as we shall see.

A Case Study: Kratie province

Further gradual displacement of traditional band leaders by

revolutionary forces, with the aid of the Viet Minh, occurred in Kratie. By late 1949, a former monk named Kruu Oum had emerged at the head of a hundred rebels in Kratie, including a group led by 'the bandit Mak Sun Heng'.[71] But, according to the French: 'The activities of [Oum's] band consist almost entirely of banditry, and the Cham inhabitants of Krauchhmar who are subject to its exactions sometimes offer vigorous resistance.'[72]

Besides provoking racial violence Oum's troops also clashed with both the government forces and the Viet Minh; after retreating to a remote area on the Kompong Thom border, they suffered a split in June 1950.[73] The effective neutralization of this traditional Issarak group was made clear in the governor of Kratie's report of February 1952. Although he now commanded two hundred troops,[74]

'The incursions of Oum's elements are not serious and could be rather easily suppressed. On the other hand, the Viet Minh effort is serious. . . The rebels estimate that, of 24 subdistricts in the province, 17 are liberated, 7 being considered occupied by the legal authorities: this intelligence demonstrates well the depth of their work and achievements. The propaganda of Oum has little significance. On the other hand, the Viet Minh propaganda is more clever and dangerous . . . taking Khmer names, forcing their auxiliaries to speak Khmer. . . they rebuild the villages according to a considered urban plan. They oblige the inhabitants to develop their crops and their stock, and give courses in hygiene and organize clinics. In the river bank areas, the Viet Minh find many accomplices, in particular among the Vietnamese and Chinese, even among certain Cambodians.'[75]

A July 1952 police report on Kratie mentions 'a band estimated to number 120 men (a Vietnamese [sic], Cambodians and Chams) in military uniform and armed with three machine guns, three submachine guns, six grenade-launchers and rifles'.[76] Whether or not such groups could be fairly described as 'Viet Minh', they *were*, as the governor feared, 'serious'.

The radicalization of the independence movement worried the colonial government. In July 1951 King Sihanouk coined the term 'Khmer Vietminh'. 'We can affirm that this situation of insecurity is provoked by the infiltration of the Viet Minh, with communist loyalties. These disruptive foreign elements, by pressure or lying propaganda, have managed to win to their cause a great number of our compatriots. Most of the Issarak bands, which call themselves nationalists to deceive us, are nothing else but Khmer Vietminh. . . We must scorn them and collaborate with the forces of order.'[77]

The communists, meanwhile, liked to call Sihanouk 'the Fascist novice'[78] because he had been placed on his throne in 1941 by the Vichy French Governor-General. The Viet Minh's *Voice of Nambo* said: 'King Sihanouk, already gone to fat, who shamelessly makes use of sensuous perfumes. . . must not rule'.[79]

The Revolution Organizes

By the end of 1949 the communists claimed to have control of 418 villages in forty districts of ten provinces.[80] In Kompong Chhnang during that year, Chan Dara had raised '3,600 followers', according to his own estimate, and he claims to have equipped seven battalions with guns he bought on several trips to Thailand. They then joined forces with '2,036 fully armed men' led by four Khmer Krom battalion commanders — Meas Vong, Meas Vannak, Monea Ba, and Dara's own son Chan Serei.[81]

These claims may not be greatly exaggerated. The figure of 2,036 at least, is not far off that of 2,300 (including '300 Khmer Issarak and Viet Minh') given by the police report of February 1949 for Issarak strength in the South-west.[82] In Takeo alone, on 7 May 1949, Meas Vong was reported by the province governor to be in command of 'about 1,300 Viet Minh and Khmer Issarak' in Treang district.[83] Two weeks later, the Khmers Nhem Sun, Meas Vong and Chea Keo took seven hundred guerrillas into Tram Kak district.[84]

At a mass meeting of three thousand people, including fifty seven officers of the eleven battalions, Chan Dara claims he was nominated Commander-in-Chief of the Khmer Issarak throughout Cambodia. However, he declined, saying: 'When we have a general assembly and invite all the Khmer Issarak, then we could decide to appoint a provisional government and all the heads of Ministries. . . We should not just seize power or all the unity of the Khmer Issarak would be destroyed.' Chan Dara says he proclaimed: 'I will make every effort to invite all the Khmer Issarak leaders to come to a meeting in the near future'.[85] From other sources we know that in February 1950, the KNLC sent a delegation — composed of Mé Muon, Hong Chhun, and Achar Duong — to south Vietnam. According to French intelligence, its mission was 'to study the formation of a pro-Viet Minh Cambodian government'.[86]

Unsurprisingly, Chan Dara writes that 'the Viet Minh lent their support' to his project.[87] In February, at the ICP's Third Central Committee conference, Vo Nguyen Giap had called 1950 a 'year of leaping forward' in Kampuchea and Laos. He advocated 'active construction of independent Lao and Kampuchean armies, helping those armies to become hard-core forces, and mobilizing the great masses of Lao and Khmer people to participate in the liberation'. Although he anticipated 'big victories' on the battlefields there, he was also in favour of breaking down large concentrations of forces (which as we have seen characterized the Issarak movement up to this point), and adopting a guerrilla warfare strategy to 'create a broad political base'.[88] The Issarak movement adopted these tactics with some success in the ensuing years.

According to French intelligence, Son Ngoc Minh and other Khmer communist leaders met with Ho Chi Minh's representative Le Duc Tho, various Viet Minh leaders from the South, and the commander of the 'Vietnamese Troops to Help Cambodia' (Nguyen Thanh Son), at a ten-day conference in Hatien beginning on 12 March.[89] Plans were co-ordinated for the 'First National Congress of the Khmer Resistance'.

This took place on 17 April 1950, when some 200 delegates, 105 of whom were Buddhist monks, assembled at Kompong Som Loeu in south-west Kampuchea.[90] At the end of a three-day meeting, the Congress decided 'unanimously'[91] to establish the Unified Issarak Front (UIF; in Khmer, *Samakhum Khmer Issarak* — literally, 'the Khmer Issarak Association'), based largely on Son Ngoc Minh's Liberation Committee. It was headed by a National Central Executive Committee under Son Ngoc Minh and including Chan Samay (Deputy), Sieu Heng (Secretary), and military commanders Chan Dara, Meas Vong, Meas Vannak, Chau Yin, Nhem Sun, Sok Saphai, and Ngin Hor.[92] Other Committee members included Keo Moni, Ney Sarann, a representative for Phnom Penh (presumably Keo Meas), and 'two representatives of Cambodians from abroad', probably Meas Vong and Meas Vannak, who were Khmer Krom.[93]

Of these fifteen leaders, only five were definitely members of the ICP (Ney Sarann joined in 1950).[94] Some, like Chan Dara, were only loosely aligned with it, but others such as Meas Vong and Meas Vannak may well have been members. Of course, the

ICP also had people like Mey Pho and Hong Chhun in key positions in the KNLC, which remained a separate organization for the time being, in cooperation with the UIF. A UIF flag and emblem were adopted, featuring a motif of Angkor Wat with five towers, on a red background, the same as that which had been used by the Liberation Committees for several years. (In 1979 this became the national flag of the People's Republic of Kampuchea.)

Perhaps more significant than the UIF was the Congress's establishment of a proto-government, the provisional PLCC or People's Liberation Central Committee (*Kanak Mouta Keaha Mocchim Ban Dos Asan*), which was also headed by Son Ngoc Minh. It had three vice-presidents, each representing one of three new zones: Chan Samay, deputy chief of the Liberation Committee of the South-west (under Minh); Sieu Heng, chief of the Liberation Committee of the North-west and of the UIF there, and Defence Minister in the proto-government; and Tou Samouth, deputy chief of the Liberation Committee of the East (under Keo Moni). All three were ICP members. Son Phuoc Rattana, who had deserted from the colonial armed forces and fled to Thailand in June 1949, was appointed Administrative Secretary (*protean muntir*) and another post went to a peasant cadre from the South-west named Non Suon who had a long political career ahead of him.[95] This organization may well have been the effective governing body of the UIF. It was in the name of the PLCC that, on 19 June 1950, Son Ngoc Minh formally declared Kampuchea's independence, claiming that the UIF controlled one third of the country.[96]

One reason for the strength of Son Ngoc Minh's group was the emphasis it had been placing on the training of Khmer cadres. This process had formally begun in 1949 with the establishment of a 'Canvassing Committee for the Creation of a Khmer People's Revolutionary Party'.[97] In 1950 there were still only 40 Khmer (compared with 1300 Vietnamese) members of the ICP in Kampuchea,[98] but hundreds of others had already been trained in Party schools. Krot Theam, a Khmer refugee now living in Australia, was a member of the first intake at a revolutionary training centre, in the forest of the North-west, in 1949. Theam says that 2,700 people lived and worked in this clandestine 'fortress', which was run by a Khmer political commissar and several Khmer instructors, including two former monks, Achar Pres and Achar Leak. (Pres, as we have seen, had

fled to the jungle after participating in the 1942 demonstration.)
The Khmers often brought in Vietnamese teachers to give
special lessons. Subjects studied including social deportment,
agriculture, military tactics, and politics, taught from a mimeographed Khmer-language textbook more than an inch thick.[99]

Men Chhan says he attended ICP study sessions in the forest in
the East of the country, near Memut, as early as 1947–48. Five
hundred students were taught in groups of fifty, studying
documents written in Khmer by Tou Samouth. Chan Mon, who
joined the revolution at the age of sixteen in nearby Tbaung
Khmum district, recalls attending a political school organized by
Tou Samouth in the same period. Samouth, he says, lectured
two hundred Khmers and distributed documents to them on five
subjects — 'the world situation, the situation in Kampuchea, the
class struggle, economics, and building up the women's organizations'. Mon claims that Samouth 'had very clear ideas on
classes and exploitation', but his political strategy was a rather
finely discriminating one. 'The workers were the base, the
leading class. Intellectuals, students, teachers and peasants. . .
were revolutionary classes also, and capitalists helped the
revolution as well. The non-revolutionary classes were the
reactionaries, the neutralists [apparently a reference to Achar Yi
or his Democratic Party backers], and the Free World.'[100]

Hem Chea, who was chief of the militia in Chup subdistrict in
Kompong Cham until his capture by the French in December
1951, told his captors that in 1949 he had attended a 45-day
course in a political-military school in the jungle of Krauchhmar
district. One of his instructors had been Vong Kan, 'a Khmer
who speaks fluent Vietnamese'.[101]

In June 1950, the memory of the World War Two nationalist
was commemorated when the 'Achar Hem Chieu Political
School' was established in south-west Kampuchea, with a first
intake of 140 district and village-level cadres[102]; by March 1951
the fifth intake had entered the school. A UIF military school
opened in August 1950 with an enrolment of 'nearly a hundred
Cambodian partisans'.[103] Towards the end of that year, a
fortnightly underground newspaper called *Issarak* began publication. Tou Samouth was 'political director' of this newspaper,
which in November 1951 published a report on 'The
Anniversary of the Russian Revolution'.[104] He also published
another journal, *Samakki* ('Solidarity').[105] It appears that
although Samouth did not command any of the regional

Liberation Committees, he was at least as important as Son Ngoc Minh and was perhaps even the key figure in the sense that it was he who was laying the foundations of Khmer communism. But what of Vietnamese intentions during this period?

At the founding Congress of the UIF in April 1950, Chan Dara recalls, 'Ung Sao, a Viet Minh general, suggested a conference to discuss the Lao, Vietnamese and Cambodian issues. He urged that these three countries form an alliance called "Indo-Chinese Communists" and elect a chairman and a deputy chairman.' Chan Dara replied that 'the Khmer, Lao and Vietnamese had not yet named governments for the struggle much less have more than fifty per cent [of the territory?], therefore electing a chairman and a deputy chairman of the Indo-Chinese Communist Federation would be illegal'. He claims that 'most of the Khmer Issarak rose to support' him, and 'asked to have the conference to create the Indo-Chinese Federation postponed'.[106] While Chan Dara's account seems to elide proposals for an alliance of United Fronts with a proposed fusion of governments and parties, his description of the exchange is likely to be fairly accurate. The demonstration of Khmer nationalism which it represented seems to have been important in determining future Viet Minh policy. In practice the process took another year, and only in March 1951 was the Indo-China-wide Joint National United Front 'formally founded', at a tripartite meeting (involving Ton Duc Thang, Souphanouvong, and Sieu Heng) in the mountains of northern Vietnam.[107]

It seems relevant that in early February 1951, the ICP's Second Congress had decided to dissolve itself into three national communist parties for Vietnam, Laos and Kampuchea. On 8 February, the nine 'Cadre Committees' of the ICP in Kampuchea met in a 'plenary session' called for this purpose by Le Duc Tho.[108] In this period, according to Vietnamese sources, the ICP in Kampuchea had three hundred Khmer members, organized in 27 military branches, 16 village, 12 district, 4 factory branches and a single city branch (perhaps headed by Keo Meas in Phnom Penh).[109] The small number of village branches, the fact that district branches were even fewer, and the large number of military ones, point to the Party's failure as yet to penetrate the peasantry. A Viet Minh document noted at the time that: 'The base of the party still rests mostly in the organized units and in the military. The leadership, organization and work method are not yet adapted to the situation in Cambodia.'[110]

On 30 September 1951, a Khmer People's Revolutionary Party (KPRP) provisional Central Committee (called the 'party forma-tion and propagation committee', pending the KPRP's First Congress) was established.[111] This committee of fifteen was headed by Son Ngoc Minh and included Tou Samouth (deputy), Sieu Heng, Chan Samay, and 'N.T. Nhung', as well as Keo Moni and a number of ethnic Vietnamese.[112] Mey Pho moved from the North-west to the Issarak 'Central Office' on Mount La'ang in Kampot, and became its Director of Information and Propaganda.[113]

By late 1951, according to a Vietnamese document captured by the French and labelled 'to be burnt after reading', the newly-formed KPRP claimed one thousand Khmer members, as well as three thousand Vietnamese.[114] French government sources for 1952 claim that the figures were much lower: 150 Khmers and 1800 local-born Vietnamese.[115] Although at this point the Vietnamese began to withdraw from the KPRP, and ethnic Vietnamese inhabitants of Kampuchea were now re-cruited instead into the Vietnam Workers' Party (VWP), it is clear that Vietnamese influence was still considerable. A captured Viet Minh document, dated 1 November 1951, asserted that 'the Vietnamese Party reserves the right to supervise the activities of its brother parties in Cambodia and Laos', and that 'later, however, if conditions permit, the three revolutionary Parties of Vietnam, Cambodia and Laos will be able to unite to form a single Party: the Party of the Vietnam-Khmer-Laotian Federation'.[116] Bernard Fall quotes another captured document dated 5 August 1951, a letter from the Viet Minh 'Central Intervention Committee' to its three zonal branches. It enclosed the Statutes of the KPRP, 'unanimously approved by the Cadre Committee of Cambodia', and a draft KPRP platform. Concern-ing the latter, the document said: 'We request the zones to have it translated into Khmer and to have it circulated only within the organizations. We hope that you will complete the present document with your opinions which you will transmit to the Central Intervention Committee before February 1952. The Central Intervention Committee shall then centralize all the opinion and inspire itself therefrom to elaborate the Official Political Credo of the Party, which then will be officially distributed among the people once it has been approved by the Cadre Committee of Cambodia.'[117]

From then on, large numbers of Khmers were sent to Hatien in south Vietnam to study 'police and administration' for eight months, and thus to 'consolidate and develop the Unified Issarak Front' on their return. According to a Viet Minh document: 'All these cadres must be familiar with the Statutes and doctrine of the Party without being bound by them.'[118]

On 7 June 1952, Son Ngoc Minh, Nguyen Thanh Son and others held a 'Conference for the Administrative and Military Re-organization of Free Cambodia' at Hatien. It was decided, according to French sources, to establish, in each zone of the country, a military-political school 'led by the Vietnamese but teaching in the Cambodian language ... The Vietnamese cadres, put at the disposition of the Issarak groups, must know the Khmer language which will be the sole language used in the ranks of the Cambodian resistance'.[119] By mid-July the Kampot police reported that eighty young Khmers aged between 18 and 20 had enrolled in two 'Viet Minh military instruction centres' in the province.[120]

When the KPRP Statutes were adopted in 1952, they were very similar to those of the VWP, with two exceptions. There was no mention of Marxism-Leninism or its founders, only a vague statement that 'the doctrine of the Party is the doctrine of People's Democracy'. Neither was there an anti-feudal or land reform component to the KPRP's programme. The Party simply 'unites the whole people in the Issarak Front to collaborate closely with the Vietnamese and Lao peoples. . . and to carry on a firm struggle so as to annihilate the French colonialists, the US interventionists and their puppet lackeys'.[121] Its stated goal, then, was simply independence, just as Tou Samouth stressed that 'capitalists helped the revolution'. Similarly, the UIF programme included a 'mission' recalling some of the aims of *Nagaravatta:* 'To leave to the bourgeois classes the initiative of doing the necessary work to assure the prosperity of the country.'[122]

A captured Viet Minh document dated June 1952 noted that the KPRP 'is not the vanguard party of the working class, but the vanguard party of the nation gathering together all the patriotic and progressive elements of the Khmer population.'[123] This formulation indicates that the Vietnamese party still saw the Marxist-Leninist status of its Kampuchean counterpart as relatively low. It does also stem from the fact that the KPRP had not yet officially held an inaugurating Congress, but more importantly, from the Vietnamese communist view that the working class was smaller and the proletarian movement less developed in Kampuchea, still an overwhelmingly peasant society with most of the land in the hands of its tillers, and yet to undergo capitalist development.[124] Both the Vietnamese and the KPRP accepted the need for Kampuchean modernization.

Over the ensuing months and years the KPRP was progressively built up from the base, with ethnic Vietnamese withdrawing from the lower levels, as Khmer cadres and recruits took over the old ICP cells (and established new ones) first in villages, then in subdistricts, then at the district, province and zone levels. The process involved the convening of separate congresses, without Vietnamese participation, at each stage. But ethnic Vietnamese continued to predominate at the highest administrative levels, where existing mixed Khmer-Vietnamese cells remained in place (until 1954) and were called 'ICP cells', even though the ICP had been officially abolished in 1951. But here too the number of Khmer members gradually increased,[125] as the party expanded.

Population Control and the Rebel Army

The colonial government found the rebellion increasingly difficult to contain. In September 1950, the governor of Kampot pinpointed the South-west headquarters of the UIF in the Koh Sla river valley, and proposed 'the creation of a war zone in which residence and travel are forbidden'. The Minister of National Defence agreed, and outlined the need to evacuate 'all the villages' and pagodas in the area.[126]

Two months later, the High Command wrote: 'The situation has again developed and it seems necessary to bring new changes to the present limits. . . of the free-fire zones and river banks (*rives et zones cannonables à priori*).' The list of these free-fire zones is five pages long, and ends with a 'particular case', Chea Keo's base in a subdistrict of Kandal: 'Between the Bassac and the Mekong: the important village of Prasath, stop-over for bands and temporary rebel station. The population must be advised that in case of military need, the village will be subject to artillery shelling and aerial bombardment.'[127]

The UIF, backed by three thousand Viet Minh troops, faced at first two battalions (1,000-1,200 troops) and many members of other services of the French Expeditionary Corps and (by late 1950) 8,900 Khmers in the colonial army.[128] Already in 1949, Phnom Penh's military expenditure had risen to 41 million piastres or 12 per cent of the national budget.[129] By 1951 it was 200 million.[130]

As part of the strategy of 'auto-defence', in late 1950 the government began rounding up 282,000 peasants in Takeo alone, as well as others in Svay Rieng, Prey Veng and Kompong Chhnang, and resettling them in 'large fortified villages' along the main roads. According to Jean Delvert, this proved an 'unhappy' experience in Takeo and Kompong Chhnang; those regrouped were 'deprived of the sweetness (*douceur*) of Cambodian village life'.[131]

But the massive number of peasants resettled in Takeo (53,000 house-holds) is intriguing. The displacement may have been to some extent spontaneous. As early as July 1949, taxes levied there by the Khmer communists, among them the man who was much later to become Pol Pot's military commander, Mok, had proved difficult to collect.[132] Mok had been born in the remote west of Tram Kak district, and educated in a monastery there. By 1949 he had become Issarak chief of the district. Chhun Samath, then a monk in a neighbouring part of Kong Pisei district, Kompong Speu, recalls that Mok had few followers but 'fought fiercely against Savang Vong's Issaraks — he would kill ordinary people as well as those working with Savang Vong.'[133]

The governor of Takeo had reported in June 1949, at the height of the inter-Issarak struggle, that 'rebels' were committing 'exactions against the population in the *west* of Tram Kak district' (my emphasis) — one of the few reports of such communist activities in the government archives of the war.[134] When regroupments began the next year, eight thousand households in Tram Kak, formerly scattered throughout the district, came together in 'only ninety eight villages'. This may reflect popular fear of Mok's depredations. However, the same thing occurred in Bati district, and the hamlets which had formerly been the norm in Samrong and Treang districts also became 'very large villages'.[135] It would seem that the revolutionaries there faced serious political problems, and not just because of their own exactions and killings in Tram Kak. They also had to contend with the influence of the always anti-communist and now 'semi-surrendered' Savang Vong,[136] whose mysterious defection to the rebels in 1949 had sparked off a wave of inter-Issarak conflict, and whose policy was to collaborate with the government's chief of Kompong Speu province[137] and perhaps that of Takeo as well. On the other hand, in March 1952

the governor of neighbouring Kampot wrote that three districts
in his province were off limits to government forces. 'The
situation in Kampot province, where government action is for
the moment practically restricted to the districts of Kampot,
Kompong Trach, Banteay Meas and Chhouk, is no more critical
than that in many other provinces of the Kingdom, [but] *the
contrast with Takeo province is striking.*'[138]

Tracts dated 15 October 1952 which were signed by Savang
Vong and appealed to Khmers to unite against 'the Vietnamese
enemy', were distributed in Takeo. They bore the Issarak
emblem, but its motif of Angkor was new — it had three towers
rather than five.[139] A quarter of a century later, this was to
become the national emblem of Democratic Kampuchea. But
the timing of its first appearance bears additional significance, as
we shall see.

Sihanouk has claimed that Savang Vong was a French stooge
who had deserted with French encouragement to organize a
'false Issarak' movement, presumably in an attempt to defuse the
resistance. Vong was said to have received arms and other
equipment from French officers, with whom he dined on
occasion.[140] This is possible, given the circumstances surrounding Vong's desertion and subsequent appearance in the Issarak
ranks. The conduct of his forces, too, was little better than that
of the UIF in Takeo. In one village in Vong's zone, 'the Issarak
were their own law. . . killed anyone they wanted to kill'; they did
recruit a number of the villagers but most remained neutral or
hostile, and some families fled to Phnom Penh to escape
them.[141]

The Khmer and Vietnamese communists now enjoyed virtually unhindered movement through the East and even most of the
South-west, the location of Son Ngoc Minh's headquarters on
Mount La'ang[142] in Kampot. The size of the movement now
under the hegemony of his organization and of the 'Viet Minh
Troops to Help Cambodia' can be gauged from the fact that the
surrender of a total of 3,500 Issaraks in Kampot province from
1949[143] had little appreciable impact on the security situation
there. On a fifty-kilometre stretch of highway leading west from
the province capital, no fewer than thirty bridges were destroyed
by insurgents in the same period.[144]

The National Police Commissioner's Report from Kampot in
June 1952 highlighted the ability of the UIF to operate almost at
will there. 'According to information worthy of good faith, the

rebels appear to be organizing a festival entitled 'Making War' for 20 June in all the corners of the province.'[145] (One leader named in this report was Non Suon, who had been appointed UIF chief for the South-western Zone by Son Ngoc Minh;[146] as we shall see, in the Sihanouk period Suon became the best-known legal cadre of the Kampuchean communist movement.) A series of police raids in Kampot in November and December, in which a total of 350 Khmers were arrested, was probably a sign of increasing colonial desperation.[147]

At the operational level, a police report dated September 1952 estimated rebel strength throughout the South-west at two thousand, including a concentration in Kampot of nine hundred troops commanded by a Khmer, Nhem Sun. The proportion of Khmers is unknown, but the district chief of Kampot, referring to local-level units, reported that his insurgent counterpart commanded a district guerrilla force of twenty-four men, only three of whom were 'Viet Minh'. Only in Takeo was a large rebel unit (of three hundred) reported to be commanded by a Vietnamese;[148] another source reports that Ngin Hor had moved there from the east and recruited two hundred peasant guerrillas of Khmer and mixed Khmer-Vietnamese extraction in Prey Krabas district.[149] Further, company-strength Mobile Units 160, 170 and 180 were also operating in Kampot, Kompong Speu and southern Takeo; the first was composed of Vietnamese, while the latter two, having been inaugurated in May as a single unit of a hundred Khmers, had now expanded to a total strength of 350.[150]

Closely linked to Nhem Sun's command in Kampot were Meas Vong's forces in Kompong Chhnang and North Kompong Speu, an 'autonomous and well-organized sector', according to French intelligence in May 1952.[151] By December, Vong was reported to be at the head of at least two hundred 'Khmer Viet Minh' members of Mobile Unit 140, which included a similar number of Vietnamese also under Vong's command.[152]

The situation was similar in the East. In early 1952 the governor of Kompong Cham reported that three or four hundred Issaraks and a thousand Viet Minh active there were heavily armed — 'estimating that their strength is far superior to that of the government, [they] never consider surrender.'[153]

Racial barriers as well as national borders were disregarded. A Cham activist on the right bank of the Mekong wrote in his own language to comrades among 'the Khmer Issarak Malays [Cham] of the Sivotha Unit': 'Everywhere the Khmer Issarak are getting their revenge. The Viet Minh are propagandizing widely to enlighten the Khmer Issarak and to ask for their cooperation to work together in a good cause.'[154] Another company of the Sivotha Unit was reported to be commanded by a Khmer former legionary, while a Vietnamese cadre in Chamcar Loeu district wrote: 'We delegated a Cambodian comrade to do propaganda work and form cells there. He has succeeded in his task. Nearly all the subdistricts now have cells.'[155]

But the greatest UIF successes were on the left bank of the Mekong. In December 1951 the French arrested and interrogated five Issarak cadres in Kompong Cham; the subsequent report to the Under-Secretary for National Police began: 'This information would confirm, if there was still any need to, the moulding of the population of the Suong area by the Khmer Issarak-Viet Minh Committees, and the necessity for the forces of order to recommence the purges with extreme urgency.'[156]

Figures 3 and 4 show the UIF organizational structure there, as revealed by the captured cadres. It is noteworthy that all but one of the sub-districts mentioned (Kor) straddle the main Highway 7, that all of the UIF officials mentioned were Khmer, and that the villages for which they were responsible were inhabited almost entirely by Khmer.[157] Thus in November 1951 an Issarak band which ambushed a police vehicle in this area was reported to be composed of one Vietnamese and nineteen Khmers.[158]

In May 1952, French intelligence reported that scattered UIF bands in Prey Veng were combining into a Mobile Unit.[159] By August, Keo Moni and a Vietnamese commander had merged their forces with So Phim's *Achar Hem Chieu* Unit, with the aim of launching concerted large-scale attacks on French posts in the south-east.[160] Half of the four hundred members of this Mobile Unit were Khmer, the rest Vietnamese.[161] On 24, 25 and 26 September, perhaps timed to mark the approaching first anniversary of the foundation of the KPRP, near simultaneous assaults were mounted against four French blockhouses in Prey Veng and Svay Rieng.[162] The assailants were repulsed, but the staging of such attacks kept the colonial forces holed up and on the defensive, and the majority of villages remained the preserve of the revolutionaries. On 30 September, Ney Sarann, who now ranked third on the Eastern Zone Committee after Keo Moni and Tou Samouth, transferred his forces to Prey Veng, in boats from the Plain of Reeds in Cochinchina.[163]

90

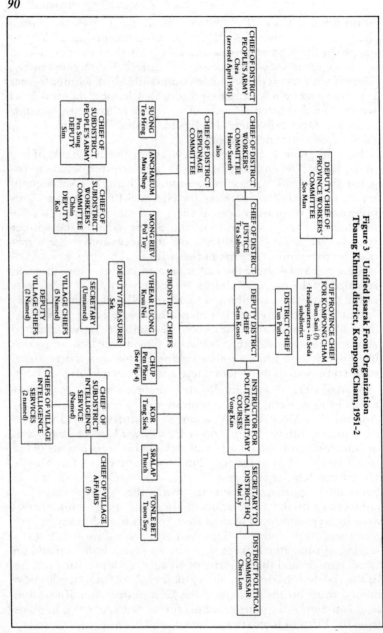

Figure 3 Unified Issarak Front Organization
Tbaung Khmum district, Kompong Cham, 1951-2

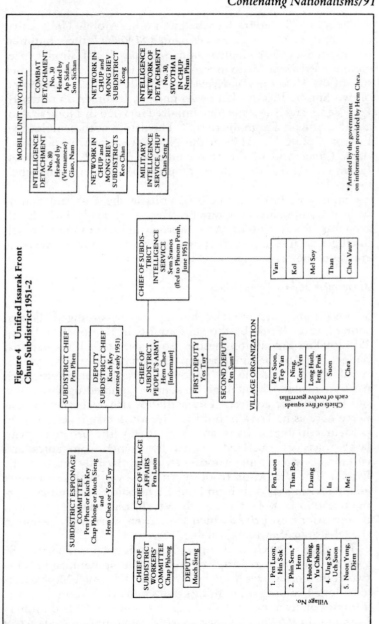

Figure 4 Unified Issarak Front Chup Subdistrict 1951–2

MOBILE UNIT SIVOTHA I

INTELLIGENCE DETACHMENT No. 80
Headed by (Vietnamese) Giao, Nam

NETWORK IN CHUP and MONG RIEV SUBDISTRICTS Keo Chan

MILITARY INTELLIGENCE SERVICE, CHUP Chan Seng *

COMBAT DETACHMENT No. 30
Headed by Ap Sidan, Son Sichan

NETWORK IN CHUP and MONG RIEV SUBDISTRICT Kong

INTELLIGENCE NETWORK OF DETACHMENT No. 30, SIVOTHA II IN CHUP Nem Phan

SUBDISTRICT CHIEF Pen Phen

DEPUTY SUBDISTRICT CHIEF Kuch Kry (arrested early 1951)

SUBDISTRICT ESPIONAGE COMMITTEE
Pen Phen or Kuch Kry Chap Phlong or Much Sieng and Hem Chea or Yos Tuy

CHIEF OF SUBDISTRICT INTELLIGENCE SERVICE Sem Sranos (fled to Phnom Penh, June 1951)

Van
Kol
Mel Soy
Than
Chea Vauv

CHIEF OF SUBDISTRICT PEOPLE'S ARMY Hem Chea [Informant]

FIRST DEPUTY Yos Tuy*

SECOND DEPUTY Pen Sum*

VILLAGE ORGANIZATION

Pen Suon, Tep Yan
Ning, Koet Ven
Long Huth, Ieng Pruk
Suon
Chea

Chiefs of five squads each of twelve guerrillas

CHIEF OF VILLAGE AFFAIRS Pen Luon

Pen Luon
Than Bo
Daung
In
Mei

CHIEF OF SUBDISTRICT WORKERS' COMMITTEE Chap Phlong

DEPUTY Much Sieng

1. Pen Luon, Hin Sok
2. Phin Sem,* Hem
3. Huot Phing, Yu Chhoan
4. Ung Sar, Uch Suon
5. Nuon Yung, Diem

Village No.

* Arrested by the government on information provided by Hem Chea.

The May 1952 report described four other Mobile Units active in the Eastern Zone: these were named *Si Votha I* (three hundred troops, led by Sok Saphai) and *Si Votha II* (of similar size, commanded by a Vietnamese) in Kompong Cham, on either side of the Mekong; *Pou Kombo* (or Mobile Unit 127, composed of two hundred troops led by an unnamed Khmer) in northern Prey Veng; and *Ang Phim* (one hundred men led by Nong Sralao, a native of Koh Thom district).[164] The names of these units, like that of Mobile Unit 140 in the North-west, which was called *Achar Chum*, and of the commander of Unit 129 in Kampot, *Okhnya Chhouk*, were those of pre-1945 Khmer anti-French heroes.[165]

Communist forces in regional units in the East and South-west of Kampuchea now numbered approximately 3,000; by all accounts about half of these were Khmer, although French intelligence was already reporting 'constant but discreet increases in the percentage of Khmer fighters'.[166]

Modernism and its Temptations

The economic war was also hotting up. According to French sources, taxes levied by the communists in Kampuchea during 1951 totalled 150 million piastres, equivalent to half the national budget.[167] (A timber merchant in Tbaung Khmum, for instance, recalls that he paid the UIF 250-500 piastres per month for each truck he owned.)[168] Intelligence sources summed up this aspect of the economic contest: 'The battle for rice is certainly not as fierce here as in Tonkin, but the Viet Minh take it seriously, in particular in Battambang and Svay Rieng [the provinces with large tracts of rice-land owned by French companies and colonists], where our troops can only partially protect the harvest. The Viet Minh troops even take over the transplanting and harvesting tasks. It is no longer a question of commandeering rice as in 1948–49. Further, the Viet Minh's takings have their repercussions on prices which have risen worryingly, while in the rebel zone they remain stable.'[169]

The scale of communist operations in Kandal can perhaps be gauged from press reports of goods and equipment captured in two French offensives there in November 1951. Viet Minh forces abandoned, among other things, 120 sampans, 70 tonnes of rice, 2 tonnes of corn, two political schools, and two 60-bed military hospitals. In 1952 intelligence sources even reported evidence of 'several autarchic agricultural enterprises, like *kolkhozes*' in Kompong Cham.[170]

An important UIF asset was its appeal in some religious circles. In February 1951, a three-day 'Khmer Buddhist Conference' was organized by Son Ngoc Minh, Chan Samay, Chan Dara and others. The program included a performance of a play about the activities of Achar Hem Chieu.[171] Minh had been joined the previous year by Prom Samith, a monk who had known him (and presumably Chieu) at Unnalom monastery in the early 1940s.[172] In November 1951, Samith, who on joining the UIF had become editor of the newspaper *Issarak,* accompanied Minh, Chan Saman and five other monks on a tour of Khmer Krom districts in south Vietnam. Speaking at a meeting of local monks and lay people there, Minh attempted to emphasize the role of Buddhism in the independence cause. 'The Cambodian race is of noble origin. It is not afraid of death when it is a question of fighting the enemy, of saving its religion, of liberating its fatherland. The entire race follows the Buddhist doctrine which places death above slavery and religious persecution.'[173]

Two months before, the French Commissioner for Cambodia, de Raymond, had described an 'Issarak Buddhist Studies School' in Vietnam's Sadec province. Thirty young Khmers were enrolled there, in what de Raymond described as 'in reality a Viet Minh spy course run by a Cambodian monk'.[174] In terms recalling the 1922 'religious demonstration' described in Chapter One, (see p. 2), the Commissioner further wrote of a revolutionary meeting during the Meak Bochea festival at a pagoda in Hatien, attended by Achar Kou (who became UIF chief for the South-west Zone when Non Suon was injured the next year), along with monks from twelve pagodas in Kampot and 'numerous Vietnamese and Khmers'.[175] The next year Son Ngoc Minh even secured the assistance of the abbots of three Kampot monasteries in advising UIF defectors to return to the movement on pain of reprisals.[176] UIF forces often attended pagoda festivals in the province;[177] Nhem Sun's political commissar was in fact an ex-monk named Achar Chiem.[178]

As we have seen, in the North-west too, people like Achar Leak and Achar Pres were playing important UIF roles. And in the East, the religious backgrounds of Tou Samouth (Achar Sok) and Keo Moni (Achar Mau) also proved significant.[179] In February 1952 forty-four monks representing pagodas of the Eastern Zone met and passed a pro-UIF resolution.[180] In October monks from three pagodas in Krauchhmar district were reported to be preparing to attend a second zone-level UIF meeting.[181] One man, who was a monk from 1946 to 1975, claims to have joined the communist movement in the late 1940s, becoming a representative of the Issarak Monks Association. In his district of Prey Veng, he says, there were twenty-four monasteries and over seven hundred monks, 'all' members of the Association. According to this man, monks could even join the KPRP itself. However, because they were considered members of an 'exploiting class', they had to serve the full nine months' candidature (others served three, six or nine months), and only two monks in the district actually joined the party.[182]

In April 1952, the Viet Minh radio station *Voice of Nambo* quoted a Khmer monk 'on a mission to Vietnam' as rejecting French 'propaganda' about the UIF and Viet Minh and claiming that the French had 'massacred' monks.[183] There is in fact little evidence of this beyond the treatment accorded Achar Hem Chieu, but such views were not uncommon among Khmer religious people at the time. On 19 June, the same radio station, broadcasting in Vietnamese, celebrated the second anniversary of Son Ngoc Minh's proclamation of Kampuchean independence, adding: 'The cause for which we fight is just, conforming to the aspirations of the Buddhist religion.'[184]

Unsurprisingly, perhaps, an article deploring these developments eventually appeared in a colonialist journal. It warned: 'The reality is this: there are monks who actively encourage the rebellion of the Issaraks, the Viet Minh and other robber bands. The pretext: the winning of liberty, of independence, which have already been achieved but are now rebaptized 'true liberty' and 'true independence', and are glimpsed through the smokescreen of an ideology which has spread throughout Asia like an epidemic.'

In terms of Buddhist participation in the communist movement, it is all the more significant that these lines were written in 1954, after Sihanouk could seriously claim to have achieved independence (in November 1953).

With apparent relief the author added: 'However not all monks are affected by the contamination of modernism and its temptations'. But enough *were* for the author to entitle his article 'The Cambodian People are More Buddhist than their Monks'.[185]

The Struggle for the Issarak Mantle in the North-West

Meanwhile, in the North-west, the KNLC was riven by a conflict between Leav Keo Moni and Kao Tak, who had been working together since early 1949 when they both broke with Dap Chhuon, taking five hundred troops with them. They seem to have suffered through Chhuon's surrender in September, however, since their combined forces then numbered only two hundred and fifty.[186] Tak was himself tempted to surrender, but remained commander, with Leav Keo Moni his principal lieutenant.[187] However, Moni, a subdistrict chief during the Thai occupation of 1941-46, seems to have had more political experience.[188] On 19 April 1950, after Poc Khun was accused of pocketing 600,000 piastres with which he had been supposed to purchase arms in Bangkok, Leav Keo Moni was elected President of the KNLC. (It was on the same day that the UIF was founded, in the South-west.) Tak became its 'President of National Defence',[189] but by the end of the year their relationship had deteriorated significantly.[190] In October, a second KNLC delegation was sent to the communist-held zones of Vietnam, to study the prospects of a close alliance. The delegates were Mé Muon, Mey Pho and Hong Chhun — all supporters of such an alliance.[191] They were accompanied on their tour by Son Ngoc Minh, Ach Saroeun and Sok Saphai of the UIF.[192] According to French intelligence: 'Tak was hostile to collaboration with the Viet Minh. For his part, Leav Keo Moni accused him of oppressing the population. The two men could not get on.'[193]

In early February 1951, Leav Keo Moni was re-elected President 'by a big majority'[194] at a meeting in Battambang attended by various leaders (including Poc Khun) and 250 troops.[195] Tak was dismissed from his post for exactions committed against the population.[196] On 13 February, according to French intelligence, 'Tak tried to draw Leav Keo Moni into an ambush at Srok Prey, but it was his band that was defeated and he himself was seriously wounded.'[197] He was condemned to death by the KNLC, but escaped capture.

The three KNLC delegates returned to the North-west in April 1951, and from that point cooperation between the UIF and the KNLC was strengthened.[198] Leav Keo Moni was again successful at the next KNLC congress, on 20 August.[199] Meanwhile, however: 'Cared for in the Royal Khmer Army post in Samrong, then in Thailand, Tak slowly recovered. He began publication of a newspaper, *Issarak*, which violently attacked Keo Moni. He designated himself Chief of the 'National Liberation Committee — First Northern Zone'.[200]

By the end of the year, Tak had managed to re-arm a force of three hundred troops with new weapons purchased in Thailand. However, Leav Keo Moni's forces outnumbered and dispersed them. Tak responded by executing fifteen local inhabitants whom he suspected of collusion with his rival.[201]

The KNLC now comprised three main bands of equal strength. Leav Keo Moni was often reported to be commanding them, but 'direct and permanent command' was said to be exercised by his three lieutenants — Achar Tumsok, Ouch Nilpich, and Thim Tralay.[202] Tralay's band was given the mission of maintaining contact with the Viet Minh, and operated with them in the south of Battambang.[203] Tumsok and Ouch were active further north.

Tumsok, a former student at the Higher School of Pali in Phnom Penh, had participated in the 1942 demonstration and then escaped to Thailand, joining the KNLC in 1949 with 150 followers.[204] Ouch, a tailor from Battambang, joined with a similar force at the same time, but his background was more complex. He had surrendered to the government in April 1951, with thirty seven troops. He had signed an accord, and then a mysterious incident had occurred: 'Ouch arrested the Captain of the Royal Khmer Army who had come to inventory his forces, as well as the officials who had accompanied him. . . However the prisoners were released several days later.'[205] Ouch had then taken off again into the jungle, with, as will perhaps become clear later, a mission.

Meanwhile, in August 1951, Sieu Heng returned to Kampuchea from north Vietnam,[206] where he had undergone a period of training. His instructor, Hoang Tung, then a representative of the VWP Central Committee, years later described Heng as 'very active and intelligent, a very capable man, more capable than Son Ngoc Minh and Tou Samouth'.[207] Heng now returned to his position as 'an influential member of the Viet Minh Command in Cambodia', becoming an 'Itinerant Commissar' in the South-west and North-west, especially the latter.[208] It was perhaps at this point that, according to Krot Theam, the Vietnamese and Khmer troops in the North-west began to divide into separate units. (One particular Vietnamese cadre had been especially cruel to those he considered 'spies for the French', even burning some of them alive, according to Theam; but now, 'the Vietnamese lost influence', and 'didn't eat in the same mess any more'.[209]) In November 1951, Heng moved permanently to the North-west with the reported aim of organizing the amalgamation of the KNLC and the UIF, 'and also the reconciliation of Tak and Leav Keo Moni'. On 1 December he was quoted as comparing the French to a tiger: 'The only way to defend ourselves and sleep in peace at night is to kill the tiger'.[210]

Heng took over all UIF and Liberation Committee operations in the North-west, and organized a 'politico-military-administrative committee', consisting of three branches — headed by Muol Sambath (military affairs), Nuon Chea (economics), and Achar Bun Kasem (politics).[211] Sambath and Chea later, as we shall see, became members of the Politburo of the Communist Party of Kampuchea. Theam concurs with Hoang Tung in that Sieu Heng was a capable man; he says, too, that on his arrival the local Vietnamese 'cooled down' and 'stopped showing off'. Heng appears to have shown some care in choosing his cadre — Muol Sambath, at least, 'refused to countenance sectarianism'.[212] So did the woman Muon, who was reported to be 'pro-Vietminh',[213] but also worked tirelessly in this period to achieve unity between the UIF, the KNLC and Tak's forces. According to French intelligence: 'Intelligent, very energetic, an experienced horse-rider, Mme. Muon enjoys great prestige in Siemreap and Battambang and must be considered a dangerous rebel element.'[214] Her cooperation with Sieu Heng helped ensure the alliance between the UIF and the KNLC, but she was eventually unable to persuade her brother Tak to participate in it.

Meanwhile, after a two-year suspension of the National Assembly, parliamentary elections in September 1951 had once again given a majority to the nationalistic, law-abiding Democratic Party. On 29 October, Son Ngoc Thanh arrived back from exile in France and was greeted at Phnom Penh airport by a hugh crowd of tens of thousands.[215] He was received there by Premier Huy Kanthoul and other members of the government,[216] and a 300-car cavalcade escorted him into the city. Earlier that same day, the French Commissioner for Kampuchea, de Raymond, had been assassinated at his official residence; a contemporary French intelligence report suggests that this may have been the work of Thanh or his supporters: 'The Viet Minh leaders were in fact noticeably surprised and annoyed by this *attentat*, for which they have since attempted to attribute responsibility to an 'Issarak patriot'.[217]

Thanh received ten years' back pay (30,000 piastres) and was even offered a Cabinet position.[218] He refused, however, and set about renewing his old contacts, especially among the more militant Democrats. In February, he travelled to the provinces with Pach Chhoeun, now Minister of Information, on his official duties. According to a French intelligence report: 'While Chhoeun, who remained rather discreet, formally condemned the Viet Minh, Son Ngoc Thanh on these occasions was not afraid to say [at public meetings] such things as: "We are not the enemy of any people. We do not want to harm any people in their march towards independence. But if the Viet Minh commit acts of banditry, they must be resisted"; which left the clear enough impression that there was no reason to oppose the 'normal' activities of those rebels.'[219]

On 11 January 1952, Thanh and his old associate Ea Sichau, who after studying in France had arrived home the previous May, established a newspaper, *Khmer Kraok* (Khmer Awake).[220] It increasingly preached revolt against 'the oppressors' and was suspended by the government the next month in response to French pressure.[221] A massive demonstration, planned for 17 February to demand total independence, was also banned.[222] Thanh became convinced that the French would make no concessions.

On 22 February, with the help of the province chief of Siemreap, Thanh arranged a secret meeting with Poc Khun and Kao Tak[223], on the pretext that Tak was in fact about to surrender. On 9 March, the seventh anniversary of the Japanese *coup* against the French, Thanh made his move. He and Sichau disappeared into rural Siemreap, accompanied by a radio operator with a small transmitter. They joined up with Tak, and about eighty students, officials and army deserters joined them. The combined forces of Tak and Son Ngoc Thanh were now reported to number five hundred guerrillas with three hundred guns.[224]

According to French intelligence, Thanh now wrote to Savang Vong and Chantaraingsey, asking them to join forces, 'along with the Viet Minh, to 'bring back peace to Cambodia'.[225] For a brief period, Savang Vong actually had an uncharacteristic, 'tense' relationship with the governor of Kompong Speu.[226] Puth Chhay, too, declared his support for Thanh. Meanwhile, Thanh's radio broadcasts promised military aid from the Viet Minh, and in early May a student defector from his camp claimed that Thanh was in correspondence with Ho Chi Minh.[227] At the same time, Muon and Sieu Heng both visited Thanh in attempts to establish unity. However, according to French intelligence, Leav Keo Moni 'hesitated', while Ouch and Tumsok 'completely refused' to work with Thanh.[228]

On 3 May 1952, the colonial forces launched Operation Lightning, which destroyed two of Thanh's camps near the Thai border. They also captured documents there which implicated the Democratic Prime Minister. Anti-French student demonstrations took place in Phnom Penh (6 May), Battambang (19 May) and again in Phnom Penh, Battambang and Kompong Cham on 26 May.

Three weeks later, obviously worried, King Sihanouk sacked the Democratic government and assumed personal rule.[229] At the same time, he promised to achieve independence within three years, temporarily throwing the entire Issarak movement into confusion. The Democratic Party, for its part, now suspended its activities, although it was difficult to believe that Sihanouk meant what he said. As one writer has pointed out: 'When the King dismissed the Democratic government he did so not only because he was at loggerheads with it but also because he was under extreme pressure — French tanks were patrolling Phnom Penh and the French Minister for Associated States, Jean Letourneau, had specifically declared that France would make no concession to a Democratic government.'[230]

Chan Dara provides an interesting account of similar confusion in the UIF ranks. Writing in the third person, he says: 'Chan Dara heard King Sihanouk's proclamation and personally took this message to the people and the Khmer Issarak. They considered it very seriously for many days, and most of the Khmer Issarak in Cambodia had a great desire for independence and agreed with the three-year plan 100 per cent. Among the Khmer Issarak [from] south Vietnam, 50 per cent agreed and 50 per cent were undecided. The Viet Minh said that King Sihanouk was absolutely swindling them and would sacrifice the Khmer Issarak.

Chan Dara told the people to be calm but ready to continue the struggle because Sihanouk had been made King by the

French. He said that King Sihanouk got along very well with the French. They would not, of course, honour his request and grant independence. Therefore, we had to unite in fighting against the French and not listen to Sihanouk. King Sihanouk and the French were using lying tactics.'

Then Chan Dara pledged that he 'could obtain independence for Cambodia on a three-year Plan, that is, 1952–54, just like King Sihanouk's. . . At that, the Viet Minh, the Khmer Krom and the Cambodians [from] Kampuchea cried Victory, and were very happy'.[231] Chan Dara soon changed his mind, however; he defected to the government with seven followers in November.[232] The rest of the UIF leadership fought on alongside the Vietnamese, but among the smaller Issarak groups many began seriously to consider putting down their arms.

Thanh's forces seem to have suffered considerable losses as a result of Operation Lightning. The then Thai deputy police chief of Surin province, who subsequently visited their head- quarters, says that Tak and Thanh 'told me they had around two hundred soldiers'.[233] They were recruiting more from the local population in Samrong district, among whom Thanh, at least, was a popular figure, according to intelligence sources in Siemreap.[234] In Battambang, however, his followers demanded on average 5,000–10,000 piastres from each village they visited,[235] by far the highest level of taxation of the population exacted by any Issarak group.

Chantaraingsey and Savang Vong, meanwhile, exchanged messages of congratulation with Son Ngoc Thanh. But neither followed what French sources say was his advice to launch 'a campaign of terrorism in the cities'. Savang Vong re-established his normal relations with the governor of Kompong Speu, and Puth Chhay again 'contacted the government with the intention of surrendering'.[236]

According to a French colonialist source, Thanh travelled to 'the Viet Minh zone' and reached an agreement with Son Ngoc Minh on 21 June.[237] Whether or not this is true, within three days of that date Tak invited UIF leader Hong Chhun to a meeting in Samrong aimed at a reaching a common accord. However, Chhun was 'busy, and postponed his date of departure'.[238] Then, a small band in Kompong Chhnang, led by Nguon Hong, defected from Savang Vong and joined Thanh's movement 'at the same time as reaching an agreement with the Viet Minh Chief Meas Vong' at the latter's Kompong Chhnang headquarters. Tak sent Hong fifty guerrillas with thirty rifles, and one of Puth Chhay's lieutenants defected to him, bringing his forces to a total of 120 troops.[239] Hong's example showed that united action was possible, but it eventually proved to be an isolated case.

A festival entitled 'Reconciliation and Unity' was planned for 13 July in a village on the border between Tak's zone and that of the KNLC. Thanh, Sichau, Tak, and Leav Keo Moni and his three lieutenants (now reported to be training three hundred new recruits) Tumsok, Ouch and Tralay were all invited,[240] but little appreciable unity seems to have been achieved; it seems that Son Ngoc Thanh was receiving more cooperation from the Vietnamese communists than from their Khmer allies. The next month, the governor of Siemreap reported that, according to 'as yet unconfirmed information from a good source', Son Ngoc Thanh had agreed to the stationing of five hundred Viet Minh troops in the north of Battambang and Siemreap, 'to reinforce his band'.[241] But 'Leav Keo Moni apparently looked on with disapproval',[242] perhaps fearing loss of his supremacy in a new reorganized KNLC. This dissension proved crucial. The Battambang police even reported: 'On 1 September 1952 there was a meeting of more than 100 rebels, presided over by Leav Keo Moni and including Achar Tumsok, Achar Bou, Achar Ren, Ouch . . . and nine Viet Minh. . . The question of the eventual surrender of the Khmer Issarak was discussed. Tumsok appears to have given the impression that he had to wait for the next proclamation of royal messages to make the final decision.'[243]

It is possible, of course, that Tumsok (and presumably Leav Keo Moni) were simply conducting a holding action in the face of pressure from those within their ranks who were arguing that Sihanouk's three-year plan for independence might be worthwhile.

In Siemreap, intelligence sources reported that Viet Minh troops were 'practising good politics': 'They help the inhabitants to locate their stolen cattle, pay for the goods they buy at the proper price, and leave the impression that they have come to help the Khmer Issarak to recover complete independence for their country.'[244]

But, in the same province, Ea Sichau is reported to have executed eight students and teachers who had found jungle life hard and wanted to return home. Five other students fled Thanh's camps. Finally, on 7 September, Dap Chhuon's troops suddenly attacked and surprised Thanh's followers; twenty two were killed and sixty wounded.[245]

The next month saw furious attempts by both the KNLC and Thanh to win control of a unified Issarak movement. Tak sent a unit of sixty men to Kompong Speu to meet with Puth Chhay, Chantaraingsey and Savang Vong 'to reconcile and unify the Khmer Issarak and Viet Minh bands'.[246] Soon after, though, Thanh's radio claimed that the USA was prepared to expose the French claims of 'independence' for Kampuchea as 'a trap' and to 'prove that there was no freedom' in Kampuchea[247] — a false hope when the US was becoming deeply committed to the French effort in Indo-China, and one that proved a serious obstacle to Issarak unity.

After a jungle meeting on 24 September involving Leav Keo Moni and his chiefs Ouch and Tumsok, a number of new Issarak leaflets were distributed in Battambang. One signed by 'the Khmer Issarak Army' noted: 'The French, backed by the USA, want to divide us, to make us kill one another. . . The Issarak movement has well understood this problem; it struggles, and if it has not obtained the anticipated results, the fault lies with the lack of unity of the Khmers.'[248] Sieu Heng's North-western Sector of Son Ngoc Minh's People's Liberation Committee, for its part, announced that it had 'joined forces' with the KNLC. According to this leaflet: 'From now on, these two committees are united in solidarity with the people of Indo-China, forming a triple Lao-Vietnamese-Khmer alliance. This unification increases our forces, which have 23 million more men . . . our revolution is a member of the democratic front for world peace.'[249]

A tract signed by Nuon Chea (Long Reth), of the North-Western Sector's 'politico-military administrative committee', also attacked the 'US interventionists'.

Leav Keo Moni, in another tract entitled 'The President of the KNLC to his compatriots', claimed: 'We are certain of success, but it can be obtained only by the unity of the Khmers, Vietnamese and Lao, to struggle and drive out the French. . . Beside us stands Russia, which directs us and leads us towards a new democracy.'[250] Moni also repeated the anti-US message, while another KNLC tract stated: 'In southern Indo-China we are the neighbours and allies of our dear Vietnamese comrades.'[251]

The official amalgamation of the UIF and the KNLC was an important breakthrough for Son Ngoc Minh and the Khmer communists, who had now incorporated the organization directly descended from the first Khmer Issarak Committee into a structure dominated by KPRP members. In May that year French intelligence underlined the significance of this with an interesting description of Leav Keo Moni: 'An ardent nationalist, he enjoys great popularity among the Khmer Issarak of the North-west. Crafty and greedy, he is nevertheless renowned for his honesty and integrity. . .'[252] Another report stated: 'Some influential members of the Democratic Party in Battambang have developed relations with certain band leaders of Leav Keo Moni's National Liberation Committee.'[253] Moni now joined the KPRP.[254] These developments were not welcomed by everyone in the KNLC, particularly not by Ouch, who had increased his power by incorporating Tumsok's band, making the latter his deputy.[255]

But they were almost inevitable given the balance of forces. At a camp near Thvak in southern Battambang, Sieu Heng and a Vietnamese named Hoang were quartering no fewer than 1,000 well-armed rebels. These men were in fact part of Mobile Unit 140, described by Krot Theam, who served in it in the Thvak area from September 1950 to September 1952, as a 'Brigade' comprising bands active throughout the North-west. It numbered, he said, over 2,000 troops, less than 400 of whom were Vietnamese.[256] According to French intelligence dating from mid 1952, 500 members of Mobile Unit 140, led by Meas Vong, and of whom at least 180 were Vietnamese, were stationed in Kompong Chhnang province.[257] It would seem, then, that the 1,000 troops reported to be based at Thvak were overwhelmingly Khmer.[258] There were also KNLC troops stationed nearby at Saing Raing — 'sixty seven Khmer Issarak and three Viet Minh' led by Tralay.[259] They appear to have been officially integrated into the UIF's Mobile Unit 480 during the October amalgamation of the two organizations. Already in August, Achar Mel Van, the KNLC province chief of Battambang, had become deputy to the senior Viet Minh military commander there.[260]

Not far to the south in Maung district was Mobile Unit 507, which French intelligence described in May 1952 as a company (about 100 troops).[261] By October it included at least 130 Khmers, and was commanded by Hong Chhun.[262] Khmers enrolled in UIF regional units in the North-west now numbered around 1,600, making a national total of over 3,000, besides those in militia forces and in Viet Minh regular units. Four hundred to six hundred troops of the KNLC were now added to this. The combined strength of all the non-communist Issarak bands, on the other hand, was less than 2,500.

At a secret meeting of Issarak chiefs on 13 October 1952, Kao Tak and Leav Keo Moni reached an 'understanding'.[263] Son Ngoc Thanh again sent messages to Puth Chhay, Chantaraingsey and Sieu Heng, inviting them to send representatives to a meeting in Sisophon on 27 November.[264] But Leav Keo Moni suddenly faced problems in his own ranks. On 25 October, Ouch arrested twenty-one of Moni's followers. Moni retreated westward towards Tak's stronghold, with Ouch in pursuit.[265] Tumsok temporarily threw in his lot with Ouch, but Tralay, Achar Ren and Achar Bou remained loyal to Moni.[266] Three days later, leaflets produced by Ouch's 'KNLC Troops' appeared in Sisophon, accusing Leav Keo Moni of using 'odious means' to put Kampuchea under Vietnamese domination, and urging his overthrow. They now bore the design of Angkor Wat with three towers, *only two weeks* after it had first appeared on a Savang Vong leaflet on the other side of the country.[267] Until then, KNLC leaflets had featured a five-towered motif, like that of the UIF.

The coincidence is remarkable. Given Savang Vong's mysterious 1949 defection to the rebels (see p. 73) and his close relationship with the colonial regime thereafter, and given Ouch's equally mysterious second defection following his 1951 surrender (see p. 96), it is fairly likely that the activities of both men were now coordinated, by French agents, to maximize differences within the Issarak movement at a time when unity was being urgently discussed. (This would be ironic, in that Democratic Kampuchea later adopted the same three-tower motif.) If so, the ploy was effective. The Battambang Police reported 'a serious reduction in rebel activities'.[268] Unable to challenge Leav Keo Moni (now reinforced by Tralay and eighty of his troops),[269] Ouch now attempted to persuade Tumsok to surrender with him, but Tumsok refused 'at the last minute'.[270]

On 27 November, Son Ngoc Thanh called a meeting in an attempt to be recognized as the Issarak 'Supreme Chief'.[271] The meeting failed to achieve its purpose. Representatives of the smaller groups led by 'Puth Chhay, Chantaraingsey and Tak recognized Son Ngoc Thanh as Supreme Chief of the 'Issarak Front'. [But] Leav Keo Moni — representing Sieu Heng — tried to impose Son Ngoc Minh and the alliance with the Viet Minh, of which the others disapproved.'[272]

A second meeting in December, called by Ea Sichau with the mediation of Poc Khun, was unable to resolve the problem, and the two nationalist groups agreed simply to 'assure mutual security',[273] the basis of a relationship that persisted until the end of the war in 1954. Meanwhile, Nguon Hong's small Issarak band, which had reached agreement with both, soldiered on, 'making propaganda in favour of Son Ngoc Thanh', and also saying: 'The communists aid us with modern equipment: soon we will receive reinforcements of men to drive the French from the country. Join the ranks of the Khmer Issarak army now! The Viet Minh have already fought the French with success in north Vietnam.'[274]

This arrangement could not be generalized through the Issarak movement, however. Thanh was unwilling to come to terms with the leaders of the largest Khmer nationalist movement, presumably because of their superior strength and organization, while they in turn were suspicious of him, presumably because of his personal popularity, pro-Japanese background, and faith in the USA. But from what had seemed his unchallengeable position as Kampuchea's leading nationalist in 1945 (and even in 1951), Thanh had lost considerable ground. The results were disastrous for the potential modernization of Khmer politics. By 1954 Thanh's representatives had received the US military attaché from Bangkok, and the scene was set for clandestine US funding of his forces through the Thai Police-General, Pao Siyanon, and the CIA.[275]

Notes

1. Archives D'Outre-Mer (AOM), Aix-en-Provence, France. Cambodge 7F 29 (2), *Note sur l'organisation politique et administrative du Viet-Minh au Cambodge,* (hereafter cited as *Note*). Direction des services de sécurité du Haut Commissariat en Indochine, December 1952. Annexe 1.

2. *Ibid.,* p.8.

3. Archives Nationales, Bibliothèque Nationale, Phnom Penh. Ministère de l'Intérieure, Divers (henceforth MID). *Rapports sur la situation politique de divers khets, fin décembre 1948 à fin 1949* (henceforth *Rapports. . .*) Report by the Governor of Takeo to the Ministry of Interior, 28 July 1949.

4. AOM, Cambodge 7F 29 (7), *Etude sur les mouvements rebelles au Cambodge, 1942–52*, (hereafter cited as *Etude*) 136 pp., at p.56.
5. *Ibid.*, pp.56–57.
6. *Ibid.*
7. *Ibid.*, p.34.
8. MID, *Rapports. . ., op. cit.*, report from Kompong Speu, 29 December 1948.
9. *Ibid.*, reports from Prey Veng, 17 January and 10 May 1949; and from Kandal, 12 January 1949.
10. The governor added: 'The situation remains unchanged in the other contaminated districts — Loeuk Dek, Kien Svay and Koh Thom.' *Ibid.*, report from Kandal, 1 February 1949.
11. *Ibid.*, *Rapport Confidentiel sur les bandes de Khmers Issarak et de Viet Minh au Cambodge*, par le Commissaire de Police du 3e Arrondissement, 28 February 1949, 5pp.
12. *Ibid.*, pp.1.
13. *Ibid.*, pp.1–3.
14. MID, *Rapports. . ., op. cit.*, Governor of Prey Veng to Ministry of Interior, 19 July 1949.
15. MID, *Rapports. . ., Rapport Confidentiel, op. cit.*, p.3.
16. MID, *Rapports. . .*, Governor of Takeo to Ministry of Interior, 21 April, 4 May, 1 June, 9 and 23 July 1949. (See also Chandara Mohaptey, 'A Khmer Issarak Leader's Story', typescript translation by Timothy Carney of Chandara's autobiographical sketch written in 1974, 8 pp., at p.5.).
17. *Ibid.*, *Rapport Confidentiel*, pp.3–4.
18. *Ibid.*, pp.4–5.
19. *Ibid.*, notation dated 12 March on covering letter from the Governor of Phnom Penh City to the President of the Council of Ministers, 5 March 1949.
20. MID, *Rapport. . ., passim.*
21. *Ibid.*, report from Prey Veng, 24 January 1949.
22. *Ibid.*, 21 March 1949.
23. *Ibid.*, 10 May 1949.
24. *Ibid.*, 30 April 1949.
25. *Ibid.*, 10 May 1949. 'Several Viet Minh' only were reported to be among them.
26. *Ibid.* Tou Samouth was said here to have decided on the same course.
27. V.M. Reddi, *A History of the Cambodian Independence Movement, 1863-1955*, Tirupati, Sri Venkatesvara University, 1973, p.159.
28. Chandara Mohaptey, *op. cit.*, p.3.
29. MID, *Rapports. . .*, report from Kompong Chhnang, 18 July 1949 (?).
30. Chandara Mohaptey, *op. cit., passim.*
31. Author's interview with Chea Soth, Phnom Penh, 22 October 1980.
32. MID, *Rapports. . .*, Governor of Kandal to Minister of Interior, 3 June 1949.
33. *Ibid.*, reports from Prey Veng, 10 May and 5 July 1949, and *Etude, op. cit.*, annexe, p.15.
34. *Etude, op. cit.*, pp.13–14.
35. MID, *Rapports. . .*, Governor of Kandal to Ministry of Interior, 3 June 1949.
36. *Etude, op. cit.*, p.14.
37. *Ibid.*, pp.14–15.
38. MID, *Rapports. . .*, Governor of Prey Veng to Ministry of Interior, 5 and 19 July 1949.
39. *Ibid.*, 5 July, 10 May and 19 July 1949. The Vietnamese chief of a mixed Khmer-Vietnamese Committee formed in a village in Prey Veng district in

April recruited fourteen Khmers and three Sino-Khmers, armed them with muskets, and trained them in military exercises each morning. *Ibid.,* 11 June 1949.

40. *Etude, op. cit.,* p.16; annexe, p.15.

41. 'Looking Back at Cambodia' *Westerly,* 4, December 1976, pp.14–28, at p.16.

42. *Le Cambodge,* 10 January 1951, p.2.

43. Phouk Chhay, *Le pouvoir politique au Cambodge: Essay d'analyse sociologique, 1945–65.* Unpublished thesis, Phnom Penh University Faculté de Droit et des Sciences Economiques, 1966, p.157. Quoted in Anthony Barnett. 'The Impact of Diem's Overthrow in Cambodia', forthcoming in *Pacific Affairs.* I have been unable to consult the thesis of Phouk Chhay.

44. It is worth noting the following report in the BBC Summary of World Broadcasts, quoting the CIA's Foreign Broadcast Information Service, 27 February 1950: 'According to Paris, Ho Chi Minh's representative in Thailand said on 13 February that the Vietnamese would fight the Chinese communists if the latter invaded Indo-China. He told journalists that Ho Chi Minh welcomed military aid from any quarter, but foreign troops were not wanted.'

45. MID, file 'Divers 2', folder labelled 'Takeo', *Bulletin Quotidien de Renseignements,* undated (1952?).

46. AOM, Cambodge 7F 29 (4), *Etude sur l'évolution de la politique intérieure et les partis politiques khmers (1945 à 1 juillet 1951),* pp.23–24.

47. *Etude, op. cit.,* p.13, annexe p.15.

48. MID, *Rapports . . .,* Governor of Kandal to Ministry of Interior, 2 February 1949.

49. *Etude, op. cit.,* p.57.

50. MID, *Rapports. . .,* Governor of Takeo to Ministry of Interior, 11 March 1949.

51. *Etude, op. cit.,* annexe, p.33.

52. *Etude,* p.57, and MID, *Rapports. . .,* Governor of Prey Veng to Ministry of Interior, 11 June 1949.

53. *Etude,* p.57.

54. MID, *Rapports. . .,* Governor of Kandal to Ministry of Interior, 10 June 1949.

55. *Ibid.*

56. *Ibid.,* Governor of Prey Veng to Ministry of Interior, 19 July 1949.

57. *Ibid.*

58. Pierre Christian , 'Le Viet-Minh au Cambodge', *Indochine Sud-Est Asiatique,* February-March 1952, p.73; and author's interview with Pham Van Ba, who was a member of the Viet Minh's command staff in Kampuchea and chief of its administrative office from 1949 to 1954. (Ho Chi Minh City 29 October 1980.) According to the French commander, General Séta, of five thousand 'Viet Minh' in Kampuchea, half were in fact Khmer troops. See Maurice Laurent, *L'Armée au Cambodge et dans les pays en voie de développement du sud-est Asiatique,* Paris 1968, p.290.

59. Bernard B. Fall, *The Viet Minh Regime,* Cornell University South-east Asia Program, Data Paper no. 14, April 1954, pp.44, 55.

60. *Etude, op. cit.,* pp.58–59.

61. MID, *Bulletin Quotidien des Renseignements* (BQR), Sûreté Intérieure, Activités Rebelles. Report by the Service de Sécurité du Haut Commissariat (SSHC), 5 September 1952.

62. *Ibid.,* 6 July 1952.

63. *Ibid.,* report by Port National, 21 June 1952.

64. *Ibid.,* source unspecified.

65. *Etude., op. cit.,* p.49.
66. *Ibid.,* p.49–51. (See also MID, 1952. Map prepared by the governor of Kompong Speu, 7 December 1951, referring to Chantaraingsey's zone, 'où on peut circuler'.) His military adviser was a Japanese lieutenant. See Wilfred G. Burchett, *Mekong Upstream,* Hanoi 1957, pp.118–121; and MID, BQR, report from Kompong Speu military police, 12 December 1952.
67. *Etude, op. cit.,* p.61.
68. *Ibid.,* p.62.
69. MID, 1952. Map prepared by the governor of Kompong Speu, 7 December 1951, referring to Savang Vong's zone 'où on peut circuler librement'.
70. *Etude, op. cit.,* p.62.
71. *Ibid.,* p.62.
72. *Ibid.*
73. *Ibid.,* p.63.
74. *Ibid.*
75. MID, *Rapports politiques:Etude sur l'insécurité* (apparently reports submitted at a conference of province governors in March 1952, henceforth cited as *Rapports politiques*). 'Etude sur l'insécurité dans la province de Kratié', par le Gouverneur, 19 février 1952.
76. MID, *Rapports. . .,* op. cit., report from the National Police in Kratie.
77. *Cambodge,* 26 July 1951, pp. 1, 4.
78. United States, Central Intelligence Agency, *Foreign Broadcast Information Service* (henceforth FBIS), *Voice of Nambo* in Khmer, 30 June 1952.
79. FBIS, *ibid.,* 27 April 1951, p.CCC 4, *Voice of Nambo* in Vietnamese, 'The Vietnam-Laos-Cambodia Bloc', 19 April 1951.
80. Tan Huyen and Pham Thanh, *Dat Nuoc Campuchia,* Hanoi 1980, p.119. Contemporary communist claims were that the Khmer revolutionary forces increased by 700 per cent during 1949. FBIS, *ibid.,* 2 January 1951.
81. 'The Viet Minh, Rin Tin and Sao Ly, had taken him to south Vietnam. The Khmer Krom supported him and he rose to command Battalion 105.' Chandara Mohaptey, *op. cit.,* p.3.
82. MID, *Rapports. . ., Rapport Confidentiel, op. cit.,* p.3.
83. MID, *Rapports. . .,* report from Governor of Takeo, 17 May 1949.
84. *Ibid.,* 1 June 1949.
85. Chandara Mohaptey, *op. cit.,* p.4.
86. *Etude, op. cit.,* annexe, p.5.
87. *op. cit.,* p.4.
88. Quoted in Porter, 'Vietnamese Communist Policy towards Kampuchea, 1930–1970', in David P. Chandler and Ben Kiernan, eds., *Revolution and its Aftermath in Kampuchea,* New Haven 1983, p.67.
89. *Note, op. cit.,* p.9.
90. Burchett, *op. cit.,* p.113; Non Suon, *Karnei Vet niw krosuong kasekam rot* ('The Affair of Vet in the State Agriculture Ministry'), confession in Tuol Sleng, Phnom Penh, dated 24 November 1976. For photographs of the monks at this meeting, see Pierre Christian, 'Le Viet Minh au Cambodge', *Indochine Sud-Est Asiatique,* February-March 1952, pp.73–77. Christian calls them 'indoctrinated false monks'. See also photo no.14, opposite p.282, below.
91. Chandara Mohaptey, *op. cit.,* p.5.
92. *Ibid.*
93. Robert Olivier, *Le Protectorat Français au Cambrodge,* thèse de doctorat du 3e cycle, University of Paris, 1969, p.320c. Chan Dara, however, says that Chau

Yin (not to mention Son Ngoc Minh and Chan Samay) was also a Khmer Krom.

94. Author's interview with Nguyen Xuan Hoang, Hanoi, 4 November 1980.

95. *Etude, op. cit.*, p.81, and 'Khmer Communist Rallier Keoum Kun', unclassified Airgram to Department of State from US Embassy, Phnom Penh, 13 January 1972, p.6.

96. *Note, op. cit.*, pp.9-11. For the text of Minh's proclamation, see Olivier, *op. cit.*, pp.320c-320g.

97. Fall, *op. cit.*, p.55.

98. *Note, op. cit.*, annexe III, translation of a captured Vietnamese-language document, section 6, part l.

99. Author's interview with Krot Theam, Melbourne, 2 December 1976. A copy of a 60-page UIF instruction manual is extant in MID, Bibliothèque Nationale, Phnom Penh.

100. Author's interviews with Men Chhan, Phnom Penh, 25 September 1980, and Chan Mon, Suong, 7 August 1980.

101. MID, Department of Justice, *Arrestations*, 'Dossiers du no. 1 au no. 28': Chief of SSHC to Minister of National Police, 29 December 1951, enclosing 'Déclaration de Hem Chea'.

102. David J. Steinberg, *et al.*, *Cambodia: Its People, Its Society, Its Culture*, HRAF Press, New Haven, 1959, p.107. 'A number of other cadres from north-east, south-east and north-west Cambodia' were also reported to have attended. (See also FBIS, report of a radio broadcast, 3 August 1950.)

103. *Ibid.*, and FBIS, 26 March 1951, quoting *Voice of Nambo*, 20 March 1951.

104. *Issarak*, no. 18, 30 November 1951. Author's copy of the original in MID, Divers 5.

105. *Note, op. cit.*, p.24. Bunchhan Mul refers to yet another Khmer communist newspaper, published in the Dangrek mountains on the Thai border in 1949. It was called *Rumdoh* ('Liberation'). See Ben Kiernan and Chanthou Boua, eds., *Peasants and Politics in Kampuchea, 1942-81*, London 1982, p.121.

106. Chandara Mohaptey, *op.cit.*, p.6.

107. *Vietnam Information*, no. 370/VNS-R, 26 January 1951 (quoted in Reddi, *op. cit.*, p.178) reports a 'preparatory conference' in November 1950. The formal foundation is reported in no. 385/VNS-R, 28 April 1951. For the resolutions adopted at the meeting, see no. 386/VNS-R, 4 May 1951.

108. *Note, op. cit.*, p.19

109. Tan Huyen and Pham Thanh, *op. cit.*, p.119

110. *Note, op. cit.*, annexe III, translation of a captured Vietnamese-language document, section 6, part 1.

111. *Summary of Annotated Party History*, by the Eastern Zone Military-Political Service of the Communist Party of Kampuchea, 1973, translated captured document de-classified by the US Government in 1978, p.1, 8.

112. *Ibid.*, and Nguyen Xuan Hoang, *op. cit.* Other members may have included such former Khmer members of the ICP as Mey Pho, So Phim, Prasith, Ney Sarann, Hong Chhun, Non Suon, Muol Sambath and Keo Meas.

113. Nguyen Xuan Hoang, *op.cit.*, and Chea Soth, *op. cit.*

114. *Note, op. cit.*, annexe III, translation of a captured Vietnamese-language document, section 6, part 1.

115. F. Joyaux, *La Chine et le règlement du premier conflict d'Indochine, Genève 1954*, Paris 1979, p.222. According to one former Issarak in Battambang, 'nearly all' the Viet Minh active in the country were Khmer speakers. 'They came from

Kompong Cham, Siemreap, Svay Rieng and Kratie where their families had established themselves a generation or two before'. Account of Ouk Samith, in *Cambodge: La Révolution de la Forêt*, by François Debré, Paris 1976, pp.47-58, at p.54.

116. 'Remarks on the Official Appearance of the Vietnam Workers' Party', US Mission in Vietnam, *Captured Documents Series*, no. 2. The document was captured in South Vietnam at an unknown date; the translation is prefaced by the note that it 'appears authentic' and that, although its 'exact origin and addressees are unknown', it 'has been accurately translated'. Another translation renders the second passage: 'later on, *when* conditions permit ...' (my emphasis). See P.J. Honey, *Communism in North Vietnam*, p.170.

117. Fall, *op. cit.*, p.56.

118. *Etude, op. cit.*, p.98, and *Note, op. cit.*, p.21. According to French intelligence: 'Until August 1951, the Cambodians admitted into the Party were few in number. From that date, a larger place was made available to them. The recruitment and training of cadres nevertheless proved difficult, because the candidates demonstrated simultaneously lack of comprehension, nonchalance and indiscipline'.

119. *Note, op. cit.*, p.21.

120. MID, BQR, report from National Police in Kampot, 16 July 1952.

121. Fall, *op. cit.*, pp.56, 37.

122. *Note, op. cit.*, p.10. The programme was broadcast on 26 May 1950.

123. Translation of a captured document dated 24 June 1952, from 'The Committee of Foreign Affairs of the Committee of Cadres of Cambodia to all Zones, to Phnom Penh, to the companies contacting the Chinese', *Official Telegram* no. 749-S.D.C.S. Copy in the Wason-Echolls Collection in Olin Library, Cornell University.

124. A Viet Minh document comments on the reason for dividing the ICP into three parties as follows: 'Although Vietnam, Laos and Cambodia, which form the Indo-Chinese peninsula, have a common enemy — French colonialism — their degree of evolution differs in all respects: economic, political, cultural, social ... That is why the character and principles of the Vietnamese revolution differ from the revolutions of Laos and Cambodia, although all three have the same gaol: ousting the imperialists and puppets. The mission of the revolution in Vietnam is to liberate the Nation, consolidate and develop the people's democratic regime towards Socialism. But the revolutions of Laos and Cambodia aim at liberating the nation and establishing an anti-imperialist government in order to achieve popular democracy. Because of these distinct characteristics and principles, there must be separate parties.' 'Remarks on the Official Appearance of the Vietnam Workers' Party', *op. cit.*

125. Author's interview with Pham Van Ba, Ho Chi Minh City, 28 October 1980, and Gareth Porter, *op. cit.*, p.90.

126. MID, file 'No. 48 à 52', *Zones de Guerre*, part 1.

127. *Ibid.*, part 2, 'Rives et zones cannonables à priori', Etat-Major, 3e Bureau, 11 November 1950.

128. Maurice Laurent, *op. cit.*, p.52. Laurent puts the total French commitment in Kampuchea at over 10,000 troops and support personnel, a figure surpassed by that of Khmers in the Royal Army only at the end of 1952. (Also author's interview with Nguyen Thanh Son, Ho Chi Minh City, 28 October 1980.)

129. *Ibid.*

130. Reddi, *op. cit.*, p.42.

131. Jean Delvert, *Le Paysan cambodgien*, Paris, Mouton, 1961, pp.208-209.

132. MID, *Rapports ..., op. cit.*, Governor of Takeo to Ministry of Interior, 1 July 1949, naming 'Meas Vong, [Chau] Yin and Mok' as commanders of 'the Viet Minh and Khmer Issarak bands... in Prey Krabas district'. All three were of course Khmer. In another report, the Governor pointed out that 'the Cambodian Seng Pok', a native of Prey Krabas, 'appears to have been named chief of the Viet Minh Committee' there. *Ibid.*, 11 June 1949.

133. Author's interview with Chhun Samath, Kong Pisei, 17 September 1980. Samath said that Mok was born in Trapeang Thom subdistrict, in the Damrey Romeal mountains.

134. MID, *Rapports ..., op. cit.*, Governor of Takeo to Ministry of Interior, 25 June 1949. The Ministry of Interior file on 'Exactions commises par le Viet Minh' contains a single dossier, a letter in Khmer to the King written by inhabitants of Kompong Yaul subdistrict of Takeo and signed with one thumbprint. MID, *Soumissions, Correspondances, Divers*, file no. 28.

135. Delvert, *op. cit.*, p.208.

136. *Etude, op. cit.*, p.38.

137. *Ibid.*, p.61.

138. MID, *Rapports politiques*, 'Notes sur la pacification de la province de Kampot', par le Gouverneur, 22 March 1952. My emphasis.

139. MID, BQR, SSHC report, 27 October 1952.

140. Reddi, *op. cit.*, p.197, note 86. Reddi cites André François Mercier, *Faut-il abandonner l'Indo-Chine?* Paris 1954, pp.147-48, in corroboration.

141. May Ebihara, *Svay: A Khmer Village in Cambodia*, Ph. D. dissertation, Columbia University, 1968, pp.541-42. This village, where Ebihara lived in 1959-60, was 30 Km. south of Phnom Penh near Kompong Kantuot (p.7), in Savang Vong's former zone of operations: see MID, 1952, maps prepared by the Governors of Kompong Speu (7 December 1951) and Kandal (11 July 1952).

142. Author's interview with Sok Khem, a former UIF cadre, in Kampot, 27 August 1980.

143. Reddi, *op. cit.*, p.162.

144. *Les Paroles de Samdech Preah Norodom Sihanouk*, Phnom Penh, Ministry of Information, October-December 1968, p.585. Speech at Tonle Bet, 10 October 1968.

145. MID, BQR, Sonn Pailinn, Commissaire de la Police Nationale, to Ministry of Interior, Kampot, 20 June 1952. No. 625/C, Confidential.

146. *Chamlaiy Dop Pir* ('Reply of no. 12'), confession by Non Suon in Tuol Sleng prison, 29 November 1976, p.3.

147. MID, BQR, SSHC report, 18 November 1952, and National Police report from Kampot, 11 December 1952.

148. MID, Divers 7, chief of Kampot district to Governor of Kampot, 25 October 1951; and MID, BQR, 'Distribution of Rebel Forces in Southern Cambodia', report by National Police in Takeo, 19 September 1952.

149. Author's interview with Seng Horl, Creteil, 3 December 1979. Horl, a native of Prey Krabas, said that Ngin Hor was of Vietnamese extraction; but the report by the governor of Prey Veng, quoted earlier, refers to an Issarak band whose members included 'several Viet Minh and also Ngin Hor'. MID, *Rapports ...*, report from Prey Veng, 10 May 1949.

150. *Etude, op. cit.*, p.75, and MID, BQR, National Police reports from Takeo, July 1952, 18 and 19 September 1952.

151. *Etude, op. cit.*, p.74. In August 1951, insurgents simultaneously attacked four government positions in Krakor district of Pursat. *Le Cambodge*, 18 and 19 August 1951.

112

152. MID, BQR, SSHC report, 26 August 1952; Battambang, National Police, 20
August 1952; and Capitaine Aron, chef du 2e Bureau, to Ministry of Interior, 9
December 1952. In French usage, the term 'Khmer Viet Minh' referred to a
fully Khmer force. For instance, *Le Cambodge*, 28 July 1951, p.4, reported that
'one Viet Minh and one Khmer Viet Minh' had been captured. See also the 24
February 1953 issue of the same paper for a similar use of the term.
153. MID, *Rapports politiques*, report by the governor of Kompong Cham.
154. MID, BQR, SSHC report, 13 December 1952.
155. *Ibid.*, 17 November 1952 and 15 October 1952.
156. MID, file 'Dossiers du No. 1 à No. 28', Department of Justice, *Arrestations*;
Chief of SSHC to Minister of National Police, 29 December 1951.
157. The ethnic Vietnamese rubber plantation workers, who lived in quarters on
the Chup plantation in the area, are not referred to in this Sûreté report. They
appear in another document, captured from the Viet Minh two months
earlier, in which about 2,000 of 8,000 Vietnamese workers in all the rubber
plantations in Kampuchea are said to have been members of communist
organizations, including 335 of the 2,000 Vietnamese at Chup. MID, *Divers 5*,
Bulletin de Soit communiqué, 'Documents saisis sur les V.M.'; table 2,
'Effectif du personnel et des membres du *cong-doan* des plantations du
Cambodge'.
158. See note 156 'Déclaration de Hem Chea', 'Déclaration de Tea Heng', and
'Déclaration de Chan Loeung alias Chan Seng'. Also author's interview with
a former timber merchant from Suong, who knew Tea Heng in this period;
Melbourne, 30 May 1982. And *Le Cambodge*, 20 November 1951.
159. *Etude, op. cit.*, p.98.
160. MID, BQR, National Police report from Prey Veng, 16 July 1952.
161. *Ibid.*, 4 October 1952, gives figures of 50 Khmer Issarak and 50 Viet Minh for
one company; *Le Cambodge*, 24 February 1953, gives a figure of 30 'Viet Minh'
in another unit of 60 rebels of the Achar Hem Chieu force, which totalled
about 400 troops in this period (see note 162).
162. MID, BQR. National Police reports from Svay Rieng, 25 September 1952,
and Prey Veng, 25 and 27 September 1952. The total number of rebels
reported involved in the attacks is 400.
163. *Ibid.*, SSHC report, 19 October 1952.
164. *Etude, op. cit.*, pp.74–75, and map, 'Implantation rebelle au 15 mai 1952'; *Note,
op. cit.*, p.15; MID, *Rapports ... op. cit.*, Governor of Prey Veng to Ministry of
Interior, 11 June 1949, and Governor of Kandal, 2 March 1949 (on Nong
Sralao). On Sok Saphai, author's interview with Tea Sabun, Phnom Penh 23
August 1980, and with Sang Lon, Kandol Chrum, 7 August 1980. On the
commander of the Pou Kombo Unit, author's interview with Chim Chin, 28
July 1980. In 1949, this Unit had had only 22 Khmer and 8 Vietnamese
members (*Le Cambodge*, 20 January 1953, p.4).
165. According to Krot Theam, *op. cit.*, Achar Chum was cited as a colleague of
Achar Hem Chieu, who had become an Issarak 'military tactician', although
no other information is available on his activities after 1945. Theam said
Chum was not the same man as Achar Khieu Chum, who also took part in
the 1942 demonstration against the French. The name 'Okhnya Chhouk' is
that of one of the leaders of the 1885–86 uprising.
166. *Etude, op. cit.*, p.72.
167. Laurent, *op. cit.*, pp.45, 47.
168. Interview with author in Melbourne, 30 May 1982.

169. *Etude, op. cit.*, p.90.
170. *Ibid.*, p.87, and *Le Cambodge*, 27 November 1951, p.1.
171. FBIS, 15 March 1951.
172. Chea Soth, *op. cit.*
173. FBIS, 28 November 1951. See also 15 November, and 5, 6, 7, 11, 13, 19 December 1951.
174. MID, Divers 2, de Raymond to the President of the Council of Ministers, 12 September 1951, no. 1806/AP/X.
175. *Ibid.* On Achar Kou, see *Chamlaiy Dop Pir*, Non Suon, *op. cit.*
176. MID, BQR. National Police report from Takeo, 10 October 1952.
177. *Ibid.*, Sonn Pailinn, Commissaire de la Police Nationale, to Ministry of Interior, Kampot, 20 June 1952. No. 625/C, Confidentiel. For another example, see MID, *1952*, report from Kompong Trach district office to Governor of Kampot, 5 May 1952.
178. Author's interview with Sam Nang, Melbourne, 2 December 1976.
179. In April 1951 a meeting of seventy UIF personnel at Mong monastery in Tbaung Khmum was attended by the abbot and five other monks. MID, file 'Dossiers du no. 1 au no. 28', Department of Justice, *Arrestations*, 'Déclaration de Tea Heng'.
180. Copies of it were distributed by Prak Sarin's UIF forces in Svay Rieng, signed by an abbot, a deputy abbot, and nine other monks. MID, *Divers 2*, captured document published by the 'Executive Committee of the Issarak Association of Romeas Hek district', 21 May 1952.
181. MID, BQR, SSHC report, 31 October 1952. The meeting was scheduled for 27 October at a location unknown to the intelligence service.
182. Author's interview with Puk Soum, Prey Veng, 8 August 1980.
183. FBIS, 16 April 1952.
184. *Ibid.*, 23 June 1952.
185. Upasaka Purusakara, 'Le Peuple cambodgien est plus bouddhiste que ses bonzes', *Indochine Sud-Est Asiatique*, 31, July 1954, pp.25–31, at pp.30, 31. In March 1951, Sieu Heng said: 'Since 1945, Buddhist monks have been the most active elements in supporting the Resistance ...' *Vietnam Information*, no. 386/VNS-R, 4 May 1951, p.4.
186. *Etude, op. cit.*, pp.46-47.
187. *Ibid.*
188. *Ibid.*, annexe, p.26. Unlike Tak, Moni had also held a post in the KPLC.
189. *Ibid.*, pp.26, 47. The date is also given as 19 April 1951, but this is chronologically impossible, since in February 1951, Leav Keo Moni 'was *re*-elected by a big majority' (p.27). See also annexe, p.20, which gives the April 1950 date.
190. *Ibid.*, p.47.
191. *Ibid.*, pp.27, 40, and annexe, pp.10, 24,27.
192. Chea Soth, *op. cit.*
193. *Etude, op. cit.*, p.47.
194. *Ibid.*, p.27.
195. *Ibid.*, and MID, BQR, undated report of the assembly, which also included the leaders Ouch, Tralay and the KNLC's province chief for Battambang, Achar Mel Van. They gathered at Bay Damram on 30 January 1951.
196. *Etude, op. cit.*, p.27, which continued, noting: 'but more likely because several of his lieutenants seemed ready to surrender'.
197. *Ibid.*, p.47.

198. *Ibid.*, p.27.
199. *Ibid.*
200. *Ibid.*, p.47.
201. *Ibid.*, pp.47–48.
202. *Ibid.*, pp.44–45.
203. *Ibid.*, annexe p.29.
204. *Ibid.*, p.44.
205. *Ibid.*, pp.45, 27.
206. *Ibid.*, p.74.
207. Author's interview with Hoang Tung, Hanoi, 31 October 1980.
208. *Etude, op. cit.*, p.74.
209. Krot Theam, *op. cit.*
210. *Etude, op. cit.*, annexe, p.25. (And New China News Agency, 1 December 1951, quoted in BBC Summary of World Broadcasts, 5 December 1951.)
211. *Ibid.*, and Krot Theam, *op. cit.* According to one report, Nuon Chea was a nephew of Sieu Heng; Kao Thao and Virayuth Puckdinukul (son of Kao Tak and son-in-law of Leath Muon), interview with author, Bangkok, 19 August 1981. Both Chea and Muol Sambath were former CPT members.
212. Krot Theam, *op. cit.*
213. *Etude, op. cit.*, p.40. At the same time, she was reported to be in charge of Son Ngoc Thanh's intelligence service (p.42).
214. *Ibid.*, annexe, p.24.
215. Reddi, *op. cit.*, p.182, gives a figure of 10,000. Other sources give the size of the crowd variously at 5,000 (P. Christian, 'Son Ngoc Thanh', *Indochine Sud-Est Asiatique*, October 1952, p.49), and 300,000.
216. *Ibid.*
217. *Note, op. cit.*, p.18.
218. Reddi, *op. cit.*, p.183, and *Etude, op. cit.*, p.35.
219. *Etude, op. cit.*, pp.33–34.
220. Reddi, *op. cit.*, pp.183–84.
221. *Ibid.*, p.186, and *Etude, op. cit.*, p.33.
222. *Etude, ibid.*, p.33.
223. *Ibid.*, p.34, and annexe, p.20. According to French intelligence in May 1952, since 1949 'the provincial police and the men of the Royal Khmer Army have fraternized with Tak's Khmer Issarak, no doubt in part because of their antipathy for Dap Chhuon'. *Etude, op. cit.*,p.47.
224. *Etude, op. cit.*, pp.34–39.
225. *Ibid.*, p.62.
226. *Ibid.*, p.38.
227. *Ibid.*, p.40. The same source adds: 'Contradictory information indicates that Son Ngoc Thanh has met Son Ngoc Minh in Kampot ... or that the latter has set out to meet Thanh ... What is more certain is that emissaries of these two rebel Chiefs have established fairly regular links between their zones of activity'. (p.40).
228. *Ibid.*, pp.28, 38, 45.
229. *Ibid.*, pp.35–37.
230. Martin Herz, *A Short History of Cambodia*, New York, 1958, p.87. Quoted in Reddi, *op. cit.*, pp.191–92.
231. Chandara Mohaptey, *op. cit.*, p.7.
232. This, he wrote in 1974, was because he 'understood that Vietnamese communist doctrine clearly aimed to destroy Laos and Cambodia.' It is

interesting to compare this view with the recollections of Thao O, a Lao nationalist who had an equally chequered career with the Lao communists, as a senior official, before defecting in 1957. Ten years later he said that the Vietnamese 'did not want to replace the French and dominate Laos. They would be satisfied with the Communist Lao.' *Ibid.*, p.8, and J.J. Zasloff, personal communication.

233. Author's interview with Chana Samudavanija, Chiengmai, 14 August 1981. Chana says he visited Thanh's headquarters 'many times' in this period.

234. MID, BQR. Undated intelligence report referring to Samrong district.

235. MID, BQR. National Police report from Battambang, 19 June 1952.

236. *Etude, op. cit.*, p.38.

237. P. Christian, *op. cit.*, p.49. The French were, of course, constantly trying to tar Thanh with a communist brush.

238. MID, BQR. National Police report from Battambang, 24 June 1952. No. 591, P.S.

239. *Ibid.*, SSHC report, 15 September 1952, and 4 and 26 August 1952.

240. *Ibid.*, SSHC reports, 15 July 1952.

241. MID, *Soumissions, Correspondances Divers*, No. 16, 'Comité Mouvement Son Ngoc Thanh', Governor of Siemreap to Ministry of Interior, 26 August 1952.

242. MID, BQR. National Police report from Battambang, 7 August 1952.

243. MID, 1952. National Police report from Battambang, 12 September 1952.

244. MID, BQR. National Police report from Siemreap, 16 September 1952.

245. MID, *Soumissions, Correspondances Divers*, no. 16, 'Comité Mouvement Son Ngoc Thanh', BQR (Spéciale), Sûreté report, 25 September 1952. This report claimed, however, that Ea Sichau's death in the clash was 'confirmed'; in fact Sichau escaped.

246. MID, BQR. SSHC report, 9 October 1952.

247. *Ibid.*, SSHC report, 5 November 1952.

248. *Ibid.*, SSHC report, 7 October 1952.

249. *Ibid.*

250. *Ibid.*, SSHC report, 7 October 1952. (On Nuon Chea, 14 October 1952.)

251. *Ibid.*

252. *Etude, op. cit.*, annexe, p.26.

253. AOM, Aix-en-Provence, Cambodge 7F 29(4), *Etude sur l'évolution de la politique intérieure et les partis politiques khmers (1945 à 1 juillet 1951)*, p.34. The same source adds: 'If this situation develops, it could place the future Assembly, and by extension, the government it produces, heavily in debt to the rebellion.'

254. Nguyen Xuan Hoang, *op. cit.*

255. MID, BQR. SSHC report, 25 June 1952.

256. Krot Theam, *op. cit.*

257. *Etude, op. cit.*, p.75, and MID, BQR, SSHC report, 26 August 1952.

258. According to Krot Theam, the military commander of Mobile Unit 140 was a Khmer named Chey Samreth (*op. cit.*). Samreth had previously been KPRP Secretary in Kampot. Non Suon, *Chamlaiy Dop Pir Leuk Ti Pram: Royeak Mun Rotpraha 18.3.70* ('The Fifth Reply by No. 12: The Period Before the 18 March 1970 Coup'), confession in Tuol Sleng, 7 November 1976, p.1.

259. MID, BQR. National Police report from Battambang, 21 November 1952.

260. *Ibid.*, 7 August 1952. The Viet Minh commander of Mobile Unit 480 was named Ong Nguyen.

261. *Etude, op. cit.*, map.

262. MID, BQR. National Police reports from Battambang, 14 October 1952 (two) and 14 June 1952.

263. MID, 1952. National Police report from Siemreap, 5 November 1952.

264. MID, BQR. SSHC report, 12 December 1952.

265. *Ibid.*, SSHC report, 3 November 1952.

266. Author's interviews with Kao Thao and Virayuth Puckdinukul, relatives of Kao Tak and Leath Muon, Bangkok, 19 August 1981 (on Achar Saren). Achar Huot Bou was killed by government forces while campaigning for the 1955 elections. ICSC, Command Papers, *Cambodia No. 1, 1957, Cmnd. 253*, pp.27 ff. Tumsok soon returned to the UIF fold, as we shall see.

267. MID, BQR. SSHC report, 14 November 1952.

268. *Ibid.*, National Police report from Battambang, 26 October 1952.

269. *Ibid.*, Sûreté report, 4 December 1952.

270. *Ibid.*, 22 November 1952.

271. *Ibid.*, SSHC report, 12 December 1952.

272. *Ibid.*, 16 December 1952.

273. *Ibid.*, and MID, *Soumissions, Correspondances Divers*, no. 16, 'Comité Mouvement Son Ngoc Thanh', report from the Cambodian chargé d'affaires in Thailand, 9 February 1953.

274. MID, BQR. SSHC report, 11 December 1952. Hong was based in Kompong Thom.

275. Chana Samudavanija, *op. cit.* General Chana arranged the meeting with the US attaché on the Thai-Kampuchean border, which took place some time before February 1954.

Urban Politics

Son Ngoc Thanh's real strength inside Kampuchea lay in the cities, as the massive welcome he had received at Phnom Penh airport testified. The communist Committee for Phnom Penh, established on Son Ngoc Minh's initiative in August 1950,[1] could not claim any such success. Although it had made significant gains among Vietnamese — a single agent recruited 150 ethnic Vietnamese workers into 36 cells within a year[2] — the Committee complained in a document dated 11 September 1951: 'Contrary to what they promised us, the monks have not yet presented any Cambodian candidates. We have addressed a letter to R.L., a progressive element in the city, but we have received no reply. The plan to infiltrate into the city Issarak members from Sa'ang has not been implemented. The latter always claim family problems in order to defer their departure ... We are not yet able to find, on the spot, Issarak leaders able to be sent on missions into the city ... Of our plan to create the Issarak movement (there), we are able to implement only one aspect: propaganda.'[3]

The unresponsive R.L. was almost certainly Ray Lomuth, editor of the newspaper *Reastr Khmer* ('Khmer Commoners'), which had been suspended in July for its anti-French campaigns. Such repression may have been one reason why Lomuth's 'Three Stars' Party had gained no seats in the elections on 9 September, but if French intelligence can be believed, he was also 'a shifty character, not very intelligent, with no serious political culture'.[4]

The serious political culture in the cities, at least among Khmer patriots, was monopolized by Son Ngoc Thanh. The student demonstrations in May 1952 were almost entirely organized by Thanh's supporters in the militant wing of the Democratic Party. The demonstrators, who included future communist leaders Hu Nim (in Phnom Penh) and Vorn Vet (in Battambang), protested against 'Operation Lightning' and distributed leaflets 'supplied by Son Ngoc Thanh'.[5] To be sure, leaflets signed by Son Ngoc Minh, congratulating the students on their efforts, did appear in Phnom Penh,[6] and workers in a Pursat distillery were discovered in possession of a UIF statement praising the students of Battambang.[7] But, in Phnom Penh at least, the UIF was unable to gain much ground.

Further, Vietnamese communists had to compete with Chinese communists for influence among the capital's non-Khmer workers. In 1949 the Viet Minh had created a 'League of Chinese Residents for Liberation', and in May 1951 the cadres responsible for Chinese residents in the Eastern Zone established a provisional committee for those in Phnom Penh. In September, 'apparently on orders from above', this was transformed into a branch of the League, perhaps to ensure tighter control; party work within it was entrusted to a Vietnamese.[8] At the same time, according to French intelligence: 'a cell of the 'Chinese Emigré Youth Movement', independent of the Viet Minh, was established in Phnom Penh in December 1951. It appears directly subordinate to the 'Overseas Chinese Commission' in Swatow (China).' The same source did point out, however: 'If in fact the Chinese Communist Party plays the part of a powerful elder brother of the ICP, and if its militants are unwilling to be placed under the orders of those of the Viet Minh, on the other hand out of necessity they have to work in the tow of the stronger and better organized Vietnamese organizations.'[9]

But in July 1952, after the arrest of many members of the Committee for Phnom Penh, the leaders of the Kandal/Prey Veng/Svay Rieng Interprovince decided to dissolve it and to assume direct responsibility for affairs there.[10] The Phnom Penh Committee was later re-established, under Keo Meas, but even by 1954 the Khmer communist movement was so negligible in the capital that it was open to a relatively easy takeover by a small outside group more at home there.

Prince Youthevong, a 'cultivated mind' according to French intelligence, had joined the Socialist Party in France, and after his return home to found the Democratic Party in 1946 he took advice from a resident French lawyer and member of the Socialist International.[11] He had even brought back from France what was apparently the first copy of the Communist Manifesto to find its way to Kampuchea, and distributed it to a number of students in Phnom Penh. But the seeds of an intellectual Marxism fell on infertile soil in Kampuchea, and largely disappeared from the scene with Youthevong himself; the radicalism of the nationalist educated class, apart from those such as Mey Pho who abandoned it, remained the rather amorphous 'National Socialism' of Son Ngoc Thanh. It was only in France that some Khmer students developed an affinity for Marxism-Leninism in this period. And even among these students, interpretations of its significance for Kampuchea varied.

In 1950, a small group of Kampuchean students in France had formed a 'Marxist Circle', apparently affiliated to the French Communist Party (PCF) as its 'Khmer-language section'; its leaders were Rath Samuoeun and Ieng Sary,[12] who later pursued widely divergent political paths. Members included Hou Yuon, who in a number of discussions found himself in disagreement with his fellow student, Saloth Sar (later known as Pol Pot); both of these, however – the first because of a devotion to his studies and the second because of a 'retiring personality' — initially played only a minimal role in the group, as did Keng Vannsak, an older man who had studied for a year in London. More active were Thiounn Mumm, Touch Phoeun, Mey Mann and Mey Phat (apparently cousins of 1945 coup-maker Mey Pho), Chi Kim An and Sien An,[13] who all played important — and later opposing — roles in Kampuchean left-wing politics over the next thirty years.

Saloth Sar wrote home to Phnom Penh occasionally, usually asking his brother Suong for money; but one day, Suong says, a letter arrived asking for the Protocol Director of the Palace to send him a short biographical account of the life of King Norodom Sihanouk. Suong presumably suspected republican motives, and he replied advising Sar to concentrate on his studies and not to get involved in politics. Sar did not heed his brother's advice — he was probably already affiliated to the PCF — but few who knew him thus far, in Phnom Penh or in Paris, would have disagreed with Suong's statement that he 'would not have killed a chicken then'.[14] All sources from this period descibe Sar as a gentle, shy and rather charming young man. Although he failed his course two years in a row, he did not lack intelligence. In this period he fell in love with Mey Pho's cousin Khieu Ponnary, who was eight years his senior and the first Khmer woman to obtain the Baccalauréat.[15] As we saw in Chapter One, Ponnary came from an elite background; her younger sister Khieu Thirith was the first Khmer to graduate in English Literature, and soon married Ieng Sary. In 1951, Ponnary returned to Phnom Penh and began publishing *Neary* ('the monthly magazine for Cambodian women'), which featured cooking recipes and articles on fashion and beauty care, as well as on social questions such as child-rearing ('Should Children be Educated in Freedom or Oppression?'), and also translations of French fables such as 'The Ploughman and his Children'. *Neary* was sold at a Phnom Penh shop called 'Petit Paris'.[16]

In mid 1950, Saloth Sar had spent a month of his holidays in a work brigade in Yugoslavia[17] — an interesting choice for someone connected with the French Communist Party, which was still avidly pro-Stalin two years after the latter's break with Tito. (In September 1950 the French communist review *Democratie Nouvelle* carried an article entitled 'Yugoslavia, Advance-post of the American Capacity for Aggression'.) It may be incorrect to read much significance into this first glimpse at socialism, although in the light of the Democratic Kampuchea experience it is intriguing that the Yugoslav Party was at that point pursuing severe and voluntarist economic policies. At first the party sponsored massive labour mobilization on capital works projects and favoured agricultural prices at the expense of urban living standards, and then, in 1949-50, it exercised the enforced collectivization of farming. By the time Belgrade reverted to a policy of fostering private peasant agriculture, Saloth Sar was back in Paris.[18]

Perhaps more significant is the fact that during the same period Ieng Sary made a point of studying Stalin's writings on policy towards minority nationalities in the Soviet Union.[19] He and Saloth Sar may well have found the early Vietnamese concept of a 'Union of Soviet Republics of Indo-China' unsatisfactory, and sympathized with Yugoslavia's independence. (If so, they were ignoring its pluri-ethnic character just as they later ignored the cultural peculiarities of Kampuchea's own ethnic minorities). They may also have seen the harshness of Yugoslav policies at the time as justified by the need to develop economic independence, e.g. from the USSR. Nevertheless Ieng Sary is reported by Keng Vannsak to have been attracted to Stalin's technique of controlling the organizational structure of the Communist Party by 'holding the dossiers'.[20]

The fact that anti-royalist, nationalist rather than socialist sentiments still dominated the revolutionary politics of the 'Marxist Circle' is also suggested by its praise, as late as mid 1952, for 'our real heroes, in particular Son Ngoc Thanh'.[21] This came in a protest message, signed by Hou Yuon as President of the Khmer Students' Association in France, to King Sihanouk after he had dismissed the Democratic Party government in June. The message linked the monarchy with French repression, but made no mention of the UIF or of events in Vietnam or Laos. This was the case despite the fact that in August 1951 the members of the 'Marxist Circle' (apart from Thiounn Mumm and Hou Yuon) had attended the International Youth Congress in East Berlin, where they met Viet Minh delegates, and had returned to Paris with a number of communist documents.[22]

But some of the 'Marxist Circle' strayed well beyond Thanh-ism. An article written by Saloth Sar in his own handwriting (Keng Vannsak had yet to invent the Khmer typewriter) in the August 1952 issue of the Association's mimeographed newsletter *Khemara Nisit*, is signed the 'Original Khmer' (*Khmaer daem*) – revealing, perhaps, a racial-historical preoccupation on Sar's part. By contrast, other contributors chose to sign themselves 'Free Khmer' (*Khmaer serei*) and 'Khmer Worker' (*Khmaer nghia*), pseudonyms with a definite modernist stamp. Sar's article does discuss the French, Russian and (1924) Chinese 'democratic' revolutions but again makes no mention of Vietnam or Laos,[23] as Son Ngoc Thanh would have done. Hou Yuon came just a little closer, in a letter to the students at home in which he praised the May demonstrations: 'These positive developments have become normal throughout the world, whether in the European countries or the Asian ones, and especially in the countries where independence is being sought.'[24]

Two years of participation in a 'Marxist Circle' in Paris had brought few of the students involved close to the fundamental motivations of the Khmer communists at home. There, as we have seen, the movement was one of non-elite composition, which had had experience in organizing the peasantry although it was pledged to working-class leadership, and which had developed a very concrete internationalist programme of cooperation with the Vietnamese. Saloth Sar, in particular, may have been furthest of all from such a stance at the time when he returned home. For instance, he set out for Phnom Penh well before his colleagues and did not have the opportunity to meet the UIF's Keo Meas, who attended the People's Conference for Peace in Vienna in December 1952;[25] nor was he in Paris when Hou Yuon and Khieu Samphan began writing their doctoral theses analysing the social and economic problems of Kampuchea.[26] (Two colleagues who *were* there but did not exhibit particular academic merit — Ieng Sary and Son Sen — later become Sar's closest associates.)

Sar failed his third year of study in mid 1952. According to his account: 'As I neglected my studies, the authorities cut off my scholarship.'[27] This seems accurate enough. While French educational records confirm that it was for clear *political* reasons that Hou Yuon suffered this fate (twice), as did Ieng Sary, Son Sen, Chi Kim An and Thiounn Mumm, the only comment in the relevant column of Saloth Sar's file is a concise '28,000 f.'[28]

He left France by ship in December and reached Phnom Penh on 14 January 1953.[29] The day before his arrival, King Sihanouk had dissolved the National Assembly, declared martial law, and imprisoned at least four Democratic parliamentarians (including Bunchhan Mul and Khieu Ponnary's cousin Im Phon). Sihanouk declared: 'I am the natural ruler of my country, the people know but the King, and my authority has never been questioned ... If the French left Indo-China, we shall have independence, true, but for how long? I therefore collaborate in the military sense with the French for the defence of our liberty.'[30]

But the adverse public reaction, beneficial to both Son Ngoc Thanh and the UIF[31] soon changed Sihanouk's mind; as V.M. Reddi comments: 'If he was to retrieve his waning popularity and safeguard the throne, it was necessary, and perhaps urgent, that he should work openly for his country's freedom.'[32] On 9 February 1953, the king left for France to plead with President Auriol for Kampuchea's independence. It was his first real contribution to the nationalist cause and the effective beginning of the 'Royal Crusade for Independence'.

Saloth Sar, like many others at the time, saw little significance in this, and along with his newly returned colleagues Sien An, Keng Vannsak[33] and perhaps Yun Soeun, Chi Kim An and Rath Samuoeun, he attempted to coax the Democratic Party to adopt a more left-wing position — not a hopeless cause in the circumstances, and one in which Vannsak was largely successful two years later. But an air of despair had enveloped both Democrats and Thanhists. For instance, Sar's journalist brother Saloth Chhay, who had joined Son Ngoc Thanh's forces in the Dangrek mountains, now left their camp and made contact with the UIF. He made several visits to the UIF's Eastern Zone headquarters on the Vietnamese border in Kompong Cham. It was Chhay who paved the way for his younger brother and Yun Soeun to move there in August 1953, and begin *their* first experience of the struggle for independence. They presented themselves as members of the French Communist Party.[34]

Chea Soth was there to meet them. He recalled in 1980 that Saloth Sar 'said he came to take part in the struggle and learn from us, but in fact he came to see if there really were Khmers carrying out the revolution or not. He said that everything should be done on the basis of self-reliance, independence and mastery. The Khmers should do everything on their own.'[35]

The two former students remained in the revolutionary headquarters, Saloth Sar joining an 'ICP cell', consisting of ten Khmers and ten Vietnamese, in the administrative office of the National Central Executive Committee. Pham Van Ba, secretary of the cell, was the leading ICP cadre in the Eastern Zone. (Years later he became Vietnam's ambassador to Democratic Kampuchea.) In a 1980 interview, he told me that he had instructed Sar how to 'work with the masses at the base, to build up the Issarak committees at the village level, member by member.'[36]

According to Sar's own account, which ignores this training , he also took part in a production unit. It may well have been his first such experience. While Vietnamese supervision undoubtedly rankled, at least as irksome was inadequate recognition of his status as an 'intellectual'. A 1980 Democratic Kampuchea statement recalls that in this period: 'Patriotic intellectuals returning from France and other countries were kept in the background. Instead of receiving political and ideological training so that they might become cadres and leaders, they were given tasks that had absolutely nothing to do with their skills; kitchen chores and the transport of organic fertilizers for crops, among other things.'[37]

This 1980 statement betrays the deep resentment on the part of Saloth Sar and others at their failure to be promoted as 'cadres and leaders', for it is fraught with irony, given the fact that they themselves treated in an identical or worse fashion patriotic intellectuals who returned from France after 1975.

Of course, Sar had worked with the UIF for only a year; but the unimportance of his role in the movement during that time contributed to his later decision to erase this early period from Kampuchean communist history.[38]

In May 1954, Sar was joined by a student from Battambang named Sok Thuok (Vorn Vet),[39] who had not been to France but whose experience of the resistance was a little broader. Vet had also fled Phnom Penh in August, when his uncle, a member of the National Assembly, was gaoled by Sihanouk. He spent the next three months in Savang Vong's zone. Unimpressed, he eventually met a UIF cadre and attempted to leave with him but was arrested en route by Savang Vong, and gaoled for four months. He then crossed into the Eastern Zone and reached Tou Samouth's camp only two months before the war ended. This was too short a period for Vet to gain much knowledge of communist politics as practised there, and within a year he had become a close associate of Saloth Sar. Nevertheless, Vet's political experience up to that point resembled — albeit in compressed form — that of the UIF leaders, and he later displayed a slightly more practical bent than Sar. This meant, ironically, that he was less contemptuous of other intellectuals, and a greater understanding of Vietnamese realities sometimes tempered his implementation of anti-Vietnamese policies (see p. 332). Vet was purged and executed in late 1978. In his Tuol Sleng 'confession' written shortly before his death, Vet looked back on this brief period when he had worked with the Vietnamese communists, and wrote of past sentiments that Saloth Sar is unlikely to have shared: 'At that time I studied revolutionary documents many times, and I learnt directly, getting a greater and greater understanding of the revolution, and I was very happy. At this time I did not understand anything about the problem of Vietnam: I was happy with their propaganda that they had come to help. In every place there were Vietnamese filling important roles; as for we Khmers, we just helped them. I was not interested in any of this, because they talked of international consciousness, about Khmer-Vietnamese con- sciousness, and I considered it reasonable.'[40]

The Unified Issarak Front, 1952–54

Saloth Sar had found himself in an expanding organization. As with the KPRP, the process of construction from the base upwards also took place within the UIF armed forces. The recruitment of all-Khmer guerrilla and regional units had begun at the level of militia (village and subdistrict forces) and was gradually being implemented at the district, province and (by 1954) Zone levels, although the process never reached the stage where an integrated national-level regular army was created.

By 1952 the French Expeditionary Corps in Kampuchea had been increased to approximately seven combat battalions (4,000 troops) and a large number of members of other services; only at the end of that year did the number of Khmers in the Royal Army (13,000) exceed that of French Union troops in the country.[41] The commitment was one that Paris could ill afford with so many of its soldiers tied down in Vietnam, where the colonialists were in much deeper trouble. Further, the French forces in Kampuchea never operated at battalion strength, thereby effectively leaving large tracts of the countryside to the UIF.

In 1952 the UIF established a Khmer Resistance Government, with Son Ngoc Minh as President and Chan Samay as Vice President.[42] Ministers included Tou Samoth (Interior), Keo Moni (Foreign Affairs), Chau Yin (Education), Sieu Heng (Defence), Leav Keo Moni (Ethnic Affairs), and Sos Man (Religion).[43] But the main emphasis was still on training and military affairs. From July 1953 to April 1954, Keo Moni, Sos Man, Mey Pho, Ney Sarann and Non Suon studied at the Tay Nguyen guerrilla warfare school in central Vietnam. They graduated with the rank of major or above.

The Vietnamese official most closely connected with the Kampuchean communists in later years, Nguyen Xuan Hoang, claims that by 1951, '59 out of 109 districts had been liberated' by the UIF and Viet Minh.[44]

Contemporary French intelligence agrees. Large-scale detailed maps of all thirteen provinces in 1952 show that the French considered more than three fifths of the entire country 'insecure'.[45] (See Fig. 5.) The map of Kandal province, which surrounds Phnom Penh, indicates one quarter of its area to be 'insecure': only one fifth was 'accessible', and slightly more than half 'accessible with an escort'. (We may assume that 'insecure'

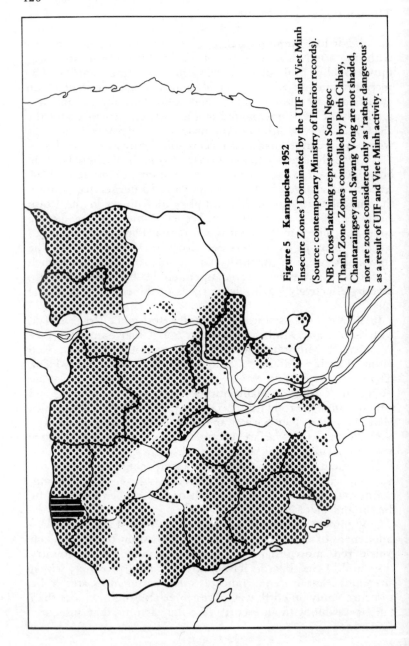

Figure 5   Kampuchea 1952
'Insecure Zones' Dominated by the UIF and Viet Minh
(Source: contemporary Ministry of Interior records).
NB. Cross-hatching represents Son Ngoc
Thanh Zone. Zones controlled by Puth Chhay,
Chantaraingsey and Savang Vong are not shaded,
nor are zones considered only as 'rather dangerous'
as a result of UIF and Viet Minh activity.

meant inaccessible even with an escort.) Five of Kompong Cham's ten districts, three fifths of Battambang, half of Kompong Chhnang, and four fifths of Kompong Thom and Kampot were all 'insecure'. So was the northern two thirds of Siemreap (partly controlled by Son Ngoc Thanh and Kao Tak); the rest of the province, patrolled by Dap Chhuon, was considered 'dubious'. One fifth of Prey Veng was 'dangerous', and another fifth 'rather dangerous'. Four fifths of Stung Treng and Pursat, half of Kratie (excluding Mondolkiri), and the northern fifth of Svay Rieng were all 'insecure'. The exception was again Takeo, where a 'dangerous' zone snaked around its boundaries with other provinces and with Vietnam.

These intelligence maps also distinguish between the various Issarak factions in Kompong Speu, where only the province capital and Highway 4 fifteen kilometres beyond it were administered from Phnom Penh. Two fifths of the area was the 'very dangerous Viet Minh zone'; one fifth was the 'dangerous Puth Chhay zone', which also extended into some parts of Kandal and Kompong Chhnang; one fifth was the 'Chantaraingsey zone where travel is possible', and one fifth the 'Savang Vong zone where unhindered travel is possible'.[46]

In order to neutralize the impact of UIF territorial advances, in July 1952 the government began another large regroupment programme in Kampot (30,000 people) and in Kompong Cham (35,000). In the latter province, the programme involved a number of 'excesses' according to Delvert,[47] and the UIF in Tbaung Khmum even considered the possibility of pre-empting it by evacuating the population towards the South.[48] (In Kampot, Nhem Sun ordered the burning of three new fortified villages.[49]) But the colonial forces proved stronger, and new encampments were systematically established: 'The peasants of each abandoned subdistrict were grouped together in a big rectangular village, surrounded by palisades and divided by two perpendicular tracks. The pagoda was brought in with the inhabitants. Forty or so wells were dug. For a period the peasants of two out of four subdistricts had to abandon their too distant rice-fields, and live miserably as coolies or by burning off new land.'[50]

By April 1953, the French claimed that nearly 300,000 Khmers had been 'put out of reach of the Viet Minh',[51] which is probably an exaggeration.

Despite these setbacks, it is probable that when Saloth Sar

arrived in Kompong Cham in August 1953, about one sixth of Kampuchea's subdistricts were under more or less regular UIF administration, and that a skeletal or underground structure existed in about half the subdistricts of the country. This would mean that about six hundred thousand of the four million Kampucheans, and about one third of the territory, were under some form of daily UIF control, while up to another two million lived in villages, covering half the territory, where the UIF was active, if only by night. It is inconceivable that a force of three thousand Vietnamese could have achieved this without very considerable Khmer participation and acquiescence. In May 1952, French intelligence noted that while 'a glance at the map shows that no Cambodian province remains unscathed', the Viet Minh "invasion'... has never been confronted with any serious reaction by the Khmer and Vietnamese populations in general'.[52]

As we saw in Chapter Three, by the end of 1952 the number of Khmers in UIF regional units exceeded three thousand. The UIF militia, for its part, was estimated by French intelligence to muster only eight hundred guerrillas in May 1951, but a year later the figure had 'seriously increased' — 'since that time numerous militia units have been established in 'strategic' districts and subdistricts. Some of these units are armed secretly, in the case of localities near the zones where our troops operate.'[53]

In Prey Veng province, for instance, the twenty one villages of South Smong subdistrict by 1953-54 each had a militia unit of ten to fifteen guerrillas, armed with knives and 'one or two guns' per village, a participant claims.[54] In Kompong Cham, Chup subdistrict had at least five squads of about twelve men each, and possibly more at the village level.[55] In Kompong Speu, O subdistrict had four hundred men in guerrilla units, twenty in each village.[56] In Kampot, the Kompong Trach district force numbered two hundred fighters.[57] All these areas formed part of much larger 'dangerous zones' according to French intelligence, and by 1954 the total number of Khmers in UIF militia units may well have exceeded twenty thousand. But most were recruited only after 1951, and lacked experience.

The UIF administrative apparatus, according to French intelligence in May 1952, was 'found at the province, district and subdistrict levels'.[58] As we have seen, in some areas such as Tbaung Khmum, the village-level apparatus was also extensive, although how this fared when half the district was regrouped later in the year is unknown.[59] At the province and district levels, the UIF hierarchy consisted of president, vice-president, head of the office (*protean muntir*), treasurer and secretaries. At the subdistrict level the third post did not exist.[60] Excluding the village level, the UIF administration thus seems to have involved a staff of more than two hundred people in each province, or several thousand for the country.

Within these military and administrative structures the Khmer People's Revolutionary Party expanded. At the national level the KPRP interim Executive Committee included seventeen Khmers of a total of 'several dozen' in 1954, according to Pham Van Ba. The few ICP cells that remained, like the one Saloth Sar joined, also comprised roughly equal numbers of Khmers and Vietnamese.[61] By July 1954 the party had 1,862 Khmer members, according to Nguyen Xuan Hoang.[62] This figure does not seem inconsistent with that of a thousand Khmers in the KPRP by 1952, or with the claim that the Khmer communists were working in 136 KPRP cells[63] (compared with sixty in 1951[64]) throughout Kampuchea; that is, there were about ten cells per province, and an average of more than one (comprising about thirteen members) per district. Although French diplomatic sources in 1954 put the KPRP's Khmer membership (Vietnamese membership is not mentioned) at only four hundred,[65] it seems unreasonable to attach any more weight to this than to the more detailed communist claims. The true figure may well have been somewhere in between, perhaps about 1,100. Both sides agree that the number of Khmer party members doubled between 1952 and 1954; and even if the French figures are taken at face value, the KPRP had more Khmer members than Son Ngoc Thanh, for instance, had troops.

Below the party structure was the KPRP's Youth League headed by Chan Saman. According to Pham Van Ba, its membership had reached 20,000 by 1954;[66] perhaps it was the Youth League that former UIF member Keo Chenda had in mind when he said that 'the party had 20,000 members'.[67] Or he may have meant the UIF itself, whose membership probably overlapped significantly with that of the Youth League; both organizations essentially formed the Party's recruitment base. Vietnamese sources claim that the UIF had 150,000 members (and the League for National Salvation of Vietnamese Residents of Kampuchea, 50,000) as early as 1950.[68]

However, national membership of the UIF probably only

totalled some twenty thousand, even by 1954. In conjunction with the UIF armed forces and militia, this still represented probably the largest political organization in Kampuchean history; but only its inner core of KPRP members received much political training, and many others probably drifted away after independence was attained, and their leaders went underground in 1954.[69] The same would seem to be true in the case of the Issarak Monks Association.

I have, however, been unable to consult intelligence records, which remain unavailable in both Kampuchea and France, dating from the 1953-54 period. Vietnamese sources (Nguyen Thanh Son and Pham Van Ba) maintain that UIF strength increased in those two years, as do most Issarak veterans I have interviewed.[70]

For his part, General Seta, who commanded French Union forces in Kampuchea, has divided the final stage of the war into two periods: from June 1952 to November 1953, when Sihanouk succeeded in gaining the attributes of political independence, and from November 1953 to July 1954, when independence was secured by the Geneva Conference and French forces finally withdrew from the country. During the first period, Seta says, 'Viet Minh and Khmer Issarak recruitment diminished'.[71]

Even so, in February 1953 the UIF scored a major propaganda victory when thirty Khmer and thirty Vietnamese members of So Phim's Achar Hem Chieu unit ambushed and killed the governor of Prey Veng.[72] However, there does not seem much connection with the political activities of Sihanouk, whose serious efforts at independence had only begun. On the other hand, the French and Royal Army military operations in this period, code-named 'Loyalty', 'Come and Eat', and 'Sugar-coated Pill', undoubtedly contributed to the rebels' problems.[73] This was the period when Chan Dara rallied to the government (November 1952), while the Son Ngoc Thanh camp was rent by discord.

In late 1952, Ea Sichau (like the KNLC before him) accused Kao Tak of pillaging the population, and relations within the Thanh camp are unlikely to have improved when Sichau attempted to win the support of the Chinese communists through their representatives in Bangkok. At any rate the Chinese, according to intelligence reports, 'decided that the Issarak movements were not yet strong enough to warrant recognition or support'.[74]

In January 1953, Sichau and six students broke with Tak and

THE FIRST GENERATION OF KHMER COMMUNISTS

1. Keo Moni (1912-1976)

2. Keo Meas (1926-1976)

3. Non Suon (1927-1976)

4. Ney Sarann (1928-1976)

5. Son Ngoc Minh (d. 1972)

6. Tou Samouth (d. 1962) addressing monks in the early 1950s

7. Saloth Sar (Pol Pot, 1928-) addressing a meeting in Phnom Penh after victory

8. Son Ngoc Thanh (1908-1976) in the forest, 1953

10. Keng Vannsak addressing a Democratic Party meeting, 1955

9. Left to right: Kao Tak, Son Ngoc Thanh, Hang Thun Hak, Ea Sichau

11. Son Ngoc Minh addressing the foundation conference of the Unified Issarak Front, April 1950. Behind him are the Vietnamese, Khmer and Lao communist flags, now the national flags of each country

12. Khmer communist agents arrested by colonial forces in the early 1950s

left for Bangkok, where they apparently entered pagodas;[75] at any rate from that point Sichau played little part in the resistance.

Sihanouk began his 'Royal Crusade for Independence' in February 1953. Most of the small, non-communist Issarak groups soon dissolved. Puth Chhay, Ouch and Kruu Oum all laid down their arms in May and June; Chhay became a major in the Royal Khmer Army, and Ouch a captain. Two who remained outside the direct control of the government, Chantaraingsey and Savang Vong, had long reached accommodations not with Sihanouk but with the French; their decision to hold out suggests that, like the UIF and the Thanhists, they did not believe that Sihanouk would oblige the colonialists to abandon the country. But all these groups underestimated the King's ability to establish himself as an effective national leader even as he remained the figure least hostile to French influence. Further, the seriousness of the French position in Vietnam would soon force the colonialists to abandon their military aims in Indo-China completely, and they would have to select a Khmer regime to succeed them.

The King met with French President Auriol but was unable to obtain satisfaction of his demands for independence.[76] He pursued diplomatic initiatives in the US, Japan and Thailand, but failed to convince the leaders of those countries that an independent Kampuchea under his leadership would constitute an effective anti-communist bulwark. In June 1953 he established his Cabinet in internal exile in Siemreap, but his north-west military command was still headed by the Frenchman Seta.[77]

During June and July, six officers and over six hundred colonial troops defected from their units and moved to Battambang. Railway guards abandoned their posts. To ease sensibilities, the French withdrew their officers from some Khmer battalions, but brought three infantry battalions and three tank units into the country as reinforcements.[78] Tension reigned in Phnom Penh as Puth Chhay's forces stirred up racist feeling against African members of the French forces, who were quickly replaced.[79] In several incidents involving Chhay's men in mid August, a French gendarme and a Khmer clerk were assassinated, and a grenade thrown into a dance-hall caused one death and several casualties.[80]

A week later Sihanouk displayed his strength. On 23 August, a grand parade was held in Battambang; the loyalty of traditional officials was mobilized, and thirty thousand members of the Royal Army, police, provincial forces and militia were displayed.[81] Over the next few months, negotiations between the Royal Government and the French led to the transfer of political power to Sihanouk, symbolized by a military parade of departing colonial troops in Phnom Penh on 9 November. Sihanouk dates independence from this successful conclusion of his Royal Crusade.

However, three largely Khmer battalions and ten companies remained under French control, and France retained operational command east of the Mekong; its own forces, numbering six thousand, were based in Kratie.[82] This situation was not altered when, according to one source, 'military authority' was surrendered by the French on 10 March 1954,[83] two weeks after Chantaraingsey and Savang Vong had finally put down their arms. Those Khmers who had fought hardest for Kampuchean independence, the Thanhists and the UIF, date it from the signing of the Geneva Accords in July 1954, when French forces withdrew completely.[84]

According to Seta, Viet Minh and UIF activity 'continued or increased' after November 1953.[85] The Royal Khmer Army launched a series of military operations against the rebels: 'Wild Boar' in Kompong Speu, 'Thunder' in Takeo and Kampot, 'Attempt' and 'Teal' in Svay Rieng, and finally 'Samakki' (Unity), which began in Battambang on 17 December 1953. These achieved 'only limited success' according to a French source.[86] Operation Samakki was headed by Sihanouk but 'organized', according to his own account, by the French General Seta, and involved nearly five thousand regular troops including elements commanded by Lon Nol, Dap Chhuon, and Puth Chhay, as well as 'thousands' of paramilitary forces, supported by French military aircraft.[87] Still, from April to July 1954 (after the siege of Dien Bien Phu had begun on 13 March), 'Viet Minh and Khmer Viet Minh activity increased significantly', according to Seta.[88] Lon Nol's 2nd Infantry Battalion attempted to re-supply the town of Pailin from Battambang, and was surrounded by combined Viet Minh and UIF units, presumably those led by Sieu Heng and Leav Keo Moni. In the East, what Seta says was the only fully Vietnamese Viet Minh unit to fight in Kampuchea, the 436/101 Battalion, crossed from southern Laos in late March. It attacked its way into the French operational sector at Stung Treng and Kratie, seizing five small towns. Mixed Khmer and Vietnamese units crossed from south Vietnam into eastern Kampuchea and attacked the French-led 9th Infantry Battalion, decimating one company.[89]

On 20 May 1954, the US Government's Intelligence Advisory Committee produced a report on 'Probable Military and Political Developments in Indo-China Over the Next Thirty Days'. It was unwilling to make a firm prediction concerning Kampuchea's fate: 'Barring the unlikely event of a large scale Viet Minh invasion, Laos and Cambodia will probably retain their present uncertain political stability during the next thirty days ... The Cambodian government will probably retain control.'[90]

Two weeks later, a US *National Intelligence Estimate on Laos and Cambodia* gave details of the strength of 'Viet Minh' forces in Kampuchea. These were said to total 8,700, of whom 2,200 were regular troops.[91] According to Seta, 'Viet Minh' troops, including regulars, in Kampuchea at this time numbered 5,000; but he says half of these were actually Khmer.[92] Seta gives no figure for 'Khmer Viet Minh' (UIF) forces but says they were 'mostly Khmer'.[93] French troops in Kampuchea thus outnumbered Vietnamese communist troops there by two to one. A Hanoi source concurs with these estimates, giving a figure of 3,000 Vietnamese in Kampuchea.[94] Khmers fighting in UIF or Viet Minh units therefore numbered 4,500 to 5,700, excluding village militia. Although the Royal Khmer Army mustered 33,000 troops, its superiority over the UIF depended on French officers such as Seta and on continuing large quantities of French equipment and supplies. According to the *National Intelligence Estimate* of 1 June 1954: 'If, as a result of a negotiated agreement with the Communists covering all of Indo-China, French and Viet Minh regular units were actually withdrawn from ... Cambodia (leaving Viet Minh irregular forces still operating [there] ...), native forces could probably preserve for some time approximately the present degree of security and stability in Cambodia ... *provided French cadres and the present scale and nature of French material aid remained available.*'[95]

The same document then gives a bleak picture of what would happen should the 6,000 French troops withdraw without a guarantee that the 2,200 Vietnamese regulars would do the same: 'However, such an agreement with the Communists would be extremely difficult, if not impossible, to implement and police, and in these circumstances the [Royal Khmer Army] could probably not for long successfully resist the Viet Minh without increased outside support ... on a scale larger than the French could provide ... If any additional support were not quickly forthcoming, the resistance of ... Cambodia to Communism would collapse.'[96]

The fact that the Viet Minh were soon to implement such a guarantee, while a thousand UIF cadres were to withdraw indefinitely from Kampuchea with them, was obviously of enormous importance for the future of the country — not least because it enabled the Royal Government to stand without the 'increased outside support' already proffered by the USA. Over the next few years, a statement made in September 1953 by Sihanouk's Prime Minister Penn Nouth (addressed to the Viet Minh but then signifying rather an attempt to pressure the French to concede independence) was in fact to become a corner-stone of Vietnamese-Kampuchean government relations: 'It is not up to us to contest your right to occupy Vietnam. We are only asking you to leave us to live our lives.'[97]

This was not an outcome that the UIF, or any other political movement, considered likely at the time. On 20 March 1954, Keo Moni said: 'In view of the increasing development of the Cambodian Liberation War, the American imperialists intervene more and more in Cambodia. Furthermore, the American imperialists pull the wires behind the puppet Sihanouk to make him play the farce of independence so as to evict, little by little, the French and to directly take over the war.'[98]

This statement was made on the day the French Chief of Staff told President Eisenhower that only massive US intervention could save Dien Bien Phu.[99] However, it proved quite inaccurate. Sihanouk's government was far more popular than that of his Vietnamese counterpart Bao Dai; it was not in danger of immediate internal collapse.[100] But the Khmer communist movement had shown itself to be capable of mounting a serious political challenge to a government not seen to be completely independent. It was partly for this reason that Sihanouk had launched his 'Royal Crusade for Independence', and that within a year he saw the need to consolidate that independence, and to under-cut potential opposition, by refusing to join any alliance with the United States and adopting a foreign policy of neutrality. Kampuchean waters were sufficiently troubled to make it worth Sihanouk's while to provide security guarantees to neighbouring communist fishermen.

Notes

1. Archives d'Outre-Mer (AOM), Aix-en-Provence, France. Cambodge, 7F 29(2), *Note sur l'organisation politique et administrative Viet-Minh au Cambodge* (hereafter cited as *Note*), Direction des services de securité du Haut Commissariat en Indochine (SSHC), December 1952, p.13.
2. *Ibid.*, p.17.
3. *Ibid.*
4. AOM, Cambodge 7F 29(7), *Etude sur les mouvements rebelles au Cambodge, 1942-52* (hereafter cited as *Etude*), annexe, p.17.
5. *Ibid.*, pp.36–37.
6. Archives Nationales, Bibliothèque Nationale, Phnom Penh. Ministère de l'Intérieure, Divers (henceforth MID). *Bulletin Quotidien des Renseignements* (BQR), Sûreté Interieure, Activités Rebelles. P.S., August 1952. The leaflets were found in the suburb of Beng Keng Kang, congratulating students on the demonstration of 6 May 1952.
7. *Ibid.*, SSHC report, 11 August 1952.
8. *Note, op. cit.*, p.16.
9. *Ibid.*
10. MID, BQR, SSHC report, 19 November 1952.
11. AOM, Cambodge 7F 29(4), *Etude sur l'évolution de la politique intérieure et les partis politiques khmers (1945 à 1 juillet 1951)*, p.8.
12. Keng Vannsak, interviews with the author, Paris, 27 November 1979 and 2 February 1980.
13. *Ibid.* And Mey Pho was himself a cousin of the Khieu sisters.
14. Author's interview with Suong, Phnom Penh, 9 July 1980.
15. Keng Vannsak, *op. cit.*
16. See the advertisements in *Le Cambodge*, 2 and 3 August 1951, p.4, and 18 September 1951, p.4. Interestingly, one of Ponnary's collaborators on the magazine was Mme. Son Sann, Treasurer of the Association of Cambodian Women and wife of Son Sann, who was to found the *Banque Nationale du Cambodge* in 1955 and become leader of the main right-wing Kampuchean political grouping in 1979. Mme. Son Sann appears to have taken over *Neary* after the appearance of its sixth issue, in September 1951. The new-style seventh issue includes an article entitled, perhaps cryptically, 'The Cambodian Woman is Neglecting her Toilet', but no overt political pieces, apart from a Khmer translation of 'The Goose that Laid the Golden Egg'.
17. *Interview of Comrade Pol Pot... to the Delegation of Yugoslav Journalists in Visit to Democratic Kampuchea.* Democratic Kampuchea, Ministry of Foreign Affairs, March 1978, mimeograph, p.23. This visit is confirmed by Keng Vannsak, who says it was merely a holiday. *Op. cit.*
18. Michael Vickery, *Cambodia 1975–82*, Boston 1984, pp. 275–78.
19. Keng Vannsak, *op. cit.*
20. *Ibid.* Sary and the others were probably who influenced by Stalin's prestige in the PCF at the time. See *Demoncratie Nouvelle*, April 1953, pp.221-4, for 'L'humanisme stalinien'.
21. 'Lettre de l'Association des Etudiants Khmers en France à sa Majesté Norodom Sihanouk', 6 July 1952, 8pp., at p.4.
22. Keng Vannsak, *op. cit.*
23. *Khemara Nisit*, no. 14, August 1952. (Sar's article 'Monarchy or Democracy' is reprinted in French translation in Serge Thion and Ben Kiernan, *Khmers*

Rouges! Matériaux pour l'histoire du communisme au Cambodge, Paris 1981, pp.357–71.)

24. *Ibid.,* 'Message from the Khmer Students' Association in France to all students in the Khmer land' by Hou Yuon.

25. Robert Olivier, *Le Protectorat français au Cambodge,* thèse de doctorat de 3e cycle, University of Paris, 1969, p. 320i.

26. Completed in 1955 and 1959 respectively. For translations, see 'The Peasantry of Kampuchea: Colonialism and Modernization' in Ben Kiernan and Chanthou Boua (eds.), *Peasants and Politics in Kampuchea, 1942–81,* M.E. Sharpe, New York, 1982, pp. 34–68; and Khieu Samphan, *Cambodia's Economy and Industrial Development,* translated by Laura Summers, Cornell University South-East Asia Program Data Paper No. 111, 1979.

27. 'Interview of Comrade Pol Pot. . .', *op. cit.,* p.21.

28. *Controle des étudiants boursiers: Carnet no. 1, France (1946–50),* copy kindly supplied by Stephen R. Heder.

29. *Ibid.*

30. V. M. Reddi, *A History of the Cambodian Independence Movement, 1863–1955,* Tirupati, Sri Venkatesvara University, 1973, pp.195–6. (He cites *Le Monde,* 18–19 January 1953.)

31. *Ibid.,* p.197.

32. *Ibid.*

33. Keng Vannsak, *op. cit.,* and author's interview with Pham Van Ba, Ho Chi Minh City, 28 October 1980.

34. Author's interviews with Loth Suong and Chea Soth, Phnom Penh, 9 July and 22 October 1980; and Pham Van Ba, *op. cit.*

35. Chea Soth, *op. cit.*

36. Pham Van Ba, *op. cit.*

37. 'Half a Century of Expansionist and Annexationist Designs of Hanoi', Press Release of the Permanent Mission of Democratic Kampuchea to the United Nations, No. 077/80, 30 September 1980, p.2.

38. From 1977, Pol Pot claimed publicly that the Communist Party had been founded only in 1960, the year he achieved membership of the Central Committee. Phnom Penh Radio, 28 September 1977, translated in BBC *Summary of World Broadcasts* (SWB), 1 October 1977, FE/5629/C2/1ff. See David P. Chandler, 'Revising the Past in Democratic Kampuchea: When was the Birthday of the Party?', *Pacific Affairs,* 56, 2, 1983, pp. 288–300.

39. The information that follows comes from Vorn Vet's confession in Tuol Sleng prison, December 1978, 54 pp., at pp. 1, 2. Copy kindly supplied by Timothy Carney. The translation is mine.

40. *Ibid.,* p.2.

41. Maurice Laurent, *L'Armée au Cambodge et dans les pays en voie de développement du sud-est asiatique,* Paris 1968, p.52.

42. D. J. Steinberg, *et al., Cambodia: Its People, Its Society, Its Culture,* New Haven, HRAF Press, 1959, p. 108; and Bernard B. Fall, *The Viet-Minh Regime,* Cornell University South-East Asia Program Data Paper no. 14, 1954, p. 56. Roland Olivier, *op. cit.,* p.320i, on the other hand, gives the date as 1951.

43. Chea Soth, *op. cit.*

44. Author's interview with Nguyen Xuan Hoang, Hanoi, 4 November 1980.

45. MID, *op. cit.* See Fig. 5. Olivier, *op. cit.,* p.344, concurs, referring to 'the kingdom's sombre situation: three fifths of the territory in the hands of the Issarak and Vietminh; the people longing for peace and independence, exhausted by the war and the exactions, more and more susceptible to the

rebels' propaganda; eighty per cent of the monks and the elite considered Son
Ngoc Thanh as the only man who could realize their wishes. . .'

46. Olivier, *op. cit.*, p.344, confirms the 'pact' between Savang Vong and the
French. See below.
47. J. Delvert, *Le Paysan cambodgien*, Paris 1961, p.209.
48. MID, BQR, military report, 1 July 1952.
49. *Ibid.*, report by Police Nationale, Kampot, 20 October 1952.
50. Delvert, *op. cit.*, p.209.
51. *Le Cambodge*, 1 April 1953, p.4.
52. *Etude.*, *op. cit.*, p.71.
53. *Ibid.*, p.72.
54. Author's interview with Kol Kon, Komchay Meas, 9 August 1980.
55. See Chapter 3, Fig.4.
56. Som Nhep, *op. cit.*
57. Author's interview with Yos Por, who joined the Kompong Trach district
'battalion' in March 1953. Phnom Penh, 11 September 1980.
58. *Etude, op. cit.*, p.97.
59. In December 1952, the Sûreté arrested three Khmers and three Chams from
the area who had all been playing important local roles for the UIF. 'This is
the first time that rebel agents have been uncovered and arrested in the
regrouped villages of Kompong Cham. Reinforcement of surveillance over
these agglomerations is prescribed for the relevant posts.' MID, BQR, SSHC
Report, 3 December 1952.
60. *Etude, op. cit.*, p. 97.
61. Author's interview with Pham Van Ba, *op. cit.*; and Gareth Porter,
'Vietnamese Communist Policy Towards Kampuchea, 1930–1970' in David P.
Chandler and Ben Kiernan (eds.), *Revolution and its Aftermath in Kampuchea*,
New Haven, 1983, p.90. Porter cites his own interview with Pham Van Ba, Ho
Chi Minh City, 12 November 1978, for the figure of 17 Khmers on the
Executive Committee.
62. Nguyen Xuan Hoang, *op. cit.*
63. *Ibid.* For the 1952 figure, see Chapter 3, p.83, above.
64. *Dat Nuoc Campuchia*, by Tan Huyen and Pham Thanh, Quan Doi Nhan Dan,
Hanoi 1980, p.119. See Chapter 3, p.82, above.
65. Francois Joyaux, *La Chine et le règlement du premier conflict d'Indochine, Genève
1954*. Paris 1979, p.222.
66. Author's interview with Pham Van Ba, *op. cit.*
67. Author's interview with Keo Chenda, Phnom Penh, 21 October 1980.
68. *Dat Nuoc Campuchia, op. cit.*, p.119.
69. See Chapters 5 and 6.
70. An exception is Hem Samin, a member of subdistrict militia forces in Kratie
in 1952. Late in that year, he recalls: 'The enemy attacked strongly. Our base
had to disperse and our militia was dissolved. I joined the Mobile Unit
Sivotha I in Kompong Cham, led by Kat Ngoun (a Khmer), from Svay Rieng.
There were 195 men in Ngoun's unit, but we ate nothing but leaves for three
months straight in 1953. Some went back to their homes, and only 95 of us
could continue the struggle.' Author's interview with Hem Samin, Phnom
Penh, 28 September 1980.
71. Laurent, *op. cit.*, p.286.
72. *Le Cambodge*, 24 February 1953, p.1.
73. Reddi, *op. cit.*, p.195.
74. MID. *Dossiers du no. 1 au no. 28*, Département de la Justice. 'Comité

Mouvement Son Ngoc Thanh', report by the Kampuchean chargé d'affaires in Bangkok, 9 February 1953.

75. MID, 'Comité Mouvement Son Ngoc Thanh', *op. cit.*, Penn Nouth to Foreign Minister, 6 February 1953. This followed a report of 10 January claiming that there was 'no evidence of discord between Tak and Ea Sichau'.

76. See the discussion in Reddi, *op. cit.*, pp.199–202.

77. Norodom Sihanouk, *Souvenirs doux et amers*, Paris 1981, p.196.

78. Laurent, *op. cit.*, p.57.

79. Olivier, *op. cit.*, p.365.

80. *Ibid.*

81. Laurent, *op. cit.*, p.56.

82. *Ibid.*, p.58; 'National Intelligence Estimate on Laos and Cambodia', 1 June 1954, in John P. Glennon (ed.), *Foreign Relations of the United States, 1952–54*, Vol. XVI, *The Geneva Conference*, Washington, Department of State, 1981, pp. 1023–29, at pp.1025, 1029. This source noted that: 'Cambodian armed forces are heavily dependent on the French for finance, equipment, training and advice. . .' (p. 1025). See also the map of areas under French command in Fall, B., *Vietnam Witness, 1953–1966*, Pall Mall, 1966, p.18.

83. Wilfred Burchett, *Mekong Upstream*, Hanoi 1957, p.148.

84. Michael Leifer has written that France did not transfer 'residual economic powers' to Kampuchea until as late as December 1954. *Cambodia: The Search for Security*, London 1967, p.49.

85. Laurent, *op. cit.*, p.286.

86. *Ibid.*, p.64.

87. *Ibid.*, p.290; and Sihanouk, *op. cit.*, p.207. Seta says that the KNLC's Tralay was captured and executed by Lon Nol in late December 1953. Laurent, *op. cit.*, p.290. However, after the war the International Commission for Supervision and Control (ICSC) reported that Thim Tralay, a former major in the Khmer Resistance Forces in Battambang, had been arrested by the authorities in August 1955; the ICSC recommended a pardon and amnesty for him, but it is quite possible that he was then quietly executed. Command Papers, *Cambodia No. 1, 1957, Cmnd. 253*, p.27 ff. See the next chapter on the 1955 elections.

88. Laurent, *op. cit.*, p.287.

89. *Ibid.*, pp.287, 289, 65.

90. John P. Glennon, (ed.), *op. cit.*, pp.872–73.

91. *Ibid.*, p. 1029.

92. This figure of 5,000 includes the 1,000 Vietnamese in the 436/101 Battalion. Before its entry into Kampuchea in late March 1954, then, 2,500 of the 4,000 'Viet Minh' in the country were Khmers, according to Seta's figures.

93. Laurent, *op. cit.*, p. 289–290. Seta says that most of the UIF commanders were Vietnamese who had adopted Khmer pseudonyms, but that 'it has never been possible to accurately establish' this. As we saw in Chapter 3, commanders of large units like Nhem Sun, Sieu Heng, So Phim, and Meas Vong were all Khmer.

94. Author's interview with Pham Van Ba, *op. cit.*

95. Glennon, *op. cit.*, pp. 1027, 1029. My emphasis.

96. *Ibid.*, pp.1027–28. Even with the continuing French presence, the military situation in Kampuchea was described as 'fluid'. *Ibid.*, US Delegate to Department of State, 17 June 1954, p. 1176.

97. Olivier, *op. cit.*, p.367, and Reddi, *op. cit.*, p.211.

98. Radio *Voice of Bac Bo*, 26 March 1954. Quoted in Fall, *The Viet-Minh Regime, op. cit.*, p.57.

99. George McTurnan Kahin and John W. Lewis, *The United States in Vietnam*, New York 1969, p.37.
100. The US report of 20 May 1954, quoted above, noted that it was 'possible that the Vietnamese Central government will disintegrate' within thirty days.

5

International Supervision

The Geneva Conference

In June 1954, the Royal Khmer Army and militia, supported by French troops and aircraft, pushed into the North-east of the country; after two battles in Kratie with the Viet Minh's 436/101 Battalion, the latter moved south across the border into Vietnam. A French source describes this as a Viet Minh 'retreat'.[1] Hoang Tung, who was then with Son Ngoc Minh in the highlands of central Vietnam, claims the explanation was different. The Geneva Conference had opened on 28 April, and Dien Bien Phu had fallen on May 7, the day before negotiations on Indo-China began. The communists, Tung says, planned to send two divisions of Viet Minh troops to 'create a free zone' under the control of the UIF, whose negotiating position would thereby be strengthened. (So too, of course, would the Vietnamese position, in relation to both France and China.)[2] But, according to Tung: 'This project was killed by a telegram from Zhou Enlai in Geneva, saying that such a move would sabotage the Conference. We did not realize that the Chinese plans were merely to establish peace on their borders, a zone of security, and northern Indo-China was enough for them.'[3]

This is one view of China's policy towards the states to its south. On the other hand, it had also been alleged that the Viet Minh were responsible for the 'betrayal'[4] of the Khmer revolutionaries. According to this view: 'The Vietnamese sacrificed the Kampuchean communist movement at the Geneva Conference in 1954, when the Vietnamese delegation abandoned demands for representation of the Khmer communists at the Conference and for the establishment of regroupment zones for their forces within Kampuchea.'[5]

In order to assess these claims and counter-claims, and to analyse Vietnamese and Chinese policies towards Kampuchea in this period, it is necessary to look at the background to an important meeting between Zhou Enlai and Ho Chi Minh on the Vietnam-China border on July 5, 1954.[6]

In early March, preparations for the coming Indo-China sessions of the Geneva Conference concerned the issue of who would be represented. It was still possible that France, Britain, the USA, China and the Soviet Union would be the sole participants. The three established governments of Indo-China, known as the Associated States, were not assured of a role. As the US chargé d'affaires in Paris cabled the State Department on 2 March: 'French position is that question should be avoided at all costs in order to avoid undesirable counter-demand that representation of Associated States would have to be balanced by representatives of Viet Minh, 'free' Laos Government [and the UIF's 'Khmer Resistance Government'] . . . Viet Minh is in no sense a government. . . We are under impression that this position was shared by Associated States Governments and for this reason they are not pressing at the moment for participation at Geneva.'[7]

This document seriously challenges the argument that the UIF was excluded from Geneva simply because Sihanouk had already achieved independence. Rather, there was apparent agreement in Indo-China that a natural consequence of the Royal Khmer Government's participation in the Conference would be similar representation of the Khmer Resistance Government of Son Ngoc Minh. But this did not prove to be the case: with US support all three Associated States took part, while on the communist side only the Viet Minh gained admission. In this respect, China and the Soviet Union clearly failed to press the advantages that all Indo-Chinese revolutionaries had gained on the battlefield, and which their opponents privately acknowledged.

The French position had probably hardened when on 23 April, according to the French Foreign Minister Bidault, the US Secretary of State John Foster Dulles 'ask[ed] me if we would like the US to give us two atomic bombs'.[8]

When the Viet Minh delegation arrived in Geneva early in May, the UIF's Keo Moni and Mey Pho came with them.[9] After the opening address in the first session on 8 May, the Viet Minh delegate immediately took up the cause of their participation. In the 'telegraphese' of the Chief of the US Delegation, Walter Bedell Smith: 'Viet Minh Vice-President Pham Van Dong. . . devoted virtually entire speech [to a] plea for invitations to Pathet Lao and Khmer Issarak along strictly communist lines (they represented struggle of those peoples for independence from foreign imperialism, etc.). He ended with formal motion [to] invite these two.'[10]

Smith recorded that the Soviet delegate, Molotov, launched a 'harangue' and 'alleged these regimes controlled much . . . territory and were leading wars of national liberation'. Zhou Enlai, however, was apparently less enthusiastic; according to Smith he supported the Viet Minh motion merely on the procedural grounds that the Conference had 'the right to discuss its own composition'.[11]

Zhou was no doubt aware that Dulles had the previous evening in Washington devoted a 'Radio and Television Address to the Nation' to the negotiations at Geneva. Dulles had said: 'The situation may perhaps be clarified as a result of the Geneva Conference. . . we would be greatly concerned if an armistice or cease-fire were reached at Geneva which would provide a road to a communist takeover and further aggression. If this occurs, *or if hostilities continue,* then the need will be even more urgent to create the conditions for united action. . . President Eisenhower has repeatedly emphasized that he would not take military action in Indo-China without the support of Congress.'[12] The next morning, before the Conference opened, Dulles cabled Smith: 'We assume that the French will have gotten the point and realize that we are ready to talk with them about internationalizing the war.'[13]

Smith had previously cabled Dulles, saying that he had met Bidault and told him that 'some form of South-East Asian NATO was necessary but that would take time. Could French provide it?'[14] Smith now told Dulles: 'He got the point and it had, I think, a great deal to do with stiffening his position.'[15]

Conversely, Dulles' speech probably had something to do with *softening* the position of the Chinese (threatened much more than the Soviet Union by creation of a 'South-East Asian NATO'), who dropped the question of Khmer Issarak and Lao Issara participation. Zhou Enlai's fear of US intervention in Indo-China, and of the Conference being used as a delaying tactic to provide time to organize it, led him, over the next two months, to make a series of further concessions that largely banished the UIF from the Kampuchean political scene. As we shall see, it became Zhou's aim to prevent the establishment of US military bases in Kampuchea; his delegation was simultaneously threatened with a US presence there and coaxed with promises of Kampuchean neutralism. In the process the UIF were progressively deprived of their military gains, a regroupment zone, recognition as a Khmer entity, and a role in on-the-spot negotiations with the Royal Government. These concessions were made by Zhou in private meetings with Western representatives, while Pham Van Dong, and to a lesser extent Molotov, continued to demand that the UIF and Pathet Lao be invited to the Conference.

The main strategy of the Western powers and the Associated States now was to discuss Kampuchea and Laos separately from Vietnam. In the absence of representation for the two local resistance movements, the Royal Governments would be able to negotiate with the Viet Minh as invaders, without considering the French as such. In the Second Plenary Session on 10 May, the Viet Minh delegate proposed 'the withdrawal of all foreign troops' from each of the three countries, and the convening of 'advisory conferences of the representatives of the governments of both sides in Vietnam, Khmer, and Pathet Lao in each of the states separately'. He also called for 'free elections to establish a unified government in each country; while interference from outside should not be permitted'.[16]

But behind the scenes the Royal Khmer Government was determining its own bargaining position. In a meeting with US delegates on 11 May, the Royal Khmer Foreign Minister, Tep Phan, told Smith that he aimed to press for 'the withdrawal of the Viet Minh aggressors and the French battalions which the Cambodian Government had called in to help fight against the invaders'.[17] Apart from the reversed chronology, this differed little from the Viet Minh proposal for 'withdrawal of all foreign troops' from the country. However, according to Smith, Phan 'warmly sympathized with Secretary Dulles's proposal for a mutual defence pact for South-East Asia', and asked for *direct* US arms aid 'instead of through France as heretofore'. Smith suggested that Phan neglect no opportunity to proclaim that Kampuchea was fully independent; Phan 'heartily agreed',[18] and in the Fourth Plenary Session three days later, he observed that 'Cambodia had made its own independence with France'. He than claimed, incorrectly of course, that French troops had 'already withdrawn from Cambodia'.[19]

Phan and his delegates maintained this position even after Bidault, for the first time in a Plenary Session, indicated the next day that the French were willing to withdraw their troops from Laos and Cambodia 'under certain conditions'.[20] At a private meeting of the six anti-communist delegations on 18 May it was agreed, according to the US representative, that 'nothing would be said about elections except as a retreat position', and that 'when Communists raise questions of withdrawal of French forces, the Cambodians amd Laotians will suggest they withdraw except as provided by respective treaties or to the extent the two countries request them to remain.'[21]

This would have been no major concession. Yet, in the Second Restricted Session that afternoon, Smith records that the Royal Khmer delegate again claimed that 'French troops had already been withdrawn'.[22] With the Viet Minh also refusing to admit that any of their troops were in Kampuchea (unless agreement was reached to withdraw 'all foreign troops' from all three countries), there was obviously little common ground.

For weeks hardly any progress was made, and 'internationalization' of the war loomed. On 12 May, Dulles cabled Smith: 'Ambassador Bonnet called on me today at his request. He referred to our talk May 8 when I told him US was prepared to sit down and talk with French about 'internationalizing' war in Indo-China. He said French government believes time has now come to have such discussions ... French government cannot wait until outcome of Geneva to know US attitude since by then military situation may have so deteriorated that Indo-China would be lost ... I told Bonnet we were prepared to begin discussions with French. Question then arose as to where discussions should held.'[23]

The next day, the British representative, Foreign Minister Anthony Eden, suggested, according to Smith, that he 'see Molotov and/or Zhou Enlai' to tell them they were 'playing a dangerous role in abusing US *and to a lesser extent France* ... Things cannot continue on present basis.'[24] The nature of this warning is revealing; according to Smith, Eden told Zhou of the 'dangers if Ho Chi Minh persisted in asking too much. He might feel that he could get it, and he 'might even be able to get it', however wider considerations should be borne in mind or [the] position could become dangerous.'[25]

This was a direct threat to the Chinese to pressure the

Vietnamese to abandon admitted communist gains in Indo-China, in what both Eden and Zhou perceived as Chinese security interests.

Molotov quickly became aware of the implications. In the next session, he noted with some prescience that 'termination of hostilities in Indo-China cannot be transformed into [a] shrewdly arranged respite for one side which would like to use it to prepare for extension of war'.[26] But he does not seem to have given ground. Smith cabled Dulles: 'Our willingness to take concrete steps [to] retrieve Indo-China position itself, expressed primarily through deeds rather than words, would have salutary effect in bringing Communists to their senses. [I] appreciate that strong US position might be viewed in some non-Communist Asian quarters as having 'colonial' or 'imperialistic' implication.'[27]

On 17 May, Eden cabled London recommending the 'immediate start of five-power military staff talks' in Washington.[28] Smith outlined Eden's proposals for the terms of reference: '[To] undertake military planning studies in order to recommend possible courses of action to enable an effective line of resistance to further communist aggression or infiltration in South-East Asia to be established. They would examine all possible courses of action.'[29] It was these 'wider considerations', and not events in Indo-China itself, which led China to abandon the UIF.

At the Third Restricted Session on 19 May, the Viet Minh representative claimed that the Khmer Resistance Government controlled large areas 'not only along the Vietnamese border but in other parts of the country'. Zhou supported this statement,[30] but in a meeting with Eden the following day he made the next political concession on Kampuchea on the part of the communists. The context was a discussion touching on Western military mobilization. According to Smith: 'Eden had said West denied so-called resistance movements in Laos and Cambodia had any existence whatever. *Zhou had said they might be minorities*, but they existed and could not be swept out of [the] countries ... Eden subsequently told me that he had warned Zhou again that the Indo-China situation was dangerous and might lead to unpredictable and serious results. Zhou had said he was counting on Britain to prevent this happening. Eden had warned him not to do so, since even though Britain desired moderation, in the event of a showdown, she would stand with the United States.'[31]

Smith met Molotov two days later; his report to Dulles

indicates that the Soviet Foreign Minister was less willing than Zhou to engage in debate on the subject, but apparently more confident of the UIF's potential. At any rate, he gave less ground than Zhou had. According to Smith: 'He had arrived at the impression that the governments of the two countries actually controlled only about half their territory, and that all of their troubles were not by any means due to external causes ... the governments of both states were weak.'[32]

In the Sixth Restricted Session, on 25 May, the DRV demanded 'recognition of the principles of readjusting areas under [the] control [of] each state'. Smith replied that partition of Vietnam, Laos or Kampuchea was unacceptable and only in Vietnam could 'regroupment' be considered. However, he cabled Dulles that the communists were 'not yet prepared to compromise'.[33]

Others were. After a meeting with British and French delegates the next day, Smith cabled Dulles:

> Eden wondered at what point we are going to stand on Cambodia and Laos. Their problem was separate but complementary to that in Vietnam and he saw no reason why a simultaneous cease-fire was in itself objectionable. He thought an acceptable formula would [be]: (1) cease-fire (2) withdrawal of troops into areas near frontier (3) withdrawal of all foreign forces within six months ...
>
> Chauvel said France did not consider the proposal of a simultaneous cease-fire throughout Indo-China to be one which we could oppose in principle ...
>
> I agreed [but said that] we must assume bad faith on Communist side.[34]

This proved unnecessary. In the Seventh Restricted Session the following day, the Chinese delegation, while proposing 'appropriate readjustments of the area of their occupied zones', conceded separate treatment for Laos and Kampuchea, and suggested: '*The States participating* in the Geneva Conference undertake to guarantee the implementation of the agreement. The question as to the nature of the obligations to be undertaken by the states concerned is to be examined separately.'[35]

This proposal allowed the Khmer Resistance Government no role in separate negotiations concerning their country, even on-the-spot negotiations at home, and broached the possible consequence that the Royal Government's obligations under an Agreement would be minimal, falling far short of those of the Vietnamese Government.

Soon afterwards, the Royal Khmer Government began to consider a position more attractive to the Chinese. Its delegate told a US representative on 31 May 'that until Viet Minh troops were evacuated from Cambodia, Cambodia could agree to no restrictions on Cambodia's right to introduce reinforcements and weapons.'[36] The target for a possible agreement along these lines became evident in the Twelfth Restricted Session on 4 June, when the Royal Khmer delegate claimed that his country faced the Viet Minh with its Chinese 'foreign armament', in the alleged 'absence of French troops' in Kampuchea. At the same time, he was prepared to give a 'commitment not to permit the introduction of foreign troops into Cambodia'.[37] The continued false denial of the French military presence there, but with the promise of neutralism, unveiled the strategy of making conces- sions to Chinese security goals in return for Chinese pressure on the Viet Minh, but no concessions to the Viet Minh, let alone to the UIF. Whether or not the promise of neutralism was at this stage genuine, the young Khmer state was showing early signs of the diplomatic mastery for which Sihanouk was to become renowned. For US policy was fast moving in the opposite direction, in the confidence that victory was possible and that only the costs needed to be weighed up. The Coordinator of the US Delegation, U.A. Johnson, told Smith on 6 June: 'If we succeeded in winning in Indo-China without bringing on World War Three our position in Asia would be enormously enhanced. However, if World War Three did result, Asia would blame us and turn against us.'[38] The latter point was perhaps reinforced by Tep Phan when he told Eden two days later that his government now had 'no intention of allowing military bases to be established on her territory'.[39]

But in the negotiations, both sides maintained the fallacy that no foreign troops were involved in Kampuchea, and little progress was made concerning Vietnam or Laos. Dulles's impatience grew. On 10 June he wrote: 'I agree that Geneva is getting us nowhere on Indo-China except backwards ... As regards internationalization, it should be made clear to the French that our offer does not indefinitely lie on the table to be picked up by them one minute before midnight.'[40]

He complained that the British had rejected 'collective action ... while Geneva was going on'. More troubling to the US, though, were 'underground military talks' between the French and the Viet Minh, being held at the same time as official military staff negotiations. Chauvel had informed Smith of the Viet Minh position to the effect that 'there was no chance of [France] getting anything on Vietnam if the French position on Laos and Cambodia [was] maintained'.[41] The Vietnamese communists thus appeared prepared to sacrifice gains they had made at home in return for some guarantees for their Khmer and Lao allies. Smith cabled Dulles informing him that in the Thirteenth Restricted Session held the same day, Pham Van Dong had 'insisted that basic fact of situation was existence of liberation movement in each country. His delegation was ready to discuss problems on this basis ... if no progress were made he doubted whether any good purpose served by conference continuing to debate unresolved questions.'[42]

But the Viet Minh, however determined, could not fight on without at least public Chinese support, and the US posture was about to ensure that such support would not be forthcoming. That night Dulles cabled Smith saying: 'It is our view that final adjournment of the Conference is in our best interest ... [and that there is] no adequate reason for further delaying collective talks on South-east Asia defence.'[43] In a second cable five minutes later, Dulles expressed fear that the 'underground' talks between the Viet Minh and the French would achieve a separate settlement. 'We would not wish to be in position where this subterranean negotiation between French and Viet Minh might have result our being suddenly faced with terms proposed settlement which we would not feel able accept and from which we might have to dissociate ourselves.'[44]

It was not long before the impact of the US stand was felt by the Vietnamese communists. A French negotiator told one member of the US Delegation that he was convinced the Viet Minh were 'anxious for a cessation of hostilities (on their terms) and that they fear the development of Chinese control over their actions, present and future'.[45]

The next morning, 16 June, Zhou Enlai met privately with the British delegation. The proposals he outlined formed the basis of the eventual settlement. According to Smith: 'Zhou indicated that he understood UK position respect Laos and Cambodia and its relation to the British position in Malaya. Said Chinese did not desire anything in Laos and Cambodia and were willing recognize 'Kingdoms of Cambodia and Laos'. Major Chinese worry is that US is attempting to establish bases in Laos and Cambodia ... for assault on China.'[46]

The Chinese offer to recognize the Royal Governments was significant. Not even the 'Colombo Powers' in Asia (India, Pakistan, Burma, Indonesia, the Philippines and Ceylon) had recognized Sihanouk's government, a fact that caused embarrassment to the Royal Khmer delegation at Geneva when Molotov had stressed it in order to ridicule its claim to independence.[47] Further, Zhou distinguished Kampuchea from Laos, a neighbouring country and thus more important to Chinese security. 'Zhou said that in case [of] Cambodia resistance forces were small and all that was necessary was a political settlement by the present royal government with them 'which could easily be obtained'. In case of Laos, the resistance forces were larger, and it would be necessary recognize this fact by formation of regrouping areas along the border with Vietnam and China.'[48] Eden expressed his personal view that Zhou wanted a settlement, but Eden had 'some doubt with regard to degree of control he exercises over Viet Minh'.[49] The next morning, in what Smith said was the 'first direct contact'[50] between the Chinese and French delegations, Zhou met privately with Bidault, repeated what he had told Eden, and added that the Viet Minh 'must withdraw' from Laos and Kampuchea.[51]

The difference in the sizes of communist forces in Laos and Kampuchea, as described by Zhou, was correct; US intelligence estimated Viet Minh strength in Laos at 18,800 and in Kampuchea 8,700. But as we have seen, about two thirds of the 'Viet Minh' troops in Kampuchea were actually Khmer, while there were more Vietnamese units in Laos.[52] It is clear that Chinese security interests, and those of the Viet Minh when they – also in Chinese interests – were obliged to accept North-South partition of their country, played a greater role in the final Agreement than guarantees of safety for local combatants.

There is little surprising either in this, or in the fact that the Viet Minh pursued an essentially Indo-China-wide strategy. From a neighbouring country, the Viet Minh would be expected to defend, more fiercely than the Chinese, the cause of the Khmer revolutionaries. Further, the Viet Minh's potential 'sphere of influence' was limited to Indo-China; for a Chinese regime, naturally, much more was at stake. For Beijing, the effect of US escalation would be as damaging as that of a communist victory throughout Indo-China would be limited. (It is possible, moreover, that the Chinese were not enthusiastic about the emergence of a bloc of countries allied to one another, communist or not, on their southern border.)

It was not greatly to Kampuchea's advantage, either, for UIF members to be accorded a regroupment zone on their own territory. But nor was there any guarantee of their political rights. It is ironic that an increasingly pro-Chinese faction of the Khmer communist movement, led by Pol Pot, later argued that it was the Vietnamese communists who had betrayed their movement at Geneva. In fact, partly as a result of what had happened there despite their effort, the Viet Minh — for the same reasons of geographical proximity which again did not apply to China — soon found their options concerning Kampuchea extremely limited.

The Fourteenth Restricted Session took place on 16 June, the afternoon of Zhou's meeting with Eden. Tep Phan stressed the Royal Khmer Government's willingness to commit itself to banning foreign troops and bases from its soil, and its desire to refrain from interference in the affairs of its neighbours. He concluded: 'Let Cambodia not be reproached tomorrow for seeking to defend itself by no matter what means when justice has been refused her and everything has been done to prevent her from living in a state of neutrality, freedom and peace at home.'[53] Here were the threat and the promise that led to the Agreement. Then followed an interesting series of speeches from the communist representatives. Zhou stated that conditions in each of the three countries of Indo-China were 'not the same' although native resistance forces in Laos and Kampuchea had to be taken into account, and foreign forces withdrawn in accordance with the original Viet Minh proposal of 10 May. He stressed that no foreign bases must be allowed in Indo-China. Then the Viet Minh delegate, according to Smith, 'spoke at some length' on the necessity of recognizing the importance of the national liberation movements in Laos and Kampuchea, which the Viet Minh 'wished to do everything possible to help'. He then added that he supported the Chinese motion. The French delegate expressed pleasure at this latter statement, and emphasized the assurances given by the Royal Governments on the issue of foreign bases. Finally, the Soviet delegate 'could not agree' that the situation in Vietnam was different from that in Laos and Kampuchea; the Conference, he said, had heard the views of 'only one of the belligerents' in each of those countries, since their resistance movements had been excluded. He said that the Chinese proposal 'might form the basis' for a settlement, but added that he supported the Viet Minh proposal.[54] In this roundabout way the Soviets, like the Vietnamese, expressed not only their differences with the Chinese proposal but also the reluctance of their agreement to it.

At the Fifteenth Restricted Session two days later, similar differences emerged. The Royal Khmer delegate, still apparently unwilling to admit the presence of French troops in his country, took issue with the Viet Minh's support for the 'so-called resistance government'. According to Smith: 'He added Zhou En-lai's proposal was not far off [on] some points from Cambodian position and expressed satisfaction at spirit of conciliation shown by Chinese.'[55]

For his part, Pham Van Dong attacked the Royal Government delegates for denying the existence of the resistance governments and hoped they 'would yield to reason'. But he was obliged to admit the presence of Viet Minh 'Volunteers' in Laos and Kampuchea, saying that 'if today there are such forces they will be withdrawn' and demanding that no foreign country should establish military bases in Indo-China.[56] The communists were by no means assured even of this *quid pro quo*, however. Bidault had reported to Smith the previous day that 'both Molotov and Zhou are obviously greatly concerned over any break-up [of the] Indo-China Conference ... Bidault said they clearly want to keep the conference going.' Smith added, in a cable to Dulles: 'Bidault and I agree (Eden did not comment) that it was important we do nothing [to] dispel Zhou's worries over US bases in Laos and Cambodia.'[57]

Bidault's views, at least, were irrelevant, since the French government had fallen that very day victim to its problems in Indo-China. Nevertheless, on 23 June, Zhou met the new Prime Minister, Pierre Mendès-France, in Berne, where they agreed on the division of Vietnam at the 17th Parallel. According to a recent study of the French diplomatic correspondence, Mendès-France now cabled his embassies in London and Washington to the effect that 'China had not sought the slightest compensation for the concessions which she had made regarding Laos and Cambodia'.[58] Zhou left for Beijing. In his meeting with Ho Chi Minh on 5 July, he thus presented the Vietnamese leader with what was virtually a *fait accompli*.

At the last session of the Conference on 20 July, the Royal Khmer Government's delegate, Sam Sary, reversed its previous stand and insisted on Kampuchea's right to permit foreign military bases on its soil. Late that evening, in the absence of Zhou Enlai, the Soviet delegate conceded the point in a meeting with French and British representatives, and agreed to insert a clause permitting such bases in Kampuchea 'in the case of threats to its security', and even in Laos.[59] The aggressive posturing of the United States, combined with skilful hard bargaining on the part of Sihanouk's representatives, and the disarray in the communist ranks, had left the latter with far less at the negotiating table than they had actually won on the battlefield. Although Sihanouk did not in the end allow foreign military bases in his country,[60] it was not surprising that many UIF members, being asked to lay down their arms and participate in national elections organized by the Royal Government, now feared for their security.

Non Suon was one of them. He had been summoned to northern Vietnam by Son Ngoc Minh for a 'Conference of the Khmer Resistance Army', and was told by Minh that UIF representatives had been sent to Geneva. Years later, as a prisoner of the Pol Pot regime, Suon wrote that a few days after the Agreement had been signed: 'I met Vo Nguyen Giap who asked me whether I was happy to see the end of colonialism in Kampuchea. I said I was, but not happy to have the Khmer Resistance under the domination of Norodom Sihanouk. Siha-nouk would arrest us, and so on. He said that they [the Vietnamese communists] would not break the Geneva Agreement because the International Control Commission was observing the cease-fire in Kampuchea.'[61]

At home, UIF members in Kompong Cham reacted similarly. Men Chhan recalls: 'We had liberated three provinces; why was Keo Meas [sic, Moni] not allowed to attend the Conference? There was trouble among the Issaraks after that; the debates lasted seven days and seven nights. We finally decided to destroy all our weapons so that our troops would not be able to use them to loot the goods of the people. The weapons and ammunition were all collected and destroyed in Kompong Cham. I was not happy about that decision.'[62]

In Prey Veng, monks who had joined the Issarak movement played an important role in persuading the rank and file to lay down their arms.[63] But so did the leaders: according to a member of a village militia unit, it was So Phim — one of the most aggressive and ruthless UIF commanders — who 'collected all the guns we had and put them away'. The same informant continued: 'But there was still a national liberation movement. It was called the Democratic Party and the Pracheachon Party; they published newspapers in the city to pursue political struggle, to resist the French imperialists, the capitalists and the feudalists like Sihanouk.'[64]

The Khmer communist leaders now took their movement into a totally different world, embracing a limited 'political struggle' and relying on tactics with which they were quite unfamiliar. They were not greatly successful; many of their supporters regarded 'the end of colonialism' as the end of the struggle and, like others who were unwilling to risk challenging the government unarmed, soon went back to their farms. But their organization did not dissolve, and when the situation changed again more than a decade later, the legacy of the UIF proved invaluable — to a new leadership.

The 1955 Elections

Non Suon made his way back to Kampuchea. 'When we arrived in Svay Rieng, we organized that Joint Commission, with Khmer Resistance members. Sihanouk's people did not agree at first, only after an argument.'[65] In fact, the Royal Government representatives refused to meet with a UIF delegation, which had to be included on the Viet Minh side of the Joint Commission for the Implementation of the Geneva Accords. It was led by Nguyen Thanh Son, and its Khmer members were Non Suon, Keo Meas, Sok Saphai, Meas Samay, Nop Bophann, Penn Yuth, Chou Chet, and former Paris students Sien An and Chi Kim An.[66] The Commission's purpose was to ensure the smooth withdrawal of Viet Minh and French forces from Kampuchea. The legal and political rights of UIF members, particularly with regard to the general elections scheduled for the next year, were in theory to be protected by the International Commission of Supervision and Control (ICSC), consisting of delegations from Canada, India and Poland. But there was little confidence among UIF leaders that their safety would be guaranteed. In October 1954, Non Suon continues: 'a telegram came from Son Ngoc Minh telling us all to withdraw to North Vietnam, or we would be destroyed by the enemy in Kampuchea. Keo Meas and I refused to go ... I argued with Thanh Son that we should stay on to carry out political struggle in the elections, etc. I sent a telegram to Son Ngoc Minh who agreed. It was decided that Keo

Meas, Chi Kim An and Sien An would remain in the Joint Commission while Penn Yuth and myself got a house in Phnom Penh. From that time on, I was cut off from the bases.'[67]

Suon spent the next two months in a *wat* in the capital. 'I had to be very careful; I had no identification card, and no work', he wrote. Only when Keo Meas, protected by the International Commission because of his official position, managed to get him an identification card did Suon venture to 'ride a bicycle around to see the city'. Penn Yuth was able to start teaching at Kambuboth High School, and in January 1955, thanks to sympathizers in the Public Works Department, Suon found employment at the airport. However, he quit the job the next month, because 'I was afraid to work at the airport where there were many military and foreigners, and if there was an incident I would be the first to get into trouble'.[68] One gains the impression of a man who had never before been to the city and who for political reasons was living in considerable fear of the administration. He had no real chance to prepare for the forthcoming elections, which were scheduled for April 1955, only two months away, in the Kampot seat where he had been nominated as a candidate.

Meanwhile, about a thousand Issaraks, fearful of being 'destroyed by the enemy in Kampuchea', left the country with the departing Viet Minh troops, and were taken from the Mekong Delta to Hanoi on Polish ships under the auspices of the ICSC. One third of these people were military personnel of the Khmer Resistance Forces, and 190 were KPRP members,[69] mostly those best known to the population in their area of activity and therefore most vulnerable to Royal Government repression. So those who regrouped tended to be the most valuable of the local KPRP cadres. They also included leaders such as Nuon Chea, So Phim, Ney Sarann, Leav Keo Moni, Prom Samith, Sos Man, Hong Chhun, Nhem Sun, Chea Keo and Chan Samay. Son Ngoc Minh was already in northern Vietnam; Mey Pho and Keo Moni went there from Geneva. Sieu Heng, probably because of his seniority, was evacuated there, on an ICSC plane with the Vietnamese commanders, on 24 October.

After a few months, however, Heng decided to walk back home down what later became the Ho Chi Minh Trail,[70] and was accompanied by Nuon Chea, So Phim and Ney Sarann.[71] It is difficult to know why these people returned to Kampuchea: after Geneva a KPRP 'temporary Central Committee' had been formed inside the country, consisting of Sieu Heng, Tou Samouth, Son Ngoc Minh, So Phim and N.T. Nhung. A 1973 Party history later described this Committee as having been established 'not in conformity with the Party's conditions',[72] and it is possible that Son Ngoc Minh was originally expected to follow the others on their secret trip home. He may have changed his mind when the first signs emerged of Sihanouk's neutral policy in foreign affairs, signalling a trend which he and the Vietnamese leaders would have wanted to do as little as possible to disturb. On the other hand, Sieu Heng had been named Secretary of this 'temporary Central Committee', [73] and Son Ngoc Minh may have intended merely to take charge of training cadres abroad.

Those who removed to Hanoi also included four of the French-trained Khmer students who had joined the maquis in 1953 — Yun Soeun, Hem Phan, Haing Narin, and Rath Samuoeun, co-leader with Ieng Sary of the 'Marxist Circle' in Paris. Pol Pot and twenty of their fellow students, however, were allegedly smuggled back into Phnom Penh by Pham Van Ba, who was travelling in the capacity of liaison officer in the Joint Commission for the Implementation of the Geneva Accords. Ba says Pol Pot entered the capital disguised as his 'aide-de-camp' and was replaced by a Vietnamese officer for the Viet Minh leader's return trip.[74] Pol Pot and the other ex-students quickly became involved in the KPRP's Phnom Penh Party Committee, headed by Keo Meas.[75]

When the work of the Joint Commission was completed, Nguyen Thanh Son recalls, Pach Chhoeun secretly came to visit him. 'Of his own accord he broke down and cried, saying that Sihanouk had betrayed the country and followed the French'.[76] This incident foreshadowed a period of close identity of views among the more modernist-oriented nationalists — former Thanhists returning from the jungle, increasingly leftist Democrats, and Khmer and Vietnamese communists. By April 1955, for instance, the Vietnam News Agency in Hanoi was describing the Democratic Party as a 'powerful democratic movement' enjoying 'mass support' and which had already succeeded in 'impeding American plans' to undermine Kampuchean neutralism.[77] But this coalition of sympathy was based as much on anti-monarchical and personal hostility towards Sihanouk as on anti-colonial feeling, and Sihanouk had only to launch a fiercely independent foreign policy to scatter it to the four winds.

But there was no sign of flexibility on Sihanouk's part in the immediate aftermath of Geneva, and royal repression struck all opposition groups indiscriminately. On 30 September 1954, Son Ngoc Thanh went into Siemreap town to pledge his loyalty to the government. On 2 November India's Pandit Nehru even stopped over there for a brief meeting with him. But Sihanouk refused outright to give Thanh an audience, and on 19 November he withdrew to the border again.[78] This decision effectively marginalized Thanh, and made him more dependent on US and Thai support. Then, in February 1955, Kao Tak was lured into a trap by Dap Chhuon and executed. The traditionalist combination of monarch and warlord thus virtually erased Thanh's influence from the domestic scene.

In Prey Veng, a local informant recalls, former UIF cadres 'were arrested and mistreated in searches for arms and rice that the revolutionary organization had put away after the war. One man from my village of Santei, called Nan, was arrested, escaped, and then committed suicide. About thirty people from Ampil, Doh Kdaong and Kbou villages were killed at that time.'[79]

In November 1954 thirty-six inhabitants of a village in Krakor district, Pursat, who had been members of the UIF forces, were all imprisoned for 'forming an association of malefactors, offences against the King, and the spreading of false news'.[80] Six months later, as the election campaign got under way, Sihanouk complained to the ICSC that Viet Minh forces had been staging 'harassment and attacks' near Voeunsai in the North-east of the country. According to Roger Smith: 'Following an investigation, however, the Commission said it could not uncover evidence that 'regular units of the Viet Minh forces' had been in the region; instead, it reported that several former members of the Khmer Resistance Forces and one 'allegedly Viet Minh area organizer' had formed a band of men, with a strength variously estimated between 178 and 400, which was spreading anti-government propaganda and generally creating disturbances in the area.'[81] This, it seems, would not do during a general election.

In Phnom Penh meanwhile, Keo Meas, Non Suon and Penn Yuth had attempted to form the 'Khmer Resistance' (*Khmer Toosu*) Party to contest the elections.[82] The Royal Government, however, threatened to withhold even registration of it, until Keo Meas successfully appealed to the ICSC. The government still insisted that the communists drop the reference to their anti-French struggle, and the name *Krom Pracheachon* ('Citizens Group') was finally agreed on in early 1955. Its leaders were named as Meas, Suon and Yuth, but of course it was a front organization for the Khmer People's Revolutionary Party (KPRP). Nuon Chea now moved to the capital from his base in Battambang to take Meas's place as Secretary of the Party's Phnom Penh branch. ('In order to deceive the enemy', according to Suon, 'he worked in business').[83] In 1976, Suon wrote that Pol Pot had also played a role in setting up the Pracheachon: 'I think perhaps the present Secretary of the [Party] Centre was involved in helping to prepare the statutes and political programme, because I saw him a lot at Keo Meas's place. He wore a white short-sleeved shirt, and drove a black Citroen 15, but I did not know his name then and did not ask Keo Meas.'[84]

Pol Pot's education, and the fact that he was quite at home in Phnom Penh, were already beginning to outweigh his lack of revolutionary seniority, as the former resistance leaders (all from modest rural origins) tried to feel their way in an environment completely new to them. Pol Pot's major task at that time, however, was liaison between the Pracheachon and the newly revived Democratic Party, which was developing favourably for the left. Suon says that Pot was instrumental in getting the Democrats and the Pracheachon together, to 'exchange views' and to agree not to stand competing election candidates in areas where one was clearly the stronger. Further, he 'performed great services for the Party, that is, he gathered progressive elements in the city into the Democratic Party in order to defeat the People's Movement [*Pracheachollana*], that is, Son Ngoc Thanh's group, and force them out of the Democratic Party, isolating them. At that time the big shots ran out and joined [Sihanouk's] Sangkum Reastr Niyum. The only one who remained was the stubborn Um Sim and some of his hangers on.'[85] One of the latter was the 24-year-old law student Hu Nim, who ended as well as began his political career in opposition to Pol Pot.

In the second half of 1954, the leadership of the Democratic Party was assumed by a group of young radicals who had returned from their studies in France but had not joined in armed resistance to the French. By February 1955 these people, led by Keng Vannsak and Thiounn Mumm, former members of the 'Marxist Circle' in Paris, had a majority on the Party Executive Committee. Prince Norodom Phurissara became

Secretary-General, and leftists filled six of the remaining eleven positions;[86] one of them was Mey Pho's brother Im Phon. Radicals also gained control of the Phnom Penh branch of the Democratic Party, headed by Ping Say and Keng Vannsak.[87] The Party now took positions quite similar to those of the Pracheachon on major issues, as did the returned Thanhists. In the words of one writer, all three groups 'emphasized the importance of the Geneva Conference in securing Cambodia's independence, the undesirability of American aid, the dangerous situation in Vietnam and 'imperialist' responsibility for it, and the necessity for free elections as guaranteed by Geneva.'[88]

If previous election results were any indication, the Democratic Party could look forward to a comfortable victory, or at least to the opportunity of forming a coalition government with the support of the Pracheachon.[89]

It was this prospect of a left-wing government which forced crucial realignments on the right, beginning in October 1954 with an alliance of four small parties (including Lon Nol's 'Khmer Renovation' Party and Dap Chhuon's 'Victorious North-East' Party), which proclaimed that they were 'rightist, monarchist, traditionalist and in principle opposed to party politics'.[90] In February 1955 this alliance was broadened by the formation of the *Sangkum Reastr Niyum*, or Popular Socialist Community, which under the leadership of Norodom Sihanouk was to rule the country for the next fifteen years. On 2 March, Sihanouk abdicated in favour of his father, Suramarit, and moved openly into the political arena.

In order to buy time for the Sangkum to establish itself, the elections were postponed until September. Six months of unprecedented political turbulence followed, especially after May when the government signed a military aid agreement with the US. Sihanouk claimed that the Sangkum was not a political party, but required that members of political parties resign before they could join it. This proviso hurt the Democrats in particular. Other groups suffered direct repression. The Thanhists, filtering back from the Thai border in groups, set up four different newspapers, which were banned one by one after publishing a few issues.[91] The newspaper *Pracheachon* started publication on 1 April and lasted nineteen issues, until 10 June; its editor Chi Kim An was incarcerated. A second attempt, *Samakki* ('Solidarity'), was banned ten days later, and its editor, Pol Pot's brother Saloth Chhay, was gaoled for his opposition to the military agreement with the United States.[92] (At first he escaped arrest and hid in his brother Suong's house. Police slept outside and kept the house under surveillance for a week. They then threatened to arrest Suong and other members of the family, and finally King Suramarit ordered that Chhay be handed over to the police.)[93] On 24 June, the Pracheachon started another paper, *Pracheacheat* ('The Nation'), which lasted until 25 October under the editorship of Penn Yuth; it was then banned and Yuth was gaoled. In August, Chi Kim An, Saloth Chhay, and the editor of the Thanhist paper *Teu Mukh* ('Forward') were each sentenced to three month's gaol. The charges were: 'claiming that independence had been obtained at Geneva through the efforts of the whole populace, *lèse-majesté*, and false statements about US military aid'.[94]

The Democratic Party newspaper *Pracheathipateiy* ('Democracy') lasted throughout the campaign. But one Party candidate, Sarinn Tong, spent most of it in gaol, and another, Keng Vannsak, was fired at by government agents at a rally on the eve of the poll, and gaoled during the voting. The Party's office in Battambang was ransacked and its Phnom Penh headquarters surrounded by police.[95] Thiounn Mumm fled the country and returned to France (where he remained for sixteen years). Likewise, three Pracheachon candidates spent most of the campaign in gaol, and according to the ICSC twenty Pracheachon members were arrested over the same period, including the KNLC's Tralay, and the former commander of the Sivotha I Mobile Unit, Son Sichan.[96] In an incident in Chhouk district in Kampot, six others were apprehended by government troops and two of them shot dead.[97] 163 alleged 'Viet Minh' were also detained, mostly in Kompong Cham gaol.[98] After the elections, in October, two more Pracheachon members were shot and killed by local authorities in Kompong Speu. 'The motive appeared to be [their] success in the elections', reported the ICSC, without giving any details.[99] The ICSC also noted three other incidents in Kompong Cham, and one in Kampot, of authorities shooting at former members of the UIF instead of allowing them to participate in the electoral process.[100] Partly as a result of this harassment, the Pracheachon was able to field candidates for only 35 of the 91 seats. The Democrats stood candidates in all seats, and between them the two leftist parties provided 62 of the 108 candidates under the age of thirty-five. The conservative Sangkum candidates were nearly all older.[101]

During the campaign in southern Battambang, where Achar Mel Van, the former KNLC province chief, was the Pracheachon candidate, his colleagues Achar Bou and Chuon Pralit were shot dead by soldiers while campaigning; a third Pracheachon propagandist was shot at but managed to escape unhurt.[102] Despite this repression, Van won an acknowledged 2,910 votes (41 per cent of the total, officially the highest opposition vote in the country) in a constituency the Democrats had won in 1951 with 1,931 votes.[103]

Voters themselves were often intimidated by the authorities. Election abuses were regularly reported in all the non–Sangkum newspapers at the time. 'Villagers were threatened with punishment, including death, if they did not vote for the Sangkum. People were coerced into taking out Sangkum membership cards, and then told that if they voted for any other party they would face punishment. Another technique was to force villagers to take an oath to supernatural powers that they would vote for the Sangkum, after which they would not dare do otherwise.'[104] As Michael Vickery points out, if such reports had been false, they would almost certainly have figured in the charges laid against the editors of the banned newspapers. They did not, 'and it may be inferred that the government didn't consider it expedient to make an issue of them'. The local Agence France-Presse correspondent reported that observers 'had some reservations about certain aspects of the voting process: unusual deployment of police forces, absence of opposition voting slips, and arrests of left-wing leaders'.[105]

Finally, ballot boxes were tampered with after the vote, to eliminate candidates of the left. According to the official figures in Memut electoral district, where Khmer Issarak and Viet Minh forces had been well-established since the late 1940s and enjoyed considerable support among the rubber plantation workers, the Sangkum candidate registered 6,149 votes, compared with 99 for the Democrats and 0 for the Pracheachon.[106] It is not necessary to assert that the Pracheachon candidate, Sok Saphai, would have won a clear majority in a fair contest, to see the official count as a laughable one. In neighbouring Krek, also a centre of rubber plantations, less zealous government officials conceded 2,855 votes, or 24 per cent, to Prom Thiounn Mealea, the Pracheachon candidate,[107] despite the fact that, like Sok Saphai, he was in gaol throughout the campaign. Tea Sabun, a former Issarak district chief, claims that Sangkum voting slips were white in colour, and the Pracheachon ones were black. 'Everyone in Anchaeum, Lo Ngieng and Kauk Srok subdistricts voted black, but the [government] district chief, Tuon Lan, came and asked: 'Who voted black?' We answered: 'I did, because black means 'we Khmer' and white means 'the French''. So he held another election and put in new ballot slips for the Sangkum, and they won. People were afraid to complain after he had threatened to throw organized dissidents into gaol. There were troops, security forces, and police on the spot at the time.'[108]

In Komchay Meas, Prey Veng, a former Issarak who had become a monk after independence claims to have seen the process at work. He says that voters were handed coloured slips of paper representing each party as they entered the polling booths; after voters had placed the slip of their choice in the ballot box, they would come out and throw the others into a reject bin. 'But the people in control of the voting booths decided to select the ballot slips. They threw out the Pracheachon slips. This is absolutely true. In the outside box we saw many Sangkum slips and very few Pracheachon slips, so most people were voting for the Pracheachon inside. But the counters were not just, and they declared that the Sangkum had won.'[109]

The official results there still gave the Pracheachon candidate 2,457 votes, or 24 per cent of the total. Eight of his agents were gaoled during the campaign. [110] Further west, the Pracheachon candidate was Sang Lon, former UIF political commissar for Tbaung Khmum district, who had just been released after two years' imprisonment by the colonial government. He spent the last week of the campaign back in gaol, but recalls the atmosphere of the time. 'The people's feelings were not unanimous. In Cheach and Dontey subdistricts everyone voted for the Pracheachon, but in the township the parties were even... We only lost on the main highway because that is where the troops were, and there was fear of imprisonment. We did not dare have any rallies or meetings. Many people were afraid to vote. During the campaign a Sihanouk agent arrived in Kandol Chrum. His name was Ta Choeum, and people were very afraid of him. When the officials rigged the counting, three Pracheachon people — Moeun, Chon and Chin — who had been calculating the votes themselves, were imprisoned along with me... After more than a week I had to bribe my way out of gaol. It cost me 8,000 riels, which I borrowed from a Chinese and had to pay back afterwards, by handing over most of my harvest... I got about 35 per cent of the vote.'[111]

The official count gave him none at all.[112] Sihanouk implicitly admitted the fraud three years later, when he described both this area, Tbaung Khmum, and Memut (where the Pracheachon had also officially received a zero vote) as "red" or "pink" districts *on the basis of the 1955 voting*. He also placed in this category a district of Svay Rieng where Ney Sarann had allegedly received only 87 votes out of 8,000.[113]

Vickery concludes his discussion of these events by saying: 'The International Control Commission certified the election as 'correct', which only shows how little such inspection may mean'.[114] It is impossible to know what would have been the overall result in a freely-conducted, scrupulously-counted poll, but a safe estimate would certainly give the Pracheachon at least six or seven seats, with the possibility of holding the balance of power between the Democrats and the Sangkum. But Sihanouk later described as 'red' or 'pink' thirty nine of the country's hundred-odd districts,[115] and the three main parties might well have gained roughly equal numbers of seats, which would undoubtedly have led to a Democrat-Pracheachon coalition government.

There seems no compelling reason to distinguish the popularity of the Pracheachon from that of its Lao counterpart, the communist Neo Lao Hak Sat (NLHS); in what was probably the only relatively democratic poll in post-1945 Indo-China, the May 1958 partial elections for one third of the seats in the Lao National Assembly, the NLHS won nine of the twenty-one seats, and its ally, the Peace and Neutrality Party, another four.

The official count gave the Sangkum all 91 seats in the National Assembly, with a total vote of 630,625 (or 82 per cent). The Democrats recorded 93,919 (12 per cent); identifiable members of the Party's radical faction (as distinct from its moderate and Thanhist wings) received an average of 20 per cent in five constituencies in Phnom Penh and Kandal. Keng Vannsak topped the Democratic Party's list with 25 per cent in the capital, and other former members of the Paris Marxist Circle, Touch Phoeun and Mey Phat, received respectively 25 per cent and 24 per cent in Kampot and Kompong Cham constituencies. The Pracheachon officially recorded 31,034 votes (4 per cent), including more than one third of the vote in three constituencies, and an average of over 10 per cent in the 35 seats they contested.

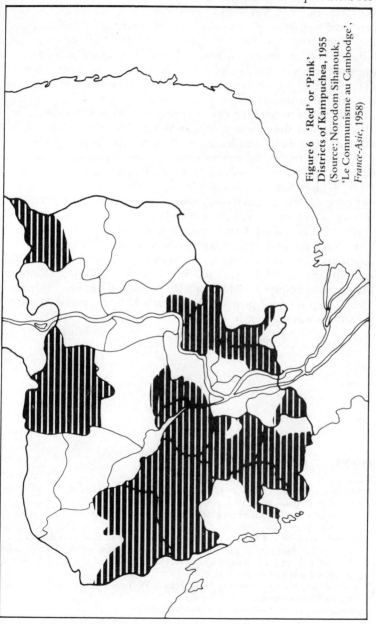

Figure 6 'Red' or 'Pink'
Districts of Kampuchea, 1955
(Source: Norodom Sihanouk,
'Le Communisme au Cambodge',
France-Asie, 1958)

(In Kampot, Non Suon and Penn Yuth received 23 and 34 per cent, and Keo Meas got 20 per cent in Svay Rieng.) The Thanhists recorded only 794 votes.[116] Michael Leifer has written; 'To Sihanouk, these figures indicated that there was still a hard core opposed to his authority and that he would have to act cautiously to avoid providing this opposition with opportunities to enhance its political position.'[117]

It should be noted, too, that in contrast to the ICSC reports from other parts of the country, former Pracheachon members from the East are unanimous in stating that during the campaign the government forces did not resort to any assassinations. This may indicate some modicum of respect for the Pracheachon's strength there. Chum Sambor, from Komchay Meas, says people were imprisoned, 'but not for long periods. . . if you gave them a lot of money, sold your buffaloes or your land, they would let you out again.'[118] Tea Sabun, from Tbaung Khmum, reports (and Sang Lon concurs) that 'there were not yet any killings of party members. . . many were gaoled but they were freed about a month after the elections'; he recalled Sok Saphai and Prom Thiounn Mealea as examples.[119] Although Sihanouk had had his way in the elections, it was still possible that he would be prepared to allow the Pracheachon to exist.

Notes

1. Maurice Laurent, *L'Armée au Cambodge et dans les pays en voie de développement du sud-est asiatique,* Paris 1968, p.65.
2. By mid June, one of the French negotiators at Geneva had become convinced that the Viet Minh 'fear the development of Chinese control over their actions, present and future'. Note from the adviser to the US Delegation to the Special Adviser, 15 June 1954, in *Foreign Relations of the United States 1952–54,* vol. XVI, *The Geneva Conference,* John P. Glennon (ed.), Department of State, Washington 1981, p.1150.
3. Author's interview with Hoang Tung, Hanoi, 31 October 1980. The 'free zone' was to be in north-western Kampuchea, Tung said, but this is unlikely since the activity of the 436th Battalion was limited to the north-*east.*

4. Stephen Heder. 'The Kampuchean-Vietnamese Conflict', *South-East Asian Affairs 1979*, Singapore, Heinemann, 1979, pp.157–186, at p.170.
5. *Ibid.*
6. Wilfred Burchett, *The China-Cambodia-Vietnam Triangle*, London, 1982, p.43.
7. *The Geneva Conference, op. cit.*, pp.428–29. The US chargé in Paris to Department of State, 2 March 1954.
8. Bidault's 1965 autobiography, quoted in Chalmers M. Roberts, 'Ike and Indo-China: To the Brink and Back', *Guardian Weekly*, 7 August 1983. Roberts quotes John Prados's *The Sky Would Fall. Operation Vulture: The US Bombing Mission in Indo-China, 1954*, to the effect that 'the Americans did say something that at least could have been construed as such.'
9. Author's interview with Nguyen Thanh Son, Ho Chi Minh City, 28 October 1980. Thanh Son recalls; 'On 6 or 7 May 1954, Gromyko received us at the airport — [Pathet Lao delegate] Nouhak, Keo Moni, Mey Pho and myself.' It is interesting that the Vietnamese brought two Khmer representatives with them, but only one Lao.
10. *The Geneva Conference*, op. cit., pp.734–36. US Delegation to Department of State, 8 May 1954.
11. *Ibid.*, p.735.
12. *Ibid.*, pp.720–726, at p.725. My emphasis.
13. *Ibid.*, p.728. Dulles to Smith, TOP SECRET, 8 May 1954, cable 'drafted by the Secretary of State'. The statement added a condition: 'if they come to the conclusion that this is preferable to the harsh terms which no doubt Communists will seek to extract'.
14. *Ibid.*, p.713. Cable dated 8 May 1954.
15. *Ibid.*, p.737. Cable dated 9 May 1954.
16. *Ibid.*, p.753. Smith to Dulles, 10 May 1954.
17. *Ibid.*, p.768.
18. *Ibid.*
19. *Ibid.*, p.798. Smith to Dulles, 14 May 1954.
20. *Ibid.*, p.819. Smith to Dulles, 15 May 1954.
21. *Ibid.*, p.838. Special Adviser to US Delegation to Smith, 18 May 1954.
22. *Ibid.*, p.839. Smith to Dulles, 18 May 1954.
23. *Ibid.*, p.786. Cable dated 12 May 1954.
24. *Ibid.*, p.792. Smith to Dulles, 13 May 1954. My emphasis.
25. *Ibid.*, p.820. Smith to Dulles, 16 May 1954.
26. *Ibid.*, p.828. Smith to Dulles, 17 May 1954.
27. *Ibid.*
28. *Ibid.*, p.837. Smith to Dulles, 17 May 1954.
29. *Ibid.*, p.841. Smith to Dulles, 18 May 1954.
30. *Ibid.*, pp.855–56. Smith to Dulles, 19 May 1954.
31. *Ibid.*, p.864. Smith to Dulles, 20 May 1954. My emphasis.
32. *Ibid.*, p.896. Smith to Dulles, 22 May 1954.
33. *Ibid.*, pp.922–25. Smith to Dulles, 25 May 1954.
34. *Ibid.*, p.931. Smith to Dulles, 26 May 1954.
35. *Ibid.*, p.948. Smith to Dulles, 27 May 1954. My emphasis.
36. *Ibid.*, p.983. Heath to Smith, 31 May 1954.
37. *Ibid.*, pp.1031–32. Smith to Dulles, 4 June 1954.
38. *Ibid.*, p.1047.
39. *Ibid.*, p.1078. Smith to Dulles, 8 June 1954.
40. *Ibid.*, pp.1117–18. Dulles to Department of State.

41. *Ibid.*, p.1132. Smith to Dulles, 14 June 1954.
42. *Ibid.*, p.1140. Smith to Dulles, 14 June 1954.
43. *Ibid.*, p.1146. Dulles to Smith, 14 June 1954.
44. *Ibid.*
45. *Ibid.*, p.1150. Adviser to US Delegation to its Special Adviser, Geneva, 15 June 1954.
46. *Ibid.*, p.1171. Smith to Dulles, 17 June 1954.
47. *Ibid.*, pp.1073, 1112. Smith to Dulles, 8 and 10 June 1954.
48. *Ibid.*, p.1173. Smith to Dulles, 17 June 1954, giving additional details of the meeting between Zhou and Eden, as reported by UK delegation member Dennis Allen, to Johnson.
49. *Ibid.*
50. *Ibid.*, p.1174.
51. François Joyaux, *La Chine et le règlement du premier conflit d'Indochine, Genève 1954*, Paris 1979, p.231.
52. *The Geneva Conference, op. cit.*, pp.1024, 1029. 'National Intelligence Estimate on Laos and Cambodia', 1 June 1954, claims the Viet Minh in Laos were 'predominantly Vietnamese'.
53. *Ibid.*, p.1157. Smith to Dulles, 17 June 1954.
54. *Ibid.*, pp.1157–61.
55. *Ibid.*, p.1181. Smith to Dulles, 18 June 1954.
56. *Ibid.*, pp.1182–83.
57. *Ibid.*, p.1173. Smith to Dulles, 17 June 1954.
58. Joyaux, *op. cit.*, pp.240–41. Zhou Enlai evidently told Mendès-France that he was urging 'the Viet Minh to become reconciled not only with France but also with the Vietnam of Bao Dai', a statement which Joyaux describes as an 'astonishingly new remark'. It certainly betrayed some Chinese interest in dividing Vietnam.
59. Burchett, *op. cit.*, pp.34–36. See also Bernard Fall, *Vietnam Witness, 1953–66*, London, Pall Mall, 1966, p.258. Fall says that partition of Kampuchea was at this stage still an issue; however, Zhou's concessions during his meeting with Eden on 16 June had already ended any UIF hopes of a regroupment zone; see above, pp.148–9.
60. Sam Sary himself was to flee Phnom Penh to join Son Ngoc Thanh's US-sponsored forces four years later.
61. *Chamlaiy Dop Pir* ('Reply by no. 12'), Non Suon's confession in Tuol Sleng, dated 29 November 1976, pp.4–5.
62. Author's interview with Men Chhan, Phnom Penh, 25 September 1980. Chhan answered his own initial question by remarking; 'The Russians did not dare to help us get recognition, because the Chinese were on the front line.'
63. Author's interview with Chum Sambor, Prey Veng, 12 July 1980.
64. Author's interview with Prak Sovan, Kranhoung, 9 August 1980.
65. *Chamlaiy Dop Pir, op. cit.*
66. *Phnaek Ti Pir; Royea Mun Rotprohar 18.3.70* ('Section 2; The Period Before the Coup of 18 March 1970'), Non Suon's confession in Tuol Sleng, dated 7 November 1976.
67. *Ibid.*, and *Chamlaiy Dop Pir, op. cit.*
68. *Ibid.*
69. Author's interview with Nguyen Xuan Hoang, Hanoi, 4 November 1980, and *Far Eastern Economic Review*, 16 February 1984, p.20, quoting the Vietnamese journal *Communist Review*, November 1983. On the reason for their departure, see p.153, above.

70. Author's interview with US State Department Officer Andrew Antippus, who interviewed Sieu Heng in 1970. March 1980.

71. Author's interview with Chea Soth, Phnom Penh, 22 October 1980.

72. *Summary of Annotated Party History,* by the Eastern Zone military political service, 1973. Translated captured document declassified by the US government in 1978, p.12.

73. *Ibid.*

74. Author's interview with Pham Van Ba, Ho Chi Minh City, 28 October 1980.

75. Author's interview with Nguyen Thanh Son, Ho Chi Minh City, 28 October 1980.

76. *Ibid.*

77. Gareth Porter, 'Vietnamese Communist Policy Towards Cambodia, 1930–70', in David P. Chandler and Ben Kiernan (eds.) *Revolution and its Aftermath in Kampuchea,* New Haven, 1983, p.71. Porter cites the Vietnam News Agency in English, 4 April 1955.

78. Author's interview with Thai provincial police chief of the time, Chana Sumadavanija, Bangkok, 14 August 1981. See also Michael Vickery, *Cambodia 1975–82,* Boston 1984, pp.253–56.

79. Author's interview with Kol Kon, Komchay Meas, 9 August 1980.

80. Reports of the International Commission of Supervision and Control (ICSC), Command Papers, *Cambodia No. 1, 1958, Cmnd. 526,* p.12.

81. Roger Smith, *Cambodia's Foreign Policy,* Ithaca, Cornell University Press, 1965, pp.167–68.

82. Author's interview with Chim Chin, Prey Veng, 28 July 1980.

83. *XII Via Niyiey Ompi Bang Bang Muoy Chomnuon Khnong Angkar Duknoam* ('No. 12 Talks about Some of the Brothers in the Leading Organization'), Non Suon's confession in Tuol Sleng, dated 21 November 1976.

84. *Phnaek Ti Pir, op. cit.,* p.6.

85. *XII Via Niyiey, op. cit.*

86. These six were, apart from Keng Vannsak and Thiounn Mumm: Sin Khmen Ko, Im Phon, Tat Heng and Chey Chum — the last described by Keng Vannsak as 'centre-left'. Keng Vannsak, interviews with author, Paris, 22 November 1979 and 2 February 1980.

87. *Ibid.*

88. 'Cambodia 1973; The Present Situation and its Background', by Michael Vickery. Unpublished typescript, p.17.

89. One Democratic supporter, So Nem, wrote to Keng Vannsak's French wife in August 1955; 'Whatever happens he will win these elections. . . His prestige and fame are soaring and no other could ever compete with him.'

90. Michael Vickery, 'Looking Back at Cambodia', in Ben Kiernan and Chanthou Boua (eds.), *Peasants and Politics in Kampuchea, 1942–81,* New York 1982, pp.89–113 at p.97.

91. 'New Khmer' was closed down in February 1955; 'Forward' in May (and its editor imprisoned); 'Khmerism' in early June after two issues; and 'Moving Forward' in mid June. Vickery, '*Cambodia 1973*', *op. cit.,* The Khmer names for these newspapers were *Khmer Thmey, Teu Mukh, Khmer Niyum,* and *Daor Teu Mukh,* respectively.

92. *Ibid.,* and Carlyle Thayer, personal communication.

93. Author's interview with Loth Suong, Phnom Penh, 9 July 1980.

94. Vickery, 'Looking Back at Cambodia', *op. cit.,* p.99.

95. Philippe Preschez, *Essai sur la democratie au Cambodge,* Foundation Nationale des Sciences Politiques, Paris. Serie C, Recherches, no. 4, October 1961, p.62.

168

Also Keng Vannsak, *op. cit.* And Pokambo (pseudonym) 'Cambodge: Coup de force de Sihanouk', *Democratie Nouvelle*, Paris, no. 10, October 1955, pp.632–33.

96. Carlyle Thayer, personal communication, information drawn from the US *Foreign Broadcast Information Service* (FBIS): 'Chan Sichan — 1954 a colonel in the Khmer people's liberation army: October 1955, reported still under detention by government authorities.' On Tralay, see note 97.

97. ICSC Reports, *op. cit.*, *Cambodia No. 1, 1957, Cmnd. 253*, p.27 ff. (On Tralay), p.34 ff.

98. *Ibid.*, *Cambodia No. 2, 1955, Cmnd. 9534*, p.19 ff.

99. *Ibid.*, *Cambodia No. 1, 1957, Cmnd. 253*, p.34. The victims were Men Suon and Proum Lao. See also *Cambodia No. 1, 1958, Cmnd. 526*, p.11.

100. *Ibid.*, *Cambodia No. 2, 1955, Cmnd. 9534*, p.19 ff.

101. D. J. Steinberg, *et al.*, *Cambodia: Its People, Its Society, Its Culture*, New Haven, 1959, p.97.

102. ICSC Reports, *op. cit.*, *Cambodia No. 1, 1957, Cmnd. 253*, p.27 ff.

103. *Journal Officiel*, 22 September 1955. I am grateful to Michael Vickery for drawing my attention to the official election figures.

104. Vickery, 'Looking Back at Cambodia', *op. cit.*, p.98.

105. *Ibid.*, p.99, and Pokambo, *op. cit.*, p.633, quoting A.F.P.

106. *Journal Officiel*, 22 September 1955.

107. *Ibid.*

108. Author's interview with Tea Sabun, Phnom Penh, 23 August 1980.

108. Chim Chin, *op. cit.*

110. Author's interview with Puk Soum, Prey Veng, 8 August 1980; and *Journal Officiel*, 22 September 1955.

111. Author's interview with Sang Lon (Chen Lon), Kandol Chrum, 7 August 1980. Lon added: 'There were no shootings though.'

112. *Journal Officiel, op. cit.*

113. *Ibid.*, and Norodom Sihanouk, 'Le Communisme au Cambodge', *France-Asie*, vol. 15, no. 144, 1958, pp.192–206. and no. 145, pp.290–306. See p.201, note 1. Ney Sarann stood in Svay Teap district.

114. Vickery, 'Looking Back', *op. cit.*, p.99.

115. Sihanouk, *op. cit.*, p.201, note 1. Sihanouk wrote: 'One day I will publish the list, province by province, of 'red' villages, with the number of votes obtained by the Pracheachon candidates [in 1955]. But I can say now that in the subdistricts, the communists rarely obtained a majority...' He then went on, however, to give a list of 'red' or 'pink' *districts*, which seems to imply his recognition of the lack of validity of his view of the 1955 count. See Figure 6.

116. Preschez, *op. cit.*, p.62, Sihanouk, *op. cit.*, p.200, and *Journal Officiel*, 22 September 1955.

117. *Cambodia: The Search for Security*, New York 1967, p.70.

118. Chum Sambor, *op. cit.*

119. Tea Sabun, *op. cit.*. He was also aware that Keng Vannsak had been gaoled.

6

The Changing of the Vanguard: 'Political Struggle', 1955–1966

If I deal extremely severely with the Non Suons, I do not on the other hand hesitate to adopt certain socialist ideas. For example I saw the correctness of our 'reds' when they pointed out to me the abuses of the private industrial enterprises which obtained patents only to profit from the brand-names for illicit business purposes. I also think they are right on the issue of the anti-imperialist struggle, and you know that our country lags behind nobody on this issue.[1]

Norodom Sihanouk, 1966

Peaceful Co-existence, 1955–62

Sihanouk moved quickly to consolidate his new-found domination of Kampuchea's political scene by pursuing moves, already hinted at before the elections, to adopt a more neutralist stance in foreign policy. At the Bandung Conference of Afro-Asian Nations in April 1955, Sihanouk had privately assured Zhou Enlai and Pham Van Dong that US military aid to Kampuchea would not mean an American military presence, and that he did not want the protection of the anti-communist South-East Asia Treaty Organization (SEATO). In March, soon after the announcement that a military aid agreement with Washington would be signed, Sihanouk had visited New Delhi and signed a joint statement with Nehru in support of the five principles of co-existence.[2] Hanoi's response was guarded, however; the Vietnam News Agency reported that the people of Vietnam 'earnestly hope that their statement will be quickly materialized', while the Vietnamese Lao Dong Party newspaper soon demanded that the arrests and intimidation marking the Kampuchean election campaign 'must end immediately'. Further, when the election results were proclaimed, Hanoi accused the Royal Government of having 'seriously violated' the Geneva Accords by holding elections 'without democratic freedoms'.[3] Sihanouk's immediate reply was to offer to exchange political missions with

the Democratic Republic of Vietnam. The Vietnamese, obviously taken by surprise,[4] took two weeks to respond. They
welcomed the offer on October 6, asking the ICSC to convey to
Sihanouk Hanoi's desire 'to implement as early as possible the
policy of good neighbourly relations through practical deeds'.[5]
Sihanouk did not follow this up, but in January 1956, during a
visit to the Philippines, he publicly rejected pressure and
inducements to join SEATO; the next month he visited China,
where he signed a Sino-Cambodian Friendship Declaration, and
his country became the beneficiary of the first grant-in-aid ($22.4
million)[6] given by the Chinese People's Republic to a non-
communist country. This produced a temporary but concerted
economic embargo on Kampuchea by Thailand, South Vietnam
and the USA. On March 3, Hanoi Radio claimed that 'American
manoeuvres to involve Cambodia in an aggressive policy have . .
. met with failure'.[7] According to one observer, this was 'the real
turning point in the Vietnamese view of Sihanouk'.[8] The Khmer
communists seem to have followed suit. In April, at the Third
Sangkum Congress, the Pracheachon even proposed a coalition
government to include itself, the Sangkum and the other
political parties.[9]

By May 1956, Non Suon, Keo Meas and Nop Bophann had
re-established the *Pracheachon* newspaper on a weekly basis. In
addition there was a 'left-wing neutral' weekly paper, *Wat
Phnom,* and a thrice-weekly one called *Meatophum* ('Mother-
land'). The latter was described by American sources as
'independent',[10] but its editor, Son Phuoc Tho, had in fact
joined with Touch Phoeun and another former member of the
'Marxist Circle', Hou Yuon (who had returned from France in
January), and also Pol Pot's brother Saloth Chhay, to form a
'Committee to Defend His Majesty's Neutrality Policy'.[11] Recently having been released from gaol, Chhay was respected in
Pracheachon circles; a monk sympathetic to the UIF veterans
recalls that at one stage Chhay had even smuggled a gun to the
monk's Prey Veng *wat,* to be passed on to KPRP leaders.[12] The
Committee's activities were above-ground, however; in 1956 it
published a Khmer translation of Hou Yuon's doctoral thesis on
colonialism and peasant problems, under the title *The Co-
operative Question.*[13] Presumably modelled on the 'Committee in
Defence of Peace and the Geneva Agreements' set up in Saigon
in August 1954 by the future NLF leader Nguyen Huu Tho, the
Khmer Committee fared much better than its Vietnamese

counterpart. Tho and his Committee members had been gaoled after a police raid in November 1954, and their Committee banned.[14] In Kampuchea in January 1957, by contrast, the Sangkum officially adopted neutrality as its foreign policy, at its Fourth Congress, which attracted a crowd of 15,000 and at which Hou Yuon was one of the main speakers.[15]

It was in this period that Non Suon reported to Sieu Heng and Tou Samouth, underground leaders of the KPRP in the country-side: 'There are places (in the capital) to do secret work. The enemy has not yet become very concerned. There are houses where we can live and easy communication routes.'[16] The pressure was off, for the moment. And there were encouraging signs: as it turned out, Sihanouk had by no means 'betrayed the country and followed the French', as Pach Chhoeun had protested; to this extent the struggle for independence had been rewarded. The struggle for socialism was something else, but at least in the sphere of foreign policy Sihanouk had taken a leaf out of the socialist book. Therein, however, lay serious problems for the KPRP. Its members, if they went by the party statutes, had been primed merely 'to carry on a firm struggle so as to annihilate the French colonialists, the American imperialists and their puppet lackeys'.[17] The fight must now have appeared to many of them to have been won, and hundreds went back to their villages and tried to settle down. Worse, Sieu Heng, the leader of the KPRP 'temporary Central Committee', had returned from North Vietnam with the firm view that 'the struggle was over', and unbeknownst to other party leaders he had made secret contact with Defence Minister Lon Nol in 1955.[18] Perhaps as part of a deal guaranteeing his future personal security, he was now prepared to inform on his comrades. The malaise probably affected other leaders as well. Non Suon wrote that in 1956 he and Keo Meas 'began to distrust Penn Yuth because he had a mistress and wrote articles we did not like' in *Pracheachon*.[19]

The period was therefore characterized by the unexpected but welcome development of Sihanouk's increasingly independent stance, and by the dampened revolutionary enthusiasm which resulted naturally from this in conjunction with the election defeat and the KPRP's lack of ideological preparation for class struggle. The 1973 Party History summed up, I believe correctly, as follows:

After Geneva, we transformed armed struggle into political

172

> struggle. . . above all during the 1955 election and with regard to the Cambodian-American military agreement (sweeping away the American strategic bases), to introduce the policy of neutrality to Cambodia. We fought unarmed behind and within the enemy's centre of power. . . This changed the political atmosphere in the country and at the level of the people. . .
>
> However, our Party, only three years old, lacked the following three things: ideology, policy and organization. With this state of affairs, the temporary Central Committee, with Sieu Heng as Secretary, foundered. Around 1956, this committee headed in the direction of urban movements; some bad activities took place.[20]

It was in this atmosphere that Son Sen and Ieng Sary returned from Paris (in May 1956 and January 1957 respectively), leaving the leadership of the Union of Khmer Students in France in the hands of another Marxist, Khieu Samphan. They joined Pol Pot and the fifteen or so former fellow students now heavily involved in the KPRP's Phnom Penh branch, increasingly the major focus of the Party's activities. (According to American sources, there had been a number of 'serious student strikes' in the capital in 1955 and 1956, during which 'some students threatened to follow their professors in rebellion against the government'.[21])

In the meantime, Pol Pot had introduced to the Phnom Penh Party Committee two other former students with less orthodox radical backgrounds. One was Ping Thuok, who had joined the right-wing Issarak movement led by Savang Vong, and then the UIF in the latter stages of the war, and was now working as a customs official. Thuok was brought into the Party by Pol Pot in December 1954.[22] The other was Sok Khnaol, who had joined the UIF on his return from France but had defected to Son Ngoc Thanh in 1954 (perhaps out of reluctance to abandon armed opposition to Sihanouk) and had led an attack on a village in Battambang three days after the elections.[23] He, too, apparently joined the KPRP in this period. Both men were soon to rise rapidly in the Party hierarchy alongside Pol Pot and Ieng Sary. Thuok, later known as Sok Thuok or Vorn Vet, became a member of the Politburo; Khnaol, under the pseudonym Peam, became administrative secretary of the Party's Eastern Zone branch in the 1960s. In the meantime, other returned students who had joined the UIF and maintained their links with its veteran leaders, for example Chi Kim An and Sien An, were down-graded in the key Phnom Penh Party branch.

Around the middle of 1956, a new KPRP Central Committee

was formed. According to the 1973 History: 'This gave rise to a rural committee, responsible for rural action throughout the country. It was composed of three persons, with Sieu Heng as chairman. The urban committee, secretly or overtly responsible for all cities throughout the country, was composed of four persons, with comrade Tou Samouth as chairman.'[24] The two committees appear to have been organized autonomously, in mutual isolation and with apparent disregard for the obvious links between rural areas and provincial capitals. Thus, in the ensuing period, Tou Samouth's urban committee, probably including Nuon Chea, Non Suon, and Keo Meas (or perhaps Pol Pot), 'succeeded in forming a few committees in cities which did not yet have any',[25] while the rural organization became immobilized. Whether or not Pol Pot was actually a member of the Party's national urban committee, he was increasingly influential in its Phnom Penh branch, which served to enhance his position in the Party as a whole, as a result of three factors.

Firstly, Tou Samouth was apparently not usually present in the capital; nor was he directly involved with activities there, at least until October 1956, when Keo Meas sent Non Suon to the Vietnamese border in Svay Rieng, to report to Samouth and Sieu Heng 'on the situation in Phnom Penh City'.[26] The fact that the chief of the KPRP's urban committee was absent from Phnom Penh meant that control of activities in the city was left more and more to those, such as Pol Pot, who were able to work securely there.

Secondly, Keo Meas (and to a lesser extent Non Suon) was in an exposed position because of his open role at the time of the Joint Commission; his activities were therefore hampered, and he may even have deliberately kept himself uninformed of the secret side of Party work, in case he should be arrested and interrogated. Cadres who were more discreet in their activities, such as Nuon Chea, who used the disguise of a businessman,[27] or whose bourgeois backgrounds afforded them some degree of protection, such as the returned students led by Pol Pot, soon came to wield enormous influence over the Party's urban network. This state of affairs assumed added importance in August 1957, when the Democratic Party dissolved itself 'after its leaders were called to the Palace for a friendly conference with Sihanouk and then were beaten up on departure by Lon Nol's soldiers';[28] political options for educated radicals and republicans were now sharply reduced.

Finally, in the words of the 1973 Party History, 'from the middle of 1956, the committee in charge of the rural movement, headed by Sieu Heng, committed worse misdeeds after its betrayal of the Party'.[29] The committee in charge of the urban movement slowly became the *de facto* Central Committee, despite the overwhelming predominance of rural membership within the Party and the fact that its implantation in Phnom Penh had been extremely recent. This development was probably a crucial factor in Pol Pot's rise within the Party.

Information on developments in the rural areas at this time is extremely patchy. There were still localized cases of repression. In September 1957, forty-eight inhabitants of a village in Chhouk district, Kampot, complained to the ICSC that the authorities were persecuting them for their past membership of the UIF and accusing them of having 'spread troubles' in the pre-1954 period.[30] Such incidents probably reflected a subdued form of class struggle, as the traditional structure of local authority was gradually reimposed on the peasants in areas that had been under UIF control during the war. The KPRP's policy in the face of this was one of restraint, and of emphasis on the common ground between it and the Sihanouk regime. This much is implied by a second incident in Kampot, also in September 1957: the ICSC received a petition bearing the thumbprints of fifty-four people from Banteay Meas district adjacent to Chhouk. The petition expressed concern at the fact that the country's frontiers were being threatened by South Vietnam and that the Diem authorities were continuing to build up military posts and forces there. It stressed compliance with the Geneva Accords and, warning of the threat to 'peace, independence and neutrality', urged the ICSC to 'maintain peace in the country, South-East Asia and the world'.[31] Pol Pot and others, however, were already coming to regard this restrained KPRP stand as a betrayal of the revolution, and soon began a determined effort to reverse it. (Ieng Sary's 1974 version of the Party History was to alter the section on the post-Geneva period from 'Our Party engaged in political struggle with the enemy', to 'Our Party engaged in *life-and-death* struggle with the enemy'.[32])

The repression, in fact, was tailing off, at least in the East. So Phim and his wife had attempted to settle down on a farm in a remote border subdistrict of Prey Veng, but after a year the authorities had come in search of him. The couple split up and disappeared into the forest. After meeting again on the other side of the Mekong, they were once more identified, and Phim fled to the capital and got work building houses in the suburb of Tuk Laak. He finally slipped out of Phnom Penh and settled down again in Prey Veng.[33] Similarly, Phuong, who had been a UIF deputy district chief there and had stood as Pracheachon candidate in the elections (he was later to become Deputy Secretary of Phim's Eastern Zone Party branch), went back to his native village and settled down with his family. The senior UIF leader, Bun Sani, took a job as a technical supervisor at the Chup rubber plantations.

In the North-West, the UIF Zone military commander, Muol Sambath, took up a farm plot with some of his followers in southern Battambang. A monk at nearby Wat Thvak recalls that in the ensuing years they were 'still talking politics', but, it seems, doing little else. Another former UIF leader took a job looking after the electricity generator at a *wat* in Pailin.[34] In the North, one man's experience later assumed special significance. Ke Vin, who had joined the UIF at the age of fifteen when French forces had attempted to round him up in his home village in Baray, Kompong Thom, took advantage in 1954 of what his relatives described as 'Sihanouk's call to come back home'. Several months later, however, he was arrested and sentenced to six years' gaol. Released after three years in Kompong Thom and Phnom Penh prisons, he returned home again in 1957 and married a woman from a nearby village, where he, too, settled down and started a family.[35] Fifteen years later — after he had once again been driven into the forest by the authorities — Ke Vin, under the pseudonym Pauk, became commander of the Northern Zone and quickly established a reputation as the most brutal of all the figures of Pol Pot's regime. (See Chapter Eight below.) But in the late 1950s there was no hint of such developments. Both repression and unrest in the countryside gradually subsided, and as Michael Vickery has written, so did the traditionally endemic rural banditry. These were 'a few years of complete peace and internal security, something the country had not known within living memory. . . By 1960 . . . one could truly travel anywhere without danger or hindrance from the authorities.'[36]

Ieng Thirith has provided an interesting account of the situation in the cities following her return from Paris in 1957.

Back at home we faced opposition from Sihanouk who was in

power at that time. Both myself and Ieng Sary were forced to work in free [private?] schools so as to force us to earn low wages. I worked for two years in Phnom Penh and underwent a hard time. We were also shouldering our underground revolutionary activities. However, Sihanouk gave me official employment in a government high school.

This was at a time when there was a change in Sihanouk's approach. He started relying more on national bourgeoisie, rich farmers and on intellectuals. He even asked me to become a member of the National Assembly. However, as our Party advised against it, I politely refused the offer. I knew Sihanouk very well, and both our families were in acquaintance with each other.[37]

Hardly a case that bears out her husband Ieng Sary's claim of 'life-and-death struggle'. Similarly, when her sister Khieu Ponnary married Pol Pot on Bastille Day 1956, two officials of the Phnom Penh municipal government arranged for the couple to obtain a nice block of land near Chamcar Mon (later the site of Sihanouk's official residence). The two officials were Chi Kim An, a former member of the 'Marxist Circle' in Paris, now a surveyor, and Ponnary's cousin Chhan Sokhom (later a leading member of the Lon Nol regime). It was of course much harder for non-elite Party members. But it was precisely because Sihanouk's regime, in the 1956–66 period, was *not* characterized by severe and brutal repression of dissidents that the KPRP leadership was able to remain in the capital, with some of its most senior cadres publicly active and known. As we shall see, this in turn enabled the urban-based Pol Pot group to take control of the Party on their own ground. Had the communists been forced into a clandestine, defensive (or even offensive) *rural* war much earlier, this could never have happened.

Ney Sarann moved into Phnom Penh and started teaching at the privately-run Chamroeun Vichea high school. So did Vorn Vet and another leftist, Siet Chhe (later a member of the general staff of the army of Democratic Kampuchea). Pol Pot himself became a history teacher there. Son Sen and his wife Yun Yat began teaching at Sisowath High School. Then, Sen was appointed Director of Studies at the Teachers' Training College (*Sala Keruvichea*), also in the capital; other teaching staff there included Paris-trained leftists Chau Seng, Uch Ven and Ros Chet Thor. (Two of their students in this period, who later became important figures on the left, were Phouk Chhay and Mam Nay.) Son Sen was later assigned to the prestigious US-funded Kompong Kantout Teachers' College on the outskirts of the city, and Thiounn Thioeunn eventually became Dean of the country's Medical Faculty. Hou Yuon became Director of another private high school, Kambuboth, and employed a number of left-wing teachers. One of these was Penn Yuth; another was Ieng Sary, who after a period at Sisowath High School moved to Kambuboth, where he taught history and geography; a third was a former Issarak medic of peasant origin, Suas Nau, who under the name Chhouk became a ranking member of So Phim's Eastern Zone Party Committee in the 1960s.[38]

Over the next ten years, graduates from these four schools provided a large proportion of the country's left-wing militants. Many became teachers in rural schools, and roused the political awareness of students there (Mam Nay, for instance was appointed principal of Balaing College in Kompong Thom in 1958); but perhaps more significant is the fact that it was through these educational institutions in the capital that Khmer communists first began to penetrate middle-class Phnom Penh circles. Apart from the rural centres of wartime communist influence, it was here that anti-royalist sentiment was strongest, provoked in part by the events of the 1955 elections and by the suppression of the Democratic Party. In some ways, too, the field was left open to the communists by Son Ngoc Thanh's refusal to return to Phnom Penh and his increasingly open alliance with the United States, by the opportunist defection of some former Democrat leaders to Sihanouk's Sangkum, and by the political inactivity of others such as Pach Chhoeun, who took up a post as Director of the National Library. Keng Vannsak, for his part, now regarded political change as impossible because, as he saw it, 'Khmers were too passive in the face of royal authority'; he too abandoned the political scene and began to devote himself to a long-term effort at cultural reform, which he hoped would 'change the mentality' of his people and provide the basis for eventual political modernization.[39]

Certainly, a strong undercurrent of modernity was already emerging in Khmer cultural life, and its political thrust was radical. The traditional establishment had good reason to fear and circumscribe it. As Christopher Pym wrote of the late 1950s:

The first Khmer play I saw was performed by a group of orphans in a converted cinema outside the capital. Members of the

National Theatre were keen to give their support to the production, so we all cycled out into the night to find the place. The play, which had been specially written and produced by the students, was called *The Awakening of the Khmer Conscience*. It treated boldly of social themes, in particular the gulf, so wide in Cambodia, between rich and poor. This theme was illustrated by a scene in which a beggar and a large dog (live) competed for crumbs thrown from a rich man's table. The Khmer people were portrayed digging for roots in the forest and praying for rain. . . The orphans' play was really a series of sketches with running commentary by an old Khmer servitor. When he repeated such maxims as, 'All work is good', and, 'Science is the great thing', there were approving whispers among the audience and even applause when one of the characters said: 'I learnt geography at the lycée, but I never knew till now how the peasants really lived.'[40]

Twenty years later another group of intellectuals made two of these maxims very widely known throughout Kampuchea. But by this time, not only were they driven home with brutal force, but also their meaning had become distorted, and the respect for modern science had largely been abandoned along the way. ('All work is good', and 'the rice-field is your diploma', were slogans repeated *ad nauseam* by cadres of Democratic Kampuchea after 1975.)

As the year 1958 began, most of the leaders and members of the KPRP had settled down in stable pursuits. Those in the countryside were no threat to the Sihanouk regime, and were now much more likely to be left alone by the authorities than in the immediate post-Geneva period. If they did feel threatened, they could find safe refuge in Phnom Penh, as had Vietnamese communist leaders such as Le Duan (in 1957)[41] and even the Cao Dai Pope, Pham Cong Tac, who had been *officially* accepted as a political refugee from South Vietnam in 1956.[42]

Meanwhile, most of the thousand Khmers who had resettled in Hanoi, a group which included a dozen or so women, had completed courses in the Vietnamese language and now began extensive training in political and military spheres (the latter including flight, naval and armoured training) and in various technical fields such as engineering, agriculture and medicine. Some, however, notably the leaders, took up administrative positions in the Democratic Republic of Vietnam. Son Ngoc Minh was named in one Vietnamese Communist document as President of the People's Liberation Committee of the Nambo

Region (southern Vietnam). Chan Samay, who like Minh was perhaps considered a Vietnamese citizen because of his Khmer Krom origins, was named 'Director of Ethnic Minorities' in Hanoi. Less senior figures took up various other responsibilities, in much the same way as many European communists did in the Soviet Union in the 1920s. Over a hundred Khmers graduated as officers and became military instructors in the Vietnam People's Army. One was posted to the Son Tay military academy, where he instructed Vietnamese officers who were about to set out down the Ho Chi Minh Trail, in the 'complexities of jungle travel and jungle combat'. Another, who was jokingly described as an 'all-weather cadre', worked in a range of jobs, including one as Secretary of a provincial vocational school, and was finally attached to the foreign relations department of the Vietnam Workers' Party, headed by Xuan Thuy. Chea Keo, who was already fluent in Thai, Lao, French and Vietnamese, added English, Chinese and Russian to his repertoire.[43] Others performed tasks abroad. Leav Keo Moni, formerly of the KNLC, spent most of the 1954–70 period working with the Pathet Lao and in liaison with the Thai communists.[44] About fifty Khmers (including Mey Pho, Rath Samuoeun, Yun Soeun, and So Phim's nephew Sa Bin) were sent for several years' political study to China, apparently in three groups. (None went to the Soviet Union, however.) One member of the first group, Chea Soth, worked with the Beijing Radio foreign broadcasting service.[45] All Khmers were given a variety of responsibilities and types of training, apparently in an attempt to broaden their political and military experience. Nearly all were eventually admitted to the Khmer People's Revolutionary Party. They were forbidden to receive mail from home, but Khmers held regular meetings, at which people were informed about the situation in Kampuchea on the basis of foreign news reports and messages received from Tou Samouth. In one sense these people were hostages to the nexus between the policies of Sihanouk and Hanoi. But in the final analysis there seems no reason to doubt their loyalty to the cause of revolution in Kampuchea.

At home, 1958 was a year of mixed blessings for the Khmer revolutionaries. The *Pracheachon* newspaper, edited by Nop Bophann, had attained a circulation of 3,200 and two new companion papers, *Mittapeap* ('Friendship') and *Ekapeap* ('Unity') were publishing another 4,500 copies per week. A fourth communist organ, *Samleng Kommakor* ('The Workers' Voice') also began distribution but closed down after achieving a circulation of 1,500.[46] In all, this represents for the communist papers about 20 per cent of the total readership of Khmer-language newspapers at the time.[47] (The circulation in this period of the other leftist paper, Son Phuoc Tho's *Meatophum,* which appeared three times a week, is unknown.) Anti-communist sources conceded that the Pracheachon press was 'rather significant' in this period.[48] This was no mean feat, given that only four years previously Khmer communist influence in the capital had been negligible, and that most supporters were illiterate peasants in remote areas, to which distribution of newspapers was difficult and subject to sporadic police confiscation. Sympathetic monks were usually relied upon to carry bundles of newspapers to villages, where they would be distributed free. At the same time, the Pracheachon published a number of booklets, also in Khmer. These included several 'Declarations' on national issues, and the Group's own political programme, but also pamphlets on 'National Culture', 'The Democratic System', and 'The Sino-Khmer Minority'. It also organized a trade union, the Transport and Portage Workers' Association (*Samakhum kommakor li saing duk noam*), with an office in the capital.[49] The KPRP, for its part, engaged in clandestine propaganda work through two journals called *Kommakor* ('Worker') and *Yuvachon Chhean Mukh* ('Progressive Youth').[50]

Elections for a new National Assembly were held in March 1958. According to Charles Meyer: 'Prince Sihanouk personally designated the sixty-two candidates for the sixty-two seats. . . Only the Pracheachon dared to stand five candidates against them, in Phnom Penh, Kampot, Battambang, Svay Rieng and Takeo, but the poor devils were never able to hold public meetings nor even publicize their programme. Only one, Keo Meas, held out in the capital, obtaining 396 votes.'[51] This appears to highlight the communists' vulnerability in the rural areas, if they offered a direct political challenge (it is revealing that no Pracheachon candidate was even nominated in Kompong Cham), and the relative safety of the capital in those conditions. Interestingly, given the silencing of the Pracheachon and the extremely low turnout of urban voters in contested national elections, Keo Meas's share of the vote was far from negligible: in the 1966 elections, for instance, a Phnom Penh seat was won with only 1,066 votes.[52] Nevertheless, Meas apparently saw little use in his remaining in the city, and went underground in the countryside soon afterwards. Pol Pot became Secretary of the Phnom Penh Party branch, which according to his own account meant that he was 'in charge of liaison with the countryside',[53] and so was obviously a key post in the organizational sense. He soon brought Vorn Vet into the City Party Committee, with responsibility for 'workers and the city population'.[54]

At the same time, Sihanouk set out to co-opt young members of the left into the Sangkum. As a result, Hou Yuon became Minister of Commerce and Industry in the new Cabinet; Hu Nim, who had moved steadily towards a socialist position after the dissolution of the Democratic Party, also won a seat in the assembly elections and became Under-Secretary of State in the Office of the Prime Minister. Other French-educated leftists, Uch Ven and Chau Sau, won seats also. Chau Sau held senior ministerial posts for the next four years, Hou Yuon for the next two years, and Hu Nim minor ones for sixteen months.[55] Over the next nine years, Yuon and Nim in particular also developed for themselves a solid base of popular support in the districts they represented, in Kompong Cham province. Hu Nim organized fund-raising for two *wats* there, and also set up a new high school at Prey Totoeng[56] (which ironically was the venue for his eventual exit from the open political scene).

The position of the left in Kampuchea in 1958, then, was not like that of the Communist Party of Indonesia (PKI), to which the allocation of important roles in a multi-party 'Guided Democracy' had already been foreshadowed by Sukarno; but neither was it similar to that of leftists in neighbouring Thailand, who, after a period of relative liberalism which was halted by successive coups in 1957 and 1958, were now hunted down in large numbers — let alone that in South Vietnam under Ngo Dinh Diem. Nor was the situation in Kampuchea analogous to the increasingly ravaged neutrality of Laos. There, agreement had been reached in 1957 on a coalition government of leftist and rightist forces, and partial elections the following May gave the left thirteen National Assembly seats; but by August 1958 Pathet Lao Ministers had been excluded from the government, and there then followed a purge of leftists in the administration. In January 1959 martial law was proclaimed; then, in May, Pathet Lao units in the army were surrounded and all Pathet Lao leaders in the capital arrested, and in December military forces sponsored by the CIA staged a coup. By early 1960, therefore, the Lao communists had 'switched from political struggle into the armed struggle and combined the two forms'.[57] There seemed little need even for such a carefully calibrated change in the strategy of the Kampuchean communists, who had something to show for their restrained attitude towards Sihanouk.

But despite Sihanouk's firm neutralist posture there were nuances in his policies towards the left to which the KPRP may have been at a loss to respond. On the international scene, he recognized the People's Republic of China in July 1958. He did sign a trade agreement with Hanoi four months later, but held off establishing diplomatic relations, and it should have been clear that he was attempting to bring Chinese pressure to bear on the Vietnamese communists and on their much closer relationship with the KPRP leaders. Early in the year Sihanouk said: 'As for the Vietminh, they don't have the same scruples as the Chinese towards us (nor the same sympathies). If they could, they would eagerly and rapidly control our destiny. They utilize all their tenacity, their guile, their craftiness to 'guide' those of our compatriots who, through weakness or ambition, accept their counsel.'[58] This strategy of prising a diplomatic wedge between Hanoi and Beijing was to remain one of the cornerstones of Sihanouk's foreign policy. It was, of course, a strategy that eventually fitted in with Chinese aims in the region — in the late 1950s, Zhou Enlai went as far as encouraging Sihanouk to lay claim to what was then undisputed Vietnamese territory.[59] And once the cracks had begun to appear in the world communist monolith, China both pressured the Vietnamese communists to reduce support for the KPRP and at the same time cultivated the emergence of a new Kampuchean communist leadership which, partly in reaction to what it saw as Hanoi's abandonment of the movement, would align itself with Beijing.

Secondly, on the domestic scene, Sihanouk favoured the younger, French-trained radicals over and above the Vietnamese-trained KPRP veterans in the Pracheachon Group. He hoped that the younger group would become 'bourgeoisified', and he was aware that they tended to scorn their peasant comrades. As he remarked a few years later: 'Our 'left and progressive' intellectuals do not like a very extensive promiscuity with the not very intellectual former servants of the Vietminh.'[60] It is true that the two groups were still closely linked and that the inclusion of members of the former in the Cabinet no doubt encouraged the latter to refrain from anti-government activities;

however, the result of according the younger militants physical security and a modicum of power, while subjecting the veterans to sporadic repression and contemptuous alienation, was also to be divisive, and to strengthen the relative position of the former. It is ironic that the veterans, with their longer political experience, were, as we shall see, more able to cope with their rejection by the regime. The youthful militants were less able to withstand either the temptations offered by their relative proximity to power or the resultant disappointment with Sihanouk's refusal to allow them complete authority to modernise the country as they saw fit. Thus, their attitudes hardened, whereas the veterans tended to roll with the punches, as people of peasant origin often have to do. There were exceptions in each leftist group (Notably Hou Yuon among the younger ones, Nuon Chea and Mok among the older) but these may be said to prove the rule.

The leftist balance in Sihanouk's international and domestic neutralist scales was thus constructed to divide the domestic and international left. Of course there were other factors such as Sihanouk's need for educated ministers. However, by pinning down that section of the left most inclined towards political moderation, and promoting the section more prone to be hotheaded, he eventually effected a transformation of the local communist movement from a Vietnamese-oriented group led by former peasants, displaying patience and caution in both political and social demands, to a Chinese-oriented one led by intellectuals, advocating social and political upheaval. Sihanouk's mistake was to underestimate the strength of the left in his country, and to believe that buying off individuals and creating internal dissension would destroy it. (In one sense, of course, this belief was vindicated, but only after the communists had actually achieved state power.)

The KPRP's analysis at this stage is clear enough. Sihanouk's personal popularity among peasants, even in remote areas, was assured, now that he had proved himself a patriot. Leaving aside the question of the depth of peasant devotion to the monarchy *per se,* the removal of the French colonial presence had allowed peasants to cease paying taxes on their crops, and collections effectively lapsed.[61] (Of course, this was also partly a result of the destruction of numerous subdistrict and district official records by the rebels during the war.) Further, in 1959 the government passed a law providing for the election of subdistrict chiefs and committees, which made for an unprecedented extension of local democracy — although the provincial administration did retain a veto over the candidates.[62] At the same time, the repression of the Party during the 1955 elections had dealt a shattering blow to its morale, and its leaders were virtually excluded from any role in the established political structure. The KPRP leaders privately held Sihanouk just as responsible for this as other figures of the regime who had more direct control of the security forces, such as Lon Nol, Dap Chhuon and Kou Roun; but they nevertheless regarded the Prince's stand on independence as having the potential eventually to divide the country's ruling circles to the advantage of the Party. Thus, in its political propaganda, the Pracheachon distinguished Sihanouk from the others, and emphasized that the communists wished to 'advance the Prince's task of independence and democratization' and to strengthen his neutralist posture. He was a 'national hero', but pictured as vulnerable and in need of support in the struggle against 'foreign saboteurs'.[63]

This position was consonant with the policies of Hanoi, designed to encourage Sihanouk's independence from the US. In March 1958, Vietnam News Agency reported with approval the words of Sihanouk's Premier Penn Nouth, when he 'called on Cambodian youth to rally around the Throne and support the country's neutral policy'. As Gareth Porter has pointed out, this report indicated that Hanoi now accepted the link between neutralism and the Throne.[64]

The KPRP position also received encouragement from further afield. In 1956, according to a Pol Pot regime document: 'The Soviet Party publicized the resolution adopted at the Twentieth Congress. . . Touch Phoeun, Chi Kim An, Keo Meas, Ya (Ney Sarann), Sien An, Chey Suon (Non Suon) and others fully supported it as they believed that the Soviet Party was older and thus was more experienced. Class division in Kampuchean society was non-existent. The Kampuchean people needed peace and should not be led to war. Sihanouk was a progressive king with whom we should continue to unite.'[65] Non Suon himself later 'confessed' that 'In early 1959, the Pracheachon Group used the declaration of the Moscow Conference of 81 Parties for study and for the instruction of cadres. This was not only the Vietnamese project, but Soviet revisionism was also influential.'[66] If the Khmer communists had moved to a formal posture of 'peaceful coexistence' with capitalism, for their part the Chinese and Vietnamese communists never accepted this 'revisionist' doctrine of Khrushchev's, and the 1973 Kampuchean Party History noted that this 'period of revisionism . . . abroad. . . destroyed our Party'.[67] In fact, however, the policies of all four parties on Kampuchea were similar because of Sihanouk's neutrality, which took up where peaceful coexistence left off.

In August 1958, Non Suon spent a month as a member of a press delegation in China, North Korea and North Vietnam, where he met Son Ngoc Minh and was given a letter to deliver to Party leaders at home.[68] Its contents are unknown, but they most probably expressed support for current KPRP policy. The next year Son Sen, who was to join the KPRP in 1960, visited Czechoslovakia to study educational and youth training facilities, while Hu Nim and Son Phuoc Tho visited Poland, Czechoslovakia and East Germany. Tho reported on the visit in *Meatophum*, and Nim in the Sangkum organ *Réalités Cambodgiennnes* and in another paper, *Pracheaserei* ('Free People'). Khieu Samphan returned from his studies in France and in September 1959 began publishing yet another left-wing paper, the French-language *Observateur;* he also took a job at Chamroeun Vichea high school. The next year, Ieng Sary's wife Ieng Thirith established an English-language high school in Phnom Penh. One teacher she employed was Leng Sim Hak, the wife of a young radical educationalist named Tiv Ol, who like Sen joined the KPRP that year, as did also a reporter for *L'Observateur* named Koy Thuon. National political life remained relatively open and the left still benefitted from 'easy communication routes'.

It is significant that no evidence exists to support Pol Pot's statement many years later that nearly half the Party's membership were killed or apprehended by government forces in the 1955–59 period,[69] prior to his appointment to the Central Committee. The repression that occurred was sporadic and localized. In Krek, Kompong Cham, in 1957, what a local informant described as 'Lon Nol people' arrested eleven women married to former UIF personnel and held them for five months in a military base.[70] In nearby Tbaung Khmum the next year, Mat Ly, a UIF cadre who says he had been tortured by the French, was once again arrested and held for twelve months.[71] In these and later years, such arrests and several assassinations by government forces certainly played a role in keeping many Party cadres inactive (or in the words of the 1973 History, in 'destroying' the Party), but so too did the knowledge that

Sihanouk's regime was moving in a fairly progressive direction, in economic as well as foreign policies.

In October 1959, Son Ngoc Thanh, now established in Saigon, published 'The Manifesto of the Khmer Serei [Free Khmer] Movement'. He claimed that Sihanouk was allowing the 'communization' of Kampuchea, and drew the Prince's attention to the 'pupils, high school and normal-school students, porters and dockers who have transferred to North Vietnam to join the Khmer communist army at Hoa Binh'; but his description of communist work in Kampuchea itself revealed no armed activity whatsoever. In Battambang, Pursat and Kompong Cham, Thanh wrote, members of various Khmer communist cells were engaged in 'recruitment, liaison and propaganda', in Kampot in 'becoming farmers in order to recruit the Cambodian peasants', and in Kratie in 'becoming teachers'. 'Some communists are Ministers' in the government, Thanh lamented.[72] In fact the Khmer revolutionaries were not at all on the offensive, but neither were they in the process of being annihilated.

Problems in the Party leadership *did* hamper its activities. In 1958, according to Non Suon: 'Tou Samouth. . . warned me about confusion in Sieu Heng's stance and consciousness. He said that if I met Sieu Heng by chance I was to act naturally and get away.'[73] While Heng undoubtedly undermined much of the KPRP's effectiveness in his four years as a Lon Nol agent, the drawn-out suspicion of him was probably even more damaging in terms of disunity and demoralization. In 1959, Heng openly defected to the authorities. The 1973 Party History criticizes him for teaching 'the people. . . that there was no struggle between the social classes' and for following 'the ruling class with Sihanouk at its head', *but also* for thinking 'only of money', for suspending 'the indoctrination, criticism and self-criticism sessions on organization', and for his failure to join an undisclosed 'struggle' (led by Tou Samouth) against the January 1959 anti-Sihanouk coup attempt made by right-wing plotters Dap Chhuon and Sam Sary.[74] Such a contradictory array of positions suggests that Sieu Heng was simply tired of politics. Satisfied perhaps, with the progress he had seen in the country since taking up the independence struggle in 1944,[75] or at least unwilling to run the risks involved in attempting to achieve more, Heng went back to growing rice in his native Battambang. Although he was probably alone in being prepared to buy his security by informing on his comrades, his motives were perhaps not dissimilar to those of his comrade N.T. Nhung. Nhung, in the words of a sympathetic Vietnamese communist, 'was much terrorized, and abandoned the Party line to lead an ordinary life'[76] — an option that was not open, incidentally, to terrorized communist cadres in neighbouring South Vietnam. Nor for that matter would Heng's motives have been dissimilar to those, in the words of the 1973 History, of the '90 per cent of the cadres and Party members [who] had become passive, and carried out no heroic acts', and of 'a number of regional committees [who were] submissive to the enemy'.[77] The second phase of the KPRP's existence, after its expansion from 1951 to 1954, was plagued by a serious loss of momentum. But there had been gains, and the alternative strategy — that of armed struggle after the gaining of independence — would have isolated the Party as effectively as it did Son Ngoc Thanh's movement.

With Son Ngoc Minh in Vietnam, the KPRP's temporary Central Committee now consisted of only Tou Samouth and So Phim.[78] Samouth was indefatigable. Sang Lon recalls him making a secret visit to eastern Kompong Cham in 1957, and attempting to raise the morale of cadres. 'He called six or seven of us, one or two from each sub-district in the area, to go into the forest and study politics with him, at night. He told us: "You must wake up and struggle. Who will struggle for us if we don't? We ourselves are the masters. If we do not struggle, we would be serving the US imperialists. We cannot just let things happen, we must get up and struggle again."'[79] Samouth's emphasis on 'self-reliance' is similar to that of later Pol Pot decalarations, but the target he identified — US imperialism — suggests that, just as in the early 1950s when the 'anti-feudal' struggle was played down, Samouth did not accept the view that the Sihanouk regime was the primary enemy of the Party. (Certainly, Pol Pot's regime was in 1978 to describe Samouth as a Vietnamese 'puppet', and the KPRP as having 'existed only in name';[80] Pot himself claims to have begun, in 1957, two years of 'preparations for the founding of the Communist Party of Kampuchea'.[81])

The right-wing coup attempt was foiled (not by the left, but by Lon Nol) in January-February 1959. Dap Chhuon was killed, and Sam Sary fled to Thailand and joined up with Son Ngoc Thanh. Coming after the June 1958 South Vietnamese incursion into Stung Treng province, and soon followed by CIA-South Vietnamese attempts to assassinate Sihanouk, it had the overall effect of strengthening the Prince's anti-US feelings. On the domestic scene, Lon Nol now emerged as one of the most powerful figures of the regime, and although there is no reason to distinguish him from Sihanouk in this period, increased repression followed. Chan Dara, who had been growing rice in Kompong Chhnang since his defection from the UIF in 1952,[82] was rounded up along with several former Democrats and Dap Chhuon supporters, and gaoled for three years. A vindictive provincial governor told Chan Dara's wife and daughter that he had been doused with petrol and burned alive after being sentenced to death by a Phnom Penh court; Chan Dara himself says that as a result they 'were so shocked that they became ill and died'.[83] Dap Chhuon's brother and one other prisoner were sentenced to death. Then on 11 October 1959, the editor of *Pracheachon*, Nop Bophann, was shot dead outside a military barracks in the centre of Phnom Penh.[84]

The 1973 Party History claims that repression now reached a crescendo: 'Towards the end of 1959 the enemy violently attacked the revolution in the countryside. Numerous bases were invaded by the enemy, who slaughtered everyone there.'[85] However, I have been unable to find corroborating evidence for this statement. It may refer to 'bases' in the remote North-East of the country, about which little information is available. (In 1959, according to one writer, two new provinces, Rattanakiri and Mondolkiri, were created there, and put under military administration.[86]) But there is in any case a question-mark beside this passage in the margin of the original party document.[87]

In fact the KPRP was in *internal* disarray. With the open defection of Sieu Heng, Tou Samouth's urban Party committee was officially 'named the committee in charge of the country's general affairs', and was charged with the task of 'organizing the Second Congress towards the end of 1959'. A three-year period of organization began, and the Congress was postponed until September 1960, when it would bring together 'representatives of all branches of operations, overt as well as secret, in the cities and the countryside.'[88]

The ambivalence of the KPRP's status on the national political scene justified its strategy of distinguishing between different sections of the ruling class, but at the same time it kept the communists off balance. In February 1960, for instance, Sihanouk praised Khieu Samphan's *Observateur* for treating 'us with some fairness in recognizing that the progress we have sponsored is without precedent in our history'.[89] Then on 13 July, Khieu Samphan was beaten up in the street, by members of Kou Roun's security services.[90] In mid August, about thirty leftists were arrested and interrogated in the capital; eighteen of them were detained, including Khieu Samphan, Non Suon, Chou Chet (who had replaced Nop Bophann) and most of the staff of *Pracheachon, Mittapeap* and *Ekapeap*.[91] Non Suon was beaten up in gaol. All four left-wing newspapers were banned; one reason given was Pracheachon opposition to Sihanouk's plans to teach French in primary schools. Sihanouk said he would prosecute the newspapers for treason, and his government produced a book of 'treasonous' articles they had published, but no charges were laid and the prisoners were all released on 21 September.[92] The editor of *Ekapeap* was briefly interrogated by the police the following month. But the veterans adhered to their stand, which they had published in June 1960 in the following 'Declaration of the Pracheachon Group':

> . . . imperialism, neighbouring countries, and treason are preparing mortal aggression against neutral, independent, peaceful Cambodia. . . Imperialism will try to eliminate the Prince, our Head of State, by any means. . . It will try to break the unity of the Khmers . . .
>
> In these grave circumstances, the Pracheachon Group appeals to its members and the entire Khmer people. . .
>
> — not to be intimidated by the imperialist threat to cut off aid or to stage an economic blockade, following the example of the Cuban people who are not for one second influenced by the imperialists. . .
>
> — to have confidence in these words of Samdech Preah Upayuvareach [Sihanouk's royal title]: 'We are not afraid of the difficulties of an economic blockade. . .'
>
> — to maintain intact national unity around Samdech Preah Upayuvareach, and raise high their consciousness of struggle, increase their vigilance, and prepare to give their lives in confronting, under the leadership of Samdech Preah Upayuvareach Norodom Sihanouk, all enemy aggression against our policy of neutrality and our national leader.[93]

Some of this was of course mere rhetoric, the slavish expression of loyalty that was necessary to keep the movement from being smashed. But had the KPRP and Pracheachon leaders not believed a good deal of it, they would not have remained in the capital, exposing their members through legal activities, but would already have taken to the jungle in armed insurgency as had other communist parties in South-East Asia who *were* confronted with pro-American governments. Sihanouk, however, does not appear to have agreed.

But the Party was evidently capable of weathering the outbreak of repression, for a week after the detainees were released, in a room at the Phnom Penh railway station, began the Party's Second Congress.[94]

The twenty-one KPRP leaders who attended included seven representatives of the urban movement. But the meeting did not represent a turning-point in the Party's activities. Its name was changed to the 'Workers' Party of Kampuchea' (*Pak Polakor Kampuchea*),[95] following the lead of the Vietnamese Party but also signifying the assumption of equal Marxist-Leninist status, with the Party as the vanguard of the *working class* and not simply of the nation.

The Congress elected Tou Samouth as Party Secretary, and Nuon Chea as his deputy, effectively maintaining the pre-1954 leadership. Pol Pot was elected to the No. 3 position and to membership of the Politburo. The Central Committee was completed by a French-educated teacher known as Moong (perhaps the man later known as Koy Thuon, who had just joined the Party), Ieng Sary, Keo Meas, Son Ngoc Minh (absent), So Phim and two candidate members, Prasith and Non Suon.[96] It is significant that students who had returned from France, through their influence on the Phnom Penh Party Committee — easily the largest urban committee in a Party many of whose rural committees had ceased functioning — had emerged in positions 3, 4 and 5 in the hierarchy. If 90 per cent of the KPRP's membership had in fact 'become passive', then active Party cadres would now have numbered about one to two hundred;[97] at any rate, overall membership was sufficiently small and scattered for twenty or so educated and confident young militants, concentrated in the capital and represented by a third of the participants at the Congress, to exert considerable influence. The promotion to the No. 4 position of Moong, if indeed he *was* Koy Thuon, then a teacher in Kompong Cham, signalled an important tendency in the Party's recruitment policies. Ouch Bun Chhoeun, a student in Memut at the time, recalls that 'Thuon was called a 'mobile cadre' then. . . he was in charge of students and sowing [the revolutionary 'seed']'.[98]

What distinguished most of the French-educated radicals from the veterans of the independence struggle was, as before, their conception of the Sihanouk regime. The Pol Pot group tended to be implacably opposed to it, as a backward, dictatorial monarchy; as younger militants they wanted to strike back against repression, and being more middle-class in background they were particularly infuriated by Sihanouk's 'feudal' characteristics, his personalized autocracy, and the fawning praise of him that was required of everyone in public life. The veterans, on the other hand, were much more inclined to see Sihanouk's neutrality and his increasingly anti-imperialist stance as positive factors in an Indo-China-wide struggle for socialism, while at the same time also giving the Prince credit for maintaining the country's independence, a goal for which they themselves had sacrificed much in the past. It is also likely that, through their closer relationship with the rural masses, they appreciated the fact of Sihanouk's popularity, and the fact that independence did actually mean something concrete for the peasants, in particular, perhaps, *de facto* cessation of government taxation of the rice harvest and an end to rural insecurity. Non Suon suggested this sixteen years later when he told his Pol Pot regime interrogators that 'the propertyless people follow economics as well as principles' (by the latter presumably meaning theoretical dogma). Discussing the reasons for the existence of the Pracheachon Group, he said he 'felt that the fate of the Kampuchean people and revolution required that the propertyless should lead, not the intellectuals from France — persons who are of the upper class. . . propertyless people do not [just] follow principles.'[99]

The 'principle' of national independence was a major issue at the 1960 Congress. Pol Pot said in 1977: 'At that time, Cambodia was a satellite of imperialism, of US imperialism in particular. This means that Cambodia was not independent. . . This was one analysis. Did this analysis generate any conflicting opinion? Yes, it did. There were conflicts within our ranks and within elements inside the national community. There were a number of factions which thought that Cambodia was independent. Some said it achieved independence in 1949 while others claimed it was independent in 1954 through the Geneva agreement. . . However, through our analysis we found that Cambodia was not independent.'[100] Pol Pot's omission of the year 1953 (when Sihanouk claimed to have achieved independence) as a date worthy of consideration exemplifies the nature of the conflict within the Party. (Few members would have given consideration to the year 1949 in this context.) Although they dated independence from 1954, the veteran Khmer communists did believe that Sihanouk's regime was an independent one with whose nationalism they could make common cause, if only for tactical reasons. According to the Pol Pot regime's *Black Book*, in this period 'the Party had not yet achieved its unity throughout the country', a situation which it blamed on 'certain elements' of the Pracheachon Group, among others.[101]

Just as the Pol Pot regime later advanced the Party's founding date, and that of its First Congress, from 1951 to 1960, so too it pushed subsequent decisions back in time in order to erase memory of the policies that delayed them.

This explains its claim that the 1960 Congress adopted a strategy of 'combined political and armed struggle' to build a revolutionary army,[102] whereas it was in fact the veterans' position of political struggle that prevailed. ('Combined armed and political struggle' was not adopted until 1967, as we shall see.)[103] Chou Chet, for instance, set up another newspaper soon after his release from gaol; its title, *Pancha Sila*[104] (the 'Five Principles' of Peaceful Coexistence), indicates continuing party emphasis on the value of Sihanouk's neutrality and on political struggle within the framework of his regime. Even among the returned students, Hou Yuon, as we have seen, recognized this as the immediate priority. Khieu Samphan, too, had even dedicated his PhD thesis to Sihanouk the year before; in it he quoted with approval Sihanouk's views on the problems associated with the acceptance of US military aid,[105] and wrote that 'the struggle for peace in South-East Asia and against military pacts belongs in the framework of our economic development efforts,'[106] a clear acknowledgement of the importance of regional developments and of Sihanouk's foreign policy, not just for independence but also for domestic progress. It would take more than one dose of official repression to change Samphan's stance. Ngo Dien, then a journalist for the Vietnam News Agency, worked in Phnom Penh from 1959 to 1962; he recalls: 'I knew Hou Yuon, Khieu Samphan, Ieng Sary, Ieng Thirith, Non Suon and Chou Chet. They were all having a difficult time with the treason of Sieu Heng and Sihanouk's repression. Hou Yuon harboured a certain bitterness about it but did not blame us Vietnamese. Khieu Samphan was quite reasonable also, but Ieng Sary and Ieng Thirith were very tough-minded.'[107] (A 1981 Democratic Kampuchea statement even claimed that the Communist Party of Kampuchea had been founded in 1960 'in order to fight the Vietnamese'.[108])

The line actually adopted at the Congress was probably the one described by Non Suon in his 1976 confession. According to a verbal summary by his Pol Pot interrogators of his statements about this period: 'He said his Party follows the path of the Vietnamese Party; if other people scold him as Viet Minh or a Vietnamese slave, let them scold. But his Party holds the principle of independence, not like the Lao who let the Vietnamese control state power along with them. His group takes Vietnamese experience, but with the Khmer holding state power.'[109] The reference to Laos would seem to express a distinction formulated only much later, since Non Suon did not see the 1960 Congress as a breakthrough in the Party's independent development; in fact, he describes it merely as 'the study-session in the railway station'.[110] The choice of the name 'Workers' Party', along with the fact that the Congress took place less than three weeks after the Vietnam Workers' Party Third Congress had decided to form the National Liberation Front, brings home the attachment of the Khmer communists in this period to what they continued to see as both independence *and* solidarity with Vietnam.[111]

For the Pol Pot group, though, the significance of the 1960 Congress was that they were now in a position to launch initiatives. Pol Pot claims to have been 'elected' Deputy Party Secretary the next year,[112] replacing Nuon Chea. Party cadres in the East of the country, at least, were apparently unaware of this, and describe him as still being Tou Samouth's 'administrative secretary' (*protean muntir*) in 1962.[113] This does not mean that the promotion did not occur, but it raises questions about the secretive nature of Pol Pot's rise to power. Also in 1961, according to a US intelligence source, Ieng Sary 'travelled from Phnom Penh to outlying provincial areas with the intent of regrouping and reorganizing the defunct cells'[114] of former UIF cadre. As part of the same process, it seems, a network of 'secret defence units' were established, made up of youths whose task was the physical protection of cadres.[115] July 1961 saw the inauguration of a secret Communist Women's Organization, headed by Pol Pot's wife, Khieu Ponnary, and in February 1962, the secret Alliance of Democratic Kampuchean Youth (*Sampoan Yuvachon Kampuchea Pracheathipateiy*) was established. A later CPK document notes that 'the Party began... the combat movement of youth. . . in 1962'.[116]

On the open political stage, 1961 saw a continuation of the ambivalent status enjoyed by the left. A dispute with Thailand flared up over its support for the rightist Khmer Serei, and led to Sihanouk severing diplomatic relations with Bangkok in October.

Hu Nim was now Deputy President of the National Assembly, and was chosen to represent it alongside Sihanouk at the First Summit of the Non-Aligned Nations in Belgrade, and as a member of the UN Fourth Committee on decolonisation. However, in August, Sihanouk called a Special National Congress for the purpose of denouncing the 'treason' of the Pracheachon Group. He claimed to have demonstrated his case when Non Suon reaffirmed the resistance veterans' past and present ties with Vietnamese communism.[117] Sihanouk then said of him: 'We have too many memories in common which unite us. I cannot bring myself to lose an old enemy. I therefore prefer to allow the Pracheachon to continue to subsist.'[118] There were no charges laid and no arrests. Soon after, Sihanouk took offence at domestic criticisms voiced in *Pancha Sila*, and after a radio debate with him, Chou Chet apologized and asked for forgiveness.[119] In December the Pracheachon paper was formally allowed to recommence publication. Chou Chet left *Pancha Sila*, which now became a weekly, in the hands of associates and resumed the editorship of his old masthead.[120]

One evening that December, Pracheachon Group leaders Keo Meas, Non Suon, Ney Sarann, Chou Chet and Um Neng met at Sarann's house in the capital to plan tactics for the National Assembly elections scheduled for June 1962. According to Suon: 'In my view, this was a continuation of the Group's 1955 committee. . . Keo Meas said he had the Party's agreement from Tou Samouth, and I knew he was in close contact with the Party. I believed that close co-operation with Vietnam was to continue, against the common enemy, imperialism. . . This was never discussed in the Group, it was accepted by all.'[121] However, it seems that, unknown to Suon and perhaps to Tou Samouth at the time, the Pol Pot group had decided that since Sihanouk's political system had to be overthrown by armed rebellion, the Pracheachon should not contest the 1962 elections. Thus, those present at the meeting were years later accused of attempting to form a new 'Pracheachon Party' whose programme was 'internationally pro-Soviet'; Suon was considered a traitor and was forced to confess that his 'big mistake was relying on Vietnam, on their armed forces in case of war'.[122]

For its part, the 1973 Party History celebrates 'the struggle against the enemy secretly or overtly in the elections', not just those of 1955 and 1958, but those of 1962 as well.[123] Regardless of the political significance of this as further evidence of Party views different from those of Pol Pot, the statement is untrue. The Pracheachon did *not* contest the June 1962 elections.

On 10 January, fourteen members of the Pracheachon were arrested at Suong in Kompong Cham. The detainees, mostly locals, allegedly told police that they were under orders from Non Suon to collect military and political intelligence in the area. Suon was then arrested in Phnom Penh, and all were charged with plotting against the state, and committed for trial before a military tribunal. The charges seem contradictory; on the one hand, the accused were said to be part of a 'spy network' gathering information about military posts along the Viet-namese border; on the other hand, according to an article on the subject in the semi-official *Réalités Cambodgiennes:* 'In fact, on the eve of the poll the Pracheachon is intensifying its intoxication campaign not only to secure the best possible chance for the election but also to justify itself in the eyes of its foreign masters.'[124] However, assuming that the first charge was not trumped-up, the Pracheachon may well have been consistently pursuing its traditional solidarity with the Vietnamese commun-ists — both in its espionage, and in its decision to accept the framework of the Sihanoukist state by contesting the elections.

On 26 January, a *Pracheachon* editorial written by Chou Chet accused the Ministry of National Security of 'carrying out all kinds of activities to make life hard' for the Pracheachon Group. Chet was already in trouble with the police over his claims that the government had suppressed its anti-corruption bureaux, for which he was liable to be charged with 'criticism harmful to government action' and sentenced to a gaol term of between one month and one year. So when he pursued his attacks on the Security forces for their 'absolute shamelessness which is proper to imperialists' he and a colleague were arrested and placed in detention, and *Pracheachon* was closed down by the government.[125]

The Party's reaction to these events seems finely distinguished but again clear. Firstly, a new newspaper was established, *Samleng Apyiakrit* ('The Voice of Neutrality'), whose title indicates continuing emphasis on the value of Sihanouk's foreign policy for the revolutionary cause. Another communist-oriented paper, *Yuvamitt* ('Young Friends') soon appeared, with a weekly circulation of a thousand.[126] But for the first time, there was no real chance of even contesting the elections. According to documents captured by Sihanouk's police soon after they had been 'introduced into Kampuchea by the famous Setha [Tou Samouth][127] on his return from Vietnam': 'In the upcoming elections there is no need for us to present candidates, since the results of these elections are known in advance and cannot evidence the power of our movement, given the fact that the people are undergoing the oppression of Sihanouk's police and Army and will be unable to clearly demonstrate their support.'[128]

According to the Prince, the 'Sangkum fortress' was described in the documents as 'a traitor to the Khmer people', and accused of masterminding the repression. On the other hand, however, the 'enemy' was described as being 'the feudalists and *national* reactionaries', who are similar to 'colonialists and *foreign* imperialists' only in the sense that they 'do not capitulate easily' and 'are presently struggling ferociously to safeguard their privileges'. There was no accusation of foreign control over Kampuchea, or of a lack of national independence. On the contrary, note was taken of 'the solid implantation of Sihanouk's party on Kampuchean soil' as an unfortunate fact that had to be recognized. The document ends with a recommendation for continuing restraint, and confidence in the revolutionary developments in Laos and Vietnam, where victories would lead 'immediately after' to victory in Kampuchea. 'Sooner or later, our just cause will triumph. . . Our cadres and people should thus arm themselves with a little patience. For the moment they should remain relatively discreet. . . Our interest, therefore, is to make the confidence of the young intellectuals who sympathize with our movement, who have been successful in introducing themselves into the Sangkum and who will be chosen to be their 'deputies'.'[129]

This restrained approach was not without its successes. A non-socialist Western observer, one of the few students of Kampuchean domestic politics in this period, wrote in early 1962: 'The only party to retain its identity outside of the popular ruling movement has been the Pracheachon, which has now not only become the focus of dissent within the country but also has the reputation of being a young party. Moreover, its left-wing (pro-communist) leanings have aroused sympathy, particularly among the student population.'[130] In the eyes of Pol Pot, on the other hand, in this period 'the movement for the implementation of the Party line. . . had not yet taken great leaps'[131] — largely because what he had in mind was not yet the Party line.

Sihanouk's cracking down on the Pracheachon augured badly for the country in that there was no longer a specific 'focus of dissent', let alone one that seemed prepared to support many of his policies even as the government was 'making life hard' for it. This incidence of Sihanoukist autocracy proved to be pure folly.

In May 1962, Non Suon and the others arrested with him were condemned to death; the sentence was later commuted to life imprisonment. Chou Chet and his colleague received one-year gaol terms. Around the same time, Son Sen was transferred from his job at the Teachers' Training College, after being accused of spreading anti-monarchical and anti-Sangkum ideas among students there. He was, however, then appointed principal of a government high school in Takeo.[132] Sihanouk's distinction between the different generations of radicals — and its potential to both encourage and divide them — became even clearer in the June elections.

Entering the 77-member National Assembly as the representative of a seat in Kandal province, Khieu Samphan now joined the 'young intellectuals who . . . have been successful in introducing themselves into the Sangkum'. There were no opposition candidates; all the deputies were personally selected by Sihanouk, despite his description of those on the left as 'climbing the ladder of the Sangkum to work for its downfall'.[133] Uch Ven stood down, but Hou Yuon and Hu Nim were re-elected in Kompong Cham, and three new deputies who could be described as 'moderate leftists' — So Nem, Son Phuoc Tho and Chau Seng — also gained seats. Further, in the new Cabinet, Hou Yuon became Minister of Finance and Hu Nim Secretary of State for Commerce, a post in which he was replaced by Khieu Samphan in October.

But by that time, although these developments largely vindicated the posture of the veteran communists towards the Sihanouk regime, their leader Tou Samouth was dead. He disappeared on 20 July 1962 after being kidnapped from his safe house in Phnom Penh, and was almost certainly assassinated immediately afterwards.[134] The most likely explanation for this murder, which occurred despite the appointment of bodyguards for cadres the previous year, is that Samouth fell victim to intra-party conflict. The Pol Pot group have never explicitly denied responsibility, and all the evidence, although circumstantial, points to their involvement.[135] Pol Pot became Acting Secretary-General of the Party,[136] and Vorn Vet Secretary of its Phnom Penh branch.

Red Light for the Pink Prince, 1962–66

With the change in the Party leadership, three developments over the next four years brought Kampuchea to the brink of civil war. These were: first, a gradual but sporadic increase in government repression of the left, which coincided with and was (in part) provoked by an increasingly rebellious Party posture, and finally the escalation of US involvement in Vietnam. All three factors combined to narrow the options of both Sihanouk and Hanoi, as well as to drive the bulk of the Khmer communist movement into dissidence, and into conflict with the strategy of the Vietnamese Party. This outcome was also quietly fostered by the Chinese Communist Party, as we shall see.

A new Cabinet, 'the youngest in Kampuchean history', took office after the June elections. According to Laura Summers: 'Khieu Samphan's views on the economy were well known . . . It is also apparent that [his doctoral dissertation] *Cambodia's Economy and Industrial Development* was something of a blueprint for the new government. In his investiture speech, Prime Minister Prince Norodom Kantol presented a strategy for reform similar in appearance to the second half of the dissertation. . . Such proposals were a striking departure from the neo-colonial, commercially-oriented norm; Prince Sihanouk was even obliged to inform financial and commercial groups. . . that he was not putting 'the young ones' in power only to embarrass them or to allow 'the old guard' back for another chance.'[137] In the ensuing months, as Samphan prepared detailed proposals for dealing with the country's economic ills, he received firm backing from Sihanouk, especially in early January 1963 when the Prince insisted that the Cabinet have a free hand and that it deserved a motion of confidence. (This was in spite of his private remarks that he thought the Cabinet's approach was too 'theoretical'.)[138] It was also at this point that Sihanouk commuted the death sentence that had been passed on Non Suon and his fourteen associates, and that Chou Chet and his colleague were released from gaol.[139]

The communist press underwent a re-organization. *Samleng Apyiakrit* was replaced by *Damnoeng Thmei* ('New Information') and *Yuvamitt* by the daily *Sahamitt* ('Friendship and Co-operation'), edited by the Paris-trained Ok Sakun, with a total circulation of 4,000. *Meatophum* was now a daily also (circulation 3,600). With Chau Seng's *La Dépêche* (3,000 to 3,300), left-wing papers now represented over half of the total Khmer- and French-language daily newspaper circulation. These high figures are those circulated by the Sihanouk government itself.[140] In the meantime, the young left-wing law student Phouk Chhay published his doctoral thesis at Phnom Penh University, arguing that the country should refuse American aid, on the grounds that it benefitted the rich but rarely the poor.[141]

During a visit to India and then China in February 1963, the Prince did intervene in economic policy by sending back to Phnom Penh a list of proposals for which he desired immediate attention, but this appears to have been rather a display of royal whim than a deliberate campaign to undermine the Cabinet's reform measures. For instance, he also urged the government to 'act to stop price rises, eliminate middlemen, stop waste. . .'[142]

At any rate, this intervention quickly became forgotten in mid February when a riot broke out in the city of Siemreap, the first of the three serious crises that erupted (the others were in 1967 and 1970) while Sihanouk was out of the country. As Laura Summers tells it:

> A local policemen, widely suspected of smuggling activities, had been harassing lycée students and school children about riding their bicycles on certain paths at night. He beat his own nephew for disobedience. Two days afterwards, a schoolboy was found beaten to death. Students accused the police of brutality and murder, but local authorities defended the officer. . . With this, student meetings were called to organize protest demonstrations. These finally resulted in the sacking of the local police headquarters, the removal and desecration of Prince Sihanouk's portraits from all public buildings, and the brandishing of placards reading 'The Sangkum is rotten', 'The Sangkum is unjust', and 'Down with the Sangkum'. When two members of the Cabinet, the provincial governor and other officials arrived on the scene to discuss the situation with students based in Siem Reap Lycée, they were forced to march around town by demonstrators who were armed with clubs and stones. Local cyclo (bicycle-cab) drivers were observed to be in support of the student movement. Student appeals for support from other colleges and lycées around the country resulted in more demonstrations in most of the country's

urban centres. With the situation manifestly out of control, the Cabinet, including Khieu Samphan, resigned *en masse*.[143]

On his return at the end of February, Sihanouk blamed Keng Vannsak, who had recently been to Siemreap to give lectures to students there, and Son Sen.[144] Former members of the Marxist Circle in Paris, both men were virulently anti-Sihanouk, but evidence of their involvement in this affair is sparse. The Assembly, however, did not accept the Cabinet's resignation, and it was withdrawn.

But the effect of these events on the communist movement was decisive. Although there seems to have been no connection between the Siemreap outbreak and any Party involvement there, the rioting spread to Kompong Cham, where the left certainly did have strong influence among the teaching corps, and it is likely that committed activists played some role. Then, on 20 and 21 February, the Third Party Congress was held at a secret location in Phnom Penh. It seems to have been convoked mainly in order to confirm Pol Pot in his post as Secretary-General (while promoting many of his associates among the returned students) and, quite possibly, to do so by taking advantage of the current anti-government turmoil.[145] According to a Vietnamese source, Vorn Vet's Phnom Penh Party Committee insisted on calling the meeting at short notice.[146] There is no information about any substantive decisions made there. The 1973 Party History says it adopted 'a new operational direction' but is otherwise strikingly vague about the 'Third Congress', whereas the revised 1974 version distributed by Ieng Sary (in which it is referred to as the 'Second Congress') adds only that it organized 'a new Central Committee'.[147] More significantly a 1971 version, also distributed by Sary, says the Congress merely 'decided to choose a new Comrade Party Secretary'.[148] Of the twenty or so delegates who attended, Vietnamese sources maintain,[149] only a few were rural-based, mostly from provinces close to the capital. According to Tea Sabun, who appears to have been one of the rural representatives present,[150] So Phim stood against Pol Pot for the post of Secretary-General. He was defeated 'not by a vote but by opinion', although the result of a vote might well have been the same, if the assembly was heavily weighted in favour of the French-trained urban-based militants.

Nuon Chea again became (or, perhaps, was bypassed but confirmed as) Deputy Party Secretary, with Ieng Sary, So Phim and Vorn Vet completing the Politburo. Moong, Prasith, Muol Sambath, Mok, Phuong, Son Sen and Son Ngoc Minh made up the rest of the Central Committee of twelve.[151] Former students thus moved into positions 1, 3, 5, 6 and 11, while Keo Meas and Non Suon were dropped from the hierarchy altogether. The retention of Son Ngoc Minh seems to have been a mere sop to the veterans, since he had little opportunity of influencing policy while still in Hanoi. The exclusion, from an *enlarged* body, of Keo Meas, still active in the country and until then No. 6 in the Party, makes little sense unless he was one of those not notified of the Congress in advance. Perhaps he had seen policy changes approaching and opposed them. Non Suon, too, was in the country, and although in gaol he was hardly less accessible than Son Ngoc Minh. (In his confession he describes how messages were smuggled to him at this time in cigarette packs.) Perhaps his problem was that he might have been released: as we shall see in Chapter 8, Non Suon was alleged by Party leaders before his release in 1970 to have 'rallied to the enemy' while in gaol.[152]

Equally significant was the failure of other prominent veterans to be included in the enlarged Central Committee — Chi Kim An, Ney Sarann, Um Neng, Chou Chet, Tea Sabun, and all the candidates in the 1955 and 1958 elections were passed over. At the same time, a youth activist named Keu, who had come to the notice even of Vorn Vet as late as 1961, was made Vet's deputy on the Phnom Penh Party Committee,[153] and thus occupied what was probably as high a post as all those just mentioned.[154] It was probably argued by the Pol Pot group (given the circumstances of the moment) that the time had come for extreme secrecy, even that the revolution was on the way, and that a whole generation of leading cadres, who had followed Party policy by taking part in open political struggle within the framework of the Sihanouk regime, were now disqualified from holding high rank because they were too well known to the enemy. (It would seem clear that the new leadership had a close interest in committing the Party to an underground posture involving outright opposition to the Sihanouk regime.) Of the veterans who *were* on the Central Committee, Nuon Chea, for one, was prepared to work with Pol Pot. (He had either agreed to step down as Deputy Secretary in favour of Pot in 1961, or, at this 1963 Congress, declined to stand against him.) Another, Mok, now benefitted greatly, perhaps because, in Phnom Penh as a member of the Higher School of Pali,[155] he had developed a close relationship with Pol Pot.[156] Mok appeared on the Central Committee, while his apparent superior, the Party Secretary of the South-Western Zone, named Mar (alias Nhim),[157] who was to vanish without trace in a few years' time, did not. The other four veterans were dispersed in the most remote regions of the country — So Phim and Phuong on the Vietnamese border in the far east of Prey Veng, and Prasith and Muol Sambath on the Thai border in the Cardamom ranges of Koh Kong and Battambang. More importantly, So Phim was the only member of the Politburo to be assigned limited geographic responsibility, as Party Secretary of the Eastern Zone. The others — Pol Pot, Nuon Chea, Ieng Sary and Vorn Vet — now effectively made up the Party 'Centre', with responsibility for national activities. In three months' time, Pol Pot and Ieng Sary were to move to the countryside. Future meetings of the Politburo and the Central Committee, which were to adopt key decisions, would be unlikely to involve much debate.

By an amazing coincidence, the Prince now published, on March 8, a list of thirty-four leading 'subversives', comprised almost entirely of leftist urban intellectuals;[158] the sole exception was Chou Chet.[159] In the National Assembly, Khieu Samphan was confronted with this accusation of subversion, but according to a witness was physically unable to utter a response. He eventually cried out that the allegations were false and that there was nothing he could say against them.[160] Nevertheless, Sihanouk accepted the government's withdrawal of its resignation, and the Cabinet — including Samphan and Hou Yuon, who was also on the list — resumed office. According to Sihanouk's English-language secretary of the time, Donald Lancaster, the Prince rejected a proposal by Lon Nol for a policy of cracking down totally on the left because he wanted people in the government 'who understood how China worked'.[161] Other reasons are given by Laura Summers, who says Sihanouk rejected the repressive option '. . . partly in order to maintain the weak left as leverage against his competitors in the aristocracy and in business, and partly out of continuing conviction that the young progressives held the key to sorting out the country's economic mess.'[162] Again the traditional Party line on Sihanouk and divisions in the ruling class had been vindicated, and this after what was probably the most severe political crisis since 1955. If the list of thirty-four really was a 'hit-list' drawn up in advance by Lon Nol (as Ok Sakun, who fled to France after his name appeared on it, and was soon joined by Thiounn Prasith, certainly believed[163]), it was those who saw little chance of it being implemented under Sihanouk who read the political situation correctly.

Sihanouk acted almost as if hypnotized by the Party veterans' analysis of his regime. He saw the Siemreap riot as the culmination of the views of the middle-class French-trained urban left, and he acted, probably for the first time since 1955, so as to give them a severe shock. But he went no further than naming them, and calling thirty-two of them to a meeting where he harangued them for not taking responsibility for their actions, and rhetorically insisted that they form the government. Sien An was gaoled later in the year, but none of the other people on the list was harmed; they continued their activities relatively unharassed, as they had been doing since 1955 (with the exception of the 1960 incident in which Khieu Samphan had been beaten up in the street).

This could not be said of the grassroots leftists (most of whom were omitted from Sihanouk's list just as they were from the Party Central Committee). Nop Bophann was dead, and Non Suon and his comrades behind bars. Nor could it be said of the leftist Foreign Minister of Laos, Quinim Pholsena, who was shot dead by rightists outside his Vientiane home during these very weeks (actually on 1 April), an event which led to the military's destruction of the 1962 neutralist coalition and the flight of communist Ministers from the Lao capital in May. Did the educated young militants of Kampuchea feel their lives to be similarly in danger? Or, on the contrary, did they see the Siemreap riot as the opportunity they had been waiting for, the sign that they could take the offensive, that a rising tide of popular unrest was destined to carry them to power? Perhaps it was a combination of the two. At any rate, the crisis soon subsided. In May 1963 Pol Pot and Ieng Sary disappeared from their jobs in Phnom Penh and moved to the border area of Kompong Cham.[164] Son Sen went underground in Phnom Penh, following them a year later (as did Ney Sarann and Nuon Chea). The wives of the three joined them, apparently in September 1965.[165] The three were rumoured to have been secretly killed by the police, which of course was untrue, although the rumour may have contributed to later disappearances of genuinely frightened intellectuals.

Sihanouk must have known about the disappearances, but

unsurprisingly he does not seems to have been greatly concerned. If Pol Pot is to be believed, the authorities were unaware of his position in the communist movement: 'I was not very well known to the public. But the Lon Nol police followed my activities. They knew me but they did not know exactly who [what?] I was.'[166] His wife Khieu Ponnary, head of the secret Communist Women's Organization, remained on the staff of Sihanouk's official magazine *Kambuja* for another two years.[167] Hu Nim, too, was a member of the staff of the Sihanoukist daily *Neak Cheat Niyum* ('The Nationalist'); he now visited China, North Korea and North Vietnam. His Beijing hosts entrusted him with forming a Khmer-Chinese Friendship Association, and in Hanoi, Nim later wrote, 'Ho Chi Minh welcomed me and promised me that he would allow me to live in Hanoi if I was unable to live in Phnom Penh any longer'.[168] Whether or not this is true, neither Beijing nor Hanoi was yet interested in supporting an underground struggle in Kampuchea.

However, at home, right-wing members of the National Assembly were attacking the policies pursued by Khieu Samphan and Hou Yuon; commercial circles were proving recalcitrant, while Sihanouk's reforming enthusiasm had lagged. But so had Samphan's. What Laura Summers calls 'the general disorganization and administrative weakness of the Sihanouk regime',[169] although in some ways beneficial to the left, made any serious policies difficult to implement, or at least too difficult for Samphan to pursue. Thus, even though he survived a no-confidence motion in the Assembly in mid June, and retained the support of the rest of the Cabinet, he 'resigned abruptly' on 1 July. By contrast, Hou Yuon had lost a no-confidence motion (his refusal to follow Sihanouk's own proposals rigidly enough was considered a case of lèse-majesté), and had had little choice but to resign.[170] Samphan's voluntary exit, after such a short period as Minister, suggests either a lack of nerve or an inability to deal with a difficult situation by means of judicious compromise. (It is possible, though, that he was instructed to abandon attempts at reform by Pol Pot, who had taken to the jungle about six weeks before.) It is ironic that Yuon, who, as we shall see, seriously believed the government could effect worthwhile reforms and devoted his energies to a political struggle to bring them about, was sacked by the government; whereas Samphan, who had the confidence of both the Assembly and the government to go ahead, took the view that the state was unreformable.

Although Khieu Samphan was apparently not one of those who saw their significance at the time, events in South Vietnam were already dwarfing those in Siemreap and developing into the most serious crisis in Indo-China since Geneva. The NLF had shown its strength at the battle of Ap Bac early in the year, the Buddhist unrest burst in on the scene in May, and in the ensuing months Saigon troops launched a series of incursions into Kampuchean territory in pursuit of NLF forces. In mid August came the sudden commencement of clandestine Khmer-language radio broadcasts made by the CIA-backed Khmer Serei forces of Son Ngoc Thanh, attacking the Sihanouk regime. Thus on August 28, barely two months after Samphan's resignation, Sihanouk broke off diplomatic relations with South Vietnam, signalling a shift to the left and an escalation of his regime's hostility to the US. In this climate, in September, Chou Chet and a group of other leftists were able to establish a new newspaper, *Smardey Khmer* ('Khmer Consciousness').[171]

The US role in the assassination of its own protegé, President Ngo Dinh Diem, in Saigon on November 2, caused Sihanouk to speculate fearfully about the plans the Americans might have in store for militant neutralist figures such as himself. (Such speculation was perhaps fuelled by Hu Nim's review of Andrew Tulley's book, CIA — *The Inside Story,* which examines the Agency's undercover role in Laos, in the pages of Chau Seng's leftist newspaper *La Dépêche du Cambodge* on 5 November).[172] Immediately the NLF launched proposals for a cease-fire and free elections in South Vietnam, which would then 'form, together with the Kingdoms of Cambodia and Laos, a neutral zone on the Indo-Chinese peninsula'. On 10 November, Sihanouk suddenly announced the nationalization of the import/export trade and of the banks, claiming that the Chinese, French and Anglo-Saxon international capitalists were a 'fifth column' hostile to neutrality. Imports of luxury goods were to be restricted, in line with the recommendations of Khieu Samphan only two months previously. In his 1959 thesis, Samphan had advocated restriction of foreign banking activities and control over imports and exports.[173] This too would now be implemented. Samphan's reaction however, was to complain about the costs of compensation, which Sihanouk fiercely attacked him for exaggerating.[174]

Hou Yuon, on the other hand, enthusiastically supported the reforms, and Sihanouk assured him that there would be no turning back. He noted with approval that Yuon 'can easily understand that the vital interests of the throne and of the Sangkum, 'my personal interests' according to him, command me to evolve my country in this way'.[175] Hou Yuon had no time for royalty *per se*, and was quite open about this (in January 1964 he claimed Sihanouk was using scarce electric power to light his own street),[176] as a result of which he was the target of personal tirades more furious than Sihanouk's attacks on any other politician. But Yuon still saw Sihanouk as a nationalist, and the Prince acknowledged this as well.

A week later, Sihanouk paraded two former Khmer Serei personnel before a National Congress; the crowd, after hearing evidence from them of the activities of their American-sponsored movement, voted to execute one of them, and to expel the US military mission from the country and terminate all US aid. Sihanouk's adoption of Samphan's proposals was thus now complemented by the implementation of policies advocated by the leftist student Phouk Chhay. The following day, Sihanouk called for a reconvening of the Geneva Conference, to guarantee Kampuchea's neutrality.

And the new leaders of the Kampuchean communist movement had *abandoned the political scene,* having already decided that an armed struggle to overthrow the Sihanouk regime was the only way to win 'true independence' and socialism. In the words of Pol Pot's *Black Book*, the Vietnamese had now 'lost control of the revolutionary movement in Kampuchea'; but it was not just for this reason that, according to the same source, the year 1964 was to see 'attacks' on the new CPK leadership 'by leading cadres right in the heart of the Party's leading organs'.[177] Some of them must indeed have felt that the Party had missed the bus.

In March 1964, large-scale government-sponsored demonstrations were mounted against the American and British embassies in Phnom Penh. As Anthony Barnett has pointed out, 'A year before, school students had been demonstrating against the Sangkum; now its radicalism was theirs, if momentarily.'[178] Although Pol Pot later claimed that the urban radical upsurge was partly a result of pressure from the alleged 'struggle in the countryside',[179] it is quite clear that the demonstrations were organized by Sihanouk's Ministry of Information, and by above-ground urban leftists such as Chau Seng and Hou Yuon. The importance of the latter group's independent actions became clear in May when Sihanouk lamented the 'increasing indiscipline and insubordination among the pupils in most of our schools' (particular mention was given to Sisowath High School); and again when further demonstrations in August incurred the Prince's displeasure: 'I must deplore the spirit in which yesterday's demonstrations in the capital were planned; their aim is to serve the cause of communism and strike a blow at *our union in the Sangkum'*, indicating that the protests were directed at rightists within the Sangkum, rather than at the Sangkum itself. Sihanouk continued: 'These demonstrations are the work of our pro-communist Khmers, who have not hesitated to press even our monks to parade in the streets, thereby infringing the fundamental discipline of their apostolate.'[180]

Divisions were indeed appearing in the Sangkum. Songsakd Kitpanich, a Sino-Thai businessman with undercover American connections, who had established the Bank of Phnom Penh, fled to Saigon in a private aeroplane (taking most of the bank's assets with him). On the other hand, former Pracheachon representative Sien An was now released from prison; although he remained temporily under house arrest, he later went on to become a 'high official'. Also in this period, the communists began publishing another new newspaper *Chadomuk* ('Four Faces'). Unrest was developing, too, among workers in the French-owned rubber plantations at Samrong, in Memut, fostered by about twenty Party members in the district.[181] The 1973 Party History may have been correct in saying that 'as of 1964, the Party had a great deal of influence', but it had little to do with the policies of the new Party leadership.[182]

Symptomatic of the ironic situation was the move by a new generation of urban student activists, led by Phouk Chhay, to establish a national students' union in 1964. Some of them approached Khieu Samphan (now a teacher at Chamroeun Vichea High School) for help, but were turned away and advised to 'do what Lenin advises us in *What is to be Done!'*[183] Samphan apparently saw the situation as analogous to that in Russia before 1905. Phouk Chhay, however, did not. He founded the General Association of Khmer Students, and the next year took up a position in the state bank and was appointed Deputy Commissar-General of the Royal Khmer Socialist Youth.

Chhay's attitude was shared by Hou Yuon, who began working on a 200-page revision of his 1956 book *The Co-operative Question*, which was published in November 1964.[184] One of a handful of serious works on politics, economics or sociology that were allowed to be published in the Khmer language during the Sihanouk period,[185] the book formally proposed an alliance between socialists and Sihanouk's regime. Yuon approved the Prince's militant stand against US intervention in Indo-China; more significantly, he also argued that the domestic reforms of late 1963 ('the royal form of nationalization') created 'the possible means to build up the national economy in the interests of the people'. He proposed the use of existing institutions, such as the co-operative body OROC ('Office Royal de Co-opération') and the nationalized banks, as well as the creation of new ones such as labour-pools and mutual aid teams, to raise the living standards of the peasantry by reducing land-rents and providing them with low-interest credit facilities which would bypass exploitative money-lenders. Co-operatives would need to be democratically organized and free of corruption. All this, he argued, would be needed to strengthen the resolve of the peasants to defend their country's independence, by giving them more of a stake in the system; things could not continue indefinitely under a system whereby 'cities and market towns actively oppress the rural areas — 'the tree grows in the rural areas, but the fruit goes to the towns'. These characteristics do not motivate or support production; they are obstacles to national economic progress.'[186]

Significantly, however, Yuon qualified his urban/rural dichotomy with another point later openly rejected by the Pol Pot regime: 'This does not mean that 'city workers oppress poor peasants in the rural areas' or that cruel capitalists in the cities and landowning peasants in the rural areas do not oppress the workers and the poor peasants.'[187] He also made it clear that the system was not at the point of revolutionary explosion. Rather, 'the economic and financial reforms have given a new lease of life for national capitalism to progress cleanly in the interests of the nation and the people', while bringing 'bright new changes for the farmers and the workers in general'.[188]

Signs of this had already emerged. 1963 had seen a record rice harvest, which was exceeded in 1964; rice exports soared; in 1964 the country's balance of trade was positive for the first time since 1955, and in 1965 National Bank deposits recovered from a long decline. The reforms were clearly an economic success. It was only from 1966, after escalation of the Vietnam war, that large amounts of Kampuchean rice were smuggled across the border and taxable rice exports fell by two thirds, so that the Sihanoukist state plunged towards bankruptcy.[189]

Thirteen years after Hou Yuon's book had appeared, a CPK document complained of the influence on the Party of such reformist ideas, which it blamed on foreigners, clearly the VWP: 'On the outside, from 1957 there were some who did not agree that Kampuchean society was already clearly divided into classes. Even by 1965 they still did not agree. . . They had great influence, they just had to say one word and some others inside the country would listen. This meant that on the outside we had to struggle. In addition, there was also a theory that the national capitalists could lead the revolution.'[190]

This is of course a parody of the opposing position, but it is true that Hou Yuon rejected the revolutionary strategy of underground opposition already adopted by the Pol Pot group. He wrote: 'We must understand that class conflict should be resolved by a method that will not damage the unity of the nation against the American imperialists.'[191] But the CPK leaders rejected the united front strategy out of hand: 'Some people told us that if we took the clandestine form as the basis, it would endanger the revolutionary forces. Only when we have *forces of broad strength* [they said], can we defend our forces. But we had our explanation [sic] which was: we must take clandestine struggle as the basis.'[192]

Finally, Hou Yuon's discussion of 'national capitalism' recalls the ICP view that by the 1930s Kampuchea was a country of 'nascent capitalism'. (See pp.17, 84.) The Pol Pot group, on the other hand, were increasingly attracted to the CCP view of pre-1949 China, as 'semi-feudal, semi-colonial' — a description they were to apply to Kampuchea, as we shall see in Chapter 8. This distinction was in fact a crystallization of the major differences within the left over the nature of the Sihanouk regime.

Like earlier Pracheachon statements, Yuon's book contains much probably insincere pro-Sihanouk rhetoric, of the kind then required of all politicians; but again, there would have been no need for him to have written anything at all had he believed the state was unreformable and/or doomed. The same stance was adopted by Hu Nim in his doctoral thesis completed the next year, in which he wrote: 'Before the 1963 reforms, general opinion had it that 'the nature of the market is such that the peasant is robbed when he sells his products and held to ransom when he buys the goods that he needs'. This is because he was

exploited by merchants, comprador businessmen and usurers. . .
It is in order to resolve this serious problem that the Government
has set up a company to collect and package agricultural
produce.'[193]

Interestingly, Hou Yuon anticipated the issues about to burst
on the scene in the Chinese Cultural Revolution a year or more
later. The leaders of new peasant co-operatives, he said, must be
'simmering with' both political awareness and technical exper-
tise. However he warned of the necessity to 'avoid smothering
technology with politics, causing technology to shrink and pale
in a political mould, unable to fulfil its role.'[194]

What Yuon did not anticipate was that even as he wrote, the
US government was planning massive direct intervention in
Vietnam, in a determined and costly attempt to reverse the drift
of events in Indo-China. Sustained bombing of North Vietnam
began in February 1965, and was followed in May by the landing
of US regular troops in the south. The next three years, as we
shall see, were critical. As the US built up a force of half a million
men, Sihanouk gradually became convinced that they were there
to stay. They forced thousands of Vietnamese guerrillas to take
refuge in sanctuaries across the border; as these became
increasingly permanent Sihanouk became convinced that they,
too, had come to stay. His options, in other words, narrowed
with the war's escalation from 1965. Sihanouk began to look
sideways at his local left, and again trimmed his neutralist sails to
the prevailing winds. Hou Yuon was politically marooned, his
analysis outdated and his proposals ignored. At the same time,
the US build-up brought the Vietnamese communists closer to
Moscow, as they increasingly required the heavy weapons that
Moscow, after the 1964 overthrow of Khruschev, was now much
more willing to supply. This in turn caused serious strains in
Hanoi's relationship with Beijing, where Pol Pot, during his
1965 visit there, would find *sub rosa* encouragement for his own
anti-Vietnamese posture. Nevertheless, this posture was also —
indeed at this stage probably *primarily* — anti-Sihanouk; and
when the Prince became aware of this, in early 1966, he began to
give Lon Nol a much freer hand to crack down on the urban as
well as the rural left, and thus threw the initiative within
Kampuchea's communist movement into the lap of the Pol Pot
group. The critical stage in the drawing of Kampuchea into the
Vietnam War was about to begin. But more of this later.

It is ironic that in 1964 Pol Pot himself, and other members of the Party Centre, were quartered in 'Office 900', just across the border in a liberated area of the South Vietnamese province of Tay Ninh. 'The Vietnamese protected the Office completely', Vorn Vet wrote years later, adding that Pol Pot's administrative secretary Ney Sarann enjoyed close relations with them.[195] For their part, Pol Pot and Nuon Chea are reported to have developed close ties with the Deputy Party Secretary of the Eastern Zone's Region 21, a former Issarak guerrilla named Seng Hong (alias Chan). According to Ouch Bun Chhoeun, the two leaders regularly stayed in Chan's house and gave him political instruction: 'They trusted Chan more than So Phim.'[196] This is at least suggested by events in the Eastern Zone in the 1970s, as we shall see in Chapter 8.

Whether, by deciding to begin preparations for an armed struggle against Sihanouk's regime, the Pol Pot group had misjudged his capacity to sponsor or tolerate left-wing activity, or simply decided to take advantage of it, they now faced a new situation. According to an internal security service report prepared in 1978: 'In [late] 1964, the meeting of the Party's Central Committee decided to prepare to counter any eventual coup by the Americans.'[197] In other words, the Centre had now *accepted* a distinction between Sihanouk and more pro-American elements in his regime such as Lon Nol.

But there was to be no return to the former united front posture of the Party. Ouch Bun Chhoeun, then a Party cadre in Memut, recalls how the line was disseminated over the next year: 'In 1965 we spread the news that Lon Nol proposed to stage a coup that year. We carried out internal Party education, raising two principles: 1) If Lon Nol stages a coup and kills Prince Sihanouk, we will launch an armed struggle, 2) But if Lon Nol takes over Kampuchea [in more subtle fashion, presumably with Sihanouk's backing] we would combine politics with arms'.[198] The distinction between Lon Nol and Sihanouk was, it seems, valid only if the latter were dead, or at least removed from the political scene: there was no acknowledgement of any improvement in his policies, or of his ability to hold on to power himself, or of his political following, nor any willingness to bolster his position to hold off the potential coup. Having prematurely escalated the communist struggle in mid 1963, the CPK leaders now did so again. They realized that armed activity on their part would *increase* the likelihood of a move by rightists already alienated by the late 1963 reforms, and believed that the resultant political destabilization 'could only be positive for the revolution'.[199]

Sihanouk, however, continued to lump together his enemies of both left and right. In May 1964, he had announced: 'Son Sen, reputedly a pro-communist, has taken flight to join up with (Son Ngoc) Thanh in Saigon.'[200] He could hardly have believed this himself, but a tactic he often used to discredit his various enemies was that of publicly associating them with one another. Interestingly, he made this statement shortly after returning from a visit to Ratanakiri province, where Khmer Loeu tribesmen had recently killed a government soldier and two local militiamen. The fact that social tension already existed in this frontier area, as a result of the establishment of rubber plantations and colonies of settlers, does not preclude the possibility that this may have been a premonition of the civil war between 'Khmer Rouge' and the Sihanouk regime. Again Sihanouk blamed the deaths on South Vietnamese incursions, although he may have had information that Son Sen had recently arrived in the area.[201]

At any rate, before the year was out Lon Nol and the security forces were to launch an extensive effort to hunt down revolutionaries in the countryside, at about the same time, it seems, as the word from Pol Pot reached the revolutionaries to take to the bush. So Phim, for instance, seems to have disappeared from his village in late 1964, without being driven out by police or by military harassment. He camped by a creek near Samrong, in Dauntey subdistrict in the south-eastern corner of Kompong Cham, where he had ready access to the NLF-controlled zone of Vietnam's Tay Ninh province.[202] On the other hand, the signal to take flight had evidently not reached Ke Vin, for instance. Vin had settled down on his release from prison in 1957, had fathered at least six children and according to a local informant was 'making a living selling alcohol and buying chickens, and doing political work' in his native district of Baray, Kompong Thom. Now, in 1964, Vin was 'attacked by police and driven into the forest'.

The same informant continued: 'I saw fifty-four men and women attend a meeting in Bos Pauk forest. They had only two carbines. They all came from the nearby village of Koki Thom, and people from there brought medicine and supplies.'[203] Ke Vin would later assume the revolutionary name Pauk, in memory of this place of refuge. He would also become notorious for the bloody revenge he took on anyone who was associated, however loosely, with the political system that had driven him there; notorious also for the difference between his policies and those of So Phim, whose move into the forest was much more politically motivated and less traumatic; and for his bitter rivalry with Phim which ended in the latter's suicide in 1978.[204]

Another later rival of Pauk's, Koy Thuon, took to the jungle in the same period (as also did Chou Chet). According to Ouch Bun Chhoeun: 'In 1963 to 1965 the enemy's activities were very strong. Sihanouk arrested cadres who had formerly been involved in the struggle. Many were gaoled. However at that time imprisonment was not very dangerous – you would be released after a period. Koy Thuon, now Party Secretary for the Northern Zone, had to leave. I met him when he came to ask So Phim for his opinion. From 1964 to 1965 he came during the dry season to teach students in the forest.'[205]

Phuong, Phim's deputy in the Eastern Zone, felt threatened too. According to a monk who joined the movement, 'from late 1964 the police were looking everywhere for 'Khmer Rouge', and so Phuong had no choice but to flee.[206] According to an older cousin of Phuong's, 'He was working as a carpenter with me, but he would go to Phnom Penh every month for secret meetings. He ran into the forest in 1964 or 1965; he couldn't stay because they were arresting people. We had the plans drawn up for three houses in Svay Rieng and Kompong Trabek, and suddenly we heard that Sieu Heng had just been captured and he was responding to interrogation. Phuong had been at secret meetings with Sieu Heng, and his face was known. He couldn't stay. He left immediately, that night; he didn't even wait to collect any money. He just went off on his new bicycle to join So Phim.'[207] It is interesting to note that Sieu Heng, according to his own account, had been in contact with Lon Nol since 1955, and openly defected from the Party in 1959. He was *not* 'captured' in 1964. Perhaps Lon Nol had just decided to make more use of him. Or perhaps the official reason given by the Party to its cadre to explain the new policies was an allegedly recent 'capture' of the one-time Party leader.

Certainly the government effort to 'look everywhere' for 'Khmer Rouge' was not always enthusiastic or effective. After Phuong's disappearance, his cousin continued: 'Later the district chief called for me. I was working on my house as usual, when a letter came from him asking me to go to the Tribunal in Prey Veng city. There were police vehicles to escort us. At 11 pm, I arrived at the district office, and asked why they wanted me to go. The district chief said he didn't know, the Tribunal had summoned me. I said that they were calling in all the old revolutionaries from the resistance, to put them in gaol. I asked a police sergeant and he said he didn't know either. Then I asked Nuon, the subdistrict chief. He also said he didn't know, the big people would decide what to do, it was up to them. I said they were going to gaol all the revolutionaries, [who] would never come back ... I said I wouldn't go. He said, do whatever you like. The next morning I told my wife and children, and that evening I was in the forest. I didn't go to Prey Veng.'[208] Perhaps he would have gone there, had he not heard the story about Sieu Heng. Perhaps he would not have come back, or perhaps he would have been treated more like Chan Mon, another former Issarak, in Tbaung Khmum district of Kompong Cham, who recalled: 'From 1965, Sihanouk's troops started persecuting me in every way, pushing me around, accusing me of being a Khmer Rouge. I was watched all the time.'[209]

In the same year, police colonel Kouroudeth approached Suas Nau (alias Chhouk), who was teaching at Kambuboth High School in the capital, and asked him to spy on Hou Yuon and Hu Nim. Already a Party member, Nau was unwilling to collaborate with the police, and yet afraid of arrest. He told Hou Yuon what had happened and asked for permission to leave his job. He was nominated Party chief for Region 24 (southern Prey Veng) in the Eastern Zone, and took to the countryside. His wife returned to her native village, where police regularly questioned her about her husband's whereabouts, but it was only five years later that the couple were reunited.[210] In northern Prey Veng in the same year (1965), another colonel arrested nine former UIF cadres, including one woman. Even as they were waiting to be shot, Puk Soum, a local monk who had been a member of the Issarak Monks' Association and still worked actively with the Pracheachon, managed to secure their release after a visit to the colonel and payment of a 20,000 *riel* bribe.[211]

It seems clear that the increased surveillance and harassment of former revolutionaries, although it still rarely involved violence, combined with initiatives and directives of the Pol Pot group in the same period, to send many of them back into the jungle.

A good illustration of this is the 1965 disappearance of Muol Sambath, the former UIF military commander of the North-Western Zone. According to another local informant, Sambath, who had been growing rice with some of his followers near Thvak pagoda since 1955, was harassed by troops sent by the governor of Battambang, and had to move five times from one village to another; he managed to elude the soldiers and meet up with his old comrade Nuon Chea, who had presumably come from Phnom Penh for the purpose of getting him to take to the bush anyway.[212] The two immediately began to reorganize their followers and engage in recruiting and propaganda activities. They were joined in mid 1965 by Keu, who had been transferred from Phnom Penh after 'the enemy arrested many youths and closed down the newspaper *Chadomuk*'.[213] Keu soon became Party military chief for the North-Western Zone.[214]

The horses of left and right on which Sihanouk was attempting his standing ride were now beginning to diverge. Unrest continued in the tribal North-East. Sihanouk made a second visit there in January 1965, and tried to cope with its intractable problem (the settler colonization of an area of nomadic agriculture) by further imposition of central control: 'I ask you to live in groups and not dispersed as before. In doing that you will receive better rewards from the administration which will then be better able to protect your villages and your possessions, in your interest. Be guided by the competent provincial offices who will advise you on the choice of sites to establish your villages, land appropriate for your crops, etc.' His approach was also one of further paternalism, as Phnom Penh Radio made clear: 'Smiles of emotion and joy appeared on everyone's lips when Samdech took from their packages the superb and so coveted gifts which he had had brought for his dear Khmer Loeu Companions; necklaces of artificial pearls, bracelets, earrings and various other articles from Paris of which the beauties of Mondolkiri are so fond.'[215]

But this was no solution to the problem of conflict over land tenure which was emerging in some parts of the country. In February, Sihanouk claimed that 'Companion Hou Yuon has taken up the defence of bad citizens who have risen up against a government decision to redistribute in the most equitable way possible disputed lands in Kompong Cham province, and who want all this land for themselves. These persons were arrested for the troubles that they created.'[216]

A relative of Hou Yuon, interviewed in 1977, gave a different version. Peasants in Yuon's circumscription of Saukong wished to protest against the expropriation of their land by absentee landlords. They elected ten representatives who went to Phnom Penh to ask Hou Yuon for assistance, staying in his house while he pursued their case.[217] This version would fit with Hou Yuon's position in *The Co-operative Question*, where he suggested government intervention for more equitable land distribution; it is unlikely that he opposed it if it did take place. Yuon claimed that there was 'so little democracy', and said the arrests showed that freedom of speech no longer existed. 'One can no longer say anything without risk of being thrown into prison and tortured', he added. Sihanouk replied with a characteristic personal attack, which he nevertheless sweetened slightly by saying: 'If I have on the contrary protected Hou Yuon, it was because I have taken his intellectual qualities into account and have wanted to allow him the chance to become a good nationalist.'[218]

On the other hand, Sihanouk's statement that 'Companion Kou Roun has told me on his honour that the police have never tortured anyone' was perhaps a veiled warning to future 'offenders', and foreshadowed an increase in the activities of the security services.[219]

Still, the prisoners were apparently released, since according to Yuon's relative they won their case over the land. Several months later Phouk Chhay drew attention to the land problem, which was to cause difficulties for Sihanouk for the remainder of his reign, and was eventually to contribute to Pol Pot's rise to power. Writing in the semi-official government newspaper *La Dépêche*, Chhay claimed that peasants were increasingly abandoning their land, because of the ever-diminishing size of family holdings, land-grabbing by large landlords, and exhaustion of the soil. Sihanouk commented lamely that he 'agreed completely' with the first and third reasons, but not with the second. 'The presence of big landowners has never forced the peasants to leave their land', he claimed, echoing his similarly implausible statement about the police.[220]

On 29 January, Ly Sae, a nephew of Ney Sarann teaching in Pursat, was arrested along with three colleagues, for distributing leaflets, and sent to the Military Police gaol.[221] At the same time police arrested a number of students found sticking posters on trees in Phnom Penh and on the walls of educational institutions. The posters accused Lon Nol and Sirik Matak, among others, of being traitors and selling out the country to the United States. Sihanouk ordered the students' release after questioning, while threatening to send their 'masters and teachers', who he claimed were plotting 'a threat to the security of the national government', before a Military Tribunal. He saw Hou Yuon as one of these, and disregarded the fact that the posters did not attack himself. 'These Khmer Rouge, with Hou Yuon at their head, want only one thing: to overthrow the Monarchy. Hou Yuon was born with anti-royalism in his blood. When he meets a Prince he sees red (it's true) ... [the word] Yuon moreover means 'Vietnamese'.'[222]

Three days later, *La Dépêche* claimed that the plot allegation was a 'lie', and Sihanouk dropped it, but attempted, as usual, to have the last word on the matter: 'I would point out to Hou Yuon that he owes it to me that he has not had his 'portrait torn down', for many Khmer nationalists of the Sangkum, civilians and military, have asked me to allow them to inflict good punishment on the intolerable Hou Yuon, who is always full of pride, arrogance, and scorn for everyone and everything that is not 'red'. Not wishing to make a martyr of him, I have always refused to agree to this, and have been content to reply in writing and in speeches to the attacks or perfidious insinuations of our left wing, leaving to the people and to the youth the task and the freedom to judge both sides ...'[223] Neither the content nor the language of this statement was new. But the next sentence sounded a more hysterical note: 'But given the rising anger of virtually the entire nation, these reds cannot continue their sabotage activities in the country without running the risk of one day being lynched by the people whom I am no longer in a position to restrain. In that case I would be exempt from any responsibility.'[224]

At the end of March 1965, a youth who had been arrested in Kompong Cham after being discovered distributing leaflets and putting up posters, was found dead, hanging by the neck in the bathroom of the local police station.[225] This was probably the first murder of a Khmer leftist by the authorities since that of Nop Bophann in 1959. Sihanouk claimed the youth had been arrested against his orders,[226] and the incident led to a series of what he called 'most unfair demonstrations against the Sangkum'.[227]

Nevertheless, the 'reds' still refrained from attacking Sihanouk himself. They accused the Sangkum of increasing taxes, and said that 'voluntary' contributions for the building of public welfare institutions were in fact obtained by coercion. They continued to name Lon Nol as their arch-enemy. Sihanouk proclaimed: 'I warn the Khmer Rouge that I will leave them to go about their filthy business freely so long as it does not threaten the vital interests of the nation. But the movement of disorder and disunity which they have started is tending to spread. It has now reached the provinces, where our youth are much less preoccupied with their studies than with distributing tracts ...'[228] The political attacks on Lon Nol and others continued,[229] however, and so did the arrests. A week later, youths being interrogated by the police for distributing tracts, would answer only with the following tight-lipped formulation: 'It is useless to ask us questions, just deal with us as you see fit, since from now on it is obvious that the small, the weak and the poor must lead their lives in neglect and silently endure what is imposed on them by the big, the strong and the rich.'[230] These teenage students were now an important element in the make-up of the left. For them at least, the battle-lines had already been drawn. But by whom?

In February and March 1965, Sihanouk hosted the Conference of Indo-Chinese Peoples in Phnom Penh. Represented were the Sangkum, the Fatherland Front of North Vietnam, the NLF and a neutralist organization from the South, the Pathet Lao's political wing, and the Resistance Front of Kampuchea Krom. Although the Vietnamese representatives were unhappy with Sihanouk's invitation to the Khmer Krom 'White Scarves',[231] and although this made a permanent impression on Sihanouk's mind, the Conference did mark a significant shift in Sihanouk's foreign policy balance in the direction of Hanoi, partly because China was not directly involved in the proceedings. It foreshadowed a proposal by Sihanouk in January the next year for an 'organization of Indo-Chinese states ... just a 'little UN' for our Indo-China ... an organization of solidarity and co-operation'.[232] The Conference called for the re-convening of the Geneva Conference in order to guarantee Kampuchea's neutrality, for the withdrawal of the US from Vietnam and for the 'liberation' of the South.

In May 1965, as US troops landed in South Vietnam, Sihanouk broke off diplomatic relations with Washington. From his prison cell, Non Suon sent the Prince a letter of 'warm congratulations'.[233] Despite the irony of this, it is true that the left retained a degree of influence on the domestic front. So

Nem, a moderate leftist, was Secretary of State for Commerce, and Chau Seng was Director of Sihanouk's Cabinet. On 17 July, Phouk Chhay led a Royal Khmer Socialist Youth (JSRK) delegation of ten members on a visit to China.[234] On 9 August, he cabled Sihanouk from Beijing, informing him of the part work, part study system of education there, which he said was intended to 'create a type of new man in China ... [and] suppress the superiority of intellectual labour over manual labour'.[235] Sihanouk's response was a public speech replete with significance for the future, in which he said: 'We must follow this example if we want our society and our country to progress ... We have until now followed too slavishly the paths traced by Western civilization, and that has caused us certain social problems, that of unemployed intellectuals, that of pure intellectuals who are much less competent citizens than the new men who are being formed in China ... there is a necessity for a thoroughgoing reform ... I ask the leaders of our National Education to take the bull by the horns and definitively attack this very important and pressing problem. The interests of the country and of our youth depend on it.'[236]

Ten days later, Sikanouk announced the establishment of a JSRK agricultural co-operative, at Stung Kranhoung in Battambang province. He said a 'mixed (Khmer-Chinese) enterprise for agriculture and pastoral activity' would be created there, after earth-moving equipment had been sent to build an access road.[237] It was ironic, and indicative of the gulf separating different groups on Kampuchea's left, that this JSRK co-operative, sponsored by Phouk Chhay, was to be the target of the first shots fired in the civil war that began in 1967.[238] In September and October 1965, Sihanouk visited China himself, and relations between the two countries reached their peak.[239] On 20 September, Hu Nim arrived in Beijing for a month's visit, on the eve of the Cultural Revolution.[240] Neither he nor Phouk Chhay (nor even the forty Khmers from Hanoi then studying in China), let alone Sihanouk, appears to have been aware that *Pol Pot was in Beijing at the time of their visits*. For both the Chinese and Pol Pot, it was essential that the Prince (and others suspected of being too sympathetic towards him) be kept in the dark about their relationship.

Around late 1964, Pol Pot, accompanied by Keo Meas, had crossed the border into Laos and begun travelling up the Ho Chi Minh Trail on a trip that was to take him to Hanoi, Beijing and

Pyongyang. He is reported to have spent 'many months' in Hanoi,[241] where his policy of armed struggle encountered opposition. Gareth Porter has summed up the two versions of the VWP's attitude to Kampuchea: 'The Vietnamese delegation led by Le Duan, according to Pol Pot's account, called on the Khmer Party to 'renounce revolutionary struggle and wait for the Vietnamese to win their victory, which would automatically produce victory in Cambodia.' [Hanoi's version is that the line of the Vietnamese Party was that the] KPRP should 'support Sihanouk while criticizing him, and maintain a political but not a military struggle.'"[242] Pol Pot also met the leaders of the Khmer communists based in Hanoi. According to one of them, Chea Soth, 'He outlined to me the question of the Party's name. He asked our opinions. Some wanted it to be called the People's Revolutionary Party, others the Workers' Party, others the Communist Party of Kampuchea.'[243] The latter choice was that of Pol Pot; it implied, of course, that the Kampuchean communist movement was, in historical and ideological terms, more 'advanced' than the Vietnam Workers' Party.

Very little is known about Pol Pot's visit to China (he has never explicitly conceded that it occurred), or about the Chinese attitude to the deepening rift between his party and that of the Vietnamese. But bearing this in mind, the context of the visit is suggestive. The Chinese were on excellent terms with Sihanouk, and as Stephen Heder has pointed out, in 1961 they had attempted to persuade the Burmese communists to play down their struggle against the similarly friendly neutralist regime in Rangoon, advising them to employ political and legal tactics rather than military ones.[244] On the other hand, however, the Chinese Party's relations with most South-East Asian countries has usually been complicated by the distinction Beijing makes between 'State to State' and 'Party to Party' relations. More importantly, the significance of Kampuchea for Beijing was quite different to that of Burma. The Kampuchean Party was most probably seen in terms of the growing tension between Beijing and Hanoi that resulted from the latter's rapprochement with Moscow. A party that was traditionally aligned with Vietnam, but whose leadership was showing signs of resentment towards it, could not have been ignored by the Chinese, who were at that time sponsoring anti-Soviet breakaway parties aligned with themselves in nearly every country of the world. The Burmese communists, like the Malayan CP, went over to

Beijing wholesale. Obviously the position of the Kampuchean Party, which was not led by ethnic Chinese, was more complex because of the Vietnamese-sponsored training of most of its *membership*, and its new leaders would need more encouragement. (In particular, tactics would need to be adopted that would lead the party's membership to the conviction that the new line was correct, and prevent a split.)

The Thai communist party would also need encouragement (although to a lesser extent), since some of its members were at that stage training in Hanoi as well as in Beijing. The difference here was that Bangkok, unlike Phnom Penh (and Rangoon), was openly aligned with Washington in a military pact, and the interests of Hanoi and Beijing converged in opposing that alignment; US troops arrived in Thailand in 1962 and in August 1963 the CPT Politburo 'adopted a resolution to start preparations for creating revolutionary bases in the jungle areas'. 'The first victorious guns were fired ... on 7 August 1965', while Pol Pot was in Beijing, where the echoes would have been resounding.[245] Many CPT leaders were based there. In May 1965, Sihanouk announced the capture in Koh Kong province of communist documents, some of them written 'in Thai!', revealing that 'our Khmer Rouge have received orders from their foreign masters to activate our people and our youth and alienate them from the Sangkum and myself. These masters are not happy with the measures I have taken in the interests of the country such as the nationalization of the banking and foreign trade sectors, and rejection of US aid, for the good reason that these measures (which Marxism itself could not have disavowed) tend to make their seizure of power and the expulsion of the Sangkum more difficult, by, in their own words, 'cutting the grass from under our feet'.[246] Rather than being encouraged by Sihanouk's domestic reforms and his neutralism, the Pol Pot group were worried that these very moves were going too far. Domestic as well as nationalist demands were now in danger of being *headed off* by being moderately satisfied, and Kampuchea would remain relatively stable, while the flames of revolutionary war lit up all neighbouring countries. Pol Pot knew that for a revolution to succeed, Kampuchean society had to be destabilized. (On the other hand, the Vietnamese communists needed a stable buffer state there, to succeed in their aims at home.)

The relationship with the Communist Party of Thailand was to be a longstanding one. It had probably already been sealed by that between Pol Pot and Nuon Chea, a former member of the CPT[247] and perhaps the intended recipient of the captured documents that apparently originated from Pol Pot in Beijing. At least, it is known that Chea was in the Cardamoms on the Thai border at the time.[248]

According to an informed Vietnamese source, Pol Pot spent four months or more in China, including a period when the then CCP Secretary-General Deng Xiaoping worked with him.[249] It is known that it was Deng and President Liu Shaoqi, rather than the leaders soon to be associated with the Cultural Revolution, who held the positions in the Chinese Party appropriate for them to have been responsible for receiving the Kampuchean Party delegation.[250] The significance for them of Sihanouk's presence in Beijing, where he praised China as Kampuchea's foremost friend, and of his attendance at China's National Day rally on 1 October, may well have been tempered by the events in Indonesia with which they coincided: the abortive coup on 30 September and the massacre, according to the CIA, of 800,000 communists and others which immediately began. Any lingering doubts in the minds of Pol Pot and the Chinese leaders as to the wisdom of preparing for an armed struggle in Kampuchea may have been dispelled by these developments, which demonstrated Sukarno's powerlessness to defend his communist allies.[251]

The fact that Sihanouk was unaware that the head of the Khmer communist movement was in Beijing at the same time as himself is of great significance. Sihanouk's confidence in Chinese willingness to deter communist activity in his country was considerable; but it was based not only on China's size and distance from Kampuchea, but also on the mistaken belief that the Khmer communist leaders were aligned with Hanoi. A knowledge of the direct Chinese interest in advancing their movement might well have altered his conviction that it was the Vietnamese, and not the Chinese, who were playing a double 'State and Party' game with his country. This misconception of Sihanouk's was a key asset to Pol Pot and the Chinese, and pains were taken to reinforce it, as we shall see. It demanded the utmost secrecy, a tactic for which the CPK Centre later became notorious, to the point where according to a 1977 Party document, secrecy itself was 'the basis' of the revolution.[252] There is also good reason to believe that in the ensuing years the Pol Pot group were little more forthcoming to the Vietnamese Communists than they were to Sihanouk. The 1978 *Black Book* implies, for instance, that Hanoi was not told of the Centre's view of it: 'As early as 1966, the Communist Party of Kampuchea *judged* that it could only have state-to-state and other public relations with Vietnam because there was a fundamental contradiction between the Kampuchean revolution and the Vietnamese revolution.'[253]

While in Beijing, Pol Pot is likely to have been asked by the Chinese, as by the Vietnamese, to refrain from outright armed rebellion against Sihanouk. But Chinese policy interests also lay in alienating the Kampuchean Party from the Vietnamese one, and for this reason Pol Pot probably did receive encouragement for his adoption of a hostile posture towards Sihanouk. Without actually threatening his regime, this would provoke sufficient repression of the legal left to render critical co-operation with him an unworkable policy, and thus would alienate the Khmer communists from the Vietnamese sponsors of that policy. This strategy would be termed 'combined armed and political struggle'.[254]

As Pol Pot prepared to leave for home (after a secret visit to Pyongyang,[255] again unknown to Sihanouk who had also been there), the Chinese Party sponsored a banquet for the Kampuchean delegation to which Vietnamese representatives were invited. On this occasion, according to the same Vietnamese source, Mao himself made a particularly effusive speech about the merits of the Kampuchean Party, causing the Vietnamese guests to believe that he had had important discussions with Pol Pot and had for some reason been rather impressed.[256] The Chinese message was clear: the new leadership of the Kampuchean Party enjoyed their protection. So was its secret nature: even thirteen years later, the *Black Book*'s account omitted any reference to Pol Pot's visit to China, mentioning only the debates in Hanoi, as part of his trip 'abroad'.[257]

Pol Pot left China before the Cultural Revolution began and arrived back in Kampuchea early in 1966, a year that was to prove a turning point for the CPK (and also for the country's history). As the *Black Book* again notes, in a curious ending to its discussion of events in 1955: 'In 1966, the Communist Party of Kampuchea consolidated and strengthened its position of independence, sovereignty and self-reliance, and clearly discerned the true nature of the Vietnamese.'[258] It is difficult to believe that Pol Pot's visit to Beijing had not aided him in his discernment. The Vietnamese seem to have sensed something of the kind; they now created a special unit, called 'P-36' and directly answerable to VWP Politburo member Le Duc Tho, to train an increased number of Khmer cadres.[259] But Hanoi still could not afford either to alienate Sihanouk or to see his regime destabilized, and the trainees, most of whom were apparently Khmer Krom, remained in Vietnam.[260]

On Pol Pot's return, the Party established a clandestine newspaper, *Reaksmei Krahom* ('Red Light').[261] Intriguingly, it was a name with the same meaning as that of the journal produced by Deng Xiaoping in France in the 1920s (*Chiguang*);[262] equally intriguingly, a radical Khmer student magazine in Paris in the early 1950s had been called *La Lumière* ('The Light').[263] The new name was also in the same tradition as those of the organs of other newly-established pro-Chinese parties in this period (such as *L'Humanité Rouge* instead of *L'Humanité*, in France). Vorn Vet made clear the impact of Pol Pot's return from China; in early 1966, he wrote in his confession, 'the Party raised the line of struggling for strength in the towns, and *preparing for armed struggle in the countryside*'.[264]

February 1966 saw the arrest of several members of the Pracheachon in Kompong Cham and a number of secondary school instructors elsewhere;[265] copies of *Reaksmei Krahom* were found in their possession. Although Pracheachon members were still publishing two above-ground papers, *Preah Vihear* (named after the tenth-century temple that Sihanouk's government had succeeded in regaining from Thailand in 1962) and *Damnoeng Thmey*, still Sihanouk regarded their group and the rest of the above-ground left as responsible for the contents of *Reaksmei Krahom* and other captured documents. On 20 February, he published a heated 'Message to the Pracheachon Party'[266] and delivered a long diatribe against it on the radio. He said it had abandoned 'the normal legal activities of a duly authorized political party'.[267] Noting that 'subversion' had recommenced 'after a retreat, a certain period of calm',[268] and that it was marked by 'pretentious so-called 'anti-Americanism'',[269] he quoted *Reaksmei Krahom* as saying that 'Norodom Sihanouk is a secret agent of the United States'.[270]

The captured documents began with three other points: that the Khmer resistance forces (not Sihanouk) were responsible for the achievement of independence; that the Sangkum was an oppressive organization and should be countered by mobilizing around the slogan 'Khmer people, stand up, overthrow Sihanouk and save Kampuchea';[271] and that Sihanouk supported and favoured only the corrupt and dishonest who stole the people's money – 'He is the accomplice of Songsakd whom he publicly pretends to condemn'.[272]

To the last point, Sihanouk aptly replied: 'I leave it to people whose brains are constructed normally to judge this accusation ...',[273] but the other points worried him more, in particular because for the first time elements of the left were attacking him personally, as well as the Sangkum as a whole. 'You have depicted me in a cartoon (appearing in *Reaksmei Krahom*) as a fisherman bringing a fish (representing the Khmer people) out of the water and throwing it into the 'American and French frying pans'; the message of the cartoon is 'Sihanouk deceiving the Khmer people and leading it to slavery and death'.'[274] He pointed out that 'all our intellectuals, even those of the left enshrined in the daily *La Dépêche*' shared his own attitude to France whose aid was considered acceptable because it was 'absolutely unconditional'. So was Chinese aid, he went on. 'Would you dare show your disapproval [to China]?' He then gave his reading of the significance of the documents: 'Since the 1950s you have always done your best to make Kampuchea the colony of a red Vietnam'. He referred to 'the advanced state of Vietminhization of the minds' of the documents' authors, who he said deserved the 'just appellation Khmer Viet Minh'.[275]

Of course, this was precisely the appellation that Pol Pot and his colleagues did *not* deserve. True, the documents emphasized the struggle of the 'Khmer Vietminh', but only before 1956, when the communists had taken account of the change in Sihanouk's policies by dropping their bitter opposition to him. Pol Pot was returning to the Party's positions of that era, despite his private claim that they had led to a failure born of dependence on Vietnam, and despite what had happened in the meantime. Thus, Sihanouk had been a US agent, according to *Reaksmei Krahom*, 'since 1955',[276] when he had signed the military and economic aid agreement with Washington. Sihanouk protested that this had taken place before the Sangkum was founded, that neutrality was 'a creation of the Sangkum', and that 'I have broken off all relations between Kampuchea and the Americans'.[277] But this was nothing but a feint, a deception, according to *Reaksmei Krahom*; Sihanouk cherished US aid but had been forced to reject it under popular pressure, and further he had waited until the last minute to break off diplomatic relations.[278]

As Sihanouk countered that he had waited until 'only one Khmer' death had occurred at the hands of US and South Vietnamese forces after his last warning to them, it was clear that the nationalist stakes were being raised.

The Pol Pot group were unwilling to support any of Sihanouk's policies; even the ones they obviously considered capable of attracting nationalist or left-wing support were to be rejected because they 'cut the grass from under our feet'. It was not the policies themselves, but the fact that it was Sihanouk who implemented them and got the credit, that they found objectionable. Several months later, when Sihanouk released the Pracheachon detainees, this was seen merely to reflect his acknowledgement that 'crime does not pay'.[279] A clandestine pamphlet entitled *Tung Krahom* ('Red Flag') captured in Kompong Cham in May, proclaimed: 'Cambodia is apparently calm but this demonstrates the need for an intense struggle against the ruling classes ... We must not count too much on Sihanouk ... He realizes that crime does not pay in the face of political consciousness, of the determination of the struggle of the masses of the people and of the democratic forces. *This attitude of duplicity is dangerous because it sometimes bears fruit.* Each member must get this into his head: remember that the Khmer people today live in terror of the feudalists and the imperialists led by Sihanouk ... In the current circumstances, Sihanouk and his supporters are not a part of the national unity organism.'[280] *Tung Krahom* denounced 'these lackeys who bawl out at length that they are the pioneers of anti-imperialism',[281] and announced the redefinition of Kampuchean nationalism. Ironically, the origins of the Pol Pot group's opposition to Sihanouk's regime lay in part in his pre-1963 failure to implement domestic reforms, and they had then considered his foreign policy irrelevent if not a sham. Now, however, given their intent to launch an armed struggle for radical social revolution, they found it expedient to *outdo* Sihanouk's nationalism. It was a revealing comment on which particular political issue was seen as most capable of mobilizing the Khmer people. 'Genuine nationalism', from now on, would be a nationalism far more tenacious and severe than that of Sihanouk.

Pol Pot and his group would have been extremely careful to avoid giving Sihanouk any indication of their differences with Vietnam and, potentially, with most Khmer resistance veterans. Had he been aware of these, he might have been tempted to provoke a split, by reducing pressure on the traditionally Vietnam-oriented left and cracking down more severely on those more attuned to the policies of the new Party leadership. This would have been disastrous for the latter. Hence the lead statement in the new propaganda offensive: the resistance forces were responsible for the achievement of independence.[282] Partly because of the element of truth in it, this touched a raw nerve. Sihanouk's reply to this 'accusation' was rabid and long-winded, and he undermined his own case by stressing the foreign patronage he had received at Geneva from the 'Great Powers'.[283] But the effect of the statement was double-barrelled. Not only did Sihanouk take the bait in blaming the Pracheachon and 'Khmer Viet Minh' for 'this new awakening' of subversion,[284] so that he was more inclined to launch a new wave of repression against them and thereby either neutralize them or drive them underground and into the organizational embrace of Pol Pot. The effect was *also* to encourage former resistance veterans to believe that their experience had not in fact been discounted by the new Party leadership and that they would be welcome participants in a new struggle if they were inclined or driven to join it.

Five days later Sihanouk attempted a public explanation for all this. 'It is surprising that the Pracheachon have chosen as the time to attack the Sangkum again the very moment when we are resisting the US imperialists and their lackeys more fiercely than ever. We even kicked out the Asia Foundation ... [The US is] the common enemy of Sangkum Cambodia and of their communist 'gurus', who approve of us, congratulate us, offer us aid.' He said that this 'strange phenomenon' could be explained only by the fact that the local communists had been fervent supporters of Son Ngoc Thanh when they were studying in France, and that Thanh's recently declared war on his regime coincided with 'this new 'awakening'' of left-wing subversion. 'It is therefore clear that these 'reds' serve the interests of Thanh', said the Prince.[285] And certainly, since Geneva, only the Thanhist and Pol Pot groups had evinced much determination to overturn Sihanouk's regime and 'remake' Khmer society.

In April Sihanouk analysed the significance of the new left-wing posture. In 1956, he said, 'when it noted, on the one hand, that the entire socialist camp had firmly decided to adopt Sangkum Cambodia as a friend for a long period, and on the other hand, that the Sangkum would never fall into the trap of pro-Americanism or pro-'Nekolim' [neo-colonialism], the 'Pracheachon' Party lowered the tone of its propaganda in a very understandable and logical way. In certain periods, it even stopped its 'discreet and whispered' subversion and gave its support to Sihanouk's 'policy of national union, peace, independence, neutrality and progress' although without the least reference to the Sangkum and the Throne ... This 'harmony' in the relationship between the crypto-communist party and the Sangkum lasted from 1956 to 1965.'[286]

However, other developments already afoot were to prove at least as signficant for the country's future. The war in Vietnam was settling down for the duration, and in 1966 it began to have a serious impact on Kampuchea's economy. In that year, forty per cent of the rice crop was smuggled across the border into Vietnam.[287] As early as November 1965, according to a US intelligence report the next month: 'Sihanouk indicated that the Viet Cong had approached Cambodian economic chief Son Sann in an effort to buy Cambodian rice. Without indicating whether any decision had been made on this overture, Sihanouk said that the illicit traffic in rice from Cambodia to Vietnam – where the price of rice is much higher – was resulting in a considerable loss of revenue to the government.'[288] Black market circles in Saigon were also involved in the smuggling.[289]

Equally important, the Vietnamese communists were resorting increasingly to the use of Kampuchean territory for sanctuary from American attack. At the end of 1965, according to the US report, they had established 'clandestine and probably temporary facilities' there, which 'have played only a small part in the overall Communist effort in South Vietnam, and in no respects compare to the extensive guerrilla base areas located in South Vietnam itself'. The report also noted: 'Various reports indicating that the guerrillas have built tunnels in the immediate border area suggest, however, that the Communists have sought wherever practicable to take advantage of the border without actually crossing into Cambodia. When they do cross, the Communists have been careful to avoid contact with Cambodian border outposts, taking advantage of a *laissez-faire* policy adopted unilaterally by some Cambodian border forces.'

However, this was increasingly difficult as the war escalated. 'The picture is quite different in other areas. Some eight instances of fire fights between Cambodian border forces and the Viet Cong have been noted this year. On several occasions

Cambodian forces have also launched clearing operations against suspected Viet Cong intruders. This conflicting picture of the VC-Cambodian border relations suggests that there is no Phnom Penh-directed policy.' And here was an important point: 'If Sihanouk is not fully aware of the situation along the border ... Lon Nol is. Lon Nol is reliably reported to have been chagrined that the Communists 'in small numbers' took advantage of Cambodian territory during the battles near Plei Me.'[290]

At the time this report was written, there was still a significant difference between the domestic political approaches of Lon Nol and Sihanouk. But 1966 was the year in which they began to converge, for reasons that should now be clear. By the end of that year, Lon Nol would become Prime Minister, with Sihanouk's backing.

Nevertheless, some leading members of the left retained the conviction that the system could be reformed from within, and in 1966 they still wielded considerable influence in national political life. Apart from Hou Yuon and others, there was Chau Seng, who remained editor of the daily, *La Dépêche*, which had a circulation of 4,000. Son Phuoc Tho's private newspaper, *Meatophum*, had become a daily with a circulation of 7,000. It regularly published translations of articles taken directly from the pages of a local NLF-sponsored Vietnamese-language daily, *Trung Lap* ('Neutral'), which itself had a circulation of 6,200. The figures for the weekly papers *Preah Vihear and Damnoeng Thmey* are unknown, but would most likely have been no more than a few thousand. The private-enterprise daily, *Phnom Penh Presse*, on the other hand, sold about 1,200 copies.[291]

In the sphere of governmental affairs, in 1966 Phouk Chhay was appointed Director-General of the state-owned National Import Company, SONAPRIM.[292] In May, an 'Important Seminar on Economic Problems' was held in the capital; according to the official government summary of the proceedings, So Nem presented a report on agriculture, Chau Seng was commissioned to contact French businessmen for the purpose of selling the coffee crop, and Hu Nim 'gave advice and suggestions on certain particular points, in order to throw more light on the questions at issue'.[293] The left now enjoyed a clearly subordinate position, but it was still able to operate relatively freely in what was, perhaps, since the institution of the military government in Indonesia in March 1966, the most open and politically tolerant society in Southeast Asia.

Even among the underground left there were serious misgivings about the strategy of armed rebellion. Vorn Vet wrote: 'My standpoint was to resist the preparations for armed struggle in the countryside. For one thing it was my personal standpoint: I saw that it would not work ... In mid 1966 So Phim came from the base to rest in the house of Se, the courier ... Phim wanted to go to Siemreap to see Angkor and come back through Battambang. I accompanied Phim on his trip ... Phim raised with me the question of the armed struggle – it had to be resisted [he said], the people did not want to spill blood ... In the Eastern bases, there would be real difficulties in the event of an armed struggle ... I replied that it would not pay, with our hands empty like that; the enemy would exterminate us first and we would disappear and not be able to rise again.'[294]

But the misgivings would soon disappear. According to Charles Meyer: 'In fact it was around the middle of 1966 that government repression began against the forces of the left.'[295] Almost simultaneously came one of the first indications that the Pol Pot group was reaping some success in convincing members of the Pracheachon that the time had come to begin the struggle for social revolution. In June 1966, *Damnoeng Thmey* published an article which stated in part that 'the feudalists hope to preserve the rough joke regime which allows them to oppress the workers and farmers.'[296] At the same time, Pracheachon members in Kompong Cham complained about the French who were running the rubber plantations there, and accused Sihanouk and other figures of the regime of being 'lackeys of the French neo-colonialists'.[297] In May, the underground pamphlet there, *Tung Krahom*, blamed 'Sihanouk's directives' for the activities of the Khmer Krom 'White Scarves, lackeys of the imperialists'. They had been unmasked by 'the Party' — an unprecedented reference which also signalled its switch onto the offensive.[298] In July, Harrison Salisbury wrote what was probably the first Western report of the activities of Pol Pot, Ieng Sary and Son Sen when he said that tribal dissidence had begun in the North-East of Kampuchea.[299] It is impossible to say whether the government repression was the immediate cause or the immediate effect of these first signs of the civil war; deteriorating socio-economic conditions also played an important part.[300]

At this stage, the Prince still seems to have played some role in alleviating repression: Ney Sarann's nephew, Ly Sae, was released from Prey Saor prison in 1966, 'by Sihanouk's decree' according to his wife. Sin Song, a young peasant from Prey Veng who had joined the secret Communist Youth of Kampuchea organization in 1965, recalls: 'In 1966, I was arrested by Lon Nol agents and imprisoned in Prey Veng for three months. We were struggling against exploitation, for rights and freedoms, struggling over produce and land, and especially against the district chief of Peam Chor, who had embezzled state funds designed for the people, after they had all put their names down in order to form a co-operative. A popular demonstration was held at the district office in order to demand my release, and a letter was sent directly to Sihanouk. Sihanouk ordered them to release me and my six companions.'[301] In general, however, the military and security forces were able to act either independently of Sihanouk or with his implicit backing, and it was at this point, according to all sources, that *violent* repressions became the norm. In Komchay Meas district in Prey Veng in 1966, 'Lon Nol people' killed a former Issarak activist, and gaoled a Buddhist monk for his sympathy with the revolutionary underground.[302] In Koh Kong in the same year, 'mopping-up operations by the forces of order' forced local communist leaders, who were headed by Prasith, to flee temporarily into Thailand.[303] In Kompong Speu, six members of a mobile traditional orchestra in a former Pracheachon stronghold near Oudong were arrested by soldiers, disembowelled and their livers exhibited outside the local military post.[304]

In Phnom Penh, Sihanouk published a series of articles in the monthly *Sangkum*. He asked: 'Why do our reds ... call on the people, the intellectuals and the youth to rise up against us?'[305] Part of the answer, namely the nature and politics of the leadership of the communist underground, became clear the next month when Sihanouk published extracts from one of its leaflets. The leaflet was entitled 'On the struggle to eliminate passivity, timidity and the adherence to tranquillity among our followers, who must prepare a violent revolution'. It stated:

> Today's society is corrupted and won over by the cult of the individual, which we must abolish at all costs. We live in a sick society since the return to peace.
>
> All brave and honest children of the fatherland must join the revolutionary party in order to move the country towards communist socialism.
>
> The capitalists who live in affluence at the expense of the working class and the masses, do not hesitate to resort to grand

methods to obtain luxuries and gratify their passions.

The masses live in misery, bled by them.

The aim of the revolution is the liberation of the people from the capitalists and feudalists. To succeed it is necessary to resort to force.[306]

The ideas expressed here are similar to those of the stridently 'Marxist–Leninist' parties that broke away from mainstream Moscow-oriented communist bodies throughout the world in the early 1960s, aligning themselves with China *before* the Cultural Revolution. (It is worth noting the leaflet's rejection of the 'cult of the individual': this is of course a reference to Sihanouk, but had there been any consuming attraction for Mao's Cultural Revolution on the part of the author it would likely have brought more circumspection to this point.)

In September 1966, just as the last of Sihanouk's articles, which were entitled 'The Behaviour of the Khmer Communist Party towards the Sangkum Reastr Niyum',[307] was published, what the Party later described as a meeting of its Central Committee was convened, and indeed, took the ('provisional') decision to change its name from 'Workers' Party' to the 'Communist Party of Kampuchea'.[308] The CPK now considered its struggle to be ideologically more advanced than that of the Vietnamese communists, and of course at the same level as that of the Chinese.

Also in September 1966, elections for the National Assembly gave a majority of seats, and power, to the right led by Lon Nol. In August, under increasing pressure from the representatives of the business and land-holding classes, and increasingly disinclined to protect the position of the left in the political system, Sihanouk had abandoned his previous policy of nominating only one single Sangkum candidate in each electoral district.[309] 425 candidates were then nominated for the eighty-two seats, and left-wing deputies now had to compete with leaders of the traditional elite, who were able to turn their political and economic status in most localities to good electoral advantage. Only forty-two of the seventy-seven incumbent deputies stood for re-election. On the left, Son Phuoc Tho, who had fallen out with Sihanouk, did not stand for re-election; nor did So Nem. Chau Seng, who had resigned his seat in 1965, also declined to stand again. Only Hou Yuon, Hu Nim and Khieu Samphan took up the challenge, which was made more difficult when Sihanouk campaigned actively and specifically against them. The three were re-elected by large margins (Hou Yuon received 78 per cent of the vote in his Kompong Cham electorate), and one other 'leftist' won a seat in Kratie; but throughout the rest of the country conservative candidates prevailed, usually by low margins over similar candidates, in a poll characterized by vote-buying and the manipulation of pervasive patron-client networks. Only twenty-six deputies won by a clear majority, and there were charges of irregularities in fifty-six of the eighty-two electoral districts.[310]

Some sections of the underground left also participated in the elections. During the year, Hu Nim made a secret visit to So Phim's base area on the Vietnamese border, and also met many other leading Eastern Zone cadres.[311] Further, in his prison confessions ten years later he recalled the help he had received from Koy Thuon (Khuon), Party Secretary of the Northern Zone, and his CPK deputy, Sreng, a former student follower of Nim in his electoral district: 'The 1966 election campaign was very tense. The Chum Sarum, Sos Saoun and Var Kim Ton groups, who were the candidates standing against me, controlled everyone with power, from the subdistrict chiefs to the district chief (Chey In) to the province chief (I Thuy), as well as the police, intelligence services and the military ... [But] Sreng organized the people and the youth to go from house to house through the villages and subdistricts, distributing my leaflets and propagandizing the people to vote for me. In the end, because the leaders of Sreng's group and their movement to support me was successful from start to finish, I then won the election, even though the opposition used their power and all kinds of cruel tactics. The election success made me believe in Sreng's group and movement.'[312] It is interesting to note in passing that according to local informants, Sreng was still working openly at this stage (although the authorities clearly had little indication of his CPK role); he went underground only in 1968.[313]

In the East, too, an associate of Chou Chet and Non Suon and former manager of *Pancha Sila* press, Chuon Ya Ngan, stood for election in Krek. With the help of two known 'partisans of the Viet Minh', Ngan managed to win five thousand votes, finishing second in a field of five.[314] At the same time, however, in Memut, the CPK underground began to infiltrate the subdistrict militia in an attempt to get control of their weapons.[315]

On 22 October, Lon Nol became Prime Minister. One

member of his new Cabinet was Kou Roun, former head of the security police. As Sihanouk said soon afterwards, the 1966 elections were in general 'a victory for the former members of [Lon Nol's] Renovation Party and for the non-left younger generation'.[316]

Perhaps alarmed by the subsequent refusal of members of all sections of the left to accept offers of Cabinet portfolios under such people, Sihanouk set up a left-wing 'Counter-Government' whose function was to monitor and criticize the activities of the Cabinet. But pressure from the right proved too strong, and Hou Yuon, Khieu Samphan and Hu Nim were quietly deprived of their positions in this body. Moreover, Sihanouk removed Chau Seng from his post as *chef du Cabinet*.[317] He did accept the *fait accompli* when Seng, in 'an after-dark raid' on the office of *La Dépêche,* took control of the newspaper and renamed it *La Dépêche du Cambodge;*[318] but when, in an editorial, Seng asked him to take over the Prime Ministership personally, Sihanouk declined, preferring simply to rub salt in the wound: 'The left. . . knows, in effect, that with Sihanouk, it can exercise effective pro-socialist subversion, in particular among the youth, which it would not be able to do easily with General Lon Nol.'[319] This was to prove true and false (Lon Nol was certainly an easier target, even if more repressive.) Sihanouk advised the left not to worry; in 'twelve years' time' they would win power.[320] He overestimated only by three years, but it was a different left that won power in 1975. By that time, the left that Sihanouk had been addressing in 1966 had been crushed between the Scylla and Charybdis of Lon Nol and Pol Pot.

Some members of this ill-fated left may have foreseen such an outcome. But there was little they could do as the process was about to begin. When eight students were arrested for handing out leaflets calling for the dismissal of the Cabinet and for new elections, 'demonstrators surrounded the police station where the eight were held, demanding their release. When they were refused, they attacked the station, destroying furniture and office supplies and injuring one policeman.'[321]

A week later, Sihanouk levelled the charge that Hu Nim and his supporters in Kompong Cham were attempting to set up a 'counter-government' seated in Nim's electoral district there.[322] The final blow, however, came in December. The Pracheachon papers *Preah Vihear* and *Damnoeng Thmey* apparently published articles stating that it was the 'Resistance Forces' who had been responsible for obtaining national independence in 1954. A tactless move by people whose veteran leaders were in gaol or in hiding, this was too much for Sihanouk, and again he played into Pol Pot's hands. According to Don O. Noel, he threatened libel suits against the editors of the two papers, and then called them before a National Congress in which he confronted them personally. The two were publicly humiliated; when they apologized to the Prince, he turned and 'then ridiculed them for not having the courage of their convictions'. Noel continues: 'The next day, both men were beaten up in a dark street. The papers closed, and the men disappeared. There is no evidence that the beatings were in any way inspired by Sihanouk but it seems likely that they were made possible by his actions.'[323]

The die was cast. The last remnants of the veteran grass-roots left, represented by the Pracheachon, had been driven underground, and most of the educated left were soon to follow, as a civil war began.

In 1977, a CPK document looked back in triumph on this period. It discussed the dissident views of Touch Phoeun, Ney Sarann (both of whom had just been executed) and others who had 'said it was necessary to live together in the world [i.e. with the Vietnamese, and] live together with Sihanouk inside the country'; it then went on: 'If our analysis had failed, we would have been in greater danger than [the communists] in Indonesia. But our analysis was victorious, because our analysis was agreed upon, because most of our cadres were in life-and-death contradiction with the enemy; the enemy sought to exterminate them constantly.'[324] To a certain extent, however, the 'analysis' had been self-fulfilling, as had Sihanouk's prophecies about communist tactics.

Notes:

1. *Les paroles de Samdech Preah Norodom Sihanouk,* Phnom Penh, Ministry of Information, October–December 1966, p.764. Speech in Phnom Penh, 4 November 1966. (Henceforth *Les Paroles.*)
2. See Gareth Porter, 'Vietnamese Communist Policy Towards Kampuchea, 1930–1970', in David P. Chandler and Ben Kiernan (eds.), *Revolution and its Aftermath in Kampuchea,* New Haven, 1983, p.72.

3. *Ibid.* Porter cites the Vietnam News Agency in English, 6 and 29 April 1955, *Nhan Dan,* 23 August 1955, and the Vietnam News Agency in Cambodian, 21 September 1955.

4. A post-Geneva analysis by the Directing Committee of the Vietnam Workers' Party had described Kampuchea in the following context: 'Nambo [southern Vietnam], *the last enemy base,* is located next to Cambodia, whose government is feudal, reactionary, and pro-American.' Interestingly, this captured document suggests that Kampuchea was nevertheless not a target of VWP ambitions. (Emphasis added.) US MISSION IN VIETNAM. . . CAPTURED DOCU-MENTS. Item 200, 'Viet Minh Policy Document on Post-Geneva Strategy', p. 13.

5. Porter, *op. cit.,* pp.91–92, citing Vietnam News Agency, 6 October 1955.

6. Michael Leifer, *Cambodia: The Search for Security,* New York 1967, p.74.

7. Porter, *op. cit.,* p.72, citing the Voice of Vietnam in Cambodian, 3 March 1956; also 11 February 1956, and Vietnam News Agency in Vietnamese, 9 February 1956.

8. *Ibid.*

9. Leifer, *op. cit.,* p.79.

10. D. J. Steinberg *et al., Cambodia: Its People, Its Society, Its Culture,* New Haven 1959, p. 294, Table 4.

11. Hou Yuon, *Pahnyaha Sahakor* ('The Cooperative Question'), Phnom Penh 1964, p.6.

12. Author's interview with Puk Soum, Prey Veng, 8 August 1980.

13. Hou Yuon, *op. cit.,* p.6.

14. Bernard B. Fall, *Vietnam Witness, 1953–66,* London 1966, pp.236–37.

15. Wilfred Burchett, *Mekong Upstream,* Hanoi 1957, pp.199–205. Burchett quotes Hou Yuon as saying 'If we are really neutral other powers should respect this. The USA should not cut off its aid because of this. But if she does, we have powerful friends to whom we can turn for help'. (pp.202–203.)

16. *Kar Teak Tong V.N.* ('Contact with Vietnam'), Non Suon's confession in Tuol Sleng, dated 7 November 1976, p.2.

17. See Chapter 3, p.84, above.

18. Author's interview with US State Department officer Andrew Antippus, who interviewed Sieu Heng in 1970. Washington, March 1980.

19. *Phnaek Ti Pir: Royea Mun Rotprohar 18.3.70* ('Section 2: The Period Before the Coup of 18 March 1970'), Non Suon's confession in Tuol Sleng dated 7 November 1976, p.9.

20. *Summary of Annotated Party History,* by the Eastern Zone Military Political Service, 1973. Translated captured document declassified by the US government in 1978, 37 pp., at pp.12–13.

21. Steinberg, *op. cit.,* p.97.

22. Vorn Vet's untitled confession in Tuol Sleng, December 1978, 54 pp., at pp.1–2.

23. Carlyle Thayer, personal communication. He cites a radio transmission monitored by the US Foreign Broadcast Information Service, referring to 'Sok Nguol'.

24. *Summary of Annotated Party History, op. cit.,* p.13.

25. *Ibid.*

26. *Kar Teak Tong V.N., op. cit.*

27. See Chapter 5, p.157 above.

28. Michael Vickery, 'Looking Back at Cambodia', in Ben Kiernan and

Chanthou Boua (eds.), *Peasants and Politics in Kampuchea, 1942–81,* New York 1982, p.99. This information was obtained by Vickery from the papers of Prince Monireth.

29. *Summary of Annotated Party History, op. cit.,* p.13.
30. Reports of the International Commission for Supervision and Control (ICSC), Command Papers. *Cambodia No. 1, 1958, Cmnd. 526,* p.13.
31. *Ibid.,* p.17.
32. Compare the 1973 *Summary of Annotated Party History, op. cit.,* p.12, with *Prowatt nei Pak Kommyunis Kampuchea* (1974, 23 pp.), p.7. The latter was distributed by Ieng Sary in 1974, and is largely a reproduction of the 1973 version, but with significant additions and deletions. See Chapter 8, Fig. 9, pp.364–7, below, at p.366.
33. Puk Soum, *op. cit.*
34. Author's interview with Krot Theam, Melbourne, 2 December 1976.
35. Author's interview with members of Ke Vin's family, in their village in Baray, 15 October 1980.
36. Vickery, 'Looking Back at Cambodia', *op. cit.,* p.103.
37. 'Interview with Madam Ieng Thirith', by Mukundan C. Menon, New Delhi, November 1979, 10 pp. (no publication details), p.5.
38. The preceding information is derived from various interviews with Khmers who attended these schools, and also from written sources such as the confessions of Non Suon and Vorn Vet, *op. cit.*
39. Author's interviews with Keng Vannsak, Paris, 27 November 1979 and 2 February 1980.
40. Christopher Pym, *Mistapim in Cambodia,* London, 1960, pp.155–56.
41. *Livre Noir: Faits et preuves des actes d'aggression et d'annexion du Vietnam contre le Kampuchea* (henceforth *Livre Noir*), Phnom Penh, Ministry of Foreign Affairs of Democratic Kampuchea, September 1978, 112 pp., at p.26. Two other Vietnamese leaders, including Nguyen Van Linh, now a member of the Politburo of the Vietnamese Communist Party, were also said to have taken refuge in Phnom Penh in this period. *Livre Noir* adds: 'In neutral and stable Kampuchea, the Vietnamese found security'.
42. Pierre Bernardini, 'L'Implantation caodaïste au Cambodge en 1969', *Actes du XXIXe Congrès international des Orientalistes: Asie du Sud-Est Continentale,* Paris 1976, vol. 1, pp.1–6, at p.2.
43. Most of the preceding information is taken from interviews with a number of these Khmers who defected after 1970 to the Lon Nol regime, or back to Vietnam. See 'Khmer Rouge Rallier Keoum Kun', unclassified Airgram to Department of State from US Embassy, Phnom Penh, 13 January 1972, 12 pp.; 'Conversations with Khmer Rouge Rallier Ieng Lim', from the same source, 30 November 1971, 4 pp.; 'Defectors Recount Disaffection with Communists', AFP, Hong Kong, 1 April 1974, in US CIA *Foreign Broadcast Information Service* (FBIS), Daily Report, Asia and the Pacific, 4 April 1974, pp.H3–H5; and 'La Terreur au Cambodge', *Problèmes Politiques et Sociaux* (Paris), no. 373, 12 October 1979, pp.5–7. Also author's interviews in Phnom Penh, 1980 and 1981. On Son Ngoc Minh, See *US Mission in Vietnam. . . Captured Documents, op. cit.,* item 204, Vol. 4, document dating from mid-1956, p.3.
44. Charles Meyer, *Derrière le sourire khmer,* Paris 1971, p.389.
45. Author's interview with Chea Soth, Phnom Penh, 22 October 1980.
46. Norodom Sihanouk, 'Le Communisme au Cambodge', *France-Asie,* vol. 15,

no. 144, 1958, pp.192–206, at p.201.

47. By comparison, in 1952, the Democratic party newspaper had had a bi-weekly circulation of nine thousand, in a period when it was the only organ tolerated by the authorities that presented non-establishment views. (Steinberg, *op. cit.,* p.143.) Much later, in 1967, when all communist papers were banned and both the absolute population and the proportional literate audience had greatly increased, the largest Khmer daily, *Sochivator* ('Civilization'), was selling about sixty thousand copies per week, and the leftist *Meatophum* about forty thousand. See Don O. Noel., 'Cambodia: The Mass Media', New York, Alicia Patterson Fund, 17 April 1967, 32 pp. at p.18.

48. See for instance André Tong, *Sihanouk, La fin des illusions,* Paris 1972, p.68.

49. *Sekkedey srong pi sapordamean Ekapeap Mittapeap ning Pracheachon* ('Report on the Newspapers *Ekapeap, Mittapeap* and *Pracheachon*'), Phnom Penh 1960, 158 pp., at p.152–53 and 115.

50. Timothy M. Carney, *Communist Party Power in Kampuchea,* Cornell University South-East Asia Program Data Paper no. 106, 1977, pp.32–33.

51. Meyer, *op. cit.,* p.140.

52. Bureau des Elections, Ministère de l'Intérieur, Royaume du Cambodge, 1966. Copy of the election statistics, in possession of the author.

53. *Interview of Comrade Pol Pot. . . to the Delegation of Yugoslav Journalists in Visit to Democratic Kampuchea,* Phnom Penh, Ministry of Foreign Affairs, March 1978, 23 pp., at p.22.

54. Vorn Vet's confession, *op. cit.,* p.9.

55. Michael Vickery, 'Cambodia 1973: The Present Situation and its Background', 50 pp. unpublished typescript, at p.21.

56. Author's interviews with Achar Kong Son and others who knew Hu Nim well in this period. Prey Totoeng, 4 August 1980.

57. FBIS, 24 March 1976, p.16, quoting Vientiane Radio, 23 March 1976. I am grateful to Stephen Heder for bringing this reference to my attention.

58. Roger M. Smith, *Cambodia's Foreign Policy,* Ithaca 1965, p.169. Quotation form *Réalitiés Cambodgiennes,* 15 March 1958.

59. Norodom Sihanouk, *Souvenirs doux et amers,* Paris 1981, p.311; see also Wilfred Burchett, *The China Cambodia Vietnam Triangle,* New York 1981, p.163, who relates an incident that he says occurred in 1956, which may or may not be the same as the one Sihanouk dates at 1960.

60. *Le Sangkum,* April 1966, p.12.

61. David P. Chandler, personal communication, based on an interview with Sihanouk's close aide Nhek Tioulong, in Bangkok, August 1981.

62. Meyer, *op. cit.,* p.140.

63. Norodom Sihanouk, 'Le Communisme au Cambodge', *op. cit.,* p. 202.

64. Porter, *op. cit.,* p.73. He cites Vietnam News Agency in English, 7 March 1958. The link, however, did not extend beyond neutralism. Political cadres in Hanoi continued to stress the incompatibility of 'kings and communism'. See 'Khmer Rouge Rallier Keoum Kun', *op. cit.,* p.2.

65. *Ompi Pankar Ruom Chong Kraoy* ('On the Last Joint Plan'), 24 pp., written by officials of the Democratic Kampuchea security service, 1978. Translation by US Embassy in Thailand, 27 pp., at p.17.

66. *Pankar Vietnam chumpuoh Kampuchea niw peel chup bainh niw Indochen thngay 20.7.54* ('The Vietnamese Plan for Kampuchea at the Time Fighting Stopped in Indo-China on 20 July 1954'), undated confession by Non Suon in Tuol Sleng, 8pp., at p.6.

67. *Summary of Annotated Party History, op. cit.,* p.16.
68. *Kar Teak Tong V.N., op. cit.*
69. See the translation of Pol Pot's long historical speech in BBC *Summary of World Broadcasts* (SWB), 1 October 1977, FE/5629/C2/1 ff.
70. Author's interview with Kol Kon, Komchay Meas, 9 August 1980.
71. Author's interview with Mat Ly, Phnom Penh, August 1981. For Mat Ly's role in the UIF, see Fig. 3, Chapter 3. Colonial records do not confirm that he was tortured by the French, merely saying that 'paralysed in both legs, he is being cared for in Chup hospital'. Bibliothèque Nationale, Phnom Penh. Ministère de l'Intérieur (MID), Bulletin Quotidien de Renseignements (BQR), *1952,* SSHC report, 27 July 1952.
72. 'Manifeste du mouvement Khmer Serei', in *Documents et écrits se rapportant au 'Khmer Serei',* copy in the Wason Collection, Cornell University Olin Library.
73. *Phnaek Ti Pir, op. cit.,* p.12.
74. *Summary of Annotated Party History, op. cit.,* pp.14, 16.
75. See Chapter 2, p.48, and Chapter 3, p.97 above.
76. Author's interview with Nguyen Xuan Hoang, Hanoi, 4 November 1980.
77. *Summary of Annotated Party History, op. cit.,* p.14.
78. In 1954 it had consisted of Sieu Heng (Secretary), Tou Samouth, Son Ngoc Minh, So Phim and N.T. Nhung. Their initials are given in *ibid.,* p.12, with 'S.V.' for So Phim's alias So Vanna. See p.366, below.
79. Author's interview with Sang Lon (Chen Lon), Kandol Chrum, 7 August 1980.
80. *Livre Noir, op. cit.,* pp.23, 24, 29, 43, 44.
81. FBIS, 4 October 1977, p.H–38, text of an official biography broadcast over Pyongyang Radio on 3 October 1977.
82. See Chapter 3.
83. 'A Khmer Issarak Leader's Story', typescript 1976 translation by Timothy Carney of Chan Dara's autobiographical sketch, 12 pp., at p.11.
84. See introduction by Laura Summers to Khieu Samphan, *Cambodia's Economy and Industrial Development,* Cornell University South-East Asia Program Data Paper No. 111, 1979, p.9.
85. *Summary of Annotated Party History, op. cit.,* p.17.
86. Smith, *op. cit.,* pp.169–70. Philippe Preschez, however, says Rattanakiri was created in June 1958, and Mondolkiri in June 1960. *Essai sur la démocratie au Cambodge,* Paris 1961, p.104.
87. *Summary of Annotated Party History, op. cit.,* p.17.
88. *Ibid.*
89. Laura Summers, *op. cit.,* p.9.
90. *Ibid.*
91. *Ibid.,* p.10.
92. *Ibid.,* p.11. For the book, see *Sekkedey srong, op. cit.*
93. See *Khmers Rouges! Matériaux pour l'histoire du communisme au Cambodge,* by Serge Thion and Ben Kiernan, Paris 1981, pp.47–48 for a more complete text, which was published in *L'Observateur,* 17 June 1960.
94. This is the term used in the 1973 Party History. A revised 1974 version, distributed by Ieng Sary, calls it the 'First Congress'. *Summary of Annotated Party History, op. cit.,* pp.17–18; and *Prowatt nei Pak Kommyunis Kampuchea, op. cit.,* p.8. See pp.364–67, below.
95. A third Party History (*Prowatt Pak*) given by Ieng Sary to Khmer cadres in Hanoi in January 1971, makes this point; it is confirmed, according to

240

Timothy Carney, by a Lon Nol regime intelligence assessment, *Synthèse particulière*.

96. *Summary of Annotated Party History, op. cit., p.18; and Nguyen Xuan Hoang, op. cit.*

97. Membership in 1954 was probably 1,000–2,000. See Chapter 4, p.129.

98. Author's interview with Ouch Bun Chhoeun, Phnom Penh, 30 September 1980.

99. *Sarop chamlaiy moat totee rebos Chey Suon dael sarapeap dambong dai niw Ingiec minh* ('Summary of the verbal answers of Chey [Non] Suon in his initial confession yesterday evening'), Tuol Sleng document dated 17 November 1976, signed by Pon, 2 pp., at p.A.

100. FBIS, 4 October 1977, p.H-10.

101. *Livre Noir, op. cit.*, p.36.

102. *Ibid.*; and speech by Nuon Chea, translated in FBIS, 19 January 1977, pp.H1–6, at p.H3.

103. See Chapter 7, pp.253–55, below.

104. 'Biographical sketches of Khmer Communist Leaders', US Embassy, Phnom Penh, March 1975.

105. Khieu Samphan, *op. cit.*, pp.45–46.

106. *Ibid.*, p.30.

107. Personal communication from Ngo Dien, now the Vietnamese Ambassador in Phnom Penh, 22 October 1980.

108. Democratic Kampuchea, Permanent Mission to the United Nations, Press Release, 11 December 1981, p.2. I am grateful to David P. Chandler for drawing this to my attention.

109. *Sarop chamlaiy moat totee, op. cit.*, pp.A, B.

110. *Phnaek Ti Pir, op. cit.*, p.14.

111. According to Laura Summers and Ong Thong Hoeung: 'The Congress in 1960 represented a new start. With Vietnamese support and approval, the faltering KPRP was upgraded and reorganized as a separate national communist party ... the anti-imperialist struggle continued to be the most important task of the Party ... Vietnamese support of this Congress [is] not acknowledged in the official revisionist histories of the CPK.' But even Nuon Chea has provided confirmation of the above analysis. See W.B. Simons and S. White, eds., *The Party Statutes of the Communist World*, The Hague 1984, pp.237–8, 241. It is also worth mentioning that in 1981 the ruling (pro-Vietnamese) Kampuchean communist party, headed by Heng Samrin, accepted the 1960 KPRP meeting as its own 'Second Congress', while in 1976 the Pol Pot regime had launched a secret purge of supposed members of an allegedly traitorous 'Workers' Party'. (There is no evidence to support Pol Pot's public claim that the 1960 meeting marked the turning-point, or rather the *beginning*, of the Party's history, any more than 1955 marks a turning-point for the Lao People's Revolutionary Party as the year of its official First Congress, after *its* official foundation in 1951.) See p.405, note 289, below.

112. *Interview of Comrade Pol Pot, op. cit.*, p.22 ; FBIS, 4 October 1977, p.H–38.

113. For instance, Ouch Bun Chhoeun, *op. cit.*

114. 'Biographical Sketches of Khmer Communist Leaders', *op. cit.*

115. Nuon Chea, *op. cit.*, FBIS, 19 January 1977, p.H-3: 'After 1961 we began to organize secret defence units'.

116. Carney, *op. cit.*, p.33.

117. Smith *op. cit.*, p.170.

118. Quoted in Leifer, *Cambodia: The Search for Security, op. cit.,* p.201.

119. Michael Leifer, 'The Cambodian Opposition', *Asian Survey,* April 1962, pp.11–15. He cites *Réalités Cambodgiennes,* 3 November 1961.

120. 'Biographical Sketches of Khmer Communist Leaders', *op. cit.*

121. *Sekkedey sarapeap rebos dop pir; chomhor ti 6* ('Confessional report of XII: part 6'), Non Suon's confession in Tuol Sleng dated 28 November 1976, 10 pp., pp.1–2.

122. *Ibid.*

123. *Summary of Annotated Party History, op. cit.,* p.15.

124. *Réalités Cambodgiennes,* 26 January 1962.

125. See *Ibid.,* 2 March 1962.

126. US Army *Area Handbook for Cambodia,* April 1963, pp.206–207, table 5.

127. *Des Mouvements Anti-Gouvernementaux au Cambodge,* Deuxième Bureau, Khmer Republic, 20 July 1973, 45 pp., at p.5.

128. Norodom Sihanouk, *Le Cambodge et ses relations avec ses voisins,* Phnom Penh, Ministry of Information, 1962, pp.59–61.

129. *Ibid.*

130. Leifer, 'The Cambodian Opposition', *op. cit.,* p.13.

131. *Livre Noir, op. cit.,* p.37.

132. Michael Vickery, personal communication.

133. *Réalités Cambodgiennes,* 22 March 1962.

134. *Summary of Annotated Party History, op. cit.,* p.19.

135. This event did not become public knowledge, and was perhaps a secret confined to Indo-Chinese communist circles alone, until 1978. In March of that year Pol Pot publicized it — without mentioning Samouth's name — in order to explain his assumption of Party leadership; he stated that 'the enemy', by implication Sihanouk and/or Lon Nol, was responsible. (*Interview of Comrade Pol Pot, op. cit.,* p.22.) However, seven years later, Lon Nol reported that Tou Samouth was 'President of the clandestine Khmer Communist Party', which suggests that the government was still unaware of his demise. (See *Le Sangkum,* November 1969; *New York Times,* 19 April 1970, and *Far Eastern Economic Review,* 6 August 1970.) Further, in the aftermath of a March 1977 purge of Som Chea, until then Party Secretary for Kandal province, blame for Samouth's death was laid on Chea by officials at local public meetings. In the 1960s Chea had been a courier for the Party Centre. He was again accused of having 'killed Tou Samouth' in an early 1978 secret report on internal enemies compiled by the regime's security service; also accused were Ros Mau, who was purged as Chief of Staff on the North-Western Zone Committee in June 1977, and Sieu Heng. The Sihanouk government was not mentioned; nor was Lon Nol. (*Ompi Pankar Ruom Chong Kraoy, op. cit.*) Pol Pot's *public* claim in the same period that 'the enemy' was responsible must therefore be regarded as disingenuous. The executions of Som Chea and Ros Mau the previous year may have been motivated by Pol Pot's desire to cover his own tracks. Finally, the sole public reference to Tou Samouth by name, on the part of the Pol Pot regime, which described him as a Vietnamese 'puppet' (*Livre Noir, op. cit.,* pp.43–44, and elsewhere) was self-consciously suppressed in the widely distributed second edition, along with several other politically revealing paragraphs. (Cf. the English translation, *Black Paper,* pp.29–30, for instance.) Similarly, the 1973 internal Party History's reference to Samouth's disappearance, namely that it was 'great grief for the Party which had just been reorganized' was deleted from Ieng Sary's 1974 version.

(*Summary of Annotated Party History*, *op. cit.*, p.19, and *Prowatt nei Pak Kommyunis Kampuchea*, *op. cit.*, p.8). See Fig. 9, in Chapter 8, pp.364–67, which details this deletion and that of all other references to Samouth's role in the Party.

136. *Interview of Comrade Pol Pot*, *op. cit.*, p.22.

137. Laura Summers, *op. cit.*, p.12.

138. *Ibid.*, p.16.

139. *Journal Officiel*, 13 February 1963, p.644.

140. Royaume du Cambodge, Départment de l'Information, 'Liste des journaux paraissant au Cambodge', 1962–63, 4 pp. I am grateful to William Willmott for passing this material on to me.

141. Don O. Noel, 'Cambodian Politics II: The Man to Get', New York, Alicia Patterson Fund, 25 January 1967, 12 pp. at p.9.

142. Laura Summers, *op. cit.*, p.16. See also note 40 on pp.16–17, *ibid.*, which suggests that the Prince was later embarrassed about the support he had given the Cabinet at the time.

143. *Ibid.*, p.17.

144. *Ibid.* Summers describes Sen as a 'Siem Reap socialist'. There is no other evidence for this, but his wife came from there.

145. One source has described it as an 'emergency Congress'. Laura Summers, 'Democratic Kampuchea', in B. Szajkowski, ed., *Marxist Governments: A World Survey*, London 1982.

146. Pham Van Ba, interview with the author, Ho Chi Minh City, 28 October 1980.

147. *Summary of Annotated Party History*, *op. cit.*, p.19; *Prowatt nei Pak Kommyunis Kampuchea*, *op. cit.*, p.9.

148. *Prowatt Pak*, *op. cit.*

149. Pham Van Ba, *op. cit.*

150. I must confess I failed to ask him. Author's interview with Tea Sabun, Phnom Penh, 23 August 1980.

151. Nguyen Xuan Hoang, *op. cit.*

152. Vorn Vet's confession, *op. cit.*, p.30. (On the other hand, Khmer communists in Hanoi regarded Suon as 'one of the most important Khmer communist cadres in the party'. See 'Khmer Rouge Rallier Keoum Kun', *op. cit.*, p.6)

153. *Ibid.*, p.15.

154. *Ibid.*, p.16, notes that Keu participated in a Party 'Centre' meeting in late 1964 along with Pot Pot, Vorn Vet (and probably the rest of the Politburo), Keo Meas and Ney Sarann.

155. Author's interview with Nou Mouk, Oudong, 26 August 1981.

156. In 1978, Vorn Vet, too, wrote, that 'I personally had a liking for Ta Mok as we had been friends from the beginning'. See Chapter 8, p.327, below.

157. Hu Nim's confession in Tuol Sleng, says Mar was South-Western Zone Secretary, at least from 1966–1968. Draft translation by Chanthou Boua, p.18.

158. The thirty-four 'subversives' named by Sihanouk were: Keng Vannsak, Hou Yuon, Son Phuoc Tho, Uch Ven, Son Sen, Chau Seng, Tep Chhieu Kheng, Touch Phoeun, Thiounn Prasith, Sim Son, Saloth Sar, Ong Borey, Ieng Sary, Duong Sarinn, In Sakhan, Sien An, Tiv Ol, Siet Chhe, Sok Lay, Chou Chet, Thach Kim Son, Ream Yossar, Yi Yong, Im Ron, Keat Chhon, Keo Sum Sipha, So Nem, Hu Nim, Monh Moeung, Khieu Samphan, Ping Say, Chi Kim An, Thach Nhuong, Ok Sakun.

159. *Phnom Penh Presse*, 8 March 1963. See also *La Vérité*, 6 March 1963.

160. Author's interview with Chea Theng, Phnom Penh, 14 February 1975.

161. Quoted in Laura Summers, *op. cit., p.18.*

162. *Ibid.*

163. *Ibid.*

164. *Des Mouvements. . . op. cit., p.43.*

165. Carney, *op. cit.,* pp.4, 44; and author's interview with Sam Ngae Heang, widow of Ney Sarann's nephew Ly Sae. She said Sarann left Phnom Penh in late 1964. (Tuk Khleang, 27 September 1980.)

166. *Interview of Comrade Pol Pot, op. cit., p.22.*

167. Carney, *op. cit., p.4.*

168. Hu Nim's confession, *op. cit.*

169. Summers, *op. cit., p.19.*

170. *Ibid.*

171. 'Biographical Sketches of Khmer Communist Leaders', *op. cit.*

172. See Anthony Barnett, 'The Impact of Diem's Overthrow on Cambodia', forthcoming in *Pacific Affairs.*

173. See Laura Summers' introduction to *Cambodia's Economy and Industrial Development, op. cit., p.7.*

174. *Principaux Discours. . . de. . . Norodom Sihanouk,* Phnom Penh, Ministry of Information, 1963, p.444. Cited in Barnett, *op. cit.*

175. *Ibid.*

176. *Les Paroles, op. cit.,* January-March 1964, p.74. Speech by Sihanouk in Phnom Penh, 31 January 1964.

177. *Livre Noir, op. cit., p.37.*

178. Barnett, *op. cit.*

179. SWB, 1 October 1977, FE/5629/C2/1 ff.

180. *Les Paroles, op. cit.,* July-September 1964, p.98. Speech in Svay Rieng, 12 August 1964. My emphasis.

181. On Sien An, see P. Brocheux, 'Points de vue', in *Vietnam* (Paris), no. 4, 1982, p.171, and J. C. Pomonti and S. Thion, *Des courtisans aux partisans: la crise cambodgienne,* Paris, 1971, p.282. On Memut, Ouch Bun Chhoeun, op. cit.

182. *Summary of Annotated Party History, op. cit., p.19.*

183. Laura Summers, *op. cit., p.19.*

184. *Pahnyaha Sahakor, op. cit.* See the partial translation in Chapter 6 of Kiernan and Boua, *op. cit.*

185. Meyer, *op. cit., p.181.*

186. *Pahnyaha Sahakor, op. cit., p.64.*

187. *Ibid., p.62.*

188. *Ibid., pp.2, 3.*

189. See the table, 'Critical Economic Indicators, 1955–56' in Summers, *op. cit.,* p.13 (Note 84, above.)

190. *Rien saut daoy songkep nu prowatt chollana padewatt Kampuchea kraom kar duk noam rebos Pak Kommyunis Kampuchea* ('Abbreviated Lesson on the History of the Kampuchean Revolutionary Movement led by the Communist Party of Kampuchea'), undated (1977?), Phnom Penh, 23 pp. typescript, p.6.

191. *Pahnyaha Sahakor, op. cit., p.11.*

192. *Rien saut. . ., op. cit.,* pp.11–12. This refers to 1965. (My emphasis.)

193. *Les services publics économiques du Cambodge,* University of Phnom Penh, 1965. For a partial translation, see Kiernan and Boua (eds.), Chapter 2, pp.77–78.

194. *Pahnyaha Sahakor, op. cit.,* pp.174–75.

195. Vorn Vet's confession, *op. cit., p.17.*

244

196. Ouch Bun Chhoeun, *op. cit.*
197. *Ompi pankar ruom chong kraoy, op. cit.*, p.18 of translation.
198. Ouch Bun Chhoeun, *op. cit.*
199. This is the formulation used in *Livre Noir* in reference to 1969 (p.47). See p.286, below.
200. *Les Paroles, op. cit.*, April-June 1964, p.158. Speech in Phnom Penh, 18 May 1964.
201. *Ibid.*, p.125. Speech in Rattanakiri, 8 May 1964. During 1965, US aerial photography detected 'a concentration of newly-constructed huts in the extreme north-east salient of Cambodia'. See US CIA, Directorate of Intelligence, 'Cambodia and the Viet Cong', 22 December 1965, 17pp., at p.10.
202. Author's interviews with Puk Soum, *op. cit.*, and Tith Sou, Prey Veng, 12 July 1980.
203. Author's interview with Sau Huot, Baray, 15 October 1980.
204. See Ben Kiernan, 'Wild Chickens, Farm Chickens and Cormorants: Kampuchea's Eastern Zone Under Pol Pot', in David P. Chandler and Ben Kiernan, eds., *Revolution and its Aftermath in Kampuchea,* Yale University South-East Asia Studies Monograph No. 25, 1983, pp.136–211.
205. Ouch Bun Chhoeun, *op. cit.*
206. Puk Soum, *op. cit.*
207. Tith Sou, *op. cit.*
208. *Ibid.*
209. Author's interview with Chan Mon, Suong, 7 August 1980.
210. Author's interview with Chhouk's widow, Phnom Penh, 12 August 1980.
211. Puk Soum, *op. cit.*
212. Krot Theam, *op. cit.*
213. Vorn Vet's confession, *op. cit.*, p.17.
214. Stephen Heder's interview with a ranking CPK member, Chantaburi, Thailand, 12 March 1980, claims he became Zone Deputy Secretary.
215. *Les Paroles, op. cit.*, January-March 1965, pp.149, 152. Speech in Mondolkiri, 29 January 1965.
216. Ibid., p.166. Speech in Kampot, 4 February 1965.
217. Author's interview with Ung Bunhuor, Sydney, 21 November 1977.
218. *Les Paroles, op. cit.*, January-March 1965, pp.165–66. Speech in Kampot, 4 February 1965.
219. *Ibid.*
220. *Ibid.*, April-June 1965, p.485. Speech in Phnom Penh, 7 May 1965.
221. Sam Ngae Heang, *op. cit.*
222. *Les Paroles, op. cit.*, January-March 1965, pp.174–79. Speech in Kompong Speu, 7 February 1965.
223. *Ibid.*, pp.191, 96. Speech in Phnom Penh, 10 February 1965.
224. *Ibid.*, p.197.
225. *Ibid.*, p.412. Speech in Phnom Penh, 30 March 1965.
226. *Ibid.* He also claimed it was a case of suicide.
227. *Ibid.*, April-June 1965, p.424. Speech in Phnom Penh, 5 April 1965.
228. *Ibid.*, pp.414–16. Speech in Phnom Penh, 30 March 1965.
229. *Ibid.*, p.412. Kou Roun was among the others.
230. *Ibid.*, April-June 1965, p.423. Speech in Phnom Penh, 5 April 1965.
231. Sihanouk later called them 'genuine Khmer patriots fighting all Vietnamese', while the Pracheachon and the Vietnamese communists regarded them as 'traitors and valets of the imperialists'. Meyer *op. cit.* pp.269–72.

232. *Le Sangkum*, No. 6, January 1966, p.5.

233. *Ibid.*, April 1966, p.10.

234. *Etudes Cambodgiennes*, No. 3, August–September 1965, p.7.

235. *Les Paroles, op. cit.*, July–September 1965, p.719. Speech in Phnom Penh, 9 August 1965.

236. *Ibid.*, pp.719–20.

237. *Ibid.*, p.748. Speech in Battambang, 18 August 1965.

238. See Chapter 7, p.250, below.

239. Meyer, *op. cit.*, p.248.

240. *Etudes Cambodgiennes, op. cit.*

241. Author's interview with Hoang Tung, Hanoi, 31 October 1980; and Chea Soth, *op. cit.*

242. Porter, *op. cit.*, p.76.

243. Chea Soth, *op. cit.*

244. Stephen Heder, 'Kampuchea's Armed Struggle: The Origins of an Independent Revolution', *Bulletin of Concerned Asian Scholars*, Vol. 11, No. 1, 1979, pp.2–23, at p.7.

245. It was not until the next month that the Political Bureau of the Thai Party adopted a resolution 'to embark on armed struggle in every zone where the necessary conditions existed', but Pol Pot would almost certainly have been aware of the preparations made since the 1963 resolution. See the 1977 CPT History, in *Thailand: Roots of Conflict*, Andrew Turton *et al.* (eds.), Nottingham 1978, pp.158–168, at pp.164–65.

246. *Les Paroles, op. cit.*, April–June 1965, p.519. Speech in Phnom Penh, 23 May 1965.

247. See Chapter 2, p.59, above.

248. Krot Theam, *op. cit.*

249. Author's interview with Kieu Minh, Phnom Penh, 22 October 1980.

250. Timothy Carney, 'The Unexpected Revolution', forthcoming.

251. A 1977 CPK document was to say of this period: 'If our analysis had failed, we would have been in greater danger than in Indonesia'. *Rien saut. . ., op. cit.*, p.5. (The CIA estimated 800,000 died there. *Harpers*, September 1984, p.42.)

252. *Ibid.*, p.12.

253. *Livre Noir, op. cit.*, p.42. My emphasis.

254. *Toosu noyobay ruom som avuth.* See Chapter 7.

255. *Prowatt nei Pak Kommyunis Kampuchea, op. cit.*, p.9, handwritten entry on the original. This entry also records Pol Pot's visit to China.

256. Kieu Minh, *op. cit.*

257. See *Livre Noir, op. cit.*, pp.37–39. See also Note 255.

258. *Ibid.*, p.33.

259. Carney, 'The Unexpected Revolution', forthcoming. The American equivalent of Hanoi's 'P-36' was called 'B-57', which was 'a highly secret Special Forces unit. . . reponsible for conducting anti-Sihanouk intelligence operations inside Cambodia' in this period. 'One former senior officer of the unit. . . says that [B-57] used only ethnic Cambodians in its operations. . . deep inside Cambodia.' S. Hersh, *The Price of Power*, New York, 1983, p.178–79.

260. According to a Kampuchean then in Hanoi: 'Hundreds, thousands of Khmer Krom cadres studied with us. They studied in technical fields, and were sent back to South Vietnam after three or four years' training. They were under the authority of the Vietnamese state'. Author's interview with Hem Samin, Phnom Penh, 28 September 1980. A 1971 US intelligence study

reported, on the basis of the account of a south Vietnamese communist defector, that large numbers of Khmer trainees did indeed return to the South: 'Between January 1968 and April 1970, the rate of returnees was said to be about eleven to twelve daily.' *Communist Infrastructure in Cambodia*, DIA Intelligence Appraisal, 8 July 1971, p.3.

261. *Les Paroles, op. cit.,* January-March 1966, p.189. Speech in Phnom Penh, 20 February 1966, reproduced on pp.177–198. The title *Reaksmei Krahom* also began to appear on clandestine leaflets.
262. Philip Short, *The Dragon and the Bear*, London 1982, p.196.
263. V.M. Reddi, *A History of the Cambodian Independence Movement, 1863-1955*, Tirupati, Sri Venkatesvara University, 1973, p.193.
264. Vorn Vet's confession, *op. cit.,* p.20. My emphasis.
265. *Les Paroles, op. cit.,* January-March 1966, pp.177–78.
266. *Ibid.,* pp.199–201.
267. *Ibid.,* p.177.
268. *Ibid.,* p.183.
269. *Ibid.,* p.192.
270. *Ibid.,* p.189.
271. *Ibid.,* p.183.
272. *Ibid.,* p.187.
273. *Ibid.*
274. *Ibid.,* p.193.
275. *Ibid.,* pp.193–96.
276. *Ibid.,* p.190.
277. *Ibid.,* p.197.
278. *Ibid.,* pp.191, 198.
279. *Ibid.,* April-June 1966, p.522. Speech in Kompong Speu, 27 June 1966.
280. My emphasis. *Ibid.,* pp.528–31. Speech in Phnom Penh, 27 June 1966. (Also *Le Sangkum*, September 1966, pp.4–5. The article in *Tung Krahom* was entitled: 'On Politics, the People's Struggle and the Strategy of the Revolution'.)
281. *Ibid.,* p.530.
282. *Ibid.,* January-March 1966, p.180.
283. *Ibid.;* see in particular pp.180–81.
284. In his 'Message to the Pracheachon Party', Sihanouk denounced 'this cowardly method of subversion of which your underground magazine *Reaksmei Krahom* is the principal organ'. *Ibid.,* p.200.
285. *Ibid.,* pp.218–29.
286. He added that the 'subversive' activities of Non Suon and others, in 1962, were the 'sole interruption' to the 'harmony'. *Le Sangkum*, No. 9, April 1966, p.10.
287. Rémy Prud'homme, *L'Economie du Cambodge*, Paris 1969, p.255, Table 12, note a.
288. 'Cambodia and the Viet Cong', *op. cit.,* p.7.
289. Gerard Brissé, 'Que penser de la guerre au Cambodge?', *L'Année politique et économique*, Paris, July 1970, pp.251–52.
290. 'Cambodia and the Viet Cong', *op. cit.,* pp.11, 9, 12, 13.
291. Don O. Noel, 'Cambodia: The Mass Media', *op. cit.,* pp.13–20. The largest-circulation daily paper, *Sochivator* ('Civilization'), which was relatively non-political in tone, sold between 8,000 and 11,000 copies, and a similar paper, *Souvannaphum* ('Golden Country'), sold 7,000 copies per day.

292. Don O. Noel, 'Cambodian Politics II: The Man to Get', *op. cit.,* p.9.

293. *Les paroles, op. cit.,* April-June 1966, pp.439–441. Phnom Penh, 2 May 1966.

294. Vorn Vet's confession, *op. cit.,* p.20.

295. Meyer, *op. cit.,* p.191. In June of that year a sixteen year old boy named Hor joined the revolutionary movement in Kandal province. Eleven years later, as a supervisor of inmates in Tuol Sleng prison, Hor was to sign a death-list bearing the names of Hu Nim, Phouk Chhay and 125 others — all executed on a single day. See *New Statesman,* 2 May 1980, which features a copy of the list.

296. *Les Paroles, op. cit.,* April-June 1966, p.528. Speech in Phnom Penh, 27 June 1966. There is a possibility, given the context of Sihanouk's quotation from the newspaper, that the reference is in fact to events in another country altogether. The quotation is extremely brief, and cannot be checked since all newspaper runs in Phnom Penh's Bibliothèque Nationale were destroyed during the Pol Pot period. However the reference to 'feudalists' may well have entailed an oblique comparison to Sihanouk, which was his main point.

297. *Ibid.,* p.531 (and July-September 1966, p.507).

298. *Ibid.,* p.530 (and *Le Sangkum,* September 1966, p.4.) Another communist leaflet in this period was more explicit: 'The Marxist-Leninist doctrine calls for revolution to create a healthy society with equality of rights and obligations. To achieve this, a merciless struggle, and solidarity among the oppressed classes, is necessary. The members of the revolutionary Party must face all the trials and evils imposed by the lackeys of the imperialists and by the ruling class. These trials are not eternal, the revolution will win, we must act like the Russian Bolsheviks at the time of Marx [sic] and Lenin. In spite of the accusations of these lackeys of the imperialists who call the reds traitors and the leftists saboteurs, none of our members must be discouraged. We must never give in to the arbitrary demands of the current rulers. The wish of each of our members must be *not to count too much on Sihanouk.* Cambodia, which is apparently calm and peaceful, demonstrates the need for an intense struggle against the classes who rage on the domestic scene. Progressives and intellectuals are arbitrarily maltreated. Each member of the Party must keep his cool in the struggle for the revolutionary cause.' (Quoted by Sihanouk in *Le Sangkum,* July 1966.)

299. *Ibid.,* July-September 1966, p.532. Speech in Kompong Chhnang, 29 June 1966. I have been unable to locate Salisbury's article.

300. One tribal village in the North-East had had to be re-located twice by 1966 as a result of 'profound changes' wrought by the the establishment of plantations in the area. J. Matras-Troubetzkoy, 'L'Essartage chez les Brou du Cambodge',*Etudes Rurales,* 1974, 53–56, Jan-Dec., pp.421–37, at p.421.

301. Author's interview with Sin Song, Phnom Penh, 12 August 1980.

302. Kol Kon, *op. cit.*

303. *Réalités Cambodgiennes,* 8 March 1968, p.25.

304. *Khmers Rouges!, op. cit.,* p.90.

305. Meyer, *op. cit.,* p.191.

306. *Ibid.;* and *Yearbook on International Communist Affairs,* 1968, p.68.

307. *Le Sangkum,* September 1966, pp.4–5.

308. Carney, *Communist Party Power, op. cit.,* p.56; and *Prowatt Pak, op. cit.* The Khmer Communists in Hanoi (the 'Committee of Liberation') were notified, and perhaps had little choice but to go along with this, although 1951 was retained as the Party's official founding date, if that was yet an issue. *Summary of Annotated Party History, op. cit.,* p.1.

309. Milton Osborne, *Politics and Power in Cambodia,* Melbourne 1973, p.93.

310. Don O. Noel, 'Cambodian Politics I: Gently to the Right?', New York, Alicia Patterson Fund, 15 January 1967, 16 pp., at pp.7–9. See also my discussion of these elections in 'The 1970 Peasant Uprisings Against Lon Nol', in Kiernan and Boua *op. cit.,* pp.208–209, 220. On the Kratie result, see M.E. Osborne, *Before Kampuchea,* Sydney 1979, pp.178-9.

311. Chan Mon, *op. cit.*

312. Hu Nim's confession, *op. cit.*

313. Author's interviews with inhabitants of Prey Totoeng, 4 August 1980.

314. *Bulletin du Contre-Gouvernement,* 4 June 1969, no. 775, p.5. Also copies of the official election results, in possession of the author.

315. Ouch Bun Chhoeun, *op. cit.*

316. *Les Paroles, op. cit.,* October–December 1966, p.774. Speech in Phnom Penh, 5 November 1966.

317. Don O. Noel, 'Cambodian Politics I: Gently to the Right?', *op. cit.,* pp.14–15.

318. Don O. Noel, 'Cambodian Politics II: The Man to Get', *op. cit.,* p.5.

319. *Les Paroles, op. cit.,* October–December 1966, p.775. Phnom Penh, 5 November 1966.

320. *Ibid.,* p.777.

321. Don O. Noel, 'Cambodian Politics I', *op. cit.,* p.15. The demonstration had begun at Hou Yuon's private school Kambuboth, although Yuon's views at that time were still in part reformist. One former Issarak from Tbaung Khmum recalls: 'In 1966, Hou Yuon sent us a document which he had written out by hand called 'Pooling the Strength of the Masses' (*Pramoul Kamlang Mahachun*); it outlined his proposals for various associations such as a 'Plates Association' to provide for popular festivals, associations to pool money for people to assist one another's funerals, and consumer co-operatives to buy food to sell (cheaply) to help the people; it also urged resistance to landlords who seized the people's land.' Chan Mon, *op. cit.*

322. *Les Paroles, op. cit.,* October–December 1966, p.816. Speech in Phnom Penh, 18 November 1966.

323. Don O. Noel, 'Cambodia: The Mass Media', *op. cit.,* p.23.

324. *Rien saut. . ., op. cit.,* p.5.

7

The First Civil War
1967–70

Due to the difficult situation, the Cambodian government has not officially declared its support for the Front, even though it has greatly respected it … The Cambodian government has recently shown its good will to help us.

Vietnamese communist document
captured by US forces in March 1967
during Operation Junction City near
the Kampuchean border.

The rebellion that first broke out at Samlaut in southern Battambang in April 1967 raises many of the issues facing the historian of modern Khmer communism. Firstly, it was, as Donald Kirk says, 'a prelude, in a microcosm, of the conflict that would sweep across the country three years later'.[1] Secondly, erupting as it did at the height of the Chinese Cultural Revolution, it raises the question of the foreign connections of the Kampuchean revolutionaries. Thirdly, it was the only real test of strength between the Sihanouk regime and the communists, and the first such test for the new CPK leadership headed by Saloth Sar — of its ability not only to select a viable strategy for the long march to power, but also to impose such a strategy on a scattered and heterogeneous movement. I have discussed elsewhere the social context of the Battambang rebellion, and its impact on the national political scene.[2] I will concentrate here on the course of the rebellion and on its significance for the Pol Pot leadership; this lies mainly in the realignment and ultimate polarization of the country's political forces.

The picture that emerges is that of a nationally-organized CPK-led rebellion in early 1967, in part provoked by the government, but which failed to achieve momentum. Repression was fierce, but so was urban unrest, and this led to a moderation of government policy and to the removal of Lon Nol from the Prime Ministership in April. However, the CPK Centre was unwilling to associate itself with military failure, and later denied its own involvement. It also denied, or was prepared to jeopardize, the *political* gains that had been made. It planned another uprising for January 1968. Although it provoked the final eclipse of the urban left, and saw Lon Nol's return to the Cabinet, the 1968 revolt was more widespread and successful. It nevertheless failed this time to involve the Eastern Zone communists; this was the first sign of regional disunity in the CPK. So Phim's Eastern Party branch finally joined the revolt eight months later, in August 1968; but it mounted only a limited military campaign, and, unlike the Centre, maintained close contact with the Vietnamese communists. Nevertheless it was politically well entrenched in the Zone.

By 1969 the CPK faced an impasse, being unable to make further headway against Sihanouk's prestige and nationalism. A secret decision was taken by the Party Centre to prepare for a *public* alliance with the Prince. This involved a repudiation of previous Centre policy. But the Centre did not abandon its long-term enmity towards Sihanouk, his followers, or the Vietnamese who had long argued for such a policy revision.

Mutual Premeditation

The insurrection was clearly organized in advance, and on a national scale. The earliest reports of fighting date from April 1967, at both the western and eastern extremes of the country. It was during that month that Ieng Thirith was sighted at Samlaut; on 2 April the (Chinese model) JSRK farm at Stung Kranhoung nearby was attacked and burnt, four army posts stormed, and two soldiers killed.[3] Two weeks later, seventy armed followers of So Phim penetrated the eastern town of Kandol Chrum in Kompong Cham, killed a former subdistrict chief, and wounded a police agent.[4] In other parts of the country, notably Kompong Thom[5] and northern Kompong Speu,[6] underground organizations launched anti-Sihanouk propaganda campaigns in the same period. As we shall see, the CPK leaders, with most of the grass-roots Pracheachon Group having abandoned legal 'political struggle', had launched a 'combined political and armed struggle' (which, as we have seen in Chapter 6, they later backdated from 1967 to 1960). On the other hand, much of the urban left that remained active – in particular Hou Yuon, Hu Nim and Chau Seng – still regarded the Sihanouk regime as one within which they could work. But this perspective could not withstand both the outbreak of rural rebellion and the rising tide of Cultural Revolution fervour in the cities.

As in 1966, the violence itself was initiated by the authorities. In early January 1967, Sihanouk left the country for two months' medical treatment in France. Almost certainly with Sihanouk's prior approval,[7] Lon Nol appears to have chosen this period to launch a massive escalation of the repression, perhaps in an attempt to nip in the bud CPK plans for armed insurrection. According to the (internal) 1974 Party History: 'beginning in 1967, the enemy, led by Lon Nol, started to destroy, kill, make arrests and put people in chains on a large scale, both in the towns and in the countryside'. After a number of arrests and executions in Kompong Cham and Takeo, the document continues, 'the second armed struggle began':

> In February-March 1967 the enemy started the civil war in Battambang, forcing five thousand people to flee into the jungle. Then in March Lon Nol declared open war on our people. He brought in five thousand troops from Oddar Meanchey, Battambang, Pursat and Phnom Penh to sow destruction with airplanes, artillery, tanks and infantry, commanded by Nhek Tioulong with the French Lieutenant-Colonel Léon Leroy as adviser. By that time our Party was already properly organized with a good network from the bases to the Centre. It is quite true that our Party had not yet raised the principle of armed struggle, but in the face of this massive civil war by the enemy, our Party had to fight back with arms.[8]

Some details in this passage (e.g. 'Léon Leroy') cannot be corroborated, and the disclaimer of an offensive CPK policy is, as we shall see, disingenuous; but the thrust of the account does ring true. In January Lon Nol established his own headquarters at Battambang,[9] as part of a nationwide campaign to ensure government collection of the rice crop, 40 per cent of which had been smuggled to Vietnam in the previous year,[10] depriving the government of needed revenue from export duties. The prices the peasants now received for their rice were as low as one third of black market prices.[11] Sihanouk later described this programme, rather glibly, as 'the collection of paddy at the most advantageous price, and the elimination of middlemen'.[12] More importantly, he directly connected it with the suppression of left-wing dissidence: 'Their programme [of subversion and sabotage] ran into even more difficulty when Companion Lon

Nol multiplied the Action Committees for the collection of paddy in the districts, subdistricts and even villages, Action Committees which also represented a nationalist Sangkum presence and made life difficult for the 'Pracheachon' cells which had until then not been bothered, and could carry out their activities with impunity.'[13]

Sihanouk said Lon Nol's campaign had been 'launched on my instructions'.[14] Moreover, soon after his return in early March, he made a revealing speech, containing strong hints that he had secretly authorized repression of the left. (This repression may have been a salutary measure, which, because it occurred in Sihanouk's absence, was intended to encourage the left to see him as their protector against Lon Nol and so restrain their newly-launched opposition to him.)

> Do not forget either, *Messieurs les rouges* – and this is a reminder to you and not a threat – that it is Sihanouk to whom you owe the privilege you enjoy at present of carrying out all your activities without fear of ending your days. Is there any need to remind you that in Indonesia there was no great difficulty in wiping out seven hundred thousand communists, and to point out that it is enough for me, not even to give the order but simply to remain silent and you, who are only a few hundred, will disappear even more quickly? [Laughter and applause] We do not lack our Suhartos and Nasutions in Cambodia [more applause].
>
> I would also inform you that I have other radical methods of destroying your illusions, namely if I leave the country – temporarily – and leave you face to face with our Suhartos and Nasutions [more laughter]. Leaving the country without anyone knowing is something I am also capable of, since *I have tried it* – successfully – by flying out two months ago without your knowledge [more laughter].[15]

If this was indeed 'a reminder and not a threat', the *urban left* had not forgotten. The speech was made in response to a demonstration organized by them the previous day, involving students and Buddhist monks;[16] the rally called for the withdrawal of troops from the Pailin (southern Battambang) area, and accused the army of 'assassinating the Khmer people' there. The protestors also demanded the dismissal of the Lon Nol government and new elections, for which Sihanouk would choose the candidates as he had done in 1958 and 1962.[17] Sihanouk noted (albeit with suspicion) that the urban leftists 'attack only Lon Nol in their demonstrations',[18] and that they also demanded 'that we arm the Vietnamese living in our frontier regions'[19] – an indication of continuing emphasis on Sihanouk's value to the Vietnamese communists' struggle against the USA.

But *in the countryside*, new battle-lines had already been drawn. Sihanouk refused to withdraw the troops, and by now (in early March) rebel tracts in Battambang were accusing him, as well as Lon Nol and Nhek Tioulong, of treason. In Sihanouk's words: 'They even featured us in popular theatre performances, portraying us with the characteristics of traitors. Songs have also been composed to pursue these accusations.'[20] In the mountainous Tpong district of Kompong Speu, rebels told the population that Sihanouk must be driven from power because he 'thinks only of going to live the good life in France'[21] at their expense. In April, the attacks on Sihanouk, first voiced in *Reaksmei Krahom* and *Tung Krahom* a year before, now found almost simultaneous echoes in leaflets and at secret meetings not only in rural Battambang and Kompong Speu but in Kompong Cham and Kompong Thom as well.[22]

In Kompong Cham, tensions had been rising for some time. In late 1966 or early 1967, Bos village, So Phim's former home in Krek district, was subjected to particularly brutal repression, According to a villager who was in the forest with Phim at this time: 'They came looking for me ... the Sihanouk soldiers came here and killed twenty-six revolutionaries in the village.'[23] Another source claimed that the victims were beheaded and their livers extracted by the soldiers.[24] A third Eastern Zone cadre, a native of Bos, continued: 'That is why the [leaders of the] revolution held a meeting and decided to take up arms against the enemy, in February 1967. Before that we had been politically active but unarmed. Now we took out our guns, and *the combined political and armed struggle began*. We used both military and propaganda cadres, attacking only where the enemy were stretched thin, at small posts, and setting ambushes along back roads. We also cleaned up active enemy agents in a few villages [and] in Kandol Chrum.'[25]

In nearby Tbaung Khmum, Chan Mon, whom troops had begun to 'push around' in 1965, was now gaoled for over a month, and one of his comrades was executed in a village.[26] Repression may have been more widespread in remoter areas, however. According to two sources, thousands of people fled villages near Memut rubber plantations in March 1967.[27] Two hundred inhabitants of Phneou village took flight after six activists had been killed there. There were also shootings in three villages in Damber district.[28] Two former Issarak leaders, May Pho and Kuong Chhum, who had slipped back into the forest three years before, assumed leadership of the 'resistance' in Memut.[29] They were joined by a young student from Wat Tuk La'ak in Phnom Penh named Hun Sen (who in 1984 became Prime Minister of the PRK). Sen fled the capital when an older CPK member, with whom he was secretly working, was arrested and then disappeared; Sen became a courier for the local communist leader.[30] Two communist sources, cited in Chapter 6, who note that previously 'imprisonment was not very dangerous', and that 'if you gave them a lot of money they would let you go', each point to a change in the situation from 1967, when they say prisoners taken by the army were usually shot.[31]

In Baray district in Kompong Thom province, twenty-one 'communists' were officially reported to have been arrested in April. They seem to have formed a rudimentary local network, with a 'President' (named Mak Sean) and a 'Vice-President' (Net Pon). These people had distributed leaflets claiming that Sihanouk and Lon Nol were 'men of straw' who had 'sold out their country to the United States'; in direct repudiation of reformism, they asserted that the State Co-operative body, OROC, had been 'created to deceive the people'. The rebels had appealed to villagers to join their struggle, promising to distribute to them important adminstrative positions and to end all state taxation after victory.[32]

The twenty-one men arrested on 11 April in the Northern Zone apparently did not include Ke Pauk, the young ex-Issarak who had been driven from his nearby home in 1964. But it seems likely that Pauk was involved in the latest agitation, and the fate of his senior comrades may have indirectly favoured his rise to leadership of the CPK's Northern Zone over the next ten years. Mak Sean, Net Pon, and their nineteen local supporters disappeared after being apprehended. Within days, anti-government leaflets were distributed in Baray and two other districts in Kompong Thom, but the police were unable to discover the identities of those responsible.[33] The treatment meted out to suspected rebels may also have reinforced Pauk's bitterness towards authority. The wife of a local schoolteacher recalls one incident in this period: 'In Kravar market the government forces held thirty to forty men from Andaeuk village, along with their wives and small children. I saw them all tied up, mistreated and beaten. This was going on all over the market place.'[34]

The worst violence was taking place in Battambang. In the first three weeks of April, two hundred rebels were captured there and nineteen killed, and the revolt continued to spread.[35] There were reported to be two thousand 'Khmer Viet Minh' rebels throughout the country.[36] This label was ironic, and so was the fact that Sihanouk blamed the urban left — specifically Hou Yuon, Khieu Samphan, Hu Nim, Chau Seng and So Nem. Faced with calls for their execution by rightist members of the Assembly, and with the prospect of facing a military tribunal, Yuon and Samphan took to the jungle on 24 April. Their disappearance, however, gave rise to widespread suspicion that they had been murdered by the secret police, and provoked a severe political crisis. Within a week Lon Nol resigned as Prime Minister, ostensibly to undergo medical treatment as a result of a car accident eight weeks before. This ushered in a period of political relaxation. On May Day, 1967, student demonstrations organized by Phouk Chhay to protest against the presumed execution of Yuon and Samphan involved fifteen thousand people from Phnom Penh, Kandal and Kompong Cham.[37] Sihanouk described the scene: 'Along with the young Vietnamese and Chinese reds our young Khmer reds sang and danced the *ramvong* for subversive ends: they distributed leaflets bearing cartoons insulting to the Sangkum.'[38]

Sihanouk complained that the left was 'more daring than ever',[39] but brought Chau Seng and So Nem back into the Cabinet along with two other leftists (one of whom, Keat Chhorn, from 1979 to 1982 served in the exiled Democratic Kampuchea cabinet). At the same time, a new left-wing daily newspaper, *Soriya* ('The Sun'),[40] was established by a Khmer Krom named Sok Lay, who had worked with Chou Chet years before on *Pancha Sila*;[41] Sihanouk described it as a 'reincarnation' of *Pracheachon*.[42] The change in the political climate also seems to have been recognized by the CPK Centre. The 1974 Party History records these events as follows: 'The enemy plan of attack was to destroy us completely in six days, but in actual fact they extended this period by many months. Yet again they were shamefully defeated ... *The armed and political struggle of our Party in that period* won an important victory when the Cabinet had to be completely replaced, as did the Chief of the 3rd

Military Region and the [Battambang] province chief.'[43] Years later Hu Nim wrote that this 'victory' had caused him to change tactics: 'Khieu Samphan and Hou Yuon left [for the jungle] before me. Four or five days later I also left. Then I met brother Vorn [Vet] who persuaded me to come back, because by then Sihanouk had replaced Lon Nol ...'[44]

Nim returned to Phnom Penh where he continued his political activities, without his brief absence being noted by the authorities. Part of his assigned task may have been to take advantage of the relaxation, but to maintain the political pressure by continuing to demand that the authorities return the missing parliamentarians — 'living or dead', in the words of one group of demonstrators soon afterwards.[45] He certainly continued to advance radical views, but the ensuing events suggest he still saw a need to co-operate with Sihanouk to some extent; his regular proclamations of complete loyalty to Sihanouk were almost certainly insincere, but were demanded of everyone in public life and were no different from the 'political struggle' tactics of Hou Yuon or the Pracheachon in previous years. This stance in fact distanced him from the Party Centre, but at this stage he may not have been fully cognizant of the implications.

By then, of course, it would have been impossible to reverse the drift of events in the countryside, even if the Centre had wanted to. When Sihanouk visited Samlaut in early May, rebels there continued to level at him 'the grossest and most revolting insults'.[46] As he arrived in Tpong a few days later, it was claimed that he 'aimed to make Cambodia a satellite of US imperialism'.[47] He appealed to the local inhabitants: 'Among you there are some who have abandoned their homes and taken refuge in the forest, perhaps for fear of being accused of complicity with the Khmer Rouge. I affectionately ask them to return home; whatever reasons drove them to join the maquis, I will pardon them completely.'[48] But the country's political forces were already locked into the mentality of civil war. A combination of three factors — the rebellion itself, brutal military repression, and the burgeoning Chinese Cultural Revolution — would, over the next few months, move Sihanouk to choose between the two sides.

It was in May that, according to local CPK cadres, the rebellion began in earnest in Battambang. A man who lived in the area in 1976 recalls: 'They talked of Phnom Veay Chap, a hill area eight kilometres square, with a small lake that could provide water for twenty thousand people. It was an old base of the Khmer Rouge, which they built up and organized in May 1967, as part of their struggle against Lon Nol.'[49] In 1977, the CPK chief of the North-West Zone, Muol Sambath, told Hu Nim: 'I regard Phnom Veay Chap as a mountain of heroes, because the people and troops who fought on that mountain were very patriotic. They fought the enemy, who had plenty of weapons such as tanks and airplanes. Then we broke out of the enemy's encirclement and victoriously withdrew from the mountain. Even though a number of troops and people sacrificed their lives, their sacrifices were very valuable becasue they provided important experience in armed struggle.'[50]

One of those who 'victoriously withdrew' was a former monk from Phnom Penh's Wat Langka named Chan Chakrey. According to one account: 'The situation was very tight, really tight. Lon Nol had sent a regiment of troops to encircle the forest ... They were there more than three months. They penetrated the forest and fired at Chakrey. There was no respite. In the end Chakrey ran out and surrendered to the enemy, bringing two or three guns with him.'[51] He was spared by the authorities, and then made his way east and eventually to Vietnam. Nine years later, this incident — in which he was alleged to have killed two comrades, including one of Sambath's couriers, and used their weapons to negotiate his release — was used with devastating effect to divide the CPK: Chakrey's arrest in April 1976,[52] when he had become Deputy Chief of the General Staff of the Revolutionary Army, was the first of a series of massive purges which led to that of Sambath himself two years later.

On 18 June, Sihanouk proclaimed that the rebellion had ended. 'Thousands of families' had returned to their villages in Battambang, he claimed.[53] However, according to Charles Meyer: 'This was the moment chosen by the army and the provincial guard, undoubtedly without Sihanouk's knowledge, to launch punitive operations! Hamlets were surrounded, their inhabitants machine-gunned, houses pillaged and burnt ... Hundreds of peasants, with their wives and children and led by their Buddhist monks, fled back into the forest.'[54] It was apparently at this point that, on the other side of the country in Prey Veng, a peasant cadre named Heng Samrin, who had joined the revolutionary movement in 1959[55] and was to become President of the PRK in 1979, took to the forest. A woman from Komchay Meas, Prok Sary, asserted in 1980 that her husband, father and brother, former Issaraks who had resumed political activity in 1962, had all been killed by government troops in June 1967. She continued: 'Then the revolutionaries came to get me and I went into the forest with them. We all took to the forest at the same time, including Heng Samrin and Chea Sim. There were six or eight of us from each of twelve villages in Cheach subdistrict, including women and children, and even a few monks, but the Organization sent most of them to the Vietnamese border with the troops because the enemy was looking for us. I had no children so I stayed with the cadres who were moving from village to village.'[56]

Two weeks later, the first attack was mounted against the government militia in the area. But participants report fighting only with 'axes, knives and a few guns' (and in Krek, to the north, with 'ancient rifles and bows and arrows');[57] the thrust of the eastern struggle was still agitation and propaganda. As a CPK cadre from the Memut area recalls: '1967 to 1970 was the period of combined political and armed struggle, meaning that we were not just engaged in political struggle but had not yet adopted armed struggle as the line. We just had some guns ... only a few.' The same source outlines the impact of the 1967 repression as follows: 'Sihanouk was the enemy of the democratic revolution. In our leaflets we even had pictures of Sihanouk with a dog's tail, because he was a feudalist, a representative of the interests of the exploiting classes. Lon Nol was a representative of the interests of the capitalists and imperialists. We dealt with [*vichey*] both of them: Lon Nol from 1955, *Sihanouk from 1967–1968* when we saw the move to kill a lot of people.'[58] In August 1967, for instance, one of So Phim's couriers was captured by the army and executed along with his three children.[59]

The Cultural Revolution

Unrest had begun to affect many of Kampuchea's schools in January 1967. According to an official report made by the Minister of Education in May, three student demonstrations took place in various towns in January, three in February, and five or more in March. Interestingly, there were none reported in April, when violence exploded in various rural areas, which may suggest an absence of involvement of the CPK Centre in the urban unrest. Then, on 4 May, students at Choeung Chnok College in Kompong Cham invaded the school office; they beat up the principal and two teachers, forcing them to flee, and then posted leaflets on the walls demanding the dismissal of five staff members. When the abbot of the local *wat* attempted to intercede, 'the students were disrespectful towards him'. The report concluded: 'Unfortunately such cases are frequent in the current circumstances ... the students tend to want to carry out justice themselves, without reference to the regulations and the responsible authorities.'[60] In Kompong Thom in early May, students accused Sihanouk of having allowed Khieu Samphan and Hou Yuon to be murdered; according to the Prince, cars were burnt and merchants physically attacked.[61] This phenomenon, described in the report as a series of 'collective and brutal demonstrations against the administration as well as the educational authorities',[62] certainly appears to betray the influence of similar events then occurring in China.

The Cultural Revolution had been brewing since November 1965, *after* Saloth Sar's departure for home. In August 1966, at the Eleventh Plenum of the CCP Central Committee, Liu Shaoqi and Deng Xiaoping, the leaders with whom Sar would have had the most contact, were downgraded.[63] It may be worth recounting the experiences of Yos Por, one of the forty Khmers from Hanoi who had arrived in China in 1963 for four years' political training, which he says involved 'Mao Zedong Thought and nothing else'. In 1979, Por became Secretary-General of the PRK's United Front for National Salvation of Kampuchea; in an interview with the author the next year, he said:

I was in Chungking, in Szechuan province, with over thirty Khmers and a number of other foreign socialist students from Latin America. During the Cultural Revolution, we saw Chinese workers, students and peasants killing one another, crashing their trucks, to 'defend Mao Zedong Thought'. There was fighting in the streets, cars ran over people, some 'capitalists' were killed, others committed suicide. Most of Mao's supporters were young school students – they beat up older people. Liu Shaoqi won support from the workers, and there was also the Lin Biao faction.

The Cultural Revolution was no good, so we went back to Vietnam in 1967.

Despite some schematizing with the benefit of hindsight and in accordance with the demands of political convenience, Por's account is of course authentic and his repulsion genuine. Still, it betrays little appreciation for the general political issues, such as the criticism of bureaucracy, that fuelled the turmoil. Perhaps this was in part because, as Por says, 'we were not allowed freedom of movement during the Cultural Revolution'.[64]

In the jungles of Kampuchea's North-East, Saloth Sar and his colleagues are even more unlikely to have been kept abreast, by Radio Beijing's Khmer-language broadcasts or by other sources accessible to them, of the momentous changes occurring in China and the ideological issues at stake.[65] Compared with the urban Khmer left, they were far less susceptible to the new version of Chinese radicalism. One student, who took to the jungle the next year, found it virtually ignored there, partly in favour of the slogans of Maoism in its *pre*-Cultural Revolution phase. In the jungle, he said, 'We listened to Radio Beijing and picked up slogans from China, such as 'Paper Tiger', 'surrounding the cities from the countryside', 'from small to big'. However, there was no talk or training concerning the Cultural Revolution nor any study of Mao Thought. The major part of the line was protracted struggle with difficulties but certain ultimate victory. There were lots of Mao's translated works in the cities, but not in the countryside.'[66]

In fact, from early 1967, when control of China's Foreign Ministry passed temporarily into the hands of an ultra-left faction (headed by a Chinese diplomat who had returned from Jakarta), the shock waves of the Cultural Revolution began to be felt in many Asian cities, leading to Beijing's rupture of diplomatic relations with Rangoon and to crises in relations with Kathmandu and Phnom Penh, even though all three capitals had until then been on good terms with China. (In India, meanwhile, Chinese support was given to the Naxalites.) Such Chinese action was, of course, probably in line with the aims of the CPK leaders, but there is no evidence that the ideological underpinnings were accepted or the resultant urban upheaval welcomed in those quarters. It is even possible that these developments were seen as a threat to the Party leadership's control over the revolutionary movement.

Towards the end of June a group of youths, enraged by criticisms of China published by the rightist daily *Khmer Ekareach*, sacked the newspaper's offices and printing press. The destruction was estimated at over a million *riels*; also damaged was an apartment belonging to the Crown, while a photograph of Sihanouk was torn from the wall and a statue of Buddha overturned.[67] Student unrest was mounting, especially in the private schools, two thirds of which were Chinese. The *Little Red Book* was widely distributed, and the Khmer-Chinese Friendship Association, led by Hu Nim, So Nem and Phouk Chhay, was extremely active. However, there were still elements among the urban left, perhaps even including all these three, who saw Sihanouk's role in a relatively positive light, especially after he had extended full diplomatic representation to the Democratic Republic of Vietnam in June. On 27 July, for instance, the following article appeared in a leftist Phnom Penh newspaper:

> The policy of the Americans and their lackeys has been and remains that of the 'big stick' ... The escalation in Vietnam and the 'peace proposals' of Johnson and his clique are part of this policy. They resort to the same procedures with regard to other countries of the Third World. For their ultimate aim remains the same.
>
> But with anti-imperialist Cambodia under the vigilant leadership of Prince Companion, our enemies of all stripes nourish such hopes in vain. Our country has indeed experienced enough lessons of this kind not to be taken in by the same trap, which has been tried and has failed.[68]

If this was also a last-ditch appeal to Sihanouk to stop the repression, it was almost immediately undermined by leaflets distributed in Kompong Thom, that blamed Sihanouk for the disappearance of Hou Yuon and Khieu Samphan and called on the people to 'rise up' in rebellion.[69] Their author was reported to have been Mam Nay, then principal of the local Balaing College.[70] (Ten years later he was to supervise the torture, interrogation and execution of Hu Nim, Phouk Chhay and many others from the urban left of this period.) The College deputy principal, a Sino-Khmer named Kaing Khek Iev, later became Nay's superior in the CPK; under the name Deuch, he was to run the Pol Pot regime's security apparatus. In this period, he was a leading figure in an incident in which rioters burnt a bus outside a police station in Prey Totoeng, Hu Nim's electoral district.[71]

Sihanouk now turned on Hu Nim. This was despite the fact that, protesting his loyalty, Nim said he did *not* hold Sihanouk responsible for the disappearance of his two colleagues, and took pains to oppose plans for by-elections to replace them in the Assembly. Knowing the two were alive, he may have wanted to keep open the possibility of their return to legal activity. But his failure to reveal publicly what he (and Sihanouk and Lon Nol and the CPK Centre) knew about them made his position untenable. He was unwilling to state that the two were not in fact dead but with the rebels – perhaps partly because of an agitational assignment received from Vorn Vet, and partly out of fear for his own safety. (The government reaction to such an authentic revelation would have been quite unpredictable.) The fact was, it now seems, that Hou Yuon and Khieu Samphan were of more use to the CPK Centre if they were considered to have been murdered by the government. Yet the government was unable to concede the more immediately dangerous fact that they had joined the rebels. Hu Nim, who knew the truth, was nevertheless caught between these two positions.

Sihanouk used his advantage on the public stage cleverly. At a special Press Conference on 7 August, he complained: 'How does Hu Nim know ... that we should wait for them [to come back]?'[72] He put Mam Nay and Hu Nim in the same category, but ironically described Nim as 'the most dangerous because he is the most hypocritical of them all'.[73] He said that other leftists had 'appeared satisfied' with the fall of the Lon Nol Cabinet, but singled out the 'pro-Chinese left' for 'continuing its subversive work'.[74] This was of course true of both the rural CPK and the restive students, but less so of other elements of the urban left; and the relationship between all three groups was not as simple as Sihanouk apparently imagined.

On 2 September, after another attack on Hu Nim, Sihanouk banned the Khmer-Chinese Friendship Association.[75] This action, and the reaction from both China and the CPK underground, spelt the end to any hopes that remained for a truce between the Sihanouk regime and the left.

The news of the ban was telegraphed to Beijing by Hsinhua the same day.[76] Nevertheless, on 4 September, the China-Cambodia Friendship Association (which was controlled by the Chinese Foreign Ministry, itself still in the hands of the ultra-left faction) sent a cable to its now defunct Khmer counterpart, congratulating it on the third anniversary of its foundation. The message said in part: 'Imperialism, revisionism and reaction [all] fear and hate this friendship and solidarity, seeking a thousand and one ways to sow discord and sabotage. In doing so they stupidly 'lift a rock to drop on their own feet' ... They are bound to fail.'[77] Sihanouk understandably saw this as 'an extraordinary interference in the internal affairs of a sovereign state' and as a thinly veiled criticism of him for 'reaction'.[78] Nevertheless, his faith in China was such that he maintained: 'China is our friend and I still consider it as such'.[79] He banned the local *Hsinhua* bulletin, but reserved the full weight of his anger for local leftists such as Phouk Chhay, who had published the Chinese telegram in *La Dépêche* on 9 September. He banned Chhay's General Association of Khmer Students, sacked So Nem and Chau Seng from the Cabinet, and suspended all private newspapers, even rightist ones.[80]

Within days, Zhou Enlai had re-established control over the Foreign Ministry in Beijing. On 14 September, as one of his moves towards setting its house in order, he called on the Kampuchean ambassador there and expressed his continuing admiration for Sihanouk. He also emphasized his traditional view that 'Cambodia occupies an important position in Indo-China and in South-East Asia'.[81] Sihanouk in fact seems to have been rather chilled by this latter statement, which he said 'hardly reassures us – we would prefer to remain the Cambodia of no importance for the Chinese communist world'.[82] But it was clear that Sihanouk had Zhou's backing so long as his own domestic position was secure, whereas Zhou's support for the CPK was limited to what was necessary to distance it from the Vietnamese communists. A future member of the 'Gang of Four', Yao Wenyuan, also repudiated the ultra-left policy (and coincidentally that of Pol Pot). In a speech in Shanghai soon afterwards, he said that although Sihanouk was 'a reactionary through and through [and] we must fight against the reactionary regime in Kampuchea ... we [however] must never forget that the situation in that country is different from the situation in India, Burma and Indonesia...', countries where Beijing was sponsoring armed insurgencies. He instead compared Kampuchea to Nepal, where he said, 'we have to intensify our political fight against the monarchy' but the 'fight must be very strictly controlled'.[83]

But the CPK was now set on a different course. Hu Nim's prison account of the ensuing events reveals the role played by the Party underground, in particular its Northern Zone leader, Koy Thuon (Khuon): 'Khuon and Sreng pushed the situation further, and made it more tense, by presenting a motion of protest from the people of Prey Totoeng, demanding that Sihanouk re-establish the Khmer-Chinese Friendship Association. Sihanouk was very angry with me ...'[84] In fact, Sihanouk had discovered that the seven hundred villagers who put their thumb-prints on this petition had believed it to be a request for a dam in the area.[85] It seems Khuon and Sreng had collected the signatures under false pretences and taken them to Hu Nim in Phnom Penh. As a local resident explained: 'It became a political controversy ... The people were angry with Hu Nim and asked him why he had done that. He replied that it was not his doing; he had simply received the petition in Phnom Penh 'from the people' and passed it on to the Assembly.'[86] Given Nim's own interest in the Khmer-Chinese Friendship Association, this appears disingenuous, but it is interesting that ten years later, in a Pol Pot prison, he told the same story. It does seem unlikely that he would have risked his tenuous and exposed position with a clumsy forgery involving his own constituents.

On 30 September, Sihanouk called a special meeting at Prey Totoeng High School in order to denounce Hu Nim in front of his electors. The same resident, who witnessed the occasion, recalled: 'Sihanouk's entourage were all there on the platform, all the important people. Kou Roun and the district chief were there, waiting for Hu Nim to come up, but he didn't, he stayed down below amongst the people. He had been followed all the way from Phnom Penh ... Then Sihanouk stood up and saw Hu Nim, and began insulting him, saying that he had a face like a Vietnamese or a Chinese.'[87] The attack was indeed virulent. Sihanouk said:

> Phouk Chhay is the fiercest amongst this handful of people who aid China. The most dissolute and dishonest is Hu Nim ...[88] 'Companion' Hu Nim is a little hypocrite ... a specialist in the art of being all honey on the outside and all venom inside. His voice has the tone of a monk at prayer, his words carry the scent of honey, but he hides his claws like a tiger ...
>
> If you were a sincere and committed communist, if you had the courage of your convictions, if you had any courage at all, if the fire that devours you was not that of ambition but that of the ideology you proclaim, you would not be afraid to struggle in the light of day for the triumph of that ideology, you would have dared to assume full responsibility for it and face all the consequences alone.[89]

He concluded that 'Hu Nim and his associates have excluded themselves from the national community', and advised them to go and live in China.[90] Even if he was correct in holding Nim responsible for the fraudulent petition, Sihanouk was speaking with the voice of the true autocrat who feels genuinely threatened by public dissenters but who has no sense of the bravery required of them. When he said to Nim: 'Your 'courage' consists simply in working in the shadows',[91] the remark would have been better addressed elsewhere on the left.

Two days later, Hu Nim received instructions from Vorn Vet to prepare to take to the jungle on 7 October.[92] It was a timely warning: in Prey Totoeng, the Party Centre was already distributing leaflets bearing the title *Reaksmei Krahom*, which proclaimed that Kou Roun was a protégé of Sihanouk and was 'taking the opportunity to oppress and trample on the little people without daring to attack the capitalists and the bourgeoisie. Khmer people, Khmer youth, rise up and overthrow the corrupt, dictatorial, anti-popular regime!'[93] Perhaps because of his inability to pinpoint the indeed shadowy '*Reaksmei Krahom* group',[94] as he called them, Sihanouk's response was to decry once more 'the double-dealing, the cowardliness, and the monstrous acts of Hu Nim.'[95] On 5 October he announced: 'I consider Hu Nim and his associates as traitors, and they will be subjected to the military tribunal and the execution block ... I warned them that if they did not go to China ... You persist in defying me, Hu Nim.'[96]

Two days later, Nim left for the Cardamom mountains, from the Phnom Penh house of his brother-in-law and chauffeur. 'It was raining ... Comrade Kun came to meet me and asked me to cover my head with a raincoat and walk right across in front of the intelligence agents who were sheltering near the house.'[97] Police arrived at the house soon afterwards. Nim's brother-in-law died in the military hospital, allegedly after pouring petrol over his clothes and setting fire to himself as they approached.[98] Phouk Chhay was gaoled on 9 October, while his associate, Van Tep Sovan, was killed in the Security Police headquarters. Soon afterwards, Mam Nay, Kaing Khek Iev, and four other teachers and two students from Balaing College were gaoled. According to a student at the time, from Kompong Cham:

> Sihanouk gave orders for the execution of many teachers and students who were suspected communists. They were arrested and brought in from very distant places, and killed in a special place in Kong forest near Skoun. I saw them being taken there.
> People were denouncing one another, people they did not like, as communists. In fact they were just teachers who were explaining modern lifestyles in the classrooms.[99]

Another seven suspected 'red' school teachers were reported to have been massacred at Trapeang Kraloeng in Kompong Speu.

It was not surprising that for the next three years Hu Nim, like Hou Yuon and Khieu Samphan, was widely believed to have been murdered as well.

In his 1978 confession, Vorn Vet recalled that amid the turmoil, 'The political base of the Party increasingly hardened. The Party pushed this movement further. At that time the Party instructed me to select youths and teachers who were still carrying out further secret work, to free them for the country-side. At that time I got the Tiv Ol group [of leftist teachers] to leave for the countryside together.'[100] They included, he said, Thuch Rin, who later played an extremely important role in the CPK's South-Western Zone, as we shall see in the next chapter, and Khek Penn, who was to become a leader of the North-Western Zone. Tiv Ol himself left in November for the Party Centre's headquarters. In this two month period, at least forty known leftists, including the last of the urban-based Pracheachon veterans, took to the forest.[101] Meanwhile, Lon Nol quietly reappeared on the political scene in October, 'fully recovered and ready to resume his own bid for power'.[102] All the opposing forces were now in place. With the urban left – including its moderate elements – totally destroyed, the CPK Centre now prepared for its second attempt at armed insurrection.

One notable feature of the 1967 rebellion is that there was little activity in the South-Western Zone (Takeo and Kampot), later the stronghold of the Pol Pot regime, and apparently none in the previously unsettled tribal North-East, where Pol Pot was based at the time. Along with the confused political developments in the urban areas during that year, another possible reason for Pol Pot's later disowning the 1967 revolt (which he dismissed as a spontaneous peasant rising limited to Battambang[103]) is the fact that the other Zone Party Committees (of the North-West, North and East) were more successful in mobilizing the population. With their Issarak backgrounds, they had, of course, had more experience in doing so than the French-trained intellectuals who made up most of the Party Centre. The implications of this, in particular for zonal autonomy, may have been considered ominous, especially if it is true, as Pol Pot later claimed, that 'the Party was there to assume leadership of the movement and decided to suspend provisionally the armed struggle in Battambang region [until 1968].' As we have seen, no such suspension was implemented. It was allegedly ordered 'so that the whole country could complete its preparations. If Battambang alone launched the struggle, the enemy would have been able to concentrate all its forces to annihilate the revolutionary forces there.'[104]

As we have also seen, the 1967 rebellion was not by any means limited to Battambang; even there, Zone Party Secretary Muol Sambath later complained that 'the Party was not interested and did not mention [the 1967 struggle on Phnom Veay Chap] in its history'.[105] It is likely that the *failure* of the 1967 revolt is the main reason why the Centre later disowned it; the Centre's clear involvement at the time, in terms of the unmistakeable national co-ordination, was made more embassassing by an even poorer showing in the zones most closely linked to it. Pol Pot's official (1977) version is that 'the Party decided' only in mid 1967 to launch a concerted uprising, early the next year;[106] his deputy, Nuon Chea, in another 1977 speech on the history of the 1967 Revolutionary Army, gave scant attention indeed to the 1967 resistance: 'At the beginning of 1967 the traitorous Lon Nol clique waged a civil war, repressing, shooting and killing innocent people and Cambodian patriots and revolutionaries in the most ferocious manner in large scale and systematic actions. On 17 January 1968 [we responded with] *our first armed exploit.*'[107] It is clear that the issue has caused confusion in the Party. The 1973 Party History, published by the Eastern Zone Branch, says that the policy of 'conducting politics with the support of arms [was] proclaimed since 1968 (?)'[108] [sic].

It also seems clear that the confusion was related to differences between the CPK Centre and the Vietnamese communists, who were preoccupied with the fear of upsetting Sihanouk's neutralism. According to the Pol Pot regime's *Livre Noir*, published in 1978: 'In 1967, an armed insurrection broke out at Samlaut ... The Vietnamese were seized with panic and redoubled their attacks on the CPK. A little later, when there was a certain calm, they rejoiced and felt a bit relieved ...'[109] The same source later gives an added indication as to why the Vietnamese may have been so encouraged. Also in 1967, 'The Vietnamese sent Nguyen Van Linh alias Muoi Cuc and a general named Tran Nam Trung alias Hay Hauv to meet the CPK to persuade it against continuing [sic] the armed struggle. *The Kampuchean side replied that it had to fight Lon Nol*, the lackey of US imperialism, because he was leading a campaign of annihilation against the Kampuchean revolution.'[110] The point is that at that stage, *Lon Nol had been removed from the political scene* (or was soon after). If the CPK had told the Vietnamese that its armed struggle was limited to resisting him, then the Vietnamese had good cause to 'rejoice'.[111] But as we know, the CPK Centre was really bent on the overthrow of Sihanouk; if we rule out deliberate deception, it is possible that the unnamed representative of 'the Kampuchean side' in these discussions was not one from the Party Centre, but rather So Phim from the East. But more of that later.

1968: Kampuchea's Tet Offensive

In 1968, Pol Pot personally assumed the post of Secretary of the North-East Zone Party Committee,[112] but he still maintained responsibility for CPK national activities. Again, as in 1967, the first fighting broke out in Battambang; and again, it was followed not long afterwards by concerted uprisings in every zone but one.

In mid January, several wooden bridges near Samlaut were burnt by rebels. On 18 January, a rebel ambush took the lives of three provincial guards; after a successful attack on the important army post at Banan, rebels stole thirty-two rifles.[113] A week later, they killed several more guards and stole fifty rifles from the Thvak post, at the foot of Phnom Veay Chap.[114] Government forces later discovered that over fifteen jungle camps and caches had been established in southern Battambang.[115] The rebels 'succeeded in rounding up' five hundred families, who then followed them into the forest.[116] In late January, Sihanouk replaced the governor of Battambang for the second time in less than a year.[117] In contract with the previous year, however, he now *brought Lon Nol back*, as Inspector-General of the Armed Forces with the prerogatives of a minister.[118] But after another series of guerrilla attacks, Sihanouk complained on 9 February that the army had been 'soundly beaten by the rebels' in Battambang,[119] who were said to number five hundred, two hundred of them well-armed.[120]

The first signs of tribal unrest for two years now emerged in the North-East. Rebels assassinated a number of 'loyalist elements', and planted defences of poisonous *punji* stakes around villages.[121] Charles Meyer has described the causes of the Rattanakiri rebellion: 'Its origins lay in the violence suffered by several Brao villages ordered to abandon their land for the State Plantation at Labansiek. The inhabitants formed a delegation and went to protest to the provincial authorities, but were brutalized and driven away. Returning to their villages, they clashed with the Cambodian troops who were pillaging and destroying their homes after having driven out the inhabitants. These proud and hardy people immediately took up arms – swords, spears and the fearsome crossbow; they dug bamboo stakes along the tracks, and mounted ambushes. The first government soldiers to be surprised at their posts by the invisible enemy were massacred.'[122] The government noted that 'the hill people seem much less interested in ideological struggles than in their isolation, which they have jealously tried to preserve so far'. Nevertheless Sihanouk went on to proclaim that 'the danger in this region is not subversion but underpopulation', and that roads should be built and 'numerous colonists' sent to settle there.[123] Those who *were* 'interested in ideological struggles' would soon benefit greatly from that very response to the unrest. As Meyer has noted, in contrast with the previous year, Sihanouk had now become directly associated with the military option: 'Sealed off in his ivory tower, inaccessible to counsels of moderation, surrounded by his entourage and the intransigent right, the Chief of State now gave the green light to repression, without realizing the treadmill he was getting onto.'[124]

On 25 February 1968, the Khmer Rouge launched their most widespread and successful campaign yet. Sihanouk later described it as 'a concerted operation against our isolated troops; the same movements, the same tactics', he said, were employed in Battambang, Takeo, Kampot, Koh Kong, Kompong Chhnang and Kompong Speu; 'the blow of 25 February', as he called it, was 'an operation ordered and co-ordinated by the Khmer Rouge command, which is exercised by a few intellectuals'.[125] In a single day, rebels seized fifty rifles and even some machine-guns in various parts of the country.[126] During the next fortnight, guerrilla attacks were mounted throughout the North-West and South-West. In Koh Kong alone (the seat of a 'very active' communist organization, headed by Prasith), all seven of the subdistrict chiefs, and a number of their deputies, were assassinated.[127] The successful uprisings elsewhere in the South-West were probably the work of Son Sen, now reported to be 'chief of the political committee for Kampot, Takeo and Kompong Speu',[128] and perhaps of Mok, who was soon to take over as Zone Secretary. Most importantly, more than ten thousand villagers in Battambang, Kompong Chhnang and

Kampot took to the forest on the initiative of the rebels, who were reported to have lost seventy-six dead during February.[129] In early March Sihanouk proclaimed: 'And so you see, it is total war ...'[130]

But not quite. This time, unlike in 1967, the CPK's Eastern Zone branch exhibited tardiness in going on the offensive. This was an important development for the CPK's future, and the evidence for it comes from a combination of sources. According to Pol Pot's 1977 public account: 'In March 1968 we rose up in the East, but did not capture any weapons. The Zone Committee was preparing a meeting to map out tactics for capturing weapons as in the South-West. But *the enemy withdrew their weapons before we attacked.* The enemy there mistreated the people and harassed the revolutionary movement for months. We rose up in March and the enemy kept harassing us throughout the subsequent period of more than three months. Our bases were destroyed and our people were killed or driven away. Only in July could we strike back. In an attack on an outpost we crushed the enemy and seized seventy guns.'[131] However, the secret 1974 Party History reveals that the CPK Centre, perhaps represented by Pol Pot himself, had had to intervene before the eastern attack was mounted: 'In late February 1968, the enemy attacked Kompong Cham, the right bank of the Mekong and the Eastern Zone. This time we were in readiness, but the area is one of flat plains criss-crossed with roads, and there was no refuge, leading us into difficulty [in facing] the enemy. Therefore *the Centre went down to observe and adopt a plan* to prepare to seize the majority of guns from the enemy first. The enemy all ran away; the situation became easy for us once again.'[132]

At yet another remove, in the oral account of a loyal CPK member then active in the South-Western Zone, the details become even clearer: 'In 1968 there was already talk of Vietnamese perfidy. When the Central Committee sent down the circular telling everybody to start capturing weapons, everybody in all the Zones did so except in the East, where they agreed with the Vietnamese who said: 'Don't do anything, we have plenty of weapons we can give you'. *Then Sihanouk started pulling weapons out from insecure areas* leaving the East with no opportunity to capture weapons.'[133] Now as we shall see, this last statement is untrue. The eventual eastern attack, which apparently occurred only in August, took the lives of ten members of the militia from several posts in Prey Veng near the Vietnamese border.[134] It provoked Sihanouk to highlight Vietnamese involvement with the rebels in the East. He also said that the Khmer communists responsible had then withdrawn to Vietnamese territory.[135] Most importantly of all, though, it was only now that Sihanouk went on to recommend 'that the number of small outposts be reduced, and that those remaining be manned by regular troops instead of local forces'. He added that this was because, up to then, 'the militia forces [were] prone to selling their rifles on the local markets'.[136]

It should now be clear that what Pol Pot in 1977 publicly alleged to have occurred in March ('the enemy withdrew their weapons before we attacked') – a statement contradicted by the internal CPK History of 1974 – *in fact* occurred only after August, and that despite later claims it could not have been the reason for the failure of the Eastern Zone communists to join in the uprising early in the year. Rather, the 'Zone Committee' meeting held at the time appears to have resolved of its own accord to refrain from doing so, probably partly at the behest of the Vietnamese, thereby forcing the Party Centre to override the Zone decision later in the year. Other reasons for the Eastern Zone's hesitancy about armed struggle probably included the unsuitable topography — 'flat plains criss-crossed with roads' — and So Phim's view, as expressed to Vorn Vet in 1966, that 'the people did not want to spill blood'. (See page 230.) The story of the withdrawn weapons appears to have served to cover up the Centre's embarrassment over this.

There seems to be a faint echo of these events in the wording of the 1973 Eastern Zone Party History, which hints at less than total unity with the Centre: 'Our Zone (the Eastern Zone) *worked to cooperate* with this *political movement supported by arms* in the country from 1968 to 1970 ...'[137] The divergence is clearer in the Pol Pot regime's later description of 1968-70 as a period of 'all-out people's war'[138] — although, as will become evident later, even the Centre did not consider it such at the time. The Eastern Zone leaders, as we have seen, had conferred in February 1967 and decided on a 'combined political and armed struggle', in accordance, I believe, with what was then the policy of the Centre.[139] But the fall of the Lon Nol government, and the apparent intercession of the Vietnamese, may have caused them to downgrade even this to a 'political movement supported by arms' in 1968 – at least until they were overruled by the Centre and again provoked by the government; but even then differences with the Centre persisted, as we shall see.

In the meantime, fighting had intensified in other Zones. In February, Sihanouk had replaced the governors of Pursat, Kampot (for the second time), and finally Battambang (for the third) with high-ranking military officers,[140] while Lon Nol again called in the air force to bomb rebel camps, less than 40 kilometres from Phnom Penh itself.[141] During March, a hundred and six rebels were reported killed and a hundred and eight captured, while in Battambang alone over two thousand people who had followed insurgents into the forest surrendered to the authorities.[142] Then, on 8 April, at least a thousand troops stormed Phnom Veay Chap, killing eighty-nine rebels; they captured another thirty-two along with more than seven hundred local people who were hiding out there, and seized huge stocks of arms and supplies.[143] The army pursued its advantage with a series of 'important operations' in the area;[144] soon afterwards, military intelligence reported that a group of forty-four rebels from Phnom Veay Chap were moving southeast in five or six groups, in the hope of linking up with their comrades in Pursat, Kompong Chhnang and Kompong Speu.[145] Mopping-up operations continued in Battambang at least until August,[146] however, when one of the rebel leaders (with 300,000 *riels* on his head) was captured and then executed along with his family.[147] (Muol Sambath, for his part, had 90,000 *riels* on his head.)

The rebel leader in Kompong Chhnang, Sou Yim, was killed in March;[148] a replacement (Ou Lum) and his political commissar were captured and killed in May.[149] But the area of greatest success in the government's breaking up of 'insurgent concentrations and base areas' was apparently the South-West.[150] In his prison confessions, Hu Nim recounted the difficulties faced by the revolutionaries in Kompong Speu:

> After the armed attack on 25 February 1968, brother Mar (alias brother Nhim), Party Secretary of the South-Western Zone, ordered me and comrade Hem [Khieu Samphan] to go and live in Prey Thom with village guerrillas who had just staged an insurrection ... [One day] the enemy arrived at Prey Thom and surrounded the lake, so that we could not fetch water. Comrade Sau led a group of fighters to the village to look for rice and salt; he returned with nothing. With a sad expression on his face, he rested on a hammock, swinging it up and down fiercely as he used

to do ... [He said:] 'Today the situation is not good ... The enemy are surrounding the lake ... But this problem is not serious; our friends have surrounded them and are fighting back ... But in the village we were defeated; we did not get a single can of rice because Hiem [the name of a soldier], whom we appointed to collect rice, has already defected to the enemy'. At that moment Comrade Sau saw darkness, and said: 'It seems as though our struggle is not easy.'[151]

Hou Yuon, for his part, was then at remote Phnom Aural, further north in the same province. According to a student from Kompong Chhnang, who had taken to the jungle in late February 'because of the influence of my teachers' and found his way to Phnom Aural: 'Life there was very difficult. Many were sick and many died. We got rice from the people and from foraging. People around the mountains were very poor. They loved us but did not have any food to give us.' There were about a hundred guerrillas at this base in 1968. Hou Yuon led their propaganda work among the villagers; the same student outlined how Yuon's view of Sihanouk had changed as a result of the 1967-68 repression: 'We explained the tax problem, standard of living problems and opposition to the Lon Nol policy of strategic hamlets ... Sihanouk was opposed ... as a great murderer of patriots. Phnom Veay Chap in Battambang was used as an example, and Kravar in Kompong Thom, and also Koh Kong.'[152] In the latter two provinces, a fierce struggle was in fact continuing, as Sihanouk explained in May: 'The rebel movement has been strangled. Now there are only two hot theatres of operations, one in Kompong Thom, the other in Koh Kong.'[153]

During June, twenty-one rebels were killed and eighty-eight captured near Baray in Kompong Thom.[154] In August, Sihanouk said that the army was still 'conducting mopping-up operations in Koh Kong';[155] several days later though, he admitted that the rebels were 'intensifying their activities' there.[156] Prasith, No. 7 in the CPK Central Committee, and his ethnic Thai lieutenants Nava and Prachha,[157] were proving the most effective of the rebel commanders.

The repression was perhaps fiercest in the North-East; here it seems the militia *had* 'withdrawn their weapons before we attacked'. According to Pol Pot in 1977: 'In the North-East, we rose up on 30 March 1968. Only four or five guns were seized from the enemy. Coupled with the four or five guns we had for the protection of our Central Committee headquarters, we were armed with less than ten guns with which to face the enemy in the North-East'.[158] But the heavy-handed repression, in combination with the rugged terrain, ensured that the CPK had free movement in Rattanakiri. As Meyer has written: 'The Brao, Tampuon and Jarai tribes went into rebellion, and the Cambodian command had to evacuate all the small military posts scattered around the province to concentrate forces around the headquarters. Significant reinforcements were rushed in to subdue the revolt, aircraft attacked the villages, tanks tried to reopen roads which had been cut by felled trees, and ground troops undertook mopping-up operations. In these unfamiliar regions of thick forest, the Cambodian soldiers were weakened by malaria and at an obvious disadvantage in combat against a people of different culture, torn from their hunting but sustained by fearsome jungle spirits. They were extremely brutal when [rebel] bands that they came across fell into their hands, but about two thirds of the province was soon out of government control.'[159]

Ieng Sary was later to claim that 'the revolution began in the North-East',[160] a statement which is of course false (unless he was referring to the 1966 unrest there), but is perhaps predictable, given his own involvement and that of his colleagues Pol Pot and (by 1970) Son Sen, and the success they had had from 1968. According to a witness, Ieng Sary said in 1976 that the north-eastern 'hill-tribes people — Brao, Tampuon and Stieng — were faithful to the revolution, not commercially oriented, and they had class hatred'.[161] It seems that Sary was distinguishing them from the lowland peasant majority.

In April 1968, as roads and bridges were cut in Rattanakiri, Sihanouk accused Vietnamese and Lao communists of inspiring the tribes to expel all the Khmers from the province.[162] The next month however, the rebels were reported to be 'inciting people to boycott schools and hospitals and *leave the towns*':[163] it may not be merely a case of reading later events back into the past to suggest that their inspiration came from a very different communist source. At any rate, Sihanouk did now accuse the Khmer Rouge, who he said 'gave rifles to the Khmer Loeu and ordered them to fire on the national forces'. He went on: 'I could not allow this and took stringent measures which resulted in the annihilation of 180 and the capture of 30 ringleaders, who were subsequently shot ... I do not care if I am sent to hell, ... And I will submit the pertinent documents to the devil himself.'[164]

However, perhaps predictably, the rebellion only intensified and in August Sihanouk reverted to blaming outsiders: 'General Lon Nol yesterday gave me some bad news — foreigners have infiltrated Rattanakiri and established themselves in nearly half the province [and] in Mondolkiri ... Pathet Lao troops are trying gradually to infiltrate Siempang in Stung Treng province. A few days ago, we caught over forty Laotian Reds of the Pathet Lao. The only solution is to send them all to hell.'[165] The next day, though, Sihanouk abandoned this accusation and admitted that the prisoners were in fact 'Khmer Reds'.[166] He went on: 'They have been shot. Now that these forty Reds have been shot, the situation is quiet for the moment in Stung Treng.'[167] He said that another 'nine Khmer Red leaders who pretended to be Laotians' had also been executed.[168] In the meantime, however, he had made clear his attitude to suspected Vietnamese communists captured by the army. In May he said of one such group: 'I ... had them roasted. When you roast a duck you normally eat it. But when we roasted these fellows, we had to feed them to the vultures. We had to do so to ensure our society.'[169]

Partly because of Sihanouk's statements, the north-eastern rebellion has long been considered NLF-led.[170] On the other hand, Ieng Sary privately told Khmer sympathizers — as early as 1972 — that the forces of the CPK Centre had in fact clashed with Vietnamese communists in this period. An account of perhaps the first battles of the Vietnam-Kampuchea conflict, which erupted into full-scale war in the late 1970s, was given by Sary at a 1972 closed meeting in Albania. According to a Khmer student in Yugoslavia who attended: 'We knew about the Vietnamese and the Khmers ... Ieng Sary was [military] commander for the North-Eastern Zone. There was strong defence against the Vietnamese before the 1970 coup ... When the Viet Cong came in and out without permission, Ieng Sary's troops attacked them and drove them back into their country ... They defended the area from all enemies, before the coup.'[171]

Whether or not this is true, the major Vietnamese concern was still the increasing destabilization of the Sihanouk regime (whose benign neutrality was now more valuable than ever, after the losses the communists had suffered in the Tet Offensive). The Prince's violence was eroding the magic of the 'oasis of peace' in domestic political circles as well. In June, members of the National Assembly, mainly from Kompong Chhnang, alleged that innocent people 'who were not red at all' were being arrested and executed 'contrary to the Constitution and international law'.[172] The next month, rebels in Koh Kong committed their first large-scale atrocity. Thirty men, led by Nava and Prachha, and armed with automatic weapons, ambushed a busload of civilians, killing five, and robbed them of all they possessed.[173]

However, more systematic violence had already occurred in Kompong Thom's Baray district. Phnom Penh Radio announced that on the night of 14 April, about thirty rebels had killed seven peasants in three villages there.[174] This report seems to have been the first occasion on which government sources gave serious attention to rebel violence against civilians outside the administration. It is not known who was leader of the Baray group, but these killings may have marked the beginning of the violent career of Ke Pauk.

Meanwhile, in Kompong Cham, the provincial governor Nhiem Thien was organizing witch-hunts for suspected communists. In Kandol Chrum, a friend of So Phim named Mon was arrested and forcibly taken to Bos to help in the search for Phim. When this proved fruitless, Mon attempted to escape but was recaptured, beheaded and disembowelled.[175] Elsewhere, according to a witness, provincial officals were ordered to take part in beating innocent peasants to death; another witness reports that two young children in Prey Totoeng, accused of acting as couriers for the guerrillas, had their heads sawn off with palm fronds. In Kampot, forty school teachers, suspected of subversive activity, were on Sihanouk's orders bound hand and foot and thrown from the cliff at Bokor.[176] The traditional violence 'behind the Khmer smile', last seen in the exploits of Dap Chhuon, Puth Chhay and Achar Yi, had again been unleashed.

In Phnom Penh, Chau Sau, Director of the National Credit Bank, was gaoled in July on a charge of supplying rebels in several provinces with money and medical equipment.[177] His assistant directors, Uch Ven and Poc Deuskomar (who was in fact part of Vorn Vet's urban network),[178] immediately took to the jungle. Also gaoled were Phung Ton, the Rector of Kompong Cham University, Keng Vannsak, a number of journalists including Khieu Samphan's brother Khieu Sengkim,[179] and So Nem. (Chau Seng had already fled to France, abandoning his post as Director of State Warehouses, after being told by Sihanouk in January 'to prepare to flee'.[180]) In

August, there were shoot-outs in the streets of the capital, leading to the capture of forty underground activists, mostly students or officials, who had been propagandizing among workers and distributing tracts. The authorities concluded that this organization was anticipating 'large-scale operations'.[181] Its leader was said to be Phieuv Hak, whom Sihanouk called 'one of the big bosses of the Khmer Rouge'; Hak was arrested and, it seems, quietly executed.

Vorn Vet later revealed that the government had come very close to netting even bigger fish: 'In July Sihanouk's spies arrested some of my urban people and this spread to important networks and even me. At that time I was staying at friend Kac Sim's house; he covered me so I could run away. He shot at Sihanouk's spies, wounding one and killing one, and then ran out after me ... I ran to tell my wife to evacuate sister Yim [Khieu Ponnary], the wife of brother No. 1 [Pol Pot].' Kac Sim was killed in another shoot-out in early September, and six of his comrades were executed by the police; a dozen or more teachers were gaoled. But the urban underground was still active a year later when, for the first time, a militant movement erupted among the workers in the Chinese-donated factories. According to Meyer it was 'smashed by the immediate sacking of all the supposed 'Maoist' elements ... Nevertheless, according to officials of these factories, underground worker organizations existed there and were preparing to take action'.[182] Such organizations were undoubtedly linked with Vorn Vet's network.

Meanwhile, Lon Nol's fortunes had been rising rapidly. On May Day, 1968, exactly a year after the widespread demonstrations against his then Cabinet, he was officially appointed Minister of Defence; in July he became Deputy Prime Minister, and on 5 December, Acting Prime Minister.[183] If he had not enjoyed Sihanouk's wholehearted backing during the previous year, he did now.

As the right strengthened its hold on power, new social problems began to develop. In 1969 a conservative Khmer economist explained how the period of the 'gap' between harvests had been capitalized upon in business circles: 'Around September 1968, following the intervention of a certain number of capitalists, the Royal Government authorized a small increase in the price of rice, to favour, it was said, the agricultural producers. The effect was in fact the opposite. It was the merchants and rice-sellers who profited from the price-rise, while the peasants who had sold everything by September were obliged to pay more for rice to feed their families.' A year later, the *riel* was devalued at the time of the 'gap', and the price-rise it provoked had similar effects, which according to this writer were 'fiercely resented in the countryside'.[184] It was in 1968, too, that Sihanouk put through legislation giving the central government power to appoint subdistrict chiefs, thus returning local administration to the system of the pre-1959 and colonial periods.[185]

Although the Vietnamese communists must have been concerned about the developments within the CPK, they still had more reason to worry about the Party Centre than about its branches and members. In the South-West, for instance, Hou Yuon and the rebels at the Phnom Aural base adopted this attitude to the Vietnamese failure to assist their struggle: 'Vietnam was a friend, but an unreliable one. Vietnam was not considered an enemy. On the other hand, there was already criticism of Soviet revisionism. The Soviet Union was already considered an enemy. China was little mentioned in this connection.'[186]

This view epitomizes the position which I have described elsewhere as that of revolutionary 'independents',[187] although it may in fact have been the view of the majority of CPK cadres, at least by the mid 1970s. But until then a large number of veteran communists maintained the view that solidarity with Vietnam, if not — in this period of severe repression — paramount, was still an important ingredient of the Khmer revolution. This was particularly the case in the Eastern Zone; the terrain there, unsuitable for the establishment of independent 'liberated zones', reinforced this tendency towards cross-border cooperation.

I have already discussed the case of Prok Sary, who took to the jungle with Heng Samrin and Chea Sim in Prey Veng in June 1967. The married women, children and monks who had accompanied them were, she said, 'sent to the Vietnamese border'. Sary described the activities of those who remained behind as basically agit-prop work: 'There were sixty people in my group, which was divided into several sections. At 7.00 or 8.00 pm each evening we would go into a village to temper [*bangrin*] the people, returning to the forest at 3.00 or 4.00 am. All the people in Komchay Meas district believed in us. They wanted to be liberated from Sihanouk's oppression. The people helped us with rice, other food, and whatever we needed for the struggle.' Sary said that her group clashed with the police or militia on only five occasions over the next three years. Another local source, a former Issarak who became a monk, has described the 1968 flight of Kung Sokun (alias Tuy), a senior cadre in the Eastern Zone in the 1970s. Tuy had been an Issarak monk himself, but had left his *wat* to study, and then, after returning to his rice farm, 'joined the secret political movement': 'In 1968 he ran into the forest again, when they came to arrest him. Several times three or four Sihanouk soldiers came to his house from the post nearby. He couldn't stay, so he ran into the jungle, where there were hundreds of people who had fled for the same reason. They split up into small groups of six or eight, and moved from place to place to hide themselves.'[188]

Other cadres, including So Phim himself, spent much of the period in NLF zones in South Vietnam. One of Phim's closest comrades recalls: 'The Vietnamese let us conduct study sessions in their territory, near the border. The teachers were Khmers, like [Eastern Zone Deputy Secretary] Phuong, and Lin.'[189] According to two first-hand accounts, during 1968 Phim lectured cadres on politics, military strategy and tactics; he emphasized cooperation with the Vietnamese against US imperialism, and displayed portraits of Marx, Lenin and Ho Chi Minh.[190] One of his students was Chhouk, the former Issarak medic turned teacher, who had fled Phnom Penh in 1965, becoming underground chief of the CPK's Region 24 (southern Prey Veng). Chhouk, too, spent the late 1960s in NLF zones across the border, where he was joined by the future Zone military commander, Chan Chakrey, who had escaped from the Samlaut area in 1967.[191]

At the same time, the Vietnamese were heavily involved in the training of Khmer revolutionaries. A 1971 US intelligence study reported the recruitment of ethnic Khmers from both South Vietnam and Cambodia for courses in North Vietnam: 'An ex-Viet Cong commo-liaison cadre recently reported that he intermittently saw small groups of these recruits moving to and from North Vietnam during the period 1962 to 1970. Between January 1968 and April 1970, the rate of returnees was said to be about eleven to twelve daily.'[192] But few, if any, returned to Kampuchean territory. And in late 1968, when the Eastern Zone CPK finally took up arms, the Vietnamese refused to help them. According to one cadre, Tea Sabun: 'The armed struggle began in 1968. At first we had only a few fighters: Phuong, Chan and I myself had thirty men in Damber and Kauk Srok (in CPK Region 21 north of Highway 7), and So Phim ninety in Krabau and Bos (in Region 20 to the south). The Vietnamese communists did not aid us at all. We went to ask for help and they said: 'You should not be struggling or asking for arms. Wait until we have liberated Vietnam. Then we will fight.' But we went after guns.'[193] According to another source from Region 21, Phim himself 'never forgot' this Vietnamese refusal of weapons.[194] Nevertheless, the struggle against Sihanouk remained largely political. Another cadre, from Region 20, says that over the next year 'we did not have many guns, partly in order to cooperate with our Vietnamese brothers on the borders, and partly in order to go out and lead the people in the villages.'[195]

Further, the military struggle was not highly successful. The biggest battle fought by Eastern Zone guerrillas in 1968, on the border of Kratie province above Memut, resulted in defeat.[196] And this was in an area where allegedly 'everyone believed in the Khmer Rouge'[197], thousands of people in Memut had taken to the forest the previous year, and land-grabbing by government officials, notably Nhek Tioulong's brother, was becoming a serious problem.[198]

In the second half of 1968, Keo Meas travelled to Hanoi in an attempt to gain the commitment to the struggle of the Khmers who had been trained there. Son Ngoc Minh and the Vietnamese, still trying not to disturb their relations with Kampuchea, rejected his appeal. Meas then accused Minh of 'becoming fat in safety while the Party faithful were being liquidated'.[199] The rebellion had finally driven a wedge between the 'domestic' Khmer communist veterans and those in Vietnam. The irony was that the CPK Centre had achieved this without formally proclaiming an armed struggle, which came only in July 1969, as we shall see. The official slogan was still 'combined political and armed struggle',[200] and it is not surprising that, nine years later, the Centre *backdated* this to 1960 and the official commencement of 'all-out people's war' to January 1968.[201]

There were concomitant effects on an international level. The Chinese Communist Party had managed to come out on top in two important but potentially contradictory struggles, for the allegiance of both the CPK and the Sihanouk regime. The subtlety of its approach, and equally importantly, its geographical distance, had enabled it to overcome formidable obstacles. Although China (like the USSR) was continuing to supply Sihanouk's army — a consignment of Chinese jet fighter-bombers, artillery, machine-guns and mines was delivered in January 1968[202] — veteran CPK members like Keo Meas and others like Hou Yuon did not blame the Chinese; instead they resented the Vietnamese communists' failure to *help* them fight back. And although the Vietnamese had indeed earned such comradely resentment in their attempts to placate Sihanouk, the Prince still blamed *them* — partly because of their proximity, partly for historical reasons — for inspiring the rebellion, rather than the Chinese. While Sihanouk roasted captured Vietnamese communists, the only dangerous period in China's relations with Phnom Penh was the brief ultra-left phase of the Cultural Revolution. After that, on several occasions, Sihanouk stated his view of the insurgency as follows: 'If one day war is imposed on Cambodia ... that war could only be the work of the Vietminh or Viet Cong, who are the masters of the Khmer Rouge and who never cease to carry out to the fullest their intention to swallow our land.'[203]

Sihanouk's unwillingness to treat China and Vietnam in similar fashions at best led him into confusion, even when he did perceive that a rebel movement more closely linked with Beijing was endangering the neutrality that both he and Hanoi valued. This confusion was expressed in a speech he made at the height of the crisis in February 1968, when Vietnamese communist energies were totally consumed in the Tet Offensive. He said: 'You have to choose between having war with the Americans or having war with us. You have to choose. That is what the Maoist camp told us. I do not mean the Peking Government but the camp of the Maoists. I do not know which of them either. You may guess. Anyhow, that is that. They are driving us into a corner.'[204] Sihanouk chose, and sounded the death-knell of his regime. So did the Vietnamese, gambling close relations with the Khmer communists in exchange for a neutral posture on the part of the latter's enemy, a neutrality increasingly crucial to their own domestic position even as it became less and less benign. China, on the other hand, far away and with much less at stake, had the best of both worlds; a seemingly unbreakable relationship with the Kampuchean government and an even better one with its eventual successor.

However, despite the deep cracks appearing in the Sangkum

system, Sihanouk remained a legitimate figure in the eyes of many Khmer peasants; just as importantly, his neutrality, and the national independence it reflected, still commanded great popular loyalty. Over the next year or more, this legitimacy and independence was to prove a critical factor, and one that had to be recognized by the CPK. When it was, in 1969, the Vietnamese communists found their long-standing attitude to Sihanouk vindicated. This development was epitomized, perhaps, by another shift in the position of Keo Meas and other CPK veterans, including So Phim, and Hou Yuon[205] — but the Party Centre did not allow this to alter its long-term anti-Sihanouk goal, which was to prove costly indeed for Meas, Phim, Yuon and nearly all their comrades.

1969: The Rectification of Errors

Tea Sabun continues his account: 'By 1969 my forces numbered over a hundred. However we were driven out of Damber and had run out of food and medicine. We all fled into Vietnam through Memut that year ... At the border the Sihanouk forces fired upon us, and so did the Vietnamese communists. But then we made contact and smoothed things over, and they let us into Vietnam, deep in so as not to let Sihanouk know. They were in touch with Sihanouk and were buying supplies from Kampuchea, and they did not want to disturb the relationship.

'So we moved about five or six kilometres inside Vietnam. There they gave us rice and pork to eat, shoes to wear, etc. After three or four days' rest they escorted us south, inside Vietnamese territory, and we met up with So Phim, at Thnaot, one kilometre from the Kampuchean border. He had a hundred fighters there, and in all there were three hundred revolutionary troops, three companies, in the Eastern Zone.'[206] By October 1969, the authorities estimated that the number of guerrillas in the East had increased to 450-500 (compared with 100-200 in October 1968).[207] They were said to be divided into four main bands, each with its own training camp in south Vietnam. By early 1970, there were apparently five companies of 100-150 men each.[208] Unlike the rebels in other zones, according to Lon Nol the easterners were based entirely in Vietnam.[209]

Ney Sarann was now reported to be So Phim's political commissar. Another leader mentioned by official circles was

Chim Saphoeun, a Pracheachon candidate in the 1955 elections.[210] At any rate, their activities seem to have been largely political – the basic unit of organization, according to Lon Nol after a personal investigation in the East, was the three-man cell 'following the Viet Cong model'.[211]

Interestingly, Lon Nol also referred to a man named Neou Pal who he said was 'directing a mobile band of sixty insurgents responsible for maintaining liaison with rebel groups operating in Cambodia'.[212] This was probably Pol Pot himself, who as we know later used the similar pseudonym 'Pol'.[213] Even more intriguing was Lon Nol's simultaneous claim that Tou Samouth was 'President of the clandestine Khmer communist party.'[214] Perhaps he simply assumed that Samouth was still alive, or perhaps he was a victim of CPK Centre counter-intelligence designed to reinforce the impression, helpful to their cause as we have seen in Chapter 6, that the Party was still under the leadership of ICP veterans.

The first six months of 1969 saw over 130 rebels killed, 100 wounded, and 60 captured or forced to surrender.[215] According to *Le Monde* in November: 'On two occasions in the course of the year, the Khmer language newspapers have published photographs showing a rifle standing on a mat, and next to the rifle, a severed head. It is noticeable that the number of rebels [reported] captured is consistently low.'[216] (The same was of course true in 1968.) In Kampot the authorities displayed three severed heads in the town market place.[217]

According to Lon Nol's report there were twenty-four incidents in the second half of September 1969. Only thirteen of the twenty-four were the result of rebel attacks, however. There had been a 'reinforcement of rebel potential' in the South-West, and a resurgence of dissidence in the North-West, but the situation appeared to be different in the East: 'The bulk of the rebels who find refuge in South Vietnamese territory, just behind the Viet Cong troops spread out along the frontier opposite Kompong Cham, Prey Veng and Svay Rieng, *do not seem to be increasing their armed actions against our forces.*' Again, it seems, the Eastern Zone CPK was concentrating on political work. Lon Nol went on: 'Scattered rebel elements are operating through villages in Kompong Cham, the north-east of Prey Veng and northern Svay Rieng, dealing with the inhabitants to ensure their complicity or their discretion (terrorism, propaganda)'.[218]

This strategy of minimal confrontation – and minimal risk – in the East was also appearing to pay off. According to *Le Monde*: 'One teacher from a small village in the north of Prey Veng province ... told us that many provincial guards prefer to disappear when they hear of the presence of armed rebels in their locality. The rebels thus have the run of the field.'[219] Meyer concurs: 'The revolutionary base in the Cardamoms and the guerrillas of Rattanakiri province were not a serious threat to the Cambodian regime. It was different in the case of the political development in the densely populated lowland regions, *in particular Kompong Cham, Prey Veng* and Kampot, and in some parts of Kompong Speu and Kompong Thom.' There, he said, small armed propaganda groups circulated 'in nearly all the villages ... [and] always tried to avoid clashes with the government troops.'[220] Despite its military caution, the Eastern Zone CPK fielded the most impressive political organization.

As for the South-Western base in the Cardamoms, Vorn Vet wrote in his confession that (despite the 'reinforcement of rebel potential') the revolutionaries were still encountering the hardships described by Hu Nim in 1968. In November of that year, Vet says, he went there only to fall ill with malaria, which badly debilitated him for many months. After eight months back in Phnom Penh, he returned to the South-West in November 1969: 'At that time life was difficult, for example because of Lon Nol's destruction. I was sick in the mountains for over two months. Only in March 1970 could I walk, and did I go back to Phnom Penh. At the time of the coup of 18 March 1970 I was still very sick.'[221] It is difficult to support the contention that direct armed confrontation had paid off in any significant measure.

In his 1969 report, Lon Nol estimated that rebel armed forces numbered only about 2,400 nationally.[222] Pol Pot himself has given a figure of four thousand troops, but organized at company level only, which may be accurate. His claim of fifty thousand guerrillas supporting them can be discounted, however;[223] both the Sihanouk regime and the CIA give a total figure of ten thousand by 1970, and Pol Pot's own figure for the number of 'regular' CPK troops in the North-East is as low as 150. All this gives the Vietnamese estimate of *Party* membership in this period, at a new low of eight hundred due to the repression, a good deal of credibility.[224]

Thus, the CPK rebellion was hardly a major military threat to Sihanouk's army — although its existence had profoundly altered the character of his regime — and it had little hope of achieving power for the CPK in the medium term. But there were other clouds on the horizon. As the Vietnam War ground on, the US became more determined than ever to rid itself of the disadvantage it faced while Vietnamese communist troops were able to take refuge in sactuaries just across the Kampuchean border. For their part, the Vietnamese, decimated in the 1968 fighting, needed sanctuaries (and the Ho Chi Minh Trail) more than ever. Most important of all, up to 80 per cent of their supplies were now apparently being shipped via Kompong Som port,[225] an arrangement that obviously depended on Sihanouk maintaining power. In March 1969, the US Air Force began the 'Menu' campaign involving secret bombardments of the sanctuaries. In June, Sihanouk signalled his return to a more genuine form of neutrality by re-establishing diplomatic relations with the USA and at the same time recognizing the NLF's Provisional Revolutionary Government. But this was also a sign that his freedom of movement was becoming limited. Both parties in the Vietnam conflict were increasing their pressure and encroachment on Kampuchea.

The direct military impact on Kampuchea was increasing. Already in 1966, Sihanouk's emissary Prince Norindeth, on a visit to Australia, had protested against US bombing and strafing of Kampuchean border areas, claiming that 'hundreds of our people have already died in these attacks'.[226] Since the early 1960s, too, US Special Forces teams had been making secret reconnaissance and mine-laying incursions into Kampuchean territory. In 1967 and 1968 about eight hundred such missions were mounted, usually by several American personnel and up to ten local mercenaries, in most cases dressed as 'Viet Cong'. One Green Beret team 'inadvertently blew up a Cambodian civilian bus, causing heavy casualties'.[227]

Then, in 1969, the number of these secret missions was more than doubled; over a thousand more were mounted before the March 1970 coup. And in the same fourteen-month period, over 3,600 B-52 raids were conducted against targets in Kampuchea, under the 'Menu' operation. In the words of William Shawcross: 'Night after night through the summer, fall and winter of 1969 and into the early months of 1970 the eight-engined planes passed west over South Vietnam and into Cambodia. Peasants were killed — no one knows how many — and Communist logistics were somewhat disrupted. To avoid the attacks, the

North Vietnamese and Viet Cong pushed their sanctuaries and
supply bases deeper into the country, and the area that the B-52s
bombarded expanded as the year passed. The war spread.'[228] In
September, Lon Nol reported a recent increase of several
thousand — to a total of 35-40,000 — in the number of
Vietnamese communist troops in the sanctuaries, an increase
which he said was 'motivated by the cleaning-up operations in
the 41st Tactical Zone, launched by the US-South Vietnamese
forces, and by flooding. In this period, nothing suggests that
these foreign units will soon leave our territory'.[229]

It was one of the major issues in Sihanouk's downfall, in which
Lon Nol was a key figure. Conversely, however, Sihanouk was to
be a key figure in Lon Nol's own downfall five years later. It is
worth quoting at length the account given by the Pol Pot regime
in 1978:

> In 1969 the situation in Kampuchea was increasingly tense. The
> Central Committee of the Communist Party of Kampuchea
> grasped the situation well and knew perfectly that the US and Lon
> Nol were going to stage a *coup d'état*. It estimated that if the US
> carried out the coup, this would drive new forces to the
> revolution's side. Thus, it was necessary to prepare to receive
> these forces. The *coup d'état* would be nothing but positive for the
> revolution. That is why the Central Committee of the Commun-
> ist Party of Kampuchea elaborated a document about the Party's
> line on the National United Front. It criticized the statements of
> the intellectuals who had joined the maquis and attacked
> Samdech Norodom Sihanouk. It considered that those statements
> ran counter to the Party's line on the National United Front, for
> they should rather have attacked the US imperialists and the traitor
> Lon Nol. The Party proceeded to the rectification of these errors
> and mobilized all forces capable of being mobilized, to fight and
> isolate the enemy.[230]

We may note the new definition of 'the enemy'. This rectifica-
tion, of errors allegedly made by unnamed intellectuals, was in
fact a change in the posture (but not the long-term policy) of the
CPK Centre itself. Vorn Vet reveals in his confession that *he* had
'organized the distribution of statements by the intellectuals ...
Khieu Samphan, Hou Yuon and Hu Nim ... attacking Sihanouk
very strongly', but that afterwards, in November 1969, he had
gone to the Cardamoms 'to study the new political line of the
Party'.[231]

13. *Above* Khmer Buddhist monks being interrogated by a colonial intelligence officer during an operation against a communist-occupied zone

14. *Left* Monks attending a Unified Issarak Front meeting

15. *Below* Tou Samouth greets a Soviet official after the 1954 Geneva settlement

18. Norodom Sihanouk chairs a meting of Khmer Rouge leaders, March 1973. Left to right: Ieng Sary, Hou Yuon, Pol Pot, Hu Nim, Khieu Samphan, Norodom Sihanouk

16. Unity in Neutrality. In July 1969, Vice-President Huynh Tan Phat of the NLF's Provisional Revolutionary Government of South Vietnam visited Prince Sihanouk's Kingdom of Cambodia. From left: Keat Chhon (later a Minister in Pol Pot's Democratic Kampuchea government), Son Sann (now head of the Khmer People's National Liberation Front), Huynh Tan Phat (now Deputy Prime Minister of the Socialist Republic of Vietnam) and his wife, Lon Nol (President of the Khmer Republic, 1970-75), and Prom Thos (Minister of Commerce, 1970-1973)

17. Hou Yuon (right) and Hu Nim in the Khmer Rouge zones, 1973 (?)

19. Left to right: Hou Yuon, Norodom Sihanouk, Son Sen (1973)

20. A French Indochina postage stamp, featuring the young King Sihanouk

Photos courtesy of General Nguyen Thanh Son (4, 5, 15), General Chana Samudavanija (8, 9), Keng Vannsak (10), Prom Thos (16), Tuol Sleng museum, Phnom Penh (7, 17), and various contemporary journals.

The CPK Centre was of course finally conceding that Sihanouk was not, after all, 'a secret agent of the United States' (see p.224), and it was now willing to join publicly with Sihanouk and take advantage of his recognized following, whatever they thought privately (or proclaimed in the villages) about him. This necessitated serious discussions with both the Chinese and the Vietnamese leaders, whose support would be essential immediately the opportunity arose. (In fact, but for *their* past cultivation of Sihanouk, in contrast with the CPK's stand, the new CPK policy would not have been workable at all.) It was for this reason that at the end of 1969 Pol Pot set out, for the second time, for Hanoi and Beijing, and so was in the latter city when Sihanouk (for the second time unaware of the fact) arrived there the day after his deposition.[232]

But it is important to emphasize that the CPK Centre made this decision of its own accord, because of the impasse it was in and the opportunities that loomed, and not as a result of Vietnamese (or Chinese) pressure. A secret version of the Party History distributed by Ieng Sary in 1971 makes this clear:

> From the end of 1967 until 1970 the enemy began a civil war. Our friends were separated from one another, contact was difficult between one another, to go from one zone to another was arduous ...
>
> In building the Party from 1967 to 1970 to the present, we were unable to have a Congress because of the difficulty; there was only an Enlarged Politburo meeting. An Enlarged Politburo meeting in July 1969 decided on a people's war to smash Lon Nol, to resist the civil war in order to prevent the loss of peace and neutrality. *We had to build up the Party in all fields once again*, in strategy and tactics once again. Considering the plan to attack the enemy, we did not move towards resisting Sihanouk at that time.[233]

The last sentence appears to be code for 'We now moved towards preparing to join in a public alliance with Sihanouk for propaganda purposes'. The testimony of a CPK guerrilla in Kompong Chhnang tallies with this interpretation of the CPK's sincerity. He reveals that locally, even though the coup was predicted, 'There was no lessening in the attacks on Sihanouk right up to the day of the coup'.[234] In Kompong Speu, an Issarak veteran serving as bodyguard for Hou Yuon, Khieu Samphan and Hu Nim describes a debate over the issue there: 'About a month before the coup, a study meeting was called by Khieu

Samphan in the jungle north of Sre Khlong. Three to five hundred people attended. He asked for opinions: 'If Sihanouk joins with us, will we allow him to join us, and if we do, will we allow him to be a king again or what?' Those who didn't really understand said: 'Let him join and be a king again.' Others said: 'No, let him break the soil like us for once.' The fighters and people who wanted to let him be a king again were in the minority, those who did not were the majority; so it was agreed that no distinctions were to be made between Khmers, who would all join together in solidarity to struggle to liberate our people and territory.'[235] That the 1970-1975 war was not fought on this basis lies at the heart of the Kampuchean tragedy.

Notes

1. Donald Kirk, *Wider War*, New York 1971, p.78.
2. See 'The Samlaut Rebellion, 1967-68', Ch. 7 of Ben Kiernan and Chanthou Boua (eds.) *Peasants and Politics in Kampuchea, 1942-81*, London 1982, pp.166-205. Henceforth, 'Samlaut'; unless otherwise indicated, detailed references are provided there.
3. *Ibid.*, p.171. On Ieng Thirith, see *Des Mouvements Anti-Gouvernementaux au Cambodge*, Khmer Republic, Deuxième Bureau, 20 July 1973, 45 pp., at p.41.
4. Author's interview with local cadre Chen Lon, Kandol Chrum, 7 August 1980.
5. *Phnom Penh Presse*, 12 April 1967, p.15.
6. *Les Paroles de Samdech Preah Norodom Sihanouk*, Ministry of Information, Phnom Penh, April-June 1967, p.133; speech at Prey Totoeng, 10 April 1967.
7. See p.252.
8. *Provatt nei Pak Kommyunis Kampuchea* (History of the Communist Party of Kampuchea), 23 pp., mimeographed, distributed internally by Ieng Sary in 1974, p.9.
9. *Phnom Penh Presse*, 1 February 1967.
10. Rémy Prud'homme, *L'Economie du Cambodge*, Paris, 1969, p.255, table 12, note a.
11. J.F. Sonolet, *Réalités Cambodgiennes*, 5 November 1971, p.15.
12. *Les Paroles, op. cit.*, July-September 1967, p.503; speech in Phnom Penh, 5 July 1967.

13. *Ibid.*, January–March 1967, p.18; speech in Phnom Penh, 12 March 1967.
14. *Ibid.*, July–September 1967, p.503.
15. *Ibid.*, January–March 1967, p.21. My emphasis.
16. *Ibid.*, p.19.
17. *Ibid.*, and April–June 1967, p.104, 3 April 1967.
18. *Ibid.*, January–March 1967, p.29, 13 March 1967.
19. *Ibid.*
20. *Ibid.*, p.104. (See also BBC *Summary of World Broadcasts*, FE/2434/A3/9.)
21. *Ibid.*, p.133, 10 April 1967.
22. *Ibid.*, pp.235, 8 (2 May 1967), 174 (22 April 1967), 104 (3 April 1967); p.133 (10 April 1967); p.112 (7 April 1967); and *Phnom Penh Presse*, 12 April 1967, p.15.
23. Author's interview with Tuot Sman, at Samrong near Bos, 6 August 1980.
24. Author's interview with Ouch Bun Chhoeun, Phnom Penh, 30 September 1980.
25. Interview with the author, Samrong, 6 August 1980. My emphasis.
26. Interview with the author, Suong, 7 August 1980.
27. Ouch Bun Chhoeun, *op. cit.*, and author's interview with Mau Met, Kompong Cham, 5 October 1980. Both men were in Memut at the time.
28. Ouch Bun Chhoeun, *op. cit.*
29. Mau Met, *op. cit.*
30. Author's interview with Hun Sen, Phnom Penh, 21 October 1980.
31. Ouch Bun Chhoeun, *op. cit.*, and author's interview with Chum Sambor, Prey Veng, 12 July 1980.
32. *Phnom Penh Presse*, 12 April 1967, and *Agence Khmère de Presse*, 12 April 1967, which reports their arrests.
33. *Bulletin du Contre-Gouvernement*, Phnom Penh, no. 183, 30 May 1967, pp.5, 6.
34. Author's interview with Sam Ngae Heang, Tuk Khleang, 27 September 1980.
35. 'Samlaut', *op. cit.*, p.172.
36. *Agence Khmère de Presse*, 11 April 1967.
37. *Réalités Cambodgiennes*, 19 May 1967, p.3.
38. *Les Paroles*, *op.cit.*, April–June 1967, p.372; 16 May 1967.
39. *Ibid.*, p.354; 13 May 1967.
40. 'Cambodia: The Mass Media', by Don O. Noel Jr., New York, *Alicia Patterson Fund*, 12 April 1967, p.20.
41. Ea Meng Try, personal communication.
42. *Les Paroles*, *op. cit.*, July–September 1967, p.593; 7 August 1967.
43. *Provatt nei Pak Kommyunis Kampuchea*, *op. cit.*, p.10. My emphasis. The replacements mentioned did indeed occur.
44. *Chamlaiy Hu Nim krosuong khosenakar* ('The reply of Hu Nim, Ministry of Information'), 29 May 1977. Archives of Tuol Sleng Prison, Phnom Penh. Translated into English by Chanthou Boua, 105 pp. typescript, at pp.15–16.
45. *Réalités Cambodgiennes*, 11 August 1967, p.4.
46. *Les Paroles*, *op. cit.*, April–June 1967, p.235; 2 May 1967.
47. *Ibid.*, p.310; 8 May 1967.
48. *Ibid.*, p.314.
49. Author's interview with Reim, Stains, 29 January 1980.
50. *Chamlaiy Hu Nim*, *op. cit.*, p.70.
51. Ouch Bun Chhoeun, *op.cit.*
52. 'Important Culprits', Document no. 2.5.24 submitted to the People's Revolutionary Tribunal, Phnom Penh, August 1979.
53. *Les Paroles*, *op. cit.*, April–June 1967, p.483; 20 June 1967.

54. Charles Meyer, *Derrière le sourire khmer*, Paris 1971, p.192. Another well-placed source relates that over four hundred bodies of peasants were discovered in a forest cave in Kompong Speu province in 1965. This may be a mis-dating of a 1967 massacre. See Kiernan and Boua, *op. cit.*, p.5.
55. *The Kampuchean People's Revolutionary Council*, NUFSK Information Service, Phnom Penh, January 1979, p.3.
56. Author's interview with Prok Sary, Prey Veng, 12 July 1980.
57. Author's interviews with Prak Sovan, Kranhoung, 9 August 1980, and Yim Sern, Kandol Chrum, 28 July 1980.
58. Ouch Bun Chloeun, *op. cit.* My emphasis.
59. Chum Sambor, *op. cit.*, and author's interview with Puk Soum, Prey Veng, 8 August 1980.
60. *Bulletin du Contre-Gouvernement*, no. 166, 10 May 1967, pp.2-4.
61. *Les Paroles, op. cit.*, April-June 1967, p.315; 8 May 1967.
62. *Bulletin du Contre-Gouvernement, op. cit.*, no. 166, 10 May 1967, p.3.
63. Jean Daubier, *A History of the Chinese Cultural Revolution*, New York 1974, pp.20, 321.
64. Author's interview with Yos Por, Phnom Penh, 11 September 1980. (See also his account in *Problèmes Politiques et Sociaux*, Paris, no. 373, 12 October 1979, pp.5-6.)
65. In 1977 Pol Pot said of this period that contact even between CPK leaders was extremely tenuous: 'Any contact required a period of a month because it necessitated a trip on foot, on the back of an elephant, and also because the enemy, who was cutting the communication routes, had to be constantly avoided.' *Discours prononcé par le camarade Pol Pot ... au meeting commemorant le 17e anniversaire de la fondation du Parti Communiste de Kampuchea*. Phnom Penh, 27 September 1977, mimeographed, p.41.
66. Stephen Heder's interview, Chantaburi, March 11, 1980. I am grateful to Heder for supplying me with a copy of this and other texts of his interviews.
67. *Les Paroles, op. cit.*, April-June 1967, p.492; 27 June 1967.
68. *Ibid.*, July-September 1967, pp.547-48; 27 July 1967.
69. *Ibid.*, p.568, 2 August 1967.
70. *Ibid.*, p.593; 7 August 1967.
71. Stephen R. Heder and Ea Meng Try, personal communications.
72. *Les Paroles, op. cit.*, July-September 1967, p.592; 7 August 1967.
73. *Ibid.*, pp.593, 590.
74. *Ibid.*, pp.588-89.
75. *Ibid.*, p.674; 11 September 1967. (See also p.652ff; 3 September 1967.)
76. *Ibid.*
77. *Ibid.*, p.675.
78. *Ibid.*, p.677.
79. *Ibid.*
80. *Ibid.*, pp.677, 679.
81. *Ibid.*, p.718; 18 September 1967.
82. *Ibid.*
83. Stephen Heder, 'Kampuchea's Armed Struggle: The Origins of an Independent Revolution', *Bulletin of Concerned Asian Scholars*, 11, 1, 1979, p.12. He quotes a report from the *Times of India*, 17 May 1968, cited in J.D. Armstrong, *Revolutionary Diplomacy*, Berkeley 1977, p.181.
84. *Chamlaiy Hu Nim, op. cit.*, p.16.
85. *Les Paroles, op. cit.*, July-September 1967, p.753; 30 September 1967.

86. Interview at Prey Totoeng, 4 August 1980.
87. *Ibid.*
88. BBC *Summary, op. cit.*, FE/2600/A3/3. (Henceforth, SWB.)
89. *Les Paroles, op. cit.*, July–September 1967, p.750–52; 30 September 1967.
90. *Ibid.*, p.761.
91. *Ibid.*, p.752.
92. *Chamlaiy Hu Nim, op. cit.*, p.16.
93. *Les Paroles, op. cit.*, October–December 1967, p.778; 5 October 1967. (It is ironic that in 1978 the CPK Centre accused 'Koy Thuon's group' of having used, in this period, 'noisy means in order to alert the enemy, thus giving it the opportunity to destroy the revolutionary movement. Apparently very revolutionary, these means acutally led to the suppression of the revolution'. As we shall see, this came true by 1969, but Koy Thuon was not solely responsible. *Ompi Pankar Ruom Chong Kraoy* ('On the Last Joint Plan'), p.16.)
94. *Ibid.*, pp.779–80.
95. *Ibid.*, p.778.
96. *Ibid.*, p.780.
97. *Chamlaiy Hu Nim, op. cit.*, p.16.
98. *Les Paroles, op. cit.*, October–December 1967, p.791; 14 October 1967.
99. *Chamlaiy Hu Nim, op. cit.*; Ea Meng Try, personal communication; and author's interviews with Suon So, Kompong Thom, 16 October 1980, and (the student) Liv Khun Leng, Strasbourg, 1 November 1979.
100. Untitled confession in Tuol Sleng by Vorn Vet, December 1978, 54pp., at p.21.
101. 'The Samlaut Rebellion', *op. cit.*, p.201; Meyer, *op. cit.*, p.192; and *Des Mouvements Anti-Gouvernementaux au Cambodge, op. cit.*, p.44 (on Tiv Ol).
102. Kirk, *op. cit.*, p.80.
103. He said it 'was started by the people themselves. At that time the Party Central Committee had not yet decided on a nationwide armed insurrection. The people in Battambang did it first, since the movement of the peasants' struggle was indefensibly fluid'. BBC *Summary*, 5 October 1977, FE/5632/C/3.
104. *Discours prononcé par le camarade Pol Pot ...., op. cit.*, p.39.
105. *Chamlaiy Hu Nim, op. cit.*, p.70.
106. *Discours prononcé par le camarade Pol Pot, op. cit.*, p.39.
107. United States, CIA, *Foreign Broadcast Information Service* (FBIS), IV, 19 January 1977, H1-6, at p.H2. My emphasis.
108. *Summary of Annotated Party History*, by the Eastern Zone Military Political Service (1973); translated captured document declassified by the US CIA in 1978, p.30. In his confession recording the conversation with Muol Sambath, Hu Nim says: 'He recalled the period of the combined political and armed struggle '1968–70' [sic]'. *Chamlaiy Hu Nim, op. cit.*, p.70.
109. *Livre Noir: Faits et Preuves des Actes d'Aggression et d'Annexion du Vietnam contre le Kampuchea*, Phnom Penh, Ministry of Foreign Affairs, September 1978, p.39.
110. *Ibid.*, p.56. My emphasis.
111. *Ibid.*, p.57. The *Livre Noir* continues that the Vietnamese claimed Lon Nol 'was the man of the French and not the Americans [and] had no money in foreign banks', and so 'could not be considered a reactionary - on the contrary, Lon Nol had rendered many services to the Vietnamese revolution'.
112. Pyongyang Radio, 3 October 1977; FBIS, IV, 4 October 1977, H38. This point in the official biography of Pol Pot is given credibility by the 1979 Heng

Samrin regime accusation that in 1968 the Party Secretary of the North-East zone was executed by the Pol Pot group. Pol Pot evidently took his place.

113. *Le Monde*, 2 February 1968, and *Réalités Cambodgiennes*, 20 December 1968. In 1977-78 this incident was to be hailed as marking the commencement of armed struggle with the foundation of the Revolutionary Army of Kampuchea. (FBIS, *op. cit.*, IV, 19 January 1977, H1-6.) Contradicting this, however, is the fact that none of the extant Party histories previously produced by the Centre — in 1971, 1972 and 1974 — even mentions the event. See extracts from *Prowatt Pak* ('The Party History') distributed by Ieng Sary on 23 January 1971, in possession of the author; Ith Sarin, 'Nine Months with the Maquis' summarizes a 1972 version of CPK History distributed by 'the Central Committee', in Timothy Carney, *Communist Party Power in Kampuchea (Cambodia)*, Cornell University South-East Asia Program Data Paper no. 106, January 1977, p.37; *Provatt nei Pak Kommyunis Kampuchea*, 1974, *op. cit.*

114. BBC *SWB*, FE/2682/A3/10.

115. 'The Samlaut Rebellion', *op. cit.*, p.182.

116. *Ibid.*, p.183.

117. *Ibid.*, p.184.

118. Kirk, *op. cit.*, p.80.

119. BBC *SWB*, FE/2706/A3/12.

120. *Réalités Cambodgiennes*, 16 February 1968, p.19.

121. *Ibid.*, p.3.

122. Meyer, *op. cit.*, p.196.

123. *Réalités Cambodgiennes*, 16 February 1968, p.3. Sihanouk's statement immediately follows the previously quoted analysis.

124. Meyer, *op. cit.*, pp.192-93.

125. BBC *SWB*, FE/2719/A3/8,10.

126. *Ibid.*, FE/2715/A3/11, FE/2719/A3/8.

127. *Ibid.*, FE/2715/A3/10, and FE/2719/A3/9. The latter reference gives Sihanouk's term *mékhum*, which means 'subdistrict chief', not 'village chief', the term I used in 'The Samlaut Rebellion', *op. cit.*, p.188.

128. 'Biographical Sketches of Khmer Communist Leaders', US Embassy, Phnom Penh, March 1975.

129. 'The Samlaut Rebellion', *op. cit.*, pp.188, 191.

130. BBC *SWB*, FE/2719/A3/9.

131. FBIS, October 4, 1977, pp.H20-21. Quoted in Heder, *op. cit.*, 'Kampuchea's Armed Struggle', p.13. My emphasis.

132. *Provatt nei Pak Kommyunis Kampuchea*, op. cit., p.10. My emphasis.

133. Interview with Stephen Heder, March 11, 1980, *op. cit.*

134. BBC *SWB*, FE/2855/A3/3,4.

135. *Ibid.*

136. *Ibid.*

137. *Summary of Annotated Party History*, *op. cit.*, p.31. My emphasis. See note 218.

138. See for instance Nuon Chea's speech in FBIS, IV, 19 January 1977, H2.

139. See page 253 above, and note 200 below, and 108 above.

140. 'The Samlaut Rebellion', *op. cit.*, pp.189, 192; *Réalités Cambodgiennes*, 22 April 1967; BBC *SWB* FE/2724/A3/7.

141. *Réalités Cambodgiennes*, 22 March 1968, p.25.

142. 'The Samlaut Rebellion', *op. cit.*, p.192.

143. See *Réalités Cambodgiennes*, 26 April 1968, p.22. After a search of rebel hideouts, troops discovered seventy-three rifles and various stocks of

ammunition, as well as food, medical equipment and documents, several granaries, 50 kg. of saltpetre, 20 kg. of powder, and 163 sacks of rice.

144. 'The Samlaut Rebellion', *op. cit.*, p.192.
145. *Réalités Cambodgiennes*, 12 April 1968, p.43.
146. BBC *SWB*, FE/2852/A3/1.
147. 'The Samlaut Rebellion', *op. cit.*, p.195.
148. BBC *SWB*, FE/2724/A3/7.
149. *Ibid.*, FE/2804/A3/6.
150. *Yearbook on International Communist Affairs*, 1969, p.96.
151. *Chamlaiy Hu Nim*, *op. cit.*, p.19.
152. Interview with Stephen Heder, 11 March 1980, *op. cit.*
153. *Les Paroles*, *op. cit.*, April-June 1968, p.325; Phnom Penh, 23 May 1968.
154. *Réalités Cambodgiennes*, 28 June 1968.
155. BBC *SWB*, FE/2852/A3/1.
156. *Ibid.*, FE/2855/A3/4.
157. *Réalités Cambodgiennes*, 20 September 1968, p.23; and BBC *SWB*, FE/3018/A3/3.
158. FBIS, October 4, 1977, pp.H20-21.
159. Meyer, *op. cit.*, pp.196-97.
160. Author's interview with a woman who attended lectures given by Ieng Sary in Phnom Penh in 1976; Paris, 1 February 1980.
161. *Ibid.*
162. BBC *SWB*, FE/2755/A3/6.
163. *Ibid.*, FE/2784/A3/2. My emphasis.
164. Phnom Penh Radio, 19 May 1968, in FBIS, 20 May 1968, pp.H1-2. Quoted in Heder, *op. cit.*, 'Kampuchea's Armed Struggle', p.14. Four days later Sihanouk repeated that 'in Rattanakiri, some two hundred rebels have been exterminated'. *Les Paroles*, April-June 1968, p.325.
165. BBC *SWB*, FE/2852/A3/1.
166. *Ibid.*, FE/2855/A3/4.
167. *Ibid.*
168. *Ibid.*
169. Phnom Penh Radio, 19 May 1968, *op. cit.*
170. See for instance Kirk, *op. cit.*, p.108. I shared this view.
171. Author's interview with Chhil Chhanno, Toul, 28 October 1979.
172. *Les Paroles*, April-June 1968, p.372; 19 June 1968. And BBC *SWB*, FE/2792/A3/1.
173. *Réalités Cambodgiennes*, 20 September 1968.
174. BBC *SWB*, FE/2776/A3/14.
175. Ouch Bun Chhoeun, *op. cit.* Another revolutionary, who was a courier for So Phim at the time, claims that in 1968 or 1969 troops in Kompong Cham arrested over a hundred people, mostly students from the province capital, and took them in four trucks to Mai Sak forest in Sralap subdistrict of Tbaung Khmum, where they were executed and their bodies buried in two large pits. The same source adds that another fifteen women, villagers and intellectuals, were executed at O Korum. Author's interview with Chan Mon, Suong, 7 August 1980.
176. See for instance, Meyer, *op. cit.*, pp.192-93.
177. *Réalités Cambodgiennes*, 2 August 1968, p.24.
178. *Chamlaiy Hu Nim*, *op. cit.*, p.16.
179. Meyer, *op. cit.*, p.196, and Ea Meng Try, personal communication.

180. BBC *SWB*, FE/2682/A3/10.

181. *Ibid.*, FE/2861/A3/1, and *Réalités Cambodgiennes*, 20 September 1968, pp.23–24.

182. Vorn Vet, *op. cit.*, p.24; *Réalités Cambodgiennes*, 13 September 1968, p.16, and Meyer, *op. cit.*, p.168.

183. Kirk, *op. cit.*, p.80.

184. Tan Kim Huon, 'Le Paysan et la hausse des prix', *Bulletin du Contre-Gouvernement*, no. 860, 15 September 1969, pp.2-3.

185. Meyer, *op. cit.*, p.140.

186. Interview with Stephen Heder, 11 March 1980, *op. cit.*

187. See my 'Pol Pot and the Kampuchean Communist Movement' in *Peasants and Politics in Kampuchea, 1942-81*, *op. cit.*, pp.227-317, at p.228. In a subsequent interview, one CPK member said that Tiv Ol, a prominent revolutionary attached to Party headquarters but executed in 1977, had told him in 1973 that Vietnam was 'a friend, but not very loyal'. Author's interview with Sin Song, Phnom Penh, 12 August 1980.

188. Prok Sary, *op. cit.*, and author's interview with Chim Chin, Prey Veng, 28 July 1980.

189. Tuot Sman, *op. cit.*

190. Yim Seun, *op. cit.*, and Tea Sabun, *op. cit.*

191. Ouch Bun Chhoeun, *op. cit.*

192. *Communist Infrastructure in Cambodia*, DIA Intelligence Appraisal, 8 July 1971, p.3.

193. Tea Sabun, *op. cit.*

194. Ouch Bun Chhoeun, *op. cit.*

195. Author's interview with Kol Kon, Kranhoung, 9 August 1980.

196. Mau Met, *op. cit.*

197. *Ibid.*

198. Hun Sen, *op. cit.*, claims that in 1969 Tioulong's brother Tok 'stole thousands of hectares from peasants in Chamcar Thmey village, Tonlung subdistrict, in Memut ... I organized a youth movement to resist this, but two carloads of police came to arrest me, and I ran off to Kratie.'

199. 'Khmer Rouge Rallier Keoum Kun', Airgram from US Embassy in Phnom Penh to Department of State, 13 January 1972, p.8. Kun, who was in Hanoi at the time, gives no date for Meas's visit, but says he then 'returned to Cambodia'. It is known that Meas came back to Hanoi at the end of 1969 (and remained there until 1975); the length of time required for the trip probably puts the first visit at late 1968, if not earlier. Yos Por, *op. cit.*, who was also in Hanoi and confirms the disagreement between Meas and Son Ngoc Minh (who 'said the situation was not yet ripe for us ... we would be in danger of defeat if we went back') puts the visit at 1967 or 1968. The 1978 CPK document, *Ompi Pankar Ruom Chong Kraoy* ('On the Last Joint Plan'), *op. cit.*, says Meas went to Hanoi 'in about 1968' (p.19). Therefore this was *before* 'an Enlarged Politburo meeting in July 1969 decided on a people's war ...' (*Prowatt pak*, 'The Party History', distributed by Ieng Sary in 1971. See below.)

200. *Prowatt nei Pak Kommyunis Kampuchea*, 1974, talks of 'the armed and political struggle of our Party in that period' (1967), p.10; see also Hu Nim's account in note 108, referring to 1968-70; finally, in August 1975 the internal CPK monthly *Tung Padevat* described the Party's mid 1967 decision 'to launch both political and armed attacks' the next year (p.37). The latter quotation is part of a speech by Pol Pot on 22 July 1975, entitled 'Long Live the Great

Revolutionary Army of the Communist Party of Kampuchea', which was printed in *Tung Padevat*.

201. Nuon Chea's speech in FBIS, IV, 19 January 1977, H1-6., at pp.H3, H2.

202. Heder, 'Kampuchea's Armed Struggle', *op. cit.*, p.12.

203. *Bulletin du Contre-Gouvernement*, no. 782, 12 June 1969, p.3.

204. BBC *SWB*, FE/2682/A3/13.

205. All three later expressed more conciliatory attitudes towards Vietnam than that of the Party Centre, and were executed in Democratic Kampuchea. See following chapter, pp.297, 340, 308, respectively.

206. Tea Sabun. *op. cit.*

207. T.D. Allman, 'Cracking a Smile', *Far Eastern Economic Review*, 26 February 1970.

208. Author's interview with Chan Mon. Suong, 7 August 1980. Mon said the 1st company was commanded by Sarun, the 2nd by Sien, and that both men were executed in 1976-77. According to another source, So Phim's overall military chief in this period was Ta Samom (alias Aom). Author's interview with Sang Lon, Kandol Chrum, 7 August 1980.

209. Lon Nol, 'Synthèse des renseignements intérieurs (16-30 septembre 1969)', *Le Sangkum*, octobre 1969, map, p.97.

210. *Yearbook on International Communist Affairs*, 1970, p.531, quoting the 27 September 1969 issue of *Cambodge*; and *New York Times*, 19 April 1970, p.26.

211. *Yearbook. op. cit.*, p.531.

212. *Ibid.*

213. Former CIA Cambodia analyst Sam Adams, personal communication, 26 September 1976.

214. *Yearbook, op. cit.*, 1970, p.531.

215. *Le Monde*, 20 November 1969.

216. *Ibid.*

217. Jean-Claude Pomonti and Serge Thion, *Des Courtisans aux Partisans: la crise cambodgienne*, Paris 1971, p.124. Thion was in Kampot at the time.

218. Lon Nol, *op. cit.*, p.96. (My emphasis.) One cadre who joined the revolution in 1966 says that the communists killed about ten government 'spies' in Dauntey subdistrict in 1969; this was one aspect of the 'political and armed struggle', which he says began only in that year; again this dating suggests tardiness in the East. Author's interview with Lim Thi, Takhmau, 15 August 1980.

219. *Le Monde*, 20 November 1969.

220. Meyer, *op. cit.*, pp. 197,199. My emphasis.

221. Vorn Vet's confession, *op. cit.*, pp. 25-27.

222. Lon Nol, *op. cit.*, map, p.97. One participant claims that there were one thousand guerrillas in the Kompong Speu-Kompong Chhnang area by late 1969. Heder interview, 11 March 1980, *op. cit.*

223. *Discours prononcé par le Camarade Pol Pot*, op. cit., p.44.

224. Pol Pot, *ibid.*, p.43; Sam Adams, *op. cit.*, and Heder, *op. cit.*, 'Kampuchea's Armed Struggle', p.14; and author's interviews with Pham Van Ba, Ho Chi Minh City, 28 October 1980, and Nguyen Xuan Hoang, Hanoi, 4 November 1980.

225. Frank Snepp, *Decent Interval*, Harmondsworth 1977, pp. 31-32.

226. *The Australian*, 15 January 1966.

227. William Shawcross, *Sideshow: Kissinger, Nixon and the Destruction of Cambodia*, London 1979, pp. 65, 24; and Seymour M. Hersh, *The Price of Power: Henry*

296

Kissinger in the Nixon White House, New York 1983, pp. 177–78.

228. Shawcross, *op. cit.*, pp. 28, 35.
229. Lon Nol, *op. cit.*, p. 95.
230. *Livre Noir*, *op. cit.*, p.47.
231. Vorn Vet's confession, *op. cit.*, p.26.
232. *Livre Noir*, *op. cit.*, pp.53–54.
233. 'The Party History' (*Prowatt pak*), distributed by Ieng Sary, dated 23 January 1971. (My emphasis.)
234. Interview with Stephen Heder, 11 March 1980, *op. cit.*
235. Author's interview with Som Nhep, Phnom Sruoch, 12 September 1980.

8

Contending Communisms:
The Second Civil War, 1970-75.

Although they did not want to join us, when the storm came they had to come and take shelter in our refuge.[1]

1970: Kampuchea Enters the Vietnam War

At the end of 1969 Pol Pot set out for Hanoi and Beijing — at a point when, in the words of the *Livre Noir*, 'the struggle between Kampuchea and Vietnam had reached its height. . . 'Friendship' and 'solidarity' were nothing but empty slogans'. But the CPK side had its dissidents. According to the same source: 'The CPK delegation was not very united and had to deal with differences in its ranks. Son Ngoc Minh, who had long lived in Vietnam, participated in the delegation also'.[2] With the support of Minh (still a member of the CPK Central Committee) and, judging from this account, others in the CPK delegation (probably including Keo Meas, who again accompanied Pol Pot),[3] Vietnamese leaders attempted to persuade Pol Pot to abandon the armed struggle, to establish relations with the Communist Party of the Soviet Union (CPSU), and to 'have confidence in the Vietnamese forces'. The *Livre Noir* claims: 'The situation in Kampuchea was getting worse and worse and was not favourable to the Vietnamese. The Vietnamese delegation was very irritated, and in spite of its efforts to maintain an attitude of diplomatic courtesy, it could not hide its violent hostility towards the Kampuchean revolution nor contain its fury with the CPK. Le Duan himself, sneak and double-dealer though he was, could not control himself. The conversations thus took place in a very tense atmosphere. . .' But the CPK stuck to its guns, believing that 'if it did not carry out the armed struggle, it would be condemned to disappear; but if it persisted in this struggle, it would be assured of continued existence'.[4]

Pol Pot was in effect counting on the fact that a deposed Sihanouk would be won over to the CPK side in spite of its hostility to him, because of what Pot *knew* would be continuing support for the Prince on the part of Hanoi, as well as Beijing. In July 1969, the PRG Prime Minister Huynh Tan Phat had made Kampuchea the object of his first state visit, and Sihanouk had been the only foreign head of state to attend the funeral of Ho Chi Minh in the North Vietnamese capital in September. Hanoi's cultivation of Sihanouk was a crucial ingredient in Pol Pot's strategy of forging a public alliance with him while continuing a clandestine struggle against him inside the country. Thus, Pot could refuse to follow such a pro-Sihanouk policy himself. He also refused to establish relations with the CPSU or even to meet the Soviet ambassador in Hanoi, a key indication of his stand in the international arena as he went on to Beijing for discussions with the CCP.[5]

'Not long afterwards', on March 19, Sihanouk arrived there from Moscow, where he had just been told of his overthrow the previous day. His first reaction was, in the words of the *Livre Noir,* 'defensive';[6] he even asked the French ambassador in Beijing if he would be granted asylum.[7] Khmer and Vietnamese communists then moved simultaneously. On 21 March, Pol Pot asked Zhou Enlai to advise Sihanouk, who he claimed was not told the source of this advice, to take an 'offensive position'. On the same day, Pham Van Dong arrived from Hanoi and put the same view to the Prince. Sihanouk then drew up a programme of resistance to Lon Nol. Again without Sihanouk's knowledge of his involvement (or even of his identity), Pol Pot claims that he 'examined and modified' this document, deleting references to 'socialist and even communist construction' which Pot considered too frank.[8] (Less frank references to the common struggle of 'our three peoples' of Indo-China, by contrast, were retained, while there was no mention of Chinese support.)[9] The programme of the National United Front of Kampuchea (*Renaksey Ruop Ruom Cheat Kampuchea,* in English, NUFK) was broadcast over Beijing Radio on March 23; it called for a general uprising against Lon Nol. Sihanouk also privately accepted Zhou Enlai's suggestion, again allegedly emanating from Pol Pot, that he would 'constantly maintain an offensive position'.[10] (That is, and this seems crucial, there were to be no negotiations with Lon Nol; victory would be achieved by force of arms and not by a political settlement which would allow the leftist forces — now more heterogeneous than ever — to emerge into the open, along with those of the Khmer right.)

But Sihanouk and Pol Pot were not the only cards in Zhou's

hand. As in the Geneva negotiations of 1954, his major concern was to prevent either the use of Kampuchea by the US military or the establishment there of bases which might conceivably threaten China. Only if Lon Nol's regime set out on that course would Zhou be prepared to sacrifice all links with Phnom Penh and sponsor a full-scale war to overthrow him. Barring this eventuality, China's interest in Kampuchea lay purely in terms of its being a 'sphere of influence', or part of a Balkanised one. For instance, Zhou may not have relished the prospect of the commitment of Vietnamese communist troops to a war there, even (or perhaps especially) on the side of his own Khmer allies. With each of the latter now separately in Beijing, and the situation on the Kampuchea-Vietnam border still uncertain, he could afford to try to maintain a relationship with Lon Nol (who had visited China as recently as October 1969), just as he had with Sihanouk when Pol Pot was determined to overthrow *him*. Vietnam's interest in Kampuchea, on the other hand, was related to its own domestic war effort, rather than to a projected geopolitical or regional goal; mere military cooperation between Lon Nol and the US-South Vietnamese forces, even without the latter becoming deeply involved across the border, was a threat to the NLF's existence. Only when the war (and the Vietnamese communists) spread irrevocably across Kampuchea, and Lon Nol was at a clear disadvantage, did Chinese policy coincide with that of Vietnam. Then, Zhou could not risk losing the support of his closest Khmer allies, when all that could be gained was continued representation with a government that from a military point of view was heavily dependent on the USA and Saigon, and likely to lose power in the medium term.

Thus, China's position was slow to take shape on each of three important issues: the interpretation of Lon Nol's coup as an 'American plot', support for Sihanouk's March 23 call for an uprising, and the severing of diplomatic links with Lon Nol. As early as March 21, Hanoi Radio declared: 'It is clear from the recent coup in Cambodia that the United States is plotting not only to counter the Vietnamese people's fight against US aggression and for national salvation, but also to subvert the independence and sovereignty of Cambodia. . .'[11] Albania, China's closest ally, released a similar statement the next day, followed by North Korea on the March 24; not until March 26 did China do so. Full support for Sihanouk's March 23 declaration was announced by Hanoi on March 24, and by the

PRG two days later, but by China only on April 5. Whereas the Vietnamese communists withdrew their diplomats from Phnom Penh on March 27, China, even while continuing to refer to Sihanouk as 'Head of State', maintained its embassy in Phnom Penh for another six weeks, until May 5. For that period, China maintained its normal double 'State and Party' relations with Kampuchea; as we have seen, it even had 'double-State *and* Party' ones — i.e. relations with Lon Nol, with Sihanouk and with Pol Pot.

There was however, no real change in Chinese policy towards Kampuchea, nor in Vietnamese policy towards Sihanouk, in or out of power. The back-pedalling was done, as we have seen in the previous chapter, by the CPK Centre.

On his way home via Hanoi, Pol Pot rejected Le Duan's proposals for a mixed military command in Kampuchea. He also arranged for the return to Kampuchea of the thousand or so former Issaraks who had been in North Vietnam since 1954. However, they were not to return immediately — in the words of the *Livre Noir,* these Khmers were a 'card' in the hands of the Vietnamese and preparations had to be made so that 'circumstances did not permit them to play it'.[12]

The Coup

Prince Sihanouk has long claimed that the American CIA 'masterminded' the coup against him. Henry Kissinger, on the other hand, has stated that it 'took us completely by surprise'.[13] There is in fact no evidence of CIA involvement in the 1970 events, but a good deal of evidence points to a role played by sections of the US military intelligence establishment and the Army Special Forces.

The most informed account of the US involvement in planning the coup is that of Samuel R. Thornton, who worked from May 1968 to May 1969 as an intelligence specialist at the US Navy command in Saigon. Thornton has told journalist Seymour Hersh that he had gained intimate knowledge of coup preparations as early as late 1968. At that point, Thornton says, Lon Nol approached US military intelligence for a commitment to provide him with military, political and economic support after his proposed overthrow of Sihanouk. The US was prepared to go further, however. It proposed to infiltrate in advance Special Forces-trained Khmer Kampuchea Krom (KKK) troops into the Kampuchean armed forces, and also, according to

Thornton, 'to insert a US-trained assassination team disguised as Viet Cong insurgents into Phnom Penh to kill Prince Sihanouk as a pretext for revolution'.

This proposal, code-named 'Sunshine Park', was approved by 'the highest level of government' in Washington in February or March 1969, Thornton recalls. However, Lon Nol rejected (as 'criminal insanity') the plan to assassinate Sihanouk. He renewed his original request for 'overt United States military support for a possible coup'. Lon Nol was then told ('unofficially') that 'he could in fact have the requested support'. Thornton, who claims he 'either helped prepare or had occasion to handle most of the pertinent documents', says that agreement was then reached with Lon Nol on the infiltration of the KKK units into Kampuchea.[14] (In May 1969, 640 such troops 'surrendered' to the government. Their commander became a Captain in Lon Nol's army, and fourteen others were appointed as officers.[15])

Part of this is confirmed by Prom Thos, a senior Minister in the Lon Nol government from 1970 to 1973. Thos told me in 1980 that planning had begun for the overthrow of Sihanouk 'a year before' the March 1970 coup. He added that around March 1969 Prince Sirik Matak had argued for the assassination of Sihanouk but that Lon Nol had been against it.[16]

In August 1969 Lon Nol assumed the Prime Ministership again. The next month he made secret contact with Son Ngoc Thanh, 'and began tentative discussions about overthrowing Sihanouk'. But only in February 1970 did Thanh assure him of material aid, in the form of the Khmer Special Forces troops still on the US and South Vietnamese payrolls.[17] In the same month, according to Forrest B. Lindley, a Green Beret captain operating near the Kampuchean border, 'I was told there would be a change of government in Cambodia'. The source was higher up the US Special Forces command system. Two companies of Khmer Special Forces troops were then sent into Kampuchea. It may have been these KKK units which apparently took part in the sacking of the two Vietnamese communist embassies in Phnom Penh on March 16, two days before the coup.[18]

While Thornton's allegation that 'the highest level' of the US government was party to the coup plans remains uncorroborated, it is clear that Lon Nol carried out the coup with at least a legitimate expectation of significant US support. The coup was primarily the work of disaffected members of the Kampuchean government. But their disaffection, over the economic crisis and the communist sanctuaries, and the outside encouragement they received, arose in large part from the deep US involvement in neighbouring Vietnam.

Domestic Repercussions

Two days after Sihanouk's call for a general uprising, large-scale popular demonstrations in his favour began in Kompong Cham, and others on March 28 in Takeo-Kampot. I have discussed these events, and CPK involvement in them, elsewhere — the Lon Nol military killed hundreds of the protestors and arrested at least a thousand in a week.[19] But it may be worth adding to this record three eye-witness accounts from the areas of unrest.

Tam Eng, an ethnic Chinese woman from Ang Tasom in Takeo, describes the events on 28 and 29 March:

> Hundreds, thousands of peasants took over the district office. They supported Sihanouk, and were shouting 'Long Live Samdech Euv!' They had only knives and sticks, but police or troops attacked them; maybe five or six were killed, I'm not sure.
>
> The next day, there was another demonstration, of thousands of people — young, old, men and women from many villages around. Then soldiers arrived from Takeo city, commanded by Lieutenant-Colonel Nim. Tanks flattened the people, two or three hundred died. I rode my bicycle there and saw all the bodies. Some people were not yet dead, and were lying there, waving flags and their hands, saying 'Long Live Samdech Euv'. Then soldiers brought tanks and flattened them all [again].
>
> Nim was cruel, a barbarian. He shot people himself. He didn't tell the people first: 'Please go home, together we'll solve the problem later. Demonstrations in favour of Sihanouk are forbidden'. Nothing like that, no announcements were made. He just brought in guns and tanks.[20]

As a student in Kompong Cham, Sia had been involved in the 1964 demonstrations, and then became a worker at the French-owned Chup rubber plantation in Kompong Cham, where former Issarak leader Bun Sani was employed as a technical supervisor. Sia says he had no contact with the communists, however, until 23 March 1970, the day of Sihanouk's appeal, and even then there were 'no leaders—we were just angry with Lon Nol'.

> All the rubber plantation workers joined the demonstrations. We went all the way to Chrui Changvar [the bridge leading into

Phnom Penh], arriving early in the morning. The Lon Nol troops fired on the crowd. I saw about thirty people killed.

About two hundred of us workers drove back home in three trucks belonging to the plantation. We were fired upon once at Trao, and again at Prey Totoeng, where those who were still with us abandoned the trucks and scattered, fleeing across the Mekong and home. There I went to say good-bye to my parents, and joined the revolution. I was so angry after being shot at; I wanted to take to the forest and build a new country. I went to Damber, and met Phuong. Phim was there. . . and five companies of fighters, people who had just enlisted, were already in the forest there. I became a soldier.[21]

Pon, a student from Kompong Cham city, joined columns of demonstrators which he said had arrived spontaneously from various northern provinces at the crossroads town of Skoun. There, he says, the crowd was told by army representatives that 'Sihanouk had come'; they were asked to wait while the soldiers distributed weapons to them, impliedly for an attack on the government. 'We were happy to hear that, and then they fired on us. Hundreds were killed. . . I ran away with my teachers and fellow students. Some of us went into the jungle; fifty or sixty of us met up later at Kompong Thmar, and went to work with the Vietnamese communists. We hated the troops, for what they had done, and we wanted to fight back.'[22]

Nevertheless, the overthrow of Sihanouk also unleashed a formidable movement among urban students and youth. The Lon Nol army grew from a force of 35,000 to as many as 150,000 by the end of the year,[23] almost entirely as a result of voluntary enlistment. Another result of the coup was the re-emergence of former Issaraks and Democrats like Pach Chhoeun and Bunchhan Mul, and of republican intellectuals like Keng Vannsak and Phung Ton. After long years of enforced political inactivity, these people welcomed Sihanouk's demise and participated in the new regime. Mul, for instance, became Minister of Cults and Religion. Nor was it long before Son Ngoc Thanh returned to Phnom Penh for the first time since 1952. On 17 June 1970 he officially became 'an advisor to the head of government'.[24] Thirty years of struggle seemed to have been rewarded when Sihanouk was condemned to death the next month, and the Khmer Republic proclaimed on 9 October.

However, other former Democrats, after years of exile in Paris, now returned to Kampuchean politics via a different route. Immediately after the coup, Thiounn Mumm and Thiounn Prasith transferred their activities to Beijing. Mumm soon became Minister of the Economy in Sihanouk's exiled government, and Prasith was named 'Minister in charge of the Co-ordination of Struggle for National Liberation'.[25] The second Kampuchean civil war promised to be a bitter one; the deep social and political divisions that had been suppressed (but also exacerbated) by Sihanouk's rule now emerged to exact their toll across the entire society.

Invasion

In the international controversy surrounding Kampuchea's entry into the Vietnam war in 1970, it has often been claimed that the war's expansion began with the combined US-South Vietnamese invasion of Kampuchea, which started on April 29 and was described by President Nixon as 'not an invasion, but a necessary extension of the Vietnam War'.[26] Doublespeak aside, there *is* a logic to Nixon's description. The Vietnamese communists had been moving deeply into Kampuchea throughout April — for over four weeks beforehand. By the same token, a related factor largely ignored is the fact that South Vietnamese forces had begun shelling the communist sanctuaries in Kampuchea as early as March 16.[27] This was the day after the expiry of Lon Nol's unrealistic demand, made on March 13 (the day he suspended sales of rice and other supplies to the NLF), that the communists quit the sanctuaries within forty-eight hours.[28] Nol's armed forces are reported to have requested this South Vietnamese support,[29] and there is little doubt that the Vietnamese communists feared they would be pinned down from two sides.

In Saigon, President Thieu, who had apparently had advance warning of the coup in Phnom Penh, remarked on the day it was carried out that the two countries would now cooperate to 'drive the Communists out'.[30] On March 19, the US command in Saigon directed its military advisers near the border to try to establish radio links with the Lon Nol army. The next day, Major-General Nguyen Viet Thanh, commander of South Vietnam's IV Corps area, authorized his units 'to provide forward artillery spotters for the Cambodians if they requested it'.[31]

On March 20, only two days after the coup, and before

Sihanouk had stated his position, all protagonists in the Vietnam War moved simultaneously. KKK troops began full-scale attacks on the communist sanctuaries in Kampuchea. South Vietnamese troops and US advisers pushed into Svay Rieng in an 'un-announced operation' later revealed by Saigon military spokesmen.[32] In Kandal on the same day, South Vietnamese fighter-bombers attacked communist positions 'a few miles' across the border, while an NLF company in the same area attacked a Lon Nol outpost, whose commander radioed for South Vietnamese help. It was immediately forthcoming: South Vietnamese howitzers shelled the NLF force, which withdrew. A second radio call enlisted the aid of a US spotter plane, which sighted the communists again, and a third radio call brought renewed South Vietnamese shelling. On March 23, fight-bombers again attacked communist positions inside Kam-puchea; US fighter-bombers followed suit the next day. A US command spokesman described this as the fifth such US air attack inside Kampuchea since the beginning of the year in exercise of an 'inherent right of self-defence'.[33]

On March 27, a South Vietnamese ranger battalion, in a 'major ground operation' planned with Lon Nol forces on March 23 and supported by US helicopter gunships, drove two miles into Kampuchea and carried out a sweep of an NLF sanctuary; fifty-three communists were reported killed. The next day Colonel Ernest Terrell Jnr, the senior US adviser in Kien Tuong province, met with a Lon Nol commander 'a few miles' across the border.[34]

It was against this background that, according to Bernard K. Gordon and Kathryn Young: 'The Vietnamese Communist armed forces both intensified and widened their military operations [in Kampuchea], beginning just prior to March 31. During the next two weeks the very small and ill-equipped Cambodian government forces were shown to be unable to prevent the movement of the Vietnamese forces.'[35] The response was the massacre of several thousand Vietnamese residents.[36] On March 30, according to the same writers, Lon Nol had already begun to suggest privately that aid 'from all sources' would be welcome. Son Ngoc Thanh, who as noted above had been in cooperation with Nol since at least February, was already touring Khmer areas in South Vietnam on a recruiting drive.[37] Then, 'several weeks' before April 26,[38] the US command began preparations for its full-scale intervention, which involved 32,000 US and 40,000 South Vietnamese troops, and was to take place at the end of the month.[39]

It does in fact seem as if the Vietnam War escalated across the border almost of its own accord, as a direct result of the coup and, more importantly, of the perceptions of its significance on all sides. Of course, the war's effects had long been felt in Kampuchea – in particular the Vietnamese communists' resort to use of sanctuaries there, and the US 'Menu' bombings of them. Just as important was the economic drain on Kampuchea, especially in terms of declining government revenue, which had begun in 1966 and set the scene for Lon Nol's rise to the Prime Ministership late in that year, his intensification of government repression, and the consequent successful mobilization of the Kampuchean left by the CPK. It was almost unavoidable that the long-term commitment of over half a million foreign troops to the Vietnamese civil war (with all the implications for their 'inherent right of self-defence') would have immense effects on a neighbouring country; this was especially so in the case of Kampuchea, whose destiny geography has linked closely with that of Vietnam. In this sense, the Kampuchean conflict of the 1970s was indeed 'a necessary extension' of American intervention in Vietnam.

Vietnamese communist troops and their Khmer allies (probably including Chhouk) crossed the border into southern Prey Veng on March 20 and 21, according to villagers from Krachap, about fifteen kilometres inside Kampuchea. In response to Sihanouk's call, broadcast two days later, seven hundred people in the subdistrict of Peam Montea joined the National United Front of Kampuchea. They formed an insurgent battalion, with a Khmer commander and three Vietnamese instructors.[40] But Sihanouk was not the only asset the revolutionaries had, for their enemies came with them.

In late April, the South Vietnamese 9th Division pursued the communists through Krachap with sixty-two M-113 armoured personnel carriers and helicopters, killing three villagers as they did so. They were followed by infantry, who 'did nothing but rob the people'; nearly four hundred head of cattle–three quarters of the village herd–were carried off over the next six months by ARVN troops, causing another fifty locals to join the revolution.[41]

A labourer from Svay Rieng who briefly worked with the South Vietnamese troops in this period, says they were 'just bandits': 'Later they killed a monk at Wat Krassang in Svay

Rieng, shot him dead. They accused him of being a traitor, because he was looking after the belongings of some women who were afraid the Thieu troops would steal them. They defrocked two other monks as well. They were led by a young American, but did not allow him to see what they were doing — they just told him they had arrested two 'enemies'.'[42]

Elsewhere the US infantry was directly involved, as in the destruction and looting of the town of Snuol in Kratie, by the 11th Armoured Cavalry Regiment. Further, by the end of the summer 'much of the country was a free-fire zone for United States aircraft. . . Pilots had far more liberty than in Vietnam to bomb any target they wanted'.[43] But the US ground troops withdrew to Vietnam two months after the invasion, and it was the South Vietnamese armed forces, who remained in Kampuchea for another two years, that did the most damage, both to the population and to the anti-communist cause. William Shawcross, using CIA documents and other official sources, has given many examples of their depredations.[44] In part they were avenging the massacres of Vietnamese residents by Lon Nol's army, and in part they were demonstrating the same lack of discipline they showed in their own country — with similar results.

In Kompong Speu, according to a CIA report, 'By maintaining tight discipline and carefully avoiding actions which might antagonize the local population, the Viet Cong/North Vietnamese have been able to convey the impression that they have the true interests of the peasants in mind.' The village of Chbal Mon in the same province was pillaged by South Vietnamese troops in June and July. Shawcross summarizes a subsequent report by the CIA's Phnom Penh station: 'When the North Vietnamese won control of it in September, they reminded the villagers that they had never had to worry about South Vietnamese looting before Sihanouk's removal and promised to help them defend themselves in the future. Communist efforts, according to the station, had already won at least a hundred recruits in this one village alone.'[45] (Chbal Mon later became the headquarters of CPK zone leader Chou Chet.)[46]

Although there were 'reports of undisciplined acts by VC/NVA troops',[47] the generally contrasting behaviour of the two Vietnamese protagonists, Sihanouk's domestic appeal, and the fact that (as a Lon Nol intelligence report conceded) 'aerial bombardments against the villagers. . . caused civilian loss on a large scale',[48] were all factors that combined to give the communists the crucial advantage in Kampuchea within months of the Lon Nol coup.

In August the US embassy informed Washington that Lon Nol was 'getting increasingly fed up' with the South Vietnamese army. According to Shawcross, Kissinger then suggested that Thailand send troops, whereupon 'Cambodian Assistant Chief of Staff, General Sak Sutsakhan, told a Filipino officer who was a CIA agent that the Lon Nol government feared that South Vietnam and Thailand were trying to annex the territory each had claimed for years'.[49] It was an ironic statement given Sihanouk's successful diplomacy in this regard, and Lon Nol's original aim, which was to evict the *enemies* of Saigon and Bangkok — the Vietnamese communists — from Kampuchean soil.

Inter-Party Struggle

Meanwhile, in Pol Pot's absence, CPK Deputy Secretary Nuon Chea had met with Vietnamese communist leaders some time in late March.[50] Chea, the only former ICP member in the Party Centre, agreed with the Vietnamese proposals to occupy large areas of the country that would serve as a sanctuary for the Vietnamese and as a resistance base for the war against Lon Nol.[51] According to the *Livre Noir*, Chea sent a 'telegram' to Hanoi for Pol Pot, informing him 'that he had had talks with the Vietnamese, and that the two parties had come to an agreement to act in solidarity and to cooperate in the struggle against the US imperialists'. Chea had weighed up the pros and cons before deciding in favour of cooperation[52] (while probably leaving open the question of a mixed military command), a decision for which Vietnamese leaders would continue to describe him as 'correct line' for years to come.[53] Hou Yuon, for his part, reputedly favoured Vietnamese intervention also.[54]

But other members of the CPK Centre were less cooperative. Ieng Sary and Son Sen, for instance, were then 'responsible for the North-Eastern Zone'. In early May they met with Vietnamese regional leaders who, according to the *Livre Noir*, pushed for the establishment of a mixed command (allegedly claiming that Pol Pot had already agreed to it), and offered them a 200-bed military hospital with medical personnel, the use of Vietnamese cadres below province level, and technical advisers.

Sary and Sen responded 'that Kampuchea needed nothing and that they had not received directives'[55] from Pol Pot on these questions. The latter were not left open: 'Kampuchea was master of the situation'. Ieng Sary added that 'in the period of the struggle against the French colonialists, the Vietnamese monopolized everything and the Khmers had no idea', which is unlikely to have been the view of Nuon Chea and many other veterans of that struggle. One Vietnamese envoy, a General Minh, 'obstinately refused to leave' Sary and Sen's camp. The Vietnamese then went to meet Pol Pot on his way down the Ho Chi Minh Trail, and allegedly told him that Sary had 'agreed with the Vietnamese proposals and only awaited his decision'. But Pol Pot refused to agree; when the envoys insisted, they were turned away by his Vietnamese escort. When Pot reached Rattanakiri and met up with Sary, they jointly rejected the proposals, leaving the Vietnamese 'very unhappy' with Pol Pot, whom 'they did not bother to accompany' further.[56]

In the absence of a Vietnamese communist account of these negotiations, we may take the Pol Pot version at its face value, especially since the *Livre Noir* makes clear that when their pressure and tactics proved fruitless, the Vietnamese gave up and acknowledged the authority of the CPK Centre. There was no mixed command. Sary and Sen also held off a Vietnamese offer to establish a military training school in the North-East Zone. It is interesting, however, that even in the North-East, then the heartland of the Centre, the Vietnamese 'had their agents there...in particular [and] managed to achieve a certain amount of grafting' of an alleged 'parallel state power' over the next twelve months.[57]

Pon, the student who had participated in the March demonstrations, was one of those 'grafted'. With over fifty other Khmer students and teachers, Pon arrived in the town of Kratie in June 1970.[58]

The Lon Nol soldiers had fled, but there were no Khmer communists in the town yet; just a battalion of Vietnamese who were running the place, appointing those who could speak Vietnamese to local positions. The people there treated the Vietnamese like monks; they cooked food for them, they were so happy that the Vietnamese had come to help Sihanouk. They liked them one hundred per cent. The Vietnamese, who were from the North, did not rob people, even of fruit. They would ask for something, and if people did not give it to them they would buy it. We stayed in the hotel. Town life remained as before, there were restaurants, etc.

After two or three months we were taken into the thick forest near Phnom Santuk on the Kratie-Kompong Thom border. We trained in combat drill, and studied tactics, and Vietnamese. Our group of ten or twelve trainees held daily meetings in which we discussed our ideas, in Vietnamese. I also taught some of the Vietnamese to speak Khmer. The forty or so others who were not learning so quickly were sent off to fight at Taing Kauk,

where Lon Nol had launched Operation 'Chenla I' to clear the road to Kompong Thom. This was in fact part of the Northern Zone, and from October 1970 Pol Pot established his headquarters not far away, near a bend in the Chinit River.[59] Ieng Sary, for his part, left for Hanoi at about the same time; he was to be Pol Pot's representative abroad, and would be dealing both with the Vietnamese communist leaders and with Prince Sihanouk in Beijing.

In the East, the Vietnamese allegedly 'tried the same manoeuvres' as in the North-East.[60] The *Livre Noir* does not claim that a mixed command was established there or that Vietnamese were employed as local cadres, but neither does it claim that the Zone Committee was hostile to such measures, as it does in the case of the North-East. The comparative brevity of this section of the *Livre Noir* suggests that So Phim's Zone Committee, and the Vietnamese, merely accepted the Centre's ruling on this.

But the Vietnamese did, we are told later, arm 'two battalions' there ('and the same in the South-West'), and also established military, medical, radio-telegraphic and administrative schools.[61] The *Livre Noir* goes on: 'At first, the CPK was not aware of all these activities because in the Eastern Zone there were several hundred thousand Vietnamese [sic] and a certain number of Khmer elements who had belonged to the ICP who carried out clandestine activities. It was only in the middle of 1971 that the Central Committee became aware of these activities. [It] then issued directives to all zones to close all these schools... Applying the directives of the Central Committee, the Eastern Zone closed the Vietnamese schools...'[62] Reading this account (written after So Phim's death in 1978), one would not guess that the CPK Eastern Zone Secretary was even a member of the said Central Committee, let alone No. 4 in the Party's Politburo. We have here an example of how the label 'Central Committee' (and even 'CPK') was used to cover the decisions of the Centre, a much smaller body of quite different composition, while the Politburo was ignored. Phim, for his part, seems to have assumed that although a mixed command was unacceptable to his Party, there could be no objections to Vietnamese involvement in the technical training of members of his organization.

Over the next year or more, before the training centres were closed, one intake of medical personnel and two of military — among them Heng Samrin and Hun Sen — graduated from them. They made the Eastern Zone forces the most effective CPK combat units; other military and medical schools run by the Centre, in the words of the *Livre Noir*, 'devoted more time to political education than to technical training'.[63]

At any rate, Phim was again, as in 1968, overruled by the Centre; again, however, this followed his prior accession to Vietnamese pressure, as Tea Sabun makes clear:

> In 1970 when Lon Nol carried out the coup, I was with So Phim at Thnaot [across the Vietnamese border]. We were in the middle of a meeting of about a hundred cadres from all regions and districts of the Eastern Zone, when we heard the news. We sent out twenty messengers to instruct all cadres on the spot to organize an offensive; meanwhile Sihanouk arrived in Beijing and confessed [or 'rallied' – *sarapeap*], and called on the people to rise up against Lon Nol. Everyone joined the resistance.
>
> The Vietnamese communists moved into Kampuchea to fight Lon Nol, and liberated a lot of territory. They met with So Phim and asked him first, but in the beginning we did not agree, because it was our country. We just asked them to give us guns. However, they said that if we did not agree it would be harmful to their country, and they would go in anyway. They said that without their help we would not be able to liberate our country.
>
> From then on we were very close to the Vietnamese, we went everywhere with them, getting the guns they seized, for our soldiers. We raised whole brigades.[64]

More so than in 1968, and more than in other zones now, Phim's organization thus benefitted greatly from his accession to local Vietnamese pressure (apparently without either local party knowing that Nuon Chea had formally given Vietnamese leaders the green light). But Phim's initial reluctance, and the fact that he was unable to foresee such an outcome (unlike Chea), were signs of a lack of *political* acumen and initiative that marked his career and eventually spelt his downfall. But his Khmer patriotism is not in question, and he probably felt slighted by the Vietnamese pressure on him.

At this stage, and for many months to come, communication between CPK leaders in various zones was minimal, and regional autonomy remained strong. One of the earliest signs of this was the Eastern Zone's use of a different Khmer term for 'unity' in the title 'National United Front of Kampuchea', which was rendered there as *Renaksey* Ekapeap *Cheat Kampuchea* (see p.298).[65] The difference has no political significance, except that the Eastern Zone CPK apparently paid little attention to Sihanouk's March 23 radio broadcast (edited by Pol Pot), and seem to have relied instead on their own translation from the Vietnamese. And certainly, 'unity' for them soon acquired a different meaning from what Pol Pot's group had in mind.

On 7 October 1970, Vietnamese communist leaders met with their Khmer counterparts in the Eastern Zone. A Vietnamese document emanating from the meeting, subsequently captured by the Lon Nol forces, gave clear instructions to the troops about standards of behaviour towards the Khmers; interestingly, it was also able to assure Khmers serving in the Vietnamese ranks that 'when the liberation of the country is achieved, they will participate in the unified Khmer government'.[66]

In the same month, on the other hand, the *Livre Noir* claims that the CPK 'Central Committee' met in plenary session;[67] again, this is contradicted by a Party History distributed privately by Ieng Sary in early 1971, which says that the only body able to meet since 1967 had been the 'Enlarged Politburo'.[68] It is not known whether So Phim attended, but according to the *Livre Noir*, those who did were 'unanimous that the Party, the United Front, the Army and the Government should hold firm in all respects to the position of independence and sovereignty, of relying on their own forces and of responsibility for their own destiny; ... with Vietnam, solidarity would be carried out from a position of independence, sovereignty and constant vigilance...'[69] At a week-long inter-Party summit meeting in November, relations worsened; the Vietnamese were warned 'not to try to carry out subversive activities among the Kampuchean people and Revolutionary Army'.[70]

Whether or not either of these accounts of the two apparently very different meetings between Khmers and Vietnamese is reliable, the short-term effect was probably the same: Khmer communist strength was rapidly increasing. Vietnamese assistance was becoming less of a necessity, whether or not it was viewed with suspicion. According to a US State Department source, 'late in 1970, Vietnamese advisors to NUFK Committees were instructed to assume a lower profile': 'In some cases, it is said that the NUFK administrators let it be known that the Vietnamese cadre would henceforth be 'tolerated only as advisers', while other sources ascribe hesitant transfers of decision-making responsibility to a Vietnamese initiative.'[71]

The CPK Organization

Meanwhile, in early April 1970, Lon Nol had released several hundred political prisoners gaoled by Sihanouk's regime; they included Non Suon and the other Pracheachon prisoners, and Phouk Chhay. These people quietly left for the countryside, but a small number of other leftists were sufficiently impressed by the urban euphoria that followed Sihanouk's overthrow to remain in the capital, hoping to encourage the government to pursue real domestic reforms. One of them was Pol Pot's brother Saloth Chhay, who had been gaoled in 1969. With Penn Yuth he soon formed a revamped 'Pracheachon Party' to contest national elections. Phouk Chhay, too, before having second thoughts and taking to the jungle, wrote an exposé of 'The Socio-Economic Legacy of the Old Regime' for the inaugural issue of a new Lon Nol government publication.[72] The last years of the Sihanouk regime had been too disastrous for most members of the left to contemplate simply returning the Prince to power, irrespective of which side they had chosen to fight on. This issue soon divided people like Chhay and Non Suon from the Vietnamese communists, who were much more sympathetic towards Sihanouk and considered that more moderate reforms would effectively come to terms with his legacy. Such a view is likely to have been resented as unwarranted interference.

Non Suon, for his part, quickly made secret contact with Vorn Vet in Phnom Penh, meeting him for the first time. But Vet recorded in his 1978 confession that Suon was already distrusted by Pol Pot: 'I did not yet know what network he was in, and I regarded him as a revolutionary. But I knew from the Organization that . . . Suon had rallied to the enemy [*sarapeap khmang*]. Because we had just met for the first time I did not dare pursue the matter with him personally.'[73] But Non Suon would have realized he was out of favour soon after his arrival in the

South-Western Zone; he was put to work in the 'mass movement', in Vet's parlance.[74] Suon's failure to obtain a Party position was a severe demotion for this former candidate member of the Central Committee and (in the Issarak period) chief of the Zone itself; only in September, five months later, was he appointed CPK Secretary of Region 31 (Kompong Chhnang province);[75] Phouk Chhay, by contrast, became political commissar of the Zone armed forces,[76] an extremely important post which he perhaps owed to a background untainted by any Vietnamese connection.

The situation in the South-West seems to have been rather complex, with important ramifications for the future. (After 1975 this zone was the heartland of the Pol Pot government.) There is little agreement, in either oral or written sources, as to which of three leaders was the senior Party figure there after 1970. The CPK South-Western Zone Secretary until 1968, Mar alias Nhim,[77] had disappeared. His former deputy Mok [78] was now reported by several sources (including Vorn Vet) to be Zone Secretary, even though his rank on the Party Central Committee (No. 9) was inferior to that of the Zone Deputy Secretary, Prasith (No. 7).[79] Moreover, to compound the confusion, other sources describe Chou Chet as Zone Secretary, and Mok as his deputy,[80] even though Chet was not even (until 1971) a member of the Central Committee.[81] What is perhaps the most reliable source gives Chou Chet's position as Zone 'Chairman' (*protean*);[82] possibly the post was specifically created in this case (it did not exist in other zones) because of Mok's promotion and resultant confusion or rivalry.[83] The post of Chairman may have been less powerful than that of Secretary (*lekha*), but there is at least agreement on Chet's responsibility for political/administrative affairs (Mok was military commander), which would indicate higher authority in a normally functioning Communist Party. The CPK was not such a Party, however, and by 1975 (as in all other zones but the East, *after* 1975) it was military commander Mok who would emerge triumphant from a fierce struggle with the political leadership.

Other members of the South-Western Zone Committee in this period included Prasith and Sangha Hoeun[84] (a former Issarak leader from Kompong Speu), the two men reported to have been most active in the area in the late 1960s; and Thuch Rin, a former teacher and Humanities graduate from Phnom Penh University, who was chief of the national Party Youth organization and of the Zone Culture and Information Service.[85] The Zone was divided into at least ten Regions, as shown in Fig. 7.

The East, with roughly the same population but smaller in area, was apparently much better organized. It was divided into five Regions and its leadership remained stable for the next five years. The Eastern Zone Executive consisted of Phim (Party Secretary), Phuong (Deputy) and Chhouk (Secretary of Region 24).

Little is known about the North-East (including Regions 101 to 105) Party branch in this period. It was administered directly by the CPK 'Central Committee',[86] and Son Sen was most likely still in charge there. In Kratie, however, Tiv Ol became province chief; according to Charles Meyer, he reopened the school and the hospital after the communist take-over of the province, and began some agrarian reforms.[87]

The other major zones, the North (including Regions numbered 31, 32, 35 and 36 — perhaps another sign of limited communications, given the use of the *same numbers* in the South-West) and the North-West (Regions 1 to 7), were headed by Koy Thuon and Muol Sambath respectively. Thuon was assisted by Sreng (Deputy Secretary) and Ke Pauk (military commander); Sambath by his deputy Khek Penn, a former Phnom Penh teacher who had taken to the jungle several years before, and Keu (military commander), a one-time youth activist recruited by Vorn Vet in 1961. (As noted, years later the military commanders Pauk and Keu rose to control these zones at the expense of the four political leaders.)

But the organizational structure was still skeletal. At the district, subdistrict and village levels, the revolutionary administration was essentially the creation of the Vietnamese communists and of Khmers working closely with them; thousands of armed propaganda teams roamed the countryside proclaiming loyalty to Sihanouk and opposition to the USA, and organizing elections for new village and subdistrict chiefs. According to an American State Department official, Kenneth Quinn:

> From everything stated by refugees, it appears that such elections were open and honest. . . In each village an assembly was first called and chaired by three NUFK cadre from the district administration who announced the establishment of a new government which would be constituted through elections. They

316

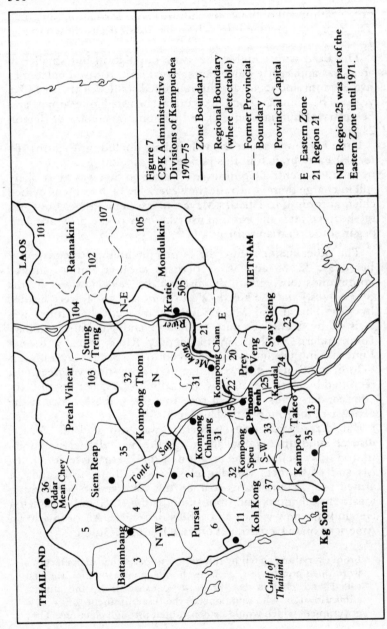

Figure 7
CPK Administrative
Divisions of Kampuchea
1970–75

— Zone Boundary

— Regional Boundary
(where detectable)

– – Former Provincial
Boundary

● Provincial Capital

E Eastern Zone
21 Region 21

NB Region 25 was part of the
Eastern Zone until 1971.

then called for volunteers to run for the post of [subdistrict] chairman and a secret ballot election was immediately held with each villager casting a single vote. The candidate with a plurality won. All of the candidates were local residents and none were members of the NUFK or [CPK]. The newly-elected village chief was empowered to select the remainder of his staff: a deputy, secretary, economic commissioner, cultural commissioner, and health and social welfare commissioner. The above election process was repeated at the [village] level to elect a chairman, who in turn appointed a deputy and economic commissioner.[88]

Of course, many of those who would normally have held these posts — members of the traditional or economic elite — had already fled to the towns.[89] Nevertheless, captured Vietnamese documents stipulated that persons of 'prestige', including monks, should be encouraged to stand.[90] These were in fact the first free local elections in Khmer history. The successful candidates' authority was limited, according to one Vietnamese document, by a proviso that should they prove politically unsuitable, the communists were to 'accept them temporarily and later use the authority of higher echelon to dismiss them'.[91] On the other hand, a subsequent circular, dated 1 May 1970 and issued by the Standing Committee of the Party Civilian Affairs Committee of South Vietnam, warned: 'Every repressive action should have the concurrence of the Party branch and the Kampuchean people, or should be taken by the latter people in accordance with our suggestions or guidance. Under no circumstances should our cadres take their place in performing this task, or take action directly'.[92]

Nationalist supporters of Sihanouk who were prepared to work with the Vietnamese communists quickly filled most of the positions in local rural administration, and the Vietnamese hoped that they would be amenable to the Khmer communists as well. In the words of another captured document: 'The Party of our friendly country [i.e. the CPK] has good experience in struggling and is closely co-ordinating with our Party to destroy the enemy. The majority of the Khmer people side with Sihanouk. . .'[93] Pro-Vietnamese forces, who adopted the title *Khmer Rumdos* ('Liberators'), were commonly seen as 'Sihanouk-ists'. However, the CPK had other ideas. A Lon Nol intelligence report described what happened to one subdistrict committee established in this period: 'Having affirmed that they had come to bring Sihanouk back to power, [the Vietnamese communists] distributed small Sihanouk badges to the seven members of this Committee. When the Khmer Rouge arrived they shot the seven members of this liberation Committee, whom they considered traitors.[94] The lack of a CPK presence in the villages and subdistricts created problems for the Party Centre, and this was compounded by the arrival of new candidates for political influence.

In June 1970, as Pol Pot arrived back in Rattanakiri, the first of the thousand Khmers in North Vietnam had begun to follow him home down the Ho Chi Minh Trail.[95] Their departure was organized by Keo Meas, who had remained in Hanoi. A few days after the Lon Nol coup, Son Ngoc Minh had called a mass meeting of 'hundreds of Party members', which Meas attended.[96] Minh told the returning Khmers that 'their exact mission would be given to them by the 'Party' in Cambodia',[97] indicating that he accepted Pol Pot's authority. However, some of the Khmers took a study-course organized by the Vietnam Workers' Party prior to setting out on the three-month trip.[98]

Taing Sarim, a Khmer cadre who helped organize the dispatch of the convoys, says they departed in groups of roughly a hundred each, and that their journey was dangerous. 'In my group there were 120. Some of us fell ill on the way, and there were only 63 or 68 of us on arrival ... Some rejoined us later.'[99] A later group of seventy, which set out in November, was reduced to fifty by bombing and malaria.[100] Another of the same size saw thirty of its members die on arrival in north-east Kampuchea, allegedly as a result of 'poison dropped by the US'.[101]

Pol Pot and Ieng Sary usually made a point of greeting new arrivals. They punctiliously referred to Sihanouk as 'Prince' (*Samdech*) but, according to two of the new arrivals, were 'already presenting him at internal Party meetings as the enemy of the revolution'.[102] These newly-returned Khmers say there was little hint of *intra-Party* factionalism: 'the first meetings were relaxed and easy', partly because those who had returned were 'considered the best instructed ... the local Khmers needed them'.[103] But others recall that on arrival: 'We were all asked to sign a circular saying that we wanted to change from membership of the 'Vietnam Workers' Party' to the 'Communist Party of Kampuchea'; Pol Pot did not recognize the Khmer People's Revolutionary Party'.[104]

One of the first to return was Leav Keo Moni, former head of the KNLC, who became a CPK district chief in his native area of

Siemreap. Keo Moni was known to the locals from his Issarak days and even before, when he had been a sub-district chief there. The Lon Nol district chief has recalled the problems he faced in waging psychological warfare against the communists after 1970:

> Leav Keo Moni came into insecure areas and explained to the people there about revolution, liberation, the abolition of land taxes, freedom, justice, and eliminating oppression. He said Sihanouk would come back to the country and organize a loose [*thou*] system as before. Some of the locals joined him in the forest; they were given guns, and went off to propagandize further ... When they wanted to take an important position, they brought in Vietnamese troops to help them ... I learned and saw that the locals who believed in the reds would spy on us. The reds would sometimes pick fruit or something, and leave payment at the foot of the tree; the locals would think that the reds were very fair to them. In 1970-71, the reds did not kill people; if they captured soldiers they would tell them to desert and let them go home as part of their propaganda.[105]

Relatively few 'Hanoi Khmers' were given political responsibility. Rath Samuoeun played a co-ordinating role with the Lao and Vietnamese communists.[106] Taing Sarim, who in 1979 became a Minister in the People's Republic of Kampuchea (PRK), was initially appointed CPK Secretary of a district in the Northern Zone. He recalls: 'I threw myself wholeheartedly into the task of establishing contacts and setting up all kinds of organizations. I created cells, and bases for the army, the Party and the mass movements. I trained cadres, and propagated the [CPK] line.'[107] By the end of 1970, Sarim had become a member of the CPK Committee for Region 31. Two of his colleagues in the same region took charge of organizing village committees and training army recruits in Baray district in Kompong Thom.[108] In the East, two others took charge of the Zone's Commerce and Logistics departments; Pol Pot's one-time fellow student in Paris, Yun Soeun, became CPK Deputy Secretary of Region 22 (southern Kompong Cham), and another returned Khmer, So Pum, was appointed Secretary of Region 25 (southern Kandal); in the South-West, Yos Por was appointed a member of the Kampot province (Region 35) Committee, in charge of Information and Education there.[109] Nhem Sun was put in charge of an important cadre training school at Amleang in the same zone.[110]

Mey Pho was employed at the CPK Central Committee Office in Kompong Thom.[111]

However, these were exceptions. Others were given only logistical responsibilities; former UIF Eastern Zone leader Keo Moni apparently became a village chief in Kompong Thom.[112] But most of the 'Hanoi Khmers', who included two nephews of So Phim in the East,[113] were assigned combat positions — usually platoon- or company-level commands in a rapidly expanding military apparatus. Ieng Lim, who had been a military instructor in North Vietnam, resented such demotion, and soon became convinced that 'the local Khmer Rouge disliked the NVA [and] the Khmers trained in the North'.[114] Still, it was impossible for the CPK Centre to neutralize these Khmers completely; 822 of them were now Party members,[115] comprising probably half the CPK's strength in 1970. There were probably at least two in every district of the country.[116] None were admitted into the Central Committee (let alone the Party Centre), even though Keo Moni, Mey Pho, Yun Soeun and perhaps Rath Samuoeun had all been members of its overseas branch in Hanoi. To the Pol Pot group, these highly trained cadres were a serious threat to the line it had adopted in the 1960s.

Perhaps the best illustration of this were the developments in Region 25, then part of the Eastern Zone bordering the South-West. At first there was 'constant conflict' between Khmer and Vietnamese communists in this area, according to a local schoolteacher. 'But then a former Khmer Issarak named So Pum arrived from Hanoi, and resolved these problems. Pum became Party Secretary of Region 25. He brought several other 'returnees' with him. By 1971 the problems had been resolved. I joined the revolution in that year; I had been a leftist since 1967 and many of my friends were also. About ten of us teachers, including one woman, responded to So Pum's call and went to work with him. He got on well with educated people, and liked to discuss politics with us. When anything happened he would ask for our opinions. He was not that well-educated himself, but he was quite literate and eager to learn from us. We enjoyed working with him.'[117]

A second local teacher agrees that the racial conflict, which had apparently not become violent, had been resolved: 'then there was solidarity' between Vietnamese and Khmers, he says. According to this man, there were now more than twenty Khmer intellectuals working from Pum's headquarters, in the Region

Economics and Education/Propaganda services.[118] Both teachers claimed that in this period the revolutionaries were popular, and attracted many volunteers for their armed forces. One probable reason for this was the moderate land reform that So Pum's followers enacted. A peasant from a village in Koh Thom district has recalled: 'In 1970-71 they gave land to the poor people who had none. In our village the poor were organized into three five-family groups who farmed the land and divided the produce among themselves. The rich were not forced to join such groups.'[119]

A Region administration was established, comprising Hanoi-trained cadres like Sien San, the Region military commander, and local communists such as Sok Buth Chamroeun, the Region Economics chief. Chamroeun was said to be a distant relative of the royal family, but had had considerable revolutionary experience; he had also been a builder's labourer[120] and then a typesetter for *Pracheachon* in the 1950s. First introduced to politics by Non Suon, he was also close to Keo Meas and Chou Chet. Other local members of the Region 25 Committee included a former teacher named Sok, who had been recruited by Ney Sarann in 1959, and Huot Sei, who had been trained by So Phim before 1967. During 1971, Chamroeun, Sok and Sei got involved in a violent dispute with a cadre named Kiet who was apparently close to the CPK Centre. The issue at stake is unknown, but Kiet was killed, and the incident would—years later—have serious repercussions for the three men.[121]

There were clashes elsewhere as well, particularly in Kompong Thom, the new location of Pol Pot's headquarters in Santuk district. According to a CIA report, during a September 1970 assault on the provincial capital, CPK troops fired on Vietnamese communist forces from behind.[122] And the next month a Vietnamese circular warned: 'In no circumstances are we to permit our troops to encircle and open fire on [Khmer communist] troops, as was done by a unit in the Xang Tuc [Santuk] area.'[123]

On the whole, however, the war against Lon Nol was going well; by late 1970 about fifteen thousand Khmers were fighting in regular communist units—in September there were already twenty Khmer battalions and five mixed ones.[124] (Vietnamese communist troops in the country numbered approximately forty thousand, as did South Vietnamese forces there.[125]) A further sixty thousand Khmers had enlisted in guerrilla and regional units.[126] Also in September, Lon Nol's operation 'Chenla I', involving six thousand elite troops, failed to achieve its goal of breaking the siege of Kompong Thom when it was halted at Taing Kauk by two thousand Vietnamese regulars and, presumably, the Khmer auxiliaries who had enlisted with Pon.[127]

By January 1971 the Khmer communists boasted twelve well-trained regiments,[128] and by June, according to the CIA's then Cambodia analyst, Sam Adams, their regular and guerrilla forces had reached a total strength of 125,000,[129] exhibiting a growth similar to that of the NLF in the early 1960s. The next month, a US Defence Intelligence Agency appraisal concluded:

> The Communists have found some backing among the Khmer peasantry, and the Chinese and Vietnamese minorities ... It is estimated that the Communists control some two to three million people in Cambodia out of a total of about seven million ... For the most part, however, the Vietnamese communists have apparently acceded to Khmer demands for autonomy ...
>
> Khmer Communist cadres have resorted where necessary to coercion, intimidation and assassination. Some have used their new positions to settle old scores with government officials who formerly opposed them when they were 'bandits' under the Sihanouk regime. On the whole, however, they have attempted to avoid acts which might alienate the population, and the behaviour of Vietnamese Communist soldiers has generally been exemplary when compared with the South Vietnamese.[130]

In most of Kampuchea's countryside, the political war had already been won. The Lon Nol government was secure only in the towns and their outskirts. Sihanouk and the Vietnamese, for so long opposed by the CPK, had proved to be valuable allies indeed.

The National Democratic Revolution, 1971-73

But they were considered to be enemies. CPK documents dating from early 1971, including copies of the newspaper *Pracheachon Padevat* ('Revolutionary People') edited by Thuch Rin, which were captured by Lon Nol forces in the South-Western Zone, are striking in their failure to mention any Vietnamese assistance to the Kampuchean revolutionaries.[131] A hand written document transcribed into a cadre's diary, entitled 'The Strategic Standpoint of the National Democratic Revolution', noted that:

Our revolutionary struggle must go through a long period of difficulty and hardship, confusion and indirectness, lows and highs, self-reliance and dependence on our own forces as the important ones even if in accompaniment *bondaer* [with others], the revolution gradually steps up towards seizing victory right until victory at the very end ...

After this period of exercising mastery over the revolutionary group(s) in every way, we can gradually win the victory. On the other hand, if we do not, if the people do not, and think only of reliance on the forces of *those other people* [*neak dotei nuh*], our revolution can not step towards seizure of victory, and we will only have difficulty and hardship for a long time in the future. *We want to and must get a tight grasp, filter into every corner*, and rely on the strategy of our revolution.[132]

It is clear from this that not only was Vietnamese assistance regarded with suspicion, but that also a *protracted* struggle was in the CPK Centre's interest; it represented a small minority of the vast movement that had been unleashed in 1970, and would need time to 'filter into every corner' and win 'mastery over the revolutionary group(s)'. Early victory—or a negotiated peace— would not serve this aim.[133]

Social Analysis

Two other important points emerge from these 1971 South-Western Zone documents. First, the social analysis: Kampuchea was considered 'a semi-colonial, semi-feudal country'. Its society was divided into five *vanna* or classes (feudal, capitalist, petty bourgeois, peasant and worker) and these in turn into various 'layers' (*sratop*), very much along the lines of the Chinese Communist Party's analysis of pre-revolutionary China. Much emphasis was placed on exploitation of the peasantry by feudal landlords (*sakdephum mchas dei*), even though, as William Willmott has pointed out, the most serious burden on the Khmer peasantry was widespread indebtedness to ethnic Chinese usurers,[134] who are not mentioned in these documents.[135] As we have seen in Chapter One, by contrast, the ICP had characterized Kampuchean society as early as the 1930s as one of 'nascent capitalism' (albeit 'with many vestiges of feudalism'), and a similar view is implied in Hou Yuon's 1964 writings, discussed in Chapter Six.

Related to this viewpoint is the documents' purely formal

adherence to the strategy of a 'worker-peasant alliance'. The working class was theoretically considered 'the leader' of that alliance, but was divided into two – 'the pure working class' and 'the partly pure working class' – while even the former was neglected in practice: 'In the countryside it is fixed to make the three lower layers of peasants the base [of the revolution]. In the towns it is fixed to make the whole petty bourgeoisie the base.' There was thus no policy of organizing the urban working class, or even the urban poor. These groups were indeed 'the base' of city society, regardless of what the Party fixed. Such CPK statements may be seen as direct antecedents of the decision to evacuate the cities in 1975. It is not surprising to read, in a 1977 Centre document discussing the history of the National Democratic Revolution:

> We decided clearly on [what were] the revolutionary forces ... The worker peasant forces were the basic force. Next were the national petty bourgeoisie and capitalists who undertook to follow the revolution.
> *Concretely*, we did not rely on the forces of the workers. The workers were the overt vanguard, but in concrete fact they did not become the vanguard. In concrete fact there were only the peasants.
> Therefore we did not copy anyone.[136]

The emphasis on the petty bourgeoisie as the urban base of a peasant revolution, to the exclusion of the working class, closely resembles the strategy then being pursued by the pro-Chinese Naxalites in India. The tactics were also similar. The leader of the Indian Maoist movement, Charu Mazmudar, wrote in 1970: 'The method of forming a guerrilla unit [should] be wholly conspiratorial ... The conspiracy should be between individuals and on a person-to-person basis. The petty bourgeois intellectual comrade must take the initiative in this respect as far as possible. He should approach the poor peasant who, in his opinion, has the most revolutionary potentiality, and whisper in his ear, 'Don't you think it is a good thing to finish off such and such a *jotedar* [landlord]?' This is how the guerrillas have to be selected and recruited singly and in secret, and organized into a unit'. The results of this individualist strategy are described by a student who was an active Naxalite at the time: '... Our movement soon became petty bourgeois in its thinking and membership, and continued to be so. Our cadres in rural areas showed impatience and adventurism, typical of the petty bourgeoisie, and went into action without proper preparation. They launched the 'annihilation' programme without first politicizing the peasant masses ... In urban areas, after finishing their actions, our cadres took refuge in petty bourgeois quarters, and not in the working class areas, because our Party had not built up a base in the working class localities.'[137]

The Naxalites were smashed, according to this student, because of their strategy and tactics. With the same strategy and tactics, however, the CPK advanced towards victory. This was partly because of assistance from the Vietnamese communists in this period, and partly because of the political weakness of the Lon Nol regime, and of its US backers, a weakness that was itself a product of the Vietnamese communists' resistance at home. International forces, therefore, were crucial to the triumph of the CPK. The irony, and the difference from the Naxalites' case, is that the CPK Centre was determined not to 'copy anyone'. This, too, may be said to stem from a 'petty bourgeois nationalism', but one whose chauvinism was, again ironically for a communist movement, rooted in the traditional *ruling* political culture, as we have seen in Chapter One. A third irony lies in the fact that this virulently 'domestic' ideology of the CPK Centre proved far more destructive of Kampuchean society than did contending ones which acknowledged more influence from abroad.

We may also note the apparent lack of emphasis on *dialectical* relationships between classes, apart from the generalized formula of 'exploitation', or on relationships to the means of production in the orthodox sense. The 1971 documents, and others detailing the CPK's class analysis, describe a series of status levels, professions, social origins and political affinities, with the words 'class', 'layer', and 'level' used almost interchangeably. (This of course is the non-dialectical sense of the original Sanskrit word *varna*.) Thus we have a 'class' of 'partly pure workers'; monks, intellectuals, and Khmers living abroad (described as a 'class apart'!) are added to later CPK texts of this kind,[138] while according to Thuch Rin and one of his subordinates in 1975, other categories included 'bookworms' (*neak kompiniyum*) and even 'petty bourgeois workers' (*kommakor anouthun*).[139] Finally, in 1978, Khmers who had returned from abroad were described by an acolyte of Ieng Sary as 'bourgeois workers'.[140]

The second point that emerges is the 'absolute character' (*charit dac khat*) of CPK strategy. Another handwritten document in the same collection, entitled 'Who Leads the People's War?', illustrates this with a veiled reference to Sihanouk:

> The exploiting classes resist the people's war to the end. Therefore they are not the ones who lead the people's war; rather they are the life-and-death enemies of the people's war. *If they use a ruse to come and take control of the people's war*, it is to kill the people and therefore to continue their oppression of the people further. Therefore the only leaders of the people's war are the layers of the people who experience the greatest oppression, the greatest pain, and have the greatest anger and are the most absolute in waging war to exterminate the exploiting classes, the imperialists, the feudalists and the capitalists. These layers of people are the toiler [*kammachep*] class. And the highest Organization [*angkar khpuos bompot*], the top general command, the vanguard force, with the boldest line of attack for the toiler class, is the toiler Party, which is adorned with the greatest brilliance of Marxist-Leninist consciousness and endowed with a political line and political standpoint of serving above all the interests of the producing class, and of the nation.

While the authors (such as Thuch Rin) of these particular documents made no mention of Vietnam, other revolutionaries in the South-Western Zone did. In 1971 subdistrict-level cadres in the Zone were summoned to a study-session in Kompong Speu. According to a participant, Phouk Chhay introduced a number of documents and talked of solidarity and cooperation between Vietnam, Kampuchea and Laos in the anti-imperialist fight. Chou Chet stressed the same theme; both men worked closely with the Hanoi-trained Khmers, called 'northern regroupees'.[141] Not present, it seems, were Mok and Thuch Rin, and no evidence exists that they shared their colleagues' view on this issue.

In fact there were clear divisions in the Zone leadership. In prison in late 1978, Vorn Vet recalled his visit to the South-Western Zone Office around February 1971: 'At that time Ta Mok was not very often at the Office; he was travelling and working in various places. Chong [Prasith] and Sy [Chou Chet] were at the Office, with their aides Troech, Hok and Kong. At that time they talked of Ta Mok and of conflicts they had with him. The atmosphere was heavily against Ta Mok throughout the Office. The one who was most involved was Chong; he was open about it. Sy did not say much but he was in conflict [with Mok] also.' Vorn Vet claims that he set about 'calming down' the two men and their aides; partly because 'I personally had a liking for Ta Mok as we had been friends from the beginning'. However, Prasith in particular 'just persisted in provoking conflict with Ta Mok and never stopped'.[142] As is normal in the Tuol Sleng confessions, there is no explanation of the nature of these conflicts. However, it is interesting that all three – Mok, Prasith and Chou Chet – had been active in the South-Western Zone during the Issarak period. As we have seen in Chapters Three and Four,[143] the movement had been least successful in Takeo, where Mok was based. Mok may well have concluded from his experience in those years that it was necessary to emulate his then rival Savang Vong, and to demonstrate complete independence from, even hostility towards, the Vietnamese — a lesson not evident in the different experience of Chou Chet and Prasith in Kampot and Koh Kong.

Vorn Vet merely notes that Prasith was going against the wishes of 'absolute ... masses and cadres'.[144] But in fact, at least some of the latter remained quite 'relative', and leaders like Prasith and Chou Chet most probably appreciated this even though they had little personal sympathy for Sihanouk, to take another issue at stake. The Zone documents I have examined above probably emanated from Thuch Rin, as did the newspaper captured with them. Their implication was such that the cadre who transcribed them into his diary, presumably at a meeting, noted down two queries that had occurred to him. The first was: 'For what reason have we joined up to serve the revolution?' The anticipated answer seemed to be, in part, in order to exterminate exploiting classes such as feudalists, because the second question was: 'Then for what reason did the despicable Lon Nol overthrow Prince Sihanouk?' It seems no answer was given, nor could any have been, so long as the CPK Centre (and Mok and Thuch Rin in the South-West), wished to capitalize on Sihanouk's appeal while continuing to target him as an enemy.

The 1971 CPK 'Congress'

In July 1971, a two-week CPK conference was held at Pol Pot's headquarters in the Northern Zone. Among the sixty or more who attended were Pol Pot himself, Nuon Chea, Vorn Vet, Non Suon, Ney Sarann, Um Neng, Chou Chet, So Phim, Phuong,

Chhouk, Seng Hong, Son Sen, Koy Thuon, Ke Pauk, Mok, Muol Sambath, Khieu Samphan, Hou Yuon, Hu Nim, some ethnic minority representatives and a number of Hanoi-trained Khmers.[145]

Several important decisions were made there. A new Central Committee was elected, consisting of about thirty members — more than double the size of the previous committee. Among the new full members were Chou Chet, Um Neng, Kang Chap, So Doeun, and Khieu Samphan; Hou Yuon and Hu Nim apparently became candidate members.[146] None of the Hanoi-trained Khmers gained admission, however; and Keo Meas failed to regain a place. The Politburo apparently remained unchanged, while the name 'Communist Party of Kampuchea', provisionally adopted in 1966, now became official.

A district cadre from the Eastern Zone, Ouch Bun Chhoeun, recalls that Deputy Zone Secretary Phuong returned from the conference with twelve booklets of documents, and passed them on to him. They contained details of resolutions on the economy ('production cooperatives, elimination of exploitation, and of markets'), culture, social action, military campaigning, and Party Statutes. A soldier who stood guard at the conference says that 'the line of the National Democratic Revolution' was proclaimed there by the Party Centre, although as we have seen, in the South-Western Zone it was already considered in process. 'It meant collectivization of land, moving people out of the towns, and expelling the Vietnamese troops. There were different viewpoints. The intellectuals — Hou Yuon, Hu Nim, Khieu Samphan — did not agree with this. Neither did the domestic strugglers who were in contact with the Vietnamese, like So Phim. There was no vote, only an explanation of the line. But there was real disagreement, for instance by Hou Yuon; he and Hu Nim and Koy Thuon were against collectivization. They wanted mutual aid teams [*krom prowas dai*] only.' Tea Sabun, who attended the conference as a participant, adds: 'For the whole day Son Sen read the documents aloud to the assembly. Then Ney Sarann spoke at length, and Hou Yuon made some criticisms of Son Sen. Khieu Samphan did not have much to say'. Sabun gives no details of what Sarann and Yuon said, but it seems that they considered the economic resolutions too radical or precipitous; the documents have not survived, but the theoretical foundations of what became CPK War Communism were almost certainly contained in them. These two men publicly dissented on such issues at a later meeting as well;[147] and Hou Yuon, officially minister of the Interior, Communal Reforms and Cooperatives in the revolutionary government, had already in 1970 'dared to scold' Pol Pot, complaining that the Party was using his name 'as a screen' by making him a 'puppet minister'.[148] He and Sarann were among the few outside the Party Centre who were educated enough to sense the economic implications of 'the elimination of markets'; among the others, too, there was probably a reluctance to question the leadership of a Party which was experiencing so many rapid advances.

A certain ambiguity shrouded other issues as well. According to Chhoeun, speaking on the basis of the documents he had read and what Phuong had told him of the proceedings: 'The resolution on foreign policy was that there could be contact with any country on the basis of equality and mutual non-interference in internal affairs. There was no real mention of China or Vietnam. There was no conflict with Vietnam, only some differences in consciousness. The Parties were not yet in conflict, but were watching each other very closely.' Sabun gives an example of this, saying that a decision was made *not* to receive an official delegation of ethnic Chinese from North Vietnam, who had asked, he claims, to 'make contact with and supervise the ethnic Chinese' in Kampuchea. 'But we said we would not be masters if they came to work with the ethnic Chinese residents in Kampuchea. The delegation received their orders from Vietnam. We disagreed with this.'

Years later, CPK leaders were to claim that the conference constituted a Party 'Congress' and that it approved a definition of communist Vietnam as the long-term 'acute enemy' (*satrev sruoch*) of the Kampuchean revolution. This is denied by both Sabun and Chhoeun. Such a decision probably *was* made, but not by the full gathering. In their confessions at Tuol Sleng in 1976 and 1978, Non Suon calls the entire event a 'national Party study-session', but Centre member Vorn Vet says the actual 'Congress' took place *after* the study-session. That an exclusive, secret meeting did then occur is also suggested by the failure of the 1973 and 1974 Party Histories to mention this 1971 'Congress', although they detail the previous ones of 1951, 1960 and 1963.[149] It seems likely that the CPK Centre, meeting on its own, passed its favoured resolutions. Then, with Ke Pauk's help, these began to be implemented in the immediate area, Region 31. (This would explain why the CPK soldier stationed there, unlike easterners Sabun and Chhoeun, became aware that a decision had been made to 'expel the Vietnamese troops'.)

Such was the isolation of the Centre from most of the rest of the CPK. The public decision on the ethnic Chinese delegation (and the exclusion of the Hanoi-trained Khmers from the Central Committee) may of course be considered the thin end of the 'acute enemy' wedge, but it is unlikely that many Party members saw it as such at the time. As in the past, international solidarity and independence were not viewed as mutually exclusive (certainly if US intelligence reports to the effect that the Vietnamese had generally 'acceded to Khmer demands for autonomy' were accurate). At any rate, few of the many new members of the Central Committee would have risked their positions by raising the question of the exclusion of the Hanoi-trained cadres, and even fewer would have realized the implications for themselves of the precedent being set by such exclusion.

The next month Lon Nol launched 'Operation Chenla II', in a second attempt to open the highway through Region 31 to Kompong Thom City. Pon, now proficient in Vietnamese, was working as an interpreter for the Vietnamese in their relations with the Khmer communists, and in this period he spent two months in the highway township of Baray, Kompong Thom. 'Large numbers of Vietnamese was billeted in big houses owned by the people there, who were all rather prosperous. The people were good to us. Then, when the Vietnamese left the town, Khmer communists came and threw grenades into the houses of those who had sheltered the Vietnamese . . . In some cases they killed entire families, in some cases the head of the family. The others all ran off far into the countryside.'[150] Lon Nol forces took Baray at the end of August. They found sixty-two tombs and mass graves, containing at least 180 corpses. Lon Nol's brother, Colonel Lon Non, told visiting journalists that the bodies were those of 'peasants or inhabitants of the area who had refused to collaborate with the North Vietnamese troops'.[151] But on 7 September, Ieng Lim defected to the government side, the first of six Hanoi-trained Issaraks to do so; *he* told debriefers 'that the local Khmer Rouge had arbitrarily executed peasants for minor infractions and that he himself had stopped the killing of civilians at Baray'. This appears to confirm Pon's account. Lim also reported serious divisions among the Khmer communists.[152]

Predictably, perhaps, Lim said he had defected because 'the war was for the benefit of North Vietnam and not the Khmer revolution', but it must have been clear to him that the tide was turning, at least in his area of operations, and he must have felt threatened by what was happening. For instance, the Lon Nol regime later published details, based on refugee reports, of fourteen 'popular demonstrations' in August against the Vietnamese communists, seven in the Eastern Zone and seven in the North. Four of these were described as having been organized or sponsored by Khmer communists; all were in the Northern Zone, and the first three in Region 31, which included both Baray and the CPK Centre headquarters (the fourth was in Siemreap or Region 35).[153] Interestingly, Koy Thuon, Secretary of the Northern Zone, was at this point based further north, in Kompong Svay district (Region 32), and apparently enjoyed good relations with ten or more Hanoi-trained Khmers there.[154]

It seems, then, that the Zone *military commander,* Ke Pauk (a native of Baray), with the support of the Centre, was primarily responsible for this first severe outbreak of CPK violence against Khmer civilians, linked as it was with an anti-Vietnamese campaign. Over the next year, regimentation of the area — but not of Region 32 — increased, and Pauk's relations not only with Koy Thuon, but with the Eastern Zone communists as well, began to deteriorate. According to Pon: 'On this side of the Mekong [the North] the Khmer Reds would not let people wear colourful clothing; on the other side [the East] they would. On this side they wanted to know why the others did not obey the rules of the Organization [*angkar*], and they would shoot people coming from there. They hated each other on different sides of the river.'[155] The CPK Eastern Zone troops, reflecting a greater degree of Vietnamese and 'Hanoi-Khmer' participation in their training and organization, were in fact already distinguishable from the black-clad Centre-organized units in other Zones, by their green fatigue uniforms and their more politicized, guerrilla-style tactics.[156] But the contrast was sharpest in the south of the country.

The 'Third Force' in the South-West: Drawing Them Over and Cleaning Them Out

Another decision made at the conference, but not *by* it, was one to detach Region 25 from the East[157] and incorporate it (along with Region 15 from the South-West) in a new Special Zone surrounding Phnom Penh. On 27 September, after a year in Kompong Chhnang, Non Suon was recalled by Vorn Vet, and spent the next three weeks with him, preparing for the change.[158] According to Suon's 1976 confession, Vet 'explained the aggressive plans of the Vietnamese and how they had invaded Kampuchea after the traitor's coup' — an interpretation little different from that of the 'traitor' Lon Nol. Vet also told Suon: 'I have been accepted as Party Secretary' of the Special Zone 'and you will be a member' of the new Zone Committee.[159] Suon continued by saying that Region 25, of which he would also become Secretary, was not in 1971 considered 'a solid base area'; 'contradictions were stronger there than elsewhere' and the situation was 'very confused', dating as far back as the pre-1954 period, when there had been conflicts (as we saw in Chapter Three) between 'Puth Chhay and Ngin Hor,[160] Khmers and Vietnamese'. 'The Organization took a great interest in Region 25', Suon wrote.

To deal with this situation Vet planned to replace the Hanoi-trained Region Secretary, So Pum, with Non Suon, intensifying the Centre's strategy, implemented at the conference, of directly playing off the 'domestic' communist veterans against their Hanoi-trained colleagues; Vet also devised a careful policy aiming to minimize potential opposition by leaving Pum's local colleagues in place. 'He told me that Chamroeun, Sok and Sei were traitors who had killed a comrade and were close to the Viet Cong: ... "Don't take action, it could endanger the war effort. Draw them over [os tieng] for now, and decide later ... Wait for our independence, and then we'll settle that. Now we must instruct them to remain with the revolution and fulfil their tasks according to their capabilities. Don't let the Vietnamese draw them over".'[161] A similar policy was to be applied in relation to 'all forces, both those who follow the Vietnamese and those who do not', and to 'all classes of the population, including monks': 'Don't let these forces be drawn over to the Vietnamese against our Revolutionary Organization', Vet said. As for the Vietnamese troops in Region 25, he went on: 'We'll solve that by inciting the population to fight them in all ways. Avoid using arms if possible; we need and must preserve our people and military forces. Use politics preferably.'[162] Vet's strategy was much more subtle than that being implemented in Baray.

Non Suon arrived in Region 25 on 15 October. According to one of the teachers working with So Pum, 'there was a conflict over the handing over of authority — Pum had not received orders to hand it over',[163] which suggests that at the Zone level, Eastern Secretary So Phim was not aware of the Centre's decision, made in July. Pum was not the only one to object. On October 18, Non Suon met Sok and told him of the new arrangements. In his confessions Suon later wrote: 'Chamroeun, Sok and Sei objected that such a transfer of authority properly required [the assent of] a Zone or Centre representative. They refused to accept it, and told me to leave while they reported to their Zone.'[164]

Meanwhile, Non Suon was establishing his own contacts in the East: 'I went two or three times to try to meet Chhouk [of Region 24] because I wanted to find Keo Meas',[165] a veteran leader whom Suon respected more than Vorn Vet. He had obviously not been told that Meas was now in Beijing, and no-one he met in the East knew this either. For the next three months or more, Region 25 was run by competing administrations, until So Phim acceded to the Centre's proposal. Non Suon and So Pum maintained separate headquarters, with most of the Khmer troops under Pum's command.[166] Suon soon managed to recruit some of the ex-teachers — including Sok, who became his military commander — while about ten others remained loyal to Pum. But as one of them says: 'Non Suon was more popular than So Pum because he was better known there; he had been very active in former times. Even though most of the teachers preferred Pum, some went to work with Suon and they soon began to call us 'Khmers in conical hats' [*khmer peak duon*]. There was no fighting however, and no killings; it was a political conflict. The northern regroupees [the Khmers from Hanoi] were keen on technology and equipment; the others were for independence-mastery [*ekareach-mchaskar*] and self-reliance; they refused all outside aid. Non Suon did not raise the Vietnamese problem — although his subordinates did — but he was more concerned with the peasantry than Pum was. He was also well-educated; he wrote and spoke well.'[167]

Chamroeun and Sei went over to Suon, and he managed to maintain cordial relations with So Pum. A teacher who worked for a year with Pum and from then on with Suon, recalls: 'I saw them get on well when they met for discussions: only from the outside did I hear of conflict between them. But I saw them solve problems together in a normal manner . . . Sok was one of the problems — he seemed to hate the Vietnamese and to resist them a good deal, even though the Vietnamese and Khmer troops got on well enough together. Some of Sok's troops were stationed with Pum, and at one point in 1972 he prepared to mount an attack on Pum. But it never came to that; Pum went to see him on a motorcycle, and the conflict was resolved.'[168] Non Suon, for his part, offered to make So Pum his deputy, in an apparent attempt to unite the two camps. But Pum would not agree to this, and by mid 1972 he had crossed the Mekong and disappeared into the Eastern Zone.[169] Chamroeun became Deputy Secretary of Region 25, in charge of the Economic Service; Sok and Sei both joined the Region Committee. Along with at least half a dozen Hanoi-trained Khmers who also retained positions of authority, they continued to 'fulfil their tasks according to their capabilities', as Vorn Vet had planned. Although the views of Sok, at least, had evidently changed radically during the dispute (perhaps bending with the wind), they would all meet the same eventual fate: death by execution in 1975. Western intelligence soon obtained reports of continuing problems between the CPK Centre (known to be headed by 'Pol') and Region 25. According to the CPK's Cambodia analyst up to 1973, Sam Adams: 'Pol, for example, always had problems on what to do with Region 25. . . and we knew of his concern that Region 25 was getting too big for its britches. . .'[170]

So Pum's departure from Region 25 was nevertheless symptomatic of more drastic changes occurring in other parts of the country, particularly in the South-West, as the CPK Centre began to make its presence felt. In neighbouring Region 13 (Takeo), where Mok's son-in-law Khe Muth was Deputy Secretary, and where in 1971 the CIA began obtaining reports of 'actual fighting between the Khmer Rouge and the Vietnamese communists',[171] a second Hanoi-trained Khmer, the military commander of two of the Region's five districts, defected to the Lon Nol regime in November of that year.[172] A local CPK member, still active in 1980, recalled that purges of such people had begun at that time, and that they had been 'completely cleaned out' by early 1972. He described using current CPK euphemisms how 'our Organization dealt with this problem': 'We called those Khmers from Hanoi to come to study and someone led them away. So really we were expelling them. . . When we began pulling them out the others did not realize what was happening. And so we were able to get rid of almost all of them. Very few realized what was happening in time and escaped to Vietnam.'[173]

In the South-West's Region 35 (Kampot), according to US State Department officer Kenneth Quinn, the Khmer communists 'forsook all allegiance to Sihanouk in late 1971'; in early 1972 they 'began their programme to communize Cambodian society' (a development we will examine presently), and simultaneously attempted to impose limitations on the movements of Vietnamese communist forces through the South-Western Zone.[174] In the other Region 35, Siemreap province in the Northern Zone, opposition to the Vietnamese was directed in the same period by a CPK cadre newly arrived from Takeo in the South-West, who became the local district chief. According to a woman from the small township of Kompong Kdei, in eastern Siemreap: 'Large demonstrations were organized against the Vietnamese troops. The demonstrators were not locals; they came from upland areas ten or twenty kilometres away, and had been educated in Red Khmer ideas — they hated the Vietnamese. The townspeople, on the other hand, just treated the Vietnamese normally; we traded with them, and they did not steal from us. The Vietnamese withdrew in the face of the demonstrations, and the Red Khmer were in charge from that point on.'[175]

As for Kampot, various sources coincide in describing the earliest phase of the implementation of the 'National Democratic Revolution' there. According to Quinn, its main theme was 'a total — though not yet completed — social revolution. . . every thing that preceded it was anathema and must be destroyed'. Writing in 1974, Quinn outlined the changes he had observed in this early period: 'doing away with the [National United] Front', and with the term *Khmer Rumdos* (the local communists now openly called themselves *Khmer Krahom* or 'Khmer Reds'), and replacement of the word 'Royal' (*Reach*) with 'Committee' (*Kana*) in the title of the revolutionary administration; destruction of most of the schools and governmental offices built by the Sihanouk government prior to 1970; replacement of the names of districts with numbers — a measure that was never adopted in other Zones, significantly, although it appears to have been decided on during the July 1971 CPK meeting; establishment of 'cooperative stores' to monopolize local trade; prohibition of 'certain social extravagances such as colourful dress'; wide-ranging land reform; and relocation of a number of villages.

Most of Quinn's information on these 1972 developments came from Kompong Trach district of Kampot.[176] It is supplemented by the account of Yos Por, a Hanoi-trained Khmer stationed there at the time (and now a senior PRK figure). Por says that in early 1972, he and his northern regroupee colleagues 'started to be relieved of our duties, and replaced':

> At study-sessions they would call us 'revisionists', 'lazy', or 'cowardly'. They carried out what was practically an overt *coup d'état*. We were transferred from our jobs; some of us were sent to grow pepper, or supervise cattle. Even a doctor was sent to raise pigs, to be 'forged'.
>
> At the time, we agreed with that, because we came from abroad and had to be forged among the people — that was correct, we thought . . . But in fact they had simply finished using us to train their forces, which had been their plan.[177]

The local communists began to say that the Party must 'beware' the northern regroupees and Sihanoukists, who together constituted a 'Third Force'. Further, Por notes that 'at that time, there were no longer any Vietnamese soldiers in the Khmer villages; their troops had regrouped in the forest. The Vietnamese were cut off from the Khmer population'.[178] In the same period, according to a local schoolteacher who had enlisted in the Lon Nol forces in Kompong Trach, the Khmer communists 'started to kill captured Lon Nol soldiers, but the Vietnamese never did'.[179] (A Lon Nol soldier who later deserted to the communist zone claims that in Region 15, north-west of Phnom Penh, an entire force of five hundred Lon Nol troops who had been captured there were all executed in 1972.)[180]

The economic changes of the National Democratic Revolution were at this stage still quite moderate. In Kompong Trach, for instance, as Quinn reports: '[Land redistribution] was carried out in all villages in 1972. . . no person was allowed to retain over five hectares of rice land and one hectare of garden land or orchard. Rice land over that limit was given to people with fewer than five hectares or to People's Associations in the village. Orchards and garden land [in excess of one hectare] were not redistributed but kept under district government control.'[181] Collective harvesting, in twelve-family groups or mutual-aid teams, became institutionalized, but land remained privately owned. Further, only a relatively small number even of rich peasants would have suffered losses under this system (five hectares per family was not low by pre-1970 standards), while Quinn notes that 'many poorer people supported [it] because they received benefits'.[182] These measures were apparently also implemented in early 1972 in other parts of the South-West, such as Region 32 (northern Kompong Speu); and in addition in Siemreap in the Northern Zone, as the woman from Kompong Kdei recalls: '[The Khmer communists] took over as village chiefs, and organized peasants into groups of ten families. They were not tough, however; I had to plant bananas one or two hours per day, to beautify some villages, but apart from such tasks people continued to work individually, and normal private trade continued.'[183]

An exception, again, was in Region 13 (Takeo), where the revolutionaries apparently managed to reduce production levels. The district of Tram Kak, the birthplace of Mok, was now run directly by his son-in-law, Region Deputy Secretary Khe Muth (and from the next year by his wife, Mok's daughter Khom);[184] a local peasant describes in apparently garbled terms the economic implications of the National Democratic Revolution in Tram Kak: 'In 1970 the communists' line was good; they did not oppress us, and there was equality. Then there was change, from one system to another. In 1971 came the National Revolution, and in 1972 the Democratic one, which meant collecting people into groups in order to live together. The people went along with this; but whereas in the old society production had been sufficient and there was a surplus to sell, now there was a shortage; there was only enough produced for six or seven months of the year.'[185] After victory in 1975, Tram Kak was named a 'model district' (*srok kumruu*) of Democratic Kampuchea.[186] A second pointer to the future occurred in Kompong Trach, Kampot, where a small number of villages were evacuated to remote areas in 1972; land in the new location was communalized.[187] In this case, however, production was high, largely for technical reasons. But the most significant innovations in this period were probably in the social and cultural field.

The CPK's Cultural Revolution

In mid 1972, according to Quinn, people living in CPK zones of Regions 13 and 35 in Takeo and Kampot were henceforth forbidden to wear the traditional multicoloured sarong; all were

now required to wear the plain black shirt and trousers normally
worn by peasants at work, which later became the uniform of
Democratic Kampuchea.[188] In the northern part of Takeo (in
Region 33) at this time, a member of a local militia unit recalls
how guerrillas were taught the following song, which was sung
in two parts, with men on one side and women on the other:

> Friends travelling through mountain forests,
> The leaves are very long,
> *Khlong* leaves and *tbeng* leaves,
> In the friends' resting place.
> In the friends' resting place.
> Your clothes are ragged because you sleep on the ground.
> Your clothes are ragged because you sleep on the ground.
> There is no-one to sew them for you.
> You sew them with your own hands.
> You sew them with your own hands.
> You depend on your grandparents
> But they are far away.
> You depend on your mother
> But your mother is at home.
> You depend on your elder sister
> But she has married a [Lon Nol] soldier.
> You depend on your elder sister
> But she has married a [Lon Nol] soldier.
> You depend on the rich people
> But the rich people oppress the poor people.[189]

The last two lines of this song make it clear that family
relationships were considered similar to class ones — unreliable
if not oppressive, and to be severed. We have here, in part of the
South-Western Zone in 1972, a portent of the fate prescribed for
family life throughout the country following victory in April
1975.

On 17 April 1972 — three years to the day before that victory
— a primary school teacher named Ith Sarin left Phnom Penh,
with a friend, for the communist zone. A month later he met the
'President of the Cultural Committee of the South-Western
Zone', Thuch Rin. Sarin was 'very disappointed' with what he
said was Rin's 'extreme leftism' and his tendency to adhere
closely to the 'Red Chinese' model.[190]

Two days after his departure from the capital, Sarin arrived at the boundary of the CPK Special Zone with the South-West's Region 33, and met with CPK military and political leaders. Although he had been an ardent supporter of the Lon Nol regime, Sarin was already treated with some confidence. He later wrote of this meeting: 'Another friend [*mit*], probably the political commissar of the battalion, discussed the problem of 'King Sihanouk' with us. He probably thought that I had worked with the Khmer Reds while in Phnom Penh, and had been involved in the movement during Sihanouk's reign, because he said: 'The Organization does not allow Sihanouk to return to Kampuchea at the moment, because if Sihanouk comes back all the people will unite behind him and we will have bare backsides'. I was very surprised to hear that. . . Another friend called him over and whispered secretly; perhaps he told him not to mention the problem of Sihanouk in front of me anymore, or perhaps he told him that I was not one of the 'core' Khmer Reds.'[191]

Not only in the 1960s was secrecy 'the basis' of the revolution. Sarin later found that the CPK was 'methodically getting rid of pro-Sihanouk cadres' and had placed Party members in charge of most subdistricts in the area.[192]

After travelling and working with the CPK, as a candidate Party member, in the South-Western and Special Zones for nine months, Ith Sarin returned to Phnom Penh in January 1973 and published a detailed report of what he had seen and heard, entitled *Sronoh Pralung Khmer* ('Regrets for the Khmer Soul'). Although he met and described dozens of CPK leaders and cadres, including Vorn Vet and Non Suon, Sarin's report contains but one single reference to the role of Hanoi-trained Khmers — 'a few. . . doctors' working in the Special Zone hospital.[193] As in Kampot, this second element of the 'Third Force' had been effectively eclipsed. By late 1972, Nhem Sun, for instance, had been removed from his post as director of the cadre school at Amleang (now headquarters of the Special Zone); he was put in charge of 'toughening' (*chumreng*) a group of twenty demobilized CPK troops who had performed unsatisfactorily in battle. One of them later explained Sun's drastic demotion: 'The Party was not happy with him because he had come from Hanoi'.[194]

The Centre's strategy of using the 'domestic' communist veterans, with their bitter experience at the hands of the Sihanouk regime in the late 1960s, in the purge of their northern regroupee (and Sihanoukist) compatriots, had had earliest success in the South-Western Zone. Sarin reported that the Centre had concentrated its 'most important leadership framework' there; he named the South-Western Zone's most influential personalities as Chou Chet, Phouk Chhay, Sieng Po Se, Thuch Rin and Mok. Only the latter two, however, would see out the war in such roles (and unlike the others would also survive unscathed the 1975–79 period): it was they whom the Centre apparently regarded as the Zone's 'framework', with their control of military and cultural affairs. Secret assassinations of Hanoi-trained cadres had already begun in the South-Western and Special Zones (as they had also, according to Pon, in Region 31 in the Northern Zone), with the exception of Non Suon's Region 25.[195] But there is also a possible hint in Sarin's report of the *next* crisis about to rend the South-West: a purge of 'domestic' Issarak veterans. Suon's former co-member of the Joint Commission for the Implementation of the Geneva Accords, Chi Kim An, who had become Chairman of the Information and Culture Department of the Special Zone, hanged himself in early April 1972.[196]

By the time Sarin arrived to work in the same department in June, he found its staff 'strict and far to the left'; nearby was the Special Zone's Arts Bureau, where about fifty children, including Ieng Sary's, learnt to perform revolutionary drama and songs.[197]

In the Eastern Zone at this time, Chi Kim An's one-time fellow student in France, Yun Soeun, who had returned from seventeen years in North Vietnam, was CPK Deputy Secretary of Region 22. With the cooperation of the Region Secretary (Siet Chhe), Soeun was planning the re-establishment of secondary education, and a number of textbooks were printed for this purpose.[198] At this point, however, the Centre intervened. Addressing a 'very divided' Zone Assembly held to discuss the issue, Nuon Chea quashed the project, and Soeun was dismissed from his post.[199] He was not purged, however; So Phim then appointed him Chief of the Zone Artisans Service — in effect he became manager of various factories in the jungle, with a workforce of over 250.[200] His demotion, on the other hand, was the first in the Eastern Zone, where, unlike in other Zones, dozens of Hanoi-trained Khmers continued to play an important role (particularly in the armed forces — Chan Saman, for instance, took command of the southern Mekong front in

Region 24 in 1972).[201] Like the more moderate policies to which the Eastern Zone cadres (for instance, Siet Chhe) seemed amenable, this did reflect the political nature of the communist movement in the East. On the other hand, as we have seen, there were also several precedents for Eastern Zone accession to pressure from the Centre.

Regional Differences

A corollary of this was the developments in Region 21 (eastern Kompong Cham). In 1971, the Region Secretary, Phuong, was made head of the Zone Economics Standing Committee. His Deputy, Chan (Seng Hong), who had allegedly developed a close relationship with Pol Pot in the 1960s, took his place.[202] A former inhabitant of Region 21 recalled in 1980: 'Then in February 1972 all the Vietnamese troops went home and none were left. The Vietnamese troops did not leave as a result of negotiations but were driven out. Then the Vietnamese residents were driven out. . . it was explained that as long as they stayed it would be difficult to expel the Vietnamese troops if they should come back to try to take over Kampuchean territory.'[203] The source affirms that this was a Zone decision, and that Phuong agreed with it. If so, it was implemented only in Region 21 in this period. Another report from the area in mid 1972 described an anti-Vietnamese demonstration organized by the CPK, in terms reminiscent of those in Baray in August 1971: 'Villagers marched around, brandishing machetes and shouting, 'We do not fear to die from bombs dropped from airplanes', and 'We all agree to die together in order to get the VC/NVA out of Kampuchea'.[204] These slogans make clear which of the two protagonists in the Vietnam War was considered the 'acute enemy' by the CPK organizers of the demonstration, probably under Chan's orders.

Similar scattered incidents occurred elsewhere. In the same period, in Region 32 in the Northern Zone, the headquarters of Zone Secretary Koy Thuon, armed conflict apparently erupted between CPK and *Khmer Rumdos* units.[205] But the latter, with their northern regroupee cadres, still vastly outnumbered the former, and the CPK Centre's views were still far from becoming widely accepted in the Khmer communist movement. When the communists' 'Easter Offensive' began in Vietnam in March 1972, just across the border from Region 21, perhaps as many as twenty thousand *Khmer Rumdos* troops fought alongside Vietnamese units during the siege of An Loc,[206] while in Region 23 (Svay Rieng) in April, another combined force overran most of the province in a few days.

The main political development for the CPK Centre and its supporters in 1972, then, was their double-barrelled campaign to 'draw over' (*os tieng*) Khmer members of Vietnamese communist and *Khmer Rumdos* units, incorporating them under direct 'Khmer' (CPK) command, and to expel the Vietnamese troops from Kampuchean soil.

By this time, the number of Vietnamese communist troops engaged in full-time combat in Kampuchea had already fallen to eight thousand or fewer (South Vietnamese troops numbered twenty thousand or so), although at least thirty thousand more were stationed in border areas and along supply routes from the North.[207] In the South-Western Zone alone there were about fifteen thousand salaried Khmer communist troops by May 1972.[208] Late in the year a CIA report noted: 'In some instances VC/NVA food and ammunition supplies were confiscated by the KC (Khmer Communists) and the VC/NVA managers of the supply sites were arrested. . . the expropriation of weapons and supplies continued at an alarming rate and had become a major problem for COSVN (the communist Central Office for South Vietnam). As a protective measure, COSVN units were advised to travel in large groups. When challenged at KC checkpoints they were not to react against the KC but were to await the liaison teams who would then take the necessary action to effect their release.'[209] This campaign was pursued by the CPK despite the fact that South Vietnamese forces were still occupying parts of the East and South-West, and were able to regain much ground for the Lon Nol regime when divisions within the communist movement presented them with the opportunity.

Such was the case in the South-West's Region 13, the scene of the earliest such divisions. In early 1972, according to a local CPK member at that time: 'We started by making appeals to Khmer forces in Vietnamese units saying that [they] should return to the Khmer Organization [*angkar*]. Then the Region Committee started negotiations with the Vietnamese big shots to get them to agree to turn over the Khmer forces to us. The Vietnamese agreed but the method of their agreement was that some Khmers were allowed to bring their weapons while others were not. . . Then in April 1972 our army started to drive [the Vietnamese] out in cases where they didn't respect our state power. In some places there was heavy fighting, in others the Vietnamese just withdrew [to the] frontier areas.'[210] Subsequently, as Quinn recounts, in the middle of the year Saigon troops there reopened Highway 2 from Takeo City to the Vietnamese border, and re-installed the Khmer Republic's 15th Brigade in many nearby outposts which had fallen into communist hands earlier in the year.[211]

In Regions 25 and 35, however, the government forces never recovered from the loss of Koh Thom and Kompong Trach district centres early in the year. It is already clear from Quinn's account of prior developments in Kampot that the CPK cadre in Region 35, led by Kang Chap, had been among the first to launch the National Democratic Revolution. It may now be useful to return to the situation in Region 25, whose cadres had proved much less enthusiastic, even after Non Suon had won control there.

A number of issues divided Non Suon and the other 'domestic' Khmer cadres in Region 25 from the Vietnamese. First were the instructions given to Suon by his direct superior Vorn Vet.[212] One source has reported that Hou Yuon 'seemed to be afraid of' Vorn Vet; if so, Non Suon is even more likely to have been under pressure. This was partly evident in July 1972 when Suon was asked to make a public declaration for radio transmission, to the effect that the Pracheachon Group had disbanded in 1962.[213] The aim was ostensibly to undercut the activities of Saloth Chhay and Penn Yuth in Phnom Penh, but the implications for Pracheachon veterans still in the revolutionary ranks were clear. (Keo Meas, for instance, had officially represented the Pracheachon at a meeting in May 1970.)[214]

Secondly, around June 1972 the combined Khmer and Vietnamese communist forces completed their campaign to drive Lon Nol and South Vietnamese troops from Region 25. The Vietnamese, about 1,300 in number, then began to use the area for rest and recuperation from the fighting[215] and also from their own 'Easter Offensive' in Vietnam, which had begun in March. The next month the local CPK began to 'draw over' those Khmer troops (still a majority) who were enlisted in Vietnamese units or under alleged 'Vietnamese' (possibly 'northern re-groupee') command; the campaign appears to have been largely successful. A third issue was the Vietnam peace talks now picking up steam in Paris; the CPK had all along refused to countenance a negotiated solution to the Kampuchean war, a stand accepted by all 'domestic' Khmer leaders, including Hou Yuon.[216] (Pol Pot as we have seen, had secured even Sihanouk's agreement to this before the NUFK was founded in 1970.) The Region 25 CPK branch took control of all Khmer troops largely by means of local negotiations with the Vietnamese communists, although in at least one case a fire-fight ensued when the Vietnamese resisted. The fourth factor, which on occasion also led to armed clashes, was an economic one. The Region 25 cadres objected to Vietnamese purchasing of draft animals, which they feared was diminishing local agricultural potential, and also to Vietnamese taxing of river traffic.[217] Fifthly, the Vietnamese presence was becoming unpopular because of US aerial bombardment, which many villagers felt would end if the Vietnamese withdrew.

These problems apart, informed local sources differ markedly in their recollections of Non Suon's own attitude to the Vietnamese communists. According to some, he described Vietnam as the 'historical enemy' of the Khmer;[218] others say he had no strategic differences with them.[219] The truth, insofar as Suon did have a consistent personal position, may lie somewhere in between; like others, he seems to have seen the Vietnamese as 'friends within contradictions'.[220] Hou Yuon, for instance, said at a public meeting in May 1972: 'At first the North Vietnamese seemed to keep us tightly reined, but since late 1971 we have managed to take the situation in hand again. We are still aware of the Vietnamese danger from both North and South. But they are our neighbours and they are helping us, so we should live with them as good neighbours'.[221] Such a view is also implied in Non Suon's 1976 statement to his Pol Pot interrogators, who reported, as we noted in Chapter Six, that Suon 'follows the path of the Vietnamese Party [but] holds to the principle of independence... [he] takes Vietnamese experience, but with the Khmer holding state power'.[222] It is significant that in Region 25 in 1972, there was still no attempt to pursue the *domestic* policy aspects of the National Democratic Revolution; neither the anti-Sihanouk campaign, nor the re-location of villages, nor the cultural and social regimentation already evident in Takeo, Kampot, and Region 31 in the North, had yet emerged in Region 25.

Nor, in fact, had they emerged in most other parts of the country, particularly not in the East, where Vietnamese communist forces remained active, unopposed by the population, and working in cooperation with local CPK and *Khmer Rumdos* organizations, while economic and social reforms implemented by the latter were moderate. In general, 1972 was a year in which the policies of the revolutionaries strengthened their hold on the loyalty of the rural population. In fact, popular approval of the liberation struggle was at its peak. Ith Sarin's companion on his nine-month trip, Kuong Lumphon, concluded after the two men had defected to the Lon Nol regime early the next year: 'The local people under their [the communists] control have enough sense to see that at the present time they have a fairly easy life and that no-one is oppressing them. . . They are grateful, they are happy, they are enjoying themselves.'[223] As Lumphon noted, however, this was partly because of the secrecy in which the CPK and its programmes (or those of the Centre) were shrouded. But it was also a result of the equitable land redistribution and other reforms, and of the continuing emphasis on cadres 'serving the people'.[224]

By the end of 1972, the Khmer communist regular and guerrilla forces totalled two hundred thousand troops and were still expanding.[225] (The Lon Nol army was only slightly larger.) About half or more of the country's population now lived in zones controlled by the insurgents.[226] Further, the communist side had achieved a more effective rural administration, by means of mass organizations. These included a Peasants' Association (*Samakhum Kasekor*) — with separate divisions for youth, men, and women; a Patriotic Monks' Association (*Preah Song Snaha Cheat*); and the secret Alliance of Communist Youth of Kampuchea (*Sampoan Yuvachun Kommyunis Kampuchea*), known as *Yuvakok*.

Mam Lon, a peasant cadre in Rolea Peir district of Kompong Chhnang (Region 31) then serving as a member of his local subdistrict committee, has given an indication of communist penetration at the village level. Lon says that the Peasants' Association, established there in 1971, had two members in his village and another thirteen in the subdistrict: all were 'poor and lower middle peasants'. The *Yuvakok* was established there in 1972; it accepted only 'poor peasants', and had two members in the village and another six in the subdistrict. The Monks' Association was represented in the sub-district but not in Lon's village.[227] On the other side of the country, in Komchay Meas district in Prey Veng (Region 20) in the East, the district head of the Monks' Association claims that by 1973 it had seven hundred members from thirty-four *wats* there.[228]

The Peasants' Association and the *Yuvakok* functioned as recruiting channels for CPK members, who had to be of 'poor or lower middle peasant' background. Lon became a candidate member of the Party in early 1972, and a full member seven months later. His description of the Party's local activities is interesting. At the district level, at least two leading cadres were northern regroupees born in Lon's village; the rest were local peasants. Sihanouk was said to be 'a leader against the US, a patriot', and emphasis was given to 'cooperation between the three countries of Indo-China to fight the imperialists together'. The latter theme was also stressed in visits to the district by Phouk Chhay and Chou Chet (although these two were also very critical of Sihanouk's defunct regime.[229]) In the same year, by contrast, when Mok came to Kompong Chhnang, he called a meeting of over three thousand monks in order to persuade them to defrock and enlist in the army (the first known example of such a CPK policy); he told the monks that Vietnamese troops were not allowed to stay in *wats* or villages, and that it was forbidden to sell food to them without written permission.[230]

1972 was also, therefore, a year of relative balance among the revolutionary factions, even in the South-Western and Northern Zones where the Centre's influence was greatest. In coastal Koh Kong, for instance, the revolution was clearly divided, with Regions 37 and 11 pursuing quite different policies. An ethnic Chinese woman who fled from the former to the latter region in 1972 later described Prasith, Prachha and the other Region 11 cadre as the 'free Khmer Rouge' (*khmer krahom serei*), because of what she said was their liberal attitude to travel and trade (Region 11 was what was called an 'Autonomous Maritime Sector'), and their good relations with the population. In Region 37, she said, the communists were much stricter. Significantly, Region 11 cadres worked closely with the Vietnamese communists, who themselves 'liked the Khmer people like their own people', and treated the inhabitants well. 'They liked the ethnic Chinese too', the woman added. Different racial groups, she said, were organized into separate 'forces', and held political meetings in their own languages.[231]

Similarly, Ith Sarin reported a revolutionary meeting in Kompong Speu in May 1972, attended by representatives of the Chinese and Vietnamese communities, as well as Buddhist monks, CPK officials, and around ten thousand inhabitants. One of the banners displayed for the occasion proclaimed: 'Long live the united force of the Kampuchean, Lao and Vietnamese peoples'. Hou Yuon addressed this meeting also; he stressed *both* self-reliance *and* 'unity with the Lao and Vietnamese people to drive the American imperialists out of Indo-China'.[232]

Finally, it is worth noting that no Hanoi-trained Khmer cadres defected to the government during 1972: more than a year passed without defections after those from Takeo and Kompong Thom in late 1971.[233] This was probably a result of contradictory factors — more systematic elimination of them in the latter areas during 1972, and consolidation elsewhere, in the same period, by more moderate elements; the latter were, at least, holding their own.

The Lon Nol Regime Founders

This was more than could be said for the infant Khmer Republic, which was not only militarily besieged but also increasingly dominated by one man in a climate described by some as 'Sihanoukism without Sihanouk'.[234] Lon Nol had promoted himself to Marshal in April 1971, and he suspended the National Assembly the following October, saying that he would no longer 'play the game of democracy and freedom'. In March 1972, after his co-organizer of the coup, Prime Minister-designate Sirik Matak, had sacked the dissident Dean of the Law Faculty, large-scale student demonstrations erupted. Lon Nol promptly ousted the Head of State, Cheng Heng, assumed the post himself, and dissolved the Assembly. Matak now declined to serve as Prime Minister, and Lon Nol appointed Son Ngoc Thanh, perhaps hoping to win back the confidence of students and intellectuals. But Thanh's collaboration with Lon Nol only ensured their complete disillusionment, and probably destroyed any chance of genuine political change. A French missionary summed up the situation at the end of March 1972: 'Youth, students and intellectuals hang their heads. The fine patriotic and republican spirit of March 1970 is broken. Their dream of social justice is vanishing in the face of reality. . . Corruption is rampant. Preoccupation with business, profit, corruption, bribery and political opportunism is openly spreading. Small groups of dissidents are joining the insurgency.' Further student demonstrations at the end of April were bloodily suppressed, and rigged presidential elections on 4 June confirmed Lon Nol in his post. When public discontent resurfaced, Prime Minister

Son Ngoc Thanh banned four opposition newspapers for spreading 'false news' and trying to discredit the Presidency. An assassination attempt on 21 August narrowly missed taking Thanh's life.

But Thanh had outlived his usefulness to Lon Nol. When new National Assembly elections were held on 3 September, all 126 seats predictably went to the Socio-Republican Party led by Lon Nol's younger brother, Colonel Lon Non. Thanh banned Sirik Matak's newspaper on 5 October, and was then himself forced to resign as Prime Minister nine days later. 'I am old', he said. 'I would like to retire in South Vietnam'. He went there soon afterwards; the longest Khmer political career, which had begun with the publication of a dissident newspaper, had come to a humiliating end.

Thanh was replaced by one of his early student admirers in Paris, Hang Thun Hak, who ironically had joined the Pracheachon in the late 1950s but was now a member of Lon Non's party. Socially progressive, Hak encapsulated the sad fate of that group of leftists who had waited so long for Sihanouk's overthrow. Lon Nol had complete backing from the US embassy for his grip on the Republic's armed forces and political institutions; impatient with Hang Thun Hak, Lon Nol pushed him aside after only six months in office.

Despite what looks like his political dexterity, Lon Nol was in many ways a traditional mystic, almost a nineteenth-century figure, inspired by his own ramshackle chauvinist ideology which he termed 'Neo-Khmerism'. He had long dreamed of the 'reconquest' of Kampuchea Krom (the Mekong Delta),[235] and outlined his hopes of 'reuniting' the Khmers in Kampuchea, Thailand and Vietnam, the Chams and hill-tribes in Kampuchea and Vietnam, and even the Mons in Thailand and Burma. He called on what he said were the historical traditions of 'holy warriors' (*yuthesel*) of the Khmer-Mon races in his crusade against the Vietnamese, and foggily looked forward to a state encompassing 'thirty million' Khmers by the year 2020.[236] Such statements fell on deaf ears. Lon Nol's domination of the foundering Khmer Republic was merely paving the way for defeat, at the hands of a culturally-related[237] but far more dynamic and tenacious chauvinism. That communist chauvinism, however, was yet to triumph over its own opposition within the CPK.

The 1973 US Bombardment

By October 1972, the US and Hanoi had reached agreement on terms for a cease-fire and US withdrawal from Vietnam. Washington dropped its demand for a North Vietnamese withdrawal from the South, and Hanoi dropped its demand for Nguyen Van Thieu's removal; both had previously been pre-conditions for a settlement. Kissinger had insisted on Hanoi securing agreement from the CPK as well, but it should have been clear to him that this would be impossible despite his stated preparedness to concentrate US air power on Kampuchea.[238] Apart from Pol Pot's antagonism to Hanoi, a cease-fire would have prevented the Centre's far-from-complete consolidation of 'mastery over the revolutionary group(s) in every way'. But Thieu was also proving recalcitrant, and it was apparently to appease him that Nixon ordered the 'Christmas bombing' of Hanoi and Haiphong in December 1972. Within a month, the Paris Agreement on Ending the War and Restoring Peace in Vietnam had been signed by all parties to the conflict there. It was to apply from 27 January 1973, and its terms were little different from those agreed in October. The US began withdrawing its remaining troops from Vietnam, but since it saw Kampuchea as an integral part of the conflict, soon switched its air arm there; it portrayed this as an attempt to force the Khmer insurgents, now on the threshold of complete military victory, to negotiate with Lon Nol. It may also have been part of a strategy designed to provoke further further divisions between the CPK and the VWP, and thus set back the latter's position in South Vietnam, in the knowledge that the CPK would *not* agree to peace talks. The then CIA Chief Strategy Analyst in Saigon, Frank Snepp, has described the ensuing massive bombardment of Kampuchea as 'the centre-piece of the Administration cease-fire strategy'.[239] Whatever its aim, the political effect was twofold: to prevent a complete revolutionary victory at a time when the CPK Centre's grasp over the revolution was still relatively weak; and to strengthen that grasp, which held the country on a course of continuing violence and warfare that lasted for the next decade.

According to William Shawcross, 'within a few months an enormous new aerial campaign had destroyed the old Cambodia forever'.[240] During the whole of 1972, American B-52s and fighter bombers had dropped 53,500 tons of bombs on targets in

Kampuchea, nearly all in the Eastern Zone.[241] From February to August 15, 1973 (when the US Congress imposed a halt), the total was 257,500 tons, and the bombs fell on all populated rural areas of the country, as Shawcross's map shows. A United Press International report in the *Boston Globe* on 1 April 1973 stated: 'Refugees swarming into the capital from target areas report dozens of villages, both east and south-west of Phnom Penh, have been destroyed and as much as half their population killed or maimed in the current bombing.' Within days of this report, the US bombardment intensified, reaching a level of 3,600 tons per day.[242]

From 1970 to 1972 the impact of the bombardment had been severe enough. As early as April 1970, a combined aerial and tank attack on the village of Chithou in Sralap subdistrict, Tbaung Khmum district, Kompong Cham, took the lives of two hundred people and killed all of the village's herd.[243] Soon afterwards, in nearby Kandol Chrum, American bombs destroyed six houses and killed seven people. A local peasant recalls: 'As a result of this, some people ran away to live far from the village. Others joined the revolution'.[244] In some cases, on the other hand, the Vietnamese communists were blamed, as the nearest possible culprits, for deaths from bombing by the remote aircraft. But the intended targets were not only communist troops. In September 1970 US intelligence reported: 'It was recently discovered that many of the sixty-six 'training camps' on which FANK had requested air-strikes by early September were in fact merely political indoctrination sessions held in village halls and pagodas.'[245] One casualty was Pol Pot's family home in Kompong Thom, which burnt to the ground after a US bombing raid in July 1970.

The bombings led to large internal population movements. By 1971, 60 per cent of refugees surveyed in the towns of the Khmer Republic gave bombing as the main reason for their displacement.[246] In the same year, another aerial attack on Kompong Cham province took the lives of fifty people in Thmar Pich village, according to a young man who joined the revolution there a few days afterwards.[247] A twenty-year-old CPK company commander told journalists on the Thai border in 1979 how his village in Pursat had been bombed eight years before, killing 200 of its 350 inhabitants and propelling him into a career of violence and absolute loyalty to the CPK, both of which he was proud to recount.[248]

Not all of this was the work of American pilots. The T-28 fleet of the Lon Nol air force, strafing and dropping napalm as well as explosives, took a toll in villages behind communist lines throughout the war. In 1971, T-28s destroyed the rice-mill and houses in Prey Chhor village of Kompong Trabek district in Prey Veng, while two hundred houses were burnt down in nearby Dong village.[249] Kbar Chen village near Oudong (Region 15) lost six civilian inhabitants in a 1971 attack and two more in a second the next year.[250] Such T-28 raids probably struck the greatest number of Kampuchean villages. A peasant from Samrong in Chantrea district of Svay Rieng recalls what he witnessed: 'One day in 1971 a T-28 arrived on reconnaissance and before leaving it fired on people growing rice – they were considered 'VC'. Three planes then returned and dropped napalm. All the trees and many houses were destroyed, and more than ten people killed.' However, the most dramatic incidents involved direct hits by US B-52s. The same peasant recalls: 'Then in 1972 B-52s bombed three times per day, fifteen minutes apart, three planes at a time. They hit houses in Samrong and thirty people were killed. There were no troops in these villages. At that time there were some Vietnamese [communist] troops on the border [nearby], but they didn't bomb the border; they bombed inside it, people's houses. The town of Chantrea was destroyed by US bombs ... The people were angry with the US and that is why so many of them joined the Khmer communists.'[251]

When troops did approach villages, the planes came again. Another peasant from Svay Rieng recalls: 'In 1972 during a fierce battle between North Vietnamese and Thieu troops right in my village, six houses and all the trees were destroyed by napalm. There were no deaths though, because the people had all run away.'[252] Attempts by the communists to avoid the bombing by lodging in villages often proved fruitless. A CIA report describes the destruction, by bombing, of three quarters of the houses in a Kompong Cham village in 1972 – the surving inhabitants expelled the North Vietnamese troops.[253] Not far away in the same province, bombs fell on O Reang Au market for the first time in 1972, killing twenty people.[254]

All but one of these examples from 1972 occurred in the Eastern Zone, where US strategic bombardment was concentrated almost exclusively at the time. But the bombing did not let up there the next year, even though it spread equally intensively

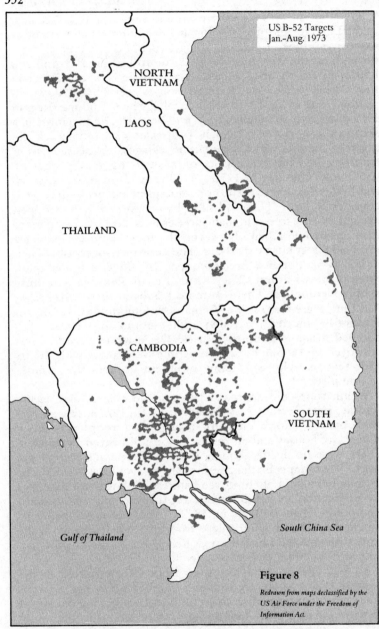

US B-52 Targets
Jan.–Aug. 1973

NORTH
VIETNAM

LAOS

THAILAND

CAMBODIA

SOUTH
VIETNAM

Gulf of Thailand

South China Sea

Figure 8

Redrawn from maps declassified by the
US Air Force under the Freedom of
Information Act.

AMERICA'S 1973 B-52 BOMBING CAMPAIGN

to the rest of the countryside as well (over all Zones but the North-West). O Reang Au was bombed twice more in 1973: the first time, the rice-mill was hit, killing another twenty people, and then it was hit again and completely destroyed along with a number of houses nearby; five more people died, including two monks.[255] Bombs also hit Boeng village in the same vicinity; it was burnt to the ground, and according to peasants from the area many people were caught in their houses and there were 'thousands' of deaths,[256] undoubtedly an exaggeration for a more accurate 'many'. Again in the same district, Chalong village lost over twenty lives when the village and its pagoda were hit by T-28s during a battle. In this case, all the monks escaped unhurt, but an inhabitant notes: 'On the river many monasteries were destroyed by bombs. People in our village were furious with the Americans; they did not know why the Americans had bombed them. Seventy people from Chalong joined the fight against Lon Nol after the bombing.'[257]

In a direct hit on Trey Chap village, Prek Chrey subdistrict, in Prey Veng, a raid by four F-111s killed over twenty people; the village was destroyed and subsequently abandoned. Meanwhile, Lon Nol's T-28s kept up their campaigns. Two kilometres away, Anlong Trea village was napalmed and bombed; three people were killed and four houses destroyed. 'Over sixty people from this village then joined the Khmer Communist army out of anger at the bombing', locals recall.[258]

B-52s also scored a direct hit on Trapeang Krapeu village, Mong Riev subdistrict, Tbaung Khmum district, Kompong Cham. Over twenty people died. Other raids destroyed hundreds of hectares of rubber plantations in the area.[259]

Near Krachap village of Peam Montea subdistrict, Kompong Trabek, in Prey Veng (Region 24), bombs killed five elderly people in 1973. A reconnaissance plane subsequently visiting the area was followed by four Dakota helicopters bringing troops; according to a local peasant woman, 'they drove our cattle away and stole *samputs*, clothes, pots and pans, everything. There was nothing left here.'[260] (As noted earlier in this Chapter, ARVN troops had already killed three of Krachap's inhabitants and stolen three quarters of the cattle herd, in 1970.)

This woman says that in 1973 she had yet to meet a 'Khmer Rouge'. The Region 24 Secretary, Chhouk, was then based in Prey Veng district to the north, in a village which his widow claims was bombed twice a month. '[The pilots] could see motorcycles coming and going and knew that an office was there. While I was there over thirty people were killed by bombs, in their houses, in the trenches, or while running to the trenches. Some entire households were killed in their homes.'[261] A cadre recalls a direct hit on the district office in Komchay Meas, in which forty people were killed. A number of other people who were foraging or trading along the roads also died in raids by B-52s, Phantoms and F-105s, he says.[262] A woman cadre from the same area says a jungle office was bombed ('there were spies inside') in the North of the district in one of many attacks, each of which took several lives.[263] Another cadre, from Memut, further north, says that O Klok village in Tramung subdistrict suffered a direct hit 'right through the village'; thirty people were allegedly killed and over a hundred wounded, and a hundred houses destroyed.[264]

In January and February 1973 the heaviest B-52 bombing was in this area (Region 21). In March it began to spread across the whole country but remained heaviest in the East. From April to June it was most concentrated in the South-Western and Northern Zones; April also saw the heaviest bombing of the North-East. Then in July and August the South-West was carpet-bombed in the most intensive B-52 campaign yet, while tactical bombing raids increased by 21 per cent.[265] The delicate CPK factional balance in the South-West up to that point merits giving close attention to the bombing's impact there.

In Chamcar Ang village, Kus subdistrict, Tram Kak district in Takeo (Region 13), more than eighty people died when B-52s hit a village and its pagoda.[266] In the same region, a CPK cadre recalled that Wat Angrun village was annihilated; only a single family survived, and 120 houses were destroyed. The cadre added: 'The army was not hit all that hard, because at that time we put our lines right up against the enemy, and most of the bombs fell behind us. This was especially true in the case of the B-52s which hit either the people or nothing.'[267] Region 13, of course, was one of the strongholds of the CPK Centre. Mok's son-in-law Khe Muth was Region Deputy Secretary and chief of Tram Kak district. Muth was now promoted to Secretary of the newly organized 3rd Zone Brigade, and his wife, Mok's daughter Khom, became CPK Secretary of Tram Kak.[268]

In Kompong Chhang (Region 31), Mam Lon, the subdistrict cadre who has described the mass organizations there, says that both T-28s and B-52s bombed his village of Prey Thom, in

Kraing Leav subdistrict, Rolea Peir district; more than a hundred people, he says, were killed or wounded. 'The people were very angry at the US imperialists'. Although he draws no connection, he reports that soon afterwards the political line hardened significantly, and a number of cadres, including himself, were soon dismissed.[269] These two examples reflect a general trend in the South-Western Zone, which will be examined in detail later.

In many cases, though, careful digging of trenches by locals was sufficient to prevent deaths. Ampil Tuk village in Oudong district (Region 15) was bombed eight times in 1973: twice by B-52s, four times by US jets, and twice by Lon Nol's T-28s. 'There were wounded but no one was killed because everyone hid in trenches', a villager reports.[270] However a man from the same Region says that, only three days before the bombing was brought to a halt: 'Three F-111s bombed right centre in my village, killing eleven of my family members. My father was wounded but survived. At that time there was not a single soldier in the village or in the area around the village. Twenty-seven other villagers were also killed. They had run into a ditch to hide and then two bombs fell right into it. The bombs seemed to be guided into it like they had eyes.'[271]

Even where no deaths resulted, as in Ampil Tuk, there were frequently subsequent arrests of villagers suspected of being 'spies' who called in the air-strikes, another example of how it was the most proximate potential culprit who took the blame. Paranoia began to plague the communist movement far more intensely than ever before. In the Northern Zone, Kun Chhay, who lived in Sankor village in Kompong Svay district (Region 32) recalls that Ke Pauk's troops now accused the villagers of 'being CIA agents and bringing in the US planes'; the people of Sankor, afraid of both US bombing and Pauk's justice, offered no resistance when Lon Nol's forces penetrated the area, 'pointed guns at us, and told us to leave for Kompong Thom City'.[272]

A CPK infantryman from Region 31 who later defected to the government has provided a vivid account of the impact of the bombing on the movement in the Northern Zone. His first battle was the siege of Kompong Thom City in early 1973, which he says progressed successfully for several months. Towards the end of that period the town's residents began to flee through the battle-lines into the insurgent zones.

But one night ... we heard a terrifying noise which shook the ground; it was as if the earth trembled, rose up and opened beneath our feet. Enormous explosions lit up the sky like huge bolts of lightning: it was the American B-52s.

In the morning we received the order to retreat at the double from Kompong Thom. The countryside was upturned, cratered with huge holes; the trees were smashed to splinters and all our trenches had been disembowelled or buried. Hundreds of our comrades had been killed. We were scarcely better off – we could no longer hear anything, and we could hardly walk straight. With the other survivors we headed by truck towards the forest of the North-West ...

In Siemreap, where Koy Thuon was now apparently based, the soldier found a much more peaceful scene. (Concentrated bombing of the province began only in May 1973.) In one place, peasants, monks, and prosperous petty traders were gathered in the grounds of an ancient temple, which also sheltered a hospital. Nearby was the Lon Nol-held province capital.

Each morning the peasants from the temples went into town by pedicab to sell their fruits and ducks and buy what could be found in the Chinese groceries. Enemy soldiers were also to be seen, dressed in civilian clothes; they came to exchange their guns for rice ... There had been very heavy fighting a year before but now no-one was fighting any more ...

Each side seemed to be waiting and to accept the presence of the adversary. In the evenings, as the sun disappeared behind the trees, the chanting of monks drowned out the noises of the forest and the smoke from incense sticks rose into the air like the mist that emerges from the earth after a heavy rain storm. Here, portraits of Prince Sihanouk were still numerous.[273]

This account seems credible, because Siemreap, and particularly the Angkor temple complex, was the focus of Sihanouk's clandestine visit (down the Ho Chi Minh Trail) to the liberated zones in March 1973; the Prince was welcomed there by Koy Thuon, who made a favourable impression on him.[274] Four years later, after Thuon's execution, the Democratic Kampuchea security services accused him of having held back the revolutionary movement: 'During the five-year period of the national liberation [war], the Koy Thuon group of Zone 304 [the North] created an atmosphere of pacifism, luxury and excitement entertained by art, girls, receptions and festivities; fostered house-alignment and the planting of banana trees along roads ...

[and] gathered tens of thousands of people to dig a canal down from Mt. Koulen, to clear the bush for planting banana trees while giving no thought to the battlefield.'[275] The internecine antagonisms that led to Koy Thuon's 1977 execution were therefore already serious in 1973. The soldier from Region 31 reports that by the year's end:

> There had been conflicts between the civil and military leaders [Koy Thuon and Ke Pauk, respectively] of the [Zone] Organization. The civil leaders claimed that the military offensive had been launched too early, and that its failure had compromised the establishment of the new administration. The military claimed that the civilians' mistakes had broken the patriotic spirit of the population who after the B-52 raids and the retreat of our forces had fled to the other side.
>
> Many villagers, peasants, and officers had been executed and the disorganized Khmer Rouge militias had been fighting one another.[276]

But this was not just a military debacle and consequent recriminations. The political issues at stake were also momentous.

The Hereditary Enemy

Early in 1973, while continuing to wage war against Lon Nol, the CPK began an intensified campaign to drive the Vietnamese communists from the country, in combination with a new purge of Sihanoukists and other dissident 'Third Force' cadres. At public meetings in Kampot, Sihanouk was accused of supporting 'the hated Vietnamese', and both were described as enemies of the same category as Lon Nol. The CPK Secretary of Kampot (Region 35), Kang Chap, told a gathering of monks at this time that Sihanouk was no more than a figurehead.[277] According to a subdistrict cadre in Kompong Speu, Mok rounded up hundreds of dissidents 'from all over the South-West' in 1973; they were allegedly forced to perform hard labour before being executed.[278]

In Region 25, Non Suon organized demonstrations against the Vietnamese as early as January 1973. Local negotiations with them had broken down in December 1972, but the signing of the Paris Agreement the next month foreshadowed a Vietnamese withdrawal in any case, and the 1,200 or so troops stationed in

Region 25 left quickly once the demonstrations began.[279] The Vietnamese likewise withdrew from Region 15 (also in the Special Zone) and from the Amleang area (Region 32) in the South-West. According to a local CPK member: 'The expulsion was organized by Ta Mok. He travelled around the area discussing the matter with district and even village cadres, instructing them to expel the Vietnamese. [Region 15 Secretary, Cheng An] also helped organize this.' The Vietnamese commanders 'agreed in principle' to leave the area, but some units allegedly proved 'stubborn and ... had to be forced out', which resulted in bloodshed. Vietnamese civilian residents were driven out as well.[280] In the North, the Vietnamese troops withdrew completely from Region 31 soon after the Paris Agreement had been signed.[281]

It was also in 1973 that the Centre's campaign to drive out the Vietnamese produced some new echoes in the Eastern Zone. There had been expulsions in Region 21 in 1972, as we have seen, and in Region 20 some CPK cadres had now begun to talk of 'wild chickens trying to scatter the farm chickens'[282] — a reference to foreigners or foreign-trained Khmers usurping their positions. However there was no mention of Vietnam as an 'enemy', and other cadres from Region 20 and Region 24 attribute the Vietnamese withdrawal not to popular or Party pressure, but to the Paris Accords and the fact that 'the Khmer revolution was now sufficiently strong to defend itself'.[283] A third cadre, then a CPK subdistrict chief in Region 20, says he was told by his superiors in this period: 'The Vietnamese must leave because we have our own army now. Our Vietnamese friends helped us fight the US when we did not have an army, and they can now leave as our army is large and our authority has developed.'[284] The withdrawal probably helped head off cadre resentment of the 'wild chickens'. By mid 1973 the number of Vietnamese communists deployed in Kampuchea had fallen to three thousand troops and two thousand political cadres.[285] (A further twenty-seven thousand Vietnamese, stationed along the Ho Chi Minh Trail in the North-East, did not take part in the war against Lon Nol.) The various Khmer communist forces, on the other hand, now numbered more than two hundred thousand, including 175 main force battalions.[286]

The sharp reduction in the Vietnamese communist commitment to the war against Lon Nol was not accompanied by any attempt to organize or co-ordinate from afar the Khmer communists refusing to cooperate with the CPK Centre, or even to 'pull them out' to Vietnam. Rather, the Vietnamese withdrawal signalled in part Hanoi's hope that a reasonable relationship with the CPK Centre could be achieved and preserved; it was, after all, one outcome of the Paris Agreement to which no objection could be expected from that quarter. This Vietnamese strategy entailed the abandonment of long-standing Khmer allies in the interests of placating the Pol Pot leadership. Those allies would now have to either seek an accommodation with the Party Centre, test their strength against it, or withdraw from political life. This fact remains true whether Vietnam's abandonment of them is considered a moral abdication, or an act of respect for Kampuchean independence.

The impact was felt even in Hanoi, where about thirty Khmer veterans remained and were working in various posts, mainly with the NUFK radio station based there and on the Ho Chi Minh Trail near the Vietnamese-Kampuchean border. Other senior cadres in Hanoi included Son Ngoc Minh and Sien An, who was RGNUK (the 'royal' resistance government) ambassador to Vietnam. However as early as 1971-72 Ieng Sary and his wife Ieng Thirith had established their political authority over the Khmers there; Thirith, for instance, was in charge of the radio. Another veteran, Keo Meas, seems to have lost his position as RGNUK ambassador to Beijing as early as March 1972. From that date he was no longer mentioned in radio broadcasts, and this was probably linked with Ieng Sary's arrival in Beijing as 'Special Representative from the Interior' in late 1971. Meas transferred to Hanoi to work under Thirith, and a new ambassador officially assumed the post in February 1973.

Towards the end of 1972, some of the cadres working in Hanoi discovered for the first time that their status in the Party was open to serious doubt. One of them, Pen Sovan, was apparently ordered by Ieng Thirith to compile a list of the names of all Khmers who had spent the Sihanouk period in Hanoi. He did so with the help of one of Thirith's assistants, a woman named Sou, whose husband, like Sovan, was among those listed. Not long afterwards, while Ieng Thirith was ill, Sou showed Sovan the resulting secret CPK report.[287] She also showed it to another veteran, Chea Soth, who claims it read as follows: 'Our Party must take a very great interest in [*yok chet tuk dak*] the revolutionaries who went abroad, or people who were not revolutionaries before but went abroad and absorbed ideas from those places. First are the people who absorbed ideas from Vietnam; second, from China; third, from France. Of these three groups, we must take the greatest interest of all in the people who have lived in Vietnam.'[288]

Around the same time, Son Ngoc Minh was sent to hospital in Beijing on Ieng Sary's request, allegedly because of 'inadequate' treatment he was receiving in Vietnam for high blood pressure. He died soon afterwards, on 22 December 1972.[289] In conjunction with the ominous implications of the CPK's 'interest' in their future, Minh's death came as a severe blow to most of the Khmers in Hanoi at the time. Keo Chenda, for instance, felt that 'there was no longer a leader'. (Chenda claims, too, that in this period he opposed the progressive dismantling of the United Front by the Party Centre; as a matter of political necessity, in his view, victory had to be won 'with Prince Sihanouk'.) Chenda, Sovan, and a small number of other cadres resigned from the broadcasting service on 1 January 1973, and claim to have immediately formed 'a new party'. Although they were soon joined by Chea Soth and several others, this 'party' was simply ignored by the Vietnamese. Further, according to Chenda, Keo Meas told the group that 'he sympathized with us but that we could not succeed in defeating the Party'. Afraid to return to Kampuchea, the dissidents soon resigned themselves to what became five years of political inactivity. Most seem to have taken low-level jobs in the Hanoi bureaucracy, but some who defected from the border area found themselves taking up farming in NLF zones of South Vietnam.[290] Ironically, the CPK was later to repay the Vietnamese for abandoning their closest Khmer allies, to its own profit, by charging that Hanoi 'entered into negotiations in 1973 in an attempt to swallow us'.[291]

It is true that the reason usually given by CPK leaders for the intensified hostility towards the Vietnamese in 1973 was their attempt, flowing from the Paris talks with the US, to get the CPK to negotiate with Lon Nol. In Kompong Speu, a subdistrict cadre reports, 'Mok told us that there had been three countries fighting the imperialists together. "Now Vietnam and Laos have negotiated with the US. Kampuchea will not." He said all cadres had to be instructed that Kampuchea would not negotiate.'[292] This speech was made two weeks after the new US bombing campaign began. The cadre who attended the meeting says that his own village had just been destroyed by B-52s, with the loss of three lives. He continues: 'And Mok said that the US had previously divided its bombing between Vietnam, Laos and Kampuchea. But now that the other two had gone to negotiate, the US was bringing all its bombs to drop on Kampuchea alone, twenty-four hours a day, *because it did not negotiate.*'[293] On the other hand, in Region 13 (Takeo), South-Western Zone cadres were proclaiming somewhat contradictorily that 'negotiations ... would lead only to a prolongation of the war'. The real point was the alleged Vietnamese perfidy, and the notion that, in the words of these cadres, CPK refusal to negotiate 'would demonstrate to the world that our Khmer Organization was independent'. Mok preferred not to stress that the Vietnamese were withdrawing from the country, or that, as was well known in the Party, 'some of our friends like China also wanted us to negotiate'.[294] One may admire the political courage of Mok and the CPK Centre, but to isolate and expose their country, alone in Asia, to the might of the American war machine was a costly decision for its people. The CPK can hardly be blamed for the bombing itself, but it is unlikely to have occurred in the event of a negotiated cease-fire like that in Laos.

The Centre may have expected the bombing indirectly to serve its aims by inflaming hatred of the Vietnamese, and as we have seen this did occur in a number of cases. But the hatred often had to be conjured up by stressing more remote issues. A woman from Region 33, for example, says that Vietnamese troops were camped 'in the forest west of my house' throughout 1973. They behaved well and created no problems, and the villagers talked without strain of solidarity, she says. But when they left at the end of the year, the CPK subdistrict chief began to talk of 'mutual enmity' between the two peoples,[295] probably following local Party documents which referred to the Vietnamese as the 'hereditary enemy' (*satrev suorpouc*) and the 'acute enemy' (*satrev sruoch*).[296]

A Hanoi-trained cadre, Yos Por, recalls a meeting in Kampot in late 1973, which was addressed by Mok and the CPK Secretary of Region 35, Kang Chap. 'They collected all of us who had studied abroad, at Wat Chhouk, and started to accuse us and Son Ngoc Minh of selling the territory to Vietnam. We had had an easy time in Vietnam, they said, and had returned home only 'after liberation'. They were instigating the breaking of solidarity with Vietnam, talking in terms of history [*prowatisat*]. Mok said that Kampuchean territory was wherever there are sugar-palms. This included Kampuchea Krom [the Mekong Delta], which

Vietnam had taken. The Kampucheans would fight to get it back, Mok said.'[297] Within months, the CPK district chief of Rolea Peir in Kompong Chhnang (Region 31), told his subordinates: 'Kampuchea Krom must be liberated; it was once Khmer territory and we have lost it all. If we do not fight the Vietnamese, we will lose the rest of our country ... Vietnam is the most acute enemy [*satrev sruoch bompot*], the hereditary enemy [*satrev suorpouc*]. After victory we aim to go and liberate Kampuchea Krom.'[298]

Underlying the anti-Vietnamese position, then, was the CPK's revival of a national chauvinism described in Chapter One. Defeat of the US and Lon Nol was only a step towards the national and racial grandeur of which young members of the traditional elite had long dreamed. In rural warlords like Mok and Pauk, the former members of the upper classes who made up the CPK Centre now had the means to put their dreams into effect.

However, there was a range of views on this issue at senior levels in the Party. For instance, in Region 13 (Takeo), according to a local cadre, 'The line was that there were two kinds of enemies; acute and non-acute enemies, and that the Vietnamese were not yet our acute enemy, which was the US-Lon Nol. But at the time, it was said that [communist] Vietnam was the No. 2 enemy.'[299] Chou Chet, for his part, did raise the subject of Kampuchea Krom, but in quite a different context — opposition to the Thieu regime and the American presence in Vietnam.[300] In the Eastern Zone, Tiv Ol addressed a six-week political study-meeting organized by So Phim in Region 21 in late 1973; he raised the issue of differences with Vietnam — the first time that many of the Eastern cadres in attendance had heard of them. He claimed that Chinese supplies coming down the Ho Chi Minh Trail destined for Kampuchea were being kept by the Vietnamese or exchanged for out-of-date equipment. He also recalled the failure of the Vietnamese to supply guns to the CPK in 1968. These issues were identified as 'problems', according to a participant, but 'Vietnam was not described as a strategic enemy — it was still a friend ... Tiv Ol said China was a good friend, while Vietnam was a friend, but not very loyal'.[301] So Phim, apparently, did not express an opinion on the matter at this point, although he probably shared that of Tiv Ol. His views, at any rate, like those of Chou Chet, were certainly far from those of Mok, and it would be many years before Eastern cadres would be exhorted to liberate Kampuchea Krom.

But there was one sign of apparent change in Phim's attitude. In September 1973, the Eastern Zone 'Military Political Service' published the Party History, in celebration of its 22nd Anniversary, which has been referred to in earlier chapters. It contains the following interesting passage about the 'Third Force' (*kamlang ti bey*), that is, the Hanoi-trained Khmers and the Sihanoukists; 'The Party took the position of strength, attacking finally and chasing absolutely the Third Force which was the obstacle; this Third Force tended to split our country's political forces in three or four directions.'[302] There are two points worth noting here. Firstly, the Third Force is considered an obstacle to unity, rather than an enemy (acute or otherwise). This suggests yet another Eastern deferral to the CPK Centre, probably out of Party loyalty and concern for unity as much as out of conviction; at the same time, the passage notes the potential or actual political following of the Third Force (and the tradition of solidarity with Vietnam, discussed below). Secondly, although by this point there are reports of the downgrading of Sihanouk, and even of clashes with the Vietnamese in parts of the East,[303] Hanoi-trained Khmer cadres there had by no means been 'attacked finally and chased absolutely': we know from other sources that many such cadres still occupied important posts in the Zone at that time.[304] This definitive statement that the problem no longer existed may in fact represent an argument *against* purging them.

This contrasts with the situation in the South-West, where as we have seen, executions of Hanoi-trained cadres had begun as early as late 1971 (in Region 13), and almost all had been purged over the next two years. Moreover, in November 1973, armed clashes broke out between communist units on the border of the Eastern and South-Western Zones. Describing these at the time, Quinn wrote that 'the two factions were at each other's throats'. The South-Western Zone forces demanded that Eastern units in Region 24, probably commanded by Chan Saman, 'terminate their policy of cooperating with the Viet Cong and North Vietnamese'. The leading Region 24 cadres (actually led by Chhouk), refused; 'the discussion grew heated, and a fire-fight ensued'. With Vietnamese help, the Region 24 troops killed forty-two South-Western Zone soldiers and drove the rest off.[305] Clashes across the Mekong between Chakrey's 1st Eastern Zone Brigade and the 11th South-Western Zone Brigade continued

Figure 9   Differing Versions of CPK History, 1973 and 1974

EASTERN ZONE

Summary of Annotated Party History

by the Eastern Zone Military Political Service, September 1973.

1. 'After World War II, followed by the second invasion of Indo-China (including our country) by the French...'

2. 'There were then few proletarians in our country. So their struggle was weak.'

3. 'Proletarian class Marxism-Leninism was injected into our revolutionary movement by the international communist movement and the Vietnamese communists. It is certain that our communist combatants were a number of Cambodians who were trained in the Indo-Chinese Communist Party, about forty men in 1951; in the French Communist Party, ten men in 1951; and in the Thai Communist Party, three or four men in 1951.'

4. 'These Cambodian communists took the following path...'

5. 'To give impulsion to the revolutionary movement of our people, especially the farmers, against the French imperialists, with the firm support of the Indo-Chinese Communist Party (new name: Vietnam Lao Dong Party) we held a conference in 1951...'

6. 'In 1951 a Party propagation and formation committee was set up, made up of (Comrades Ng.M., S.H., T.S.M. and Ch.S.M.)'*

PARTY CENTRE

History of the Communist Party of Kampuchea

by Ieng Sary, distributed to cadres in Hanoi, September 1974. (emphasis added).

'After World War II, followed by the second invasion of Kampuchea (and all Indo-China) by the French ...

'There were then *very*·few proletarians in our country. So their struggle was *very* weak.'

'Proletarian class Marxism–Leninism was injected into our revolutionary movement by the international communist movement.'

(deleted)

'The following path was taken ...'

'To give impulsion to the revolutionary movement of our people, especially the farmers, against the French imperialists *and their lackeys*

(deleted)

we held a conference in 1951 ...'

'In 1951 a Party propagation and formation committee was set up.'

(deleted)

7. 'Then a Congress of representatives from the whole country was organized in order to form a just and durable Party.'

'It was decided that when conditions were ripe a Congress of representatives from the whole country would be organized in order to decide to organize a definite and full-fledged Party.'

8. 'The Party was formed little by little, adopting the following two factors: it was a people's revolutionary movement of all social levels, above all the farmers; and education in proletarian-class Marxism-Leninism by the nucleus trained in the Indo-Chinese, French, and Thai Communist Parties and with the support of the Vietnamese Communist Party.'

'The Party was formed little by little, adopting the following two factors: it was firstly a people's revolutionary movement of all social levels, above all the farmers; and secondly, the spread of proletarian-class Marxism-Leninism among the people, especially our peasant people.'

9. 'The conditions for the formation of the Party in our country were not different in principle from those of the revolutions which formed the world's Marxist-Leninist Parties. To the best of our knowledge of France, England, the USSR, China, Vietnam, etc., all followed the same principle of revolution, that is, the people's revolutionary movement; and the people are the workers (in the industrial countries) or farmers (in the underdeveloped agricultural countries).

The formation of the Party was certainly according to Marx and Engels's 'Manifesto of the Communist Party', Lenin's disciples' Party, the Great October Socialist Revolution, China's People's Democratic Revolution, and revolution throughout the world.

During the period from 1951 to 1954, our Party developed the qualities to build the Party bit by bit. It directed the revolutionary movement little by little.

(deleted)

It surmounted obstacles to win victory over the French imperialists and their lackeys at the 1954 Geneva Conference, with the Party and people of Vietnam, Laos and the entire world.'

(deleted)

10. 'After the 1954 Geneva Conference, a temporary Central Committee, not in conformity with the Party's conditions, was set up. It was composed of S.H., T.S.M., Ng.M., S.V. [So Vanna alias So Phim], and N.T.Nh., with Sieu Heng as Secretary. After Geneva, we transformed armed struggle into political struggle. Our Party engaged in political struggle with the enemy.'

'After the 1954 Geneva Conference ended the First Indo-China War,

(deleted)

we transformed armed struggle into political struggle. Our Party engaged in *life-and-death* struggle with the enemy.'

11. 'However, our Party, only three years old, lacked the following three things: ideology, policy and organizaiton.'

'However, our Party, only three years old, lacked the following three things: ideology, policy and organization, *and that is why we encountered such great difficulties*.'

12. 'This gave rise to a rural committee, responsible for rural action throughout the country. It was composed of three persons, with Sieu Heng as chairman. The urban committee, secretly or overtly reponsible for all cities throughout the country, was composed of four persons, with Comrade T.S.M. as chairman.

(deleted)

13. 'From the end of 1954 to 1959, the committee in charge of the urban movement, with T.S.M. as chairman, continued its revolutionary activities against the enemy either secretly or overtly.'

'In the cities from the end of 1954 to 1959, we progressively built up the Party in political consciousness and in organization ...'

14. 'The committee in charge of the urban movement was named the committee in charge of the country's general affairs. It was composed of four persons, with Comrade T.S.M. as chairman.'

(deleted)

15. 'It had . . . to organize the Second Congress [of the Party in 1960].'

'The First Congress had to be organized.'

16. 'The Second Congress approved a political line, strategy, tactics and Marxist-Leninist statutes for the Party. It decided to form the Marxist-Leninist Party in Kampuchea, to wage the Kampuchean revolution continually, and to form a Party Central Committee plenipotentiary (?) [as published] to operate as leader. This committee was composed of eight persons, with Comrade T.S.M. as Secretary.'

'The First Congress approved a political line, strategy and tactics for the Party, and decided to form the Marxist-Leninist Party in Kampuchea, to wage the Kampuchean revolution continually, and to form a Party Central Committee plenipotentiary to operate as leader.'

(deleted)

17. 'On 20 July 1962 ... Comrade T.S.M., Secretary of the Party, was kidnapped by the enemy, leaving no trace. This was great grief for the Party which had just been reorganized.'

(deleted)

18. 'At the beginning of 1963, on the 20 and 21 February, the Third Party Congress was opened to study past activities and draw experiences from them in order to rectify and improve the political line, strategy, tactics, and Party statutes, and to approve a decision for a new operational direction which would correspond to the situation at that moment.'

'From the 20 to 21 February 1963, the Second Party Congress was opened. It studied past activities and drew experiences from them in order to rectify and improve the political line, strategy, tactics, and statutes, approved a decision for a new operational direction *and organized a new Central Committee* which corresponded to the concrete situation at that moment.'

NB.: Prowatt Pak ('The Party History') distributed by Ieng Sary in Hanoi in January 1971, renders this section as follows: 'On 20 and 21 February 1963, the Congress decided on the Party's programme, strategy and tactics, approved the decision of the Party, and decided to choose *a new Comrade Party Secretary*.'

★ (Son) Ngoc Minh, Sieu Heng, Tou Samouth and Chan Samay.

368

until the end of the war.[306]

Symbolizing the political differences between the Eastern Zone and the CPK Centre, is the fate of the Zone's Party History. When the Centre (through Ieng Sary) issued a Party History to celebrate its 23rd Anniversary in September 1974, much of it was an exact copy of the previous year's Eastern Zone version. However, all references to the history of solidarity with Vietnam were now deleted (as well as references to the Party's previous leaders who had followed such a policy).[307]

The Democratic Revolution, 1973–75

The Class Enemy

On 20 May 1973, as the US bombardment approached its peak, the CPK Centre launched a 'cooperativization' programme which initially involved organizing peasants into groups of ten, twenty or thirty families. This had already occurred in many areas, but now land was to be collectivized as well and the produce of the peasants' labour was to be confiscated by the authorities. In some cases, regulations concerning the destruction of religion and family life, and enforced communal eating were also implemented. This was termed the 'Democratic Revolution'.[308]

It seems clear that the increased demands of the CPK armed forces, resulting from the bombing, were partly what motivated this campaign. A CPK document dated February 1974 gave one reason for it as follows: 'Our country is at war and no mercy has been shown us. Therefore, many of our young people have gone off to the battlefield, and only the old and women are left.'[309] A CPK member later explained that by ensuring a minimum subsistence for all villagers, through collection and rationing of supplies, the communists could 'release forces' for the army and its logistical needs, notably the able-bodied who in theory were no longer needed to support their families.[310]

However, both these sources also gave a second reason, an ideological one. In the words of the CPK document: 'We must construct a clean, honest society'. What this meant was to be explained in an August 1975 issue of the internal CPK magazine, *Tung Padevat* ('Revolutionary Flags'). Its author expressed ambivalence concerning the pre-1973 situation: 'There was progress on the one hand, and the same old society on the other.

. . The state confiscated land from the traitors. . . and took control of it. . . This was a good point. . . [Secondly, however] those in possession of the land continued to keep their private ownership. Furthermore previously landless peasants, and previously landless workers now received land from the state. Therefore, land remained in private ownership in general'. This picture conforms with that available from other sources concerning the 1970-73 period, and the then popularity of the revolution. But a mixture of progress and 'the same old society' was not good enough for the CPK. The May 1973 establishment of the 'cooperatives', especially in wartime, was a break with communist practice in other countries. This was justified rather lamely, in the same article, by the suggestion that Kampuchea alone had developed a comprador class of traders: 'According to past world experience, it was common. . . to use the private sector, to use their forces. But in Kampuchea, they refused to work, because to some extent the capitalists underwent a change in their features. They transmuted and became comprador.' The allegedly unique Khmer compradors were so powerful in the liberated areas that 'Our state was their satellite'. The extreme sensitivity underlying this statement is also evident in the example given. Until 1973, we are told, 'Kratie township showed the same signs as in the old society. Honda motorcycles were speeding up and down the streets like before, while our ragged guerrillas walked in the dust. This showed that they were still the masters. . . They distributed things to the people, mostly commercial equipment. If we had followed that road, we could have gone nowhere.'[311]

So the Party Centre had to ensure that 'the state controlled everything'. Kratie was evacuated. There was to be 'no more trading, mortgaging, labour-exchanging or buying on credit'. A 'state' monopoly was decreed over rice, salt, fuel, cloth and petrol. Without petrol, private owners of trucks, boats and tractors (and presumably Honda motorcycles) 'disappeared'; the CPK state took over their equipment. More importantly, private ownership of land and of the means of production was also abolished. Needless to say, these measures were not approved beforehand by a party Congress, or even by a Central Committee meeting.

The political motivation for all this is underlined by the words of a former Eastern Zone CPK member from Region 21, who attributes the changes to heightened revolutionary zeal resulting from the progress the Party had made thus far: 'The reason was that the people supported the Khmer Reds, so the Khmer Reds decided to move on to higher-stage cooperatives'.[312] Given somewhat more than an inch by their association with Sihanouk, their aid from the Vietnamese communists, and the popular reaction to the US bombing, it seems that the Party Centre now decided to take a mile. Popular approval of relatively moderate policies became an excuse for extremist ones.

The accounts of two peasants from different parts of the country illustrate this, and undermine the claim that the cooperatives provided a better means of ensuring the subsistence of villagers. Nem, aged 46, from Kompong Chhnang (Region 31) in the South-West Zone, says that the mutual-aid terms introduced in 1972 were popular in his village; each person earned a set ration of 12 *thang* (300 kg) of paddy per year, which he says was adequate. But in late 1973, cooperatives were organized, and Nem became a cook in the communal eating hall. Rations were insufficient, popular disenchantment rose, and within a year villagers were being executed for stealing food from the common store.[313] Sang, aged 43, a peasant from Region 22 in the Eastern Zone, recalls:

> In 1972 mutual-aid teams were formed. [Land remained privately owned.] Rice production was then very high, and the living conditions of the people were really prosperous. . . The rich and poor helped one another, and production was divided up so that most of the people got most of the produce. We could raise and eat our own poultry, and so on. The poor had enough to eat, and some left over as well. If they were strong [workers] they got even more than the rich people in the old days. It was easy, no problems. . .
>
> Then in 1973 the cooperatives were formed, and difficulties began. The rice was stored in collective warehouses, and food ran short. Eventually people ate only rice gruel, with salt, water and banana stalks. We had to get permission to raise our own poultry, under pain of imprisonment.

Importantly, though, Sang noted that in Region 22 the cooperatives were not established 'all at once' in mid 1973. Rather, the local Party leaders 'selected certain good places, with good cadres' to start with, 'for fear of popular reaction', and the process was not complete even two years later, when communal eating was finally instituted. Sang described the CPK district and subdistrict chiefs up to that time in favourable terms.[314] Three villagers were imprisoned in 1974, but he reported no executions or starvation.[315] It is hard to believe that the cooperatives could have been established at all without both some degree of public confidence in the local leaders, and the fact that 'people in our village were furious with the Americans'. It was in Sang's village, Chalong, that over twenty people died in a T–28 bombardment in 1973, and seventy others immediately joined the communist army. However, this was an Eastern Zone village, and the CPK response elsewhere was far more dramatic.

The Northern Zone

After the bombing had been brought to a halt in August 1973, the soldier from Region 31 returned with his unit to Kompong Thom to find that while they had been in Siemreap, the population movement into the countryside had reversed. Fifty thousand peasants had now fled into Kompong Thom town; 'the countryside was deserted, the villages empty', the soldier recalls. This was not just because of the US bombardment of the countryside, which had stopped, or because of aggressive Lon Nol army patrolling, which had resumed. It was also because the CPK Zone military commander Ke Pauk, and probably Pol Pot's wife Khieu Ponnary (who in July 1973 was reported to have become Party Secretary of Kompong Thom[316]) had fully implemented the Democratic Revolution in Region 31. The soldier continues: 'In the Kompong Thom region the Organization [was] led by very severe men [*sic*]. . . Their discipline was terrible; there were many executions. . . Buddha statues were destroyed and pagodas secularized. . . youths forced to work very hard, especially when the villages had been reorganized and rebuilt; the Organization had not allowed the construction of individual houses; there were camps for women, children, young women and young men; meals were eaten communally and rations consisted only of rice soup without meat. . . children were forbidden to respect their parents, monks to pray, husbands to live with their wives.'[317]

In September 1973, CPK troops from Region 31 seized half of Kompong Cham city and penetrated to within a hundred metres of the governor's residence. When they withdrew, they took fifteen thousand townspeople into the countryside with them.[318]

In February 1974, Pauk's troops were committed to a drive

against Oudong and Phnom Penh, and thousands more peasants took the opportunity to flee into the Lon Nol-held province capital of Kompong Thom. Their accounts, particularly of low food rations, confirm the soldier's description. 'We were forced to work very hard, and got nothing', one of them, a former village chief, told journalist Donald Kirk soon afterwards. The wearing of black clothing had now become compulsory, and the death penalty was commonly applied, particularly for evasion of the CPK draft. Those put in charge of villages were now chosen because they were 'poor and ignorant'.[319] This description may partly reflect the bitterness of a man deprived of his traditional status; but it is unlikely that the majority of peasants, neither poor nor ignorant in the sense implied,[320] were better served by such an upheaval, even though the new opportunities and power, given to the previously most downtrodden minority, do help to explain the fanaticism of the Democratic Revolution.

The same village chief provided a further insight into the changes, which began, he said, the month after Sihanouk's visit to Siemreap. 'In April of 1973 they stopped talking about Sihanouk. . . They said that he was 'not the only man', that he was 'no good now' and that we 'do not need him any more'. . . If you still use his name and support Sihanouk, then you will be sent away, and you will never return. . . [We were told to] 'support Khieu Samphan and no others'.'[321] In Region 31, the 'state' of Democratic Kampuchea (DK) had emerged fully-grown. (And when that state was officially proclaimed in January 1976, Sihanouk was quickly replaced as Head of State by Khieu Samphan.)[322]

The corollary developments within the party are described by Pon, the former student who had been working with the Vietnamese communists in Kompong Thom since 1970. Pon reports that towards the end of 1972, after a request from Ieng Sary, the Vietnamese asked the Khmers working with them in the area if they wished to transfer to CPK units. Most volunteered to do so, but not long afterwards two of them returned with the news that the others had been executed because they allegedly had 'Vietnamese minds'. Pon concluded that the time had come for him to leave the movement. The Vietnamese were now being attacked 'every day' along the roads, by CPK forces; they had decided to withdraw, and asked Pon to accompany them to South Vietnam. Disillusioned with them, and perhaps afraid of CPK reprisals, he refused, and so a Vietnamese driver took him most of the way back to his native village; he then went on to Phnom Penh. Three of his Khmer comrades, however, did agree to go to Vietnam,[323] where they probably joined a force known as the *Khmer Sor* ('White Khmers'), who fought alongside the Vietnamese in the border regions until 1975, by which time they represented all that formally remained of the *Khmer Rumdos*. (Some of them returned to Kampuchea, again alongside the Vietnamese army, in 1979.)

Early in 1974, two Hanoi-trained Khmer veterans defected to the Lon Nol regime from Region 31. They confirmed that the Vietnamese had left the area after the 1973 Paris Agreement, and said they feared for their lives — thirty of their comrades had been executed by CPK units in Region 31 alone.[324] Another, Taing Sarim, a member of the Region Party Committee, had fled to Vietnam in late 1973 after he had been criticized and excluded from political responsibility. Sarim later recalled how another of the Hanoi-trained veterans, Rotana Keo, a battalion commander in Kompong Thom, had reproached CPK cadres for neglecting the living conditions of their troops and for nepotism. 'Rotana Keo was called to a meeting and murdered along the way.'[325] (Sarim, on the other hand, survived to become Minister of Commerce of the People's Republic of Kampuchea in 1979.)

Changes were also afoot in Siemreap. Leav Keo Moni, the Hanoi-trained veteran Issarak who had taken charge of Srei Snam disrict in 1970, died of natural causes, it seems, in late 1972, and was replaced by a much younger man. Before Moni's death, local communists had carried out their first executions — of Lon Nol soldiers, previously captured and released, who had rejoined Lon Nol's army. The communists also began burning houses and forcibly regrouping the population away from the front lines; but according to the local Lon Nol district chief, speaking in 1979, they 'rarely killed civilians'. Moni's death and the increased bombing, however, were followed in 1973 by large-scale executions of 'all' captured Lon Nol troops and militia, and also of traders, the district chief reports. 'The communists now began to evacuate whole villages, with livestock, and compile records about everyone. Rich people had to do forced labour.' At the same time, fighting broke out between the Khmer and Vietnamese communists, and the inhabitants were forbidden to give food or aid to the Vietnamese.[326]

In Kompong Kdei district in the same province, as we have seen, during 1972 the inhabitants planted banana trees for a couple of hours a day, but were otherwise allowed to carry out trade and to conduct relatively normal lives. However, some bombing of the area had already begun; and although the digging of trenches kept the number of deaths low, the appearance of US planes still inspired great fear. According to the Kompong Kdei woman quoted earlier: 'At the time it was not so hard working under the Khmer Rouge; we were afraid only of dying under the bombs.' Here as elsewhere, intensification of the US aerial campaign was accompanied by a significant hardening of communist policy. B-52 bombing of the area began in March 1973, and in that month, according to the woman, Kompong Kdei was forcibly evacuated and the market closed down; the town's one thousand families, now labelled 'upper class' (*vanna kphuos*), were sent into the forest to clear land for farming. Work was collective, organized in twelve-family groups, and the harvests were confiscated to feed the increased requirements of the army. 'They only left us with what we managed to hide away', the woman recalls.[327]

However, it is worth noting that in Region 32, between Siemreap and Kompong Thom, policies remained relatively moderate, similar to those later ascribed to Koy Thuon by the CPK security apparatus. There were 'village trading cooperatives', but communal eating was not instituted even after mid 1974 when money was abolished. At least eleven Hanoi-trained Khmers retained military positions there (but none held political authority) until the end of the war.[328]

The North-Eastern Zone

Because of its remoteness and scattered population, little is known about developments in the North-East. Ith Sarin reported in 1973 that for strategic reasons the Zone was 'under the direct administration' of the CPK Centre.[329] The cooperativization programme may have been particularly inimical to the tribal populations, and in combination with the influence of Vietnamese-trained local cadres, this may have been responsible for a communist mutiny there in 1973. According to the *Livre Noir*, as we have seen, there had been 'a certain amount of grafting' of a 'parallel state power' in the Zone in 1970-71. Vietnamese sources claim that the Deputy CPK Secretary of Rattanakiri province (Region 102), Bun Mi, and the Zone military commander and his Staff Assistant, Bou Thong and Soy

Keo (both of whom had spent the 1954–70 period in Vietnam), led a popular rebellion in Voeunsai district in 1973.[330] They were unsuccessful, and the three withdrew to the Vietnamese border, where they remained, apparently inactive, for five years. In 1974 they were joined by another Hanoi-trained cadre, Nou Beng, from Stung Treng (Region 104). The unrest may account for Ney Sarann's appointment as Zone party Secretary,[331] with Um Neng as his deputy (in 1974). These two senior Pracheachon figures may have been considered capable of preventing further defections of veteran cadres, such as Chea Keo, who was then Party Secretary of Stung Treng. Kratie province became an Autonomous Sector (Region 505), and the North-East in general receded in strategic significance for the Centre as CPK forces closed in on Phnom Penh.[332]

The South-Western Zone

But it was the South-Western Zone that saw the greatest convulsions in the revolutionary ranks. 1973 was the year that the Mok-Thuch Rin tendency, closely allied with the CPK Centre, established its supremacy over Prasith, Chou Chet and their more moderate colleagues, and completely eclipsed the Hanoi-trained Khmers throughout the Zone.

The first high-ranking victim was apparently Sangha Hoeun, an Issarak veteran and a member of the Zone Committee. A former monk from Kompong Speu (Region 33), who joined the communists in 1970, recalls:

> In 1971-72 the revolution was good; the people were not worried at all. Sangha Hoeun was friendly with the Vietnamese and never had any trouble with them. And the people liked Sanga Hoeun a lot because he sponsored theatre performances with national traditional music. Also, there were plenty of Lon Nol soldiers and intellectuals who came to the liberated zones from Phnom Penh and the province capitals, to join the revolution. Sangha Hoeun and Chou Chet re-educated and taught these people. I saw this; they did not kill them. But Mok did kill such people, and he became angry with what the other two were doing. There was a power struggle [*tumnos amnach*].
>
> In 1973 the killings began. At first there were transfers of subdistrict and Region cadres. Then Chou Chet and his followers fought with Mok's followers, at a combined Zone and Region meeting in our subdistrict, which I helped organize. The fight broke out over politics and theory, in the middle of the meeting.

Chou Chet then left for the West to discuss the question of the executions of the Lon Nol soldiers. Phouk Chhay went with him. I was told they were transferred to Koh Kong.[333]

Two weeks later, Sangha Hoeun was arrested by Mok's troops. At first they took him under guard to our village for a day and a night, and then to the Centre or Zone [headquarters]. Five trucks came to take his followers to Kompong Chhnang.[334]

Kenneth Quinn reports that in 1973 Chou Chet 'had his authority and influence. . . reduced because of his pro-NVA [North Vietnam Army] and pro-Sihanouk stands and, in fact, was even ambushed and slightly wounded by the KK [CPK forces] once in late November while travelling with some NVA soldiers on Route 16'.[335]

After his arrival in Kompong Chhnang (Region 31), Chou Chet continued to stress solidarity with the Vietnamese at political meetings.[336] A *Yuvakok* member in Upper Kompong Tralach district there claims that because Chet was an 'intellectual' he was in constant conflict with a 'forest' revolutionary like Mok. Further, despite their own experience at Sihanouk's hands in the 1960s, Chet and others like Phouk Chhay (and Koy Thuon) appreciated Sihanouk's appeal, even if to them he was only a figurehead. The *Yuvakok* member in fact says that 'the people believed in Sihanouk more than in the revolution'; problems arose when the Party began to criticize the Prince openly, and Mok's response was to impose his authority by force: 'Mok was cruel ever since 1971-72. Unlike Chou Chet and Phouk Chhay, he was fierce, a killer. The killings began in 1973, as the bombs were falling. Also, some prisoners of war were executed, and others put in re-education centres. 1973 was the year the US began bombing [the area] with B-52s, so they had to fight back hard. The killings were in accordance with regulations. This was called "strengthening the Democratic Revolution" [*bangrin padevat procheathipateiy*]. No one dared resist the changes. I know for sure, from friends who worked directly with Mok, that he was the one who ordered the killings. They took place in the forest. . . Mok had the power but he did not have much understanding of politics. Phouk Chhay was educating him [but] there was conflict between the 'forest resistance', people like Mok, and the 'internal [urban] resistance', people like Phouk Chhay who had recently arrived, since 1970.'[337]

Here again the latter seem to have lost out. The Secretary of Region 31, Chan, was replaced in 1973 by Sarun (who was still loyal to the Party Centre eight years later.) A campaign criticizing Sihanouk was launched, and according to the local subdistrict cadre Mam Lon, there was a 'change in the political line'. Lon was expelled from the Party in October, and soon afterwards one of his comrades in the *Yuvakok* was executed along with three other local officials.[338]

Quinn, who was monitoring developments in the South-Western Zone from across the Vietnamese border, reports that local elections were no longer held in the areas newly seized from the Lon Nol government; from 1973, he says, village chiefs and subdistrict officials were appointed by CPK district committees. The number of Buddhist festivals was reduced to two each year, and Cham Muslim ones were 'totally forbidden'. In Kampot in July, each Buddhist *wat* was ordered to supply ten monks to serve as infantrymen in the army's depleted ranks. Soon afterwards, in both Takeo and Kampot (Regions 13 and 35), all but four monks in each *wat* were drafted, which Quinn notes 'decimated the monk population' there. At the same time, local towns such as Ang Tasom and Kompong Trach were evacuated, and in rural areas a 'large-scale re-location process' was implemented — twenty thousand people were moved out of their villages in two districts of Kampot alone. Quinn continues: 'In parts of Takeo and Kampot, the Khmer Communists brought in a large number of new cadres to implement this programme, having lost faith in many older cadres whom they considered to be either pro-North Vietnamese or not tough enough to carry it out.'[339] Although there was no sign of such developments in Non Suon's Region 25 (Kandal), July 1973 also saw the defection to the Lon Nol regime of the Khmer communist military commander of Region 38 (Kompong Speu), who had undergone training in Hanoi in 1971.[340] (Two Khmer veterans who had spent the years 1954–70 in Vietnam, also defected in 1973, the first to do so since 1971.)

Popular unrest was also mounting. Quinn reports that fighting broke out between rival communist units in the South-West in November 1973, only three days after the clashes on the border with the Eastern Zone. He cites three incidents in Kampot (Region 35) of popular and military reaction to attempts by CPK cadres to forcibly re-locate the population and confiscate rice harvests. In one case, *Khmer Rumdos* forces 'rallied about five hundred villagers to come to their aid, and, armed with scythes, machetes and hatchets, drove the KK [*Khmer Krahom*, or official

CPK forces] off, killing nine and wounding twenty'. A fourth clash in the same area in December saw a hundred people killed and wounded, and by January 1974 'a large pro-Sihanouk force was reported manoeuvring to gain control of all of Route 16 from Tani to Tuk Meas, as well as part of Route 205 east of Tani'.[341]

In March 1974, 742 *Khmer Rumdos* surrendered to the Lon Nol regime in Region 37. They claimed to represent a total force of ten thousand who were ready to follow them if Lon Nol granted them operational autonomy to continue their fight against their CPK rivals. They were refused.[342]

(Lon Nol's own position was becoming increasingly insecure as well. March 1973 had seen an entire battalion of his troops defect to the communist side in Region 33. They had not been paid for four months, victims of the rapacious corruption that US aid had fostered and that was threatening Nol's regime with political disintegration from within. In the same month, according to William Shawcross, 'the Lon Nol government had reached its nadir'. The Marshal introduced conscription, and, after students blamed his brother Lon Non for the deaths of two of their number when secret police agents threw grenades into a meeting, he declared a state of siege.[343] Massive student demonstrations and teacher strikes in this period no doubt confirmed the CPK Centre's confidence in the 'petty bourgeoisie' in the towns, but other social movements were developing as well. In mid 1973 Associated Press (AP) reported: 'Some forty thousand production workers and coolies locked themselves in forty factories Monday and continued their sit-in Tuesday, refusing to admit the management. . . The struck factories included the partly American-owned firms of Pepsi-Cola, Esso, Caltex and Shell, the Danish-Australian-Khmer holding company Commin Khmer, and the Khmer-Australian Sokilait Dairies.' In an interview, Hy Serei, General Secretary of the 'Khmer Syndicate of Workers and Peasants', told AP that the workers were demanding an increase in their 2,500 *riels* (US$12) average monthly wage: 'Serei threatened to extend the strike to the other forty thousand Phnom Penh factory workers and said if the government still resisted he would expand it nationwide'. Like the *Khmer Rumdos,* the urban population was increasingly caught between Lon Nol and Pol Pot. When the Lon Nol government finally fell, Phnom Penh workers would discover that they were considered to be not 'the base' of an urban revolutionary movement, but members of the exploiting classes who had prospered on the backs of the poor peasants.)

In Region 13, the imposition of the Democratic Revolution sometimes provoked assassinations of cadres by enraged, recalcitrant villagers. As one local CPK soldier tells it: 'At first the Khmer Reds were popular, from 1970 to 1974. Their line was good, with no oppression. The people were prepared to follow them into the socialist revolution. In July 1973 I enlisted because I believed what they said about liberating Kampuchea from oppressors and imperialists. But persecution began in 1973-74, when everything was collectivized. Communal eating was introduced in May 1973, in groups of twelve families. [Soon] people were eating banana leaves, sugar-palm roots, coconuts, and finally weeds. Then there was nothing left at all. In the end the people rebelled, killing cadres in all villages. Here [Prey Piey village] one cadre was taken off and disappeared. So the Khmer Reds had to give in, and in 1974 private eating was once again allowed'.[344] But this district, Tram Kak, run by Mok's daughter Khom, was officially lauded by the Party as the first in Takeo to introduce communal eating,[345] which was of course resumed after victory in 1975. Meanwhile, in nearby Kong Pisei district (Region 33), two Region-level cadres were assassinated by their own couriers in 1974, after they had attempted to send out orders to implement the new measures.[346] Although it is possible that Quinn underestimated the solid base of support that the CPK had developed among the minority of poor peasants in the South-West, the thrust of his conclusion is undeniable: 'In early 1973 when the KK entered the new harsh phase of their campaign in which all rules were strictly enforced and unpopular programmes carried out, with stiff penalties for non-compliance, almost all popular feeling turned against them.'[347]

Finally, and perhaps most important of all in the political sense, came the destruction of Prasith, the Zone Deputy Party Secretary who outranked Mok on the CPK Central Committee, and of his 'Autonomous Maritime Sector' — Region 11 in Koh Kong province. The ethnic Chinese woman who was living there recounts what happened to those she calls the 'free Khmer Rouge':

In late 1973, the Vietnamese. . . were told to go back to their country and we saw no more of them. In October or November, the ethnic Chinese revolutionary cadres all disappeared as well, and the Chinese force was dissolved. Only the Khmer force remained.

In 1974, hard times began. Zone and Regional armed forces from Kompong Seila [Region 37] arrived in Koh Kong; they included many women . . . Prachha was arrested and taken away. They said he was going to study, but actually they killed him. Everybody in Koh Kong was afraid, because their leader had been taken away. Prasith disappeared about the same time. . . It got harder and harder. The Khmer Rouge began killing people; people who did anything wrong were taken away and shot. In 1974 they recruited every youth 16 years old or more into the army . . . Some who didn't go were killed.'[348]

According to Lon Nol intelligence, which confirms this account of Prasith's execution, Vorn Vet assumed control of Region 11 in mid 1974;[349] trade with Thailand now came under the CPK 'state', as did nearly all aspects of life in Koh Kong.

There was one exception. About two hundred of Prasith's followers escaped arrest and fled into the Cardamom mountains along the Thai border, where they initially set up five small bases, each of platoon strength. Led by Sae Phuthang, some of these people held out for the next six years. Abandoned by the Vietnamese communists, they constituted no threat to the CPK regime, but were occasionally aided by ethnic Khmers and local Thai officials across the border.[350]

Region 25

The upheaval in the South-West also had its reverberations in the neighbouring Special Zone. Non Suon's interrogators reported in late 1976: 'He certainly stood on the side of Sangha Hoeun, because Sangha Hoeun was from the Nine-Year [Resistance, i.e. 1945-54] group. . . When he saw Sangha Hoeun smashed, he thought that his day would come too.'[351] Suon wrote in his confession that although he had known and worked with Mok in the 1945-54 period, 'we were not close friends', and that he did try to keep out of harm's way in the 1970-75 war: 'I never interfered in the South-West outside Region 25 because I was afraid of Mok'. Suon's disagreement with and fear of Mok are also reported by Vorn Vet.[352] But the pressure on him was mounting: 'Up to the end of 1972 my feelings were no different from the Party [line]. Then in April 1973, when I met Chhouk [Secretary of the neighbouring Region 24, in the East] ... Chhouk spoke about all the former Pracheachon Group men around, and the need to develop forces. Then I began to think about [them] ...[353] From April 1973 on, Chhouk kept bringing up the matter of the Pracheachon party being in conflict with the present party. This undermined my attitude ...'[354]

In June 1973 Non Suon began to set up cooperatives, but in a cautious and non-coercive manner. CPK cadres from neighbouring Regions (13 and 15) claim that Suon accepted the 'official analysis' of the Party (that only 40 per cent of the population were poor or lower middle peasants, and 'everybody else was a class enemy'), but in fact their description of Suon's establishment of cooperatives in Region 25 provides an interesting contrast to events in others parts of the country, particularly in the North and South-West: 'At that time the rich peasants and others were not forced to join the cooperatives, but were allowed to continue to farm privately. Those poor peasants who did not want to join would be given explanations of why they should join, by the cadres. But if they remained stubborn they would not be forced to join. Anyway more than 90 per cent of the poor and lower middle peasants voluntarily joined the cooperatives.'[355] Moreover, in Region 25 there was no attempt to draft monks into the CPK armed forces, or to introduce communal eating. In early 1974 Quinn wrote that he had 'no report' from Region 25 of harsh CPK gaols for dissidents similar to ones he was able to detail in Region 35 (Kampot), and likewise his list of CPK executions of villagers and monks included examples only from the South-West.[356]

But this general picture of Region 25 needs to be refined in the case of one of its five districts. A local cadre from Koh Thom district claims that private farming *did* end in 1973. Further, 'Lists were made up, and land was requested, sometimes forcibly, from rich people, and given to groups of poor people'.[357] In this same district, according to Quinn, 'several thousand' villagers were now removed from their homes along the Vietnamese border. It was in Koh Thom, too, that CPK forces kidnapped three *Khmer Rumdos* cadres on 3 November 1973, leading to the clashes with Eastern Zone troops described earlier.[358] Now this seems politically significant: Koh Thom district was under the authority of Som Chea, a former Centre courier involved in the assassination of Tou Samouth in 1962. (See Chapter Six, p.241.) Chea had become the district CPK Secretary in 1972,[359] from which year the local cadre dates the beginning of 'the Khmer-Vietnamese conflict' in the area.[360] In a pattern already evident

in the South-West and North,[361] and often repeated in Democratic Kampuchea in later years, this was followed by local CPK
persecution of the Cham minority: according to Quinn, in 1973
Islamic practices were 'totally forbidden [and] local KK cadre
constantly threaten[ed] to destroy all mosques by the end of
1974'.[362]

It is worth comparing this development with the accounts of
Cham villagers from further north in Region 25. There, Islam
survived, and mosques remained open, until as late as mid 1976,
villagers told me in 1980. One, from the village of Cham Loeu,
said:

> In Non Suon's period [the communists] did good things, they did
> not kill people. Life was still happy then. He liked us, and
> politicized us, [moving us] to work hard ... The Chams fished for
> supplies for the troops, out of gratitude to them. In 1971-72 our
> young people were taken into the army; if one died we would be
> comforted. The military commander [Sok] really liked us; he gave
> 2,000 to 3,000 *riels* in aid to the parents of dead soldiers ...
>
> Non Suon came here once, for a festival in 1974. He called in all
> the Chams. He liked us, and let us organize religious festivals in
> the way we wished ... At that time religion was still permitted.
> Groups of ten to twenty people farmed the land collectively, but
> we lived and ate our meals privately. Money was still in circulation
> to some extent. There was no persecution.[363]

Presently I shall return to the implications of these apparent
district-level differences. But in spite of them it is clear that in
1973 Region 25 remained relatively untouched by developments
that were already common in the neighbouring South-Western
Zone.[364]

In August 1973, Non Suon attended a national CPK meeting in
the Northern Zone. He was disappointed to find that his former
Pracheachon colleagues Ney Sarann, Keo Meas and Um Neng
were not in attendance.[365] On the way home, he wrote,

> I made the trip to the Region 24 Office ... I asked Chhouk frankly:
> 'Where is Keo Meas? He never comes to the Party's annual
> study-session. How is his tendency and stance?' Chhouk said he
> did not know ... [366]
>
> Chhouk said that I should be careful; the Party was watching
> me because I was from the former Pracheachon Group.[367]
>
> I began to think I was gradually betraying the Party, through my
> lack of confidence in the Party, which did not include Keo Meas

in its [leading] Committee, although I still had some hope in Achar Sieng [Ney Sarann]. Chhouk was trusted by Keo Meas; I told him to let me know if there was any news. Later in 1973, Chhouk came to Region 25. I told him I was having trouble. The men I trusted — Chamroeun, Sok and Se — the Organization says are traitors, because they killed someone [see page 321]. If I warn them, I will be in trouble.[368]

Suon wavered: 'Sometimes I moved ahead with the Party, and sometimes I fell back away from the Party'. But finally the pressure on him seems to have proved too great: 'I decided to follow the present Party to get rid of my treason'.[369] Vorn Vet's permanent presence in Region 25 from late 1973[370] may well have contributed towards this decision.

The results are evident from the account of Kenneth Quinn, who wrote:

> While the KK [Khmer communists] in Kampot province forsook all allegiance to Sihanouk in late 1971, in Kandal province the KK found it expedient to support the Prince until the middle of 1973. In fact, as late as September 1973, KK draftees were told they were going to fight to enable Sihanouk to return to power ...[371]
>
> [Then] in December the KK in Kandal dropped the masquerade of supporting Sihanouk and publicly identified themselves as members of the Communist Party led by Khieu Samphan. In late December, they staged rallies in populated areas which affirmed the anti-Vietnamese and anti-Sihanouk character of their policy.[372]

When Suon 'confessed' three years later that 'My treason was reborn on 1 September 1973 after talking with Chhouk',[373] it is likely that he was signalling misgivings he had had about the approaching changes. It must have been clear to him, on the other hand, that failure to go along with them would have meant risking the fate of Sangha Hoeun.

In 1974, Suon wrote, 'the cadres in all four district [committees]' were removed, and put in offices near the Region [headquarters]'. An exception, however, was Som Chea from Koh Thom districts, who was now appointed CPK Secretary of Sa'ang and promoted to become 'a member of the Region Committee as well'.[374] It is clear that the personnel changes were not of Suon's making. 'The new district cadres were not yet functioning smoothly and I was not sure of their attitude towards me. Chhouk warned me: 'Don't drink as much as you used to, and avoid showing any sign of factionalism".[375]

In 1975 Som Chea would replace Suon himself. Control of Region 25 was already slipping from Suon's grasp. In Phnom Penh in June 1974, Donald Kirk interviewed a refugee, apparently from a district of Region 25, who said of the cadre he had lived under: 'He who recalls Sihanouk will be captured and shot. They say that Sihanouk must be put aside. They began this policy in February or March [1974] ... All the rice was gathered into common barns, and they gave away very little to each family ... They said they would destroy Phnom Penh ...'[376]

Premonition

On 18 March 1974 (the fourth anniversary of Sihanouk's deposition) a combined force of CPK Northern and South-Western Zone troops, led by Pauk and Mok, overran the former royal capital of Oudong, twenty-four miles north of Phnom Penh on the border of the two Zones. A few months later, Donald Kirk investigated the aftermath of this CPK victory, which had serious implications for royalism as well as for the Khmer Republic. 'There was manifestly a conscious effort on the part of the Khmer Rouge not only to overrun government outposts but to destroy the last vestiges of a civilization that appeared totally decadent and irrelevant. Thus the Khmer Rouge, after conquering Oudong, led the populace of twenty thousand persons into the nearby jungle, killed all school-teachers and government officials and deliberately razed the town, setting buildings on fire or tearing them down.'[377] A peasant from the village of Veang Cas ('Old Palace') outside the town, who had been aware of local CPK activities since 1967 and sympathized with their anti-royalist views, took part in the evacuation. In 1980 he recalled: 'Forty thousand people [sic] were sent in all directions. The Khmer Rouge burnt houses everywhere. We had to go west into Region 31, Kompong Chhnang, and were sent on and on. Uniformed Lon Nol soldiers were executed along the way ... People were split up into groups of fifty, two hundred, or three hundred and escorted by groups of Khmer Rouge. Of those sent on to Region 31, and further — to Pursat and Battambang in some cases — only one in five survived to return five years later.'[378] A CPK subdistrict cadre in the area affirms that the orders to evacuate the town population came directly from Mok; the rationale, he says, was to get them 'to grow rice in the rear bases, malaria-infested areas where there were food shortages'.[379]

Oudong was an omen, on a small scale, for the population of Phnom Penh. Equally ominous for the CPK Centre, however, was the *recapture* of Oudong by the Lon Nol army in June 1974, three and a half months after its fall – ominous in that in 1979 the Vietnamese army marched into Phnom Penh, three and a half years after it, too, had been captured and evacuated. Although the Khmer Republic was by this stage in an impossible position, news of the developments in CPK zones gave many of its troops a new burst of determination, and the war was now fought out to the bitter end.

Still, the political situation in the countryside remained complex. In terms of living conditions and revolutionary policy, the political map of rural Kampuchea still resembled a 'leopard-spot' pattern,[380] even though the combined Mok-Pauk seizure of Oudong showed that the darker spots were beginning to link up.

Chou Chet was in Kampot when Oudong was taken,[381] and on his return later in the year he adopted a dissident position on the future of the country's urban population. The subdistrict cadre quoted above recalls: 'Chou Chet told us in lectures that when we take Phnom Penh City, there will be no need to evacuate the people from it. All we needed to do was fight the Lon Nol system and the Lon Nol army, and gather up the high-ranking Lon Nol people for re-education. He did not say we should kill them.' The same cadre also reports a CPK company commander telling him in 1974 that Hou Yuon opposed evacuation of the capital. But Yuon and Chet had been out-manoeuvred, at least in the South-West. Mok and Khieu Samphan, the cadre says, were already in favour of evacuating Phnom Penh.[382] The deputy CPK Secretary of Region 37 at the time later told an interviewer: 'If we had captured Phnom Penh in 1974 there would also have been an evacuation. This had been a long-standing plan; the slogan was "Dry up the people from the enemy".'[383] Reasons given for this by Region 13 (Takeo) cadres included security problems, the need to protect the living-standards of urban dwellers when food was short in the capital, and the fact that 'people were the source of labour power'. But the possible reaction of city-dwellers to the Centre's policies loomed largest. The Region 13 cadre added: 'The main thing was that we could not be assured who the people in Phnom Penh were'.[384]

There was, however, little attempt to find out. In early 1974

Tith Nath, the CPK military commander of Region 33, ordered the rocketing of the southern suburbs of Phnom Penh, sections of which caught fire, causing many civilian deaths and much destruction.[385]

The Eastern Zone

There were some parallel developments in parts of the East. Quinn reported that over ten thousand people fled into South Vietnam from Svay Rieng province (Region 23) in June 1973, after cooperativization had begun there. The refugees also complained of the repression of Buddhism, and the 'denial of freedom of speech and the right to voice support for Prince Sihanouk'. The Prince had been described by cadres as 'a leech on the revolution'. However, Quinn continues: 'This precipitated spontaneous popular demonstrations. To make amends, the KK had to send in a second propaganda team explaining that it was all a mistake.'[386] It would be an exaggeration to conclude from this incident that 'freedom of speech' was accepted in the East. But it is clear that the CPK cadres there were still sensitive to popular feeling. By contrast, Quinn reported the accounts of refugees who had fled from the South-West in the same period: 'the climate of fear is so oppressive that even in their own homes they dared not utter a complaint against the government lest someone outside hear them and take them away to be tortured and killed'.[387]

It was only in mid 1974 that the Eastern Zone began to exhibit some of the patterns that had been evident elsewhere for several years. In August, seventy-one Hanoi-trained Khmer cadres from all over the Zone were assembled for a 'study course' in Region 21 (Kompong Cham). One of them, Hem Samin, recalls that they were lectured by Phuong and Region Secretary Chan on the 'meaningless' 1945-54 anti-French struggle (so described because 'we were just following the Vietnamese'), and reprimanded for having lived safely in Vietnam during Sihanouk's persecution of the Party. The resentment on the part of the local 'farm chickens' was genuine, as was their expression of independence; but they also harboured a certain defensiveness, fearing that their positions might be under threat from their more senior and better-trained 'wild' cousins. Phuong then informed the group that they were now in detention, and had 'to stay where we were in order to be self-reliant ... until the Organization came up with a solution so that [we] could go back to work'. Ten of the prisoners soon disappeared, allegedly taken 'to carry out duties somewhere else' - in fact quite possibly executed. The other sixty-one, including Samin, were put to work in the fields under close supervision. They enjoyed some freedom of movement, however, and Phuong's statement suggests that the Eastern Zone Executive did not wish to rule out a future role for them.[388]

By contrast, only six of their colleagues were still alive in gaols in the South-West; hundreds of others had been executed since 1971,[389] and no more than four had escaped.[390] However, several actually retained their posts in the East, including at least two district chiefs and the director of the Zone Artisans Service, Yun Soeun. Another thirty or more were quietly executed in various parts of the zone, almost certainly by roving squads of the Centre Security forces, known as the *Santebal*. One of the victims was So Phim's nephew Kim Teng. Others were gaoled by local Zone and Region security units (*Santesok*) but not executed; Chan Saman, for instance, was imprisoned by the Region 24 security forces.[391]

At the same time, the Cham 'Eastern Zone Islamic Movement' was disbanded. Its president, Sos Man, who had also spent the years 1954-70 in Vietnam, was not even gaoled but sent to 'live quietly' in a village in Region 21.[392]

So Phim's appreciation of the capacity of the Third Force to 'split our country's political forces in three or four directions' was now vindicated by the development of a Cham opposition movement in Region 21. At the end of 1974, journalist James Fenton interviewed refugees from the area in South Vietnam, and reported: 'A group called the *Khmer Saor*, or 'White Khmers', had broken away from the Khmer Rouge and taken to the forests. The White Khmers, whose leaders are former Communist officials, are mostly Cham Moslems. They support Sihanouk and oppose collectivization of property. They believe simply in the abolition of middlemen.'[393] In November or December, a Cham rebellion broke out in Trea village in Krauchhmar district.[394] Although So Phim and Phuong sanctioned its suppression, it is significant that, like the *Khmer Saor* movement and another revolt in a nearby village the next year, the scene of the conflict was Chan's Region 21. The large Cham communities in Region 22, for instance, remained quiet, partly because (like most of those in Non Suon's Region 25) they were still permitted religious freedom. This was also the case even in some parts of Region 21,[395] but it was there that conditions most closely resembled those in the South-West and parts of the North (particularly Region 31), just as it was in Region 21 that the first moves had been made in the zone to expel Vietnamese communist troops, in early 1972. (See p.341, above.)

However, the *Khmer Saor* dissidence now went beyond the Chams of Region 21. In Svay Rieng (Region 23), large numbers of communist troops went over to the *Khmer Saor*, in one case after a CPK unit commander had arrested one of his men. These troops fought alongside the Vietnamese communists in the border zones, mostly against South Vietnamese forces, but clashes with CPK units were also common.[396]

The Eastern Zone CPK had finally broken with its tradition of solidarity with the Vietnamese. As with previous Eastern concessions to the Party Centre, this break was implemented under pressure: a Centre brigade, the 280th commanded by Nhao, moved into the zone in 1974 and began driving out the remaining Vietnamese.[397] Further, the arrests of most Hanoi-trained Khmer cadres by Zone units probably saved their lives, at least for a time, by keeping them out of reach of Centre assassination squads.[398] And the repressive methods of the Eastern Zone leaders were mild enough to allow many other dissidents to escape, or even to remain in the CPK fold. As noted above, Chakrey's forces in Region 24 continued to clash with South-Western Zone troops long after the arrest of Chan Saman; Region 22 troops also displayed continuing antagonism towards the Centre.[399] In 1974 Tiv Ol, who had described the Vietnamese as 'not very loyal' friends at a Zone meeting the previous year, visited Hanoi where he wrote a poem about Indo-Chinese solidarity called *Sosar pi phnom Truong Son* ('In Praise of the Truong Son Mountains').[400] A eulogy to the range that unites (and divides) the three countries of the region, this poem may be said to express the ambivalence of the Eastern Zone cadres towards the Centre's single-mindedness on the issue, and its publication in a Vietnamese magazine is unsurprisingly alleged to have drawn criticism from Pol Pot.

The rejection of fraternal cooperation with the Vietnamese by So Phim and the other Eastern Zone leaders did not automatically mean, except in the case of Chan in Region 21, a switch to uncompromising and aggressive hostility. Most of those who had spent the Sihanouk years in Vietnam had now been dismissed, but many others, trained by the Vietnamese in the

Zone since 1970, continued to hold their posts. Such people were far more numerous in the East than in any other zone, and the Eastern Zone Executive, unlike any other in the country, both comprised exclusively Vietnamese-trained Issarak veterans (So Phim, Phuong and Chhouk), and remained intact until after the war ended. At a less political level, because of the proximity of the border and Vietnamese labourers' past participation in the rubber plantation economy, many eastern cadres were married to Vietnamese; one Region-level cadre was married to a Khmer woman trained in Hanoi.[401]

Nor did the end of political and military cooperation with Vietnam put an end to economic relations (the Eastern Zone continued to trade with the Vietnamese communists for over two years)[402] or herald a dramatic radicalization of domestic policy similar to that occurring in the South-West and in Region 31 in the North. The Democratic Revolution moved only slowly into the East. Mutual aid teams, not cooperatives, remained the norm in the Zone until the war ended. An exception was Memut district in Region 21, where in late 1974, according to local cadres, cooperativization was completed, communal eating introduced, Vietnamese residents expelled (except those married to Khmer men), and a 'secret anti-Vietnamese policy' introduced. Here Vietnam was said to be 'revisionist' because of its peace agreement with the USA and its opposition to Kampuchea's cooperatives. The former district agricultural chief claims that the new 'trading cooperatives sold clothes, salt and medicine to the people cheaply'.[403] This is not confirmed by other sources, but former civilian inhabitants state that, even here, many of the cadres had earned the respect, if not the affection, of much of the local Khmer population, and expectations of improved conditions after victory remained high.[404] That these hopes were dashed was to a large extent beyond the control of the cadres concerned, even if their positions in the new regime ensured that they would bear considerable responsibility. The Eastern Zone legacy (especially in Regions 20, 22, 23 and 24) of recalcitrance and relative moderation, and the greater popular support that flowed from it, continued to create obstacles for the CPK Centre. These obstacles were just as significant as the advantages the Centre reaped from the Zone cadres' strong sense of Party loyalty.

The year 1973 was a watershed in Kampuchean history. The US bombardment of that year had several major effects. Firstly, it decimated and even destroyed a number of CPK regular units (sixteen thousand men in all, according to the Seventh Air Force Commander.[405] The casualties were particularly heavy among South-Western Zone units during the siege of Phnom Penh in July 1973,[406] and this may have helped tip the balance of power there in the CPK Centre's favour. Secondly, the widespread loss of civilian life and property drove a large number of new recruits into the revolutionary ranks, recruits who were often motivated as much by a desire for revenge as by positive political or social goals. This was probably fatal for relatively moderate CPK leaders like Prasith, who was overwhelmed by fanatics and killed just as Chou Chet and Phouk Chhay also lost out to Mok and Thuch Rin in the crucial struggle for control of the South-West at this time. It is clear too, that Koy Thuon's position in the North, in relation to military commander Ke Pauk, was severely undermined by the impact of the bombing there. Had all these people been able to hold their ground, the history of Kampuchea in the remainder of the 1970s might well have been different.

Thirdly, many villagers saw themselves as victims not only of US policy but also of the failure of the CPK and VWP to agree on a co-ordinated strategy, and they concluded that close cooperation between Khmers and Vietnamese was no longer possible or even desirable.

Fourthly, the evacuation of towns like Kratie, Kompong Trach, Ang Tasom and Kompong Kdei in 1973 was not an abnormal measure at the height of the bombardment. (The fate of the cities of North Vietnam the previous December was a clear indication of that.) But it also provided the CPK with a precedent to push further ahead, to take advantage of this momentum and mobilize the population for war communism even after the bombardment had stopped. The 'Democratic Revolution', was both a product of, and a capitalization upon, the US aerial war. Having heard of the effects of that war, or actually experienced it in 1973, many inhabitants of Phnom Penh in 1975 were prepared to believe the first CPK troops arriving in the capital, when they announced that everyone would have to leave because the US was about to bomb the city.

The bombing sowed a whirlwind which the CPK Centre was

ready to reap. Not only did it harden the base of the movement, but it also prevented what would otherwise have been an inevitable insurgent victory in 1973, at a time when the Centre's domestic and foreign policy extremism was far from generally accepted in the revolutionary movement, most particularly in the East. Although broad United Fronts are a classic communist tactic, rarely has a Communist Party leadership encountered such resistance within its Front, both open (and violent) and, in the case even of some loyal Party adherents, passive.

Thus, had the revolution triumphed over Lon Nol as expected in 1973, it is extremely unlikely that the cities could have successfully been ordered evacuated. Further, since urban disillusionment with Lon Nol was already general, Sihanouk had regained much of his former popularity there.[407] His position would therefore have been far more secure (and might still have been strong in the countryside as well). Hundreds of Hanoi-trained Khmer cadres would not only have escaped secret executions behind the lines, but, like 'domestic' communists with a bias towards urban or working-class action, would also have had a potential base in the cities. This base would have severely restricted the Centre's freedom of manoeuvre. The strategy of 'protracted struggle', too, long recognized by the CPK Centre as crucial to 'exercising mastery over the revolutionary group(s) in every way', would have been blocked by an early end to the war. Further, the CPK-VWP conflict, also essential to that strategy, would have remained subdued, as neither cadres nor population would have regarded the Vietnamese and their peace negotiations as being responsible, as the most proximate potential culprit, for US bombing or for continued war in Kampuchea. Sihanouk, for instance, announced in mid 1973, when he realized that victory was no longer imminent, that Phnom Penh would not be taken 'for many years' because the North Vietnamese had withheld supplies after the cease-fire.[408] Those supplies would never have been needed, even given Sihanouk's refusal to negotiate with Lon Nol, had it not been for the 'centre-piece of the Administration cease-fire strategy'. Relieved of the burden of supporting a now heightened conflict with Vietnam, the Khmer people would have been spared a great deal of future suffering. Just as French domination and intransigence in the 1940s and 1950s had provoked the development of the Khmer communist movement out of a nationalist one, American intervention and bombardment contributed significantly to the movement's extremist metamorphosis in the 1970s.

But the CPK's 'cease-fire strategy' must also carry a large share of responsibility for this. The Centre rejected a cease-fire for one major reason, disingenuously expressed in the *Livre Noir*: 'If the Kampuchean revolution had accepted a cease-fire, it would have collapsed'.[409] In fact, nothing could be further from the truth. More likely, a 1973 cease-fire would have seen a political revolution in Phnom Penh demanding a left-wing-dominated coalition government. (This did happen in Laos in 1973-75.) The Lon Nol regime was at its nadir of popularity, the revolution at its zenith, as we have seen.

The possibility of the return of Sihanouk, accompanied by Hou Yuon, Khieu Samphan and other popular figures, would have sealed the fate of Lon Nol, and of the war. But the CPK Centre did not wish to win in such fashion. They saw that this would have been at their own expense, at least relatively speaking, because they stood to lose much in an open political atmosphere. Only in this sense can it be said that 'the revolution would have collapsed'. That statement, by the authors of the *Livre Noir*, is in fact a veiled but devastating admission of their extreme political isolation.

With the 1973 rejection of a cease-fire, too, the internal conflicts that eventually led to the destruction of the revolution by the CPK Centre were probably inevitable, since the Hanoi-trained cadres, approximately half the Party's membership in 1970, were already being secretly eliminated without any public intra-Party debate or discussion. Most of these executions were not even known to second-rank Party members (Non Suon's four years of attempts to discover *just the whereabouts* of Keo Meas illustrate the secrecy involved) or even to Politburo members like So Phim, until after they had occurred; this was the case whether or not such people were prepared to approve, or, in the cause of Party loyalty or their own amibition, to acquiesce in the killings. The Stalinist process of destruction of the Party's own administrative and political base, so closely reproduced in the workings of Tuol Sleng prison after 1975, had already been set in motion.

On the other hand, the same process also set the scene for the eventual overthrow of the CPK regime. Not only had small numbers of veteran Khmer communists from various zones escaped to the hills or to Vietnam; but what had driven them there — the hostility to Vietnam, along with the severe domestic policies, and the purges closely related to both — would eventually produce the successful Vietnamese reaction which was to sweep them back to power in 1979. Vietnamese silence in the meantime, about the CPK's internal policies as well as its military provocations, was a strategy of appeasement doomed to failure. Having set out on the political path it had chosen, the CPK would eventually find its popular base so small that it could not survive in power without launching the foreign adventure that its hard-core members and youthful army had been led to expect, and which promised some hope of distracting attention from domestic problems and mobilizing a Khmer national chauvinism under its banner. Only a principled even-handedness in *Chinese* policy towards Indo-China could have prevented such an adventure, and in the circumstances that would not be forthcoming.[410] When it was not, the Vietnamese sensed the danger to themselves. Like other aspects of the Pol Pot experiment, for a Khmer regime to provoke a full-scale war with Vietnam was to fly in the face of history.

Notes

1. *Rien saut daoy songkep nu prowatt chollana padewatt Kampuchea kraom kar duk noam rebos Pak Kommyunis Kampuchea* ('Abbreviated Lesson on the History of the Kampuchean Revolutionary Movement led by the Communist Party of Kampuchea'), undated (1977?) Phnom Penh, 23 pp. typescript, at p.8.
2. *Livre Noir: Faits et preuves des actes d'aggression et d'annexion du Vietnam contre le Kampuchea,* Democratic Kampuchea, Phnom Penh, September 1978, pp. 47, 40, 51.
3. Author's interview with Yos Por, Phnom Penh, 11 September 1980.
4. *Livre Noir, op. cit.,* p.48, 50.
5. *Ibid.* It is worth comparing this with a contemporary statement by the Politburo of the Communist Party of India (Marxist). In August 1971 the CPI(M) said: 'Each Communist Party should apply Marxism-Leninism to its problems, irrespective of the Chinese-Soviet differences and develop its own revolutionary movement ... We follow an independent policy like the parties in North Vietnam and North Korea'. Quoted in Dilip Hiro, *Inside India Today,* London 1976, p.142.
6. *Livre Noir, op. cit.,* p.53.
7. William Shawcross, *Sideshow: Kissinger, Nixon and the Destruction of Cambodia,* London 1979, p.125.
8. *Livre Noir, op. cit.,* pp.53-54.
9. See the text in Malcolm Caldwell *et al., Cambodia in the South-East Asian War,* New York 1973, pp.389-393.
10. *Livre Noir, op. cit.,* p.54.
11. It then added: 'We are firmly convinced that the struggle of the Cambodian people against the US imperialists and their lackeys will certainly continue to develop ... [and so will] Vietnamese-Cambodian militant solidarity'. *Survey of China Mainland Press,* 4626, 22 March 1970, p.64; quoted in Fritz Buchler, *The God-King in Peking,* B.A. thesis, University of New South Wales, 1974, 103 pp., at pp.17-18. The information in the rest of the paragraph is largely drawn from Buchler, pp.28-29.
12. *Livre Noir, op. cit.,* p.57.
13. Norodom Sihanouk, *My War with the CIA,* Penguin 1973, p.56; and Henry Kissinger, quoted in Seymour Hersh, *The Price of Power: Henry Kissinger in the Nixon White House,* New York, Summit Books, 1983, p.180.
14. Hersh, *ibid.,* pp.179-181.
15. *Réalités Cambodgiennes,* 24 October 1969. The commander was Chu Bun Sang. Another two hundred Khmer Serei had defected to the government between December 1968 and March 1969. Radio Phnom Penh, 27 February 1969, BBC *Summary of World Broadcasts,* FE/3018/A3/3.
16. Prom Thos discovered this only later in the year, and said he was unaware of any US involvement in the planning. However he said that in 1965 Long Boret had confided to him that he had been approached by an American, an agent of the CIA, and invited to work for Sihanouk's overthrow. Long Boret said he had then approached Lon Nol for his cooperation in such a plan. Lon Nol's reply, according to Boret, was neither 'yes' nor 'no', but he had asked Boret to 'maintain his contacts with the agent'. Author's interviews with Prom Thos, Paris, 12 February and 3 June 1980.
17. Milton Osborne, in the Melbourne *Age,* 12 January 1971. This article is based on Osborne's interview with Thanh's brother Son Thai Nguyen. Quoted in

Sihanouk, *My War ...*, *op. cit.*, pp.37, 49.
18. Hersh, *op. cit.*, pp.178, 181.
19. See 'The 1970 Peasant Uprisings Against Lon Nol', in Ben Kiernan and Chanthou Boua (eds.), *Peasants and Politics in Kampuchea, 1942-81*, New York, M.E. Sharpe, 1982, pp.206-223.
20. Author's interview with Tam Eng. Paris, 24 January 1980.
21. Author's interview with Chheng Sia, Suong, 5 October 1980.
22. Author's interview with Pon, Strasbourg, 1 November 1979.
23. Shawcross, *op. cit.*, p.184.
24. Léon Trivière, 'Le Cambodge en grand désarroi', Information Missionaire, M.E.P., Paris, May 1972, 22 pp., at p.10.
25. Caldwell, *op. cit.*, p.385.
26. *New York Times*, 1 May 1970.
27. Hal Kosut, ed., *Cambodia and the Vietnam War*, Facts on File, New York 1971, p.72.
28. Bernard K. Gordon with Kathryn Young, 'The Khmer Republic: That Was the Cambodia That Was', *Asian Survey*, 11, 1, January 1971, pp.26-40, at p.32. Shawcross comments: 'This was a crucial event for Cambodia. It was a ludicrous demand, one that could only be made by a man who had a tenuous grasp on reality, or had promises of external support'. *op. cit.*, p.118.
29. Seymour Hersh, however, says that it was on March 17 that 'Lon Nol authorized a South Vietnamese Army task force to cross the Cambodian border on a military sweep against Communist strongholds.' *The Price of Power*, New York, 1983, p.176.
30. Shawcross, *op. cit.*, p.123.
31. Kosut, *op. cit.*, p.73.
32. *Ibid.*, p.89. (On the KKK operation, see Hersh, *op. cit.*, p.181, citing a report to the Pentagon by Gerald C. Hickey.)
33. *Ibid.*, pp.72-74.
34. *Ibid.*, p.74.
35. Gordon and Young, *op. cit.*, p.34.
36. The *New York Times* reported 3,500 killed and 20,000 detained. 9 May 1970.
37. Shawcross, *op. cit.*, p.131.
38. See the text of a memo to Nixon dated 26 April 1970, quoted by Bruce Page, 'The Pornography of Power', in *Aftermath: The Struggle of Cambodia and Vietnam*, by John Pilger and Anthony Barnett, New Statesman, London, 1982, pp.43-53 at p.49. The memo was excised from his memoirs by Kissinger after the publication of *Sideshow*, presumably to give the impression that preparations began much later.
39. Gordon and Young, *op. cit.*, p.35; see also Kosut, *op. cit.*, p.89, who puts the US figure at a peak of 23,000.
40. Author's interview with villagers in Krachap, 9 October 1980.
41. *Ibid.*
42. Author's interview with Touc Muong, Romduol, 23 July 1980. This incident, Muong said, took place around 1972.
43. Shawcross, *op. cit.*, pp.150, 174.
44. See *ibid.*, pp.151, 174-75, 185, 222-23, 249.
45. *Ibid.*, p.249.
46. Author's interviews during a visit to Chbal Mon, 17 September 1980.
47. 'Cambodia: Can the Vietnamese Communists Export Insurgency?', *Research Study*, Bureau of Intelligence and Research, US State Department, 25

September 1970, 6 pp., at p.5. No details are given, however. (In 1971 a Khmer defector to the Lon Nol regime accused the Vietnamese communists of killing monks; see 'Khmer Rouge Rallier Keoum Kun', Airgram from US Embassy in Phnom Penh to Department of State, 13 January 1972, p.5.)

48. *Ibid.,* p.6.

49. Shawcross, *op. cit.,* pp.175, 417.

50. *Livre Noir, op. cit.,* pp.63-64.

51. *Le Monde,* 14 October 1978.

52. *Livre Noir, op. cit.,* pp.63-64, claims that Chea had first referred to 'the different positive aspects of the difficulties of the question of independence and sovereignty as well as of solidarity'; the same source claims that only the second part of the telegram was immediately passed on to Pol Pot, and the rest one day later, after the meeting with Le Duan in which Pol Pot rejected Vietnamese proposals for a mixed command. This detail of Vietnamese tactics rings true, but of course the second part of the message was the substantive section.

53. See *Far Eastern Economic Review,* 21 October 1977, p.24.

54. In his confession in 1977, Hu Nim wrote of Hou Yuon: 'After the coup in 1970 he thought that Vietnam must be asked to help in the offensive to liberate the east bank of the Mekong River'. *Chamlaiy Hu Nim krusuong khosenakar* ('The Reply of Hu Nim, Ministry of Information'). Archives of Tuol Sleng prison, Phnom Penh, 28 May and 16 June 1977. Translated into English by Chanthou Boua. 105 pp. transcript, at p.86.

55. *Livre Noir, op. cit.,* p.65.

56. *Ibid.,* pp.65-67.

57. *Ibid.,* pp.68-69.

58. Pon, *op. cit.*

59. *Livre Noir, op. cit.,* pp.70-71.

60. *Ibid.,* p.67.

61. *Ibid.,* pp.68-69.

62. *Ibid.,* pp.69-70.

63. *Ibid.,* p.70.

64. Author's interview with Tea Sabun, Phnom Penh, 23 August 1980.

65. See the Eastern Zone document reproduced in the St. Louis *Post-Dispatch,* 26 June 1970, p.1. The Centre's term was *Renaksey* Ruop Ruom *Cheat Kampuchea*; see Kenneth Quinn, 'The Khmer Krahom Program to Create a Communist Society in Southern Cambodia', Airgram from US Consul, Can Tho, to Department of State, 20 February 1974, 37 pp., at p.4. (Henceforth 'Quinn, 1974'.)

66. David E. Brown, 'Exporting Insurgency: The Communists in Cambodia', in J.J. Zasloff and A.E. Goodman, eds., *Indo-China in Conflict*, Lexington, Massachusetts, 1972, pp.125-135, at pp.130-31.

67. *Livre Noir, op. cit.,* p.70.

68. *Prowatt Pak* ('The Party History'), dated 23 January 1971. See Chapter Seven, p.287, above for a fuller extract.

69. *Livre Noir, op. cit.,* pp.70-71.

70. *Ibid.,* p.72.

71. Brown, *op. cit.,* p.129.

72. *Cambodge Nouveau,* no. 1, May 1970, pp.50-52.

73. Vorn Vet's untitled confession in Tuol Sleng prison, December 1978, 54 pp., at pp.30-31.

74. *Ibid.,* p.31.

75. Non Suon, *Phnaek ti bey: royea kraoy 18.3.70 mok pacchabon* ('Section Three: The Period after 18 March 1970 to the Present'), confession in Tuol Sleng dated 7 November 1976, 30 pp., at p.23.

76. Ith Sarin, 'Life in the Bureaus of the Khmer Rouge', in Timothy Carney, *Communist Party Power in Kampuchea*, Cornell University South-East Asia Program Data Paper No. 106, 1977, pp.42-55, at p.43.

77. See Chapter Seven, p.272.

78. *Chamlaiy Hu Nim, op. cit.*, notes that 'brother Mok was then [in 1966] Deputy Secretary' of the South-Western Zone; and Mar was Secretary, a rank he still occupied in 1968. In 1977 he was described as 'now dead'. Translation, p.18.

79. See Chapter Six, p.201; the author's interviews with Chhun Samath and Chap Hen (Kong Pisei, 17 September 1980), and Yos Por (Phnom Penh, 11 September 1980), and Stephen Heder's interviews with other Zone Party members (Sa Keo, 9 March 1980, and Chantaburi, 12 March 1980) all indicate that Mok was Zone Secretary from at least 1970.

80. Author's interviews with cadre Nou Mouk (Oudong, 26 August 1981) and a CPK soldier who said he met 'the Zone Secretary who preceeded Mok' (presumably he was referring to Chou Chet) at a conference in 1971; and Stephen Heder's interview with a CPK cadre from Region 13 (Takeo, where Mok was born), Sa Keo, 8 March 1980.

81. Vorn Vet, *op. cit.*, p.32.

82. Ith Sarin, *op. cit.*, p.43.

83. Vorn Vet, *op. cit.*, p.31. He notes: 'When we met in November 1970 at Phnom Pis I saw that Chey Suon [Non Suon] and Sy [Chou Chet] were very friendly ... They were in agreement to fight [*veay prohar*] Ta Mok. But Chey Suon did not dare come out openly ...'

84. Chhun Samath and Chap Hen, *op. cit.*; on Prasith, see Chapter Seven, p.273, above.

85. Ith Sarin, *op. cit.*, p.43; *Congress of Democratic Kampuchea on December 15-17, 1979*, Permanent Mission of DK to the UN; *Vietnamese Studies*, no. 33, 1972, pp.100-101. Until at least June 1973, Rin was 'Chairman of the Federation of Cambodian Democratic Youth'; the term 'Democratic' indicates a Party body — see Carney, *op. cit.*, p.10.

86. Ith Sarin, *op. cit.*, p.43.

87. Charles Meyer, *Derrière le sourire khmer*, Paris 1971, p.389.

88. Kenneth K. Quinn, 'Political Change in Wartime: The Khmer Krahom Revolution in Southern Cambodia', *Naval War College Review*, Spring 1976 (hereafter referred to as 'Quinn 1976').

89. Brown, *op. cit.*, p.133, refers to the 'refugee exodus of the summer of 1970, when most village officials, teachers and merchants decamped on the arrival of the VC/NVA armed action teams'.

90. *Ibid.*, p.128.

91. *Ibid.*

92. *Ten Documents illustrating Vietnamese Communist Subversion in Cambodia, August 1969 to April 1970*, n.d., Document no. 9, p.2.

93. *The Viet Cong March-April 1970 Plans for Expanding Control in Cambodia*, US Mission, Saigon, Vietnam Documents and Research Notes No. 88, January 1971; captured document no.5, dated 9 April 1970. For a detailed analysis of these Vietnamese communist documents, see *Peasants and Politics in Kampuchea, 1942-81, op. cit.*, pp.257-261.

94. *Des Mouvements Anti-Gouvernementaux au Cambodge*, Khmer Republic, Deuxième Bureau, 20 July 1973, 45 pp., at p.29.

95. 'Conversations with Khmer Rouge Rallier Ieng Lim', Airgram from US Embassy in Phnom Penh to Department of State, 30 November 1971, 4 pp., at p.3. Also, author's interview with 'returnee' Hem Samin (Takhmau, 28 September 1980), who said the first groups left Hanoi in May 1970.

96. Yos Por (a second 'returnee'), *op. cit.*

97. 'Conversations with Khmer Rouge Rallier Ieng Lim', *op. cit.*, p.2.

98. G. Boudarel, 'La Liquidation des communistes cambodgiens formés au Vietnam', in *Problèmes politiques et sociaux*, no. 373, 12 octobre 1979, p.5; this contains an earlier interview with Li Yang Duc, alias Yos Por.

99. *Ibid.*, p.7.

100. 'Khmer Rouge Rallier Keoum Kun', *op. cit.*, p.4.

101. Hem Samin, *op. cit.*

102. 'Defectors Recount Disaffection with Communists', AFP, Hong Kong, 1 April 1974; in US CIA *Foreign Broadcast Information Service* (henceforth FBIS), Daily Report, Asia and the Pacific, 4, 66, April 1974, pp.H3–H5, at p.H4. (Also Yos Por, *op. cit.*)

103. *Ibid.*

104. Hem Samin, *op. cit.*; *Problèmes politiques et sociaux*, *op. cit.*, gives Yos Por's slightly different version.

105. Author's interview with Chhing Nam Yeang, Rouen, 11 October 1979.

106. 'Khmer Rouge Rallier Keoum Kun', *op. cit.*, p.8. Kun also told his American debriefers that Samuoeun was leading an 'opposition' to the Vietnamese, an apparent contradiction.

107. *Problèmes politiques et sociaux*, op. cit., p.7.

108. 'Defectors Recount Disaffection with Communists', *op. cit.*, p.H4.

109. Yos Por, *op. cit.*

110. 'Khmer Rouge Rallier Keoum Kun', *op. cit.*, p.8.

111. Author's interview with Vietnamese general Nguyen Xuan Hoang, Hanoi, 4 November 1980.

112. Hem Samin, *op. cit.*

113. Their names were Kim Teng and Sa Bin. Sa Bin had also studied in China for four years with Yos Por and about forty others.

114. 'Conversations with Khmer Rouge Rallier Ieng Lim', *op. cit.*, p.3.

115. Nguyen Xuan Hoang, *op. cit.*

116. 'Khmer Rouge Rallier Keoum Kun', *op. cit.*, gives the names of sixteen 'returnees' active in seven districts of the South-Western Zone.

117. Author's interview with Tea Chhay Hou, Prek Ambel, 1 August 1980. French Missionary Jean Clavaud was captured 'by the Khmer Vietminh' in September 1970 and spent forty days [in So Pum's headquarters] at Talun, Kandal province. A former student of Clavaud's then vouched for him, and he was allowed to move to the student's village in Takeo, where the 'Khmer Rouge' were in control. However he soon found that the province chief, Duch, and his deputy were in favour of executing Clavaud, but the eight other members of the province committee prevailed, securing his release on 3 January 1971. (Personal communication, 23 September 1980.)

118. Author's interview with Lau Sokha, Koh Thom, 1 August 1980.

119. Author's interview with Ney, 66, Koh Thom, 1 August 1980.

120. Author's interview with Nhim Sitho, Prek Ambel, 21 July 1980.

121. Non Suon, *Phnaek ti pram: XII bainhcheak ompi batopeap konlong mok* ('Section 5: No. 12 Explains Past Events'), Tuol Sleng archives, dated 20 November 1976, 40 pp., at pp.23–24.

122. Shawcross, *op. cit.*, p.250.

123. Brown, *op. cit.*, p.131.

124. 'Cambodia: Can the Vietnamese Communists Export Insurgency?', *op. cit.*, p.iii; and personal communication to the author from the CIA's Cambodia analyst in this period, Sam Adams, 26 September 1976.

125. Kosut, *op. cit.*, p.89. According to Shawcross, *op. cit.*, p.179: 'By early September 1970, there were twenty-one South Vietnamese battalions scouring the country and fully one quarter of all air-strikes and troop lifts flown by the Vietnamese air force were committed to them.'

126. Sam Adams, *op. cit.*

127. Donald Kirk, *Wider War*, New York, Praeger 1971, p.132.

128. *Des Mouvements Anti-Gouvernementaux ...*, *op. cit.*, p.25.

129. Sam Adams, *op. cit.*

130. 'Communist Infrastructure in Cambodia', DIA Intelligence Appraisal, 8 July 1971, 10 pp., at pp.2, 5, and 7. See also, note 221.

131. I obtained a copy of these untitled documents, which had apparently been reproduced by Lon Nol intelligence, during a visit to Phnom Penh in 1981.

132. My emphasis.

133. In early 1973 a defector from the CPK wrote: 'They do not want to effect a quick victory (if they win) because they realize that the people do not yet know them ... Thus, they are preparing for a long drawn-out struggle. If they won quickly it would be meaningless.' Kuong Lumphon, *Report on the Communist Party of Kampuchea*, 46 pp., at p.43. See note 193.

134. See W.E. Willmott, 'Analytical Errors of the Kampuchean Communist Party', *Pacific Affairs*, 54, 2, Summer 1981, pp.209-227.

135. There is a brief reference to 'intermediary businessmen, [who] include the rich merchants who buy paddy cheaply and take it to be milled in order to sell it dearly, and businessmen who sell things to other people.'

136. *Rien saut daoy songkep ...*, *op. cit.*, p.7. My emphasis.

137. These quotations appear in Hiro, *op. cit.*, p.154 (citing the February 1970 issue of the CPI(M-L) journal *Liberation*), and p.164.

138. Laura Summers, personal communication. See also Timothy Carney, 'The Organization of Power in Democratic Kampuchea', forthcoming.

139. Author's interview with Ung Pech, who was lectured by Thuch Rin and his subordinate Ang. Phnom Penh, 7 September 1980.

140. Y. Phandara, *Retour à Phnom Penh*, Paris, 1982, p.114. The quotation is from Hing Un, who had 'the confidence of Ieng Sary who had known him for a long time' (p.125).

141. Author's interview with Mam Lon, Kraing Leav, 3 September 1980. The meeting took place at the foot of Mt Aural.

142. Vorn Vet, *op. cit.*, p.29.

143. See pp.86–8, 127, above.

144. Vorn Vet, *op. cit.*, p.29.

145. *Ibid.*, p.32; also, author's interview with a CPK soldier who stood guard at the Congress.

146. Vorn Vet, *op. cit.*, p.32; and author's interviews with Tea Sabun (23 August 1980) and Ouch Bun Chhoeun (30 September 1980) in Phnom Penh. Much of the information that follows is drawn from these interviews.

147. This was in 1975. See David P. Chandler and Ben Kiernan, eds., *Revolution and Its Aftermath in Kampuchea*, Yale University, 1983, pp.178-79.

148. *Chamlaiy Hu Nim*, *op. cit.*, p.86.

149. *Summary of Annotated Party History*, by the Eastern Zone military political service, September 1973; and *Prowatt nei Pak Kommyunis Kampuchea* ('History

of the Communist Party of Kampuchea'), 1974.

150. Pon, *op. cit.*

151. *L'Aggression Vietcong et Nord-Vietnamienne contre la République Khmère (Nouveaux documents)*, Phnom Penh, Ministry of Information, October 1971, 121 pp., at p.71.

152. 'Conversations with Khmer Rouge Rallier Ieng Lim', *op. cit.*, p.3. Lim defected when a North Vietnamese withdrawal exposed his flank.

153. *L'Aggression ...*, *op. cit.*, pp.99, 100.

154. Author's interviews in Kompong Svay, 15 October 1980. Thuon's head-quarters in 1971 were said to be in Sambou subdistrict.

155. Pon, *op. cit.*

156. The South-Western Zone forces, for instance, preferred more conventional military tactics. One South-Western Zone soldier later described 'the different military tactics of the Eastern Zone troops' as follows: 'We would attack and then dig trenches. They would use trees as trenches [protection] and then move up to attack.'

157. Vorn Vet, *op. cit.*, p.32, notes that after the conference: 'Before I left the Centre office Brother No. 1 told me that Region 25 would be taken away from the East ...'

158. Non Suon, *Phnaek ti bey*, *op. cit.*

159. Non Suon, *Chamlaiy XII ...* ('The Reply of No. 12'), Tuol Sleng confession dated 27 December 1976, 26 pp., at pp.22-23.

160. Ngin Hor, incidentally, had returned from Hanoi but was working elsewhere in the East.

161. *Ibid.*

162. *Ibid.*

163. Tea Chhay Hou, *op. cit.*

164. Non Suon, *Phnaek ti bey*, *op. cit.*

165. Non Suon, *Chamlaiy ti pram*, *op. cit.*, p.39.

166. Stephen Heder's interview with Non Suon's former courier, Sa Keo, March 7, 1980.

167. Tea Chhay Hou, *op. cit.* Conical hats are customary in Vietnam.

168. Author's interview with Leng Leang Y, Prek Ambel, 1 August 1980.

169. Lau Sokha, *op. cit.*

170. Sam Adams, *op. cit.*

171. Stephen Heder's interview with a Region 13 cadre, Sa Keo, 8 March 1980; and Shawcross, *op. cit.*, p.250.

172. 'Khmer Rouge Rallier Keoum Kun', *op. cit.*

173. Heder interview, *op. cit.*

174. Quinn, 1974, *op. cit.*, pp.7, 4, 5.

175. Author's interview with Ung Channa, Paris, 30 November 1979. The cadre from Takeo was named Soeng Hau.

176. Quinn, 1974, *op. cit.*, pp.4, 5, 10, 32.

177. Yos Por, *op. cit.*

178. *Problèmes politiques et sociaux*, *op. cit.*, p.6.

179. Author's interview with Ly Veasna, Caen, 7 October 1979.

180. Interview with Stephen Heder, Mai Rut, 16 March 1980.

181. Quinn, 1974, *op. cit.*, p.28.

182. *Ibid.*, pp. 29, 34. Quinn gives the following details: 'Each family was responsible for buying seed, plowing, planting and hoeing and weeding its own tract. However, at harvest time, all members of the inter-family group formed a joint crew which moved from plot to plot, cutting, thrashing and

collecting paddy which was then moved to a central storage point ... The group chairman distributed rice to each family based on a formula which allowed each person an equal amount of rice per day ... Enough rice was to be retained to feed everyone in the group until the next harvest and the remainder sold to the village government ... Money made by any inter-family group from the sale of excess rice was kept by the chairman to pay for any special needs of the group or any member, such as special medicine or certain types of farm equipment'.

183. Ung Channa, *op. cit.*

184. Stephen Heder's interview with a Region 13 cadre, *op. cit.*

185. Author's interview with Ieng Thon (Kus, 16 July 1980), who joined the CPK army in the area in July 1973.

186. Author's interview with Lieu Sarun, Kirivong, 26 August 1980. Sarun said the other model districts after 1975 were Prasaut Thmey in Svay Rieng and Upper Kompong Tralach in Kompong Chhnang.

187. Quinn, 1974, *op. cit.*, p.32.

188. *Ibid.*, p.26.

189. Author's interview with Hul Yem, Strasbourg, 31 October 1979.

190. Ith Sarin, *Sronoh pralung khmaer* ('Regrets for the Khmer Soul') Phnom Penh, 1973, 80 pp., at p.30. It is more than ironic that in 1982, when the defeated Pol Pot forces were attempting to present a moderate image, Rin was appointed their representative on the Culture and Education Committee of the exiled Coalition Government of Democratic Kampuchea. The *Age*, Melbourne, 30 August 1982.

191. *Sronoh pralung khmaer*, *op. cit.*, pp.5,6.

192. Carney, *op. cit.*, pp.39,8.

193. *Ibid.*, p.45. Sarin's companion on the trip, Kuong Lumphon, made no reference at all to any Hanoi-trained Khmers, in his 46-page *Report on Communist Party of Kampuchea*, dated 8 May 1973. I am grateful to Timothy M. Carney for providing me with a translation of this report.

194. Author's interview with Chhuong Kau, Kompong Chhnang, 1 September 1980.

195. Sarin did not visit Region 25, where Hanoi-trained former Issaraks were still working under Non Suon.

196. Carney, *op. cit.*, p.42. Kuong Lumphon, *op. cit.*, adds: 'The matter was kept very quiet. Some said he was disappointed because he had criticism from above ...' (p.27.)

197. Carney, *Ibid.*, p.44.

198. *Chamlaiy Hu Nim, op. cit.*, p.36.

199. Ouch Bun Chhoeun, *op. cit.*

200. Author's interviews with Men Chhan (Phnom Penh, 25 September 1980) and Hao Sophan (Kandol Chrum, 28 July 1980). It is possible that Soeun escaped severe treatment because of his years in France with Pol Pot, or because, in the words of a fellow Hanoi-trained Khmer, his 'narrow-minded nationalism' was more in tune with the views of the Party Centre. (Hem Samin, *op. cit.*) These factors did not spare him when he was executed by the Party Centre in 1976, but Soeun did survive longer than nearly all the other northern regroupees, partly because he was in the East.

201. Author's interview with Sin Song, Phnom Penh, 12 August 1980.

202. Ouch Bun Chhoeun, *op. cit.*

203. Stephen Heder's interview with Um Samang, Sa Keo, 10 March 1980.

204. Shawcross, *op. cit.*, p.251.

205. *Des Mouvements Anti-Gouvernementaux*, *op. cit.*, p.29.

206. *Ibid.*, p.25. The *Khmer Rumdos* are said to have suffered heavy casualties from US B-52 bombardment during the siege. A number of Khmers were also participating in a mixed Khmer-Vietnamese unit called the 'Phuoc Long Group', presumably named after the Vietnamese border province where it was active. 'Cambodia: Can the Vietnamese Communists Export Insurgency?' *op. cit.*, p.4.

207. T.D. Allman, *Guardian Weekly*, 26 August and 4 and 11 September 1971.

208. Carney, *op. cit.*, p.43: 'According to Phouk Chhay's report to a meeting at the end of May 1972, the monthly expenditures in the South-Western Zone reach over two million *riels* for Khmer Rouge military and civilian personnel, who earn 135 *riels* each per month,' Ith Sarin tells us. Simple arithmetic gives a figure of over 14,800 troops and cadres, which does not include unpaid guerrilla forces.

209. Shawcross, *op. cit.*, p.251.

210. Stephen Heder's interview with a Region 13 cadre, *op. cit.*

211. Quinn, 1974, *op. cit.*, pp.5, 6.

212. Cheng An, for instance, who was Suon's counterpart in the other Region of the Special Zone, Region 15, had in 1971 already begun to put 'diplomatic and military pressure' on the Vietnamese to leave the area, according to a local sympathizer; An 'led the struggle against the Vietnamese in the Special Zone'; he spoke at one 1972 mass meeting about Vietnamese plans to occupy and take over Kampuchean territory, and added that if necessary they would have to be driven out by force. Stephen Heder's interviews with two CPK personnel from Region 13, Sa Keo, 6 March 1980.

213. See the text, dated 29 July 1972, in *Bulletin d'Information*, Mission du GRUNC, Paris, 18 August 1972, pp.10–11, citing *Agence Khmère d'Information*, 3 August 1972. The same journal carried attacks on 'the puppet Phung Ton' (7 July 1972) and (a second) on Penn Yuth (4 August 1972), but interestingly, none of the three statements mentioned Pol Pot's brother Saloth Chhay. On Hou Yuon, see Kuong Lumphon *op. cit.*, p.21.

214. See *Peking Review*, 19 June 1970, p.33, reporting a Congress of the Peoples' Movement of United Resistance held in a liberated area on May 7 and 8, 1970.

215. Stephen Heder's interview with Non Suon's former courier, *op. cit.*

216. Ith Sarin, *Sronoh pralung khmaer*, *op. cit.*, pp.20–21. Kuong Lumphon adds: 'The Communist Party holds the position of refusing to believe that America really wanted peace, and said it was only a wheeler-dealer.' (*op. cit.*, p.42.)

217. Tea Chhay Hou, *op. cit.*

218. Stephen Heder's interview with Suon's former courier, *op. cit.*

219. Author's interviews with Tea Chhay Hou, Lau Sokha, Leng Leang Y, and Nhim Sitho, *op. cit.*

220. *Met knong tumnos*.

221. *Des Mouvements Anti-Gouvernementaux ...*, *op. cit.*, p.14. Kuong Lumphon reports this statement, which he heard, in similar terms. *Report on the Communist Party of Kampuchea*, p.36. Lumphon adds: 'I did not see the North Vietnamese do any interfering in our government, military, economic, etc. activities. I knew only that whenever there was a big fight, the Red Cambodians asked the Vietnamese to help.'

222. See p.193 above.

223. Kuong Lumphon added: 'There is certainly no liquor, [molestation of] women, gambling, or criminals; there is no bribery, robbers, court cases, or

extortion. There are no [excessive ?] taxes and even the ones there are are sought as contributions. There is no borrowing or lending on the rice crop. In commerce there is no Chinese middleman.' The insurgents, he reported, received 'help from the farmers' in intelligence-gathering. One group of peasants Lumphon met told him they 'detested capitalism, injustice, oppression, rottenness'. The emphasis on 'serving the people' may have been at least in part only a temporary legacy of Nhem Sun's cadre training programmes. But a veteran Issarak who served as bodyguard for Khieu Samphan and lived with him from 1968 to 1972, says: 'We all took turns to cook, one day each, both leaders and bodyguards. There were no distinctions. Whenever they took something from the people, they kept a record of it in order to pay the people back.'

224. Kuong Lumphon, *op. cit.*, pp.9, 18, 43, 37-41. See also Carney, *op. cit.*, pp.46, 49-51.

225. Sam Adams, *op. cit.*

226. *New York Times*, 5 November 1972, says 60 per cent of the population was living in insurgent-controlled areas.

227. Mam Lon, *op.cit.*

228. Author's interview with Puk Soum, Prey Veng, 8 August 1980.

229. Mam Lon, *op. cit.*

230. Nou Mouk, *op. cit.*

231. Author's interview with Tan Hao, Alençon, 4 October 1979. For a fuller description of Hao's experiences, see *Peasants and Politics in Kampuchea, 1942-81, op. cit.*, pp.274-76.

232. *Sronoh pralung khmaer, op. cit.*, pp.18-21.

233. The next defections of northern regroupees were those of Mom Chhen on 4 January 1973, and Pha Sophat on 18 December 1973. However, no information is available about their reasons for defection.

234. Much of what follows is taken from Trivière, May 1972, *op. cit.*, and Trivière, L., 'Le Cambodge entre la guerre et la paix', *Information Missionaire*, M.E.P., Paris, June 1973, 20 pp.; and from Shawcross, *op. cit.*, pp.229-234.

235. Meyer, *op. cit.*, p.264, notes that although Lon Nol 'in particular' harboured such dreams, in the Sihanouk period they were also shared by 'certain leaders'; as we shall see below, they were not limited to the Kampuchean right wing. See pp.414-15, below.

236. *Le Néo-Khmerisme*, par le Maréchal Lon Nol, Edition revue et corrigée, Phnom Penh, n.d. See in particular pp.2, 28.

237. A CPK speaker in 1975 told a meeting in Battambang that the Party wanted Kampuchea's population to reach twenty million by 1990. See also p.30.

238. See *Livre Noir, op. cit.*, p.90.

239. Frank Snepp, *Decent Interval*, Harmondsworth, 1977, p.61.

240. Shawcross, *op. cit.*, p.264.

241. *Ibid.*, p.272. Air force maps of the July-December 1972 bombing, obtained by Shawcross under the Freedom of Information Act, show very few targets outside the Eastern Zone.

242. Shawcross, *Ibid.*, p.297. Shawcross's 1973 map is reproduced here as Figure 8. An indication of the intensity of the bombardment can be gained from the fact that, according to a member of the US Embassy in Phnom Penh at the time, there was extremely heavy bombardment along the Mekong River south of Phnom Penh during February 1973, yet this is hardly discernible from the small-scale air force map of B-52 targets for that month. See also N.

Chomsky, *Towards a New Cold War*, 1982, p.131.

243. Author's interview with Chan Mon, Suong, 7 August 1980.

244. Author's interview with Nguon Ao, Kandol Chrum, 7 August 1980.

245. 'Cambodia: Can the Vietnamese Communists Export Insurgency?', *op. cit.*, p.4. FANK was Lon Nol's Forces Armées Nationales Khmères.

246. George C. Hildebrand and Gareth Porter, *Cambodia: Starvation and Revolution*, New York, Monthly Review, 1976, p.109, note 83. They cite interviews conducted with Khmer refugees in 1971 by the General Accounting Office, Congressional Record, 18 April 1973, p.S7812.

247. 'Bombing Turns Cambodian Villagers into Refugees', by Boris Baczynskyj, *Asian Reports*, 21 February 1972. The youth had since defected.

248. Stefan Hildebrand, personal communication.

249. Author's interview with Triet Sambath, Kompong Trabek, 8 October 1980.

250. Stephen Heder's interview with a local villager, Kamput, 11 March 1980.

251. Author's interview with Suon Sarat, Chantrea, 23 July 1980.

252. Touc Muong, *op. cit.*

253. Shawcross, *op. cit.*, pp.250-51.

254. Author's interviews with Som Yan and others, O Reang Au, 6 October 1980.

255. *Ibid.*

256. Author's interviews with Chin Chhuon, Chhai Chhoeun, Khim Veng and Yem Yiem, at Ampil Tapork, 6 October 1980.

257. Author's interview with Sang, O Reang Au, 6 October 1980.

258. Author's interviews with Song Rus and others, Prek Chrey, 7 October 1980.

259. Chheng Sia, *op. cit.*

260. Author's interview with Prak Voa, Krachap, 9 October 1980.

261. Author's interview with Suas Samon, Phnom Penh, 12 August 1980.

262. Author's interview with Chim Chin, Prey Veng, 28 July 1980.

263. Author's interview with Prok Sary, Prey Veng, 12 July 1980.

264. Author's interview with Preap Pichey, Kompong Cham, 8 August 1980.

265. Shawcross, *op. cit.*, p.297. These increases flouted Nixon's agreement with Congress that the intensity of the bombing would not be raised after July 1.

266. Author's interviews with Kus villagers, 16 July 1980.

267. Stephen Heder's interview with a Region 13 cadre, *op. cit.*

268. Ieng Thon, *op. cit.*; and Stephen Heder's interview with a Region 13 cadre, *op. cit.*

269. Mam Lon, *op. cit.*

270. Stephen Heder's interview with an Ampil Tuk villager, Kamput, 11 March 1980.

271. Stephen Heder's interview with a former inhabitant of Region 15, Sa Keo, 7 March 1980.

272. Author's interview with Kun Chhay, Kompong Svay, 16 October 1980.

273. See the soldier's full account in Francois Debré, *Cambodge: La Revolution de la forêt*, Paris 1976, ch. 12, especially pp.185-89.

274. In an interview with journalists in May 1979, Sihanouk recalled Koy Thuon as 'a very nice man'. Tape of the interview kindly provided by Anthony Malcolm.

275. *Ompi pankar ruom chong kraoy* ('On the Last Joint Plan'), 24 pp., written by officials of the Democratic Kampuchea security service, 1978. Translation by US Embassy in Thailand, 27 pp., at p.16.

276. Debré, *op. cit.*, pp.187-88.

277. Quinn, 1974, *op. cit.*, p.7.

278. Nou Mouk, *op. cit.*

279. Stephen Heder's interview with Suon's former courier, *op. cit.*

280. Stephen Heder's interviews with former CPK personnel from Region 15, Mai Rut, 15 March 1980 and Sa Keo, 6 March 1980.

281. 'Defectors Recount Disaffection with Communists', *op. cit.*

282. Author's interview with Yim Sern, Kandol Chrum, 28 July 1980.

283. Sin Song, *op. cit.*; and author's interview with Sang Lon, Kandol Chrum, 7 August 1980.

284. Author's interview with Chum Sambor, Prey Veng, 12 July 1980.

285. *Des Mouvements Anti-Gouvernementaux ...*, *op. cit.*, p.25, citing a Pentagon estimate. Snepp, *op. cit.*, p.62, gives another explanation: 'Under Soviet pressure the North Vietnamese grudgingly and gradually reduced their military presence in Laos and Cambodia', in the wake of the Paris Agreement.

286. Sam Adams, *op. cit.*, and Shawcross, *op. cit.*, p.296.

287. Hem Samin, *op. cit.*

288. Author's interview with Chea Soth, Phnom Penh, 22 October 1980.

289. See the account in FBIS, 25 September 1978, p.K8. Minh's Khmer and Vietnamese supporters now claim that he was killed by the Chinese, but this remains unclear even though an internal CPK report described his death as a 'victory in the liquidation of Party leaders' accused of working for outsiders. See 'Salut à la victoire de notre parti dans la liquidation des dirigeants du parti du Travail Cambodgien à la solde de la CIA', 1978 Democratic Kampuchea security document submitted in translation at the trial of Pol Pot and Ieng Sary, Phnom Penh, August 1979. Document no. 2.5.16.

290. Chea Soth, *op. cit.*; and author's interview with Keo Chenda (Phnom Penh, 21 October 1980). Also Yos Por, *op. cit.*

291. Shawcross, *op. cit.*, p.372, quoting Phnom Penh Radio of 24 June 1978.

292. Nou Mouk, *op. cit.*

293. *Ibid.*; emphasis added.

294. Stephen Heder's interview with a Region 13 cadre, *op. cit.*

295. Author's interview with Rat Samoeun, Kong Pisei, 13 September 1980. This woman is of course no relation to the Hanoi-trained cadre Rath Samuoeun.

296. Chap Hen, *op. cit.*

297. Yos Por, *op. cit.* Por says Mok was backed up in this view by the CPK Secretary of Region 35 (Kampot), Kang Chap, and his deputy Sa Rin. The next year Por was arrested and told he was going to be executed. He escaped to Vietnam and in 1979 became Secretary-General of the Kampuchean United Front for National Salvation in Phnom Penh.

298. Author's interview with Kim Kai, Kompong Chhnang, 4 September 1980.

299. Stephen Heder's interview with a Region 13 cadre, *op. cit.*

300. Chap Hen, *op. cit.*

301. Sin Song, *op. cit.*

302. *Summary of Annotated Party History*, *op. cit.*, pp.33–34. The document continues: 'The Party took the position of strength, rejecting absolutely the game of negotiations and arrangements under any method, form or trick.'

303. Donald Kirk, 'The Khmer Rouge: Revolutionaries or Terrorists?', unpublished 1974 paper, 18 pp., at p.17.

304. Some of these men included staff officer of the Zone command, Kat Nguon; So Phim's nephew, brigade commander Kim Teng; a second nephew Sa Bin, a Zone agricultural cadre; Chan Saman, commander of the Peam

Chor battle front in Region 24; Chuon Soth, chief of the Zone Commercial Service and in charge of the clandestine trade (mainly in rubber) with merchants in Phnom Penh; Sabou, a leading security cadre; Hien, deputy chief of Zone logistics; Sos Man, a Cham, President of the 'Eastern Zone Islamic Movement'; Prom Samith, former private secretary to Son Ngoc Minh and now a leader of the Zone Patriotic Monks' Association; Yun Soeun, chief of the Zone Artisans (Light Industry) Service; Bou Sarou, chief of the Zone Transport Service; and two doctors, Hak Sae and Chan Chhoeung, chief of the Zone Health Service. Another hundred or so held various military posts (e.g. Meas Huon, deputy commander of the Memut district forces) or technical ones (e.g. Hem Samin, director of a military vehicle workshop), and at least two were district Party Secretaries. According to Hem Samin, he had since 1971 sensed that 'something about the situation was wrong', but there were no defections or executions as in the North and South-West; and not until mid 1974 did the issue of these cadres' role in the movement come to a head in the East. (This information is based on various interviews).

305. Quinn, 1974, *op. cit.*, pp.7-8.
306. *Ibid.*, p.8; Tea Chhay Hou, *op. cit.*; and author's interview with 11th Brigade member Chhin Phoeun, Kong Pisei, 17 September, 1980.
307. These included Son Ngoc Minh, Tou Samouth, and So Phim himself. Interestingly, the Eastern Zone version had mentioned these names but not that of Pol Pot. See Fig. 9.
308. *Tung Padevat* ('Revolutionary Flags'), the CPK's internal monthly magazine, no. 8, August 1975, p.14, notes that 'we launched the Democratic Revolution from mid 1973 onward ...' Translation provided by T. M. Carney.
309. *Decisions Concerning the Line on Cooperatives of the Party in Region 31* (apparently from the Kompong Thom area), February 1974. Translation by S. R. Heder.
310. S. Heder, interview, 11-12 March 1980, *op. cit.* The same source adds that, as for those already enlisted, 'their relatives at home would be better off and more secure and they themselves would have better morale, and more to fight for'.
311. *Tung Padevat*, *op. cit.*
312. Author's interview with Mau Met, Kompong Cham, 5 October 1980.
313. Author's interview with Nem, Oudong, 18 September 1980.
314. 'They had been good people, only Pol Pot said they were no good', to which Sang attributes their disappearance in 1975.
315. Sang, *op. cit.* See note 257.
316. *Des Mouvements Anti-Gouvernementaux ...*, *op. cit.*, p.41.
317. Debré, *op. cit.*, pp.188-89.
318. Shawcross, *op. cit.*, p.312.
319. Kirk, 'The Khmer Rouge', *op. cit.*, p.9.
320. Stephen Heder's Region 13 cadre interviewee, *op. cit.*, defined a 'poor peasant' as a farmer who 'had no draft animals and produced only enough for a few months' [food]' from his/her small plot of land. This would include a tiny minority of peasants, perhaps 10 per cent.
321. Kirk, 'The Khmer Rouge', *op. cit.*, p.10.
322. This was not the last occasion on which Samphan's name was used as a cover for the CPK Centre: in December 1979 Samphan formally became Prime Minister of the exiled DK regime, in place of Pol Pot, who remained

CPK Secretary and army Commander-in-Chief. Samphan's long-term role contrasts with that of Hou Yuon, who had travelled the country in 1972 and early 1973, addressing meetings in places as far apart as Kompong Chhnang, Koh Thom, and Stung Treng. Yuon never associated himself with extremist policies, according to witnesses. However, this public life seems to have ended with the Democratic Revolution. (This account is based on interviews with a number of people who heard Hou Yuon addressing these meetings. None of them says that he advocated the extremist measures described above; he is said to have limited himself to denouncing the US and the Lon Nol regime, and to generally extolling the virtues of united effort. The last such meeting reported was in Sa'ang district of Region 25 in April 1973, when Yuon was said to have contracted fever and to be slurring his speech. Tea Chhay Hou, *op. cit.*) Although much better known in the countryside than Khieu Samphan, Yuon was never considered reliable enough to be a figurehead representative of the Party Centre.

323. Pon, *op. cit.*
324. 'Defectors Recount Disaffection with Communists', *op. cit.*, p.H5.
325. *Problèmes politiques et sociaux*, *op. cit.*, p.7.
326. Chhing Nam Yeang, *op. cit.*
327. Ung Channa, *op. cit.*
328. Kun Chhay, *op. cit.*
329. Carney, *op. cit.*, p.43.
330. Nguyen Xuan Hoang, 'Campuchia, Mot Su Kien Cach Mang Tuyet Voi', in *Hoi Nghi Khoa Hoc Chao Mung Cach Campuchia Toan Thang*, Southeast Asia Institute, Hanoi, 1979, ch. 3, pp.3,4. Bou Thong is a member of the Tapuon tribe, Soy Keo a member of the Krachak tribe.
331. Author's interview with Men Chhan, Phnom Penh, 25 September 1980. Chhan said Ney Sarann was head of the Central Committee office 'until at least 1973, when he became Secretary of the North-Eastern Zone'.
332. Chea Keo was executed in 1975, Ney Sarann in 1976, and Um Neng in 1978, but in 1979 the four rebels who had escaped emerged as leaders of the People's Republic of Kampuchea. In 1982, Bou Thong was Defence Minister, and Soy Keo was Army Chief of Staff.
333. This man insists that it was at this point that the Western Zone (Kompong Chhnang, Kompong Speu and Koh Kong) was created under Chou Chet, leaving Mok supreme in the populous heartland of the South-West, Takeo and Kampot. Other sources, however, date this from mid 1975, which may have been when such an arrangement was formalized.
334. Author's interview with Chhun Samath, Kong Pisei, 17 September 1980.
335. Quinn actually ascribes this fate to Mok, but that is impossible. Again the confusion seems to arise from the position of the leader concerned; Quinn says it was the 'Chairman' of the Zone – clearly Chet, given the evidence of Ith Sarin (see Carney, *op. cit.*, p.43). Quinn, *op. cit.*, p.7. Mok has never been described as Zone 'Chairman'.
336. Nou Mouk, *op. cit.*
337. Author's interview with Chhuong Kau, Kompong Chhnang, 1 September 1980.
338. Mam Lon, *op. cit.* In 1975 Lon was gaoled for alleged involvement in a 'Hanoi Vietnamese' spy network.
339. Quinn, 1974, *op. cit.*, pp.12, 23, 25-26, 32.
340. BBC *Summary of World Broadcasts*, FE/4734/A3/2, Phnom Penh Home

408

Service, 14 August 1973. The commander's name was Chieng Chen.
341. Quinn, 1974, *op. cit.*, p.7.
342. *Washington Post*, 8 March 1974. Their leader was named Sok Sophan.
343. Shawcross, *op. cit.*, pp.273-74.
344. Ieng Thon, *op. cit.*
345. Chhin Phoeun, *op. cit.* It was probably the first in the country.
346. Chap Hen, *op. cit.*
347. Quinn, 1974, *op. cit.*, p.34.
348. Tan Hao, *op. cit.*
349. 'Évolution de l'Organisation Politico-Administrative et Militaire des K.C. depuis Mars 1970', Khmer Republic, Deuxième Bureau, February-March 1975, 9 pp. at p.5. Vorn Vet is described as 'Ta Van' (Vorn).
350. With the overthrow of Democratic Kampuchea in 1979, a hundred of them emerged to participate in the formation of the People's Republic of Kampuchea. Sae Phuthang became Deputy Secretary of the ruling People's Revolutionary Party of Kampuchea, and two of his lieutenants became Party Secretaries of Koh Kong and Kampot provinces. Author's interview with Kampot Party Secretary Koy Luon, Kampot, 27 August 1980. See also Wilfred Burchett, *The China-Cambodia-Vietnam Triangle*, New York 1981, pp.195-96.
351. *Sarop chamlaiy moat totee rebos Chey Suon dael sarapeap dambong dai niw lngiec minh* ('Summary of the verbal answers of Chey [Non] Suon in his initial confession yesterday evening'), Tuol Sleng document dated 17 November 1976, signed by Pon, 2pp., at p.B.
352. Non Suon, *Phnaek ti pi: royea mun rotpraha 18.3.70*, Tuol Sleng confession dated 7 November 1976, p.3, and *Sekkedey sarapeap rebos dop pi* ('The Confessional Report of No. 12'), Tuol Sleng confession dated 28 November 1976, p.7. (Vorn Vet's account, in *his* confession, appears on p.31. See note 83, above, for a quotation.)
353. *Sekkedey sarapeap, ibid.*, p.3.
354. *Chamlaiy XII, op. cit.*, pp.23-24.
355. These sources added: 'It was only after the liberation of Phnom Penh that everybody was forced to join a cooperative', by which time Non Suon was no longer in charge (see below). Stephen Heder's interview with Region 13 and Region 15 cadres, Sa Keo, March 7, 1980.
356. Quinn, *op. cit.*, pp.19-20, 22.
357. Lau Sokha, *op. cit.*
358. Quinn, 1974, *op. cit.*, pp.33, 7-8. Discussing the re-locations, Quinn does not specify the district, but notes that 'a depopulated buffer zone had been established along the South Vietnamese border stretching from the Gulf of Thailand *to the Bassac River*' (emphasis added). This rules out the other district of Kandal province which he studied, Loeuk Dek. (See pp.33,1). It does, however, implicate Koh Thom district, as well as the entire South-Western Zone.
359. *Phnaek ti bey, op. cit.*, pp.25-27.
360. Lau Sokha, *op. cit.*
361. Quinn notes bans placed on Cham costumes and hairstyles in the South-West from mid 1972. (1974, *op. cit.*, p.26.) As for the North, a Region 31 CPK document dating from February 1974 states: 'Concerning fraternal Islamic Khmer, delay having them join [cooperatives] ... it is necessary to break up this group to some extent; do not allow too many of them to concentrate in one area ... Chinese foreign residents may not join cooperatives. Vietnamese may not join either. Suppose Chinese and Vietnamese want

to run away ... they are not allowed to go and if they do, all their materials can absolutely be confiscated and their families absolutely will not be allowed to leave'. *Decisions Concerning the Line on Cooperatives, op. cit.* Translation by S. R. Heder.

362. Quinn, 1974, *op. cit.*, p.24.

363. Author's interviews in Cham Loeu village, 1 August 1980. Although this village is just inside Koh Thom district, Non Suon was clearly much better known there than Som Chea. However, one of the Chams said he had seen Chea at a meeting 'when he was still at the district level', and adds that after Suon's disappearance from the Region and Chea's assumption of his post in 1975, 'Chea was good to us like Non Suon had been', apparently dating persecution only from mid 1976 as the others did. This may mean that Quinn's information is incorrect on this point, although it does not affect the general point about the differences between Region 25 and the South-Western Zone.

364. See Quinn, *op. cit.*, pp.19-20, 22.

365. *Chamlaiy XII, op. cit.*, p.24; and *Phnaek ti pram, op. cit.*, p.39.

366. *Phnaek ti pram, op. cit.*, p.39.

367. *Sekkedey sarapeap, op. cit.*, p.3. In another confession, Suon adds: 'I dared to tell him the truth about Region 25, and I trusted him in the matter of betraying the Party ... Chhouk still doubted me and did not tell me everything [perhaps because Suon had been placed in charge of Region 25 by Vorn Vet at the expense of the Eastern Zone]. But I followed his instructions in order to serve our Pracheachon Party.' Suon says he agreed with Chhouk to maintain good relations with the Vietnamese communists, and to place trusted cadres in key positions, in particular along the border, 'to avoid using too many people who might let our secrets out'. He concludes: 'Therefore my treason was reborn on 1 September 1973 after talking with Chhouk'. However, taking into account the nature of such confessional evidence, it is likely that Suon in fact acceded to Centre pressure to implement the new programme, but did so more reluctantly than ever. At any rate a real long-term conspiracy might have demanded a show of loyalty in this period. See below.

368. Non Suon, *Chamlaiy XII* (2), Tuol Sleng confession dated 22 November 1976, 9 pp., at p.1.

369. *Chamlaiy XII* (27 December 1976), *op. cit.*, pp.23-24.

370. Vorn Vet, *op. cit.*, p.36.

371. Quinn, 1974, *op. cit.*, p.7. The number of draftees involved was as many as four thousand. Communist losses under the US bombing (which ceased on August 15) had been heavy. Quinn notes that, unlike in the East and in Region 25, the CPK in the South-West were now drafting monks. (*Ibid.* p.22)

372. *Ibid.*, p.8.

373. *Chamlaiy XII* (27 December 1976), *op. cit.*, p.24. See note 367.

374. *Chamlaiy XII* (2) (22 November 1976), *op. cit.*, p.2. (And on Som Chea, *Phnaek ti bey, op. cit.*, pp.25-27. Leng Leang Y, *op. cit.*, suggests that Chea was in charge of Loeuk Dek district in this period, as well.)

375. *Ibid.*

376. Kirk, 'The Khmer Rouge', *op. cit.*, p.15.

377. *Ibid.*, p.1.

378. Author's interview with Tim, Oudong, 18 September 1980.

379. Nou Mouk, *op. cit.* (he says Chou Chet was in Kampot at the time). Mok's command of the troops that took Oudong was also confirmed by the author's interviews with Chheng Sy Leang, and with a monk who was evacuated from

Oudong and forcibly defrocked but protected by villagers. Oudong, 18 September 1980.

380. Tim, for instance, managed to slip away from the evacuation columns out of Oudong, and, accompanied by half a dozen refugee families, made his way to Region 32 (Kompong Speu). There he worked transporting food to the Phnom Penh front, until the war was over. 'It was softer there; killings were rare in Region 32', Tim says. 'Where I lived there were none.' *Op. cit.* He adds, however, that 'higher up, towards Amleang, Lon Nol soldiers with long hair were executed'. Amleang was the headquarters of Vorn Vet's Special Zone, although the surrounding area did not fall within it. For further evidence of a 'leopard-spot' political pattern in the South-Western Zone in 1975, see B. Kiernan and C. Boua, *Peasants and Politics in Kampuchea, 1942-81*, London 1982, p.276-77.

381. Nou Mouk, *op. cit.*

382. *Ibid.*

383. Stephen Heder interview, 11-12 March, 1980, op. cit.

384. Stephen Heder's interview with a Region 13 cadre, *op. cit.*

385. Heder interview, 11-12 March 1980, *op. cit.*; and Carney, 'The Organization of Power in Democratic Kampuchea', forthcoming.

386. Quinn, 1974, *op. cit.*, p.34. Interestingly, this reversal of policy parallels the temporary discontinuation of communal eating in Tram Kak districts of the South-West the same year, although the CPK there was much more violent (see next paragraph). Quinn does not mention any cases of violence in the East or specify the district of Svay Rieng in which this incident occurred, but it would be interesting to know whether it was Prasaut, which like Tram Kak was later declared a 'model district' by the DK regime. However, there is no evidence of a direct connection, as there is in the case of Tram Kak, specifically cited by the CPK as the first district to introduce communal eating. See p.379 above.

387. *Ibid.*, p.24.

388. Hem Samin, *op. cit.*, and Stephen Heder's interview with Hem Samin, 8 July 1981. Samin remarked to a fellow prisoner in 1976: 'Do we have to wait until they put us in irons before we say we're in prison?', which suggests uncertainty about the nature of their detention, even at that late date. On the 'farm chickens' and 'wild chickens', see p.358 above.

389. Author's interview with one of the six, Sok Khem, Kampot, 27 August 1980. He said there were less than ten survivors of '460' natives of Kampot who went to north Vietnam with him in 1954, and returned in 1970.

390. For an account of Yos Por's escape, see *Problèmes politiques et sociaux*, *op. cit.*, p.5.

391. Author's interview with Neang Samnang, Kompong Trabek, 8 August 1980.

392. Author's interview with Man's adopted son, Mat Ly, Phnom Penh, 13 August 1980.

393. Washington *Post*, 24 November 1974.

394. Mat Ly, *op. cit.*

395. Author's interview with Ibrahim, a Cham who lived in Region 21 from 1970 to 1979, Phnom Penh, 19 September 1980. He said: 'From 1970 to 1975 life was normal, there was no persecution yet. People believed in the Khmer Rouge then. US bombs fell on my village in 1971, burning it to the ground and killing several people. Some of the Cham villagers joined the Khmer Rouge as soldiers ... In 1974 suffering was imposed in some places, like Trea

Village. But it was not yet severe, only when Buddhism and Islam were abolished at the end of 1975 ...'

396. Kirk, 'The Khmer Rouge', *op. cit.*, p.17.
397. Author's interview with Chan Mon, Suong, 7 August 1980.
398. Hem Samin, *op. cit.*, told the author: 'If I had been taken to a gaol in Phnom Penh I wouldn't have survived'. The reference is to Tuol Sleng prison.
399. Author's interview with Khieu Sisavoun, Paris, 30 November 1979. Region 22 troops told him in 1975 about these clashes and said they 'were not very happy with the system' being established by the DK regime, although they also opposed Vietnamese intervention.
400. Keo Chenda, *op. cit.*
401. Her name was Sa'em, and her husband Sos was a member of the Region 21 Party Committee. He later became Region Party Secretary but was executed in 1978. Her fate is unknown. She may have been a sister of Heng Samrin.
402. Author's interviews with a number of Eastern Zone cadres, including a member of So Phim's administrative office. Dauntey, 6 August 1980.
403. Author's interview with Hun Sen, Phnom Penh, 21 October 1980, and Mau Met. *op. cit.*
404. This statement is based on a large number of interviews with inhabitants of the Eastern Zone who were ordinary citizens in this and later periods. See my 'Wild Chickens, Farm Chickens and Cormorants: Kampuchea's Eastern Zone under Pol Pot', in David P. Chandler and Ben Kiernan, eds., *Revolution and Its Aftermath in Kampuchea*, Yale South-East Asia Studies Monograph No. 25, 1983, pp.136–211.
405. Shawcross, *op. cit.*, p.298.
406. Carney, *op. cit.*, p.10.
407. See Shawcross, *op. cit.*, p.337.
408. See for instance, *ibid.*, p.295.
409. *Livre Noir*, *op. cit.*, p.91.
410. On 30 July 1977, Chinese Foreign Minister Huang Hua told cadres of the Foreign Ministry that Kampuchea had recently engaged in border conflicts with Vietnam, Laos and Thailand. He said China had already made clear its 'four-point stand' to the three Indo-China states. These were for (1) cease-fire and negotiations, (2) solidarity, (3) 'China will not take the side of any state', and (4) 'We support the stand of Cambodia and her people against Soviet revisionist social-imperialism and will not watch indifferently ...' The fourth point, contradicting the others, soon became China's policy. See King C. Chen, ed., *China and the Three Worlds*, New York 1979, pp.268–72.

Epilogue

In June 1974, according to Pol Pot, the CPK Central Committee met and decided to 'launch the decisive offensive to liberate Phnom Penh and the whole country'.[1] The campaign would begin on 1 January 1975. It was probably at the mid 1974 meeting that the evacuation of Phnom Penh was first discussed openly among leaders, leading to Chou Chet's and Hou Yuon's disavowal of the plan soon afterwards.[2]

In November 1974, the NUFK announced that the rubber plantations in the East and North had been nationalized. With credits obtained from China in return for the promise of supplies of rubber, the CPK bought Chinese water mines with which they intended to block the Mekong and thus to cut off the only remaining transport route to Phnom Penh. (The highways from Kompong Som port and South Vietnam had long since been cut.) The mines were delivered down the Ho Chi Minh Trail,[3] and over the next few months the Mekong became a graveyard for supply ships, with progressively fewer and fewer, and finally none, reaching their destination. This crucial part of the campaign was conducted by Chakrey's 1st Eastern Brigade.[4]

The US Administration attempted to make up for this with a massive air lift, and asked Congress for a large increase in military aid to Lon Nol. As the CIA's Chief Strategy Analyst in Saigon at the time, Frank Snepp, later wrote:

> The Lon Nol government would fall in a few weeks, they warned Congress, unless the proposed supplemental aid for Cambodia was approved at once.
> None of this, however, was very persuasive. The CIA had just completed a National Intelligence Estimate which showed that even with additional aid the Phnom Penh government would be unable to regain the military initiative in the forseeable future. CIA

Director Colby spelled out these conclusions candidly and in detail to a Congressional committee, and from that point on the Adminstration's proposed aid programme for Cambodia was doomed.[5]

And so was the Khmer Republic. It had received a total of $1.85 thousand million in US military and economic aid over the previous five years, almost exactly one million dollars per day. (The cost to the US of the air bombardment of Kampuchea was another $7 thousand million.)[6] The communist side, now poised for victory, had managed with far less foreign aid and equipment.[7] However, as CPK forces moved into position for the final assault on Phnom Penh, they brought with them, according to Snepp, 'their ultimate weapons ... captured US 105 mm howitzers that were undoubtedly a gift of the North Vietnamese'.[8]

Although the Vietnamese communists themselves overran the southern province capital of Phuoc Binh on 7 January 1975, most observers did not believe that they would take Saigon in the near future. Nor did the Vietnamese leaders themselves. On the basis of detailed and varied intelligence, Snepp summarizes the October 1974 decision of the VWP Politburo as, 'to move cautiously and gradually on the battlefield, with negotiations as a possible interim objective'. After Phuoc Binh had fallen, this aim was modified but complete victory remained a long-term prospect. Only after the fall of Ban Me Thuot on 11 March 1975 did the Vietnamese leaders move towards what Snepp calls the 'monumental shift in strategy'[9] that opened up the possibility of a quick end to the Thieu regime.

It is clear, then, that the CPK must initially have anticipated that Phnom Penh would be in their hands well before the Vietnamese communists could take Saigon. The evidence of a CPK attempt to take advantage of this by immediately attacking Vietnam is patchy but consistent, as we shall see. In this context, later CPK statements present a revealing example of psychological 'projection'. Hanoi's plan in this period, Pol Pot's radio alleged in 1978, had been to seize Saigon *and then march on Phnom Penh*: 'This time again, they were a step behind Cambodia. Cambodia won victory before them'.[10] However, it was only a matter of thirteen days, because of the disastrous miscalculation made by Nguyen Van Thieu when he decided on 13 March to evacuate the Central Highlands (Truong Son mountains), thereby precipitating the collapse of his army and administration.

Neak Leung, the last Mekong River town held by the Khmer Republic, fell to Chakrey's forces on 1 April. Lon Nol fled the country on the same day. On 12 April, Ambassador J. Gunther Dean furled the American flag and was evacuated by helicopter to Thailand. The Khmer Republic surrendered at 9.30 am on 17 April 1975.

Two days later, according to Snepp: 'For the first time Communist artillery men shelled Phu Quoc',[11] a large island off the coast of the Mekong Delta, undisputedly belonging to Vietnam.[12] Snepp does not specify who these communists were, but two weeks later elements of the CPK's 3rd South-Western Brigade (later called the 164th Naval Division) landed on the island. Their political commissar was also the new CPK Secretary of Kompong Som port, Mok's son-in-law Khe Muth.[13] According to later Vietnamese allegations, the Kampuchean troops landed on 4 May, and six days later attacked another island, Tho Chu, even further beyond the sea border claimed by Sihanouk and Lon Nol. According to Hanoi:

> The Kampuchean authorities launched repeated attacks on this island with their armed forces, destroyed villages, killed many people and abducted 515 inhabitants of the island. In spite of the protest made by the Vietnamese side, the Kampuchean troops maintained their occupation of Tho Chu island. For this reason, on 25 May 1975, Vietnamese local armed forces were compelled to use their legitimate right of self-defence to drive the intruders out of Tho Chu island and, on 6 June 1975, pursued them as far as Hon Troc [Wai island].[14]

Six hundred Kampuchean troops, as well as Kampuchea's Wai island, were captured in these engagements. But in the meantime, on 12 May, Kampuchean naval units had seized the US cargo vessel, Mayaguez, provoking a much more visible international crisis.[15] In combination with the fall of Saigon on 30 April and subsequent consolidation of VWP control over the Mekong Delta, this rendered unworkable a CPK plan, or at the very least a Mok plan with apparent Centre acquiescence, to attack and if possible seize Kampuchea Krom from the Thieu forces before the Vietnamese communists could do so themselves.

On 2 June, Pol Pot received VWP representative Nguyen Van Linh in Phnom Penh. According to the Vietnamese in 1978, Pol Pot 'argued that the Kampuchean troops' 'ignorance of local geography' had been the cause of these painful, bloody clashes'.

In August, the Vietnamese withdrew from Wai island.[16]

It is likely, however, that something more calculated than ignorance had been involved, and that the CPK was now merely beating a tactical retreat. Thon, a member of the 2nd Battalion of the 120th Regiment (the CPK's Region 13 forces), says that his regiment had been dispatched to the border 'immediately after' capturing Takeo city, on 18 April. 'The regimental commander, Soeun, said we were going 'to liberate Vietnamese territory because it is all our territory'.' On arrival at Koh Andeth, 15 kilometres from the border, Thon heard other CPK leaders announcing that 'we have to fight Vietnam because there are eighteen of our provinces there, including Prey Nokor [Saigon]'. Soeun was soon promoted to brigade commander; the new regimental commander, Pien, reiterated the irredentist claim, and the troops moved off.[17] Hanoi claims that attacks were mounted across the land border in various places 'as early as 1 May 1975 ... causing great human and material losses to the local populations'.[18] The CPK troops from Region 13, the original base of Mok and Muth, were undoubtedly among those responsible.

In neighbouring Region 33 at this time, at least two members of the Region Committee were quick to claim that Kampuchea Krom was Kampuchean territory. These two were Mok's son, Chong, former CPK Secretary of Prey Krabas district and recently promoted to Region Secretary, and Khim, Secretary of Kong Pisei district. 'Chong was the one who said this the most emphatically of all', according to a local subdistrict official and CPK member.[19]

Although publicly forecast by Mok since at least 1973,[20] the border attacks were not just a family affair, and although Mok had become the Puth Chhay of the 1970s, these attacks were closely related to Communist Party policies. According to a regimental political commissar from Region 24:

Immediately upon liberation on 17 April 1975, there was a Special Centre Assembly for Cabinet Ministers and all Zone and Region Secretaries. Eight points were made at the Assembly, by Pol Pot:
1. Evacuate people from all towns.
2. Abolish all markets.
3. Abolish Lon Nol regime currency, and withhold the revolutionary currency that had been printed.
4. Defrock all Buddhist monks, and put them to work growing rice.
5. Execute all leaders of the Lon Nol regime beginning

with the top leaders.
6. Establish high-level cooperatives throughout the country, with communal eating.
7. Expel the entire Vietnamese minority population.
8. *Dispatch troops to the borders, particularly the Vietnamese border.*[21]

Predictably, dissident voices were raised at this meeting — notably those of Hou Yuon, Koy Thuon, Ney Sarann and Chhouk[22] — and it is unlikely that Pol Pot would have divulged to such an audience the full extent of his policy towards Vietnam. But whatever that policy may have been, it is clear that the evacuation of Phnom Penh and other urban centres was not just an ideological or economic measure but also part of a strategy of *continuing warfare*. From now on the Vietnamese were not to be tempted to react by 'swallowing' Kampuchea in a strike against a vulnerable populated capital.

The two million people in Phnom Penh were scattered into the countryside. A member of the South-Western Zone's 11th Brigade was sent in 'to defend the city'. He recalls: 'We went in to Phnom Penh on 18 April to search for enemies hidden there, and to drive the people out. We were instructed to tell people to leave for three days, and that they could then return. We were told to shoot those who refused to leave. Our squad shot two or three families north of Daem Thkou market.'[23] There was to be no return in three days, of course. Perhaps as many as twenty thousand city-people died or were executed on the roads in the next month or so, and perhaps a million more died over the next four years.

On 13 September 1975, diplomatic sources in Beijing reported that China had extended to Kampuchea US $1 thousand million in interest-free economic and military aid, including an immediate $20 million gift. This was apparently described as 'the biggest aid ever given to any one country by China'.[24] At the same time China substantially reduced its aid to Vietnam. However, China was on the threshold of a political crisis, and its ideological favouritism did not signal an interest in provoking hostilities with Vietnam. In December 1975, during a visit by US President Ford, 'the Chinese exhorted him to begin improving relations with Hanoi by announcing a programme of reconstruction aid to the war-shattered country'.[25] (The Chinese argued that this would reduce Vietnamese dependence on the Soviet Union.) Ford declined to take up this suggestion. Meanwhile, probably looking over their shoulders at Beijing, the Vietnamese maintained silence about the CPK's actions and the worsening situation in Kampuchea.

The author of an article in the August 1975 issue of the CPK magazine *Tung Padevat* warned that, although the urban population had been evacuated, 'Their economic foundation has already collapsed but *their views still remain, their aspirations still remain.*'[26] (This is why, incidentally, so many of the survivors returned to recreate the capital in 1979.) It may also be said, of course, that the 'economic foundation' for the kind of society the CPK Centre was attempting to create had 'collapsed' as long ago as the eighteenth century, although the 'aspirations' of some elements of that traditional society were hanging on just as doggedly, notably in the CPK Centre. Although the ideology behind the evacuation of Phnom Penh was more diverse than that, the hope that the destruction of a city would transform the social and economic relations formed by history betrayed the same kind of stubbornness. *Tung Padevat* continued: 'Private property ... has no power to oppose us. Because we do not allow it time to strengthen and expand its forces it will collapse and disappear without fail. If we had kept Phnom Penh, it would have had much strength. It was true that we were stronger, and had more influence than the private sector when we were in the countryside. But in Phnom Penh we would have become their satellite. However, we did not keep them in Phnom Penh. Thus, private property has no power.'[27] A peasant in Region 21 later recalled: 'After 17 April 1975 the Party stopped saying that the workers were the base'.[28]

In his 1977 confession, Hu Nim revealed that Hou Yuon's opposition to this ideology made him one of the first targets of the CPK Centre: 'After liberation, when the Party abolished money and wages and evacuated the people, Hou Yuon again boldly took a stand against the Party line.'[29] He apparently survived until August 1975, when according to one report he addressed a large gathering of evacuees and others at Prek Por on the Mekong River. He spoke out strongly against the evacuation and was applauded by the crowd. Soon after leaving the meeting, according to this report, Hou Yuon was shot dead by a CPK squad, and his body thrown into the Mekong.[30]

Others, less bold, lasted a little longer. In April Non Suon was transferred to Phnom Penh to work in the National Bank. On 22

July, a ceremony in the capital marked the amalgamation of the various Zone armies under Centre control, an occasion of which Non Suon wrote in his confession: 'I was very disappointed not to see Achar Sieng [Ney Sarann] in the Politburo as I had hoped ... I was worried that the Organization did not trust me, because it had taken me away from my base area.'[31] On 5 September, Suon met with Chhouk, So Phim, and Pol Pot in the Region 24 office. 'Chhouk asked about Sok and Chamroeun. I said they had been 'taken care of'. They were immoral and in 1971 had killed friend Kiet.'[32] Suon was, it seems, unable to speak his mind about the fate of 'the men I trusted',[33] in the presence of Party Secretary Pol Pot. Soon afterwards, a member of Suon's staff revisited Region 25, and returned with the news that 'the cadres were discouraged because one by one they were being called in by the Organization and disappearing.'[34]

The Party's twenty-fourth anniversary celebration on 30 September 1975 saw the arrest of Mey Pho. The most senior of all surviving Khmer communist veterans, Pho as a young palace clerk had with six others sounded the clarion call to the struggle for independence by staging the republican coup of 9 August 1945. After his return from Hanoi in 1970, Pho had taken charge of the Central Committee's Office M-5, a depot where supplies from Vietnam were delivered. No more of those were expected, however, and Mey Pho was last seen in Boeng Trabek detention camp in the capital, by a woman whose husband was soon led away with him. No confession by Mey Pho has been discovered; like the woman's husband, he was probably summarily executed.[35] The same fate had just befallen the last of his co-conspirators of thirty years before, Thach Sary, who had served in the government army since the 1950s and was shot several days after the fall of Phnom Penh.[36]

Soon after the April 1975 victory, the South-Western Zone was formally divided into two, and a Western Zone created out of the most barren section, with Chou Chet as its Party Secretary. (Mok now held complete sway over the populous area between Highway 4 and the Vietnamese border.) Conditions in the Western Zone, partly because many evacuees were sent there, were extremely poor, and Chet predictably seems to have had less power than his military chief, Paet Soeung, the former commander of the 1st South-Western Zone Brigade who had implemented Mok's orders to evacuate Oudong in 1974. (It was Soeung, for instance, who signed the death warrants for inmates in the Zone prison).[37] Nevertheless, a CPK Centre representative, addressing a Western Zone cadre congress in July 1977, complained that a 'fair number' of cooperatives in the Western Zone were controlled by 'enemies and various classes' other than poor peasants. In some areas, former Lon Nol military personnel headed the cooperatives, and in others, former Sino-Khmer 'employers'. This was 'no way to build socialism', the Centre representative said. He went on to note that, although local traitors and dangerous Party members had been 'wiped out' in the previous six months, the backgrounds of all Party officials had to be reviewed, including those at the Zone level.[38] This amounted to an overt attack on Chou Chet. In March 1978, after he had publicly dissented from the views of another Zone Committee member over policy towards Vietnam, and then attempted to organize an armed rebellion, Chet was arrested by Soeung and taken to Tuol Sleng prison, where he was executed.[39]

Chet's former colleague, Phouk Chhay, was removed from his post as political commissar of the South-Western Zone armed forces immediately after the end of the war. He then worked at Phnom Penh airport, where he was reported to have been 'in charge of foreign contact'. Given the ultra-nationalism of the new regime, this may have been a demotion, a warning, or at least a risky assignment. Chhay was eventually arrested on 14 March 1977, in a purge that swept up his former Khmer-Chinese Friendship Association colleagues Hu Nim and Tiv Ol, as well as Koy Thuon (to Pauk's advantage in the North), Touch Phoeun, Siet Chhe, and hundreds, even thousands of others in a matter of months.[40] By 1978, a cadre greatly responsible for foreign contact was the head of the Foreign Ministry's Asia Department, Thiounn Prasith.

At the July 1975 ceremony, Chakrey's 1st Eastern Zone Brigade was transferred to Phnom Penh, becoming the 170th Division. Chakrey was appointed Deputy Chief of the General Staff (under Son Sen), but was arrested on 20 May 1976 after having allegedly 'exploded grenades behind the royal palace and fired on the National Museum';[41] if this was indeed the case, it was a less successful coup than the one on the same spot in August 1945. Two of Chakrey's regimental commanders were arrested with him. This led directly to the arrest of Chhouk on 20 August, signalling the commencement of a long series of purges of Eastern Zone cadres. Masterminded by Chan, whom the

Centre appointed Deputy Zone Secretary in late 1975, these purges finally provoked the fierce rebellion led by Heng Samrin and Chea Sim in May 1978. So Phim committed suicide on 3 June, the victim of a lifetime of Party loyalty and inability to back his own judgement.[42]

Keo Meas returned from Hanoi in May 1975 to work in the office of the Central Committee. He was arrested on 25 September 1976, five days after Ney Sarann and shortly before Non Suon (who as Minister of Agriculture was abroad at the time and was arrested at the airport on his return.) The Pracheachon Group had finally been obliterated, five days short of the Party's twenty-fifth anniversary, which the Centre now declined to celebrate or even mention because of the implied historical connection with Vietnamese communism.[43]

By early 1977, Pol Pot had purged most of the CPK's dissidents and was probably convinced that the new government in Beijing would fully back Kampuchea, in the event of a war with Vietnam. The war began again in March 1977, with renewed calls for the liberation of Kampuchea Krom by cadres in every Zone, including Chan in the East.[44] As with the 1975 conflict, the new war brought massive suffering to the Khmer population; 'higher-stage cooperatives' were introduced, communal eating generalized, rations reduced and working hours increased. Executions now occurred daily in many villages, and famine reigned despite production levels that were adequate to provide for the population, had the produce been distributed. But the rice was either exported to China in return for weaponry, or stored for the use of the army. The Party slogan, with rice 'we can have everything',[45] applied, it seems, even to Kampuchea Krom. On 17 January 1978, just after the first major Vietnamese military reaction, Pol Pot announced that the war was going well: 'We are not worried that the source of our army would become exhausted, for the people of the lower classes are very numerous.'[46]

The Vietnamese army drove his regime's remnants into the hills a year later. His colleague Thiounn Mumm found himself in charge of a group of peasant children he had been training in Phnom Penh. During the forced retreat, according to a witness: 'Six of the boys died: they were so hungry that they ate toxic tubers ... And Thiounn Mumm said, in front of these boys who were already very sick: 'That is what happens to undisciplined children'. And he said it in a very cynical fashion. That shocked everybody for we could not imagine hearing an intellectual, in a situation like that, say such things instead of helping the children.'[47]

Notes

1. *Discours prononcé par le camarade Pol Pot ... au meeting commémorant le 17e anniversaire de la fondation du Parti Communiste du Kampuchea*, Democratic Kampuchea, Phnom Penh, 27 September 1977, p.51.
2. See Chapter Eight, p.385, above.
3. Frank Snepp, *Decent Interval*, Harmondworth 1977, p.101.
4. Author's interview with Ouch Bun Chhoeun, Phnom Penh, 30 September 1980.
5. Snepp, *op. cit.*, p.125.
6. William Shawcross, *Sideshow: Kissinger, Nixon and the Destruction of Cambodia*, London 1979, p.350.
7. A June 1975 US Defence Intelligence Agency appraisal of the Khmer Republic's defeat noted that it had possessed 288 howitzers to the CPK's 15 to 20, as well as 190 naval craft and 70 attack aircraft to the CPK's none. It went on: 'Although the insurgents suffered heavy casualties ... they were able to replace their combat losses in most areas. These replacements had little training or experience; nevertheless, they performed satisfactorily in most situations ... The Government of the Khmer Republic, although outnumbering the KC [in terms of regular troops] by almost two to one, never redressed its long-standing problems ... combat losses and numerous desertions exceeded the conscription programme's ability to provide recruits ... Corruption in all segments of society also undermined the effectiveness of the military as well as the government ... Towards the end, however, supplemental US military aid assistance probably would not have changed the outcome'. DIA Appraisal, 'Cambodia: The Military Campaign that Defeated the Cambodian Armed Forces', 12 June 1975, 7pp., at pp.3-4, 6-7.

8. Snepp, *op. cit.*, p.135.

9. *Ibid.*, pp.100, 114, 146.

10. Shawcross, *op. cit.*, p.372, quoting Phnom Penh Radio of 10 May and 24 June 1978.

11. Snepp, *op. cit.*, p.299.

12. It was this island that Zhou Enlai had unsuccessfully encouraged Sihanouk to claim in 1960. N. Sihanouk, *Souvenirs doux et amers*, Paris 1981, p.311.

13. Stephen Heder, personal communication, and Timothy Carney, 'The Organisation of Power in Democratic Kampuchea', forthcoming.

14. *Kampuchea Dossier*, Hanoi, 1978, vol.l, pp.125-26. (In interviews with Stephen Heder in Thailand in 1980, some former members of the 164th Division confirmed that Kampuchean policy towards the Mekong Delta and Phu Quoc in 1975 had been irredentist, while others denied it. Stephen Heder, personal communication, 2 February 1981.)

15. Kompong Som port, oil refinery and airport were bombed by US airplanes on 15 May. Seventeen planes were destroyed on the ground.

16. *Ibid.*

17. Author's interview with Ieng Thon, Tram Kak, 16 July 1980.

18. *Kampuchea Dossier*, 1, *op. cit.*, p.125.

19. Author's interview with Chap Hen, Kong Pisei, 17 September 1980.

20. See Chapter Eight, p.361, above.

21. Author's interview with Sin Song, who was told of the meeting by Chhouk. Phnom Penh, 12 August 1980. My emphasis.

22. *Ibid.*; and author's interview with Northern Zone inhabitants in Kompong Svay, 16 October 1980. According to the latter sources, they were told of the meeting by a local battalion commander named Ret, who said that it occurred in May 1975 and that 'eleven points' were made there. Ret claimed that Koy Thuon and himself, and others 'argued for money, schools and religion'. I believe the meeting was the NUFK Special National Congress held within a week of the victory. (See Timothy Carney, *Communist Party in Power in Kampuchea*, Cornell University South-East Asia Program Data Paper no.106, 1977, p.22.) Sin Song's full account of the meeting can be found in Ben Kiernan, 'Wild Chickens, Farm Chickens and Cormorants: Kampuchea's Eastern Zone Under Pol Pot', in David P. Chandler and Ben Kiernan, eds., *Revolution and its Aftermath in Kampuchea: Eight Essays*, Yale University South-East Asia Council Monograph no.25, 1983, pp.178-79.

23. Author's interview with Chhin Phoeun, Kong Pisei, 17 September 1980.

24. *China Quarterly*, no.64, December 1975, p.797, quoting a report in *Le Monde* of 13 September 1975.

25. *National Times* (Sydney), 22-28 April 1983, p.9, quoting US 'official records that have just come to light'.

26. Emphasis in original.

27. 'Cadres, Party members, people and the Revolutionary Army must be unanimous with the Party in examining and assessing conditions in order to carry out the new tasks with soaring success', in *Tung Padevat*, no.8, August 1975.

28. Author's interview with Chan Mon, Suong, 7 August 1980.

29. *Chamlaiy Hu Nim* ..., confession in Tuol Sleng prison, 28 May and 16 June 1977. Translation by Chanthou Boua. 105 pp. transcript, at p.86.

30. Author's interview with Ros Kann, Surin, 3 March 1979. Kann said he was told of this in Kompong Cham province by a CPK cadre named Pen

Kimsruong, among others, who disapproved of what was happening and advised Kann to flee. Jean Lacouture gives a slightly different account of what was probably the same incident, saying that Hou Yuon 'was killed by one of his bodyguards a few days after the capture of Phnom Penh, as he was departing on a motorcycle from a public meeting where he had criticized the plan to turn pagodas into stables.' *Survive le peuple cambodgien!*, Paris 1978, p.117.

31. Non Suon, *Chamlaiy XII* (2), Tuol Sleng confession dated 22 November 1976, 9 pp., at pp.3-4.

32. Non Suon's confession dated 3 November 1976, 9 pp., at pp.8-9.

33. See p.383 above.

34. 'The Affair of Comrade Heang', Non Suon's confession dated 25 November 1976.

35. This information comes from the woman, named Heng. Personal communication to the author, Takhmau, 27 September 1980. For an account of Mey Pho's early career, see Chapter Two.

36. Michael Vickery, personal communication.

37. Author's interviews with Chhuong Kau, Kompong Chhnang, 1 September 1980, and Moeung Sonn, who was imprisoned in the Zone gaol, Sarcelles, 26 October 1979.

38. Timothy Carney, 'The Organization of Power', *op. cit.* He cites *Tung Padevat*, no.8, August 1977, pp.20, 24, 31.

39. Author's interviews with various people who had contact with Chou Chet in early 1978. Kompong Chhnang, September 1980.

40. See Ben Kiernan and Chanthou Boua, *Peasants and Politics in Kampuchea, 1942-81*, New York, M.E. Sharpe, 1982, p.300.

41. *Ompi Pankar Ruom Chong Kraoy* ('On the Last Joint Plan'), Democratic Kampuchea security services, 1978. Translation by US Embassy, Thailand, 27 pp., at p.2.

42. See Kiernan, 'Wild Chickens ... ', *op. cit.*, for a detailed account of these purges and their aftermath.

43. David P. Chandler, 'Revising the Past in Democratic Kampuchea: When was the Birthday of the Party?' *Pacific Affairs*, Summer 1983, 56, 2, pp.288-300.

44. On the 1977-78 conflict, see Kiernan, 'New Light on the Origins of the Vietnam-Kampuchea Conflict', *Bulletin of Concerned Asian Scholars*, 12(4), 1980, pp.61-65. As for alleged Vietnamese subversion, the Democratic Kampuchea security services admitted in early 1978: 'The name of the Vietnamese network still evaded us as we had no document to certify it'. ('One the Last Joint Plan', *op. cit.*, p.14.) The Vietnamese may have maintained some kind of intelligence network in Kampuchea, but there is no evidence even of their encouragement of opposition to Pol Pot's regime until 1978, after they had suffered a year of border attacks, the evidence for which is now overwhelming.

45. See *Democratic Kampuchea is Moving Forward*, Phnom Penh, August 1977, p.11.

46. Pol Pot, *Speech Commemorating the 10th Anniversary of the Founding of the Revolutionary Army of Kampuchea*, Phnom Penh, 17 January 1978. French version published by the Comité des Patriotes du Kampuchea Démocratique en France, p.5.

47. Marie A. Martin, 'Les écoles techniques de Phnom Penh: La dramatique épopée du massif des Cardamomes, janvier-juin 1979', ASEMI (Paris), XI, 1-4, 1980, pp.113-127, at p.122.

Glossary of Terms and Abbreviations

Achar:	a former Buddhist monk, or pagoda (*wat*) ceremonial leader.
Angkar:	'the Organisation', or Communist Party of Kampuchea, usually meaning its leadership.
ARVN:	Army of the Republic of Vietnam, the anti-communist Saigon regime (1954-75).
CCP:	Chinese Communist Party.
CIA:	US Central Intelligence Agency.
Centre:	national leadership of the CPK.
CPK:	Communist Party of Kampuchea (1966-).
CPT:	Communist Party of Thailand.
DK:	Democratic Kampuchea, the CPK regime (1975-79), headed by Pol Pot.
DRV:	Democratic Republic of Vietnam (1945-), now called the Socialist Republic of Vietnam.
ICP:	Indochinese Communist Party (1930-1951).
ICSC:	International Commission of Supervision and Control, comprising delegates from Canada, India and Poland.
KNLC:	Khmer National Liberation Committee (1949-54).
KPRP:	Khmer People's Revolutionary Party (1951-60), and Kampuchean People's Revolutionary Party (1979-).
Livre Noir:	The 'Black Book' on relations with Vietnam, published by the Democratic Kampuchea regime in September 1978.
NLF:	National Liberation Front (south Vietnamese communist organisation).
UIF:	Unified Issarak Front (1950-54), Khmer independence movement.
VC/NVA:	'Viet Cong/North Vietnam Army'.
VWP:	Vietnam Worker's Party or Lao Dong (1951-76), now called the Vietnamese Communist Party.
wat:	Khmer Buddhist temple or pagoda.
WPK:	Workers' Party of Kampuchea (1960-66).

Index